ANTINOMIES OF ART AND CULTURE

ANTINOMIES OF ART AND CULTURE

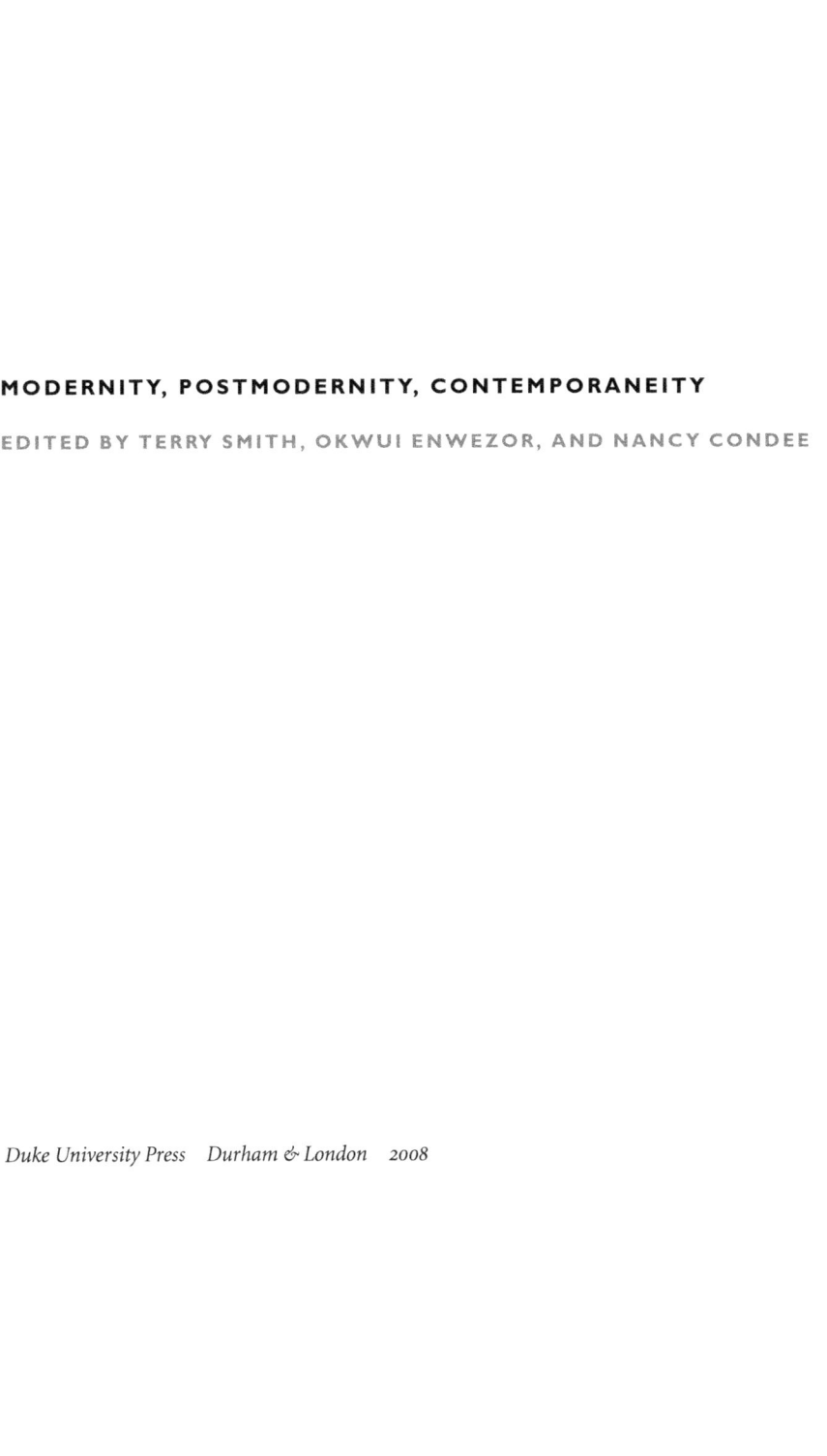

MODERNITY, POSTMODERNITY, CONTEMPORANEITY

EDITED BY TERRY SMITH, OKWUI ENWEZOR, AND NANCY CONDEE

Duke University Press   Durham & London   2008

© 2008 Duke University Press

All rights reserved

Designed by Amy Ruth Buchanan

Typeset in Minion by Keystone Typesetting, Inc.

Library of Congress Cataloging-in-Publication Data appear on the last printed page of this book.

TO JACQUES DERRIDA, 1930–2004, IN MEMORIAM

CONTENTS

ILLUSTRATIONS

PREFACE

In the aftermath of modernity, and the passing of the postmodern, how are we to know and show what it is to live in the conditions of contemporaneity?

This is a question about individual being and social belonging now, about how the relationships between them might be understood these days, and how they might be represented to others—in speech, in texts, in works of art, and in exhibitions. The editors of this book begin from the intuition that, when it comes to offering acute accounts of these relationships—in brief, of large-scale world picturing and small-scale world making—the time of postmodern doubt about modernity may appear to have run out. Does this mean that the kinds of large-scale world making and the various projects of totalization associated with modernity have returned to dominance, albeit in multiple, contingent, and contradictory forms? Or does it mean that the world has entered a condition in which overarching frameworks, however internally differentiated and skeptical, have lost their power to shape the far reaches of thought and thus their purchase on the particularities of everyday life? This would leave us naked to the present. If so, it is a contemporaneity that is riddled with as much wary doubt as it is infused with watchful hope, that seems immured in utopian appeals to the futurity of various pasts, including that of modernity, yet everywhere and always poses itself to itself as a pressing question.

The chapters in this book have been developed from papers given at a meeting of scholars, theorists, artists, critics, and curators that was convened in Pittsburgh in November 2004, two days after the U.S. presidential elections that gave George W. Bush a second term. In the twilight of postmodernism, and the resurgence of modern imperialisms and ancient fundamentalisms, three generations of thinkers came together to assess how ideas of the modern, the postmodern, and the contemporary were engaging with these apparently unparalleled circumstances. An introduction by one of the editors sets out an account of why these circumstances seem to press us to consider the question of contemporaneity, reviews key elements in the current conceptualization of modernity and postmodernity, and then introduces the main themes of the book.

Subsequent chapters are organized into four parts around a centerpiece. In part 1, "The Politics of Temporality," the main themes are posed by leading theorists, critics, and curators. The question of contemporaneity is tested against a powerful and widely influential theorization of empire and multitudes. This is followed by an analysis of an extraordinary instance of action by one of these multitudes—the unexpected defeat of right-wing forces in the 2004 national elections in India—and of the role of documentary filmmaking in this cultural conjuncture. Focus then turns to the persistence of media-specific values of artistic Modernism in the work of well-known contemporary artists. In contrast, it is argued that installation, with its capacity to declare a space of open-ended provisionality, is now an artistic genre so ubiquitous that it has become the main medium of contemporary, as distinct from Modern, art. These different emphases indicate that the time has come to see Modernism as a richer heritage than postmodernist critique has allowed, one that adds to the complications of the present, even as it recedes within them.

Part 2, "Multiple Modernities," is concerned with reconceptualizing the ways in which various kinds of artistic Modernisms were part of the development of distinctive modernities in different parts of the world during the nineteenth and twentieth centuries. It raises the question of recognition of the inventiveness of artists at the edges of empire and those consigned to the far peripheries of canonical modernist art cultures. It then probes the conditions of production and the nature of artistic modernization within colonized societies, pushing ideas of "alternative modernities" toward the recognition that, in certain circumstances, they may be seen as more subtle refractions, as "double" or even "para-modernities." Societies with powerful traditions distinct from those of the West may also be expected to have generated distinct experiences of modernity, and thus different ways of representing their experiences of them. How might these be identified without importing the at once universalist and nationalistic commitments of modern Western art history? Meanwhile, we face the legacy of the fact that colonization forced these differences together. What have been the consequences of this (we now see) bad marriage? For how long will estrangement cloud the perspectives on all sides? The chapters in this section tackle these questions in specific, closely studied situations.

The book's centerpiece—which represents the turning that is at its heart—is a work of art: Zoe Leonard's *Analogue* of 1998–2004. Deploying the high modernist devices of the framing grid and the serial sequence, Leonard turns her camera to shop fronts and warehouses in both Brooklyn and Kampala, tracking the global trail of doubly coded commodity: the transformation of discarded clothing, donated to charities in Western centers, into fashionable wear in poorer, supposedly decolonized countries. This work makes visible one concrete strand in the dense trafficking of material goods and dreams across the globe that the spectacular imagery and ideologies of globalization tend to obscure. As such, it offers up a thoroughly contemporary metaphor.

In part 3, "Afterworlds," a number of authors explore the options for artists in a global situation that can no longer be confidently understood as divided into geopolitical worlds of the First, Second, Third, and Fourth variety. Residues of this reductive structure certainly continue to exist, not least on the edges and in some of the thinking in the centers of Cold War empires. Since 1989, however, this world picture has been unraveling with increasing speed: while this has been most obvious in the former Soviet Union, another signal of its demise may be the failure of the overstretched U.S. emperium in the Middle East. At the same, the processes of decolonization have continued to unfold, not only in Africa, but indeed everywhere, precipitating the world as a whole into a "postcolonial constellation." This has led to the emergence of unexpected, hybrid state formations, most evidently in China. These developments have posed new challenges to artists; the chapters in this section trace the challenges in careful detail.

All of these deformations continue into the present, shaping its complexity as a simultaneity of antinomies. One of the most striking features of contemporaneity is the coexistence of very distinct senses of time, of what it is to exist now, to be in place, and to act, in relation to imagined histories and possible futures. Part 4, "Cotemporalities," sets out a range of pathways into this complexity. These include an overview of political principles, of different forms of governmentality; a study of how earlier kinds of radical ambition might be reinterpreted in ways useful for present purposes; a proposal about shifts in aesthetic attention, and another about forms of activist intervention, during what some label "the information age." The book concludes with an essay that returns to the question posed at the beginning and reviews contemporary artists' responses to the main currents of our contemporary condition.

All of these voices are individual. There is no party line here. Nor can there be, in a world in which parties can only be partisans of limited vision, bent on imposing their partial-sightedness on others, often as a black-and-white blindness. This collection eschews any attempt at foreclosure, and all pretence at speaking from a position of totalized knowledge. Instead, the authors recognize that—within the realms of art and culture—the questions identified here are among the most important posed by the antinomies that drive contemporaneity. We hope that these essays help clarify the terms in which these questions are being put, that they provide useful hints toward some answers, as well as raising further, sharp questions.

Terry Smith, Okwui Enwezor, Nancy Condee

ACKNOWLEDGMENTS

Our first thanks goes to James Thomas for his editorial assistance with obtaining the illustrations and permissions, to Karen Lillis for her work on the bibliography, and to Miguel Rojas. We also thank Ken Wissoker and his colleagues at Duke University Press, including Courtney Berger for taking on this publication; Molly Balikov, Maura High, and Amy Ruth Buchanan for seeing it through; and the anonymous readers for their detailed and helpful comments. We are grateful to the artists and others who have supplied illustrations and permissions, in particular Zoe Leonard for making available a wonderful set of images from her *Analogue* series of photographs.

As we indicate in the introduction, this book is based on papers given at a symposium entitled "Modernity ≠ Contemporaneity: Antinomies of Art and Culture after the Twentieth Century," held at the University of Pittsburgh, November 4–6, 2004. We thank the presenters at that symposium for their efforts in reviewing and, in many cases, substantially revising their texts for this volume. In most cases, presenters were able to make their texts available for publication. Lev Manovich was unable to present his invited paper, but has developed it into a chapter for this volume.

At the University of Pittsburgh, we are grateful for the continuing support of Professor N. John Cooper, dean of the School of Arts and Sciences, and our colleagues in the Department of the History of Art and Architecture and in the Graduate Program in Cultural Studies. We thank librarians and staff at the Frick Fine Arts Library, University of Pittsburgh; the Schaeffer Research Library, University of Sydney; and the National Humanities Center, Research Triangle Park, North Carolina.

As the 2004 symposium was the basis of the book, we would like to acknowledge those who contributed to its realization. Many have continued in support of our efforts to bring it to publication. The symposium was generously funded by the Pittsburgh Foundation, The Heinz Endowments, and the Office of the Provost and the Dean, School of Arts and Sciences, University of Pittsburgh. Additional support came from the University Center for International Studies, Graduate School of Public and International Affairs, University of Pittsburgh; the Mattress Factory; the Carnegie Museum of Art; the Andy Warhol Museum; and Labwerks. A number of individuals were pivotal to its success. These include Mark Nordenberg, N. John Cooper, Colin McCabe, Elizabeth Conforti, Dick Howe, Giuseppina Mecchia, Aparna Nayak-Guercio, Trish White, Volodia Padunov, Ilya Goldin, Barbara Vattimo, Barbara McCloskey, Kirk Savage, Miguel Rojas, and Linda Hicks; the student volunteers at the University of Pittsburgh; Renee Abrams and Linda Indovina of Renee Abrams Associates; Barbara Luderowski, Michael Olijnyk, and Jennifer Barron at the Mattress Factory; Tom Sokolowski and Jessica Gogan at the Warhol Museum; Richard Armstrong, Laura Hoptman, Marilyn Russell, Lucy Stewart, Elizabeth Thomas, and Sarah Hromak at the Carnegie Museum of Art; Judith Schachter, Susanne Slavick, and Jennifer Strayer of Carnegie Mellon University; Jessica Fest and Greg Brickl of Labwerks; Jeanne Pearlman of The Pittsburgh Foundation; Janet Sarbaugh of The Heinz Endowments; Brett Designs; and Isaac Julien, Chika Okeke, and Carlos Basualdo.

INTRODUCTION: THE CONTEMPORANEITY QUESTION

TERRY SMITH

In the aftermath of modernity, and the passing of the postmodern, how are we to know and show what it is to live in the conditions of contemporaneity?

What a loaded question! Those with an interest in knowing how big-picture concepts tie to the particularities of existence these days will immediately recognize its challenges. For those involved in showing the rest of us how these particularities resonate with more general purport—that is to say, for artists, writers, teachers, thinkers, and the many other workers on matters symbolic (recently labeled "the creative class")—it may be among *the* most pressing. This book interrogates these kinds of connections in the light of this kind of question. It explores the conditions that have startled such questions into the open, charts their impact within a variety of academic disciplines and cultural domains, and notes their polemic force in public debate. The chapters that follow offer a set of subtle and engaged readings of the most important antinomies at work in the arts and in culture at large today. There is much contestation, and some surprising points of agreement. What emerges are the lineaments of new kinds of approaches to some important issues—not least, the loaded, and of course quite contemporaneous, question of what kinds of purchase macro-descriptors such as modernity and postmodernity retain, and what implications that asking such a question might have for contemporary life, thought, and art.

In early November 2004, the contemporaneity question—its provocations and ambiguities no less naked to the gaze than its character as an entreaty—was posed to a public meeting of scholars, theorists, artists, critics, and curators at the University of Pittsburgh. The occasion was a symposium, "Modernity ≠ Contemporaneity: Antinomies of Art and Culture after the Twentieth Century," convened by the editors of this volume as a complement to the Fifty-fourth Carnegie International Exhibition at the Carnegie Museum of Art.[1] The eminence of some participants had made their names nearly synonymous with the concepts of modernity and modernism, postmodernity and postmodernism. Others, however, had become accustomed to dismissing the viability of such world picturing, or to resisting it in the name of radical particularity. Still others were active proponents of more partial, even partisan descriptors. Three generations of thinking on these matters, from widely different perspectives and from all over the globe, were represented. This book maps out the considerations that led to the posing of the question of contemporaneity, and records the extraordinary responses that it received, both at the symposium and in the papers that have been revised by their authors as chapters for this volume.

CHANGING TIME

For a number of years there have been indications of profound realignments between the great formations of modernity, and of the emergence of what may be new formations. The 9/11 moment is a recent flashpoint of both civilizational and region-to-region conflict, and it continues to be used as a justification for governments of all stripes to declare open-ended states of emergency, and as an umbrella for the imposition of repressive agendas in many countries, not least the United States. Intractable, irresolvable "events" of this kind have come to seem almost normal in the state of aftermath: the wars in Afghanistan and Iraq; the uncertain prospect of a U.S. emperium; the question of European polity, internally and externally; the implosive fallout of the Second World and the reemergence of authoritarianism and "democracy" within it; in the ex-Soviet peripheries, the suddenness of unReal states, and of the apparent extension of Europe; continuing conflicts in the Middle East, Central Europe, Africa, and the Pacific; the deadly inadequacy of both tribalism and modernization as models for decolonization in Africa; the crisis of post–World War II international institutions as political and economic mediators (United Nations, International Monetary Fund, World Bank); the revival of leftist governments in South America; the accelerating concentration of wealth in a few countries, and within those countries its concentration in the few; ecological time bombs everywhere, and the looming threat of societal collapse; the ubiquity and diversification of specular culture; the concentration and narrowing of media, in contrast to the spread of the Internet; contradictions within and between regu-

lated and coercive economies and deregulated and criminal ones; the coexistence of multiple economies and cultures within singular state formations
(most prominently, now, China); the proliferation of protest movements and
alternative networks; the retreat toward bunker architecture at the centers and
proliferation of ingenious, adaptive architecture in the border zones of swelling
cosmopoli; and the emergence of distinctively different models of appropriate
artistic practice, as manifested in major survey exhibitions, such as documenta
11 of 2002 and the Fiftieth Venice Biennale in 2003, along with the retreat into
compromise that has marked much curatorial planning since then—with some
exceptions, such as the 2006 editions of the Sydney Biennale and the Second
Seville Biennial, also in 2006.[2]

These are just some of the most obvious new formations and fissures at the
most public, political levels. Intense friction between them has set the world's
agenda since the end of the Cold War, creating a nearly universal condition of
permanent-seeming aftermath—Ground Zero everywhere—yet also inspiring
insights into adaptable modes of active resistance and hopeful persistence.
While there are many elements in a list such as this that are familiar from
accounts of modernity and postmodernity, something about the mix, the
mood, and the outcome seems to be becoming distinctive. On all levels, in every
sphere, but above all at the level of public polity, there is an evident need for
fresh ways of seeing the shape of present diversity. In the following sections I
will set out the framework of concerns that led to the posing of the lead
question about contemporaneity, situate the symposium in its immediate political context, and then introduce the chapters that make up this volume.

MAPPING MODERNITY

One of the most suggestive essays in the history of ideas—at least as that field
bears on the arts—is "Modernity and Literary Tradition," by Hans Robert Jauss.[3]
It is a subtle study of conceptions of the modern—"the consciousness, that is, of
having taken a step from the old to the new"—ranging from ordinary Latin usage
in the ancient world to the self-conscious statements of the mid-nineteenth
century. The story culminates in Charles Baudelaire's famous formulation of
1864: "La modernité, c'est le transitoire, le fugutif, le contingent, la moitié de
l'art, dont l'autre moitié est l'éternel et l'immutable" ("*modernité*, that is, the
transitory, the fugitive, the contingent, the half of art, the other half of which is
the eternal and the immutable").[4] For Jauss, writing in 1970, Baudelaire's insight
marked "the threshold of our current modernity." He was right about that.
Jürgen Habermas and Matei Calinescu are prominent among those who have

since attempted to chart the next chapter, to bring Jauss's account up to date.[5] No one has done so with the gusto and the philological precision that Jauss applied to the earlier history. In fact, much more acumen was displayed in profiling the appearance of concepts of postmodernity in cultural discourse, and doing so, in the great syntheses of Fredric Jameson and David Harvey, and in studies such as John Frow's *What Was Postmodernism?*, while it was happening.[6]

In mid-nineteenth-century Paris, Baudelaire's act of definition gained much of its force from its double nature: it frightened by insisting on the priority of the immediate, the chancy, the passing present, but it was thrilling, too, in its promise, to Modern artists of consequence, that a timeless art could be distilled from the random-seeming mobility of the contemporary. This art would be classic—perhaps eventually, perhaps soon—but in ways that neither the classical artists of the distant past nor the romantic artists of the recent past could ever have imagined. It would be new beauty, a modern eternality, whatever the future may hold. No wonder Baudelaire's doublet has attracted artists and critics, curators and collectors, ever since. It has also attracted sociologists, political scientists, commentators, and ideologues of many stripes.[7] It held out the hope of a modernist realism that would outlast its necessary (but never sufficient) contemporaneity.[8] It was the best of Modernism.

Yet modernity in the larger sense—as an ideology, a social formation, a world order—can now be seen to have developed such that it ratcheted up "the transitory, the fugitive, the contingent" as facts of experience and history to such a pitch that it gradually but inevitably obliterated the other half of the doublet. Throughout much of the twentieth century, there was an incessant cycling between the two halves, a phenomenon that defined the main features of Modern art: its play of acceptance and rejection of the elements of modern life, its mobilizing of aspects of both high and popular culture, its interlacing of traditional practices with those of the new mechanical means of reproduction, its division into a formal and a historical/critical/political avant-garde, its tracking in and out of the museum. Many of these tensions became, in time, and especially in Europe and the United States, comfortably resolved. Modern art had achieved its own immutable eternality. Yet, in the 1960s and 1970s, when larger world changes and internal tensions pushed the edifice of modernity into overload, art began to struggle to generate productive syntheses. It does so now, in the form of official Contemporary Art, as echoes of its past glories. The antithetical energy of modernity's internal contract has faded, its trading off the past for the future is no longer foundational, its ice-calm control, however dazzling, is thinning fast.

Nowadays, the idea of returning to "the eternal and the immutable," or of forging new forms of both, appears anachronistic, quaint, and feeble, or worse, infantile. More broadly, the qualities of modernity have been forced into new conjunctions. Aspects of these changes were first recognized under the label "postmodernity," and their artistic, fashion, and intellectual manifestations soon attracted the appellation "Postmodernism." The nagging concern right now is that, for all their history as outcomes of modernity, does not the evolution of these qualities amount to a fundamentally changed situation? Have not forces that preexisted modernity returned unavoidably, do they not insist on the validity of other worldviews? Modernity has not, for decades, been able to maintain its division of the world into those who live in modern times and those who, while physically present, were regarded as noncontemporaneous beings. In arguing that the global spread of information and the instantaneousness of its communication now means that the "sociotemporal world order is changing in favor of contemporaneity for all," historian Wolf Schäfer quotes a passage from Cheikh Hamidou Kane's 1961 novel *Ambiguous Adventure*, an exchange between the father of a young Senegalese revolutionary and a French teacher: "We have not had the same past, you and ourselves, but we shall have, strictly, the same future. The era of separate destinies has run its course. In that sense, the end of the world has indeed come for every one of us, because no one can any longer live by the simple carrying out of what he himself is."[9]

Increased opportunity of access has not, of course, meant equality of outcome—on the contrary—nor has it meant (contrary to early fears about globalization) homogeneity of choices. During the period of modernity's dominance, the downside of what used to be called cultural imperialism was a kind of ethnic cleansing carried out by the displacement of unmodern peoples into past, slower, or frozen time. In a mediascape characterized by such contrary forces as instant communication of key decisions by political leaders and the capacity to demonstrate against them anywhere across the globe within the same news cycle, the power to force everyone forward in broadly the same direction has been lost. In many parts of the world, consciousness is concerned with taking many steps, fast, not from the old to the new, but vice versa. Multiple temporalities are the rule these days, and their conceptions of historical development move in multifarious directions. Against this broad tide, fundamentalisms move in just one direction, implacably. In these conflicted circumstances, any appellation that ties a current world description entirely to modernity, in however conditional a manner, and however decked out with a modified version of postmodernity, will miss as much of the main point as do the fundamentalisms.

Are we at a threshold of large-scale meaning change, yet again? If so, it is one that has built its gateway around us, through indirection, and as an outcome of quite other great changes, not least the reduction of modernity to "the only remaining superpower," the evaporation of postmodernist fashions as a one-generation wonder, and, some would argue, the isolation of postmodernity as a fate of the West (or, at least, of many parts and elements of it) but not the world. Nor does postmodernity seem any longer to explain, to others, enough of what is happening in what remains of the West as the world migrates to it, everyone changing as they come and go.

In these circumstances, a number of options loom. Contributors to this volume exemplify their variety. They tend, however, in two main directions. One mainstream returns to modernity, to revised visions of its richness in the West, of its multiplicity and distinctiveness elsewhere, and of the tensions across its many borders. The presumption here is that this revisioned modernity will return to take up a paradigmatic role, hopefully one less conflicted and deadly than that which reached its apogee in the twentieth century. Another seeks a strategic deferral of the question of the nature of the contemporary world picture while the business of critique continues, along with the identification of valued particularities. The hope here is that a configuration open to the antinomies of the present will emerge, one that tends toward hope, equity, and freedom—a genuine globalism, for example, or cosmopolitan citizenship. The risk in deferral is that it leaves effective definition in the hands of those with the will and power to impose their definitions. Given the current disposition of force in the world, and the evangelical and bellicose disposition of those forces, this is a risk indeed. Surely it is time to push critique further, to grasp a more supple set of ways of being in time now, and to shift to another set of terms. There is such a set, lying close by. But first another quick detour through the modern.

THE THICKENING OF THE PRESENT

In the ancient world, around the shores of the Mediterranean, the word "modern" (*modernus*) distinguished a mood, or mode, of fullness emergent in the otherwise ordinary passing of time, and within the predictable unfolding of fashion (*hodiernus*, "of today"). This sense that the present could be pregnant with something special about itself persisted until late medieval times, when contrast with what was seen to be the past, and then several past periods, became central to the meaning of modern. An early formulation was that of Saint Augustine: "There are three times: a present time of past things; a present time of present things; and a present time of future things."[10]

In the expanded modern world, however, "modern" became the core of a set of terms that narrated the two-centuries-long formation of modernity in terms of novelty, pastness, and futurism, not least those of its definitive artistic currents, Modern Art and modernism, Modern Movement architecture, and modern or contemporary design. Despite the vibrancy of these tendencies, the "modern" aged, as its time went on, until it became, in a paradox tolerated by most, historical. Indeed, it became the name of its own period, one that would, it was presumed, become increasingly modern, without end.

In art world discourse for most of the twentieth century—especially in the 1920s and the 1960s, when modernist attitudes prevailed—"contemporary" served mainly as a default for "modern." In his proposal for the symposium, Boris Groys pointed out the main reason: "Modern art is (or, rather, was) directed toward the future. Being modern means to live in a project, to practice a work in progress. Because of this permanent movement toward the future, modern art tends to overlook, to forget the present, to reduce it to a permanently self-effacing moment of transition from past to future."[11] Nevertheless, a number of the most engaged contemporary artists are redefining what it means to live in a project, and doing so in terms that acknowledge the power of the present. Examples of their work are regularly cited in the chapters that follow. This shift has been occurring since the decline of modernism in the 1980s, and has appeared in institutional naming—of galleries, museums, auction house departments, academic courses, and textbook titles—which, however, tend to use "contemporary" as a soft signifier of current plurality. This reflects broad-scale, ordinary usage: in English, and in some but not all other European languages, in China and much of Asia—"modern" has surrendered currency to the term "contemporary" and its cognates. Saint Augustine's accumulation of presents has returned, uncannily, to currency.

REGARDING CONTEMPORANEITY

The word "contemporary" has always meant more than just the plain and passing present. Its etymology, we can now see, is as rich as that of "modern." The term calibrates a number of distinct but related ways of being *in* or *with* time, even of being *in* and *out* of time at the same time. Indeed, for a while, during the seventeenth century in England, it seemed that the contraction "cotemporary" might overtake it to express this strange currency. Current editions of the *Oxford English Dictionary* give four major meanings. They are all relational, turning on prepositions, on being placed "to," "from," "at," or "during" time. There is the strong sense of "Belonging *to* the same time, age, or period" (1.a.), the coincidental "Having existed or lived *from* the same date,

equal in age, coeval" (2), and the adventitious "Occurring *at* the same moment
of time, or *during* the same period; occupying the same definite period, contemporaneous, simultaneous" (3). In each of these three meanings there is a
distinctive sense of presentness, of being in the present, of beings who are (that
are) present to each other, and to the time they happen to be in. Of course, these
kinds of relationships have occurred at all times in the historical past, do so
now, and will do so in the future. The second and third meanings make this
clear, whereas the first points to the phenomenon of two or more people,
events, ideas, or things, "belonging" to the same historical time. Yet, even here,
while the connectedness is stronger, while the phenomena may have some sense
of being joined by their contemporaneousness, they may equally well do so, as it
were, separately, standing alongside yet apart from each other, existing in simple simultaneity. They may also subsist in a complex awareness that, given
human difference, their contemporaries may not stand in the same, or even a
similar, relation to world time as they do; yet we are all, at the same time,
touched by what is now global time—a new phase, perhaps, in what Fernand
Braudel named "world time."[12] Given the diversity of present experiences of
temporality, and our increased awareness of this diversity, it is becoming more
and more common to feel oneself as standing, in important senses, at once
within and *against* the times.

It is the OED's fourth definition of "contemporary" that brings persons,
things, ideas, and time together under a one-directional banner: "Modern; of
or characteristic of the present period; especially up-to-date, ultra-modern;
specifically designating art of a markedly *avant-garde* quality, or furniture,
building, decoration, etc. having modern characteristics." In this definition, the
two words have finally exchanged their core meaning: the contemporary has
become the new modern. We are, on this logic, emerging out of the Modern
Age, or Era, and into that of the Contemporary.

To leap to such a conclusion would be to miss an essential quality of contemporaneousness: its immediacy, its presentness, its instantaneity, its prioritizing
of the moment over the time, the instant over the epoch, of direct experience of
multiplicitous complexity over the singular simplicity of distanced reflection. It
is the pregnant present of the original meaning of "modern," but without its
subsequent contract with the future. It is the first, discomforting part of Baudelaire's famous doublet, but bereft of the comfort of the second part. If we were
to generalize this quality (of course, against its grain) as a key to world picturing, we would see its constituent features manifest there, to the virtual exclusion
of other explanations. We would see, then, that *contemporaneity consists precisely in the acceleration, ubiquity, and constancy of radical disjunctures of percep-*

tion, of mismatching ways of seeing and valuing the same world, in the actual coincidence of asynchronous temporalities, in the jostling contingency of various cultural and social multiplicities, all thrown together in ways that highlight the fast-growing inequalities within and between them. This certainly looks like the world as it is now. No longer does it feel like "our time," because "our" cannot stretch to encompass its contrariness. Nor, indeed, is it "a time," because if the modern was inclined above all to define itself as a period, and sort the past into periods, in contemporary conditions periodization is impossible.[13] The only potentially permanent thing about this state of affairs is that it may last for an unspecifiable amount of time: the present may become, perversely, "eternal." Not, however, in a state of wrought transfiguration, as Baudelaire had hoped, but as a kind of incessant incipience, of the kind theorized by Jacques Derrida as *à venir*—perpetual advent, that which is, while impossible to foresee or predict, always to come.[14]

Multeity, adventitiousness, and inequity are not only the most striking features on any short list of the qualities of contemporaneity; they are at its volatile core. Unlike Baudelaire's three initial markers of *modernité* ("the transitory, the fugitive, the contingent"), they are not the symptoms of a deeper stability, or an entry point to its achievement. In the aftermath of modernity, and the passing of the postmodern, they may be *all that there is.* This is why there is no longer any overarching explanatory totality that accurately accumulates and convincingly accounts for these proliferating differences. The particular, it seems, is now general, and, perhaps, forever shall be.

This is not a recommendation for stand-alone, singularizing particularism— rather, it is an appeal for radical particularism to work with and against radical generalization, to treat all the elements in the mix as antinomies. Global historians continue to do us great service by tracking the trajectories of large forces that unfold through lengthy durations. These include the social and ecological elements—localized, metropolitan, and cosmopolitan—of the successively expanding "human web" described by J. R. McNeill and William H. McNeill.[15] Yet it is equally important to weave into these accounts some recognition of the less visible workings of what Manuel DeLanda names "matter-energy."[16] A paradoxical outcome of recent long-term historical explanations is their unusual degree of uncertainty with regard to the immediate future.[17] While belief in the persistence through the present of ongoing formations is widespread, the forms in which that might occur seem less predictable. Obsession with the past, and concern about the complexities of the present, have tended to thicken our awareness of it, at the expense of expectations about the future. Social geographers such as Jared Diamond alert us to the prospect that societies based on guns, germs, and steel are on the verge of immanent collapse if they continue to maintain present modes of thought and organization.[18] As Wolf Schäfer (rather mildly) puts it, "coming to terms with the complexity of the present time, which results from the massive parallelism of cultural contemporaneities, is obviously one of the great challenges."[19] The most developed theorization of contemporaneity so far advanced is that of Marc Augé. Responding to the crisis in anthropology brought about by decolonization, he boldly draws out the consequences of the fact that the core object of that colonial discipline suddenly ceased to be the remote other—rather, it became the proximate other and then, precipitously, othernesses within ourselves. His insight is that what counts in contemporaneity (which he labels "supermodernity") is none of these identities-in-formation alone but their existence in relation to each other. "The world's inhabitants have at last become truly contemporaneous, and yet the world's diversity is recomposed every moment; this is the paradox of our day."[20]

By the turn of the twenty-first century, the elements of accelerated modernity picked out during the 1970s by the theorists of postmodernism had become, with a precise perversity, popular. When, in late 2004, Apple Inc. sought a slogan to market its iPod Shuffle—a portable device for playing digitalized music files installed and organized not, as in the original iPod, by the owner but by the machine itself, which plays them in a preprogramed but unpredictable sequence—it chose "Life is Random." Reading that on billboards, or seeing it on television, seemed more than tautological. During the early months of 2005, the best-selling book on the *New York Times* nonfiction list was Malcolm Gladwell's *Blink*. Subtitled *The Power of Thinking without Thinking*, it celebrated the acuity of instant, intuitive judgement, as exemplified in the attributive ability of art connoisseurs.[21] These are two widely separated but convergent instances of contemporaneity recognizing, and celebrating, itself in its most superficial manifestations.

In public discourse, "master narratives" not only persist but also have become increasingly simplified (perhaps so that they can be grasped, and believed, without thinking). They continue to promise everything from continual modernizing progress—"freedom" and "democracy" are the watchwords of U.S. expansion into the Middle East—to the return of spiritual leaders under the banner, for example, of jihad. Certainly the commanding, beguiling power of these simplifications builds followings in larger and larger numbers. But their partiality inevitably means that they do so in ways that divide each bloc of believers more and more from the others, with the net effect that they not only cast out "unbelievers" but also undermine their own future triumph. In the hearts of their spiritual leaders, there is a dawning sense that world domination by any one set of views is impossible in human affairs, that not even their fundamentalism is applicable to all human kind, that the others will, mostly, remain Other. This sense underlies, and deeply threatens, the homogenizing thrusts of certain kinds of economic globalization, obliging it to adapt to local circumstances. It also renders provisional, and often gestural, the appeals to universal rights that have been for decades an available language for negotiation between competing interests. This is dangerous. New forms of translation need to be found for channeling the world's friction.

Differences that are as profound as these do not lie side by side, peacefully, nor do they sit up separately in some static array awaiting our inspection. They are actively implicated in one another, all over the place, all the time, just as every one of us lives in them, always. Their interaction is a major work of the world, of the world on us and us on the world. We are, all of us, thoroughly embedded inside these processes. Too many of them are violently bent on the erasure of the other. Some, however, seek reconciliation within a framework of respect for difference. The Australian contemporary Aboriginal art movement, for example, is significantly driven by this impulse. All of these elements were present in events such as the 9/11 attacks on various U.S. "icons of economic and military power"—an incomplete event with continuing effects in all spheres of life. While the language of universals remains current, reflecting the global networks that actually and materially connect the world's diversity, it always arises in concrete particulars, and increasingly in the form of frictional encounters.[22]

IMMEDIATE POLITICS

One condition unavoidable in a conference about the present held in the United States (or, perhaps, anywhere else) in the first week of November 2004 was the presidential election campaign, completed just two days before. The usual clichés about this being "the most important election ever" had been advanced, at their normal, hyperbolic level. There were, however, good reasons to take such a claim seriously. Like many others, the symposium conveners had thought that the country—and all those elsewhere in the world affected by U.S. policy and actions (that is to say, most of us)—would likely be in a state of suspension similar to that which occurred in the weeks following the 2000 election, when the outcome was not clear, the will of the people so divided that its accurate expression became impossible to discern, and a partisan institutional solution was imposed, with the result that a much-vaunted political system seemed to survive by chance, through the wielding of raw power, and to subsist through blind luck. Suspension of disbelief, a sense of waiting for the fallout from events incompletely understood, dread of arbitrary punishment, fearful anticipation of obscure disaster, uncertainty with regard to both past and future—these are just some of the moods of aftermath that the symposium set out to explore. They played a key role in the 2004 campaign, which had become a pitched battle between steadfast commitment to a few simple values, a plain list of patriotic staples, and a realistic recognition that, on September 11, 2001, the world's complexity had come home to roost.

Nor was this great divide confined to the messages sent by candidates Bush and Kerry. That other global players could see its signature was evident in their comments made during the campaign period. British prime minister Tony Blair obediently explained the U.S. president's banalities in more subtle registers. Osama bin Laden addressed the American people, via video, enumerating a decades-long list of U.S. attacks on Muslims in the Middle East, to which, he claimed, Al Qaeda was reacting, and doing so with demonstrable effectiveness. Faced with the persistence of exploding planes, subway bombs, schools held hostage, and botched rescue attempts, Russian president Vladimir Putin came clean: "We have to admit that we failed to recognize the complexity and danger of the processes going on in our country and the world as a whole."[23] Nevertheless, by a sufficient majority, on November 2, 2004, the U.S. electorate accepted, as a truth or at least a tolerable fiction, the gross simplification that the world was riven by just two tendencies: globalization, led by the U.S. government and U.S. companies, was a progressive, universal good, whereas all forces ranged against it were deluded at best, or, at worst, terrorists. Along with many others elsewhere, they accepted the argument that the warring between globalization and terrorism is definitive of the present time, and that the winning of this war will define the future. Or, perhaps more accurately, they were prepared, for various quite particular reasons of self-interest, to be governed by those who held this view. As these realizations sunk in, they infiltrated the speech of the symposium in a variety of ways.

One political season, however fraught, in one country, however influential, does not in itself signal a change in the ways the world strives to understand itself. Nor does one occurrence, however traumatic its outcomes. In the months immediately following the attacks of September 11, 2001, it became a commonplace, especially among citizens of the United States, to characterize "9/11" as "The Event That Changed the World Forever." Phrases such as "Nothing Will Ever Be the Same" concretized an already existent age of anxiety, and were a plea to be led out of the strangeness through an all-out attack on fear, quickly labeled by a desperate media and an opportunist president as a "War on Terror," to be carried out both at home and abroad. Originating in genuine shock, the statement elevated specific bewilderment into an act of History; it generalized immediate affect into a cliché that recognized pain but promised ultimate comfort. Public rhetoric, so often confined to the pragmatics of average self-interest —as in the case of the phrase "It's the economy, stupid!" that swung the 1992 presidential campaign in Bill Clinton's favor—inflated itself to the stratosphere. Many critical thinkers, artists among them, were caught short.

While simplification might dominate the public rhetoric of elites across the political spectrum, and prevail in elections at major power centers, it less and less matches the everyday experience and the imaginary lives of more and more people. Voters in India in 2004 threw out a fundamentalist regime; in 2005 voters in "core" European nations refused to ratify a Constitution for Europe; petty dictators are being dislodged from the periphery of the former Soviet empire; in 2006 voters in the United States finally lost patience with the tissue of self-deception that shrouded the conduct of U.S. policy in the Middle East and called it for what it was, a colonialist enterprise being pointlessly pursued in postcolonial times; meanwhile, within Islam, a great contestation is occurring between literalist and open forms of belief, one that may dislodge the rigidity of its ruling houses and perhaps its fundamentalisms . . . condensed instances of each of these developments are not only instantly seen all around the world, and seen for what they are, but in one form or another they are felt to matter everywhere. They are the antinomies of contemporaneity: now, more than before, the services of those able to grasp complexity, and place its clarity before the people, are not only necessary but, in the longer or shorter run, may stand a chance of being effective.

ANTOLOGIES OF THE PRESENT

In the aftermath of modernity, and the passing of the postmodern, how are we to know and show what it is to live in the conditions of contemporaneity?

While few defenders of Postmodernism as a style in art or architecture remain, many still take postmodernity as the best available critical theory of global capital and its cultures in the contemporary world. Pivotal to the planning of the 2004 symposium and this volume were the theories of postmodernity as the form of "the cultural logic of late capitalism" advanced during the 1980s by Fredric Jameson and elaborated by David Harvey. Jameson continued to deepen his analyses in a number of books that warned against the hegemonic tendencies in ideas of globalization and emphasized the antinomial nature of the main forces constituting postmodernity.[24] His more recent work has been a salutary signal of the need to confront these issues in all of their stark intractability. In *A Singular Modernity* he warns against pluralist dreams of "alternative modernities," pointing out that such analyses suit the ideologues of global capitalism.[25] Against this, he sets out to confront the persistent power of modernity as a necessarily periodizing, situational "narrative category," and that of "artistic modernism," which "necessarily posits an experience of the work in the present."[26] Attacking modernity for its ideological work on behalf of capitalism, and Modernism for its incessant recursions to formalism and putative artistic autonomy, Jameson confined their usefulness as concepts to the past, and concluded that "ontologies of the present demand archaeologies of future, not forecasts of the past."[27]

The chapters in this book pursue this goal in a variety of ways. In the first, Antonio Negri poses a key question: "What does it mean to be 'contemporary' between modernity and postmodernity?" A lot rides on that "between." Negri argues for a postmodernism that escapes "the direct lineage of modernity." After carefully measuring the concept of contemporaneity against each of the elements in his own extraordinarily subtle conceptions of postmodernity and of Empire, Negri concludes that it subsists *within* postmodernity, originating at the points of its most radical break with modernity and is manifest now at its points of most radical potential. Responding directly to the ideas advanced by the symposium convenors, he states: "Contemporaneity (as you define it) is situated in postmodernity, when postmodernity is understood as a field of forces that are not only new and orbiting the global circuit, but are also innovative and antagonistic. . . . Contemporaneity is the only way to express the eternal will to resistance and freedom." As Geeta Kapur shows in the second chapter, exactly this type of will was expressed by the people of India in their vote in the 2004 national elections, as it had been in the work of a number of documentary filmmakers.

Staunch defenders of a type of Modernism that is committed to focused, exact acknowledgment of the specificities of its mediums as the only possible pathway for serious art today (explicitly in this volume, Rosalind Krauss) seem nonetheless satisfied with postmodernity, particularly that defined by Fredric Jameson, as an adequate world descriptor. Other art world voices propose that Modernism needs to be updated: in his contribution to the symposium (unfortunately not in this volume) curator Nicolas Bourriaud extended his now quite famous description of major tendencies in current art (relational aesthetics, postproduction art) by identifying what he called an *altermodernism*—the Modernism of the others, a worldwide spread of distinct but related Modernisms.[28] The installation, now ubiquitous in contemporary art exhibitions, is explored by Boris Groys, who argues that it designates a space both literal and metaphorical, in which anything from the actual world may be made at once present and provisional. Because this occurs without evoking the implied social and aesthetic narratives of modernity and Modernism, installation, he suggests, is the quintessentially contemporary art form.

Another major theme in the chapters that follow begins from the recognition that periodizing generalizations such as "modernity" and "postmodernity" were foreign to non-Western cultures, and that their imposition onto these cultures, while provocative of local Modernisms, was accomplished, as Sylvester Ogbechie and Colin Richards argue, at great and, in many cases, continuing cost. Nevertheless, as these authors, along with Monica Amor and Suely Rolnik, show, individual artists in such settings were quite capable of developing practices that absorbed and transcended the limits that others sought to impose. Jonathan Hay urges us to think of these complex exchanges and developments in terms of doubled and even para-modernities.

More broadly, Okwui Enwezor points out that decolonization has had as profound a set of effects as globalization (the latter might indeed be seen as a response to the former), not only in previously colonized cultures but also in those of the colonizers. The entire world is, from this point of view, in a postcolonial constellation. Modernity and postmodernity are seen as having diminishing relevance to other cultures at the borders of Europe and beyond the West. Nancy Condee argues modernity was always a strange hybrid in the Soviet empire, and has become a malleable, yet still astringent, relic in the aftermath of its implosion. Contemporaneity, Gao Minglu suggests, has always been a permanent condition of Chinese culture (it being tradition-directed but never futuristic), yet is being redefined, according to Wu Hung, by the recent and current engagement of Chinese artists with the contemporary art world, itself increasingly internationalized beyond East-West, North-South divisions. Just how artists working in different parts of the world are responding to the situation in their regions and to the global condition of contemporaneity is an issue to which authors in this book constantly return.

In the last section, a number of authors offer pointers toward political orientation in present conditions. Bruno Latour argues for a return to consensus building based on an ecological model: the agreement among things as to their negotiated differences. James Meyer shows that the revival of interest among contemporary artists in the strategies of political engagement proposed during the 1960s and 1970s, however nostalgic, is also a searching for a useable past. What, then, of the impact of ubiquitous new media, especially digital? Lev Manovich urges us to notice the shift to "infoaesthetics," while McKenzie Wark lauds hacker interventions into the seeming dominance of the vector class. In the concluding chapter, Nikos Papastergiadis returns to the contemporaneity question posed at the beginning of this inquiry and sums up ways in which contemporary artists are facing its challenges.

Composer Karl-Heinz Stockhausen saw the 9/11 attacks, however deplorable, as having some of the sublime qualities of the "total work of art." During the culture wars of the 1980s in the United States, passionate conservatives such as Jesse Helms labeled certain artists "cultural terrorists." If it is to be truly contemporary, rather than an update of comfortable Modernism, the art of today must respond deeply to the complex conditions of contemporaneity. Does this put at risk the assumption, widespread among artists, that the very process of making art, the lifelong struggle for insight and originality, is fundamentally redemptive? The implied contract between artists and their societies—the invitation to provide beauty, insight, and provocation in exchange for tolerance and occasional support in pursuing one's obsessions—that has been forged over the past two centuries: what will be its fate in the new world disorder?

My own description of the current situation is one that would find varying degrees of support, and some strong opposition, among the contributors to this volume. I discern four major preoccupations in most contemporary art practice and discourse: continuing work on the implications of the fundamental provisionalization of art that erupted in the 1950s and 1960s; the institutionalization of Contemporary Art as a recursive refinement of high Modernism; the accommodation of the diversification of values introduced by practitioners emergent from all over the world; and a widespread inclination toward an art of small gestures, slight interventions, imagined transformations. (These last are, however, far from unstructured: time, place, medium, and mood preoccupy younger artists—theirs is an immediate response to the turbulence of temporalities, locations, mediations, and identities that typifies contemporary conditions.) All of these themes occur in the chapters that follow, where they receive different degrees of emphasis and are combined or challenged in distinctive ways. From the broadest perspective, they might be seen as art world responses to friction between the three antinomies that have come to dominate contemporary life: (1) globalization's thirst for hegemony in the face of increasing cultural differentiation (the multeity that was freed by decolonization), for control of time in the face of the proliferation of asynchronous temporalities, and for continuing exploitation of natural and (to a degree not yet seen) virtual resources against the increasing evidence of the inability of those resources to sustain this exploitation (for these among other reasons globalization is bound to fail); (2) the accelerating inequity among peoples, classes, and individuals that threatens both the desires for domination entertained by states, ideologies, and religions and the persistent dreams of liberation that continue to inspire individuals and peoples; and (3) an infoscape—or, better, a spectacle, an image economy or "iconomy," a regime of representation—capable of the potentially instant yet always thoroughly mediated communication of all information and any image anywhere, but which is at the same time fissured by the uneasy coexistence of highly specialist, closed-knowledge communities, alongside open, volatile subjects, and rampant popular fundamentalisms.[29]

Working within but also against this general condition (contemporaneity itself), artists everywhere supply particular kinds of provisional syntheses, or provide pauses in the overall rush into the unsynthesizable, showing its flows as if in section, or as glimpses frozen into objects intended for passers in between; artists model the minutiae of the world's processes as supplements that mark out possible pathways before us. It is no accident that works such as Gego's *Retricularea*, Lygia Clark's *The Structuring of the Self*, and Zoe Leonard's *Analogue* are highlighted in this book. These kinds of artistic offerings take shape somewhat distinctively in the different regions of the world, depending on the purchase of recent history and the specific demands of locality, but they also seem to be benefiting more and more from growing experience of interrogatory cosmopolitanism, from the circulation of critical ideas and examples. Mapping, accurately, the specific frictions of this world making—the actualities, the potentialities of it—is the most pressing task before contemporary art history. Relating such maps to the larger scale frictional machinery of the current world (dis)order—identifying, again, the actualities, the potentialities—is the main challenge facing cultural theory today. The essays in this book are offered as a contribution to these urgent enterprises.

NOTES

1 According to its curator, Laura Hoptman, the exhibition profiled certain artists whose work engaged with " 'the Ultimates' . . . [the] fundamentally human questions: the nature of life and death, the existence of God, the anatomy of belief." See her "The Essential Thirty-Eight," 35.

2 See Merewether, *2006 Sydney Biennale*; and Enwezor, *The Unhomely.*

3 In Jauss, *Literaturgeschichte als Provokation.* An English translation was published in *Critical Inquiry.*

4 Baudelaire, *The Painter of Modern Life and Other Essays*, 12.

5 Habermas, *The Philosophical Discourse of Modernity*; Calinescu, *Five Faces of Modernity.*

6 Frow, *What Was Postmodernism?* and *Time and Commodity Culture.* This essay charts,

among others, the classic statements of Fredric Jameson, Ihab Hassan, and David Harvey. See Jameson, "Postmodernism, or The Cultural Logic of Late Capitalism," and his *Postmodernism, or The Cultural Logic of Late Capitalism*; Hassan, *The Postmodern Turn*; and Harvey, *The Condition of Postmodernity*.

7   For example, Berman, *All That Is Solid Melts into Air*; Hall and Gieben, *Formations of Modernity*.

8   See Nochlin, *Realism*, 25–33.

9   Kane, *Ambiguous Adventure*, 79–80; quoted by Schäfer, "Global History and the Present Time," 119; Schäfer quotation page 118.

10   Augustine, *Confessions*, book 11, chap. 20: "tempora sunt tria, praesens de praetertis, praesens de praesentibus, praesens de futuris." I am indebted to Schäfer for this reminder.

11   See www.mc.pitt.edu/overview—Resources.asp.

12   As "the trades and rhythms of the globe," for Braudel world time is "a kind of superstructure of world history"; yet he cautions, "even in advanced countries, socially and economically speaking, world time has never counted for the whole of human existence" (*Civilization and Capitalism*, 3:19–20).

13   This responds to one of the dilemmas posed by Jameson in his *A Singular Modernity*.

14   A key concept in Derrida's later work, the most relevant texts here being *Specters of Marx* and the interview following 9/11 in Borradori, *Philosophy in a Time of Terror*.

15   McNeill and McNeill, *The Human Web*, introduction and chap. 8. Attempts to relate developments in art to larger social and natural formations have a long history. See Kaufmann, *Towards a Geography of Art*. An anthology of current efforts is Kaufmann and Pilliod, *Time and Place*.

16   DeLanda, *A Thousand Years of Nonlinear History*, 227–74. Just as relevant is his effort to develop Deleuze's ideas about assemblage to the layerings of social complexity between the personal and the global. See DeLanda, *A New Philosophy of Society*.

17   See Christian, *Maps of Time*.

18   Diamond, *Guns, Germs, and Steel* and *Collapse*.

19   Schäfer, "Global History and the Present Time," 109.

20   Augé, *The Anthropology of Contemporaneous Worlds*, 89. Augé is best known for his earlier book *Non-Places*, a brilliant study of the interstices of contemporary spatial experience, seen, along the lines of David Harvey, as accelerations of the conditions of modernity. An accessible introduction to the implications of this approach for anthropology today is Augé and Colleyn, *The World of the Anthropologist*.

21   Regarding art connoisseurs, Gladwell might have profited from reading Panofsky's 1927 essay, "Reflections on Historical Time," in which it is demonstrated that such connoisseurs are actually thoroughly expert art historians, applying, in the instant of looking at a previously unseen work of art, the same skills and competencies that are at the base of their scholarly essays, and which may be found in expository form there.

22   See Tsing, *Friction*.

23   Quoted by Meyers, "Putin Says Russia Faces Full 'War.'"

24   Jameson, *The Seeds of Time*.

25   Jameson, *A Singular Modernity*, 12.

26   Jameson, *A Singular Modernity*, 94–95.

27 Jameson, *A Singular Modernity,* 215. In his comments at the Pittsburgh symposium, Jameson expressed doubt as to whether the concept of contemporaneity was adequate to this task.

28 See Bourriaud, *Relational Aesthetics* and *Post-Production,* both reviewed in *October,* no. 110 (Fall 2004).

29 For expanded versions of this argument see my *The Architecture of Aftermath,* "Contemporary Art and Contemporaneity," "World Picturing in Contemporary Art," and "Creating Dangerously." I thank Susan Bielstein, W. J. T. Mitchell, Okwui Enwezor, and James Thomas for their assistance in refining these formulations.

PART 1: THE POLITICS OF TEMPORALITY

CONTEMPORANEITY BETWEEN MODERNITY AND POSTMODERNITY

ANTONIO NEGRI

TRANSLATED FROM THE ITALIAN BY GIUSEPPINA MECCHIA

Contemporaneity: what does it mean to be "contemporary" between modernity and postmodernity? For me, the definition of "contemporaneity" raises problems. Perhaps I will be somewhat polemical in pursuing this question, but it will be worth the effort.

Looking back at the cultural history of recent years, we see that (generally speaking) we have been steeped in the construction of a concept—and an experience—of postmodernity that wished to remain in the direct lineage of modernity. Postmodernity was, in fact, constructed as exasperation with modernity and the sublimation of its qualities. The Frankfurt school was, from this point of view, the source of the gravest misunderstandings and mystifications about the linear, "hypermodern," and sometimes catastrophic configuration of modernity. The school derived this sense and destiny from the pessimistic, often desperate, and always critical perspectives of a certain brand of Marxism typical of the 1920s. These conceptions, which could all be assigned to a common critical matrix, led to the construction of a "hypermodernity" rather than to a realistic vision of the coming into being of postmodernity and of the "radical break" that it implies.

As often happened in various Marxist heresies, the concept of "trend" was used in a teleological sense, as if it alluded to a necessity. Yet already in Marx, the concept of trend denotes the contrary: a break, a scission, a discontinuity. A trend is not dialectical; it is not reconciliatory in character. It implies the objective contradictions of development, and these contradictions recompose and intersect the subjective mechanisms of class struggle through a complex play of transformations in the material conditions of consciousness.

This line of thought is paradoxical and tragic: it has determined a situation in which critical-catastrophic traditions (from Lukacs to Adorno, passing through Benjamin) and critical-reactionary traditions defining capitalist development and the imperialist state (from Max Weber to Carl Schmitt) ended up coinciding. At that point, Heidegger's synthesis found itself right at home.

Postmodernity, in contrast, when it is defined as the real subsumption of society into Capital, reveals that this subsumption is not linear with respect to modernity, but antagonistic in nature. Not only is it antagonistic with respect to modernity, it is also contradictory in itself. Contemporaneity (as you define it)[1] is situated in postmodernity, when postmodernity is understood as a field of forces that are not only new and orbiting the global circuit, but are also innovative and antagonistic. To be contemporary one has to confront the end of the 1900s, the historical upheavals that characterized it, and the counterreformation happening today (if the comparison were not too flattering, one could talk about Bush as another, "hypermodern" Cardinal Bellarmino). Being contemporary will, then, mean defining postmodernity as a break with modernity and as a field in which antagonism is expressed in the most radical way.

In the most recent debates, and in particular in the field of cultural studies and in the discussions taking place in the so-called underdeveloped countries, the categories of modernity have become associated with and opposed to antimodernity. Similarly, modernity, in its constitution and in the forward movement that it implies, has been accompanied by a linear and rigid definition: the capitalist or the socialist model of development (we should never forget that socialism always had the skeleton of capitalism in its closet) triumphed in it.

But could "another" modernity exist? Another modernity, one that did not want to be, or better, did not want to construct itself either as a return to archaic forms of accumulation or as a reproduction of static (Eurocentric and Western) definitions of value, but that would determine alternative modes of development and a different material organization in the existing social and political forms? Another modernity, one that would not appeal to paradigmatic and utopian "use values" but would raise the question of acting differently and of transforming the world—starting from productive dimensions and established ways of creating commodities in our society? Debate about this possibility was extremely lively in some of the great developing countries (China, India, Latin America); nonetheless, the weight of a rigid postmodernity, fixated on Eurocentric or Western models of continuity with modernity, has neutralized all efforts to build something "other." More important, it also prevented the finding, within the process of development itself, of nondetermined alternatives that would not be fallaciously considered necessary or constraining but that could be free, inventive, original.

The idea of another modernity arose in the debate that took place in China between the end of the Cultural Revolution in 1976 and the massacre at Tienanmen Square in 1989. On that square the demonstrators were not the defenders of the West, but people who were looking to another, original way toward development within and beyond underdevelopment.

We need to remember that a similar debate developed during the classical period, during the birth of modernity. The field of antagonism identified at that time was one on which the ontological power of the multitude was being expressed. Against the capitalistic seizing of power, an instance of liberation was posited. Both Hobbes and Spinoza commented, from different viewpoints, on these antagonistic tendencies. Alternatives of this type are often found within the debates and struggles typical of developing societies. Today, we will not find a balance, or a new hope, unless we break the teleology of modernity, that is, the command imposed by Hobbes and capitalistic transcendentalism.

When we insist, today, on the concept of "contemporaneity," I am not certain that we simply want to summarize, to find an abbreviation, a logo for the break with the teleological paradigm of modernity. If we do want to take this shortcut, I welcome the theories of "contemporaneity," but they will have to assume as their foundation that the break with the paradigm of modernity, the opening toward a spectrum of new possibilities, is based on a new potential of resistance and difference.

When we talk of contemporaneity, therefore, we have to consider it as the field of antagonism. But why is this antagonism powerful? We need to stress, first of all, that this antagonism has nothing to do with the one formerly described in modernity, because it is rooted in a new social, economical, and political context: the context of biopolitics. When we say "biopolitics," on the one hand we mean that capitalist power has invested in the entirety of social relations, but at the same time we also consider this context as a historical reality inhabited by new subjects and new political and social configurations. Empire is a biopolitical reality; it is not simply a new capitalist organization of work. It is the ensemble of forces that traverse this reality and that express the power of life.

We cannot fully assume contemporaneity if we fail to thematize it within the passage from modernity to postmodernity, within the simultaneous passage from modern to postmodern biopolitics, between the invasion and the colonization of existence by power and the antagonistic dimension of the powerful contradictions present in the biopolitical context.

This configuration implies certain consequences.

(1) We can define the biopolitical context as the place where labor antagonisms have become social. When we say "social," we mean that the paradigm of work, or better yet of productive activities, pervades the whole society while becoming immaterial and cooperative. Today, the capitalist invasion of society, its subsumption by capital, is accompanied and contradicted by the transformation of the paradigm of work. Modern biopolitics were disciplinary; postmodern biopolitics are founded on control. Our deconstruction of modernity, therefore, revisits the material conditions of the totality of existence during the modern period in order to show contemporaneity as being the context for new contradictions.

If the social composition of contemporaneity has nothing to do, anymore, with social constitution within modernity, it is because innovative transformation is actually happening in the field of labor. We are talking about the passage from the mass worker to the social worker and from material to cognitive labor, as well as the transformation of the construction of value, which is no longer a measure of the time of production, but is, rather, the innovative construction of new mediations for the value of work. Here, the new technologies (new technological environments and new machines) are closely interwoven into a new social composition. The jump is decisive. As I noted before, understanding the present in terms of postmodern contemporaneity requires us to posit a new periodization in historical development. The change in the nature of work and of technology implies an anthropological mutation. Still—and this is the true meaning of a new historical periodization—these processes are not purely technical, nor are they simply anthropological (if anthropology is predicated on the individual); they are "social passages" tying the transformation of humanity to the facts of social cooperation. Work becomes linguistic in its very expression; it is cooperative, not simply because it includes cooperation but because it expresses it, determining cooperative innovations and producing a continuous excess of signification.

(2) In the philosophy of postmodernity we have witnessed a long and laborious philosophical effort that has tried to grasp the events that have ruptured the continuity and the teleology of modernity. It might be useful to remember three great lines of development.

The first was initiated by French philosophers of postmodernity when they insisted on the complete circularity of the processes that produced both commodities and subjectivity. So-called weak thought, aesthetic conceptions of life, and Marxist heresies about a production fully dominated by capital and therefore immeasurable and out of control, on its way to catastrophe—all of this did in fact reconfigure the field of analysis. At the same time, however, it also neutralized it. Between Lyotard and Baudrillard, it would be difficult to decide who was less responsible for this.

A second group tried to find, through the deconstruction of this context (precisely because they recognized it as being neutralized and insignificant), a point of rupture: a "marginal" point of true rupture that would allude to another form of existence or at least to a capacity to renew its meaning. From Derrida to Agamben, this line of thought developed its potential with force and intelligence. But the point of rupture remained and still remains marginal; the field and the horizon where this attempt at reversal takes place are extreme and become hardly viable. They are both frail and vulnerable to extremist tendencies. Critical theory here trumps practical reconstruction: the problem is recognized; the solution escapes our grasp.

The third line of development finds its inspiration in Foucault and Deleuze: it locates the powerful production of subjectivity at the center of the constitution of the real, rooted in a resistance to the insignificant self-enclosure of the world created by the production of commodities. This conquest of a creative ontological space (also called a space of difference) is crucial: this difference, this resistance, this production of subjectivity located in the center of the metropolis, in the center of cultures, in the center of intellectual and affective exchanges, in the center of linguistic and communicative networks, this center that is everywhere—well, it is from here that an ontological alternative can be given. Not a desperate, but a constructive, one.

(3) When we implant ourselves in the biopolitical field, work becomes a social activity and vice versa. Social activity participates in the General Intellect. But the General Intellect, in a biopolitical context, is also Eros: this means, obviously, that our anthropological becoming, in contemporaneity, is a process of singularization that is pragmatic and intellectual, affective and corporeal. The production of subjectivity accompanies an affective and a corporeal singularization. When we say "general intellect" we therefore indicate that ensemble of relational, ethical, and affective activities that were once called "eros." I will give you an example: the processes of artistic innovation from Cézanne to Beuys can indicate the direction taken by the reconstruction of this ontological concretion, consisting of matter and spirit. Spinoza described this kind of process as a synthesis of complexity and ingenuity. Between material and immaterial labor, between the production of commodities and the production of

services, the workforce infuses the totality of the life experience and apprehends itself as a social activity. Living labor, and therefore the production of value, presents itself as at once an excess and a by-product.

(4) Capital and state control of technological development, reacting against the struggles and the resistance of workers and citizens (of the worker-citizens), operates essentially through the attempt to reappropriate social cooperation, and therefore through the dissolution of the commonality of life, through the colonization of affects and passions, through the commodification and the continual reduction to financial entities of the places of resistance and antagonistic cooperation. Nonetheless, the existence of apparatuses of resistance is becoming increasingly evident. Today, the expression of "living labor" is directly the "production of a residue": this expression is, therefore, in the anthropological terrain, a production of subjectivity, and, in the political terrain, a production of democracy.

I come now to my conclusion. We cannot get rid of the category of postmodernity: in fact, this category allowed us to identify—beyond the conceptions that envisioned postmodernity as a pure and simple description of the capitalist invasion of life—a field of struggle, of antagonism, of power. Postmodernity gave us the possibility of imagining contemporaneity as the place of the production of subjectivity. It made us discover, in the totality of subsumption, the permanence of antagonism. It made us imagine an ethical power that would be entirely immanent.

It is, therefore, the concept of multitude that brings us back to contemporaneity. Today, when we talk about multitude, we sometimes find ourselves in an ambiguous position: we define it as a multiplicity of singularities, but this reality of the multitude is fully inserted in the antagonistic context of postmodernity. We affirm, in fact, that the multitude is capable of a reconfiguration of the sensible; we also affirm that the figure of imagination is capable of innovation and that, vice versa, innovation is capable of constituting a context capable of imagination.

On the other hand, the multitude appears to us within a catastrophic picture. Nothing is less terroristic than this affirmation—we should not be afraid of it; but nothing is less messianic either. We only want to emphasize that the emptying of meaning typical of capitalist development finds as an alternative (as an alternative to catastrophe) the power of the multitude. This is why, today, the multitude appears as the figure of a possible recomposition of the sensible, within the catastrophe of contemporaneity. The multitude appears as a liminal figure between biopower and biopolitics, or, better, between *pouvoir* and *puissance*. Could we, at this point, reformulate an old figure of the antagonism, as did those seventeenth-century English thinkers who distinguished between power[2] and multitude?

I would define contemporaneity in Spinozist terms: as the path that unfolds between the natural *conatus* toward cooperation, and the *amor* that constructs the sensible dimensions of social, institutional, and democratic process; as the cooperative opening of living labor and of every movement of renewal. Contemporaneity has to be reconsidered within the antinomies of postmodernity, that is, it has to be seen in relation to the new figure of the contradiction between capital and labor, between power and life, which appears in postmodernity. To live in postmodernity not as utopia but as "dis-utopia" (as the pragmatic tension that crosses real contradictions; that is capable of traversing its contradictory content without bypassing it, without dreaming of its beyond, but transforming the existing state of affairs) can be understood as the struggle to reclaim the meaning of contemporaneity. This dis-utopia is the contemporary apparatus operated by the collective will to resolve (in a revolutionary manner) the contradictions of postmodernity and to have done, once for all, with capitalists and bosses. In Spinozist terms, I want to say, this means that contemporaneity is the only way to express the eternal will to resistance and freedom.

NOTES

1   This refers to the concept of contemporaneity advanced at "Modernity ≠ Contemporaneity: Antinomies of Art and Culture after the Twentieth Century" by the symposium conveners and elaborated in the introduction to this volume.

2   In the original Italian essay, the word "power" appears in English.

A CULTURAL CONJUNCTURE IN INDIA:

ART INTO DOCUMENTARY

GEETA KAPUR

INTRODUCTION: IS CULTURE WHAT ARTISTS MAKE?

The unexpected turnaround staged by the Indian electorate in 2004 released extraordinary possibilities for reexamining the coordinates of citizenship, culture, and art practice. This essay follows from that event, the implications of which continue to unfold. Challenging the flourishing right-wing ideology of middle-class India, the election demonstrated with remarkable élan the power of the democratic vote, the maturity and astuteness of the (still largely rural) electorate, the possibility of overthrowing an antipeople right-wing government, and of giving a subtle mandate that requires a long surviving centrist party to seek support from regional, undercaste/*dalit*, socialist, and left parties to form a mixed (and balanced) government. The 2004 churning of Indian democracy can be seen as reconfiguring a secular public sphere capable of exposing the vileness of a majoritarian ideology (like Hindutva), but, further, as throwing up a debate on the rights of representation within the increasingly fraught and complex paradigm of the nation.

The argument I just outlined is poised on the fragile hope that a democratic election can also change the economic destination of a nation—an extrapolation worth maintaining for the sake of its discursive potential if not its political certitude. Symbolically, the wager of the vote is that the Indian state and the government in power must return to certain key principles guaranteed in India's advanced constitution. Specifically, that economic security is an inalienable right of the citizenry and the responsibility of the state—to fulfill which, it must guide the national-global compact through and beyond a contemporary that is overdetermined by the consolidation of a new empire.

If this democratic assertion is to be read across a preceding series of political disjunctures (I mean people's resistance movements and the left parties' emancipatory pedagogy that exerts direct, even extraparliamentary, pressure on government and state), the consequent electoral change reflects the convergence of a people's representational drive. It signals the need to define a radical version of citizenship, one that goes beyond the protocols of civil society. It precipitates a cultural conjuncture in the contemporary, which, in turn, needs to be transcribed into a calibrated account of subjectivities specific to the practice of the arts. The framing thematic of the present work, its reflection on the antinomies of art and culture, is held in suspension here in order to suggest that they are both driven by the same set of contradictions in any given historical circumstance; but that they nevertheless parody the rules of interdependency. I pose a riddle to condense and problematize the relationship: *Is culture what artists make?*

There is a straight answer: culture is a field made up of opposing representational interests that need to be kept in a workable relationship of consensual norms. Traditionally a containing matrix, culture at its most persuasive acquires a hegemonic status inviting noncoercive and participatory allegiance. On the other hand, art is always made up of a set of paradoxes nurtured in the imaginary and working *with,* but also *against,* the norm—to undermine its authority in favor of a new configuration of symbolic meanings. We place artists, like other cultural practitioners, among "organic intellectuals" or the committed intelligentsia, as a "class" that can be seen to translate the people's representational drive into the norms for a civil society, and these norms, in turn, into an immanent expression of individual subjectivity. It is this last embodiment that remains the elusive part of the mediated relay. The language of the arts draws equally from a socialized as from an (existentially) estranged subjectivity; it refracts and defers and conceals meaning to mark its radical variance from instrumental reason as operative in the political domain.

If, on the other hand, we claim provocative sets of contradictions in and between art and culture, it makes the above question tendentious, but still not redundant. It is asking to be answered in the double negative, but with the slippages read into the negation serving as critical clues in a failed equation. Even traditionally, culture has seeds of dissent inscribed into its interstices that can be interpreted as confrontational cultures/cultures of protest. Modernist art, for all the autonomy it claims, acquires an avant-garde status at the juncture where it goes outside the institution of art and connects with the more radical political movements of its time or, at any rate, with the subversive aspects of the cultures in opposition.

Not wanting to repeat the methodology of contextual readings made too familiar by sociology, I propose that art can be read as an index (of the rapid process of globalization), as symbolic (of persistently hypothesized national cultures), and as a sign (of the surplus value and, with it, the unsolicited pleasures generated beyond commodity exchange). I want also to steer clear of the culturalist euphoria sometimes encouraged within cultural studies discourse; or, rather, its pointedly postmodern misrepresentations with a weak (and faulty) politics. I refer to such ruses that suppress the economic to cushion the impact of corporate globalism, that deploy a rhetoric playing on the political with the perverse purpose of celebrating failures in class confrontations and national projects.

Neither do I, for obvious reasons, want to revert to the culturalist ideologies favored in countries with rich surviving traditions, such as India. The contemporaneousness of traditions and modernities requires special alertness and flexibility on the part of cultural practitioners. For example, Modern art as an "institution" does not have a stable status within the matrix of civil society in India, which means that contemporary Indian artists have no buffer against the social, against social reality—nor, perhaps, against the ideology of the state. To compensate for this "lack" (of autonomy) the politics of civilizational plenitude and cultural synchronicity, and, in conservative times, of a homogenizing cultural nationalism, is played up. Representational drives are translated into a programmatic plotting of identities; a minority polemic that further marginalizes the culturally disenfranchised is foregrounded.

It may also be that the institutional autonomy of art, supported by the luxury of a liberalized economy, does not suffice within the postcolonial condition; that the chimera of a self-sufficient aesthetic, too quickly appropriated by the market (booming with the recent, neoliberal, turn), robs the art scene of a substantive equation: between a hypothesized institution of art and art's agonistic function in what is, in a country like India, a valid public sphere.

My riddle is posed both to counterbalance the option of (economic and political) overdetermination that I risk in this essay, as well as to ensure that we are not left with what are at once soft and spurious options for a reified (transnational/transcultural) exchange of spectacular, consumer-driven signs. This twin skepticism changes both the definition of radicalism in art and the expectation from an avant-garde—about which more as we go forward.

NATIONAL/GLOBAL DETERMINANTS

By trouncing the incumbent right-wing party in 2004, the Indian electorate (55–60 percent of the voting population, or 626 million out of a total population of 1,050 million) brought to the surface a clutch of social and economic issues that crucially concern the country's incomparably heterogeneous population—in terms of class and caste, religion and ethnicity. Most important, it brought up the question of survival that had been obfuscated through the gloss on India's metropolitan prosperity: a celebration of the "shining" top decile of the population, the upwardly mobile middle and upper classes topped by an established and upcoming bourgeoisie, that not only prevent the benefits of a rising growth rate of the economy from percolating to the people, but, in a sense, opt for virtual "secession" from the nation so as to assimilate within the extravagant phenomenon of the global.

The electorate voted in the centrist Congress Party to form a new coalition government with the participation of several other parties and the backing of the communist parties. The Congress Party recognizes that the electoral mandate was not only against right-wing communalism, but also against the inequities and deprivation produced by the neoliberal economic policies driving globalization. Its own long-standing promise to eradicate poverty continues to face a contradiction arising from its ideological choice, since the 1990s, of repudiating India's state capitalism and opening up the economy to global capital.

This agenda is undertaken in India, as everywhere else in the developing world, under the rubric of "structural reforms," known to have tragic consequences for the national economies of such countries. Liberalization—the opening up of markets, the encouragement of direct foreign investment in hitherto "protected" economies—sets off, it is claimed by mediating/controlling institutions such as the International Monetary Fund (IMF) and the World Bank, a much needed "migration" of capital from the north to the south. In actual fact, the advantage of productive capital inflows is far outstripped by the subordination of these national economies to the force of metropolitan monopoly capital and, simultaneously/successively, to international finance capital. Globalized finance, "a highly volatile force buzzing around in quest of speculative gains," is the defining feature of imperialism today.[1] It opposes any form of state activism on the part of national governments, not to speak of relief and protection for vulnerable segments of the economy. And, in order to maintain a deflationary course in the southern economies, it lets domestic deindustrialization, increased unemployment, and a depressed demand structure lead large parts of the population into a downward spiral of poverty.

The large rural population (still up to 70 percent of the total population) of India has borne the cost of these deflationary policies. The substantial improvement achieved in the agricultural sector during the first three decades after independence has been undone through a series of measures—large reductions in the government's development expenditure, progressive dismantling of structures of public procurement and distribution of goods, reduced access to institutional credit, and cuts in subsidies alongside increases in prices of inputs.

Landless agricultural laborers, small and medium farmers, and barely surviving artisanal communities have faced drought, debts, malnutrition, and hunger. The phenomenon of increasing numbers of Indians in a condition of endemic hunger has been proved with relentless logic by the economist Utsa Patnaik in her now emblematical essay "The Republic of Hunger," where she argues how, in the five years of her study (1998–2003), the population of India had been sliding down toward sharply lowered levels of per capita food grains consumption.[2] Such low levels, she elaborates, were last seen in the initial years of World War II—from where they had fallen further still (during the British-induced Great Famine that broke out in 1943 in Bengal). On the other hand, there has been a massive increase in food grain stocks: "This paradox of a country with a huge starving population undertaking massive exports at throw-away prices is a singular contribution of the deflation associated with neoliberal policies."[3]

Thus, while the growth of the Indian economy is indeed conspicuous, it is highly selective. The growth in the services sector is to be seen against a general decline in the commodity-producing sector. There is a decline in the growth rate of agricultural production with a disproportionate decline in rural employment, and there is stagnation in the organized sectors of the economy. Cuts in government expenditure affect the level of demand in the industrial sector and, together with import liberalization, precipitate recessionary conditions. The virtual disappearance of the world-famous cotton textile industry in Bombay and Ahmedabad and the absolute impoverishment of *lakhs* (hundreds of thousands) of workers mark a tragic moment in the global history of labor.

Bound by the vote to alleviate immediate conditions of social suffering, the present centrist government, while promoting neoliberal economic reforms, has thought it necessary to offer palliative measures that may in fact be progressive, even radical, in the context of a world capitulating to global capital. These measures are embodied in a mission document entitled the *National Common Minimum Programme* that was prepared in conjunction with the government's left and other allies, chaired by the Congress Party president, Sonia Gandhi. It includes a special consideration of the depressed agricultural sector with proposals for food and nutrition security and announcements of debt exemption for farmers; an Employment Guarantee Act; reconsideration of the labor policy in the face of privatization; a continuing debate on the functioning of public sector enterprises, on the equity pattern for foreign capital, and on the terms and conditions for foreign direct investment; new terms of negotiation on the G-20 front (the group of developing countries with a special interest in agriculture) and a tougher stand on trade agreements with the developed world; an effort to detoxify educational and cultural institutions from a politics of hate; and proposals to extend special consideration to women, to depressed tribes and castes, and to minorities recently subjected to fascistic assault by the right-wing forces.

The National Rural Employment Guarantee Act, adopted by parliament in mid-2005, is perhaps the first major achievement in relation to the election mandate. Broadly, this act amalgamates earlier provisions for minimum wages, food-for-work programs, and other crisis management measures. Further, by adopting measures antithetical to the dictates of global capital and in defiance of threats from the IMF and World Bank reformers, it reaffirms a national policy space within globalization. It signals to the neoliberal ideologues at home and in the global system that independent nation-states still have the mandate, and the will, to look after the needs of their people.

India's distinguished Marxist economist Prabhat Patnaik argues that the retreat of the state in countries of the South (with special reference to India) is "the retreat to unfreedom."[4] The postcolonial state, with a carefully calibrated form of the national economy, needs to be strengthened in the era of global capitalism in response to a particularly grotesque irony at play: a developed country like the United States that denounces nationally constituted economies in the developing world, pumps up its own corporate interests (U.S.-controlled multinational corporations) that are in cohoots with its ruling elite, and uses that muscle to take control of world resources and force the IMF and World Bank, the World Trade Organization (WTO), *and* the United Nations to elicit grossly immoral advantages in clubbed bargains from the rest of the world. This is not even to speak of the horrific destruction of West Asia for the loot of cheap oil.

"There is," Prabhat Patnaik states, "a fundamental contradiction between the adoption of neo-liberal policies and the preservation of democratic institutions."[5] We must remember that the threat of capital flight and of bankruptcy, brandished with ever increasing force by the global nexus, has coerced national governments to modify their propeople policies—Cuba, as we know, has been crucified, and, more recently, the African National Congress in South Africa and President Lula's Workers' Party–Communist Party alliance in Brazil have had to change course. The pressure is relentless on Hugo Chavez in Venezuela— as indeed, behind doors, on India. There is some hope, with groupings like the G-20 in the WTO, that globally persuasive nations of the developing world can represent and empower themselves. In the face of their frequent inability to withstand the sanctions-laden pressure to assimilate, the democratic upheaval of an alert polity can help to chart agendas for change. The world has witnessed protest movements against globalization (including mass gatherings in the World Social Forum), in cities as far-flung as Genoa, Montreal, Seattle, Chiang Mai, Washington, Porto Alegre, and Mumbai. This is a form of "political praxis"—a parliamentary as well as an insurgent politics within the democratic framework itself. What it adds up to is a pragmatic view that the national state is irrevocable in the era of global capitalism because it is both complicit with, and an instrument of negotiation and resistance against, the new empire.

Even as the national is critically staged in this argument to emphasize the material contradictions, the conceptual and moral dilemmas, the struggles, and the demonstrable demand for change, we have to configure a fresh argument when culture is put on the plane of inquiry. Once the relationship between the political economy of the nation-state and its multiple community formations is stated, the cultural problematic opens out for exploration. And, while we look for those adversarial notions of citizenship that challenge and transform the nation and the state, we look also for locations where new subjectivities lodge, and for creative expression that rides the metropolitan entropy and sites as a fresh horizon for the aesthetic.

ARTISTS AS CITIZENS

During the twentieth century, all through the national movement and up until the immediate contemporary, Indian artists (including, for this argument, visual artists, filmmakers, writers, and theater practitioners, with specific examples drawn from the first two categories) have represented, both euphorically and critically, the imagined community, even perhaps the state embodiment, of the nation. Deriving from the hundred-year-long national movement for independence, artists, as members of the intelligentsia, have found forms of critical affiliation with what can justifiably be called the "national-state."[6] They have devised genres and styles and figural types, as well as aesthetic strategies, for the purpose.

While, at this level, artists may identify with "accredited" members of a national elite and seek to wield power with and through institutions of the state, at another, they support the more contestatory values of a democratic polity by positioning themselves in the public sphere. When faced with assertive aspects of state power, artists, like the large, left-leaning intelligentsia of India, have tried to step outside the orbit of coercions, to recognize the changing contours of a democracy addressing itself to political dissent beyond the protocol of (a covertly state-administered) civil society. The courage and imagination of Indian artists (and I mean all the arts, including literature) were tested in recent decades during the Indian Emergency declared by the government of Indira Gandhi in 1975–1977, when the state took on authoritarian powers, cracked down on all opposition, and suspended the democratic process to combat what it called a situation of nationwide anarchy; and then during the ascendancy of right-wing parties between 1992 and 2004, when antisecular/protofascistic forces engineered riots and virtual genocide of the minorities in different parts of India. In the course of this essay, I will show in some detail how the Indian documentary took a new and brave turn at these two junctures. Visual artists, foremost among them Vivan Sundaram, Nalini Malani, N. N. Rimzon, Rummana Hussain, and Navjot Altaf, articulated the rupture in the democratic equation between the state and the polity by changing the course of what was until then a largely classical/modernist art scene. By incorporating documentary photography, by switching over to sculptural and video installations, the language-in-use, and, more important, the subject position of the artist, were made intentionally unstable, volatile, radical. Dating from the early 1990s, this body of work constitutes an important political statement.[7] Further, there is a history of artists operating from within explosive group formations, collectives, and movements and taking on a forthrightly antagonistic role. Foregrounding their view from a subaltern locus, dalit writers in particular challenge, defy, and mock the ideology of the ruling class (and caste), the hegemony of the state, and the very legitimacy of the national.[8]

On a broad plane, Indian artists, in terms of their aesthetic, have tended to function much like the "universal" moderns, with the liberty of projected identification of the "other," with a language sensitive to the ethics of such embodiment, and with strategies for displacement, subversion, and gender transgression.[9] In a more philosophic sense, they have tended to assume the privileged, if ironical, status of a sovereign subject, corresponding to but more self-valorizing than that of the citizen-subject. They have sought allegories or otherwise deconstructed signs of the national whereby they can be both inside the nation and outside the state in their interpretative rendering of the political.[10]

With globalization, new factors have emerged to alter the role of artists as citizens. The retreat of the state within a global capitalist economy means that we must look not only for new notions of citizenship but also for new subjectivities that develop among young aspirants within the urban—among, say, the new "class" of youth gambling on livelihood chances in the outsourcing economy of global capital. I am thinking of the seemingly vacuous masquerade played out by Indian youth within internationally hooked call centers, or of young cyborgs interpellated into a global network of infotechnology within altogether new space-time coordinates. Younger artists tend to identify with these expanding realms of indeterminacy and often adapt a mediatic version of the avant-garde—turning the rupture in the institutional associations of nation and state into a transsubjective "free zone" of democratic exchange.[11] Dissolution of causative trajectories of purposes and interests, a vertigo of disconnection, produces a shredding and restringing of material connectivities, a spin into a vortex of anxieties and desires, and, thereupon, an aggravated condition of metropolitan entropy. "All that is solid melts into air," and the surreal fragments of the unredeemed Real ask to be theorized (perhaps) in cultural terms, ask to be rendered (perhaps) into new aesthetic practices.

When the national-state, claiming custodianship of its peoples' economic interests, is handicapped and eventually even crippled by capitalist globalization, the widespread suffering is accompanied by the emergence of fresh affiliations in the form of affirmative or, more properly, partisan action at the grassroots, some of which is "documented" in the very process of formation by filmmakers and videographers working in solidarity with national and international nongovernmental organizations (NGOs). Covering the subterrain of a nation's neglected populace, this makes, in some ways, common cause with the idea and emergence of "multitudes," and it looks to establish human rights and good governance in the constitution of a global citizenry.

A DOCUMENTARY MO(VE)MENT

The recent groundswell in the Indian documentary scene is politically compelling in that it helps to explore how spontaneous resistance to reactionary ideologies can bestow upon scattered practitioners the status of a movement that is virtually "underground" at the same time as it is fully public.

The context is the five-year rule (1998–2004) of the right-wing government led by the Bharatiya Janata Party, which peaked in ruthless logic in 2002, when a state-supported pogrom against the Muslim community in Gujarat consolidated the Hindutva ideology as fascist. Almost a dozen films dealing directly with the Gujarat genocide of 2002 have been made; earlier riots and massacres saw hardly one or two. Documentary evidence assumes access to citizens as co-witnessing spectators. Not surprisingly, therefore, a confrontation on the censorship law became the actual occasion for the documentary movement to erupt. During a routine selection procedure for the Mumbai International Film Festival, the requirement, prescribed by the state, for all Indian films to obtain a censor certificate became a sudden rallying point and developed, in 2004, into an alternative film festival with a traveling circuit. By now nearly three hundred short and documentary filmmakers are associated with this action platform, a majority of whom have opted to exhibit their films without the censor certificate, sometimes under threat from the authorities.

After the May 2004 election the actual situation in the country is less grim. Yet the need for solidarity continues in anticipation of the need to assert the constitutional right to freedom of speech and expression (a useful euphemism to win the right of dissent and confrontation). The constitutional right is of course bracketed with other provisos that constrain that right. This well-marked battle involves legal interpretation and a complex political discourse; it involves a proactive definition of rights of representation as much as those of expression and information, and of all these in relation to theories of spectator address and reception.

We should note that the rejection of censorship arises as much from a precipitate political moment as from video and digital technology itself, which, by its immediacy/informality, constructs a different private/public interface, suggesting what it means to function in and shape a contemporary public sphere. Place this development within the twin frames of the nation and the state—both based on privileged identities, legal sanctions, and hierarchy of command—and the grant of official freedom through a censor board certificate begins to appear at best gratuitous. It is the mood of the moment to foreground these issues in disregard of, and in opposition to, the mediating institution of the state. Thus these hundreds of filmmakers seek a mandate under the title "Films for Freedom 2004."

The upsurge in the production and reception of documentary films in India has to do with "a crisis in democracy," says the filmmaker Amar Kanwar; equally or, rather, inversely, one might say that it is the result of a more extensive democratic consciousness that reveals gaps and losses and translates these into a language of intervention. "In some ways," Sudipto Kaviraj says, "it is better not to treat democracy as a governmental form. . . . A better strategy . . . is to treat it, more problematically, as a 'language,' as a way of conceiving, and in more propitious circumstances, of making, the world."[12] Indeed, if democracy, as

Kaviraj suggests, is something like a "narrative contract" between identifiable nationalities and group formations, then the documentary form confirms the contract, whether it adopts the activist mode, connected to political ideologies/ organizations/movements (such as the century-old Indian labor movement), or whether it links with anthropology-driven, grassroots politics that prioritizes the immanent nature of community structures and seeks legal visibility and self-definition within the local context. Either way, the capture of political space is sought in terms of the direct access assumed by its communicational ethics. And, while any one documentary unravels the issues piecemeal, the synergy of many eyes/hands/expositions at work with the camera provides a peculiar "narrative" positioning of the medium, in the above contractual sense of the term, at the present juncture.

If we mark 2003–2004 as a moment when the Indian documentary movement names itself, it is preceded by nearly two decades of interventionist documentary film practice. Take a major protagonist in this battle, the pugnaciously political Anand Patwardhan, who has been at the forefront of the documentary scene since the late 1970s and early 1980s.[13] He has confronted the major issues during these decades: the Emergency (*Prisoners of Conscience*, 1978); the demolition/displacement of "slum" habitation in a city like Bombay, caught between the ordering regime of urban development and devouring real estate sharks (*Bombay Our City: Hamara Shahar*, 1985); and the people's movement against the big dam project on the Narmada River that has destroyed a large (tribal and peasant) population, and the story of its decades-long opposition that finally lost to a bitterly fought juridical order (*Narmada Diary*, 1995). Here we focus on Patwardhan in the year 1992, when the Babri Masjid Muslim mosque was demolished, an event signaling the victory of the right-wing straight through to the parliamentary elections of 1998–1999. Patwardhan's *In the Name of God* (1992) was made during and after the Babri Masjid demolition. It was followed by *Father, Son, and Holy War* (1994), which traces the origin of the fascist tendency to a pathological regret over lost manhood perpetrated by the false ideology of "modernized" Hindutva.

Patwardhan's films are based on a rationalist, cause-effect dialectic; their spirit is entertaining, volatile, provocative, and their form is pedagogic and associated with avant-garde moments in culture and politics: the revolutionary vigor of the early Soviets through to the Third Cinema movement in Latin America during the liberationist decade of the 1960s (and early 1970s).[14] Patwardhan is contextualized within a documentary movement based on historical rupture on a momentous scale; a movement coming in the wake of political and cultural decolonization that proposes nothing less than a third world aesthetic

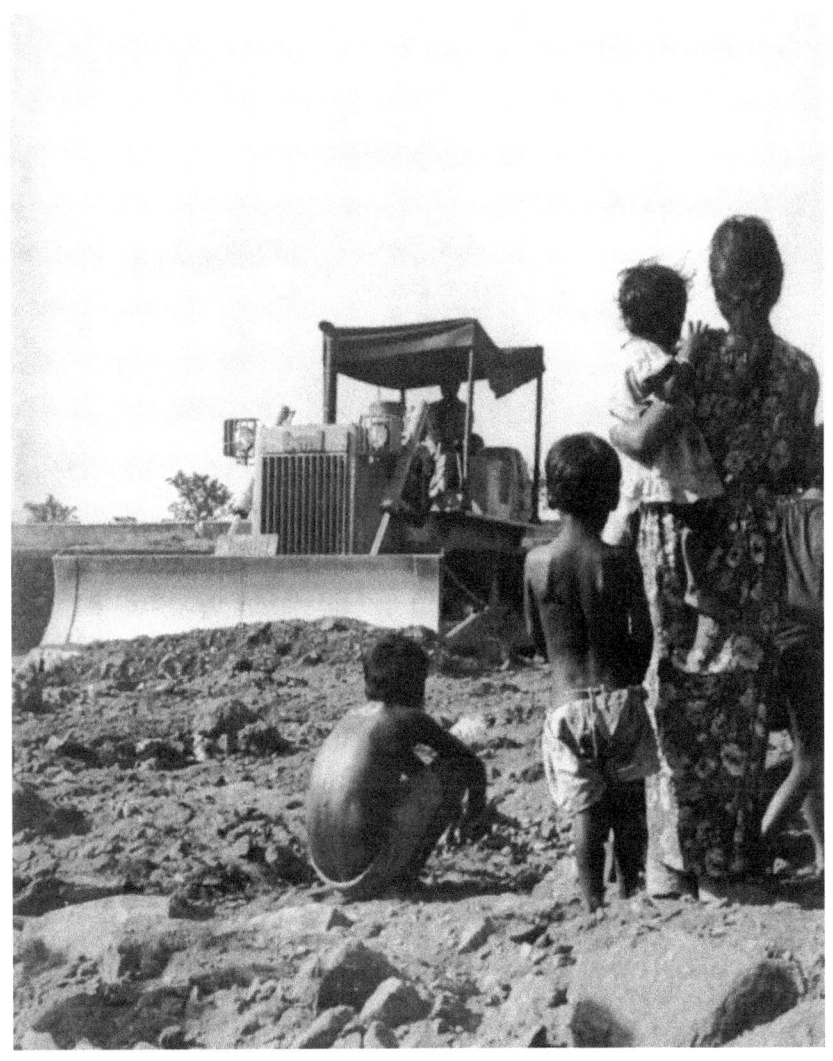

Anand Patwardhan, bulldozers in a Bombay slum. Still from *Bombay Our City,* 1985.
Courtesy of the filmmaker.

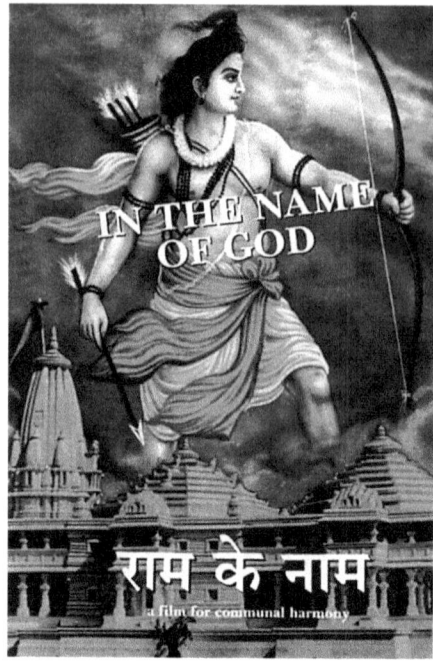

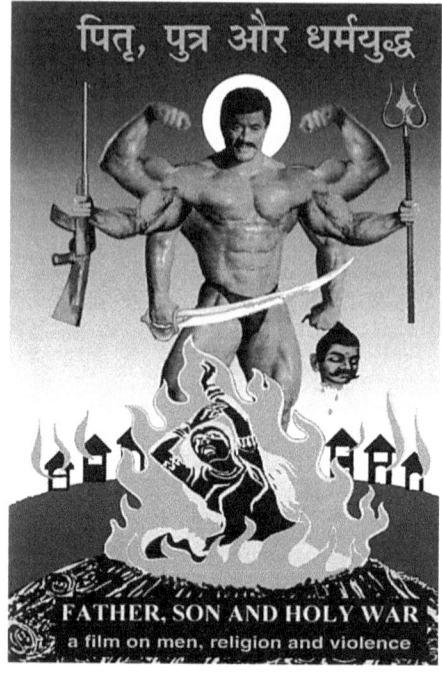

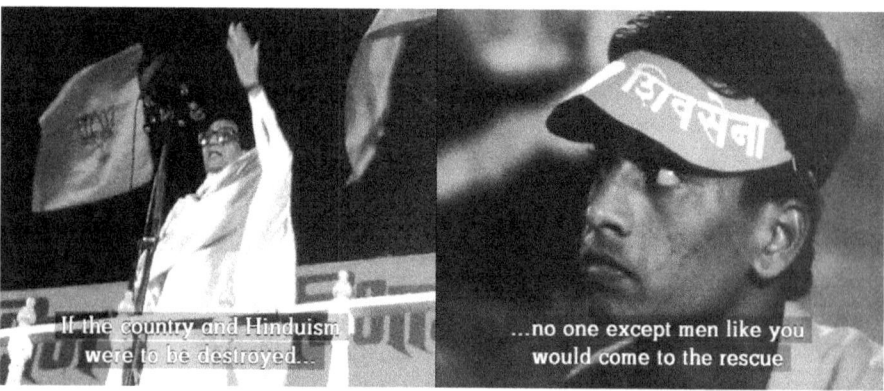

Anand Patwardhan, poster based on the campaign image of the fundamentalist Hindutva movement. Still from *In the Name of God*, 1992. Courtesy of the filmmaker.

Anand Patwardhan, *Father, Son, and Holy War*, 1994. Poster based on images in popular media. Courtesy of the filmmaker.

Anand Patwardhan, stills from *Father, Son, and Holy War*, 1994, showing the Hindu leader Balasaheb Thackeray inciting young men against Muslims in a Bombay rally. Courtesy of the filmmaker.

whereby "artists" lay simultaneous and rhetorical claim on realism, modernity, and the avant-garde, and, more specially, on documentary "truth" *as* an avant-garde strategy of resistance and renewal. Within India, Patwardhan runs into trouble with the state and fights with guerrilla tactics and legal aplomb, repeatedly claiming that the state is a reality; that it can be fought and made to bend and, at best, even taught by citizens' initiatives to rectify its ideological (mis)understanding of a living democracy.

The much younger filmmaker Amar Kanwar, in what he calls more activist documentaries such as *The Many Faces of Madness* (2000) and *Freedom . . . !* (2002), presents a morally pitched interrogation of problematized subject matter ranging from agricultural labor, dalits, and ethnic minorities, to dispossessed tribal communities fighting the devastation wreaked on their living environments by the development policies of independent India, accompanying all this with a philosophical discourse on human (and environmental/planetary) survival.[15]

Here the signal differences between Patwardhan and Kanwar emerge.[16] The "objective" interlocutor that Patwardhan foregrounds in his films is, in Kanwar, an extension of the very person of the speaking subject—the filmmaker himself. Working in the interstices of the social, Kanwar develops a "documentary" form of intersubjectivity, but through a ruse. He displaces social issues on to more philosophic, aesthetic, affective planes of thought and feeling. Using poetry and reflection above argument and dialectics as his preferred style—manifestly in his 2002 film, *A Night of Prophecy*—Kanwar advances the idea of freedom and ethics as natural correlates of film practice, and defers any programmatic definition of praxis. Kanwar's films ask that we undertake critical rethinking of the two supposedly contradictory categories of interrogation and affect. And to thereby rethink action, especially action inducing (as it often does) the specter of violence.

In *A Season Outside* (1998), the slowly materialized, sensuously held image arrests the attention of the spectator until it reaches the stage of what Walter Benjamin calls "mimetic innervation." In this film, several narratives crisscross and plot the iconic moments of valiant militancy in the communitarian identity of the Sikhs of India. Folding the medieval into the modern, the sacrifices of the legendary gurus into the community's fraught honor today, Kanwar uses visual allegory in such a way that the travesty of masculine violence is interrogated from within the beauty and pain of martyrdom. Kanwar's own vulnerable passage into contemporary history brackets the film: an autobiographical reference to his family's journey at the time of the Partition; a documentary quotation of Gandhi walking to quell communal riots at the time of the Partition.

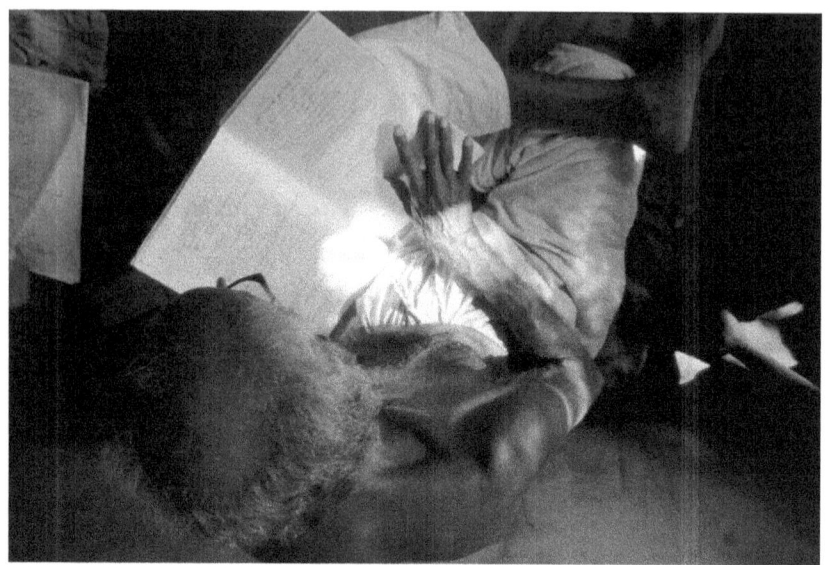

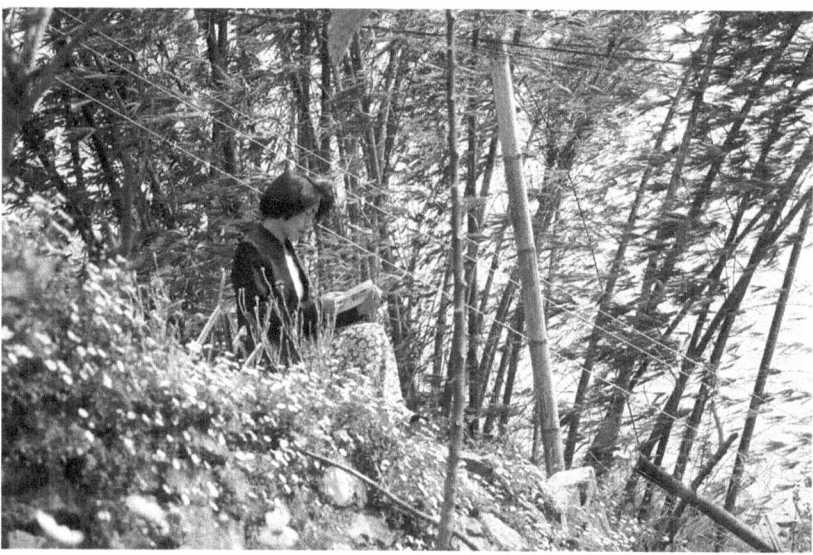

Amar Kanwar, "O Waman dada! Tell us where is the path to their hideout?" Still from *A Night of Prophecy*, 2002. Video. Courtesy of the filmmaker.

Amar Kanwar, "Bury my heart too at Wounded Knee." Still from *A Night of Prophecy*, 2002. Video. Courtesy of the filmmaker.

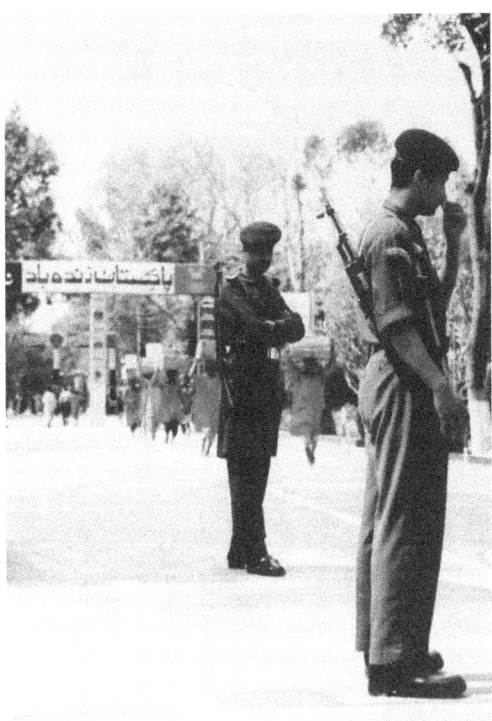

Amar Kanwar, "Each carrying
their own box of colour." Still
from *A Season Outside*, 1998.
Video. Courtesy of the filmmaker.

The film ends by consciously adopting a form of social "mourning" that becomes, by the deployment of a deliberate default, political in the manner of its
righteous reflexivity.

Thus what I schematically designate as two alternatives in documentary film
practice in India may, equally schematically, be seen as a generational change in
the nature and pursuit of politics itself. Patwardhan's courts history. Kanwar's is
an exploration of the ground reality by a filmmaker who prefers to hold a
premium on subjective knowledge, and when in doubt, delay discourse concerning means and ends set in motion by history. In an increasing number of
films, the subaltern figure is seen working with a subversive (more secessionist
than cumulative) strategy of survival, inhabiting a fragmented map of the social
that no longer coincides with that of the nation.

What is gained and lost by this change in the documentary genre and in the
genre of politics itself is arguable. Even today, beyond the successful and failed
revolutions, postcolonial realities and their corresponding cultural imperatives
continue to be crucial; and a conscious representational drive, with the dynamic of an evidentiary aesthetic, erupts in clusters across the new empire. In
any case, current ideological preferences hold no absolute privilege over the

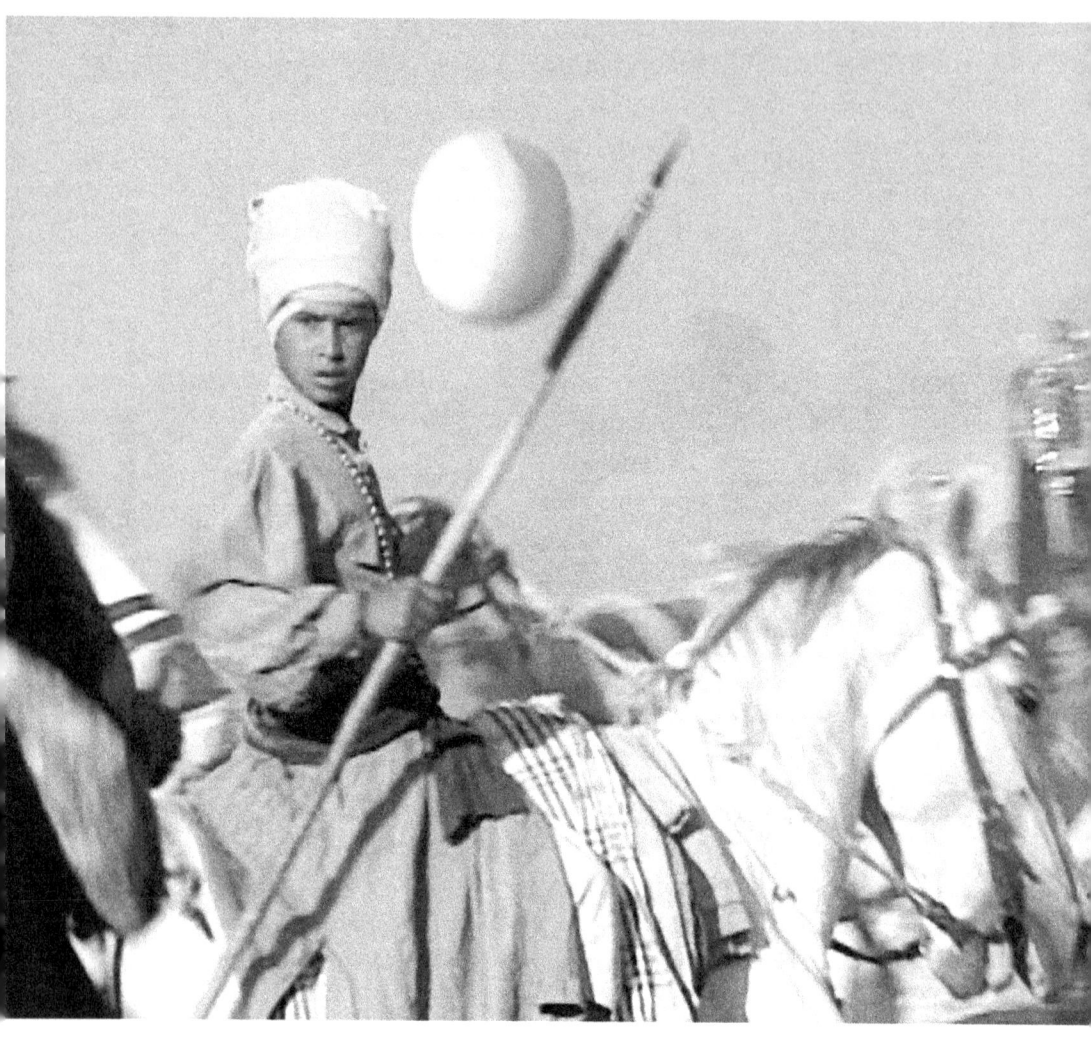

Amar Kanwar, "Then a little magician arrived in the morning." Still from *A Season Outside*, 1998. Video. Courtesy of the filmmaker.

future, and I think the balance is tipped by the degree to which different styles of cultural articulation support confrontational alternatives that are being rapidly disempowered by the consolidation of global capital.

THE SPHERE OF ART: WHERE THE COMPASS POINTS

I describe, now, what I call a full circle of manifold art practices, and position "high" art and "low" art on the polar points of a vertical axis, particularizing these rough categories as modernist art and popular art. I position a horizontal axis across the vertical and polarize two opposing categories, genre and avant-garde, particularizing genre with reference to the powerful drive for realism and the avant-garde as a contemporary site of radicality (related to but not exhausted by the 1920s historical avant-garde that spelled extreme rupture).

The vertical and horizontal axes support a full circle. Navigating the top half of the circle's circumference, a picture of sanctioned reciprocity between the categories of Realism, Modernism, and the avant-garde is obtained. Positioned at the southern pole with "low" art, I reach up, somewhat more willfully, to the avant-garde—gaining agency for the popular/urban in mockery of Clement Greenberg's puritanical separation of avant-garde from kitsch. Indeed, the two-way equation confirms, precisely, the wit exercised by avant-garde practice in drawing from high and low art at once. On the opposite side, I extend the reach of low art to the comprehensive category of genre in its realist (and quasi-realist) aspect—what the Bombay films, for example, manipulate with such élan.

In this full circle, my compass points, first, to auteur-based high art, seeing it sustaining its stakes in subjectivity, sovereignty, and utopia. Modernism in its reflexive moments has offered pedagogies for the advancement of a counterculture (as for example with Dada). And it has provided a framing aesthetic for "an immanence of the concrete" consonant with a materialistic dialectic during the revolutionary decades of the twentieth century: I am referring to the Constructivist movement in the visual arts; the insurgent cinema of the Soviet revolution; Brecht's epic form in theater that played, along with Sergei Eisenstein's montage aesthetic, a foundational role in defining what we mean by socialist radicalism in art. In a finer analysis, there is reason to separate the Soviet-led historical avant-garde from European high art designated as Modernism, but here the conjunction will hold simply as a way of designating the conceptual complexity and linguistic innovations in the advanced arts of the early twentieth century. It also explains why I so privilege the consolidated ground of high art in the spherical diagram of manifold art practices.

The compass then points, symmetrically, to the popular, which helps unpack the modernist norm, showing not only how it may end up going awry through reification within bourgeois ideology but offering, more positively, performative maneuvers in the imaginative rendering of the stratified social. Interestingly, this is done by none other than Eisenstein and Brecht (which is why the distinction between mainstream Modernism and the socialist avant-garde needs to be drawn), and then by the intrepid radical of the 1960s, Jean-Luc Godard. Further, the popular foregrounds the politics of pleasure lodged in the unconscious; it submits the symbolic to a vulgar, faux-surreal decoding procedure, and offers up an almost grossly rich signification. I am thinking of Hollywood's film noir and Bombay cinema's most affective subgenre, the melodrama, both of which also become tools used by film theorists to build a semiotic and psychosocial critique of what is considered after the 1960s as the precious culture of auteur-based art cinema.

The location of the popular is considered to be methodologically more useful in today's culturalist debates. Popular cultural studies offer a different, broadly anthropological, interpretation that is more hybrid than deemed respectable in art history proper. Placed within the frame of the postmodern, popular culture lends theory the daring to force a passage into the very obscenities of the Real, thus, as it were, blasting open the more discreet transaction between the imaginary and the symbolic conducted on the ground of a purer aesthetic. More specifically, in India, recognition of the now near ubiquitous cinema effect triggers styles of contemporary acculturation that complicates the argument in favor of popular Indian cinema's corrupt and stubborn forms of realism. And, by a kind of generic twist, this cinema offers, as film theorist Ashish Rajadhyaksha shows in his many writings, a politically canny take on shifting power relations between the citizen and the state.[17]

I am not, however, inclined to give over the ground of contestation to the anti–high art/antimodernist formations that often dominate today's cultural studies discourse. I do not believe that a people's democratic impulse must essentially be read into the consensual reception of popular forms. There is sufficient critique of the image-based culture industry and the culturalist ideology itself as it develops in late capitalism, as of the phenomenon of a fatally spectacularized culture and its strategies of subsumption, to require any reiteration here. My argument rests on the possibility of keeping up the tension in the high-low binary: to keep up the cognitive ambitions and the epistemological value of art's transformative structures in high art, and to keep alive visual and other pleasures through the subversive agency of low art. The argument suggests that a strategic makeover of modernity's utopian drive may, in certain ways, enter and imbricate the everyday common culture. But, equally, that by accommodating popular culture's ruder features, the (class) barriers between genres may come down and do some all-round good.

We are, by this stage of the argument, looking toward the avant-garde, but the compass is now volatile. Its oscillation activates the sphere's entire circumference: so, what is the message?

While the four main nodes—high and low, genre and avant-garde—are well-formed compounds, there are differentiated subcategories stretched along the arcs of the sphere's four segments. Modernist high art pushes toward the avant-garde position via conceptual art or, more broadly, the conceptual approach, which is translated today into the predominantly lens-based options of photography, film, video, and the digital. Between the avant-garde and the popular lies the more amorphous category of new media art, involving a digital, computer-based, research-and-play repertoire of intelligent games that offer mediatory transformations of the everyday.

On the opposite side, between high art and (the realist) genre, I suggest placing the critical, self-reflexive form of the documentary, carrying a mandate for raising the subjective pitch in proportion to the political partisanship of the maker. And, on the curve between realism and the popular, I place the documentary as a recording genre dominated by an information-ethnography ethics and aspiring to enrich a "common culture." Such documentaries use popular representational means and even, at times, mythologized fable structures that prod the political by decoding the icons, rituals, caprices, and prejudices of everyday culture through a playful semiotics, like that used most tellingly in Roland Barthes's *Mythologies*.

My diagram proposes—in a cunning fit that serves, let me admit, my own purposes—that radical elements are now to be drawn from all round the circumference of the sphere: as much from within the "classic" binaries of high and low, genre and avant-garde, as from the conceptual, the mediatic, the documentary, and the "mythological."

DOCUMENTARY RETAKE

Since the establishment in 1989 of a unipolar world, a substantial number of documentary "films" aim to break into routine accounts of war, disaster, torture, and genocide, as delivered by the "world news" syndrome, and to invert the gross and homogenized televisual spectacle into a discreet exposure of those multiplying targets of destruction, coercion, and subjugation that lead to the suffering of large parts of humanity within the globalizing process.[18] More ambitiously, these documentaries want to address the absolute power of capitalism as embodied by the most belligerent, blighted, blatantly criminal nation-states, led by the United States of America. The compounding of corporate, militaristic, and trade sanctions decreed upon the besieged economies of the world, the worldwide control over people's civil and political rights in the name of Western-style (neoliberal) democracy, and the abuse of democracy by these same superimperialist powers produce, above all, a desperate urgency to forge a corresponding language for oppositional "truth": for enduring testimonies, for witness accounts, for collective strategies of spontaneous resistance through people's action.[19] And for imaging/voicing the sustained work of organized political movements.

As my two examples from India show, the "new" documentary addresses the many struggles of the citizens and the populace against global capital, against national governments and their respective states, against class (and caste), and against the forces of the right that align with religious and communal violence as they do with antipeople policies in favor of the ruling classes.[20] Appropriately, the language of the new documentary is tuned to the conditions (the cultural intricacies, the contour and rhythm) of life in specific societies, just as they are, of course, to the ideology and style of the documentarist.[21]

Today, the power of the moving image and of the political pedagogy embedded in it depends on a recognition of the critical apparatus developed by cultural and creative practices (for example, the rich dialogue for and against realism in auteur cinema), and the knowledge archive, the discursive output, within history and the other social sciences since (especially) the 1960s. I have already juxtaposed Patwardhan and Kanwar in some detail; the work of Madhushree Dutta (*I Live in Behrampada,* 1993), Ramesh Sharma (*Final Solution,* 2004) and Lalit Vachani (*The Boy in the Branch,* 1993 and *The Men in the Tree,* 2002), also devoted to an examination of the communal/majoritarian ideology of Hindutva, is instructive in terms of the very definition of documentary form: is it to be (gross) mimesis or social analysis; is it to be insurgent or investigative, hostile or compassionate, polemical or reflexive? These questions exemplify the "deconstructive" nature of the new documentary.

The women's movement has provided the groundwork for a good number of feminist films: Deepa Dhanraj's film against brutal, nationwide state policy on family planning, in *Something Like a War* (1991); and Surubhi Sharma's exploration in *Jari Mari: Of Cloth and Other Stories* (2001) of the unorganized sector of small-scale industry (in Mumbai) where women's labor still earns them no working-class rights. Concerning women and sexuality, there is Reena Mohan's film on the anxieties and bad faith around female beauty in *Skin Deep* (1998); Shohoni Ghosh's witty articulation of and by the female sex workers of Calcutta in *Tales of the Night Fairies* (2002); and Paromita Vohra's take on the pop pedagogy of a postfeminist feminism in *Unlimited Girls* (2002). Rahul Roy's modest and compassionate portrait of working-class urban youth in *When Four Friends Meet* (2000) contrasts with Amar Kanwar's exploration of the vulnerable and voracious aspects of male sexuality in the Indian metropolis in *King of Dreams* (2001). The emancipatory agenda is fulfilled on a more personal and eccentric register in Ruchir Joshi's film journey with itinerant Baul singers, the "mystic" minstrels of Bengal, in *Eleven Miles* (1991); while *A Night of Prophesy* (2002) by Amar Kanwar "narrativizes" songs of protest from different regions of the Indian republic to echo an anarchist ring of liberation.

Documentarists understand that even as they work within the tropes of the document, the archive, and a verité-based realism, even as they respect the ethics of indexicality—the relationship between representation and a profilmic "reality"—the ruse of representation must be fully addressed. As also the transitive, durational, and deferred nature of the narrative fragment in the short film format. These make up the very poetics and politics of what is at stake as the bare "truth-value" of the documentary project. It follows that recognition of the inextricability of subject and history, widely accepted in critical discourse, permits contemporary documentarists to interject anxiety and memory in the everyday, to test promises and betrayals in civil society by tracking forms of mortality in the biographical (and autobiographical) mode. Wary of a political "method" and polemical pronouncements, the new documentary offers data that have a premium on the condition of indeterminacy and loss. It could in some ways hope to realize what was so poignantly addressed in one of Susan Sontag's last texts: a compact with the world *Regarding the Pain of Others*.

While the documentarist cannot, perhaps, answer to the overtaken ideal of a "people's culture" in the socialist sense of the word, it may be possible to hypothesize, on the basis of a worldwide documentary upsurge, a common culture of the "multitudes" with a "be against" slogan in the manifestos of hope that the new global empire supposedly yields—in the form of a nemesis or, indeed, as a demonstration of the dialectic.[22] This claim postulates that cultures of protest find spontaneous communicability across and beyond communitarian and national boundaries. Further, that the extrapolated forms of historical knowledge translate as collective creativity, as evidentiary articulation, pushing the promise of democracy and even perhaps approximating, in their enunciation, in their disinterested passion, to a version of an aesthetic. Can this agenda proxy for the avant-garde; can it actually be, in our time, what the vanguard was for the twentieth century: an inquiry into the wide parameters and present conditions of praxis premised at once on refusal, risk, and utopia?

MEDIATIC, CRITICAL, AVANT-GARDE

Leaving these questions suspended, my next move is to refocus on the sphere of art, to reiterate the significance of establishing, and then blurring, mediums and art historical categories.[23] To let the needle oscillate and "encompass" segments of my proposed sphere, rather than fix the direction for the avant-garde. "I have chosen to think of the contemporary work in film and video that shares . . . a kind of lifeline between the received categories of the documentary and avant-garde, each of which has been discursively and institutionally cloistered to its disadvantage."[24]

Beyond the conditions that made it a rigorous phenomenon in the 1920s, the avant-garde reinvents itself in the present through two new channels: one, the witnessing aesthetic of the documentary—verité films, as well as reflexive accounts of lived lives, autobiographical or fictional; and, two, the multiplying media technologies expanding the realm of the virtual. These tendencies are together but differently driven by the challenge global capitalism throws at existing formations of state, nation, and community; and, consequently, on culture, communication, and intersubjectivity.

If the radical documentary is infused with the courage to "undo" the righteous claim on reality and to remap the world on the basis of global deprivation, experimental media artists can be seen, on the other hand, to rework the symbolic in the light of emerging new subjectivities in the projected global citizenry. Artists will interject political issues of loss and reparation in a monologic form. Personal fictions unfold within the nonnarrative schema of, say, an ethnographic account. In terms of structure, both documentarists and artists have developed an aesthetic of the fragment—psychic fragmentation, as well as fragmentation owing to the disaggregation of life-worlds that corresponds, metonymically, to physical displacement all across the world.

This is the place to interject a hitherto deferred fact: in terms of technology, the postcelluloid media has far-reaching consequences on the meaning and effect of the moving image.[25] The ontological/indexical bond between image and reality is disturbed (if not broken), setting off what we might call specters without footprints crisscrossing the threshold of objectivity. The sanctity of Bazanian realism is relativized, affecting all forms, whether documentary or experimental, narrative or avant-garde.[26] Because of the "ubiquity, endless receptivity, and ephemerality" of video and digital media, there is an insistence on the "now."[27] Live signals, shallow and often degraded images, destabilize received settings and pitch the mediatic encounter into something of a semiotic crisis.[28] In the stake sweep of media technology, what is the relay between a formal aesthetic of the moving image, the evanescence of the virtual, and the speed on the information highways of cyberspace? To what extent does this technology yield a democratically constituted "commons" and what kind of hackers' ethics, what liberationist attitude, do media gift to youthful entrants?[29]

Unlike a classic documentarist who will, very likely, want to reestablish indexicality for the new medium, an artist will use the eminently erasable image produced by electronic and digital media for more fantastic, more elusive, purposes. The media seem to provide an interface not only between the private and the public but also between semiotic crises and extreme conditions in the social. It is not surprising therefore that these media have lodged themselves (belatedly but) so rapidly in precisely such societies as have witnessed the most radical changes in the globalized political—changes that push the fraught and fragmented narrative of national citizenship to the brink, that produce conditions for subjectivities *in extremis*. A deeply visceral response, translated into visual allegories at once sublime and cannibalistic (recalling "anthropophagia," a Brazilian "modernist" trope, which valorizes a devouring instinct to fulfill a "perverse" form of transcendence), comes across in an increasing number of videos/installations by non-Western artists, especially the Chinese.[30]

Pushing the argument further: artists as media practitioners, working out the relationship between the imaginary and the symbolic, are prepared—by the medium?—to face up to what one might call the residue of the abject, and the obscene, in the material substratum that is the Real. Think of the highly subjectivized video performances that have allowed the body in all its excess to surface via the virtual in a vision of the soul at once spectral and carnal.[31] This could be the unreconstructed self; on the other hand, it could be the estranged other, grossly designated, lovingly recuperated, in terms of class, color, race, ethnicity, and gender.[32] It is the peculiar pulse of an unstable subject-position that makes the contemporary artist function at all—and in experimental video it becomes, one might say, a mediatic compulsion, even as the odd and varied presentational formats of video installations establish a vulnerable ephemerality, a desired "unknowing," reinforced by a disorienting multiplication of monitors and screens in a maze of black-box projections within the exhibition space.[33]

But here I want to recall a counterpoint played throughout the argument. The terms of reference between documentary, narrative, and avant-garde—as between the indexical and the virtual, and between analog and digital—are so upturned that artists, as much as they may be attracted by the ineffable, are drawn, by way of compensation, to the vastly variable reality effect. When the global flux within the mediatic and the political accelerates, the stakes on the truth-value that artists are required to uphold are raised.[34] My argument thus moves toward translating the cleft genres and crossed languages now being adopted by art and media practitioners into an equation framed by the critical. "Vision, whether blind or seeing, is always invested with a function of apprehending the visual in a manner far more extensive and complex than what the eye ultimately sees. And what truth can images tell us when they are drowning in the continental drift set up by modern media industries?"[35]

Today's interactive art practices (including video/digital/new media technologies, installations, and performance) are volatile. They are driven by contradiction. At their most alert, these practices make a judicious alignment with the critical. This move provides access by proxy to the dialectic once given over to the all-conquering new that the earlier, more self-possessed, protagonists in the vanguard put forward.

Okwui Enwezor asserts: "The propagators of the avant-garde have done little to constitute a space of self-reflexivity that can understand new relations of artistic modernity not founded on Westernism."[36] He is targeting radical art that has allowed itself to be subsumed within Modernism's superior claims to artistic autonomy, and the avant-garde in general for its rigid alignment with the European grand narrative of permanent innovation. Tellingly, therefore, he entitles a section in his essay in the documenta 11 exhibition catalogue "What Is an Avant-garde Today? The Postcolonial Aftermath of Globalization and the Terrible Nearness of Distant Places." He then positions himself across the divide in the era of postcolonial globalism, which must, by historical necessity, introduce what he calls the condition of aterritorial instability, defy totalization, and encourage what he calls a nonintegrative discourse resulting from the ongoing deconstruction of Western democracy, as from the vast, diasporic displacement of populations across the continents. He demands that the avenues of postcolonial politicality structure the road map of art history in a way such that you gain direct access to the vexed issue of a citizenship ethic (complicit with/critical of the new concept of global sovereignty), and so that the springs of new subjectivities already unleashed by the great rupture of decolonization are uncovered.

Critical art privileges theory/ideology/critique of the aesthetic—and the imaginary is not suspended in such practice. The structural relationship of the imaginary and the symbolic may be weighted in favor of an interrogative mode in critical art, but the unexpected subversions nurtured in the imaginary are fully at play if we mean by critical art something distinctly other than plain discourse or polemics. Critical art bends the claim of radicality in favor of reflection through a subverting aesthetic, through formal innovation and a conceptual recoding of "artistic" materials, and it is this that sets in motion a vanguard within the contemporary.

IN CONCLUSION

To end on an ideological note: this criticality is not only what is useful for investigating the theoretical antinomies of art and culture, it is what is most forcefully deployed in interrogating the hegemonic presumptions of the West. More particularly, I refer to the confrontation between the "institution of art" serving as an invincible citadel of aesthetic and ethical value in the Western world, and the complex matrix of practices (cultural/aesthetic) produced in the still explosive conditions (as against institutions) of postcoloniality within and outside the West. To the degree that the postcolonial is both a global and postmodern phenomenon, it gives to these two brittle categories their more historical and multifaceted profiles. I therefore suggest that when we work through larger sets of (economic and social) antinomies characteristic of late capitalism, we must move to a situational analysis of cultural production within vastly heterogeneous geopolitical realities. I would thus argue for the necessity of constituting a space for self-reflexivity not only outside that of Westernism but also, indeed, in what Enwezor calls "distant places," which are, in my argument, both terribly near and terribly far. The postcolonial global in Enwezor's reckoning is characterized by the expanding diaspora; in mine, it is situated in locations geographically outside the West—Japan, Latin America, Africa, Asia—that offer at different times and for quite different reasons, a conjunctural dynamic propitious to radical, critical art that we may still choose to conjure in the form of an avant-garde.

Wary of what is now being called "transcultural extraterritoriality," I suggest we gauge the holding power of the contemporary within the global "time of now," but vis-à-vis named entities: nation-states, social and political formations, and all the territorially contained yet cruelly exposed sites of cultural production spread widely across a political topography.

In my ongoing argument, this is what provides the impetus for artists to set apace a vanguard: in dispersed locations, in displaced contemporalities. This is not to relativize the avant-garde out of existence. It is to give it a redoubled, contextual value. The efficacy of the claim on the radical, as, indeed, the worth of the praxis achieved, depends on the locus of operation, the historical moment, and the discursive position the practitioner is seen to (made to) occupy. It depends on the particular historical conjuncture and the degree of responsiveness of the "artist" in the face of exigent forces that spell the contemporary.

NOTES

1 Prabhat Patnaik, "The Meaning of Contemporary Globalization," keynote address, conference on globalization, N.R.R. Research Centre, C.R. Foundation for Social Progress, Kondapur, Hyderabad, 2004, 1.

2 Utsa Patnaik, *Republic of Hunger.*

3 Prabhat Patnaik, "The Meaning of Contemporary Globalization," 6.

4 Prabhat Patnaik, *The Retreat to Unfreedom.*

5 Prabhat Patnaik, "The Meaning of Contemporary Globalization," 11.

6 Chatterjee, in his *Nationalist Thought and the Colonial World,* and in his subsequent and ongoing work on pre- and postindependence India, characterizes the nature of state formation that has occurred in the aftermath of a national struggle for independence as that of national-state, distinguishing it from the European concept of the nation-state.

7 A consolidated frame of reference for the period 1992–2002 was foregrounded in an exhibition entitled "Ways of Resisting," curated by Vivan Sundaram for SAHMAT, a major Delhi-based platform enabling artists and intellectuals to articulate their social concerns and participate in the larger public sphere of the country.

8 I refer to literature produced by the lowest/"untouchable" members of the Hindu caste hierarchy who have assumed the term *dalit* (the oppressed) as a sign of their estrangement and defiance. The radical interrogation in dalit literature of the presumptions of universality in India's constitutional values—those of democracy, modernity, secularism—puts unprecedented pressure on what a culturally validated aesthetic could possibly mean in the deeply divided social life of India, as indeed on the national political formation itself. An account of this (almost) century-long, incomparably powerful literary movement is outside the scope of this essay.

9 For example, the late Bhupen Khakhar (1934–2003), who produced a remarkably unique iconography for gay sexuality. See also feminist articulations by artists and photographers using a wide range of materials and strategies: these include Nalini Malani, Rummana Hussain, Navjot Altaf, Nilima Sheikh, Dayanita Singh, Pushpamala N., Sheela Gowda, Anita Dube, Sheba Chhachhi, and Sonia Khurana. There are also key feminist works produced by theater practitioners and filmmakers. Together, this output marks, quite literally, the full stretch of the vanguard for cultural practice in India.

10 India's lofty tradition of auteur-based, modernist, and avant-garde cinema is well known. The limits of sovereign-subjectivity are tested to the limits in the oeuvre of filmmakers as diverse as Satyajit Ray, Ritwik Ghatak, Kumar Shahani, Mani Kaul, and Adoor Gopalakrishnan.

11 The Raqs Media Collective, a trio located in Delhi, has developed a theory and practice of documentary/video/new media art. Through their preferred tropes of migration/displacement, marginality/surveillance, they function across the transcultural zone of global art. Other young artists, mainly from Mumbai, use video and computer imaging to convert extended allegories of subversion into timely purposes: for example, Tushar Joag devises means to "facilitate" the common commuter of the Indian metropolis in navigating life in the city; Shilpa Gupta manipulates electronic

and digital forms to parody local consumer complicity in the perpetuation of global greed.

12 Kaviraj, "The Imaginary Institution of India," 33.

13 For updates on Patwardhan's films, see http://www.patwardhan.com. For an early contextualization of his film practice, see Patwardhan, "Waves of Revolution and Prisoners of Conscience: The Guerilla Film, Underground and in Exile." Patwardhan has seen himself, and been seen by film theorists such as Paul Willemen (see Pines and Willeman, *Questions of Third Cinema*), as continuing to contribute to the famous debate, initiated by critics and filmmakers Gettino and Solanas, known as "Towards a Third Cinema." See also Cubitt, "Interview with Anand Patwardhan"; Crusz and Liyanage, "Interview with Anand Patwardhan"; and Sharma, "Anand Patwardhan."

14 For a polemical discussion of liberationist cinema in the third world, see the collection of essays in Pines and Willemen, *Questions of Third Cinema.*

15 See Kanwar, *Notes for a Night of Prophecy;* Kanwar, "Not Firing Arrows"; Kierulf, *Amar Kanwar—Portraits;* Paasche, "Strong Political Filmportraits"; Saltz, "Worlds Apart."

16 Vasudevan compares the two documentarists in "Selves Made Strange." For a full discussion of the two, see Lal, "Travails of a Nation."

17 Indian film studies provide highly developed theses on contemporary cultural production and related ideologies of society and state. See, for example, Rajadhyksha's "The Bollywoodization of the Indian Cinema," "Visuality and Visual Art," "Rethinking the State after Bollywood," and *Cinema in the Time of Celluloid.* See also Prasad, *Ideology of the Hindi Film;* and Vasudevan, *Making Meaning in Indian Cinema.* Essays by Vasudevan relevant to this subject include "An Imperfect Public" and "Selves Made Strange."

18 Apropos the use of the word "film," I must clarify that I am not using an exclusively medium-based distinction between celluloid and electronic and digital media. This means, in effect, that I am not making a foundational difference between mediums on the basis of indexicality; nor restricting relational "truth" between image and material reality to the photochemical reproductive processes of the photograph and film. A relative difference will be indicated at points where it seems relevant to the argument.

19 The question of truth-value and witness accounts in the documentary genre is elaborated by Nash, "Experiments with Truth."

20 The "new" is placed in contrast to the early or "classical" documentary, which developed in the 1920s and 1930s in the Soviet Union and Britain (with their respective communist and conservative agendas for nation building). If the ideology of early documentary corresponds to the full spectrum of the modernist project (see Renov, *The Subject of Documentary,* 134–35), the new documentary (post-1960s), by its very chronology, engages with a critique of the national-modern compact.

21 Michael Renov, for example, attributes a major role to structuralist and poststructuralist thought, and, more broadly, to cumulative theoretical interventions post-1960s "that challenged certain fundamental bulwarks of Western thought"; and he sees film- and videomakers since the 1980s as having pursued "similar matters in their artistic practice, constructing historical selves that are nonetheless sites of uncertainty rather than coherence." See Renov, *The Subject of Documentary,* 104 and 109.

22 See Hardt and Negri, *Empire.*

23 I take it that there has always been an interface between art as artisanal practice (object-oriented and auratic, signatured or otherwise expressive) and the technology of vision provided by the lens (photography and film, video and the digital). This interface became, as we know, a major trope for theorizing visual modernity on the basis of a conceptual/semiotic divide between the original work of art and its re-producible doubles. I am referring of course to Walter Benjamin. From the 1960s, and especially with the emergence in the 1970s of a (feminist-led) conceptual (anti-) aesthetic, a re-vision of documentary material in the form of the photograph and, more broadly, lens-based work, takes place in Western art history. Thereon, the major entry of experimental video pulls art practice into the realm of the moving image.

24 Renov, *The Subject of Documentary,* 106.

25 There is a ubiquity of electronic and digital media, postcelluloid, and it may be simpler to refer to these in a hyphenated compound: "moving-image/media-prac-tices." For extended sets of definition and the terms of aesthetic discourse on what should strictly constitute "new" media technology, see Manovich, *The Language of New Media.*

26 Andre Bazin's foundational contribution to the concept of realism in cinema informs his entire work; for his preferred position, see "An Aesthetic of Reality."

27 Renov, *The Subject of Documentary,* 139.

28 Jameson, "Video: Surrealism without the Unconscious," characterized experimental video as offering a random play of signifiers; as providing a master trope for psychic fragmentation; indeed, as a medium constitutionally incapable of documentary value, as it is, at the same time, structurally bereft of memory. This characterization is supplemented and critiqued, among others, by Renov, *The Subject of Documentary,* 137–38 and 142.

29 In addition to Manovich's *The Language of New Media,* it is interesting to refer to an intensely interactive debate supported by the Sarai New Media Initiative, Delhi. See *Sarai Reader 03* and *Sarai Reader 04.*

30 While this is not the place to elaborate on the outburst of experimental video and video installation art by Chinese artists within and outside China in the last decade, it is relevant to my argument to mention those extraordinary examples of self-inflicted violence, of aggressive sexuality, of the comic grotesque, of macabre forms of mor-tality, that characterize the Chinese avant-garde, illustrating the deeply visceral re-sponse to a national-global fission. A brief selection of texts on recent Chinese art include Gao, *Inside Out;* Wu, *Transience;* and Merewether, "The Spectre of Being Human."

31 For example, Bill Viola's masterly oeuvre of video installations dating from the 1970s, wherein he consistently thematizes the body/self; Gary Hill's apparitional *Tall Ships* (1992) and, in radical contrast, Bruce Nauman's tragic-comic performative video *Shit in Your Hat-Head on a Chair* (1990).

32 I highlight the point by selecting some examples of artists/filmmakers working with the moving image framed within the white cube of the art space as a black-box (multiprojection) installation. Consider how a change in context, technology, and medium, how a reorientation of narrative and a changed protocol of spectatorship

complicates the representational politics of class, color, race, and ethnicity in Stan Douglas's *Le Detroit* (2000); Isaac Julien's *Frantz Fanon: Black Skin, White Mask* (1996) and its two-screen video installation, *Fanon S.A.* (1997–2004); William Kentridge's animation films like *Monument* (1990), *Mine* (1991), and *Felix in Exile* (1994); Steve McQueen's *Western Deep* (2002) and *Carib's Leap* (2002); Willie Doherty's *Nonspecific Threat* (2004); and Jayce Salloum's multiprojection, *Everything and Nothing and Other Works,* from the "Ongoing Project," Untitled (1998–2005). Consider how the theme of gender, frequently tuned to surreal modalities—erotic and introvert—is maneuvered through multiple looped and sequestered projections in Kutlug Ataman's *Four Seasons of Veronica Read* (2002) and, in strong contrast, in Araya Rasdjarmrearnsook's *Reading for Corpses* (2002).

33 See Nash, "Art and Cinema."

34 Consider just two examples: Chantal Akerman's multimonitor piece investigating the conditions of "illegal migration" on the Mexico-U.S. border, *From the Other Side* (2002), and Eyal Sivan's and Michael Khleifi's *Route 181* (2003), which unravels the history of imperialism in west Asia through a four-hour journey along the undefined border between Israel and Palestine.

35 Enwezor, "Documentary/Verité," 103.

36 Enwezor, "The Black Box," 42–55.

3

SOME ROTTEN SHOOTS FROM THE SEEDS OF TIME

ROSALIND KRAUSS

Fredric Jameson's recent book, *A Singular Modernity,* begins with something between a low moan of disbelief and a high shriek of rage. After all the years and all the words he has invested in the theorizing of postmodernism, with its demonstration of the death, the extinction, the collapse of Modernism, Jameson now finds himself looking out onto a landscape teeming with the living dead. Philosophy has found itself saddled with the returns not only of the moldy subfield of ethics but of aesthetics as well; meanwhile, within discussions of the contemporary arts, there has appeared what he describes as "the reminting of the modern, its repackaging, its production in great quantities for renewed sales in the intellectual marketplace." This "recrudescence of the language of an older modernity," as he puts it, can only be the work of "a few cantankerous and self-avowedly saurian intellectuals."[1]

Yet somehow, between the lines of his preface there is a sense that Jameson himself feels a sneaking responsibility for the resurgence of this outworn, exhausted language of autonomy and reflexiveness; and this possibility, I would submit, is to be found within his own masterly theorization of the postmodern: *The Seeds of Time.* The typological schema of postmodernism's genealogy is plotted there as setting out from an initial modernist binary in which the semes of Totality and Innovation face off one against the other within a semiotic square through which to think the contrary of each term as the logical components of postmodernity.[2] The contradictory seme of Totality will be the part or the hypostasized signifier, while that of Innovation will be repetition or Replication. From these two contraries comes, then, the postmodern binary. Working this genealogy within the sphere of architecture, Jameson finds his example of the converse of Innovation in the treatment of the architectural signifier in the work of Peter Eisenman, with its concentration on the grid as the fundamental, structural lattice of built form. His symmetrical example, combining Totality and Replication, turns to the work of Rem Koolhaas, particularly his project for the Très Grande Bibliothèque in Paris. Koolhaas's self-professed commitment to totality has been acknowledged in relation to the mammoth size of contemporary architectural projects, which he characterizes as "extra-large," and which he criticizes for annihilating any sense of human scale within the built environment.[3]

The brilliance of Koolhaas's solution to the form of the library-of-the-future was totally lost on the project's jury, which selected a banal and academic design for the commission. Koolhaas's idea was to conceive the library as something like the hard drive of a computer, entirely filled with parallel rows of shelving. Within this semisolid volume, a series of penetrations would intervene, like the holes in a block of Swiss cheese. These inner cavities would serve in turn as circulation, containing escalators, and stairways, or as functional spaces, such as reading rooms, auditoria, and administrative offices. The project as a whole, then, projects the idea of the human body, with information-filled brain invested by the organs of the lower torso—the unconscious operating below the scope of consciousness, as it were. For Jameson's seme of Totality I would here substitute the other central value of Modernism, which is that of Autonomy, since Koolhaas's building foregrounds those components of the built object that architectural discourse has separated out as constituting architecture's essence or ontology. These components are "promenade" on the one hand (otherwise called circulation) and pavilion (or built volume) on the other. Their masterful combination is to be found at the outset of architectural Modernism in the work of Le Corbusier. Although my title, with its epithet "rotten," may sound censorious, it is intended, instead, as self-critical, since I am the complete dinosaur who is not only committed to reinventing Modernism, but never admitted its eclipse by postmodernism in the first place.

Since one of the dimensions of this book is a focus on the contemporary, I will now turn to those present-day practitioners whose work is, I believe, not only the most powerful being done right now, but is as well wholly committed to the modernist project. I will take them up in sequence, but I will start with the one who represented the United States in the 2005 Venice Biennale: Edward Ruscha.

Contemporary criticism shares Fred Jameson's conviction about the extinction of Modernism and with it, the demise of the aesthetic medium, or distinct technical support for each genre of the visual arts, such as painting, or drawing, or photography. The assumption is that conceptual photography, published by artists in little pamphlets, was intended to jettison the aims of art photography with its attempts to assert the autonomy of a new aesthetic discipline, and instead, to adopt the look of photojournalism or documentary. In the context of contemporary assumptions about the obsolescence of the aesthetic medium, it is important to challenge that Conceptualist dogma about the status of books such as these and the "obviousness" of their renunciation of the aesthetic medium in the widest (but most naive) reception of them. Ruscha's case is particularly arresting since he, himself, so often invokes the concept of the medium, as when he says: "Right now, I am out to explore the medium. It's a playground or a beach so I'm going to send as much sand up in the air as I can! I think the next time I'll print with iodine. I have to be in control of the medium. The organic elements have to combine satisfactorily. What I'm interested in is the possible range; also in the use of a *processed* media."[4] Or, again, when he says: "New mediums encourage me. I still paint in oil paint. But what I'm interested in is illustrating *ideas*. I'm not interested in color, if a color suits me I use it intuitively. I'd prefer my painting to come to an end. . . . Painting for me is a tool."[5]

Ruscha is not sending sand "up in the air," so much as he is kicking it in the eyes of his admirers, who see him following the Conceptualist strategy of abandoning the traditional mediums of the visual in favor of the textual one of the book. Nonetheless one of his interlocutors recently detected a connecting thread that weaves its way through the varied directions of the books and links them as well to other parts of Ruscha's oeuvre. Addressing Ruscha, he comments: "You've said, half-seriously, I suspect, that you came to California because you like palm trees and hot rods. You've done the book of palm trees but never one of cars. It seems like cars are a missing link in the books, quite literally, since they would tie them together, be the conduit between the pools, apartments, and of course, the parking lots and gas stations. Perhaps I'm taking things too literally again."[6]

What this interviewer is suggesting here is that cars function as the "support" for all of Ruscha's practice and Ruscha himself understands that mediums are, in fact, supports for work, as when he says: "I'm painting on the book covers. I guess I'm just looking for another support. Maybe I'm moving away from the canvas, but I can't predict. I still paint on canvas, but I think there's another shift about to happen somewhere, maybe not so radical, but at least one that I know I will want to stick with."[7]

As Ruscha uses the word, *medium* can mean either the element in which color is suspended—traditionally oil—but for his "Stains," iodine, chocolate syrup, chutney, and so on; or "medium" can be the technical support for the image, traditionally canvas, but for him, book covers like taffeta, or the photography of the books' contents. Besides the extravagance of his invention of matrices—axle grease and caviar is an example—Ruscha's interest in the idea of medium as a type of support also takes shape as a set of rules, as when he remembers: "I had this idea for a book title—*Twenty-six Gasoline Stations*—and it became like a fantasy rule in my mind that I knew I had to follow."[8] So for him *medium* has less to do with the physicality of the support, than with a system of "rules." This is the system the philosopher Stanley Cavell wants to call "automatism," in an effort to get his reader to focus on the self-regulating character of traditional aesthetic mediums.[9]

The Greek word for "self," shared by the prefix for *auto*matism and *auto*mobile, not only restates the possible relation between car and medium but also turns "medium" in the direction of "medium specificity," or the medium's power to represent it*self* so central to modernist reflexivity. For Cavell, as for Ruscha, rules become necessary once the artist finds himself cut free of tradition and wandering haplessly in a field where "anything goes." In this situation the artist has to improvise, but it is only the rules—like the system of the fugue, or the resolution for the end of the sonata—that give his invention a goal, allowing him to gage whether his polyphonic improvisation on a melodic fragment or his impromptu cadenza called for by the score is successful or not.

"Auto" not only expresses the isolation of the artist, then; it also suggests that the source of the "rules" comes from within the support: the "twenty-six" of Ruscha's book title deriving from the number of gas refills necessary between California and Oklahoma City and thus referring to the demands of driving and the exigencies of the car. In good modernist tradition, "parking lots" in his 1964 project *Thirty-four Parking Lots* could refer to the flatness of the page, but it more probably marks the serial nature of the car, its existence as a multiple, like the printed book itself.

In this form "medium" is both specific, which is to say self-reflexive, and inventive, in that anything can be a medium, even the most common contemporary substance the artist—newly *auto*nomous—can imagine. In interviews with Ruscha his interlocutors ask about other aspects of Los Angeles, besides palm trees and swimming pools, that attracted him to the city. In this context they ask about the beat poets such as Jack Kerouac and Gregory Corso.

Jack Kerouac's *On the Road* is perhaps the most famous and widely read book of the beat generation. In it, its two main characters, Sal Paradise and Dean Moriarty, and their companions rocket back and forth across the conti-

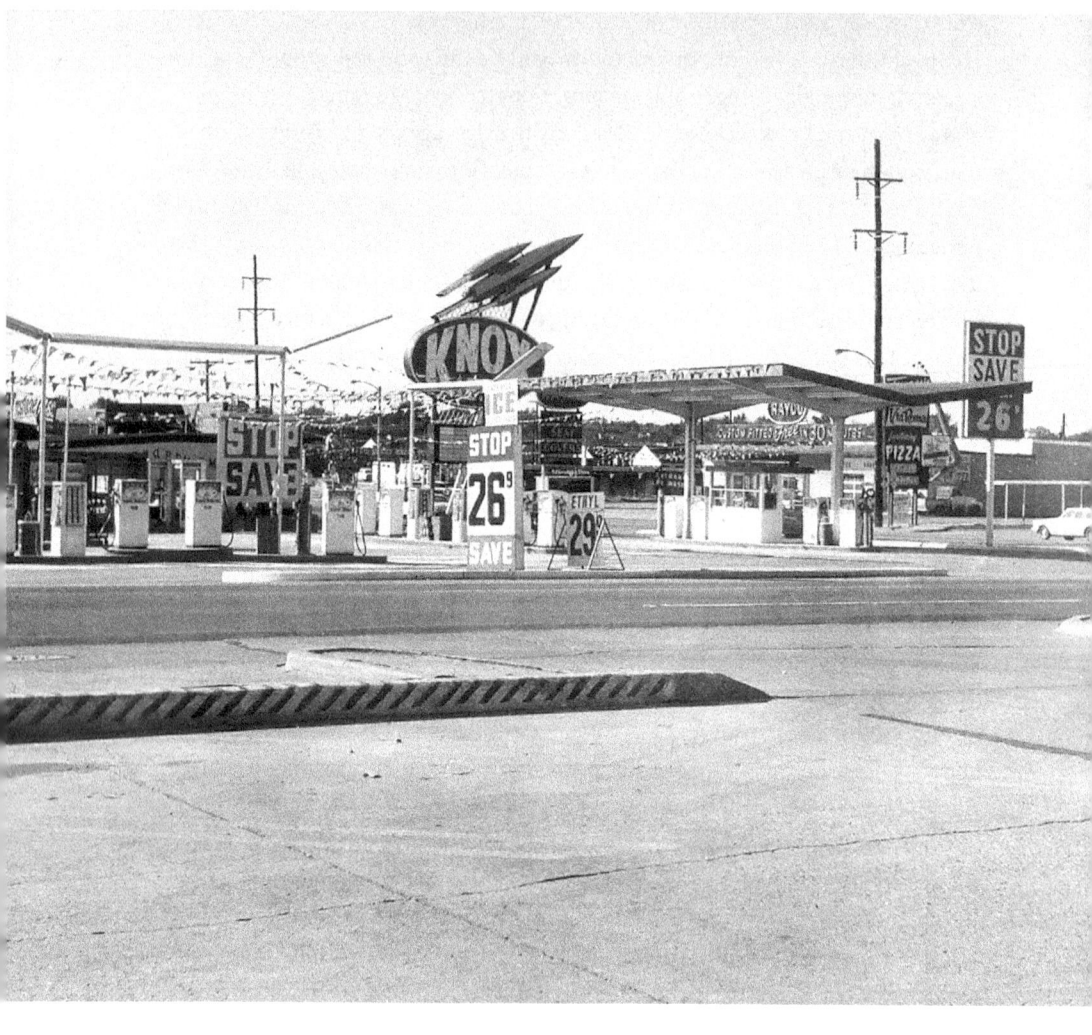

Ed Ruscha, *Knox Less, Oklahoma City, Oklahoma,* 1962. Gelatin silver print; black offset printing on white paper. © Ed Ruscha. Courtesy of Gagosian Gallery, New York.

nent, like pinballs knocking against the buffers and sides of the tray and making lights blink in the panel above. The feverish intensity of their travel, in its dogged obsession and its frantic restlessness, has the road itself as its support or what, in another way of speaking, could be called its "medium." Kerouac wrote the book on manuscript sheets taped together so as not to interrupt the flow of his language with changes of typing paper: the book forming a single track of words 120 feet long, a road of verbiage. Kerouac writes: "As a seaman I used to think of the waves rushing beneath the shell of the ship and the bottomless deeps thereunder—now I could feel the road some twenty inches beneath me, unfurling and flying and hissing at incredible speeds across the groaning continent with that mad Ahab at the wheel. When I closed my eyes all I could see was the road unwinding into me."[10]

The dislocation tracked by Kerouac and the poets who came to be known as the beat generation was measured by the cities they traversed as they hitchhiked coast to coast, each the name of another set of expectations: Council Bluffs, Shelton, Columbus, North Platte, Ogden, Cheyenne, Denver.

Peeling off the layers of Ruscha's experience from his San Francisco days in 1968, yields the names of the beat heroes, like Kerouac. "Beatniks were in," he says, "and that lifestyle seemed appealing to us all. Jack Kerouac and so on had a strong effect on all of us."[11] From 1968 to 2004 is a leap, but at a recent talk he gave at the Whitney Museum, when asked what photographic project he was then working on, Ruscha answered that he was doing a book that would interpret Kerouac's *On the Road*, this admission making the car the most enduring and specific of his concerns.

"Medium specificity" may ring strangely in the instance of Ruscha, but his very case promotes a sense of how eccentrically *medium* can be used to track this dimension of contemporary practice. If the car can become a medium, then anything might be pressed into such service. It only needs the set of rules that will open onto the possibility of artistic practice—like the musical goal in the example of improvisation. The very idea of the artist's invention of a medium and thus his or her devising a set of rules will undoubtedly make us nervous. A medium is, after all, a shared language developed over centuries of practice so that no individual initiative can either organize new sources of its meaning or change established ones. It is as though we were imagining the artist as playing a game and announcing in the middle that the bishop moves orthogonally instead of diagonally. Ruscha's inventions are arbitrary, but not as eccentric as the one just mentioned. His *Stains* exult in the exoticism of his choices (examples are blueberry extract on rayon, and cherry stain on rayon), but the very term "stains" pays homage to the recent history of painting in which staining provided what was felt to be a necessary alternative to drawing such that from Pollock to Morris Louis and Helen Frankenthaler, laying down a stain was a way of avoiding the violence of a hardened contour. The rules for "stains" are thus "invented" within the context of a set of principles for abstract painting; these latter are presupposed for the possibility and pertinence of the invention of the former.

So remote is the idea of the medium from the center of attention of the contemporary viewer that concern for the medium is often confused with very different preoccupations. The work of the Irish artist James Coleman is a case in point. The medium he has "invented" is the slide tape, a sequence of exactingly projected slides synchronized with a taped sound track. The slide tape is familiar to most of us from the advertising projections we've seen in train stations and airports. It's part of the spectacle culture so widespread in the West—a public form of commercial entertainment to distract commuters and relax shoppers. Coleman's version of the slide tape seems to have as one of its "rules" that it will acknowledge this condition as entertainment, and to this end his characters are often lined up across the visual field as though taking a bow at the end of a play. Altogether its "rules" take the form of *auto*reference; the staccato sound of the slides falling into place as the carousels turn in sequence is imitated on the sound track of the 1994 work $INITIALS$, as the narrator spells various words by rapping out the individual letters: e-s-o-p-h-o-g-u-and-s.[12]

There is another "rule" Coleman has invented, which we might miss in a casual viewing, since we so often rely on a set of familiar ideas in explanation for this vivid work. The human subject, we have been taught, is constructed, a concatenation of social, ethnic, and even gender protocols to produce the roles each of us will play. Coleman's theatricality presents this project of construction and the way individuals bend to its demands, we might think. In our reading of what we take to be the "identity politics" of Coleman's work, we might neither notice nor ask about the curious choreography of his characters, who interact by facing the audience rather than each other. If we had taken the time we would have thought of the way Roy Lichtenstein's lovers are always looking directly out of the frame even while their speech balloons project the most tender expressions toward each other. We would have realized that the syntax of film editing is open neither to the comic book illustrator nor to Coleman, since a film can jump back and forth between a speaker's face and the person to whom he or she is talking, the alternation (called "angle, reverse-angle" in ciné-speak) happening in the blink of an eye.

For Coleman to imitate angle, reverse-angle would be more "realistic" but extravagantly distended in terms of the number of images needed to enact even

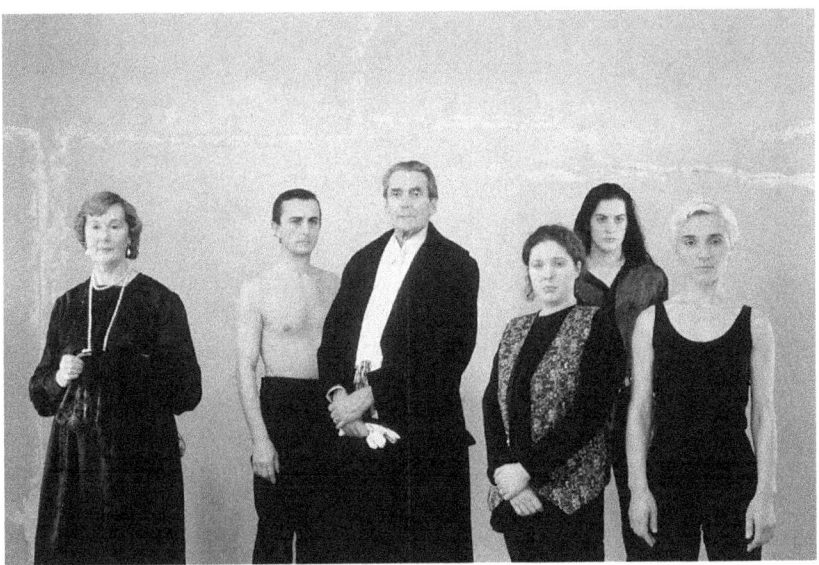

James Coleman, *I N I T I A L S,* 1994. Slide-tape, multiple-slide projection with synchronized audiotape. Courtesy of the artist and Marian Goodman Gallery, New York.

the briefest of exchanges. It is both simpler and more economical for his actors to express their most fervent emotions toward one another as they both stolidly face the camera. So one of Coleman's rules could be called the "double face-out." He takes it from other forms of visual narrative: not only comic books, but also photo novels and advertising. What it supplies him with is a reminder of the screen's surface as the underlying principle from which the "rule" derives.

Every space of projection—whether video or film—seems to supply proof that there is no field of "specificity," no surface against which to register the unity and extension of something like the picture plane. Since the picture plane had been, for many centuries, the cornerstone for "specificity," its erosion is the warrant, we believe, of these projection artists' indifference to the problem of the medium. From Coleman, our attention might be drawn to William Kentridge, a South African artist whose animated films pursue the problems of apartheid across the African veld with its mines and its slag heaps. Kentridge is another artist, however, who is inventing a set of "rules." His technique is erasure; every line is a potential pentimento, a mark to be modified, each modification recorded by a frame of film. This "rule" produces many of the sequences such as a car ride through which the view is of the landscape constantly blurred by the windshield wipers, an image of the very act of erasure. The car's interior is then the site of the traumatic memory that forms the

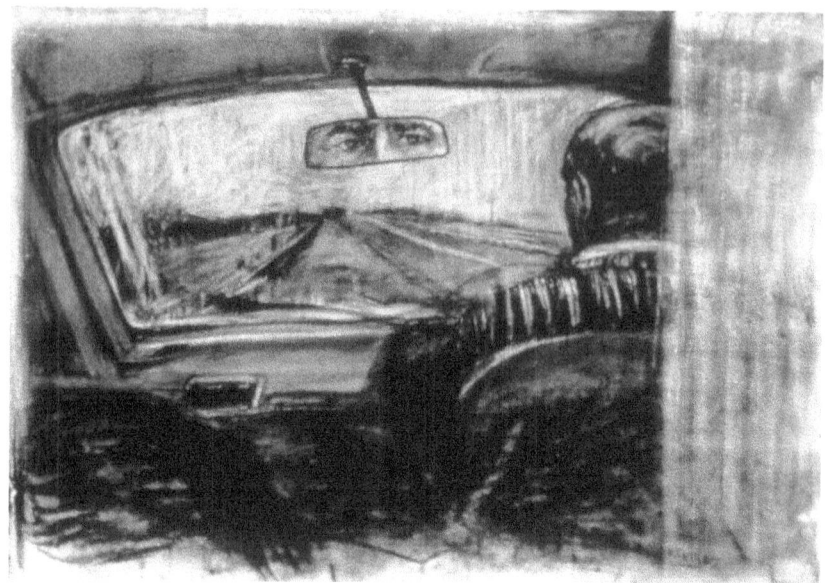

William Kentridge, *History of the Main Complaint*, 1995–96. Still from video with sound. Courtesy of the artist and Marian Goodman Gallery, New York.

narrative climax of the 1995–1996 work, *History of the Main Complaint*, Kentridge's technique constantly narrativizing his own process.[13] Erasure is to line what *Stains* is to drawing: two artists having converged within the grammar of modernist painting to discover the same set of "rules" for self-reference.

Nothing about the recoding of "self-reference" into "rules" will distract us from the poststructuralist critique of specificity with its metaphysical recourse to the "proper" or to the "self-presence" of the inherent truth of the nature of a medium.

Within modernist practice, artists will reach for signs that function as algorithms of the structural support or medium within which they occur. As the core or center of that structure, such a sign secures the unity or singularity of the work itself, a unity that in another era Walter Benjamin had named its "aura."

If the condemnation of the reflexivity of self-reference has been the message of many texts by Jacques Derrida, we also owe to Derrida its rehabilitation through his concept of the re-mark. In "The Double Session," addressing the structure of the fold or hymen within the context of mimetic repetition or redoubling, Derrida asks his audience to notice what the fold adds to the identical halves of the mirrored twins. In thinking this logic of the re-mark it is helpful, I think, to recall Roman Jakobson's question about the universal character of nursery language as found in systematically redoubled forms such as, Mama, Papa, dodo, caca, and so forth.[14] His answer, we remember, is that the infant, while playing with the random phonetic production available to the human mouth, will notice that, by doubling a given sound, he or she can retroactively mark the first sound as a signifier and thus a bearer of meaning. But this marking not only marks and thus redefines the first phoneme; it also marks the space between that phoneme and itself, adding to its mark the seme of the diacritical space of differentiality. The logic of the re-mark is, then, that in marking a mirror-object as the same as itself, it simultaneously marks itself as different, or to go the next step, as self-different.

This is the direction Sam Weber takes in his masterful discussion of the essence of television, which he names as its "differential specificity." Saying, "Above all television differs from itself," he produces an example of the medium-specific, one that escapes poststructuralist strictures.[15]

This "constitutive heterogeneity" might well define the late modernist work I've been discussing in this essay. In returning to the example of William Kentridge, we notice his reflexive strategy of mapping the image of the frames of the film we are even now watching onto the frame of the film itself. But by marking the seme of an invisible, or imperceptible element, since the cinematic frame is phenomenologically beyond us, he re-marks the space between the frames or that infrastructural visual difference that produces the sense of motion of film itself.

The dinosaur you've been reading is, indeed, an unreconstructed modernist. It seems to me the only aesthetic option open to us today.

NOTES

1 Jameson, *A Singular Modernity,* 7.
2 Jameson, *The Seeds of Time,* 133.
3 Jameson, *Seeds of Time,* 134–38.
4 Ruscha, "Ed Ruscha Discusses His Latest Work," in Ruscha, *Leave Any Information at the Signal,* 30.
5 Ruscha, "Ed Ruscha Discusses His Latest Work," in Ruscha, *Leave Any Information at the Signal,* 32.
6 Ruscha, "Ed Ruscha: An Interview," in Ruscha, *Leave Any Information at the Signal,* 213.
7 Ruscha, "Conversation between Walter Hopps and Ed Ruscha," in Ruscha, *Leave Any Information at the Signal,* 322.
8 Failing, "Ed Ruscha, Young Artist," in Ruscha, *Leave Any Information at the Signal,* 233.
9 Cavell, *Must We Mean What We Say?,* 215–23.

10 Kerouac, *On the Road,* 234–35.

11 From Paul Karlstrom's interview with Ruscha, in Ruscha, "Interview with Ed Ruscha in His Western Avenue, Hollywood Studio," in Ruscha, *Leave Any Information at the Signal,* 114.

12 *I N I T I A L S* was included in Coleman, *Projected Images.*

13 Christove-Bakargiev, *William Kentridge,* 99–102.

14 Jakobson and Halle, *Fundamentals of Language.*

15 Weber, *Mass Mediauras,* 110.

4

THE TOPOLOGY OF CONTEMPORARY ART

BORIS GROYS

Today, the term "contemporary art" does not simply designate art that is produced in our time. Rather, today's contemporary art demonstrates the way in which the contemporary as such shows itself—the act of presenting the present. In this respect contemporary art is different from Modern art, which was directed toward the future and it is different also from Postmodern art, which was a historical reflection on the Modern project. Contemporary "contemporary art" privileges the present with respect to the future and to the past. So, to rightly characterize the nature of contemporary art, it seems to be necessary to situate it in its relationship to the Modern project and to its Postmodern re-evaluation.

The central notion of Modern art was that of creativity. The genuinely creative artist was supposed to effectuate a radical break with the past, to erase, to destroy the past, to achieve a zero point of artistic tradition—and by doing so to give a new start to a new future. The traditional, mimetic artwork was subjected to the iconoclastic, destructive work of analysis and reduction. It is also no accident that the vocabulary constantly used by the historical avant-garde is the language of iconoclasm. Abolishing traditions, breaking with conventions, destroying old art, and eradicating out-dated values were the slogans of the day. The practice of the historical avant-garde was based on the equation —"negation is creation"—already formulated by Bakunin, Stirner, and Nietzsche. Iconoclastic images of destruction and reduction were destined to serve as the icons of the future. The artist was supposed to embody "active nihilism"— the nothingness that originates everything. But how can an individual artist prove that he or she is really, genuinely creative? Obviously, an artist can show it only by demonstrating how far he or she has gone along the way of reduction and destruction of the traditional image, how radical, how iconoclastic his or her work is. But to recognize a certain image as truly iconoclastic we have to be able to compare it with the traditional images, with the icons of the past. Otherwise the work of symbolic destruction would remain unaccounted for.

The recognition of the iconoclastic, of the creative, of the new requires, therefore, a permanent comparison with the traditional, with the old. The iconoclastic and the new can only be recognized by the art historically in-formed, museum-trained gaze. This is why, paradoxically, the more you want to free yourself from the art tradition, the more you become subjected to the logic of the art historical narrative and to museum collecting. A creative act, if it is understood as an iconoclastic gesture, presupposes a permanent reproduction of the context in which the act is effectuated. This kind of reproduction infects the creative act from the beginning. We can even say that, under the condition of the modern museum, the newness of newly produced art is not established *post factum*—as a result of a comparison with old art. Rather, the comparison takes place before the emergence of a new, radical, iconoclastic artwork—and virtually produces this new artwork. The Modern artwork is re-presented and re-cognized before it is produced. It follows that modernist production by negation is governed by just this reproduction of the means of comparison—of a certain historical narrative, of a certain artistic medium, of a certain visual language, of a certain fixed context of comparison. This paradoxical character of the Modern project was recognized and described by a number of the theore-ticians and reflected on by many artists in the 1960s and 1970s. Their recogni-tion of this inner repetitiveness within the Modern project led to a redefinition of it during recent decades, and to the postmodern thematization of the prob-lematics of repetition, iteration, and reproduction.

It is no accident that Walter Benjamin's essay "The Work of Art in the Age of Mechanical Reproduction" became so influential during these postmodern de-cades. That happened because, for Benjamin, mass reproduction—and not the creation of the new—constituted modernity. As is well known, in his essay Benjamin introduced the concept of "aura" to describe the difference between original and copy under the conditions of perfect technical reproducibility. Since then, the concept has had an astonishing philosophical career, largely as a result of the famous formula of the "loss of the aura" characterizing the fate of the original in the modern age. The "loss of the aura" is described by Benjamin precisely as a loss of the fixed, constant, and reconfirmable context of an art-work. According to him, in our age the artwork leaves its original context and begins to circulate anonymously in networks of mass communication, reproduction, and distribution. That is, the production of the mass culture operates by a reversal of the "high" modernist art strategy: "high" modernist art negates the repetition of traditional images but leaves the traditional art historical context intact, whereas "low" art reproduces these images but negates, destroys their original context. In the modern age you negate either an artwork or its aura, its context—but not both of them simultaneously.

Accent on the loss of the aura is, on one hand, totally legitimate, and certainly in tune with the overall intention of Benjamin's text. Nevertheless, it may be less the loss of the aura but, rather, its emergence that gives us the opportunity to reach a better understanding of the processes taking place in today's art, which operates predominantly with new media and techniques of reproduction. Concentrating on the emergence of aura might lead to a better understanding, not only of the destiny of the original, but also of the destiny of the copy in our culture. In fact, the aura, as described by Benjamin, only comes into being thanks to the modern technique of reproduction. That is, it emerges precisely at the very moment it is fading. It is born precisely for the same reason that it disappears. Indeed, in his text Benjamin starts from the possibility of a perfect reproduction that would no longer allow any "material," visually recognizable difference between original and copy. The question he formulates is this: does the erasure of any visually recognizable difference between original and copy also mean the erasure of the difference between the two as such? Benjamin's answer to that question is, of course, no. The erasure of all visually recognizable differences between original and copy is always only a potential one because it does not eliminate another difference existing between them which, albeit invisible, is none the less decisive: the original has an aura that the copy lacks. The original has an aura because it has a fixed context, a well-defined place in space; through that particular place it is inscribed also in history as a singular, original object. The copy is, on the contrary, without a place and is thus ahistorical—being right from the beginning a potential multiplicity. Reproduction means dislocation, deterritorialization; it transports artworks to networks of topologically indeterminable circulation. Benjamin's corresponding formulations are very well known: "Even the most perfect reproduction of a work of art is lacking in one element: its presence in time and space, its unique existence at the place where it happens to be," and he continues: "the here and now of the original is the prerequisite to the concept of authenticity."[1] But if the difference between original and copy is only a topological one—if it is only a difference between a closed, fixed, marked, auratic context and an open, unmarked, profane space of anonymous mass circulation—then not only is the operation of dislocation and deterritorialization of the original possible, but so, also, is the operation of relocation and reterritorialization of the copy. We are not only able to produce a copy out of an original by a technique of reproduction but we also are able to produce an original out of a copy by a technique of topological relocation of this copy—that is, by a technique of installation.

Installation art, nowadays the leading form in the framework of contemporary art, operates as a reversal of reproduction. The installation takes a copy out of an allegedly unmarked, open space of anonymous circulation and puts it— even if only temporarily—in a fixed, stable, closed context of a topologically well-defined "here and now." This means that all the objects placed in an installation are originals, even when—or precisely when—they circulate outside of the installation as copies. Artworks in an installation are originals for one simple topological reason: it is necessary to go to the installation to see them. The installation is, above all, a socially codified variation of individual flaneurship as described by Benjamin, and therefore, a place for the aura, for "profane illumination."[2] Our contemporary relationship with art cannot, therefore, be reduced to a "loss of the aura." Rather, the modern age organizes a complex interplay of dislocations and relocations, of deterritorializations and reterritorializations, of deauratizations and reauratizations. What differentiates contemporary art from previous times is only the fact that the originality of a work in our time is not established depending on its own form, but through its inclusion in a certain context, in a certain installation, through its topological inscription.

Benjamin overlooked the possibility—and thus the unavoidability—of reauratizations, relocations, and new topological inscriptions of a copy because he shared with high Modern art a belief in the unique, normative context of art. Under this presupposition, for an artwork to lose its unique, original context would mean that it would lose its aura forever, that it would become a copy of itself. The reauratization of an individual artwork would require a sacralization of the whole profane space of the topologically undetermined mass circulation of a copy—which would be a totalitarian, fascist project. That was the main problem of Benjamin's thinking: he perceived the space of the mass circulation of the copy as a universal, neutral, and homogeneous space. He insisted on the permanent visual recognizability, on the self-identity of the copy as it circulates in our contemporary culture. But now, both of these main presuppositions in Benjamin's text are questionable. In the framework of contemporary culture an image is permanently circulating from one medium to another medium, and from one closed context to another closed context. A certain length of film footage can be shown in a cinema theater, then converted to a digital form and appear on somebody's Web site, or be shown during a conference as an illustration, or watched privately on a television screen in a person's living room, or put in a context of a museum installation. In this way, through different contexts and mediums, this footage is transformed by different program languages, different software, different framings on the screen, different placement in an installation space, and so on. Are we dealing all the time with the same film footage? Is it the same copy of the same copy of the same original?

The topology of today's networks of communication, of generation, translation, and distribution of images is extremely heterogeneous. The images are all the time transformed, rewritten, reedited, reprogrammed on their way through these networks. They become visually different at every such step. Their status as copies becomes, therefore, just a cultural convention—as, earlier, was the status of the original. Benjamin suggested, as we saw, that the new technology was able to make a copy more and more identical to the original. But the contrary has become the case. Contemporary technology thinks and works in generations. To transmit information from one generation of hardware and software to a next generation means to transform it in a significant way. The metaphoric use of the notion of "generation," as it is practiced now in the context of technology, is very revealing. All of us know what it means to transmit a certain cultural heritage from one generation of students to another. The situation of "mechanical reproduction" in the context of, let us say, the contemporary Internet, looks no less difficult—perhaps it will prove to be even more so.

We are as unable to stabilize a copy as a copy as we are unable to stabilize an original as an original. There are no eternal copies, just as there are no eternal originals. Reproduction is as much infected by originality as originality is infected by reproduction. By circulating through different contexts a copy becomes a series of different originals. Every change of context, every change of medium can be interpreted as a negation of the status of a copy as a copy—as an essential rupture, as a new start that opens out a new future. In this sense, a copy is never really a copy, but rather always a new original in a new context. Every copy is by itself a flaneur; it experiences time and again its own "profane illuminations," turning it into an original. It loses old auras, and gains new ones. It remains, perhaps, the same copy, but it becomes different originals. This shows that the Postmodern project to reflect on the repetitive, iterative, reproductive character of an image is as paradoxical as was the Modern project of recognizing the original and the new. This is also why Postmodern art is able to look very new even if—indeed, actually because—it is directed against the notion of the new. Our decision to recognize a certain image as an original or as a copy is dependent on the context—on the scene where this decision is taken.

And this decision is always a contemporary decision, one that belongs not to the past and not to the future but to the present.

That is why I would argue that the installation is the leading art form of contemporary art. The installation demonstrates a certain selection, a certain chain of choices, and a certain logic of inclusions and exclusions. By doing so, an installation manifests here and now certain decisions about what is old and what is new, what is an original and what is a copy. Every large exhibition or installation is made with the intention of designing a new order of memories, of proposing the new criteria for telling a story, for differentiating between past and future. Modern art was working on the level of individual form. Contemporary art is working on the level of context, framework, background, or of a new theoretical interpretation. That is why contemporary art is less a production of individual artworks than it is a manifestation of an individual decision to include or to exclude things and images that circulate anonymously in our world, to give them a new context or to deny it to them: a private selection that is at the same time publicly accessible and thereby made manifest, present, explicit. Even if an installation consists of one individual painting, it is still an installation, since the crucial aspect of the painting as an artwork is not the fact that it was produced by an artist but that it was selected by an artist and presented as something selected.

The installation space can, of course, incorporate all kinds of things and images that circulate in our civilization: paintings, drawings, photographs, texts, videos, films, recordings, objects of all kinds, and so on. That is why the installation is frequently denied the status of a specific art form, because the question of its specific medium arises. The traditional art media are all defined by a specific material support for the medium: canvas, stone, or film. The material support of the medium in an installation, however, is the space itself. This artistic space of the installation may be a museum or art gallery, but also a private studio, or a home, or a building site. All of them may be turned into a site of installation by documenting the selection process, whether private or institutional. That does not mean, however, that the installation is somehow "immaterial." On the contrary, the installation is material par excellence, since it is spatial. Being in space is the most general definition of being material. The installation reveals precisely the materiality of the civilization in which we live, because it *installs* everything that our civilization simply *circulates*. The installation thus demonstrates the material hardware of civilization that would otherwise go unnoticed behind the surface of image circulation in the mass media. At the same time an installation is not a manifestation of already existing relationships among things; on the contrary, an installation offers an opportunity to use the things and images of our civilization in a very subjective, individual way. In a certain sense the installation is for our time what the novel was for the nineteenth century. The novel was a literary form that included all other literary forms of that time; the installation is an art form that includes all other contemporary art forms.

The inclusion of film footage in an artistic installation shows its transformative power in an especially obvious way. A video or film installation secularizes the conditions of film presentation. The film spectator is no longer immobilized, bound to a seat and left in the darkness, supposed to watch a movie from its beginning to its end. In the video installation where a video is moving in a loop the spectator may move about freely in the room, and may leave or return at any time. This movement of the spectator in the exhibition space cannot be arbitrarily stopped because it has an essential function in the perception of the installation. Clearly a situation arises here in which the contradictory expectations of a visit to a movie theater and a visit to an exhibition space create a conflict for the visitors: should they stand still and allow the pictures to play before them as in a movie theater, or move on? The feeling of insecurity resulting from this conflict puts a spectator in a situation of choice. The spectator is confronted by the necessity to develop an individual strategy of looking at the film, at the individual film narrative. The time of contemplation must be continually renegotiated between artist and spectator. This shows very clearly that a film is radically, essentially changed by being put under the conditions of an installation visit—from being the same copy the film becomes a different original.

If an installation is a space where the differentiation between original and copy, innovation and repetition, past and future takes place, how can we speak of an individual installation itself as being original or new? One installation cannot be a copy of another installation because an installation is by definition present, contemporary. An installation is a presentation of the present, a decision that takes place here and now. At the same time, however, an installation cannot be truly new, simply because it cannot be immediately compared to other, earlier, older installations. To compare one installation to another installation we have to create a new installation that would be a place of such a comparison. Which means that we have no outside position in relationship to installation practice. That is why the installation is so pervasive and unavoidable an art form.

And that is why it is also truly political. The growing importance of the installation as an art form is in a very obvious way connected to the repoliticization of art that we have experienced in the recent years. The installation is not only political because it provides the possibility of documenting political positions, projects, actions, and events. It is certainly true that such documentation has also become a widespread artistic practice in recent years. Yet more important is that fact that installation is in itself, as I suggested earlier, a space of decision making: first of all, for decisions concerning the differentiation between old and new, traditional and innovative.

In the nineteenth century Søren Kierkegaard discussed the difference between the old and the new using as an example the figure of Jesus Christ. Kierkegaard noted that for a spectator who was a contemporary of Jesus Christ it was impossible to recognize in Christ a new god, precisely because he did not look new. Rather, he initially looked like every other ordinary human being at that historical time. In other words, an objective spectator at that time, confronted with the figure of Christ, could not find any visible, concrete difference between Christ and an ordinary human being, a visible difference that could suggest that Christ is not simply a man, but also a god. So, for Kierkegaard, Christianity is based on the impossibility of recognizing Christ as God, a function of the impossibility of recognizing Christ as visually different: by merely looking on Christ we cannot decide, is he a copy or an original, ordinary human being or God. Paradoxically, for Kierkegaard this implied that Christ was *really* new and not merely recognizably different, and therefore that Christianity is a manifestation of difference beyond difference. We might say that Christ, according to Kierkegaard, was a ready-made among gods, just as Duchamp's urinoire was a ready-made among artworks. In both cases, the context decides the newness. In both cases we cannot rely on an established, institutional context, but have to create something like a theological or artistic installation that would allow us to make a decision and to articulate it.

The differentiation between old and new, repetitive and original, conservative and progressive, traditional and liberal is not, therefore, just one set of differentiations among many others. Rather, it is a central differentiation that informs all other religious and political options in modernity. The vocabulary of the modern politics shows this very clearly. Contemporary artistic installation has as its goal to present the scene, the context, and the strategy of this differentiation as it takes place here and now. That is, indeed, why it can be called genuinely contemporary. But how does the contemporary installation relate to the recent controversy between Modern and Postmodern art practices?

The iconoclastic gesture that produces the modernist artwork functions, of course, not simply as a manifestation of artistic subjectivity understood as pure negativity. This gesture had the positive goal of revealing the materiality of the artwork, its pure presence. It aimed to establish, as Malevich stated it, the "supremacy of art" by liberating art from its submission to mimetic illusion, communicative intention, and the traditional requirements of instantaneous recognizability. Too often characterized as "formalistic," modernist art can hardly be defined in formal terms alone. Modernist artworks are too hetero-geneous on a formal level to be subsumed under any purely formalistic criteria. Rather, modernist art can be characterized by its specific claim to be true: in the sense that it be present, thoroughly visible, immediately revealed, or, to use a Heideggerian term, "unconcealed." Beyond this specific claim to truth the modernist artwork loses its edge and becomes merely decorative, whatever its form might be. Precisely this claim to truth was put in question by postmodern-ist criticism: the apparently immediate presence of a modernist artwork was accused of concealing its actual repetitive, reproductive character. The mere fact that a modernist artwork is still recognizable as an artwork means that it reproduces the general conditions of recognizability of an artwork as artwork, even if it seems to be quite original in form. Moreover, the iconoclastic gesture that produces the modernist artwork can itself be described as functioning in a repetitive, reproductive manner. This means that the truth of the modernist artwork, understood as its immediate material presence, can easily be described as a lie, as a concealment of the potentially infinite number of reproductions, copies that make this "original" artwork identifiable, recognizable in the first place. Postmodernist art gives up the claim to truth that Modernism has raised. But postmodernist art does not formulate its own claim to truth, remaining exclusively critical and deconstructive. Under the conditions of Postmodernity art becomes a lie that manifests itself as a lie, finding its truth in the classical paradox of a liar confessing to be a liar. This paradox arises because a Postmod-ern artwork presents itself as merely an example of an infinite sequence of reproductions and repetitions. This means that the Postmodern artwork is present and absent, true and false, real and simulated at the same time.

With these distinctions in mind, it becomes relatively easy to characterize the place that the contemporary installation occupies in relationship to the mod-ernist claim to truth and to its Postmodern deconstruction. The installation is, as it was already said, a finite space of presence where different images and objects are arranged and exhibited. These images and objects present them-selves in a very immediate way. They are here and now, and they are thoroughly visible, given, unconcealed. But they are unconcealed only as long as they are parts of this individual installation. Taken separately, these images and objects do not raise the claim to be unconcealed and true. Quite the contrary, these images and objects manifest—mostly in a very obvious way—their status as copies, as reproductions, as repetitions. We can say that the installation formulates and makes explicit the conditions of truth for the images and objects that this installation contains. Every image and object in the installation can be seen as being true, unconcealed, present, but only inside the installation space. In their relationship to the outside space the same images and objects can be seen as revealing and at the same time concealing their status of being merely the items of the potentially infinite sequences of repetition and reproduction. The Modern artwork raised the claim to be unconditionally true, to be unconcealed. Postmodern criticism put this unconditional claim into question, but without asking about the conditions of truth understood as presence, as unconcealment. The installation formulates these conditions by creating a finite, closed space that becomes the space of open conflict and unavoidable decision between original and reproduction, between presence and representation, between unconcealed and concealed. But the closure that is effectuated by an installation should not be interpreted as an opposition to the "openness" as such. By closure, the installation creates its outside and opens itself to this outside. Closure is here not an opposition to openness but is its precondition. The infinite is, on the contrary, not open because it has no outside. Being open is not the same thing as being all-inclusive. The artwork that is conceived as a machine of infinite expansion and inclusion is not an open artwork but an artistic counterpart of an imperial hubris. The installation is a place of openness, of disclosure, of unconcealment precisely because it situates inside its finite space images and objects that also circulate in the outside space—in this way it opens itself to its outside. That is why the installation is able to openly manifest the conflict between the presence of images and objects inside a finite horizon of our immediate experience and their invisible, virtual, "absent" circulation in the space outside of this horizon—a conflict that defines contemporary cultural practice.

NOTES

1 Benjamin, "The Work of Art," 214–15.
2 On flaneurship and the aura, see Benjamin, "On Some Motifs in Baudelaire," 321–29 and 337–43. On "profane illumination" see the discussion in Benjamin, "Surrealism," 207–21.

PART 2: MULTIPLE MODERNITIES

5

ON THE CONTINGENCY OF MODERNITY AND

THE PERSISTENCE OF CANONS

MONICA AMOR

Here it becomes evident that the hallmark of the new type of researchers is not the eye for
the "all encompassing whole" nor the eye for the "comprehensive context" (which mediocrity has claimed for itself) but rather the capacity to be at home in marginal domains.
—Walter Benjamin, "Rigorous Study of Art"

While theoretical proposals critical of blind belief in the unmediated referen-
tiality of historical discourse are intrinsic to the modern—one has only to think
of Walter Benjamin's contempt for tradition, for the kind of historical tradition
that stupefies the past through a corrosive order, an approach that he countered
with a practice of violent decontextualization and deadly interpretation[1]—
contemporaneity has gone blithely further, deploying a relentless attack on the
ideological categories of history and its *grand recits.*[2] In this attempt to map the
spasmodic terrain of history, solid ground has been left behind. For art historical discourse this has meant a degree of unpredictability, a methodological
freedom somehow lacking in the social sciences. This situation might allow us
to dismiss comfortable identities—regional categories, for example—as organizing matrixes. It might enable us to attempt an understanding of neighboring
modernities mediated by artists' common interests and by artistic strategies of
aesthetic redefinition.

Canonical histories of postwar art have systematically privileged Minimalism as the most radical break with the conventions of modernist sculpture and

previous art in general.³ But recent research on the parallel occurrence of experiments with space, industrial materials, and the reductionist morphologies of geometry by artists in the United States, Europe, and the rest of the Americas constitutes a long overdue reexamination of the complex artistic landscape of the sixties, a seismic terrain that is not limited to the SoHo scene, New York. Moreover, in what is an explicit effort to expand a twentieth-century art canon currently limited to the experimental practices of Europe and the United States, the use of comparative methodologies willing to breach generational and cultural gaps might prove to be a difficult but rewarding task. This is an enterprise that does not rely on an empirical model dependent on evidence and accumulated information, but that instead operates on the basis of nuanced historical intersections, malleable subjective configurations, and dispersed and sometimes misunderstood legacies. Why not, for example, look at the work of German-Venezuelan artist Gego in tandem with that of American Eva Hesse, both of whom were Jewish women émigrés in the Americas, natives of Hamburg, who reinterpreted modernist sculpture's legacy of drawing in space while experimenting with and diverting from the prominent sculptural positions of their male counterparts: the Kineticists and the Minimalists respectively. Any such investigation would also include the work of other artists, for example, Mira Schendel (Switzerland/Brazil), Hanne Darboven (Germany), and Lygia Clark (Brazil).

A work such as Gego's *Reticulárea,* an environment made of triangular meshes and nets of metal, created in 1969 for a small room at the Museo de Bellas Artes de Caracas, generates enriching and astonishing associations when placed in dialogue with Eva Hesse's canonical *Right After,* also from 1969. Along with later, more compact installations of the seventies, the *Reticulárea* exploited the mutational potential of sculpture (a medium both Gego and Hesse contested from within) to explore space as it becomes body and vice versa, a transformation mediated not by the fictitious ideality of geometry (the current artistic language of the time), but by the indeterminacy of line. This relationship had already been explored by Gego in her drawings: in these, a sort of scriptural nothingness, a linear abyss, pointed to the possibility of line becoming form, and vice versa. If in her spatial practice Gego undermined geometrical exactitude, architectural space and its associations with enclosure, sculptural space and its associations with volume, in her drawings she layered lines in indefinite configurations that resembled a nonsensical language of graphic traces and marks while bypassing line's capacity of definition.

In the work of both artists, it is reliance on line (on drawing first, then on real space later) that one can identify as the operative element that allowed them

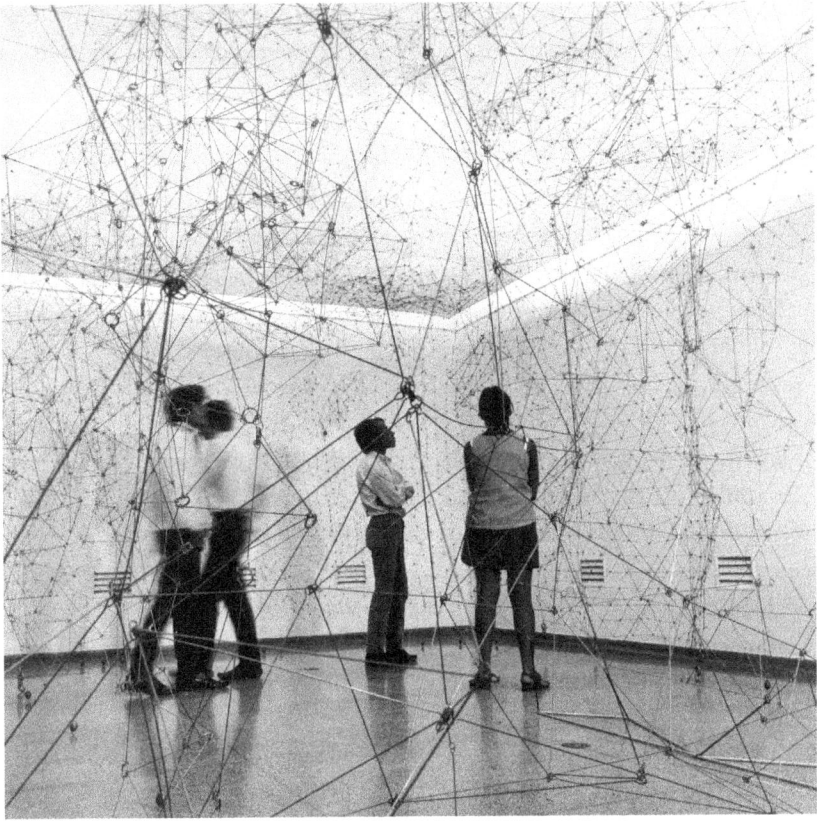

1.Gego, The *Reticulárea (Ambientación)*, 1969. Installation view, Museo de Bellas Artes, Caracas. Photograph by Paolo Gasparini. Courtesy of the author and the Gego Foundation, Caracas, Venezuela.

to undo media specificity, specifically that of sculpture. Hesse's defiant attitude toward the literalist and rigid geometric structures of Minimalism, a penchant for anticompositional all-overness, and a delight in the use of malleable materials such as papier-mâché, latex, and fiberglass, is present in her mid- to late sixties work. It parallels the linear and geometric reversals operative in Gego's work. Although much younger than her South American counterpart, Hesse was also a German émigré negotiating her position as a cultural producer within a well-established, mostly male artistic scene.

As with Gego, the line—with its multiple topological possibilities, its paradoxical capacity to order and derange, its mechanical and organic associations, its freedom and its potential to embody opposites—seems to have provided Hesse with the perfect tool to disturb the conventional supports of painting and sculpture. Later, both artists used it to disturb the smooth geometries privileged by so many artists at the time. From drawings to reliefs and then to suspended or placed objects, the transition from line into space was clear. By 1970 art critic Cindy Nemser would characterize Hesse's work as "fallen from the edge."[4] Indeed, there is no better evidence that Hesse and her work had already "fallen from the edge" than *Right After, 1969*, and its subsequent "ugly" twin, *Untitled, 1970*. Although dated 1969, *Right After*, made of long wires of fiber saturated in resin and suspended from hooks distributed across the ceiling, had been hanging in Hesse's studio for some time, unfinished due to illness. Hesse complained that in coming back to it after a year she felt that the piece needed more work. That was a mistake, she wrote, because as it was, the piece "was very, very simple and very extreme because it looked like a really *big nothing* which was one of the things that I so much wanted to be able to achieve."[5] This nothingness, to which she aspired, and later described as "non forms, non shapes, non planned,"[6] seems to have been Hesse's way out of the structural rigidity and geometric command over a world of objects that characterized the work of her Minimalist peers and sculptural representation in general. But in Hesse's work, as in Gego's, the outcome was not an oppositional one but a marginal, peripheral relationship to the monumentality and centrality of structure. In both artists' works, specifically in *Reticulárea* and *Right After*, we see construction being replaced by accumulation, layering, and manipulation. This amounts to a working method that implies a kind of bodily abandonment that stands as the Other of the rational clarity of the mind, an aspect that both artists did not so much reject as complicate. At the heart of these investigations there was an implicit critique of the separation of mind and body advocated by the gestaltic concerns of Minimalism and the optical illusions of Kinetic art.

   In some recent writing on the history of contemporary art, the comparative model—a slippery web in contrast to the structured columns with which we normally associate binary systems and dialectical models—has been contemplated by even the most Eurocentric art historians (the result usually traumatizes the canon from within). In 2000 Benjamin H. D. Buchloh found himself struggling with the comparative method when applied to the work of artists who, when they arrived in Paris in 1949, shared only a generational proximity. Discussing the pictorial practices of Simon Hantaï and Jacques de la Villeglé, Buchloh admits that "we might have to propose a third context, a more narrowly focused, more dehistoricized one" in order to attempt, in a historico-structural way, to flesh out the morphologies, histories, and parameters shared by the two artists. Buchloh's response to the comparative conundrum, one that lead him to dismiss formalist analysis and "the mechanistic principle of ideol-

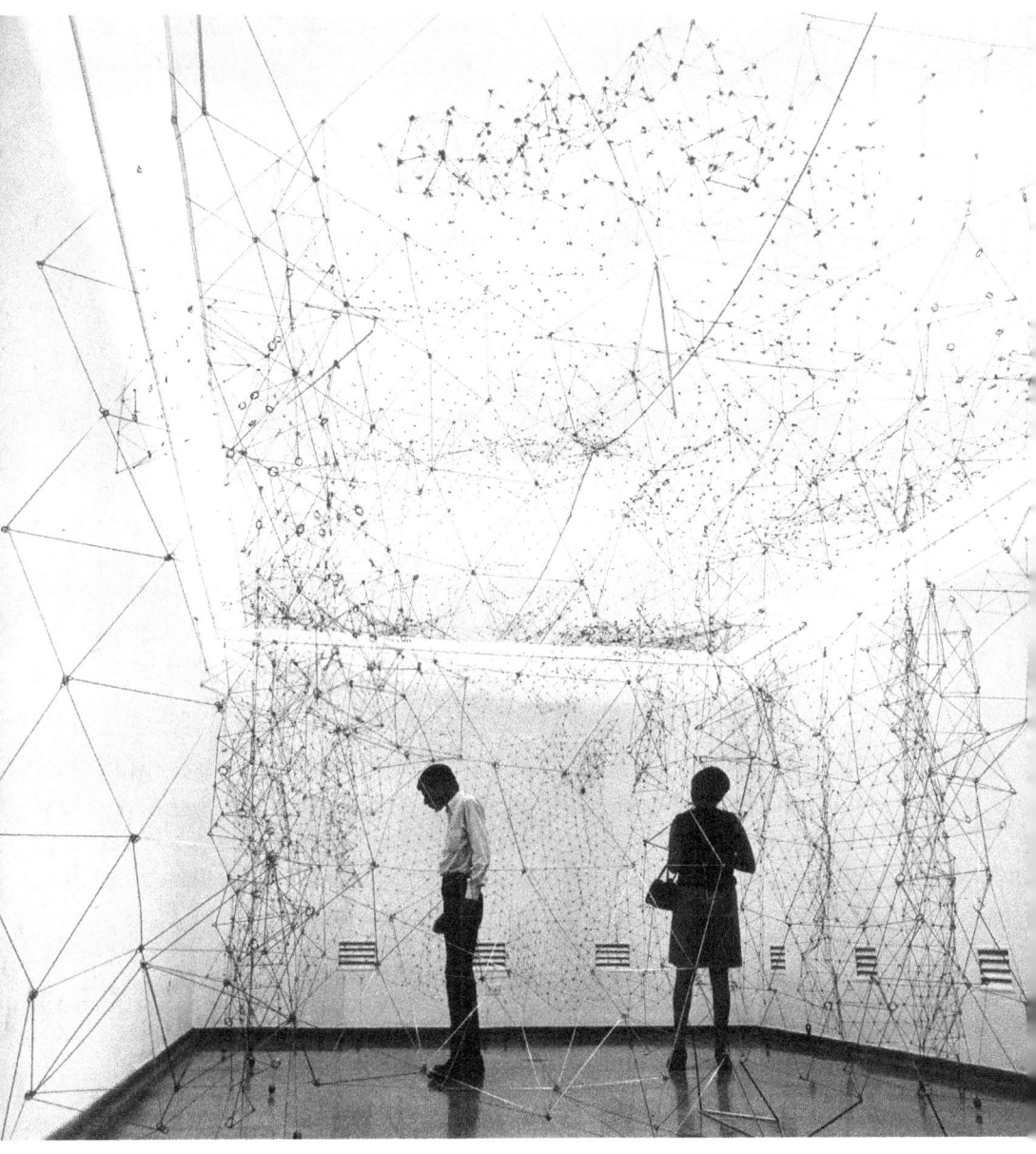

Gego, The *Reticulárea* (*Ambientación*), 1969. Installation view, Museo de Bellas Artes, Caracas. Photograph by Paolo Gasparini. Courtesy of the author and the Gego Foundation, Caracas, Venezuela.

ogy critique," is indicative of the difficulties the art historian faces when confronting the historical asymmetries and structural/formal parallels that cannot be accommodated by institutions, such as the museum, and disciplines, such as art history, that have historically been driven by the nationalistic urges. A different methodology "would yet have to be elaborated," writes Buchloh, "[one] in which the structure of the historical experience and the structure of aesthetic production could be recognized within sets of complex analogies that are neither mechanistically determined nor conceived of as arbitrarily autonomous, but that require the specificity of understanding the multiple mediations taking place within each artistic proposition and its historical context."[7]

Two years later, Carol Armstrong would suggest another ground for comparison by affiliating the photography of Tina Modotti, an Italian-American émigré working in Mexico in the 1920s, to that of American Francesca Woodman, made while she was living in Rome in the late 1970s. A generational gap and an almost insurmountable geographic distance separated the photographic production of both women. It was mitigated somewhat by the fact that Modotti was Edward Weston's model and lover. To Armstrong, the affinities of both photographic enterprises—in their subject matter, their formal and compositional strategies, their metaphorical displacement of the image, and their evocation of the material and the physical—"might flow from the cultural positioning and psychological constitution of the female subject." Unconcerned with the essentialist charge that her feminist undertaking might provoke, Armstrong, by aligning her project with that of French philosopher Luce Irigaray, underlined the subversiveness of feminism in its refusal to "utterly sever culture from biology" and thus comply with the linguistic and philosophical categories of Western logocentrism.[8]

But diffidence, in conventional art historical discourse, toward a comparative, dialogical approach—one that attempts to bridge different modernities, to bring together canonical and noncanonical works belonging to different cultural, generational, and national contexts, even when an aesthetic proposition calls for such an approach—is not uncommon. Dislodging the North-versus-South axis has proven one of the most difficult tasks, as it breaks an institutional taboo at best and might be seen as an unworthy enterprise at worst.

In a 1995 essay, art historian Keith Moxey tackles some of the real issues at stake in the discussion of canonical orthodoxy. He reminds us that syllabi are organized and classes taught around figures considered key or major in the history of art; the majority of publications and exhibitions are dedicated to a small group of artists, styles, and movements; tradition is rarely challenged; notions of quality are never discussed; the role of nationalism (or chauvinism), capital, collections, and museums in the formation of canons is ignored; and the myth of objectivity is tacitly fostered by the empirical foundations of the discipline while personal agendas are repressed. Moxey's solution to these dilemmas is to embrace a relativist and contingent notion of cultural value that implies that, following the poststructuralist gambit of social construct, "the standards involved in making . . . judgments [of artistic merit] differ according to the attitudes and interests of different historical groups and individuals."[9] The apparently benign but in my view disastrous result is that "[students] might encounter a Marxist canon, a feminist canon, a gay and lesbian canon, a postcolonial canon, and so forth."[10] This could indicate to them the ever changing possibilities of the canon, as Moxey hopes, but it could also reinforce and perpetuate hierarchical relations between a canonical (or mainstream) canon, and a peripheral (or substandard) canon.

The possibility of conceiving an art history without canons is, of course, remote. Nor is it necessarily useful. It just is the case that some intellectual strands develop in tandem with epochal events, that artistic strategies are innovated by and experimented with, in certain works, that paradigms of production and discourses of interest to the art historian are developed by both specific works and artists, providing compulsory but contingent frames of references that allow for a synchronic analysis of a historical topic. Canons are also established, produced, and institutionalized by artists, either because they become models to be defied, to be emulated, or to be challenged from within. But the opaque mechanisms (imposed by taste, professional allegiances, institutional conventions, nationalistic feelings, social habits, cultural assumptions, and political agendas) that arrest the expansion and mutation or displacement of the canon, operations that should come naturally to it if we consider its rather arbitrary nature—these should be confronted and not silenced; they should trigger responsible discussions about value judgment and the specificity of the positions that are taken.

The persistence of canons has perpetuated a history of contemporary art—in North America, Europe, and even in Western peripheries such as Slovenia and Brazil—bound, on the one hand, by the seminal status of Minimalism (which, seeking a tabula rasa, raged against the conservatism of Clement Greenberg and painterly abstraction, denying any connections to historical geometric abstraction and overlooking all other experiments with geometric sculpture taking place in the rest of the world) and, on the other, by a circuit of biennials and gallery exhibitions that determine which African or Mexican artist will make it into the next survey book of contemporary art. A recent text, David Hopkins's *Art after Modern Art*, includes examples of both: celebrated

Nigerian artist Yinka Shonibare and Mexican Gabriel Orozco. Unfortunately, however, in this text Gabriel has mysteriously reincarnated backward in time to become an important Mexican muralist from the 1930s.[11]

If the most current canon is at least bent by market forces, even our most recent histories of art resist the variables that could enrich our view of past innovations and aesthetic structural interfaces—here I am referring to works that cannot be excluded on the basis of "[a transferring of the locus of interest] to more formal or structural features,"[12] nor on the basis of stylistic and technical discrepancies. License to draw parallels between mainstream and marginal works of art is rarely granted in art history. If we want to look for disciplinary antecedents, at least in theory, the obvious frame of reference has been generated by comparative literature, which, since its constitution as a discipline, has been typified by the displacement of centers to the margins, by its antinationalist stance, and by the vagaries of (cultural and literal) translation.

Emily Apter has recently given us her account of the origins of global *translatio* in comparative literature by surveying the pedagogical practices and diasporic experiences of Leo Spitzer, a German-Jewish literary scholar in Turkish exile during the thirties. Under the sway of the Turkish Republic's modernizing agenda, which forthrightly opened its university posts to Jewish scholars, German-based philology transformed itself, perforce, by confronting Istanbul as a locus between tradition and innovation, Eastern and Western cultures, local and international intellectual agendas, "into a global discipline that came to be known as comparative literature when it assumed its institutional foothold in postwar humanities departments in the United States."[13] In Spitzer's disrespect (in his seminars and publications) for "narrowly constructed East-West dichotomies," in his deference toward Turkish as a language worthy of philological inquiry, and in his insistence (in his texts) on maintaining the opacity of the original (untranslated) citation, Apter sees an "explicit desire to disturb monolingual complacency," a willingness to confront foreignness and acknowledge what she calls the "pulse-quickening thrill of dangerous liaisons."[14] Risking the integrity of the literary/artistic sign, with its implied embodiment of a (usually nationalistic) zeitgeist, comparisons generate anxiety while retrieving the enriching vulnerability of the text/object. It is no wonder that exile, diaspora, and migrancy (of people, ideas, and objects) have become privileged loci to think transnational juxtapositions that expose the repressed counternarratives of cultural history.[15] Comparative methodologies strive toward an unavoidable lack, the impossible presence of the sign, that, never seeking to be all-encompassing but, on the contrary, to be topical, structural, tropological, and morphological. Indeed, the analysis of conceptually central but geographically displaced practices dispenses with totalizing systems and is prone to glitches and gaps that underline the unending possibilities and fictional teleology of narratives, including those bound to the politics of academia. This line of thinking calls attention, as Norman Bryson has done, to the fact that context has no "legislative force," is not naturally given, since it is something we make, something we might not be able to recover, and that pales in comparison with the persistent materiality of the works. This disposition facilitates morphological, structural, and topical interfaces across geographical boundaries that take into account the radiating structure of modernity, its ambitions, ideals, and permeable systems.[16]

Recent attempts to retrieve the work of noncanonical artists such as Gego, in the light of more visible and legible aesthetic practices such as Postminimalism, do not particularly aspire to produce a center-periphery reversal. Instead, they begin from the conceit that modernity itself is inherently discontinuous and incomplete. It is no coincidence that this project of recovery and recontextualization is, in its early stages, usually undertaken by younger art historians and critics working within the interstices of institutional permissibility. A theoretical foundation for an open-ended conception of modernity has been offered by German sociologist Niklas Luhmann. He has elaborated a systematic critique of European transcendentalism (or, in Hans Herbert Kögler's words, "of 'Old-European' habits of thought")[17] in terms of system theory, which, in its antimetaphysical and antitranscedentalist stance, opposes "natural laws," "rational principles," and "indisputable facts," instead presenting modernity as a contingent and changeable structure whose characteristics vary in time. In order to argue the latter, Luhmann introduces the activity of observation as a logical operation of modernity that enacts distinctions that are contingent rather than necessary and which oblige the observer to use one side of a distinction and not the other, thereby creating form from the making of a distinction as such. This theory of observation was inspired by G. Spencer Brown, whose work on the calculus of form, published as *Laws of Form* in 1969, developed the idea that to draw a distinction is to mark space, to establish and cross the boundary between a marked and an unmarked state. Most important, systems theory is further predicated on second-order observations, the latter being directed at first-order observations and the blind spot from which they deploy their distinctions.

Observations, Luhmann points out, are asymmetrical. In making distinctions, they differentiate one particular mark as form, differentiating it from everything else. Yet this indication, or designation, has to take into account that which has been left unsaid, unmarked. If splitting of the world into marked and unmarked states is necessary to observe, describe, and ultimately generate objects of observation/study, then "[the] unity [of the world] becomes unobservable."[18] There is, therefore, always a blind spot, because an observer observing an observer cannot observe him/herself. Furthermore, moving toward the unmarked space (observing it) implies a new distinction that severs this unmarked space. Inevitably, one reproduces the world as a unified, unobservable entity. And so on. This capacity of observation systems to create and recreate their boundaries (between system and environment) relies on "loose couplings" and "random links" with its environment. It is contingent. At the center is a "narrator who stages the narration—whether of the novel or of world history—in which he no longer appears," an observer who draws distinctions and who remains unobserved, who distinguishes what he observes from everything else, leaving that, consequently, as "unmarked space," indeed, who observes from this "unmarked space": "The person, whom one could ask: why this and not another way?"[19]

This "dual-value logic" presupposes a society of consent judged from positions of authority within the system, "that is, from the top or centre," positions of privilege that reconfigure the rest as "corruption, error, blindness."[20] To challenge these blatantly inequitable arrangements Luhmann proposes in his systems theory to operate on the basis of only one distinction: that between system and environment. Such a strategy, he claims, "calls for consistently 'autological' concepts, since the observer must also recognize himself as a system-in-the-environment as long as he carries out observations and connects them recursively. The narrator appears himself in what he narrates. He is observable as an observer. He constitutes himself in his own field—and thereby necessarily in the mode of contingency, that is, with an awareness of other possibilities."[21]

Most important, Luhmann's concept of modernity might encourage reconsideration and resignification of the vulnerable processes of production of historical narrative and canons. If we begin from the premise that each account, judgment, evaluation, model, and aesthetic structure is contingent, namely, that it is the result of a process of observation within a preestablished system we call art history, then we might be open to accepting the inextricable partiality of these accounts. What the Enlightenment posits as the various spheres of specialization and differentiation that make up modernity, Luhmann considers as social systems, which, in order to survive and proliferate, absorb change and conflict while rejecting unity, redemption, and transcendentalism, in the process constituting their fragile order. This is a challenge to art historians who might like to remain within the gratifying and reassuring confines of the canon, within the limited horizons of the discipline. And to those who remain comfortable within the prescribed perimeter of an avant-garde project whose mission remains undisturbed despite our appeal to contextuality and history. Was it not this programmatic sense of finality that forced Peter Bürger to read the avant-garde as a failure? Is it not this that leads Buchloh to finally deem the neo-avant-garde as succumbing to disappointing assimilation?[22]

Many of these questions arose as I set out to study and interpret the work of Gego vis-à-vis the dominant aesthetic models of the time. How could I consider seriously a body of work that defied the conventions of hegemonic cultural production (she was a Jewish émigré working in a cultural and geographic periphery), male artistic supremacy (she was a woman), the myth of a youthful avant-garde (she was in her fifties at the peak of her artistic career), and which in itself dismissed unity and consistency?

It was Gego's *Reticulárea* of 1969, an environment of metal wire nets and meshes that the viewer could enter, and the conditions of artistic production that framed the making of the work, which seemed to deliver a model of spectatorship that figured forth an observer caught in the contingencies of viewing and judgment. The importance of the observer for the meaning of the work is strikingly evident from the photographic record. All photographs feature visitors and their interaction with the work. The images point to the possibility that *Reticulárea* addressed not one but many spectators. But the position of these observers is important to our understanding the spectatoral model at stake. Unable to distance themselves from the work, viewers cannot occupy an unmarked space, a removed point of view from which to describe the world. If we apply Luhmann's operative figure, the observer reenters observation, "constitutes [herself] in [her] own field—and thereby necessarily in the mode of contingency, that is, with an awareness of other possibilities."[23]

Incapable of embodying wholeness, *Reticulárea*'s implicit infinity and defiance of structure prescribes this incapacity. The viewer finds him or herself inescapably occupying, while constantly unfolding, the blind spot of observation. Or, to return to Luhmann again, the system operates within the environment, but it is one that is accessible only from the inside. As David Roberts observes in a comment on Luhmann: "The World divided by a distinction gives the two sides of Form. On the one side are all the forms of the world, on the other side is the 'other' of rationality, the 'unmarked state'—God, world, chance, chaos, the unlimited."[24] It is in the artificial margin between the two that the *Reticulárea,* with its geometrics gone awry, seems to operate; thus its careful attention to site, its pliant behavior, but also its concern with an infinite effect that might suggest this otherness to the world as form.

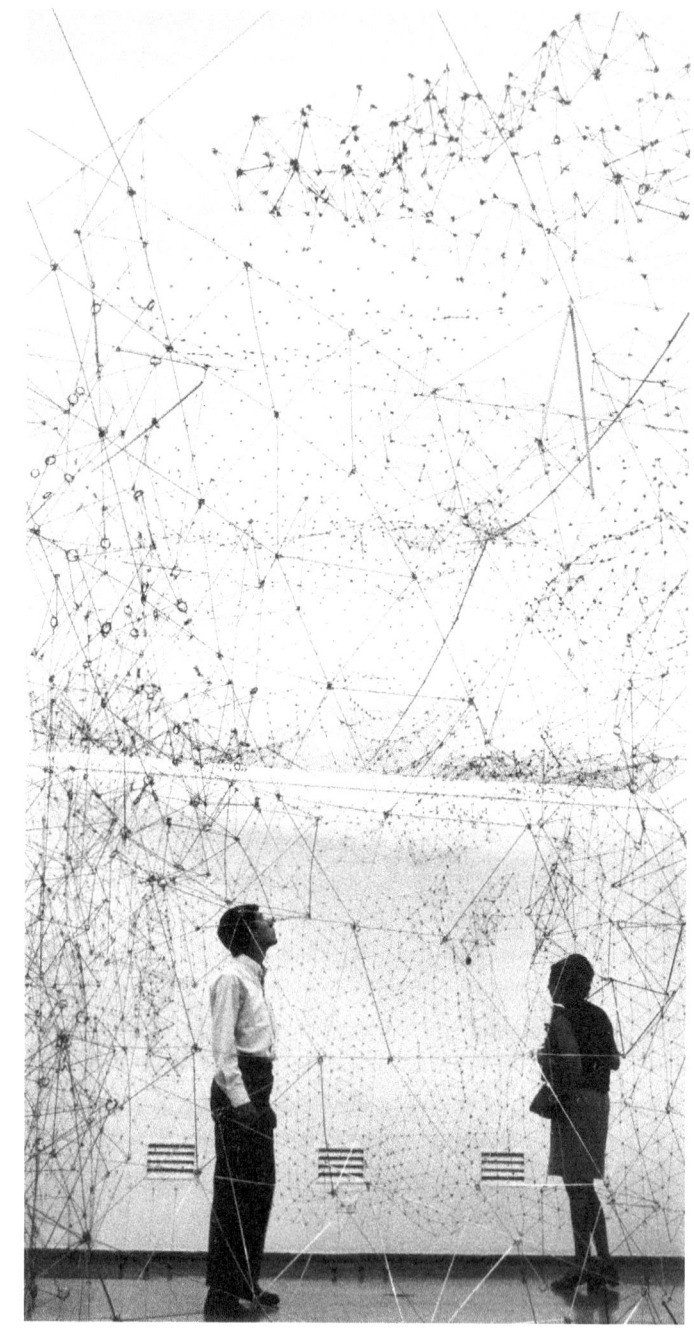

Gego, The *Reticulárea* (*Ambientación*), 1969. Installation view, Museo de Bellas Artes, Caracas. Photograph by Paolo Gasparini. Courtesy of the author and the Gego Foundation, Caracas, Venezuela.

To adopt contingency, and the politics of impure interfaces, as the foundation of our historical semantics is to revisit and resist the indisputable positions of art history: its traditions, its texts, its objects, its institutions, and its canons. It is to opt for a methodology of displacement, and to think of one's space as a permanent redefinition of boundaries. To accept the fragility of nominalism is to simply embrace the legacy of deracination in modernism and modernity: the internationalism of the avant-garde and, later, its avowed homelessness. This, perhaps, might be the destiny of the émigré who thinks of home as the space created by conceptual deterritorialization, the fluid sites of postnational dispersion, anachronism, and the pricking insistence of other possibilities.

NOTES

The epigraph is from Thomas Y. Levin's translation, interpolating the first (unpublished) and the second (final) version of "Strenge Kunstwissenschaft. Zum ersten Bande der *Kunstwissenschaftlichen Forschungen*," which appeared, under Benjamin's pseudonym Detlef Holz, on July 30, 1933.

1 See Arendt, "Introduction," 38–51.

2 See Lyotard, *The Postmodern Condition* and *The Postmodern Explained.*

3 Within contemporary art history few artistic categories have sustained the privileged and cohesive status that Minimalism has achieved. In old and new histories of the period Minimalism is posited as the sire of all subsequent artistic experiments, a role that neither Allan Kaprow's prophetic reading of "The Legacy of Jackson Pollock," which sketched an image of the heterogeneous landscape of contemporary art in the sixties, nor Rosalind Krauss's significant critique of the movement thirty-one years later in her essay "The Cultural Logic of the Late Capitalist Museum," did much to shake. More recently, two exhibitions opened up the path for a reconsideration of the uniqueness of Minimalism: "Beyond Geometry: Experiments in Form, 1940s–70s," Los Angeles County Museum, curated by Lynn Zelevansky and presented from June 13, 2004 to October 3, 2004, and "A Minimal Future? Art as Object, 1958–1968," Museum of Contemporary Art, Los Angeles, curated by Anne Goldstein and presented from March 14, 2004 to August 2, 2004.

4 In Nemser, "An Interview with Eva Hesse," 63.

5 Lippard, *Eva Hesse*, 161.

6 This is how she described *Untitled* 1970 in her diary; quoted in Lippard, *Eva Hesse*, 172.

7 Buchloh, "Hantaï, Villeglé, and the Dialectics of Painting's Dispersal," 35.

8 Armstrong, "This Photography Which Is Not One."

9 Moxey, "Motivating History," 397.

10 Moxey, "Motivating History," 400.

11 "Pollock's experiments in pictorial scale partly derived from his enthusiasm for murals by socially committed Mexican painters of the 1930s and 1940s such as Gabriel [*sic*] Orozco, David Siqueiros, and Diego Rivera": David Hopkins, *After Modern Art, 1945–2000*, 15. The correct name of the muralist is José Clemente Orozco.

12 Smith, "Contingencies of Value," 32.

13 Apter, "Global *Translatio*," 269–70. The quoted sentence ends with a footnote, where Apter clarifies that "when comp lit took root as a postwar discipline in the U.S., the European traditions were dominant, the Turkish chapter of its life was effaced. What attracted the American academics was European erudition." See also Apter, "Comparative Exile," 86–96; and Cooppan, "World Literature and Global Theory."

14 Apter, "Global *Translatio*," 278–80.

15 "One could say," writes Apter, "that the new-wave postcolonial literacy bears certain distinct resemblances to its European antecedents imbued as it often is with echoes of melancholia, *Heimlosigkeit,* cultural ambivalence, consciousness of linguistic loss, confusion induced by 'worlding' or global transference, amnesia of origins, fractured subjectivity, border trauma, the desire to belong to 'narration' as a substitute 'nation,' the experience of a politics of linguistic and cultural usurpation." Accordingly, Apter concludes, "the theorization of *Heimlosigkeit,* as a mode of critique, emerges, paradoxically as the country of comparative literature. A substitute homeland, a placeless place that is homely in its unhomeliness, comparative literature becomes the institutional and pedagogical space of not-being-there" (Apter, "Comparative Exile," 90 and 93 respectively).

16 "Extendability of context, as an idea, provides a conceptual space from which to problematize context as having any kind of legislative force. It highlights that 'context' is never naturally given; it is something we make, whether we are viewers at a Salon or art historians working in our institutional contexts" (Bryson, "Art in Context," 39).

17 Kögler, "Review of *Social Systems* by Niklas Luhmann," 271.

18 Luhmann, "Deconstruction as Second Order Observing," 770.

19 Luhmann, "European Rationality," 67.

20 Luhmann, "European Rationality," 69.

21 Luhmann, "European Rationality," 73.

22 Bürger, *Theory of the Avant-Garde;* and Buchloh, *Neoavantgarde and the Culture Industry.*

23 Luhmann, "European Rationality," 73.

24 Roberts, "Sublime Theories," 183.

6

POLITICS OF FLEXIBLE SUBJECTIVITY:

THE EVENT WORK OF LYGIA CLARK

SUELY ROLNIK

TRANSLATED FROM THE PORTUGUESE BY BRIAN HOLMES

Until the late 1990s, Lygia Clark, the Brazilian artist who lived from 1920 to 1988, was principally known for her paintings and sculptures.[1] Only then did a wider public become aware of the highly singular experimental artistic practices that she created during her last twenty-six years of work.[2] Yet, as in any artistic practice of this kind, traces of these practices are scarce. This contributes to maintaining their inaccessibility and neutralizing their disruptive force—even more so in the case of Lygia Clark, given that her work is on the order of an event, which moreover is not only artistic but also therapeutic and political. What this event consists of and what its force is are inescapable questions for research, if one wishes to grasp the artist's experimental practices in their radicality.

To meet this challenge I will focus on *Estruturação do Self* (Structuring of the Self, 1976–1988), the last and probably the most accomplished of Lygia Clark's artistic "proposals." As a beginning, we might say that this work was undertaken through a very precise device (*dispositif*), which abandoned the conventional locations of art and was developed instead in the artist's apartment. In a strange room, something between a studio and a permanent installation, "sessions" between artist and viewer unfolded, mediated by unusual objects scattered about in the space.

These objects, which the artist qualified as "relational," are made of ordinary materials, without any definite form. They have a rich variety of physical qualities, which are often contradictory within the same object—such as light and heavy, cold and hot, and so on—producing a mutable and unstable form. Indeed, in the only text the artist published about this work she makes very little reference to their visual qualities, but instead referred to the sensations they provoke through their greater or lesser body, temperature, weight, pressure, volume, density, texture, and so on.[3] Hence the name: the objects are "relational" in their very essence, since they only reveal themselves in their encounter with one's body, or more specifically, with the *viewer*'s body, in a relation with the artist and in the context of a specific aesthetic experience.

The artist comes closer to the viewer, via the objects and a protocol of experimentation. And the person who was traditionally a viewer—and who has now become a "client," in Lygia Clark's terms—comes to know the art object through the hands of the artist who places it on different parts of his naked body, caressing it, sweeping over it, massaging it, or simply letting it lie there in rest. A special kind of fecund intimacy is established between artist, object, and viewer.

Yet other characteristics of the device are equally fundamental: the absence of speech during the session, the fact that the artist only relates with one client at a time and for a long period (sometimes for more than a year), punctuated by the regularity of up to three sessions a week. The silence, the focus of attention on an experience with a single person, the affective quality of this attention, the temporality, and its rhythm—all these aspects allow the realization of what Lygia Clark offers to the participant, which she defined as a process of structuring the self.

Why did Lygia Clark call this proposal *Structuring of the Self?* The artist probably used a notion of the "self" inspired by D. W. Winnicott, the English psychoanalyst with whom she particularly identified. For him the self, or that which produces a feeling of oneself, is never unequivocally defined, but is generated in a continuous process, which happens in what he calls a "potential space," a formless zone between the I and the Other where the creative drive is convoked.[4] But Lygia Clark was not a disciplined reader in the academic sense. She appropriated philosophical and psychoanalytic concepts in her own way, when they seemed to reverberate in her intuitions and to help her to elaborate and express them. Given this characteristic of the artist, the question why she named this work *Structuring of the Self* will remain unanswered if we stick to an examination of the concept of the self in the psychoanalytic or philosophical literature. This approach should be replaced by a quite different series of inquiries. What did the notion of the self allow Lygia Clark to elaborate? What definition of this notion can be derived from her artistic practice? What did the artist mean to say by "structuring of the self," and why did she propose to do it? Why did she feel it necessary, in the late 1970s, to bring her work to bear within the dimension of subjectivity and therefore close to the borderline of therapeutic practices? In what sense would this approach also be political? Why did she choose this particular type of proposal? Finally, in what sense is this work an event? How can this event be understood in its triple nature, at once artistic, therapeutic, and political?

To respond to these questions, two detours will be necessary. The first will concern the concept of the event in its relations with the process of subjectivation. The second will set out a genealogy of the dominant politics of subjectivation that was taking form at the time when Lygia Clark created *Structuring of the Self*. Only after this inquiry will we have all the materials needed to return to her proposal and to situate the singular force with which it worked through the problems of its time.

THE EVENT

Knowing and relating to the otherness of the world as matter implies the activation of different potentials of subjectivity in its sensible dimension, depending on whether the matter world is grasped primarily as an outline of forms or as a field of forces. Knowing the world as form calls upon perception, which is carried out by the empirical exercise of sensibility; whereas knowing the world as force calls on sensation, which is carried out by the intensive exercise of sensibility. The latter is engendered in the encounter between the body as a field of forces—constituted by the nervous energies that course through it—and the forces of the world that affect it. In this relation to the world as a field of forces, new blocks of sensation pulse within the body subjectivity as it is affected by fresh experiences of the world's varied and variable otherness.

"Perception" and "sensation" refer to different powers of the sensible body. The perception of the Other brings his or her formal existence to subjectivity (an existence translated into representations that are visual, auditory, etc.), while sensation brings the living presence of the Other, which cannot be represented or described but only expressed, in a process requiring an invention that is concretized performatively: a way of being, feeling, or thinking, a form of sociability, a territory of existence, but also a work of art.

Between these two modes of apprehending the world there is an invincible disparity. This paradox is constitutive of human sensibility, the source of its dynamics, the driving force par excellence of the processes of subjectivation—

triggering the inexhaustible movements of creation and recreation of the reality of oneself and the world. Yet the paradox ultimately places the current forms of reality in check, as they become an obstacle to the integration of new connections of desire that provoke the emergence of a fresh block of sensations. The current forms of reality then cease to be the guides and conductors of the process; they are drained of vitality and lose their meaning. A crisis of subjectivity sets in, exerting pressure, arousing feelings of astonishment and dread, causing vertigo. To respond to this uncomfortable pressure, life is mobilized within subjectivity as the power of invention and action. The feeling of astonishment and dread forces the expression of a new configuration of existence, a new figuration of oneself, the world, and the relations between them—which is what mobilizes the power of creation (the artistic affect). The same feeling also forces one to act so that the new configuration can assert itself in existence and inscribe itself within the reigning map as a shared reality, without which the process cannot be fulfilled. This is what mobilizes the power of action (the political affect, both in its constructive aspect and in its resistance to oppressive forces).

The "event" is the culmination of this process. It is precisely the passage from a virtual, intensive reality to an actual, empirical one, unleashed by the disparity between those two experiences of otherness. It is the creation of a world, it is what puts the world to work.

In the relation to the world as form, subjectivity orients itself in the space of its empirical actuality and situates itself within the corresponding cartography of representations. In the relation to the world as a field of forces, subjectivity orients itself within the diagram of sensations—which are the effect of the irreducible living presence of the Other—and situates itself as a living being among living beings. And in the relation to the paradox between those two sensible experiences, subjectivity orients itself within the temporality of its vital pulsation and situates itself as *event,* its becoming-other.

This process makes any and all forms of subjectivity into ephemeral configurations in an unstable balance. Thus the politics of subjectivation are elastic, they shift and transform, and they emerge as a function of new sensible diagrams and the loss of meaning of existing cartographies. They vary therefore along with the sociocultural contexts of which they are the sensible and existential consistency. What determines their specificity is, among other factors, their politics of cognition: the place that is occupied by the two modes of sensible approach to the world, the dynamics of their relation, the status of the paradox between them.

How might these considerations be used to problematize the dominant politics of subjectivation in the late 1970s and early 1980s, the time when Lygia Clark practiced "structuring of the self"?

GENEALOGY OF THE POLITICS OF SUBJECTIVATION OF THE LATE 1970s

Answering this question requires going back in time, to the late 1960s and early 1970s, when the long bankruptcy on which the so-called modern subject had embarked—a process of decline that began at the close of the nineteenth century—reached its nadir, and provoked an important social, cultural, and political crisis. When I speak of the modern subject I am referring to the figure of the "individual" with its belief in the possibility of controlling nature, things, and oneself by will and reason, under the command of the ego. On what politics of cognition does that crisis-ridden model of subjectivity depend?

Sustaining the illusion of control over the turbulences of life depends on a certain status of the empirical and intensive exercises of the sensible. On the one hand, there is an anesthesia of the intensive exercise of the sensible; and on the other, there is a hypertrophy of the empirical exercise. Subjectivity therefore tends to move exclusively within the limits of its current existential territory and the outlines of its corresponding cartography, which are reified. The experience of the paradox between the new sensations and the current cartography is denied and repressed, and with this, the cause of the feelings of loss of meaning, astonishment, and dread becomes unknown. As a consequence, the powers of creation and action naturally brought into play by the experience of the loss of references are dissociated from sensation—that is, from the effects of the living presence of the other, the signs that they ask one to decipher, and their critical force with respect to the reigning orientations.

The result is a hypertrophy of the ego: it oversteps its primary function, which is to guide subjectivity through the meanders of the current map of representations, and claims the power of command over the processes of creating new forms of social and subjective life, of providing oneself with a subjective consistency. This gives rise to a feeling of oneself as spatialized and totalized, detached from the world and from temporality—hence the idea of the individual with its supposed interiority. With this kind of subjectivity governed by the identity principle, an anesthesia of its living dimension installs itself as the dominant politic of subjectivation that took form between the seventeenth and the nineteenth centuries.

This is the figure of subjectivity that begins to enter its decline at the end of the nineteenth century, in a process that will be completed after World War II. The causes for this breakdown have been widely studied, and I need not elaborate them here. Yet there is an aspect to be noted for our purposes: from the late nineteenth century onward, subjectivity is increasingly exposed to a greater and more swiftly changing diversity of worlds than it had formerly known, exceeding what it had equipped itself for psychically. A negotiation between the virtual and the actual becomes necessary in order to incorporate the new sensible states that are ceaselessly engendered, and that can no longer be contained in their state of repression, as they had been in the modern politics of subjectivation. A new strategy of desire begins to emerge. I will call it "flexible subjectivity" in reference to a notion proposed by Brian Holmes, which I will problematize here in terms of its psychodynamics.[5] From the end of the nineteenth century and throughout the first half of the twentieth century, this figure appeared primarily among the artistic and the intellectual vanguard.

Beginning in the 1950s, and more intensively in the 1960s and early 1970s, this flexible subjectivity overflowed the cultural vanguard to take on a palpable presence among an entire generation. A movement of massive disidentification with the dominant model of society was unleashed among broad sectors of mostly middle-class youth throughout the world. The forces of desire, creation, and action, intensely mobilized by the crisis, were invested into audacious existential experimentation, in a radical rupture from the establishment. Flexible subjectivity was adopted as a politics of desire by a wide range of people, who began an exodus in which current ways of life shifted and other cartographies were traced—a process supported and made possible by its broad collective extension.

A series of aspects characterize the new politics of subjectivation. These aspects include the activation of the intensive exercise of the sensible and the emergence of an instance of subjectivity whose function is exactly that of marking the dissonance between the effects of the two exercises of the sensible, as well as the inadequacy of empirical maps and the need to create others, each time that life indicates or requires it as a condition for maintaining its processuality. Is this not the instance that Lygia Clark calls the "self"?

With a functioning self, subjectivity is led to develop its nomadic potential: the freedom of letting go of the territories to which it is accustomed, negotiating between sets of references, making other articulations, setting up other territories. To do this the ego must also upgrade its cognitive capacity, so as to learn how to move within new cartographies. Yet there are many different politics of the creation of territories: for this process to unfold in the direction of life's movement it is necessary to create the territories on the basis of the urgencies indicated by the sensations. It is the self that orients this process through its condition as interface between the virtual diagram and the actual map, comple-

menting its function as an alarm indicating that a shift between the two registers is necessary, with its other function as the operator of this shift. In this
politics, the self replaces the ego as the guide of the processes of subjectivation—
as the organizing instance of oneself and, therefore, that which supplies subjective consistency. What forms is a type of subjectivity that embodies the paradox
that constitutes it as temporality—in other words, a processual subjectivity that
is multiplicity and becoming.

This shift in the politics of desire provoked a serious subjective, social, and
cultural crisis that threatened the existing economic and political regime. In the
face of this situation, the power structure needed new strategies to reassert itself,
to regain control. This would be achieved in the late 1970s and early 1980s, exactly
when Lygia Clark proposed the *Structuring of the Self*. The flowing fountain of
creative force mobilized by deterritorialization and crisis would be instrumentalized by capital, which seized upon the social proliferation of flexible subjectivity itself—not only its functional principle, but also the forms of critique that it
manifested and the modes of existence that it had invented over the course of two
decades. As in the martial arts of the Far East, where one does not attack the
enemy's strength but rather uses it against him, the inventions of the 1960s and
early 1970s were to serve as the formula and fuel of the new regime.

THE GLOBAL REALITY SHOW

In the late 1970s, transnational finance capitalism took on its full dimensions,
becoming what we may call, with Antonio Negri and Michael Hardt, "cognitive," "cultural" or "cultural-informational" capitalism, stressing that the labor
power from which surplus value is now primarily extracted is no longer the
mechanical force of the proletariat, but instead the power of knowledge and
invention of a new productive class, which some authors call the "cognitariat."[6]
But how is this power siphoned off?

An idea of Maurizio Lazzarato, which I will develop from the viewpoint of
the politics of desire, could help answer this question.[7] Lazzarato points to an
important difference between industrial capitalism and the entrepreneurial
capitalism that was spreading across the planet at that time. Instead of objects in
the Fordist factory, what the new regime fundamentally produces is the "creation of worlds." These are image worlds fabricated by advertising and mass
culture, conveyed by the media, serving to prepare the cultural, subjective, and
social ground for the implantation of markets. In the late 1970s, subjectivities
were exposed to an intensifying deterritorialization, principally because of a
powerful deployment of the technologies of communication at a distance and

the necessity of adaptation to a market that was changing at an ever more rapid rate. But a radical change is introduced by the particular subjective effects of deterritorialization produced by the image worlds of capital. This particular difference constitutes one of the principle aspects of the politics of subjectivation that emerged at that time.

The chain that constitutes this capitalist world-factory includes four types of producers, who are instrumentalized in their labor power of intelligence, knowledge, and creativity, but also of belief, spontaneity, sociability, affective presence, and so on. First, the creators, including a series of new productive sectors such as advertising and all the different professionals it involves (concept creators, photographers, graphic artists, designers, audiovisual technicians, etc.). Second, the consulting professionals such as business and marketing experts, headhunters, personnel managers, and the like. Creators and consulting professionals are the strategic equipment for a new kind of war that we have all been living through since that period, one that Lazzarato calls "a planetary aesthetic war." A war that takes place over the ready-to-wear worlds created by capital, in the ferocious competition between machines of expression rivaling with each other to conquer the market of subjectivities thrown into crisis. For it is not enough to create image worlds; they must also have the power to seduce, so that the subjectivities choose them as models for their remapping and concretize them in their everyday life. Indeed, in order for them to move the market, these worlds born in the form of advertising campaigns— whose reality is only one of images, a reality of signs—must ultimately be built into the performance of social life.

Here comes the third type of producers in the chain: the consumers, those who actualize the image worlds in empirical existence, and thus simultaneously become producers of the regime. They must have great cognitive agility to catch and select the plurality of worlds that never cease being released into the air all at once; an athletic mobility of the ego to leap from one world to the other; a plasticity in resculpting themselves according to the mode of being specific to each ready-to-wear world. With the labor force of these subjective powers, the consumers participate in the production of the worlds created by capital, concretizing them in empirical reality.

To this end, another whole new series of professionals comes into existence, the fourth type of producers of the capitalist world-factory: the human self-presentation specialists (personal trainers, personal stylists, clothing stylists, fashion consultants, dermatologists, plastic surgeons, estheticians, designers, interior architects, self-help professionals, etc.). Their major business consists in selling their work to the consumers, who believe it has the power to help them to achieve this new kind of flexible subjectivity.

This process gives rise to a self-for-sale that commercializes its power to signal the dissonance between the virtual and the actual in order to produce the worlds of capital, either as creator, consumer, or consultant. A showroom type of flexible subjectivity is embodied here: what is exposed to the other—reduced to the condition of spectator/consumer—are the elements of the latest fashionable worlds and the ability and speed to incorporate them into a kind of marketing or advertising campaign for oneself. In the face of this aberration, a question arises in our minds: what is so seductive about the ready-to-wear worlds created by capital? What differentiates them from actual, concrete worlds?

PERVERSE SEDUCTION

The answer to this last question leaps out before our eyes, if we can cut through the tightly woven veil of images that mesmerizes the empirical exercise of our visual sensibility and obfuscates its intensive one. We can, then, see that what seduces is the image of self-confidence, prestige, and power of the characters inhabiting these image worlds, as though they had resolved the paradox and had forever rejoined the ranks of the supposedly "guaranteed."[8] In other words, what seduces about the image worlds created by capital is, basically, the illusion they convey that there exist worlds whose inhabitants would never experience fragility and feelings of vertigo, or who would at least have the power to avoid them or to control the disquiet they provoke, living a kind of hedonistic existence, smooth and without turbulence, eternally stable. This illusion bears the promise that such a life exists, that access to it is possible, and even more, that it depends only on the incorporation of the worlds created by capital. A perverse relation sets itself up between the subjectivity of the receiver/consumer and these image characters.

The glamour of these privileged people and the fact that, as media beings, they are inaccessible in their very nature, is interpreted by the receiver as a sign of their superiority. As in any perverse relationship where the seduced idealizes the arrogant indifference of the seducer—instead of seeing it as a sign of his narcissistic poverty and his incapacity to be affected by the other—the receiver/consumer of these characters feels disqualified and excluded from their world. Identified with this image being, and taking it as a model in the hope of one day becoming worthy of belonging to its world, consumer subjectivity begins by wishing to resemble it, placing itself in a position of submission and perpetual demand for recognition. Such desire remains unsatisfied because it is unsatisfiable by definition. All hope is short-lived. The feeling of exclusion always returns and, to free itself of this feeling, subjectivity submits even more, continually mobilizing its forces to a higher degree, in a breakneck race to find ready-to-wear worlds to be embodied and concretized.

This mendacious promise constitutes the fundamental myth of integrated world capitalism.[9] Yet it is the driving force of its politics of subjectivation, the difference that it introduces in the contemporary experience of deterritorialization. The illusion that upheld the structure of the modern subject finds a new formula here. It is transvalued and attains the apex of its credibility in the religion of cultural capitalism. A monotheistic religion whose scenario is basically the same as in all the religions of this tradition: there exists an all-powerful God who promises paradise, with the difference that capital is in the role of God and the paradise that it promises is within this life and not beyond it. The glamorous guaranteed beings of the worlds of advertising and mass-culture entertainment are the saints of a commercial pantheon, "superstars" that glitter in the image sky above the heads of everyone, announcing the possibility of joining them.[10]

The belief in the religious promise of a capitalistic paradise is what sustains the successful instrumentalization of subjective powers. The feeling of humiliation that this belief produces, the hope to one day "make it" and escape exclusion, mobilizes the desire to realize the ready-to-wear worlds offered on the market. It is through this dynamic that subjectivity becomes the active producer of these worlds: a voluntary servitude that is not achieved through repression or obedience to a moral code, as in the traditional monotheistic religions where access to paradise depends on virtue. Now, the code does not exist, but on the contrary, the more original the world that the corporation conveys, the greater its power to compete—understanding originality in this context as a mere artifice of image that differentiates one world from all the rest. This difference is what seduces, since its embodiment would make the consumer into a being distinct from and above all the others—an illusion that is essential in this politics of relation to the Other, because it feeds the illusion of being nearer to the imaginary pantheon.

In this context, public life is replaced by a global reality show orchestrated by the cultural-informational capitalism that has taken over the entire planet. A kind of worldwide display screen where people jostle their way toward a possible role as an extra, a fleeting and imaginary place that has to be incessantly administered, invested, and guaranteed, against everything and everyone.

SELF FOR SALE

The contemporary politics of subjectivation thus found a way to confront and neutralize the reactivation of public life brought by the social propagation of a flexible subjectivity in the 1960s and early 1970s. It embodied the shift from an identity-based principle of subjectivation to a flexible one, but only as a more successful way to reinstate the anesthesia of the modern subject and its dissociation from the effects of the living presence of the Other. That gives way to a flexible sort of identity, the different figures of which have no link with collective life and remain marked by the illusion of unity.

On the one hand, the nonstop creation of noisy, new, ready-to-wear worlds provokes a hyperstimulation of the paradox between the two exercises of the sensible, of the crisis to which it leads and the suffering it brings. On the other hand, the dissociation of subjectivity from the cause of this anxiety is pushed to the extreme by the perverse relation established between the consumer and the market, whose driving force is belief in the promise of paradise. The self, in its function as an alarm that signals the necessity of creating new territories, is therefore instrumentalized by the market; and the ego takes over the management of the forces of creation and action that this alarm convokes in response. But the ego knows only the empirical exercise of the sensible—its primary function being, as we have seen, to guide subjectivity through the cartography of current territories. When it is placed at the command of the processes of creating the cartographies of oneself and the world, the ego has no way to know the causes of the vertigo arising from the experience of the paradox that causes it to lose its references. It tends to interpret its disorientation as the result of a collapse of its very subjectivity, not only of its current configuration. It then begins to fabricate imaginary reasons that are supposed to explain its distress— hence the feelings of inferiority and exclusion. To protect itself from its unease, it represses the feeling by constructing defensive barriers. Given that this state is mainly mobilized by the image worlds proposed by capital, the most obvious defensive strategy consists in seizing upon their images and trying to fulfill them in existence, in the hopes of overcoming anxiety.

Thus the instrumentalization of subjective forces by capital comes full circle. In fact, all the phases of the subjectivation process are used as primary energy for the production of worlds for the market: intensive and empirical sensibility; the unease of the paradox between their two exercises (which is turbo-charged by the market); the pressure that this feeling of unease exerts to realign oneself and the world; and the forces of desire, creation, and action that this pressure mobi-

lizes. A population of hyperactive zombies comes into being, one that will proliferate increasingly across the planet in the last decades of the twentieth century and
the beginning of the twenty-first, as the models of a winner-take-all subjectivity.

The experimentation that had been carried out collectively during the 1960s
and early 1970s in order to attain emancipation from the dominant pattern of
subjectivity became indistinguishable from its incorporation into the emergent
politics of subjectivation under cognitive capitalism. Many of the protagonists
of the movements of the previous decades fell into the trap: dazzled by the
celebration of their creative force and their transgressive and experimental
posture, which had formerly been stigmatized and marginalized, dazzled as well
by their prestigious image in the media and their high salaries, they became the
creators of the worlds produced by capital. But this was not the case of Lygia
Clark. On the contrary, in her event work we can find a response to this politics
of instrumentalizing the potential of art.

THE AESTHETIC, THERAPEUTIC, AND POLITICAL
EVENT WORK OF LYGIA CLARK

Now, at last, we can say why, at a precise historical moment, Lygia Clark proposed a practice that consists in structuring the self, and how the work emerges
as an event that unfolds in a zone of indiscernability between aesthetics, thera-
peutics, and politics.

Let us begin by inquiring into this work as a therapeutic event. *Structuring of
the Self* treats the three mainsprings of the politics of subjectivation under
cultural capitalism, whose psychopathological effects have been infecting the
planet like a veritable epidemic. On the basis of the description of this politics of
subjectivation presented above, one could define a common feature of these
three mainsprings: they are three sorts of misunderstandings.

The first misunderstanding is of the Other as a living reality. As we have seen,
the Other in this regime is reduced to the status of a being of representation, a
reduction stimulated by the image worlds imposed by the market. The second
misunderstanding is that of the vital pulsation and its rhythm, which tends to
lose its beat. The rhythm is composed of a continual sequence of movements,
each with its inherent temporality, punctuated by pauses: the opening of sensibility to the world to receive its effects; the intimate absorption of the resulting
sensations; the invention of a mode of expression that renders them present;
and finally, opening again to share this expression with the Other, so as to
interfere in the current cartography. The third misunderstanding is of the
inexorable character of life's processuality, in its power of differentiation, and in

the inescapable violence that characterizes it—the demolition of a world when it no longer serves to express the new sensible states that emerge in collective coexistence. If, on the one hand, this experience probably occurs more frequently in contemporaneity than in any other period of Western history or in any other civilization, on the other, the myth of the promise of paradise contributes to the negation of this active or positive cruelty of life, which is our tragic condition. It is this triple misunderstanding that creates the terrain for the perverse instrumentalization by the current economic regime of life as force of creation. The most frequent contemporary psychopathologies are symptoms of this state of affairs.

How could the structuring of the self treat this triple misunderstanding? Learning to coexist with the Other as a living reality tends to be achieved here through a device that renders difficult, or even impossible, the simple recognition of objects. At least two characteristics of Clark's "relational objects" help block this reduction: first, the fact that they do not have any defined form, and therefore cannot be apprehended exclusively by the empirical exercise of the sensible; second, the fact that these objects, the strategy whereby one has access to them, and the context where all that takes place do not correspond to any of the known aesthetic references of the territory of art, and therefore cannot be easily identified on the cartographies of that world. But this alone would not be enough to get beyond the misunderstanding, if the device did not help to reconnect the person who chooses to live out this experience with his or her body in its potential of being affected by these objects and by the context where the experience unfolds, through the reactivation of the intensive exercise of his sensibility.

This first learning experience leads to the second: learning the rhythm of the vital pulsation, which is made possible here by an initiation into the knowledge not only of virtual reality but also of its paradox with respect to actual reality. This initiation depends on certain characteristics of *Structuring of the Self* described at the beginning of this essay: not only the specificities of the "relational objects," but also the silence, the fact that the experience is offered to one person at a time, and the temporality punctuated by the regularity of sessions. Thus the device creates the conditions needed to live out the paradox, traversing the turbulence, the disorientation and crisis that result from it, but without interpreting this experience in a delirious way and repressing it through defense mechanisms. At this point we come to face the third learning experience, which concerns the tragic sense of life.

Here we approach the frontier with art and politics. Let us first examine the properly artistic nature of this event: the pathology that this device proposes to "heal" is also what contributes to maintaining the instrumentalization of the artist's force of creation, and the blockage of the spectator's aesthetic experience. This instrumentalization and blockage, as well as the fetishization of the object that derives from it, are essential features of the reigning politics of art since the late 1970s. How can the structuring of the self help to change the status of the artist, the viewer, and the object within the dominant cartography?

The device tends to feint with the instrumentalization of the artist's inventive power, given that the latter cannot be separated from the production of the event within the subjectivity of the viewer in his or her relation to the Other, where the work properly speaking is realized. The device also tends to thrust through the blockage of the viewers' aesthetic experience, given that it bears on their relation with the object, carrying out a reconnection between their drive to know and the diagram of their sensations. Viewers will only accept becoming "clients" of this kind of *ritual of initiation* if they really desire it and feel confident about it. But if they make this choice they will not be able to sneak away from living the aesthetic experience: they will be obliged to strip away their position as mere consumers of this experience, which is what they usually are as they stroll socially through the spaces destined for art. The shift in the status of both artist and viewer that is carried out by this device also establishes the conditions for displacing the fetishization of the object, conditions reinforced by the physical qualities of the "relational objects" that render their form always provisional, so that they can never be grasped solely through perception, and even less by a perception limited to vision. In this way, what tends to transform itself is the entire cartography of art that was fully installed at that period.

So, where is the political, or rather, the micropolitical nature of this event to be found? The treatment carried out by the structuring of the self helps to eradicate the virus of faith in the supposed paradises promised by cultural-informational capitalism—a myth that feeds parasitically on the most essential potentials of subjectivity. The self that Lygia Clark sought to structure tends to free itself from capture by capital: it comes to orient the creation of cartographies of oneself and the world and ceases to be a mere adjunct of the ego in the latter's management of this creation, through its reference to the worlds proposed by the market. With this reorientation, the flexible subjectivity on whose formation the artist wished to collaborate ceases to be a showroom subjectivity or a self-for-sale, producing/consuming the worlds created by capital. In its place, a subjectivity moved by the urgencies indicated in the double exercise of the sensible has a chance to come into being: a subjectivity open to otherness, able to live a shared experience and to construct itself and the world on that basis. These are the necessary conditions for the reactivation of the political and aesthetic potentials of subjectivity, but also and above all of a public life in the strong sense of the term.

Structuring of the Self seems to have prepared the subjectivity of Lygia Clark's clients to be more disposed toward this shift, even if the change is slight and subtle. But this small change is quite important before the mobilizing power of a flexible subjectivity for sale, of the type imposed by cognitive capitalism in its transnational extension.

The principal force of this proposal is that it was an artistic response, located on the frontier of politics and of therapeutic practice, to the perverse politics of subjectivation that was establishing itself at that period. It did not entail a return to the politics of identity dating back before the 1960s and early 1970s, but instead took up again the process of creating a flexible subjectivity as a collective movement, which began at that time and was interrupted and diverted from its goals through its instrumentalization by integrated world capitalism. What is most surprising is that Lygia Clark grasped this perversion at the very moment of its emergence in the late 1970s and early 1980s, and even more, was able to elaborate such a precocious path of response.

Would this not be the essential meaning of that strange encounter between the artist and the naked viewer that Lygia Clark insisted on practicing across this entire period, in *Structuring of the Self?* This singular and powerful poetic-political consultancy was the last and probably the most subtle artistic solution created by Lygia Clark to face the questions of her time. The disruptive power of this confrontation, which was certainly at work from the first to the last gesture in her trajectory as an artist, offers us a possible key to its greatest critical force.

NOTES

1   Illustrations of Lygia Clark's *Estruturação do Self* (*Structuring of the Self*), 1976–1988, may be found in a number of books and catalogues devoted to the work of the artist, and in many publications dealing with modern art from South America. For example, Rolnik and Diserens, *Lygia Clark;* and Ramírez and Olea, *Inverted Utopias.*

2   I am referring to the first retrospective and catalogue of Lygia Clark's entire oeuvre, organized in 1997. After its inauguration at the Antoni Tapiès Foundation (Barcelona, 1997) the exhibition traveled to the MAC de Marseille (Marseille, 1998), Serralves Foundation (Porto, 1998), Palais des Beaux Arts (Brussels, 1998), and Paço Imperial (Rio de Janeiro, 1998–99).

3   "Objeto Relacional" by Clark (with Rolnik).

4   See, in particular, Winnicott, *Playing and Reality.*

5   Cf. Holmes, "The Flexible Personality." Online at http://www.beavergroup.org/brian/.

6 Negri and Hardt, *Empire*.

7 Lazzarato, "Créer des mondes."

8 A notion advanced by various tendencies within Autonomia Operaia in Italy during the 1970s, subsequently reworked by Félix Guattari. See Guattari and Rolnik, *Micropolítica*, 187–90.

9 "Integrated world capitalism" (Capitalisme mondial integré or CMI) is a term coined by Félix Guattari during the late 1960s as an alternative to the term "globalization," which he considered to be excessively generic and as serving to hide the fundamentally economic, specifically capitalist and neoliberal, senses of the phenomenon of transnationalization, which began to be installed at that period.

10 See Holmes, "The Flexible Personality" and "Warhol in the Rising Sun."

7

DOUBLE MODERNITY, PARA-MODERNITY

JONATHAN HAY

A few years ago, Fredric Jameson wrote that the nonmodern "is unavoidably drawn back into a force field in which it tends to connote the 'pre-modern' exclusively (and to designate it in our own global present as well)."[1] The non-modern is the residue, then, of modernity that Jameson, following Habermas, portrays as an incomplete project of modernization. Coming at this from a non-Western perspective, and thinking about the production of art today in these terms, I then ask myself under what circumstances non-Western art making can be considered modern. It seems that non-Western art only becomes modern to the degree that it enters the field of Modernism (and its derivative, Postmodernism), to which it has to conform by adopting a set of attendant aesthetic protocols and embracing an ideology of innovation. The term "derivative" may not sit well—it effectively characterizes the postmodern break as internal to modernity—but the rest of this essay will outline a perspective in which this makes a particular kind of sense.

What I particularly appreciate in Jameson's view of nonmodernity is that he frankly acknowledges modernity's totalizing thrust, which in artistic production is embodied in Modernism (and its derivatives). In everyday parlance, this thrust is discursively embodied in the "G" words—globalization, globalism, globality, and the global—which serve to keep the non-Western world at a safe conceptual distance, as object rather than cosubject. The ideological power of the "G" words as an interrelated cluster lies in the fact that they rhetorically evoke a two-way process—as modernity extends its reach from the West to the rest of the world, the Rest also moves toward the West. This masks a fundamental asymmetry, in which the Rest attains subjecthood only to the extent that it becomes part of the West. The Rest—as the nonmodern/premodern—is assigned the false subjecthood of the traditional, which in its diverse forms either evacuates history or makes it finite (because it ends with the arrival of modernity). In these ways the West transforms the Rest into an object of knowledge, desire, and pleasure.

Against this, I want to discuss here two contrasting and unrelated artistic situations: one Chinese and one African, one canonically contemporary and the other outside any contemporary art discourse. Neither of them, in my opinion, can be fully grasped within a conceptual framework that takes for granted the totalization of "our" modernity or of Modernism.[2] I am presenting them together because in discussions of the West and the Rest, any attempt to challenge the totalizing claims of Western modernity that is made from a single point is immediately neutralized by a binary discourse, whether that be East versus West, the primitive versus the modern, or the one I have just used, the West and the Rest.[3] Within these binary frames of reference, challenge inevitably gets characterized as a claim to victimhood. My experiment with triangulation, however awkward, is an attempt to get around this problem.

The assumption here will be that our modernity can be framed in ways other than the diachronic, other than between the pre- and the after; that our modernity—which I shall now start to call Euro-American—is a particular one with an outside that can only be seized geoculturally.[4] No serious claim for any exteriority of Euro-American modernity could be made on the basis of its mere extension to other parts of the globe; if the notion of alternative modernities ultimately means variations on a Euro-American theme, then there is no escape from Modernism (and its derivatives). So the argument is for a different kind of outside, one that would imply a reconfiguration of our understanding of modernity in general. The basic point, to give it a more systematic formulation, is first that modernity is a larger phenomenon, if that seems possible, than we normally consider it to be; second, that this larger phenomenon should not be confused with its Euro-American formulation; third, that its full description requires the creation of a differentiated typology of modernities to account for its internal complexity; and fourth, that the structure of contemporary modernity lies in the relations among its particular forms and their respective histories (and the relations among these relations).[5] I am arguing, in other words, for the modernity of certain aspects of the nonmodern and the premodern as these words are currently construed.[6]

THE DOUBLY MODERN

I turn first to China, and contemporary Chinese art, on which I want to offer some very general remarks in a historical perspective. As an art historian who works on much earlier periods, I am especially aware that the sinologist's view of modernity is not necessarily the same as the contemporary art specialist's. The place where this moves from being a disciplinary issue to being a theoretical one is around the concept of the early modern. The most significant historiographic development in recent years with regard to Chinese history from the sixteenth to the nineteenth century has been the debate—still ongoing—over the possibility of characterizing those final four centuries prior to the twentieth century in terms of modernity, on an analogy with the now well accepted early modern period in Europe. I am centrally involved in the debate as a proponent of the "promodern" position, but only on the basis of a narratological argument that relativizes modernity as a diachronic frame of reference (it was one of three available temporal mediations of experience). This relativization is essential if the identification of parallels with Europe is not to turn into a facile transposition of a European frame of reference to the Chinese context.[7] What is at stake in the debate is the possibility of a modernity that does not ultimately *derive* from Euro-America, though it interacts with it. We need a term to designate this latter possibility—the possibility of incomplete projects of modernization other than our own—so I will speak here of a history of *otherly modernity* in China, from the sixteenth to the nineteenth century.[8]

This is not the place to make the case for a pre-twentieth-century otherly modernity in China—but as a thought experiment one might want to consider how this would alter one's sense of the relation between China and Euro-America.[9] It would mean that in the seventeenth-century world the encounter between Chinese and Euro-American modernities was an encounter of equals, developmentally speaking.[10] Only in the second half of the eighteenth century did a developmental dysphasia between China and Europe kick in in favor of Europe. Whereas Europe at that point underwent a moment of accelerated social and cultural process that transformed it, China did not. Not that China stopped evolving, as some would have it, but it developed more slowly than Europe, still within the older framework of its otherly modernity. A disjunction between a slow- and a fast-track modernity was then born and made itself felt over the course of the nineteenth century. In the late nineteenth century, an Enlightenment-mediated ideology conditioned by the generalization of industrialization—in other words, modernism in the broadest sense as the ideology of our particular project of modernization—was exported eastward. But the degree of dysphasia in favor of the Euro-American world rendered China's otherly modernity invisible to Westerners who needed to believe that China-men were mired in an unchanging past. More than a century later, we continue to have difficulty with the idea that a city such as late nineteenth-century Shanghai was born from an encounter not between modernity and tradition, but between two different forms of modern condition and temporality.[11] With-in China the invisibility of its own otherly modernity was ensured at the begin-ning of the twentieth century once educated Chinese opted for the Euro-Ameri-can model of the intellectual over the earlier Chinese model of the *literatus*. The adoption of the subject position of the intellectual together with its accompany-ing norms of conceptual language imposed the rhetorical assumption that modernity of any kind was a recent arrival from the outside world. In a climate of lost national confidence, Chinese intellectuals took over the prejudices of their Western mentors that consigned anything nonmodernist to the dustbin of tradition. Post-1949 the modernity tradition opposition was taken over by the Communist state.

In China today this opposition continues to structure the rhetorical dis-course on modernity among transnational artists and critics in China, obscur-ing what I take to be the reality of the situation. In the historical perspective I have offered, contemporary Chinese art can be said to be *doubly* modern in the sense that it derives from not one but two genealogies or, better, narratives of modernity. It is from this point of view that one needs to assess the contempo-raneity that is currently being obsessively pursued in art in the People's Re-public of China, as Wu Hung has written, under the name *dangdaixing*, which has more to do with achieving up-to-dateness in relation to the world beyond China than with breaking with the thinking of a previous generation of artists.[12] Dangdaixing recalls the equivalent early twentieth-century obsession with the new, *xin*, and the modern, *xiandai* or *shidai*, which have themselves too hastily been assimilated to a modernist obsession with innovation. As rallying calls, the "new" and the "modern" signified differently in Euro-America and China, and it would be my contention that their effective meaning in Republican-period China came much closer to what is now called contemporaneity, as reflected in the title of a literary journal of the time, *Les contemporains*.[13] From this point of view, contemporaneity has long been the ideology of a condition of double modernity in China.

These purely theoretical remarks need to be fleshed out more fully than is possible here, but I can at least indicate some aspects of their relevance around the question of the status of nonmodernist features in contemporary Chinese art. Here I want to make a distinction between representation and practice.

Characteristically, on the side of representation all that is not modernist or postmodernist becomes tradition. The easiest way to see this is in works where the artist uses a reference to "tradition" to create the fiction of a ground of nonmodernism from which the artwork emerges in all its up-to-dateness, as in Zhang Dali's graffiti photographs (the pre-twentieth-century building in the background) or Ah Xian's porcelain busts (covered with Ming or Qing dynasty floral designs). Works like these also offer a visual metaphor for current criticism that tends to see every modernist feature of a Chinese artwork as emerging from a ground of nonmodernism that is passive, inert, and malleable. On the side of practice, however, one gets a very different view of the question. Let me give three examples.

First, theatricality, long an important element of contemporary Chinese art, has recently been intensified by the conceptual turn that took place in art in the People's Republic of China in the mid-1990s, as can be seen in the International Center of Photography's exhibition "Between Past and Future," curated by Wu Hung and Christopher Phillips. This ushered in the paradigm of second-order representation, for which photography has provided the most common, though far from the only, technical means.[14] The effect of the layering of representation and performance is very often one of distantiation, and one can certainly view works like Wang Qingsong's *Night Revels of Lao Li* (2000), Zhao Bandi's *Chinese Story* (1999), Ma Liuming's *Fen-Ma Liuming* (1998), or Yang Fudong's *The First Intellectual* (2000) in these terms as a conceptual stylistics, heavy on the attitude. On the other hand, in a longer historical perspective what is striking to me is the very association of theatricality with self-definition, not only because this coupling has a very long history in China, but because, wherever one sees it in pre-twentieth-century Chinese art, it is a response to the instability and unbelievability of available social roles, an index of doubt and independence—and as such, a modern phenomenon.[15] From this point of view, the current landscape of short-circuited subjectivities cannot be accounted for simply in modernist terms.

A second aspect of contemporary practice, involving a thematization of the city, may be less familiar, partly because it is not specific to the particular China of the People's Republic. There is a well-known body of work that bears witness to the devastating remaking of Beijing in recent years, but here I have in mind something else, an approach to the city that can be seen here and there among artists in China, Hong Kong, and Taiwan, and among Chinese artists living in other countries. It is particularly to be found in video and photography, where it is often associated with a very slow temporality negating the speed of contemporary urban life. The surface busy-ness of the world is allowed to rush by, as in

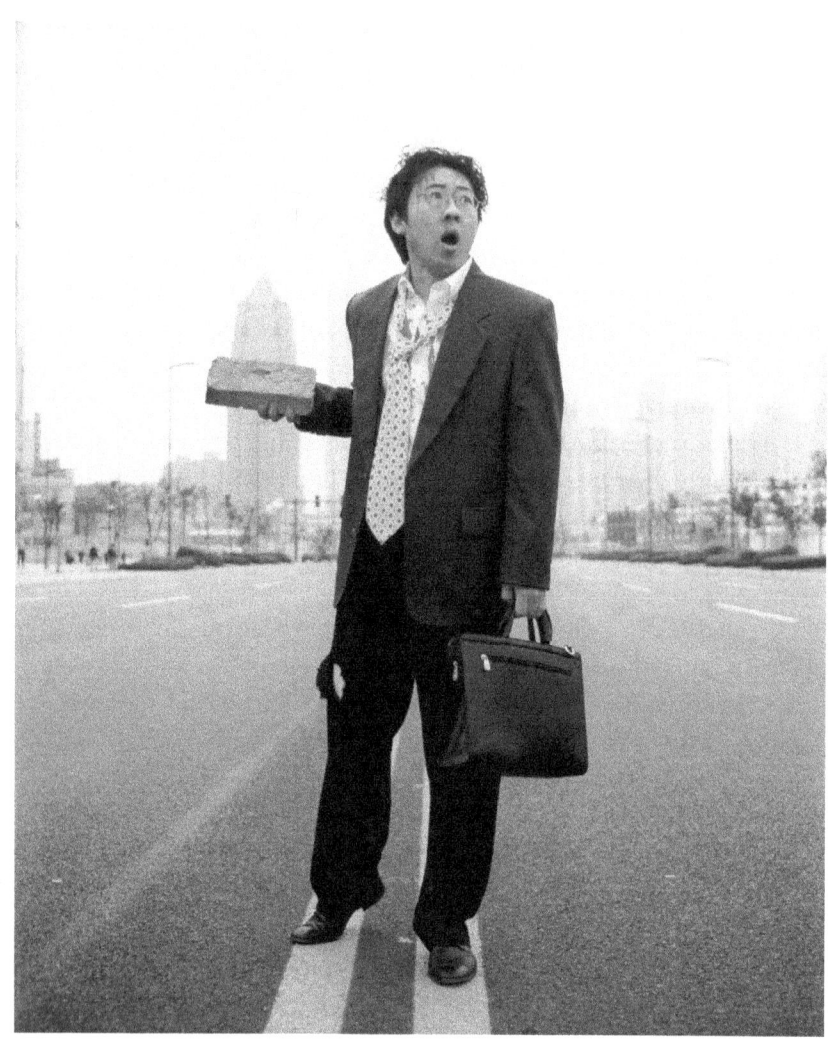

Yang Fudong, *The First Intellectual*, 2000. From a triptych of 3 C-prints. Courtesy of the artist.

Ellen Pau's *Recycling Cinema* (2001), featuring a section of a Hong Kong free-way, or is even made to disappear as in Yang Gouang-ming's *City Disqualified* (2001), where one of Taipei's busiest intersections is shown at midday, strangely deserted. The city's accompanying toxic aspects are either eliminated, as in *City Disqualified,* or take on a strange loveliness, as in Li Yongbin's *Face* series of videos, set in Beijing. What is left is the effect of an attenuated and conflicted sense of belonging. And this effect has a clear prehistory in pre-twentieth-century ink painting—not in representations of the city per se but in landscape, which was the genre into which the processing of urban experience was charac-teristically displaced in China when artists wanted to explore their relationship to their environment. This displacement had much to do with China's otherly modern need to reconcile the shallow time of the city with the deep time of the countryside. What one sees in these contemporary works is, conversely, the reinvention of urban temporality as a new kind of deep time. The city has won but there still exists a memory of something else.

Third, the last few years have seen an exciting return to ink painting and calligraphy by contemporary artists inside and outside China. What they have returned to is rather specific—a tradition of eccentric, iconoclastic self-posi-tioning that is one of the great artistic developments of the seventeenth and eighteenth centuries. One of the enduring myths about this tradition is that pre-twentieth-century artists of this independent-minded kind were uncon-cerned with politics except during changes of dynasties, whereas in fact they addressed political issues constantly, albeit obliquely for reasons of self-preser-vation.[16] So it does not seem surprising to me that painters like the New York-based Yun-fei Ji, commenting on the Three Gorges project in his *The Old One Hundred Names* series (2002), would reference seventeenth-century ink paint-ing, notably the form-generating brush trace of Shitao (1642–1707); or that the stylistic precedents for the political calligraphies of the Yangjiang group of artists lie in this same independent, individualistic tradition.[17] Sha Yeya's 2002 *Powell denied the possibility of war declaration on Iraq, saying that America won't take action without discussion with its allies* is a perfect example, its illegibility recalling the less extreme liberties taken by a group of eighteenth-century painter-calligraphers often termed "Eccentrics." With regard to the Yangjiang calligraphers, I am struck by the fact that they present their work not in the aestheticized terms of calligraphy but as a form of public writing. This position relates their work directly and confrontationally to the exploitation of calligra-phy as public writing by Communist Party leaders; however, Mao and the others were themselves following in the footsteps of the Qing dynasty emperors, who in the late seventeenth century were the first to turn calligraphy into public

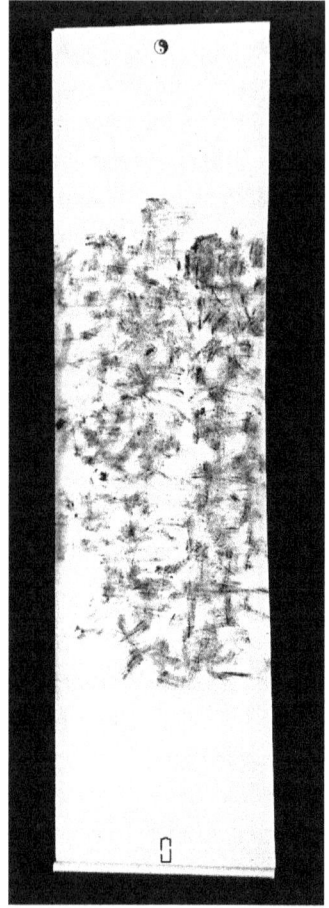

Sha Yeya, *Powell denied the possibility of war declaration on Iraq, saying that America won't take action without discussion with its allies,* 2002. Hanging scroll, ink on paper, 295 x 78 cm. Courtesy of the artist.

writing to serve as an art of political authority suited to modern circumstances of pseudocontact between political leaders and the people.[18] This history is no less relevant to New York–based Xu Bing's well-known calligraphy project, encapsulated in his nonironic *Art for the People* banner.

I do not have time here to extend the argument to the figure of the artist, other than to point out that the easy assumption of a self-legitimizing role, the reluctance to cede commercial control to others, the instinctive understanding of branding, the sharp calculation of political possibility, and the acceptance that the public responsibility of the artist-intellectual is an issue—all of these practices and attitudes of contemporary Chinese artists were already familiar features of the Chinese art world under the otherly modern conditions of earlier centuries. My last remark would be that if the Chinese world has been doubly modern for at least a century, and if contemporaneity is the ideology of that condition, then contemporaneity in a relatively strong sense has been part of the modern world for just as long. I take the claim, by the editors of this volume, of a *current* condition of contemporaneity to be a sign that this has finally become everyone's business, and perhaps also, less simply, as a sign that the doubly modern, in the various parts of the world where it exists, may be ready to move beyond its repression of its own history.

THE PARA-MODERN

I turn now to Africa. Here I speak from a nonprofessional position, as a collector of modest means. A few years ago, in a hard-hitting article, Zoe Struther challenged the nonmodern characterization of one of the canonical bodies of African masks—the twentieth-century masquerade masks of the Central Pende people of the Democratic Republic of the Congo.[19] She demonstrated that the stripping of authorship from the masks has obscured a century-long history of integration of Pende sculpture into the global market. Conversely, the restoration of authorship to the masks becomes a path to the acknowledgment of the modern condition of their production. The Central Pende sculptors are not an isolated case. Although Struther's careful research has not been widely duplicated, there is enough scattered information available to make it clear that some variant of this argument could potentially be developed for any number of well-known genres of "genuine" African art.[20] At the end of her article Struther asks, "Will the 'modern' always look like 'me'?" From my point of view, the question may not go far enough. Simply identifying the shared condition of the global market leads only to a claim for a shared modernity on such a general level that it is hard to see how a specialist of contemporary Euro-American art—or for that matter contemporary African art—might feel directly concerned.

A different way of approaching the problem is suggested by the work of Enid Schildkrout on an artistic genre that was generated by the colonial presence in the northeast of the Democratic Republic of the Congo, and which like the Pende facemasks has become part of the Western canon of "genuine" African art. Schildkrout has shown that among the Mangbetu, figural sculpture for both Mangbetu and Western patrons was part of a larger effort of cultural self-definition along ethnic lines—involving an acquisition of fixed or hardened ethnicity—that was specific to the colonial period.[21] The larger point is that encounter situations force into existence a process of cultural self-distancing or self-consciousness that changes the meaning of practices of representation, because these now become *self*-representation as well. Africanist colleagues stress that this process predates, and continues to happen separately from, the encounter with Euro-American culture.[22] So one must ask: Do the colonial and postcolonial encounter situations significantly change a preexisting intercultural calculus? I believe they do. The entry on to the scene of the juggernaut of capitalism brought with it a potentially unlimited market, with the result that the economic rewards of self-representation increased exponentially. This created the conditions for *acting* on the fact that the disparity of cultural frameworks between Africa and Euro-America created far wider latitude for self-representation. And in the face of the enormous disparity of economic and political power between Africa and Euro-America, the manipulation of Western consumer desire is hardly a politically neutral act.

I will eventually come back to "genuine" African art, but I think the issue is more easily grasped initially through its unspoken other: forgeries. These have a truly abject status in scholarly discussion, routinely being scorned and abused as a kind of aesthetic pornography. To the degree that the successful forgery wreaks havoc with historical understanding this is perhaps an understandable attitude; on the other hand, it also obscures the intrinsic interest of these artifacts. In the remarks that follow I shall consider forgeries to be works whose physical construction embodies a deceitful claim to have been produced for the purposes of ritual or other use within an indigenous context. Obviously, any such forgery involves a self-conscious representation of an aspect of African culture, and it is part of the definition of a forgery at this moment in the history of faking that the object purports to be a nonmodern/premodern artifact, either preceding or escaping the intercultural contact of the colonial period.[23] At this point I suspect that some readers may have a mental image of the low-quality examples offered on the sidewalk outside museums like the Whitney. Let me ask you to slide that image out of your mind.[24] In this discussion I am concerned with more ambitious artifacts, some of which might convince an experienced dealer or museum curator, while others, although they might not deceive someone so expert, would take in someone less experienced (like me). Some of these forgeries are copies or even replicas of specific genuine artifacts; many more, however, make reference to an artifact *type*.[25]

Forged artworks of this kind have been produced in Central and West Africa for over a century, often by artists unrelated to the people whose art they are imitating. Produced for sale to outsiders, these artifacts are sometimes very similar to objects made for indigenous use; in the early days especially they were sometimes identical except for the fact that they showed no evidence of having actually been used. It did not take long for African producers to discover that collectors prized evidence of use as an element of an aura of primitive authenticity; today, signs of wear are a feature of every ambitious forgery. The *aura* of

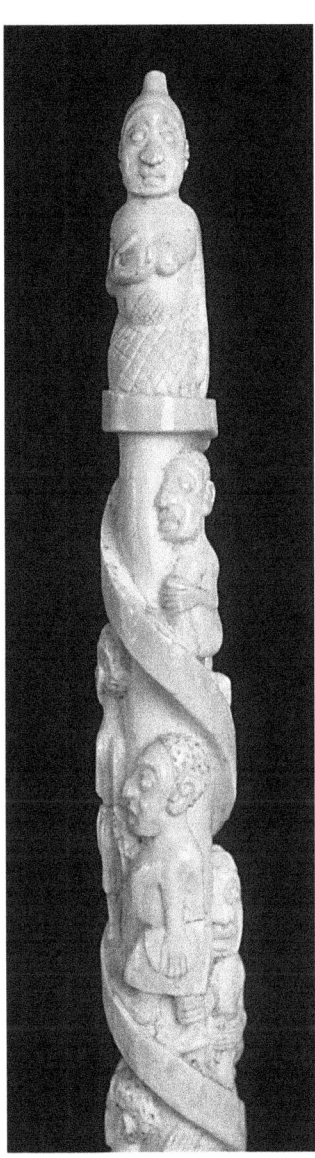

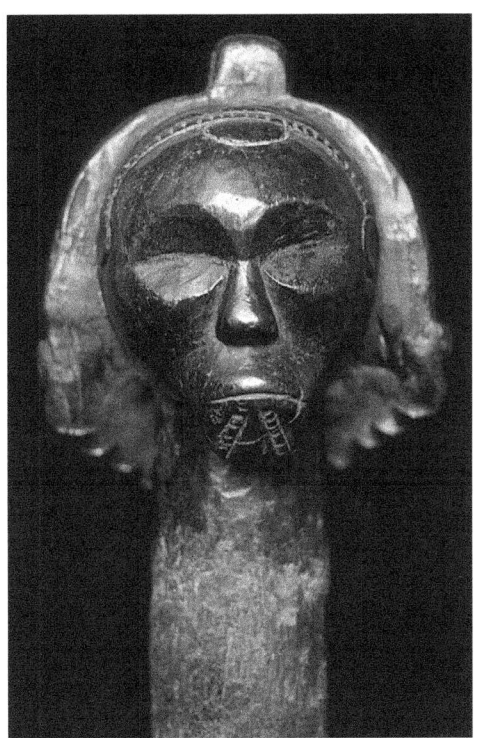

Kongo peoples, Angola, ivory tusk for the export market, carved with a procession of male figures advancing toward a kneeling female figure, late nineteenth–early twentieth century, height 21.8 cm, height of detail 15 cm. Collection of the author.

Unknown African artist (country unknown), contemporary forgery of a Fang reliquary head. Wood, height 29.7 cm. Collection of the author.

the primitive is the forger's lodestone and goal. The producers' area of creativity is the staging of an illusion of authenticity, a representation of the tribal, that reproduces or exaggerates elements of indigenous art making to meet the expectations of a partially informed outsider audience.[26] This does not preclude other kinds of adaptation of forms to outsider taste: the scale, the materials, the surfaces, and the iconography often anticipate a function of bourgeois decoration. However, the most successful forgeries are never reducible to mere decoration because they not only admit of concentrated and sustained attention, but also characteristically demand it. Even their absorption is theatrical.

Because the most ambitious examples can be strikingly beautiful or grotesque, and impressively inventive, they have made their way into collections and museums. Obviously, no collector or curator likes to be duped, but few curators and fewer collectors entirely escape this fate.[27] When forgeries go unrecognized, they are admired alongside the genuine article; but as soon as the secret is out, a profound embarrassment on the part of the duped consigns them to oblivion.[28] Although the factor of deceit might at first seem to explain the discomfort that the African forgeries cause, a more important malaise is figured in negative whenever the unmasked forgery is recognized to be too self-conscious, or indeed is unmasked *because* it is too self-conscious, because it seeks to please, and seeks to please us here in the West. What is this "too"? We are happy to accept self-consciousness when the modern African artist accepts transnational norms with regard to modes and genres and mediums of art making, and protocols of authorship. But when the medium of art making is an indigenous African one, the Euro-American audience by and large wants that aura of the primitive, and it is the lack of our own kind of self-consciousness that we look for to guarantee this aura. The transnational African artist may justifiably object that she or he does not aim to please a Western audience but to discomfit and confront it. This, however, speaks to a difference in the way self-consciousness is exploited, not to the fact that self-consciousness is shared by forger and transnational artist alike.

What, then, is the frame of reference within which the forgery might make sense and, further, be seen to deserve respect and even admiration? The forgery has a parasitic relation to both indigenous art and Modernism, and I want to understand this relation as a productive one. On the one hand, the forgery embodies a limited and qualified engagement with Modernism, through the productive distance that it takes from its own culture by anticipating modernist needs. On the other, it maintains continuity with an indigenous nonmodern relationship to time through its fidelity to the artistic medium. The forgery represents a triage of the processes and forces arriving from outside. This phenomenon needs its own name: I shall describe it as *para-modernity*.[29] Contrasting with the narrative overdetermination of the doubly modern, para-modernity claims no history, no narrative of its own; it does have a history, of course, but the *claim* to a history is not part of its self-definition.

As long as only forgeries are in play, the question of para-modernity will seem trivial or unimportant. But as the example of Mangbetu figurative sculpture showed, para-modernity can be a feature of indigenous practice as well. In fact, Zoe Struther's argument on Pende sculpture demonstrates, in my terms, not so much the modernity but more narrowly the *para*-modern dimension of large parts of indigenous practice in the twentieth century.[30] Part of the usefulness of the forgery for a theoretical argument is that it provides a bridge between this para-modern dimension of "genuine" African art on the one hand, and the vast realm of artistic genres specific to the intercultural interface on the other.[31] Let us not forget that these latter fully declared genres of intercultural encounter have a history as long as the history of direct contact between Europe, or later Euro-America, with non-Western cultures—in other words, going back to the sixteenth century. It is revealing that the names usually given to this kind of artistic production—tourist art, souvenir art, export art, and so on—define it in terms of the modern consumers of Euro-America and, nowadays, Asia as well. In contrast, a para-modern frame of reference privileges the producer's perspective, by acknowledging both the continuities of technique or style with precolonial practice and the productive distance from African culture that is absorbed from another, more thorough-going form of modernity.

The ideology of the para-modern can be described as a special form of contemporaneity: what one might call a simultaneous claim to contradictory temporalities, or temporal disjunction for short. The anthropologist Johannes Fabian has written that "radical contemporaneity would have as a consequence that we experience the primitive as co-present, hence as co-subjects, not objects, of history."[32] The para-modern frame of reference contributes to this goal, I hope, and claims a place for such art on a shared playing field with modernist and doubly modern practices without at the same time denying the fundamental differences.

In conclusion let me return to the initial question of the totalizing thrust of an undifferentiated theory of modernity generalized from the Euro-American case. Along with the tendency to totalization go two implications for artistic form. The first is that modernist and modernist-derived forms do their work of modernity solely across the categories of Modernism and Postmodernism. The second implication—the flip side of the first—is that there are no nonmodernist or nonmodernist-derived mediums of contemporary art, and that the only place for nonmodernist forms is in quotation, as fragments. The satisfyingly bothersome challenge of the doubly modern and the para-modern is that neither one can be integrated into an expanded parsing of Modernism and Postmodernism. The doubly modern resists such integration by its historical depth; even if one pursues the prehistory of Modernism back to the sixteenth century, one never reaches a point where China's otherly modernity can be derived from a Euro-American paradigm. The para-modern, on the other hand, resists integration due to its use of indigenous mediums, which goes far beyond the mere quotation of nonmodernist or nonmodernist-derived forms as fragments.

I have introduced the doubly modern through China and the para-modern through Africa. But I could have reversed this, at least partly. There is also a Chinese history of para-modernity, originally centered on its seaports and on the imperial court, and these days highly visible in the more commercial forms of cinema and contemporary art. (I generally call this "Chinaspace" to distinguish it from the transnational commitment to innovation.)[33] But even within the realm of transnational practice, the important theme of self-representation as Chinese is incomprehensible without taking into account its relation to this para-modern history. I might also mention the hostile discourse within the People's Republic that classes much of contemporary Chinese art as a form of export art.[34] I do hesitate, on the other hand, to claim an early African history of otherly modernity leading to a present double modernity in contemporary African art, but only because I am not an Africanist and am not competent to make the case. In pre-twentieth-century circumstances modernity is usually geographically highly localized; I see no reason to rule out its presence in sub-Saharan Africa a priori, and I am particularly curious about the history of Nigeria.

I hope it goes without saying that although I have not mentioned other parts of the world, I am putting these concepts forward as potentially of wider usefulness. As much as I admire the achievement of postcolonial theory, and as much as I am convinced by Dipesh Chakrabarty's attempt to provincialize Europe within Europe's own paradigm, it seems to me that this is still a more limited provincialization than is necessary.[35] I cannot myself go along with postcolonial theory's acceptance of Modernism's totalizing claims. And I want to ask speculatively, still within the parameters of the thought experiment I suggested earlier, whether it is possible that postcolonial theory itself has been created as much from a position of double modernity as from the position of Modernism.

Modernism, the doubly modern, and the para-modern: these are simply lenses that place us differently and through which one can construct different parallactic representations of contemporary art.[36] Moving from one placement to another, transversally, is not likely to leave anything looking quite the same as before, because it will no longer be fixed in one given place.[37] And this goes as much for the Euro-American world as for any other part of the globe. Perhaps more?

NOTES

1 Jameson, *A Singular Modernity*, 215.

2 In my choice of the word "situation" I am thinking of Alain Badiou's implacable philosophical critique of cultural difference as understood in identitarian terms ("Does the Other Exist?"). His argument, which I find persuasive, is that since there are only singular *situations*, the problem is not one of difference but of the Same. Yet Badiou's critique is itself open to the objection that the very singularity of the situation loses its density if alterity is denied. The price of his argument is that a place has to be found for alterity within the order of the Same—an alterity not of identity but of the situation in all its contingency. I doubt that this contingency can be grasped without the kind of differentiation of modernities for which I argue below.

3 Despite the great differences between the two artistic situations discussed here, and despite the fact that each represents a very specific case within the modern and contemporary artistic production of China or Africa, nonetheless they share something important in common. If "our" modernity finds its ideology in Modernism, these are both examples of situations in which modernity cannot so easily aspire to ideological formulation, partially so in the Chinese case and wholly so in the African example. For us, Modernism as the ideology of modernity is a problem; but in the perspective that I wish to offer, we are privileged to have it be that problem.

4 I am using the idea of an outside in Niklas Luhmann's terms as an observing position, including in it the possibility that the outside can also inhabit the inside. See Luhmann, "Observation of the First and Second Order."

5 Nothing in what I have said changes the fact that modernity itself is a problematic concept, but does perhaps justify setting aside its problems temporarily for the problem at hand. To construct a narrative of Euro-American modernity around subjectivity, consciousness, self-consciousness, or reflexivity, for example, may indeed amount to a lapse into ideology, following Jameson's third maxim of modernity. But the refusal to bring these categories to bear on the situations that I will be discussing might be considered equally ideological, albeit in a different way.

6 My grateful thanks go to the following colleagues and friends who generously offered criticism of earlier versions of this essay: Francesca dal Lago, Dorothy Ko, Joan Kee, Sarah Brett Smith, and Susan Vogel; as well as to Nancy Condee, Bruno Latour, Terry Smith, and Wu Hung, all of whom offered helpful comments following the conference presentation.

7 I should mention three points in order to clarify my position, which is somewhat atypical among proponents of a long-term history of modernity in China. First,

modernity, as I use the term, is not simply a condition but also a form of narrative representation that narrates the past, backward so to speak, from a starting point in an ever shifting present. As a form of narrative representation I distinguish it from two other forms that also have analytic purchase in the Chinese situation: narratives of belatedness, which start from one or other ideal moment in the past, and narratives of dynastic cyclical time, which have a cosmic starting point outside human time. Although one may, for the sake of convenience, speak of an early modern China, this means only that a narrative of modernity has relative precedence over the others from the sixteenth century onward; it in no sense implies that narratives of belatedness or dynastic time stop being relevant at that point in history—indeed, they continue to be relevant today. In other words, modernity belongs to a larger, disjunctive diachronics. Second, a narrative of modernity has usefulness only to the degree that its representation brings to visibility an existing condition of modernity. That condition, from the sixteenth to the early nineteenth century, had both a "hardware" and a "software" dimension. On the hardware side, the elements of a modern condition included, inter alia, the replacement (*pace* Anthony Giddens) of space by place as trade and technology (and also, one might add, increased state efficiency) broke down barriers of distance and speed; the autonomization and differentiation of businesses, professions, and spheres of knowledge; the expansion, though along pathways very different from Europe, of a discursive space of independent opinion and societal debate; the emergence of cities as a political force with which the state had to reckon; and what Bruno Latour—in his *Pandora's Hope*, 195–96—terms the increasingly intricate mesh binding the human and the nonhuman in shared collectives. On the software side, a modern condition implies among other things: the relatively greater importance of a sense of the unarguable difference (for better as well as for worse) of present-day circumstances from those of any other time; an intense awareness of social and psychic disjunction; an aspiration to autonomy in relation to the state, the market, and the community, often qualified by the desire for acceptance and legitimation; an intensified social self-consciousness, or reflexivity; a tolerance for doubt with regard to established social discourses; and the floating free of a psychophysical concept of subjecthood challenging the previously normative hierarchical social networking of the human subject. The third point that needs to be made concerns the use of a Western term, "modernity," in the Chinese context. The Chinese registered the above described developments discursively through constant recourse to two different but closely related master terms. The first, *jin*, covers a tightly focused semantic field corresponding to our words "today," "present-day," "the present." This was a term that modernity shared with the narrative of belatedness, where it also played an important role. The second term, *qi*, had a contrastingly vast semantic range, covering: the strange, extraordinary, or exceptional; the novel and the exotic; individualism and originality; and difference. The *qi* of the present brings us very close, I believe, to the idea of modernity. For a relevant bibliography on all these issues, see the following note.

8 Publications adopting and adapting the paradigm of the early modern to the Chinese situation in diverse ways include Rowe, *Hankow;* Clunas, *Superfluous Things* and *Pictures and Visuality in Early Modern China;* Hay, "The Diachronics of Early Qing

Visual and Material Culture," "The Kangxi Emperor's Brush Traces," *Shitao,* and "Toward a Disjunctive Diachronics of Chinese Art History"; and Rawski, "The Qing Formation and the Early-Modern Period." Struve, *The Qing Formation,* includes several dissenting essays.

9 It is sometimes startling to see where the absence of a concept of the otherly modern can lead. I have found Niklas Luhmann's theory of the functional differentiation and autonomization of self-creating social systems to be one of the most effective interpretative lenses through which the otherly modernity of seventeenth-century Chinese painting and society can be recognized as such. But this requires breaking with Luhmann's own assumption that, historically, modernity was a Euro-American monopoly until the franchise was opened at the end of the nineteenth century. A few years ago, in a footnote that has a Morellian revealingness, Luhmann shared his views on, of all things, Chinese painting: "We are not questioning the high artistic achievements, e.g., of Chinese painting or Indian music. Nor do we intend to look down on these accomplishments from a European perspective. We merely point out that one cannot speak of evolution in these cases, nor of structural changes heading toward an ever-increasing improbability. On the contrary, what impresses us in art forms of this kind is the constancy of the perfection accomplished. To be sure, there are developments in Chinese painting that could be interpreted as evolution—especially the shift from a linear and distinctly ornamental style of contours to a spontaneous style that expresses the unity of the brush stroke and the painterly result. But one can hardly claim that such changes lead to the differentiation of a self-evolving art system. Rather, Chinese painting is an indication of what kind of evolutionary opportunities reside in ornamental art forms" (*Art as a Social System,* 379–80, n. 78). Although Luhmann's characterization of Chinese painting as a quasi-natural phenomenon, and the portrayal of its artists as hostages to a process divorced from historical time, is, shall we say, idiosyncratic, it does give the measure, I think, of the difficulty of imagining the existence of otherly modern histories.

10 In my view, if one were to push their respective narratives of modernity back even further, to, say, the eleventh century—without here going into the arguments over the validity of viewing such early periods in a perspective of modernity—then China rather than Europe would seem the more modern society. By 1600, Europe had done no more than catch up with China.

11 Hay, "Painting and the Built Environment in Late Nineteenth-Century Shanghai."

12 Wu, "Between Past and Future," 26.

13 The journal's Chinese title was *Xiandai,* literally meaning "modern."

14 For a detailed discussion see Wu, "Between Past and Future," 25–26.

15 Hay, "The Conspicuous Consumption of Time."

16 See, for example, Hay, "Culture, Ethnicity and Empire in the Work of Two Eighteenth Century 'Eccentric Artists.' "

17 Yangjiang is a seaside town in Guangdong, which has become a center of contemporary art practice due initially to the efforts of Zheng Guogu, a native of the town and graduate of the Guangzhou Academy of Fine Arts. See the handbook produced for the occasion of the 2002 Shanghai Biennial, *2002 in Shanghai, in Yangjiang, Some Event Occurring.*

18 Hay, "The Kangxi Emperor's Brush Traces."

19 Struther, "Gambama a Gingungu and the Secret History." Struther demonstrates that the Pende have been producing masks for the Western market continuously since 1905, that this circumstance made possible the emergence of full-time professional Pende sculptors who were anything but anonymous, that the names of the masks' authors were and are systematically stripped from the masks in the course of their transfer to Euro-American collections, that the same sculptors continued to work for Pende customers, and that the sculptors had no trouble innovating within the aesthetic parameters of Pende art—innovations appreciated by foreign and Pende customers alike.

20 One example is the genre of naturalistic head crests covered in antelope skin in southeastern Nigeria that replaced earlier overmodeled enemy skulls when colonial rule cut off the supply of skulls; the new genre soon became sought after by Western collectors. See Sidney Kasfir's important article "African Art and Authenticity." Her article, though not principally concerned with forgeries, discusses many issues related to the present essay.

21 Schildkrout and Keim, *African Reflections.*

22 Susan Vogel and Sarah Brett-Smith made this point in personal communications. I would go further and argue that there is no culture without intercultural encounter.

23 Although all sorts of people can be involved in the production and distribution of fakes, including Westerners, my interest here is in forgeries produced by an African sculptor, an African middleman, or a combination of the two.

24 Those objects might be described as tourist art, though Susan Vogel suggests the category could also be termed "African home decoration," since this now provides its principal market within Africa itself in the absence of tourists.

25 Replicas are a special case, where the issue of a specific original complicates the question of aura.

26 It goes without saying that "tribal" is a highly problematic category. I refer to it here in acknowledgment of its ideological role.

27 In 1976, *African Arts,* the leading scholarly journal on African art, devoted an entire issue to the question of authenticity in response to the growing number of forgeries on the market, publishing an extensive number of statements on the question by leading scholars, curators, dealers, and others. Introducing these statements, the editor included the following anecdote: "You will be relieved to know the simple fact that virtually no museum in this country owns a fake! Long and costly telephone conversations elicited this Ripley information. The Smithsonian for example has a 1000 batting average in its collection of 20,000 pieces. No fakes occur in Philadelphia, Brooklyn, San Francisco or Boston. The curators all agree that there are large numbers of fakes all around the country but they are in private, not public collections. The owners of these dubious collections are hinted to be of wide public knowledge but of course there could be no names, on the old army adage no doubt, 'no names, no pack drill.' The UCLA museum, prodded into increasing verity by the leverage of proximity and collegiality, admits to 3 or 4 pieces out of the 10,000 acquisitions. These were 'deliberately acquired' or retained 'solely for teaching purposes.' There may well be reasons for these statistics if not for the defensive tone in which they are couched.

They could be explained by the periodic elimination of duds by a wild bonfire every equinox, or by the fakes being smuggled out in sacks on dark nights and dropped into the Hudson River (where they are no doubt rescued subsequently by all those notorious dealers we are told about, encrusted with the exquisite extra patination of that liquid slime that passes for fetish material in New Jersey). It seems rather that the whole subject is distasteful, like talking of B.O. at a tea party."

28 To the best of my knowledge, no scholar of African art has written a full article recognizing their aesthetic interest, though one can find the odd admiring comment here and there. It goes without saying that no "positive" museum exhibition of them has ever been mounted.

29 Joan Kee has reminded me of Rey Chow's concept of "para-site." As Chow puts it: "Because 'borders' have so clearly meandered into so many intellectual issues that the more stable and conventional relation between borders and the field no longer holds, intervention cannot simply be thought of in terms of the creation of new fields. Instead, it is necessary to think *primarily* in terms of borders—of borders, that is, as *para-sites* that never take over a field in its entirety but erode it slowly and tactically." From "Leading Questions," 201.

30 Struther makes her own connection to forgery when she writes: "In the African art market, it is the buyer who replaces the artist as visionary, who is able (like Marcel Duchamp) to recognize aesthetic value in the unassuming artifact. In this climate, Gabama, Nguedia, and the rest all become 'forgers' charged with the obsessive reproduction of the moment just before the Compagnie du Kasai opened its trading posts in 1903." From the side of nonmodernity, so to speak, one might comment that the conversion of named sculptors into anonymous forgers is only possible because the sculptors bring to their work a tradition of self-consciousness that lends itself to cultural self-representation. But from the side of modernity, the salient point is that the conversion of authored objects into anonymous "forgeries" is possible only because the authored objects, like fakes of the kind I have been discussing, ultimately share a common para-modern frame of reference.

31 On this, see Kasfir, "African Art and Authenticity." Some genres, such as Kongo tusks carved with figurative reliefs, obligingly distinguish themselves from the ritual practices of religious and social life every bit as clearly as the forgeries confuse the issue. Some genres (for example, those Mangbetu figurative sculptures for Westerners) have been integrated into the respectable world of the "authentic" tribal artifact. And some genres such as Kamba figurative sculptures occupy a midpoint, mixing the old and the new without any intention to deceive, and in ways that confuse our neat categories. Which in any event are not so neat; the fact that a genre was invented to serve an outside market has never prevented its simultaneous integration into the culture that produced it as a prestige object.

32 Fabian, "Culture, Time, and the Object of Anthropology," 198.

33 Hay, "Adventures in Chinaspace and Transnationalism."

34 As pointed out by Charles Merewether, "The Specter of Being Human," 61.

35 Chakrabarty, *Provincializing Europe.*

36 I have expanded on this point in "Toward a Disjunctive Diachronics of Chinese Art History" and "The Diachronics of Early Qing Visual and Material Culture."

37   Take, for example, the practice of ink painting in the People's Republic of China after 1949, which was rejuvenated by two generations of modernists who adapted to the change of political circumstances by abandoning oil painting in favor of the Chinese brush. Do we read their ink paintings from within the Euro-American paradigm as a variant of Modernism, although the medium is not a modernist one? Or do we read them from without, so to speak, as an integration of modernist principles into an otherly medium, and therefore as an example of the doubly modern? Or, from the same period, one could take the example of Zao Wou-ki in Paris. Do we read his oil paintings, watercolors, and prints from within Modernism as a modernist integration of Chinese conceptions of the trace? Or do we read them from the other side as a Chinese otherly modern engagement with modernist mediums and so as another example of the doubly modern?

8

"PARTICULAR TIME, SPECIFIC SPACE, MY TRUTH":

TOTAL MODERNITY IN CHINESE CONTEMPORARY ART

GAO MINGLU

For people from the West, it is very difficult to imagine that the meaning of modernity has been important for the Chinese, yet we have debated it, intensely, for more than a hundred years. Even at the dawn of the twenty-first century, amid rapid globalization, "modern" (*xiandai*) is still a preferred term, as evident in phrases like "modern fashion" (*xiandai shishang*), "modern metropolis" (*xiandai dushi*), "modern style" (*xiandai fengmao*), and "modern design" (*xiandai sheji*). Of course, these designations all refer to the present moment of their utterance, not to the modern era of Europe and the United States since the late eighteenth century, nor to the time and taste of Western artistic Modernism.

Meanwhile, contemporary Chinese also very frequently use the term "contemporaneity" (*dangdaixing*) as a substitute for "modernity." When we speak about Chinese contemporary art, the word "contemporary" refers to the past three decades of new artistic production, the years since the end of the Cultural Revolution in 1976. When we speak of the "contemporaneity" of Chinese contemporary art, however, we are referring to the special markers that tie this art to the particular social and cultural environment of a specific period, or what modern Chinese call *shidai jingshen,* or "spirit of an epoch." In the indigenous Chinese context, we often refer to this "spirit of an epoch" as its "modernity" (*xiandaixing*).

This "modernity" should not to be confused with "modernity" in the Euro-

American sense of a marker of temporal logic (as part of a sequence from premodern to modern and postmodern). Rather, it refers particularly to a specific time and a concrete space, and to the value choices of society at that time. This sense of the word had already emerged in the beginning of Chinese modern history, at the turn of the twentieth century. Since then, the consciousness of Chinese modernity has been determined by the idea of a new nation rather than that of a new epoch. In my 1998 essay "Toward a Transnational Modernity," I put it this way: "For the Chinese *modern* has meant a new nation rather than a new epoch. Thus Chinese modernity is a consciousness of both transcendent time and reconstructed space with a clear national cultural and political territorial boundary."[1]

In this essay, I will first distinguish Chinese modernity from its Western referential origin, and argue that the fundamental characteristic of Chinese modernity can be interpreted as a permanent condition of contemporaneity, driven by a kind of empiricism, throughout modern Chinese history. In the second part I will discuss how Chinese modernity has shaped the horizon of contemporary Chinese art, locating it within a particular spatial perspective. Throughout the discussion I will show that recognition of dislocation and displacement, in the sense of a merging of art and society by complex negotiations between various cultural domains, is essential for an understanding of Chinese modernity in contemporary art.

TOTAL MODERNITY IN THE FORM OF A TRINITY

How can we distinguish Chinese modernity from Western modernity, which has influenced Chinese art since the early twentieth century? The difficulty, in real cultural praxis, is that what we call the "essence" of Chinese modernity, and the Western concept of modernity, are in fact bound in a relation of inseparability. This difficulty, however, should not prevent us from searching for the differences between them. On the theoretical level, the best way to discover the "essence" of Chinese modernity is to compare what is considered modernity in a Chinese context with the contemporary theory of Western modernity.

As I understand it, there are two guiding principles in the Western theory of modernity. First, "modernity" is about a historical time and epoch, as Habermas indicates.[2] It divides human history into premodern, modern, and postmodern epochs. Concepts such as "traditional" and "modern" are discursive structures that originated in the West during its period of modernization, where they were associated with "backwardness" and "progress" respectively. Using these categories, the history and art of third world countries has been judged by the principle of Euro-American modernity and reduced to either old or new, past or future. As a result, negative judgments on modern and contemporary non-Western literature and art, based on this inequitable dichotomy, are ubiquitous in studies of these fields.[3]

The second principle is the theory of the two opposite modernities, which is based on a further dichotomy, that is, aesthetic modernity is set against the materialistic modernity of bourgeois society. This, too, is described by Habermas, and elaborated by Peter Bürger, Matei Calinescu, and other scholars.[4] In Euro-American modern art history, aesthetic modernity often appears as a manifestation of the criticism of the materialized modernity of capitalist society. The critical tendency of aesthetic modernity, however, can either move toward a pure aestheticizing material culture—what one may call "autonomous aestheticism," such as the formalism that Clement Greenberg advocated, or move toward a critical, conceptualized material culture—what we may call "critical aestheticism," embodied in the legacy of Marcel Duchamp and Conceptual Art of the 1970s and 1980s. Furthermore, this split between two modernities is commonly recognized as a result of the original project of cultural modernization, which emerged during the French Enlightenment, in the form of a separation into three autonomous spheres: science, morality, and art.[5]

These two principles have effectively shaped Western art history. They not only describe as a logical progress the historical line in Euro-American art history, but also fit the socioeconomic contexts of the transitional age from the early to late modern period. The dichotomy-based theory of modernity in capitalist culture has been adopted as an aesthetic foundation by revolutionary artists and critics during different periods: thus Baudelaire's consciousness of modern life in Romanticism, Adorno and Horkheimer's theory of art's negativity relative to an all-pervasive cultural industry, Greenberg's aesthetic formalism, the counterinstitutional inquiry launched by Conceptual Art, and the merging and confrontation of high and low culture in Pop Art and in the theories of the cultural logic of the late capitalist society advanced by Fredric Jameson and other scholars.

The model of periodization natural to Euro-American modernity may not fit the experience of most non-Western countries, in particular third world societies, which lack a clear historical line of progression from premodern to modern then postmodern. On the contrary, third world societies have been obliged to merge characteristics of all these periods, adopting them in hybrid forms and often using incompatible elements at the same time. These processes may also have been experienced differently in different nations and shaped according to local priorities. In some societies, such as in China, modernization has lasted for a century; in others, such as in Malaysia, only a few decades. Third world countries, therefore, have experienced modernity more through changes of their social environment and political space rather than through more abstract notions of time and epoch. Although certain terms, such as "new" and "modern," have repeatedly been used to discuss cultural phenomena in these regions, they tend to refer to the pursuit of a certain ideal environment within a Western referential model. In this situation, time and epoch are more flexible. In the terms of the Euro-American epochal sequence, they can appear in reverse order. They are always ready to be metaphorized along with the shaping of a specific social space at a particular time.

After the Cultural Revolution, for instance, when Chinese city construction began to reach its first phase of modernization, debate in the architectural field was not about Modernism, but rather about Postmodernism. Since the 1990s, however, due above all to rapid urbanization, these debates have shifted their attention to theories and controversies about modernity and Modernism. In the former case, in a society suddenly opened up to the influence of Western contemporary theory, postmodernity was considered mostly as a set of concepts, which served as the first step in a search for modernity.[6] In the latter case, modernity is being specified and merged into a true condition of Chinese urban construction in the current booming, globalized society.[7] This sequence-reversed epochal terminology suggests that the consciousness of time in China might always have been determined by the experience of a specific physical space and social environment. It is this experience that has made the consciousness of modernity in China, and perhaps in other third world countries as well, more specific, empiricist, heightened, and thus problematic compared to the Euro-American historical chronology outlined above.

Rather than instituting a split between the different autonomous spheres—religion, politics, morality, and art—the mainstream of Chinese intellectual thinking in the modern and contemporary periods tends to try to close the gap between different fields as well as between past and present. For instance, Cai Yuanpei (1868–1940), an influential educator and philosopher of modern Chinese history, in his famous 1917 lecture "Replace Religion with Fine Art," advocated that aesthetics and art practice were equal in social importance to religion and commitment to morality.[8] Chinese modern and contemporary art is fundamentally concerned with how to integrate art and social projects, and how to fuse the benefits of a modern environment with a deeper understanding of current living space, in order to create a totality.

The consciousness of modernity in China, therefore, has long been framed within what I call the project of "total modernity." This was, perhaps, best

elaborated in the theory of Hu Shi, a leading figure of the New Cultural Movement of the early twentieth century, who transformed the principles of early
twentieth-century American pragmatism into the Chinese cultural context and
combined them with traditional Confucian pragmatism. Influenced by Dar-
win's theory of "the survival of the fittest," Hu Shi once defined his new pragmatism as a principle of seeking truth in modern society. He noted, however,
"the truth is nothing more than a tool for dealing with the environment. As the
environment changes, the truth changes with it. The real knowledge needed by
humanity is not absolute principle and reason, but rather particular time,
specific space, my truth."[9]

We could legitimately take Hu's notion of "particular time, specific space, my
truth" as the principle of Chinese modernity in the form of a trinity, one that
breaks down and transcends the dichotomy formation of the Western modernity. This trinity, qua trinity, also subverts the dichotomous thought patterns,
such as subject versus object, and time versus space, emphasizing instead a
network of forever changing relations among human subjectivity, living space,
and experience. Furthermore, this trinity principle does not attempt to become
a philosophical framework on a metaphysical level; rather, it is to be embodied
in daily practice. That is to say, considered within the perspective of daily
environment and a person's choice of truth and value, time is always a particular moment (not a linear, historical construct), and space is always ongoing,
mutable, and actual. This pragmatic principle of daily experience is well illustrated by Deng Xiaoping's famous sayings, such as "Cross the river by jumping
from stone to stone on the riverbed" (*mozhe shitou guohe*), and "White cat,
black cat, as long as it catches mice, it is a good cat." Both are metaphors of
"socialism with Chinese characteristics," which is the guiding principle of economic reform initiated in 1978. Perhaps these percepts can also be seen as
illustrations of Hu Shi's trinity theory of modernity. This principle of modernity has consistently been adopted in Chinese political and cultural projects
throughout modern and contemporary history. Although history and art in
China have changed rapidly since then, this heritage of pragmatism has consistently influenced contemporary Chinese art, including the avant-garde projects
of the last three decades.

It is this total modernity that has established a permanent condition of
"contemporaneity" as the Chinese model of "modernity." By being overwhelm-
ingly concerned with space and environment during the last three decades,
Chinese contemporary art has truly evidenced the principle of total modernity.
I would offer a further argument: that the nature of "contemporaneity" in the
twenty-first century, worldwide, is also more about space than time, because it

has been shaped during the last two decades by globalization and postcolonial cultural theory. The consciousness of space in Chinese contemporary art, I have claimed, has been driven by a kind of empiricism embedded in the experience of location and dislocation, the placement and displacement of various spatial references, rather than simply by dichotomies such as internal versus external, local versus international, import versus export, and so forth. In the second part of this essay, I will develop my argument by discussing some specific art phenomena, such as Chinese avant-garde, urban spectacle, "abstract" art, and Chinese women's art as examples of these changes.

LOCALITY, DISLOCALITY, AND RELOCALITY IN AVANT-GARDE SPACE

Although the avant-garde as an energizing force in Western art died during the 1970s, and the concept of avant-gardism fell into disrepute (not least among artists), it has flourished in China since that time. This is one reason why the Chinese avant-garde needs to be discussed from the perspective of Chinese social and artistic space where a specific, local avant-garde consciousness has been embodied rather than from the viewpoint of the Western ideology of Modernism and its material culture. It is the attempts by Chinese artists to close the gulf between art and real space, rather than merely represent consciousness in materialized aesthetic space (for example, in artworks), that establish a fundamental difference between Chinese avant-garde activity and that of its Euro-American counterpart.

What about the avant-garde legacy left behind by the woodcut movement and the leftwing literature movement of the 1930s, which deliberately presented themselves as *xianfeng*, or "avant-garde" activities? What is their impact on the contemporary Chinese avant-garde? The main concern in the artworks of these earlier movements was the immediate social environment, including such subjects as the suffering of the masses, governmental corruption, and the war against the Japanese. As the Russian avant-garde participated in the October Revolution in 1917 and the Italian Futurists supported the rebellion of the Italian Fascists in the 1930s, many Chinese avant-garde artists abandoned their lives in the metropolitan centers and took the long journey to join Mao's revolutionary army in Yan'an. Unlike the Russian and Italian collaborations, however, both of which ended in splits between the avant-garde and the authorities due to the naïveté of the avant-garde ideology (that is to say, its autonomous aestheticism, which did not fit the masses' comprehension), the Chinese avant-garde of the 1930s accepted the principle of Mao's mass revolutionary art and literature embodied in Mao's "Yan'an Talk" on May 2 and May 23, 1942, during the First Great Rectification campaign. Consequently, the Chinese avant-garde artists of the 1930s not only changed their petit-bourgeois sentiments toward a proletarian stance, but also transformed their identity from artists to soldiers. In this sense, their art also became revolutionary per se.[10] In the past two decades, the space for Chinese avant-garde art has undergone a tremendous transformation.[11] The initial loosening of ideological taboos at the end of the 1970s, the cultural expansion of the 1980s, and the economic and market globalization since the 1990s have all exerted influences on the space for Chinese avant-garde art. The "space" in question refers not only to exhibition space but also to the space for art production, including artists' studios as well as forms of interaction among artists, and between artists and their audiences. It refers not only to the occupation of working space by artists but also to the conceptual space delineated by the political, academic, and commercial systems. To examine the space for Chinese avant-garde art practice is to explore the identity of avant-garde artists.

The development of Chinese avant-garde art has been linked to the political climate from the very start. Art spaces were transformed into political realms, especially before the mid-1990s. On the other hand, avant-garde ideology has also led to confrontation in the public sphere. The avant-garde of the 1980s was equipped with many different resources, including Western Modernism and Postmodernism, art movements such as Dada, Surrealism, German Expressionism, and Pop, mixed with traditional philosophy, such as Chan Buddhism, as well as Mao's revolutionary heritage, in particular the proletarian antagonistic sentiment. Needless to say, all these resources carry strong iconoclastic attitudes toward the existing orthodoxy. In contrast, autonomous, aestheticist tendencies, such as Cubism, Constructivism, Fauvism, and American Abstract Expressionism, have rarely influenced Chinese contemporary art since the Chinese art world opened to the West in the late 1970s. Rather, Dadaism, Surrealism, and Pop, which embodied the other tendency of the critical aestheticism in twentieth-century Western art, have profoundly influenced Chinese avant-garde art.

The sphere of avant-garde art is impossible to nail down, drifting as it does between art space and sociopolitical space, the official and the unofficial, the aboveground and the underground. Art has always existed in opposition to and in negotiation with social space. As a result, avant-garde art has not always moved ahead; it has retreated as well. Many exhibitions or projects have begun only to be shut down in no time, or to cause political controversy, thus converting an art event into a political affair, an art space into a political space. Two such transformations took place at the "Stars" exhibition in 1979 and the "China/Avant-Garde" exhibition in 1989.[12]

Nevertheless, the avant-garde's perception of and attitude toward the relationships between art and the exogenous social sphere have undergone different stages of change in the last two decades. In general, avant-garde artists had begun to move into the public sphere before the 1990s, but they drew back during the 1990s, especially in the early 1990s. Since 2000, the division between art and political space has slowly blurred, except in the case of certain extremely sensitive political issues and performance art. Moreover, the art world has become more diversified: where once it included only state museums, academies, and journals, it now encompasses a range of national, private, commercial, and academic institutions. This has multiplied the possibilities for artists, but the borders have thus become more ambiguous and flexible.

Some Western scholars consider the Western avant-garde to be the experiment of aesthetic modernity that resulted from artists seeing themselves as the personification of alienation. This theory of alienation in capitalist society— initiated by Marxists and developed by Existentialists—has frequently been applied by Western scholars to characterize modernist artists, especially avant-gardists, as a rebellious, decadent, and resistant minority set against the capitalist society. Among such studies, Renato Poggioli pays particular attention to Marx's idea of alienation and considers "avant-gardism as ideology and as an aesthetic myth."[13] Another important contribution to the theory of the avant-garde is Peter Bürger's research on the topic.[14] His study is based on a critique of aesthetic autonomy that tries to relocate the Western avant-garde in the historical development of institutions in capitalist society. Rather than considering the avant-garde an ideological force resulting from alienation, Bürger realizes that the avant-garde is part of the institutional framework of capitalism, and that its revolutionary rule has been the critique of the institutionality as such. The contribution of the avant-garde, therefore, is to turn the critique of institutions, especially that of Art, into the primary content of their artworks. Bürger thus attempts to bridge the gap between aesthetic autonomy (aesthetic modernity) and capitalist society (social modernity) by bonding both together as a part of the institutional structure in capitalist societies.

This theory of the institution, it seems to me, is similar to the notion of "social base" in Marx's theory. There, the social base in most situations is held to determine the form of superstructure. Although Bürger's theory attempts to transcend the dichotomy of modernity and the avant-garde, his consideration of institutions as the social base is still confined within the framework of aesthetic modernity verses capitalist modernity. The relation between the changing institutions and the avant-garde discussed in his book is in fact not an engagement of the avant-gardists with the institutional system as it operates in real social space; rather, the artists still operate within an aesthetic space. The real world remains what he calls "the object of investigation."[15] The difference between Bürger and Poggioli is that the former takes his point of departure from the latter's elaboration of the avant-garde ideology in order to develop a more refined discourse of the universal aestheticism of the critical avant-garde. This difference, however, does not conceal the fact that both Bürger and Poggioli's stances are based on the dichotomous theory of modernity and avant-garde, and that both theories set up critical aestheticism against the social modernity in capitalist societies.

It becomes unlikely, therefore, that either of these theories will work for the Chinese model of the avant-garde because the Chinese institutional system has been constructed in a totally different way. In it, both socialist and capitalist forces are influential. As well, there remain in Chinese society clear markers of cultural and political boundaries. This makes the living space of the avant-garde much more complex and multidimensional. It invites constant negotiation between avant-garde activities and the public sphere, often leading to confrontation and requiring a variety of strategies toward actions in the public space, such as the offering of offence, followed by retreat and relocation.

We may consider the Chinese avant-garde movement of the 1980s and 1990s as a response to alienation, targeting not the vulgarity and philistinism of a consumer society as did its Western counterpart, but rather the dominant, ideologically driven society as it became combined with the commercial imperatives. Chinese avant-garde artists have always embraced society when seeking individualism and creative freedom. There is no way for them to escape to an ivory tower; on the contrary, they must go onto the street and confront both the public and authority. By using the idea of "the shock of the new," an effective tool of Western avant-garde art for attacking the banal, vulgar taste of the middle class, Chinese avant-gardists created some extremely violent works. They did so not to attack the public, but rather to resist authority while trying to stimulate thought among the populace. One of the main features of the Chinese avant-garde of the 1980s was the shunning of traditional studio work by artists who were focused instead on social projects taking place in the public sphere, such as villages, factories, streets, and plazas. This was a result not only of their idealism in seeking to enlighten the masses, the enjoyment of being involved in a movement, and a sensibility growing out of Mao's revolutionary legacy, but also because of the complete absence of an art market, either local or international, in the 1980s in China.

Despite the significant differences between the Western avant-garde and the '85 Movement in terms of their different targets and acceptance, we might still find many ideological similarities on the levels of abstract spirituality and basic attitudes of rebelliousness, in what Poggioli described in his four-part typology of the Western avant-garde.[16] Even when the Chinese avant-garde made a retreat from the public space in the early 1990s, their activities still demonstrated a peculiar avant-garde spatial motivation, which turned out to be a broad social and public matter, rather than a spatial concern of privacy. Facing difficulties after the end of the Tiananmen Square incident and during the booming commercial society of the early 1990s—such as lack of acceptance of the avant-garde by both official and commercial galleries in China, being ignored by the media, lack of attention by the organizers of some Chinese avant-garde exhibitions overseas, and a paucity of financial resources—conceptual artists have had to retreat to confined spaces. Many artists in Beijing, Shanghai, and Guangzhou have been forced to do their work at home; to employ inexpensive materials in small-scale works that can only be displayed in private space; and to communicate only with a small audience of artists and interested persons. I call this unique phenomenon Apartment Art (*gongyu yishu*), which has produced a number of unsaleable and unexhibitable site-specific installations.[17] Song Dong and his wife, Yin Xiuzhen, for instance, are Beijing-based artists who lived in a room some ten meters square. Many of their projects were made in this small room, most of them sketched on paper. One of Song's projects was to practice Chinese calligraphy every day on a chunk of ordinary stone or the surface of a table, using a traditional brush dipped in clear water rather than ink. After the water characters evaporated, he wrote again.

Some of the works of Apartment Art are called proposal art (*fangan yishu*): for example, an outdoor work or a large-scale installation is presented as illustrated sketches. These proposals remain on paper and are never turned into reality. This avant-garde practice attempts to formulate a distinctive personal discourse in an admittedly polymorphous, polycentric world. It is a resistance to all totalizing ideologies in order to be free from any particular one. Yet this resistance is also a way of cultivating a private, meditative world apart from the materialistic society that has emerged since the early 1990s. Apartment Art is, therefore, engaged in responding to the double kitsch of Chinese society—the previous ideological kitsch as well as the later commercial kitsch. One may think that this retreat is similar to the attitude of Western Modernism in the first half of the twentieth century, in the terms of its isolation from outside society. The motivation of Apartment Art, however, is to use materials selected from the surroundings of the artists' own daily lives to represent the true relationship between the avant-garde art space and the social space in general. In this way, their unsaleable and unexhibitable works mirror the social environment and

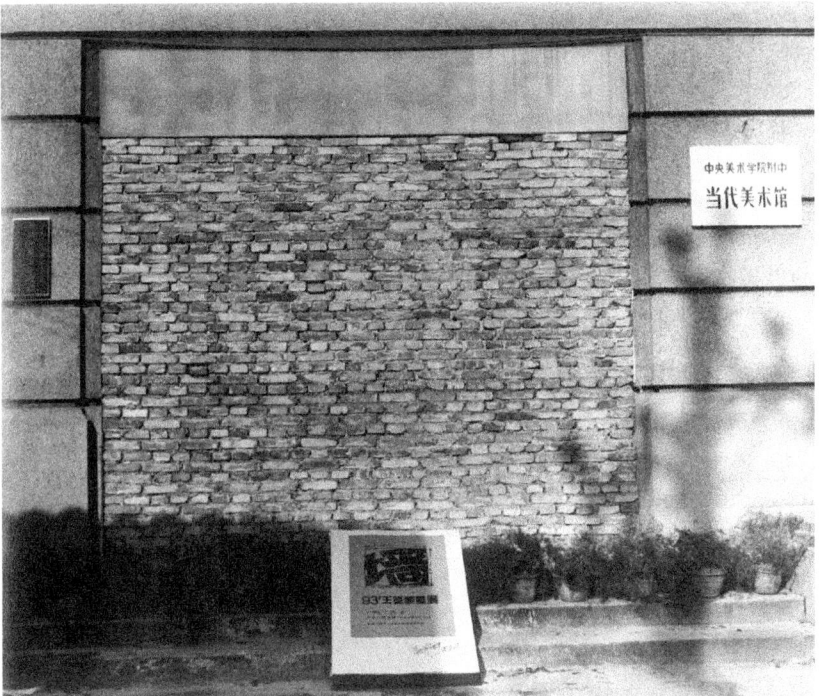

Wang Peng, *Wall*, 1990. Mixed media. Courtesy of the artist.

constitute a close investigation of the society. The works by the artists of Apartment Art are in this way the silent personal materials voicing the condition of their "inexistence" in a way of self-dematerialization. In 1990, Wang Peng and Feng Mengbo had a joint exhibition in the art gallery at the affiliated middle school of the Central Art Academy. Immediately before the opening, Wang Peng constructed a brick wall that sealed off the door to the gallery. The wall was meant to symbolize the self-confined space between the avant-garde and the official art system and market, a border behind which the artist had retreated.

It is this consciousness of environmental intervention rather than mere exploration of language or concept that has driven the new art movements of the last three decades toward an avant-garde tendency. Recently, some Chinese curators have tended to use the term "experimental art" (*shiyan yishu*) rather than "avant-garde" (either *qianwei* or *xianfeng*) to define contemporary Chinese art, expecting through this change to redefine Chinese contemporary art. This move may avoid the out-of-fashion usage of "avant-garde," or point to its dislocation in China today. Some may feel the term "avant-garde" to be too politically confrontational. Nevertheless, the notion of "experimental art," like "avant-garde," is itself a Western notion, widely adopted in the 1960s to refer to new art. I think the term "experimental art" cannot include most Chinese contemporary art phenomena of the last two decades, because, compared with "avant-garde," it sounds too passive and lacking in motivation and direction.

What is important is not the terminology of "experimentation," but rather its goal and significance. Of course, meaningful "experimentation" cannot limit itself merely to form and language but must have embedded within it a concrete critique, whether linguistic or social, especially at the present moment, when, under the onslaught of globalization and systematization, the direction of Chinese contemporary art's experimentation is far from clear. In fact, the phrase "experimental art" was introduced in the early 1990s, appearing first in the *Timeline of Chinese Experimental Art*, edited by Feng Boyi and Qian Zhijian. Later, "avant-garde" and "experimental" art were used interchangeably by Chinese critics and curators in reference to new art.

"Experimental" is a term that seems more moderate and palatable than "avant-garde," while still retaining the idea of seeking the new. Although it also has a sense of exploring boundaries and "self-marginalization," the exact aims of "experimentation" remain unstated and opportunistic, because, from the very beginning, experimentation has a subjective sense of indeterminacy, as everything hangs on the result of the experiment itself. Experimentation depends on the chance unification of subjective and objective conditions. For that reason, it is flexible. And perhaps for this same reason, it was fitted to China's rapid and chaotic internationalization and marketing in the 1990s. Nonetheless, it is inappropriate to use the term "experimental art" in reference to the Chinese art of the late 1970s and 1980s. The term also seems less than perfectly suited to the "underground" phenomenon represented by Apartment Art during the early 1990s. And it is even less suited to the "Political Pop," "Cynical Realism," and "New Generation" painting schools, each of which had an obvious eye toward real life.

By contrast, "avant-garde" seems better suited to highlight the "contemporaneity" of contemporary Chinese art. As I mentioned above, "contemporaneity" is not a term referring to a specific time, but means rather the "spirit of the time." Therefore, to be "avant-garde" is to make value choices, to adopt a specific critical direction. This critique integrates two inseparable tendencies: social critique and self-critique. Self-critique refers to the avant-garde's disillusionment with its own conservatism and corruption, with the lifelessness of artistic language and methodology. Thus "avant-garde" has a built-in sense of critique and protest.

The various uses of the term "avant-garde" by Chinese artists over the last two decades have already become a part of Chinese contemporary art history in and of itself. Moreover, from the moment Chinese artists began using this term, its meaning was already different from the meaning derived from Euro-American Modernism: the separation between aesthetics and politics implied by that earlier meaning was replaced in China by a unity of the aesthetic and the social. The tag "avant-garde" accurately described the position of Chinese artists in the social context of the 1980s and 1990s when various post-isms (postsocialism, postmodernism, postcolonialism, and postindustrialism) encountered one another in the same country, one that bore a long tradition. For the Chinese avant-garde, the "posts" mean nothing more than the end of the age, and therefore the task of the avant-garde still remains significant.

RITUALIZATION IN RECONSTRUCTING HISTORICAL SPACE

In recent years an ahistorical view has been applied, by some, to the study of Chinese contemporary art. This is the outcome of certain postmodernist theories, such as deconstructionism. To look at contemporary Chinese art from this point of view is to find that everything is contingent, transient, and lacks historical logic. In the Chinese context, however, the historical view has always been considered an important perspective in the creation of the art of the day, and the consciousness of modernity has always brought historical memory into what I call the ritualized space in which the contemporary and the past meet through certain ceremonial or monumental environments created by Chinese artists. This can be commonly found in the various contemporary art projects associated with historical architectural sites, such as the Great Wall, Summer Palace, and Tiananmen Square.

It has been very common in the last three decades for contemporary Chinese artists to turn historical sites into a symbolic medium to express modern Chinese identity. In the beginning of the new transitional era, there was an evident impulse to use historical sites. For example, around 1979, these sites emerged in the process of criticizing and reflecting upon the Cultural Revolution. As pursuing social modernization became the driving ideological force in Chinese society, the ruins of the Old Summer Palace destroyed by the Western "Joint Army of the Eight Powers" suddenly became the favorite hangout for young artists and scholars. Mourning the Old Summer Palace did not necessarily mean a longing for the old; rather, it revealed the artists' wish to excavate a new life for the nation and to achieve a Chinese modernity. The Old Summer Palace came to be a favorite topic among artists. For instance, *Newly Born*, an oil painting by Huang Rui, a member of the Stars group, aroused a great deal of resonance

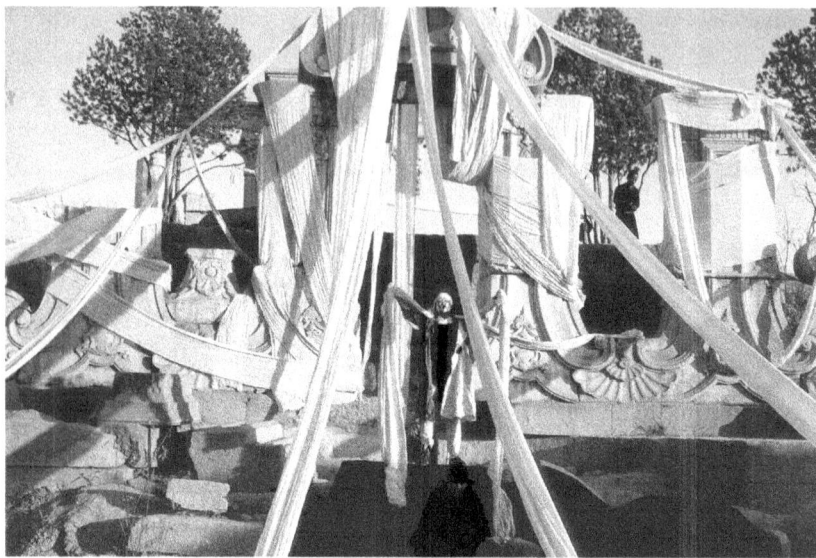

Kang Mu, Zhao Jianhai, and Sheng Qi, *Performance,* 1985. Performance, Old Summer Palace, Bei-jing. Courtesy of the artists.

among the public. Clearly, the meaning of his painting demonstrated a wish for the self-strengthening and rebirth of a weakened China caused by both foreign invasion and civil turmoil, such as the Cultural Revolution. Kang Mu, Zhao Jianhai, and Sheng Qi conducted performances for the first time on the site of Old Summer Palace in 1985. They bound up the old ruins. Their physical activities existed together with the historical existence of the edifice itself.

Many performance works have taken place on the Great Wall in the last two decades. In fact, the meaning of the Great Wall has consistently been recon-structed and reinterpreted throughout the twentieth century. Consequently, this reinterpretation itself has been formulated as an unending "discourse of the Great Wall." It has become a process of shaping or reshaping the consciousness of Chinese identity. Almost all the performance, earth works, and installations of the Great Wall projects involved certain kinds of ceremonial form.[18] Through these ritualized acts, environments, historical ruins, and stages were all part of the "ritual site." The "body" of the artist transmuted from being a symbol of the "sacrificial" in the past to being the living man mourning the "sacrificial" in the present. It is the contrast between historical memory and immediate feeling, the discrepancy between grand natural environment, historical background, and actual living situation that causes disorder in the recognition of identities. Using a memorial ceremony, a completely unreal situation and ritual, the artist

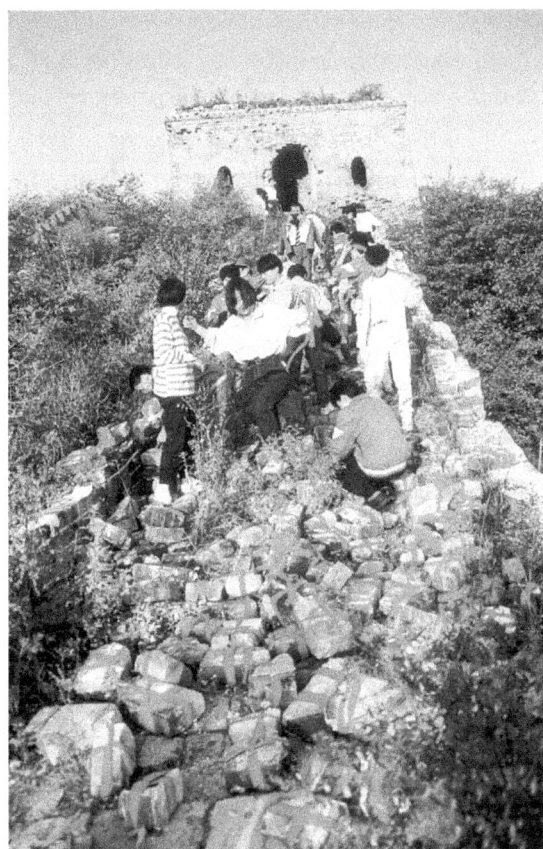

Zheng Lianjie, *Great Exploration*, 1993. Performance, Great Wall of China. Courtesy of the artist.

can turn his factual identity into an unreal but nevertheless idealized and mystic identity. For example, he could call up a spirit such as a witch, or "die" in the battlefield like an ancient warrior, or wander around like a ghost or spirit, as in the 1988 performance of the Beijing-based group 21stCentury, and in Zheng Lianjie's performance called *Great Exploration,* which took place on the Great Wall in 1993. What performance artists could become in the process is to be determined by their immediate spiritual purpose, by the sense of loss over their current identity, or by the longing for belonging (in classificatory, national, community, and even sexual terms). Regardless of differences among the various projects associated with ritual form on the historical sites, they all demonstrate the application of historical myth as a force over certain modern myths.

There have been a variety of modern myths: ideological, cultural, national, and even some relating to gender. Most artists took their performance or earth works to the Great Wall in order to make their social critique in response to national symbols and state ideologies. These include Xu Bing's *Ghost Pounding the Wall* (1991) and Cai Guoqiang's *Project to Extend the Great Wall of China by 10,000 Meters: Project for Aliens No. 10* (1993). In contrast, He Chengyao, a Beijing-based woman artist, made her Wall performance very personal, and brought the site of the Wall into a gender space in a very unusual way. On May 17, 2001, when the German artist H. A. Schult installed his one thousand "trash people," displayed like terracotta soldiers on the Great Wall at Jinshanling, He Chengyao staged her performance *Opening the Great Wall.* She suddenly took off her red T-shirt, showing herself naked above the waist, a gesture that comes from her mother's "extreme behavior of insanity." In the 1960s, He Chengyao's mother and father were fired from their jobs because she illegally became pregnant out of wedlock. Her mother subsequently suffered a mental break-down. Day and night, stark naked, she goes shouting through the streets in her hometown.[19] Whereas the other artists take their performance or earth work on the sites of the Great Wall to make their comments on the national ideology, He Chengyao reconstructed the living space of her childhood under the spatial pressure from both the Wall and the terracotta soldiers, seen as a symbol of a male-dominated patriarchal society.[20] In this case, He Chengyao undertook her ceremonial act as "imitating the insanity of her mother" in order to make her commentary on the modern myth that has ruined Chinese women's identity and life.

DISLOCATION AND DISPLACEMENT IN RESHAPING URBAN SPACE

Since China is the most rapidly changing country in the world economy today, Chinese contemporary art, it seems, should also fit the contemporary theory of globalization. In this theory, one may draw an idealistic picture of the twenty-first century, claiming that after the end of the Cold War, the world is moving toward a transnational order, one that will break down any national and local boundaries. Elaborating this transnational theory, Anthony Giddens, an influ-ential theorist of modernity, claims that one unique characteristic, already evident, is the tension between the "expansiveness" of globalization and the "privateness" resulting from the loss of individual identity. In other words, there exists an increasing interconnection between the two "extremes" of exten-sionality and intentionality, between globalizing influences and personal dis-positions in the world of the twenty-first century.[21]

The history of the last fifteen years, however, may be read as bearing witness of a move in a different direction. On the one hand, the world economy has indeed come to be bound by globalization much more monolithically than ever before. On the other hand, the world has culturally and politically been divided even more widely by concerns of national identity and local economy. September 11, the war in Iraq, and the crisis of the Middle East seem to have validated Samuel P. Huntington's anticipation of the religious conflict or "the clash of civilizations" between Christianity and Islam (with Confucianism added later) in the twenty-first century.[22] The dichotomous pattern of "expansiveness" versus "privateness" in the age of globalization, however much it may make sense in the developed countries, may have been challenged when applied to the societies of the developing countries. In the Chinese context, for instance, the major confrontation has not been confined to the one between the individual and the global, but appears more strikingly in the one that involves much more complex relations between locality and internationality, humanity and individuality, in response to the rapid environmental change. Changes in surroundings and living space have most profoundly impacted Chinese daily life as well as Chinese art during the last decades.

Although the dichotomy theory of transnational modernity may not be appropriate to the local context, this perspective has already become popular in the narratives of Chinese contemporary art. For instance, there is the belief among some critics that the more "individual" traits a work shows, the truer it is to Chinese contemporary art. Many works, in particular photographs that depict Chinese family history and private life, have captured the attention of the international art world. But this critical stance overlooks the artwork's connections both to history and to the current environment. Many critics and art historians take the "individual" narratives that appear in the art of the 1990s as essentially different from the art that preceded it. Yet if we look closely, we see that what appear to be "individual" narratives are actually to a large extent variations on and continuations of the collective. Many of the kind that carry the "individual trait," such as family pictures or photographs of personal life, are all nearly identical in subject matter, without much individual specificity, except the facial features. Most involve the period from the Cultural Revolution to the present, and are group narratives of the artist's generation and his or her parents' generation. For Chinese people, these stories are commonplace; they are attractive mostly to foreigners in the market and in international exhibitions for their exoticism.

On the other hand, in this kind of transnational narrative, it is as if globalization has brought about a global notion of what constitutes "individual identity." Accordingly, globalization threatens to turn Chinese artists into residents of a "global village," in which they speak their most intimate secrets in a standardized, international language, in particular in the works of those who have engaged in frequent travels around the world. All the dichotomous patterns listed above may turn problematic when applied to the topic of urbanization in Chinese contemporary art.

Since the 1990s, many Chinese artists have enthusiastically committed themselves to the investigation of current globalization and urbanization. I would like to argue, however, that what the artists have demonstrated in their works cannot be seen as purely the portrayal of globalization and Chinese urbanization in the terms of the dichotomies of the transnational theory; I would argue, rather, that their work serves as a commentary on the impacts of current globalization based on their close observation of their surroundings, especially the transformational process from the agricultural to the urban. Their observations have drawn attention to the dislocation and displacement that signifies the complex and mutual relations between local, international, individual, family, female and male, and so forth. This dislocation and displacement is also a metaphor for the violent change and devastation of the natural environment, and the disjuncture between material culture and the humanist spirit caused by rampant modernization. Consequently, reconstruction and the appropriation of architectural space, urban space, community space, private space, and public space have become the main subjects of contemporary Chinese artists. This not only expresses the estrangement in the current Chinese urban spectacle, but also, more importantly, becomes a means of presenting the transformation of social class and identity in urban space in the form of a powerful imagery of locality and relocality.

By 2020, the population of migrant laborers in cities in China will reach three to five hundred million, a number unprecedented in human history. In comparison, immigrants from Ireland to the United States in the hundred-plus years between the 1820s and the 1930s totaled a mere four and a half million.[23] Neither the needs of immigrants nor their impact on urban culture and the economy have been fully accounted for by China's urban planners. The conceptual photography of Wang Jin, particularly the works *100%* and *0%*, offer a visual inquiry into this social problem. In *100%*, several groups of migrant workers were asked to form a human wall, supporting a traffic overpass with their hands. In this image, their bodies are endowed with the power of steel and concrete. The workers represent the construction of the urban future, not only in terms of architecture, but also in terms of population. In *0%*, the dirty feet of peasant workers sticking out of cement pipes provide a sharp contrast to the modern skyscrapers of Beijing. One represents disorder and filth, the other rationality and grandeur. In this work, Wang Jin suggests that peasant workers are a force that is able to facilitate, as well as devastate, the urban future.

The dislocation depicted in Song Dong's work is a metaphor of the switch in

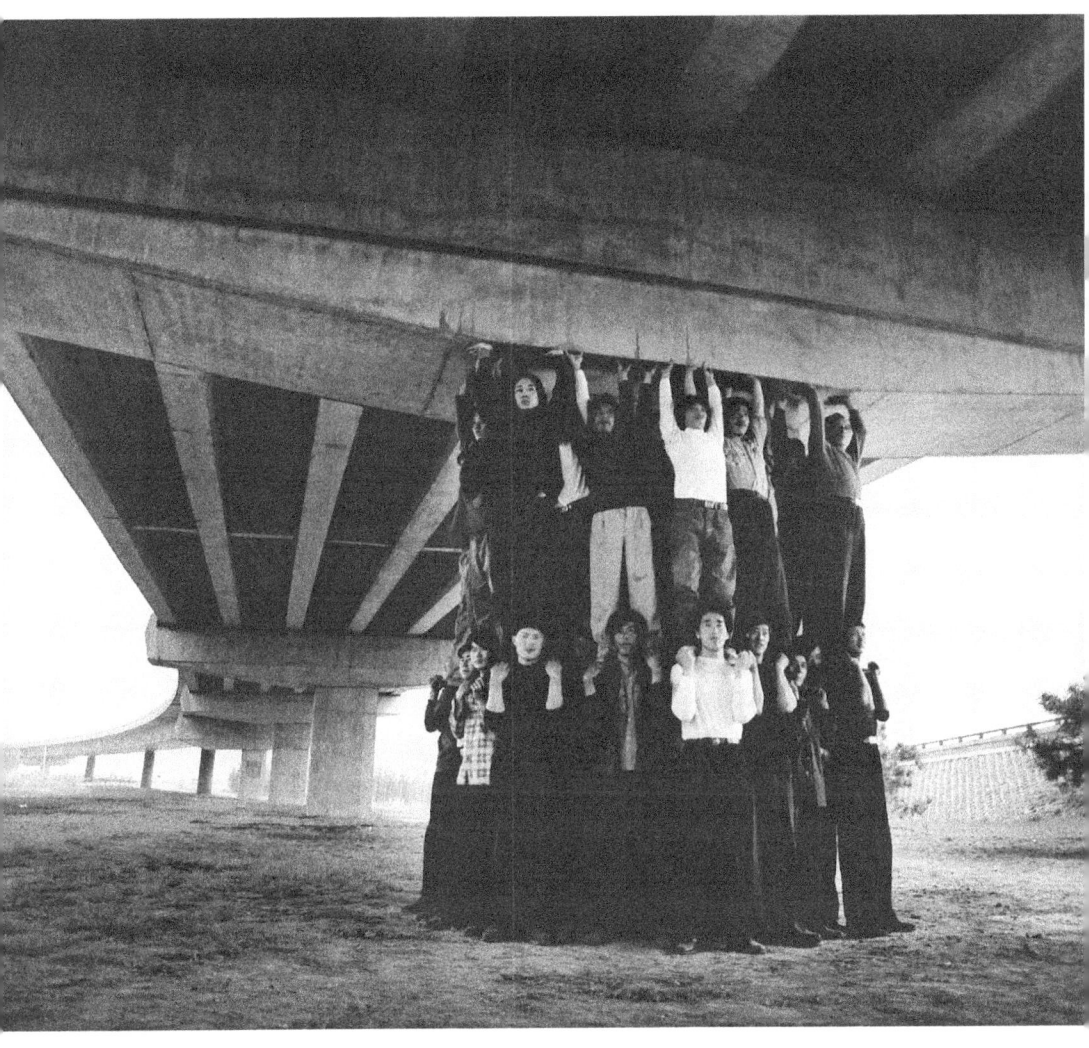

Wang Jin, *100%*, 1999. Photograph. Courtesy of the artist.

the social positions of the construction workers and urbanites. Common to almost all of Song's works is a deep involvement in the life of the alleys (*hutong*) of Beijing, where he lives. He is one of the few Beijing natives among contemporary Chinese artists. Song was also a participant in the Apartment Art movement of the early 1990s, when he was concerned with his own state of mind, his small living space, and his choice of media and materials. In his works after 2000, Song has been more concerned with class issues in the city, especially those concerning peasant workers, and has created a series of video, photograph, and installation/performance works called *Together with Farmer Workers, 2001–2005*. Song Dong regards farmworkers as an emerging class, one that is, as he states, "a human symbol of a great agricultural country's transformation into a new social form. . . . I do not wish to pay tribute to them in my artworks and idealize them. Instead, I wish to represent this important human symbol by means of both viewing them [the migrant laborers] and looking at how they view us [so-called urbanites, especially so-called upper-class people]."[24] In the photography exhibition "Humanism [*Renben*] in China," held in December 2003, in Guangzhou, Song Dong exhibited urban landscapes photographed by forty peasant workers. Cameras were provided by the museum, and the workers were encouraged to take pictures freely. The artwork furthers the concept of "seeing and being seen" and transforms the "other" in the eyes of urbanites into a subject who observes the city. Through such a shift in subjectivity, self-centered urbanites see themselves and their environment in a new light.

Zhang Dali is China's first graffiti artist, as well as the first "ruins" artist. His graffiti is mostly his self-portrait, which appears together with the tag "AK47." This can be interpreted as the devastation of human nature wrought by the violent disruption of urban construction. Zhang Dali then documents the ruined walls, self-portraits, and symbols using video and photography. Each vista that he selects has a particular significance embedded within it. Often this meaning is conveyed through comparison, for example, by juxtaposing demolished walls with the "permanent" landmark buildings of Beijing: the corner towers of the Forbidden City, Stalinist buildings among the "10 Great Construction Projects" of 1959, such as the National Art Museum of China, or newer symbols such as the Jinmao Tower in Shanghai. Zhang Dali claims the demolished walls as his own artworks, locating the walls in a larger urban landscape and creating a spectacle by contrasting urban ruins and skyscrapers.

What Zhang concentrates on in his work is not trafficking in urban anthropology or the geographical issues of urban development. Instead, he concerns himself with human nature. His project is entitled *Dialogue with Demolition* (1995–2003), which does not signify a dialogue between ruins and skyscrapers,

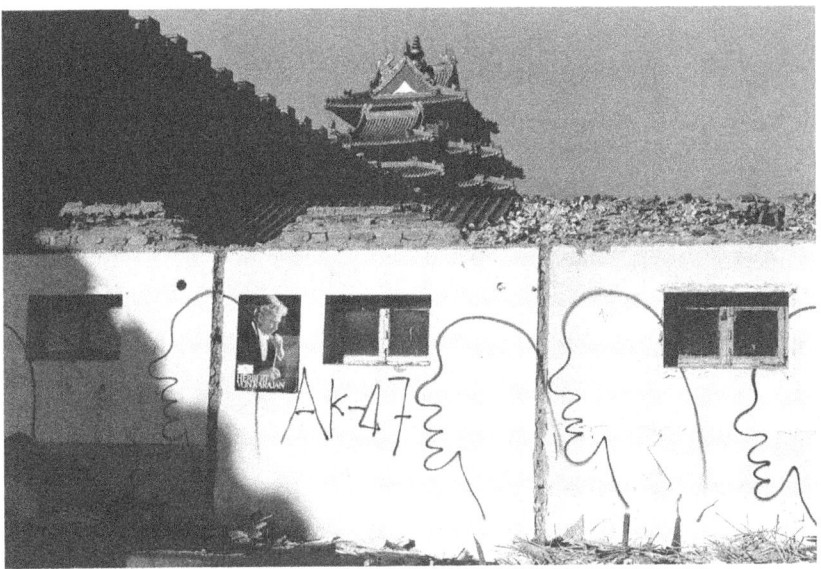

Zhang Dali, *Self-Portrait, Jinmao Tower, Shanghai,* from the series *Dialog with Demolition,* 1995–2003. Graffiti, photograph. Courtesy of the artist.

or the new and the old, but between human and concrete, or between essential human nature and urban alienation. It is, in fact, an inner monologue: "Sometimes it's impossible to think and to pass judgment on the things happening in our environment. These events influence our life, dim our sight, corrupt our soul. In the new era, reality is hidden under a beautiful cloak. . . . For a long time I have made every effort to keep myself awake, in front of the beautiful flowers, the beautiful popular songs, in the presence of the deceitful shows. I prick my anaesthetized soul, trying with the eyes of my soul to see the reality behind the appearances."[25]

If Zhang Dali uses his portrait to symbolize the triumph of the human spirit over the destruction of architecture, He Yunchang uses his own flesh to challenge mechanical power, seeing it as a metaphor of resistance to urban material culture. He said, "My life is mine, and I can play with my body in whatever way I like. I have my choice at least on this point."[26] He commonly uses his body in a contest with concrete, a metaphor that displays his faith in humanism. In 2004, in an exhibition at the 798 Arts Centre in Beijing, he sealed himself in a room made of cement for twenty-four hours, with only a small hole at the top for air. Nobody knew that he was inside until workers helped break the wall and let him out. In his work *Diary on Shanghai Water,* performed on November 3, 2000, he drew ten tons of water by bucket from the lower reaches of Suzhou Creek in

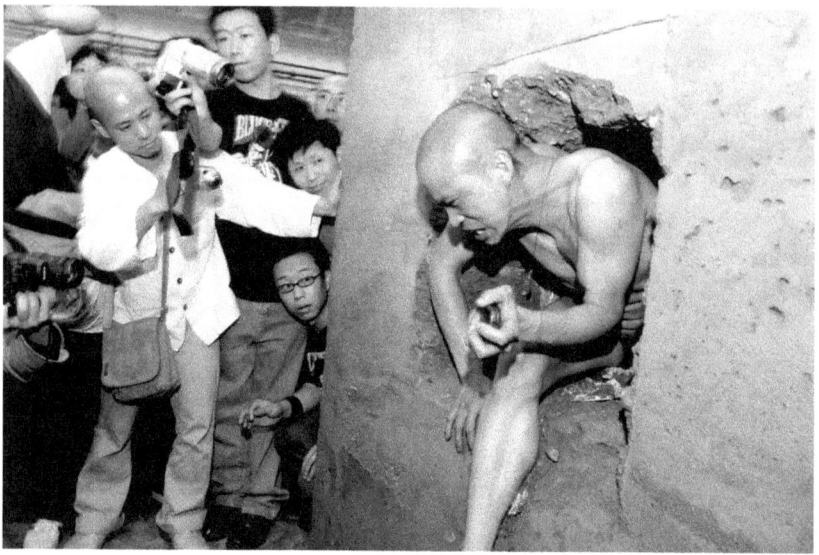

He Yunchang, *Untitled performance*, 2004. Performance, 798 Arts Center, Beijing. Courtesy of the artist.

Shanghai, then poured it into a boat and transported it four kilometers upriver, where he poured the water back into the river, allowing the water to flow back again.

Some Chinese artists comment on urbanization by substituting a beautiful appearance or modernist aesthetic taste for a horrific industrial outcome. Many viewers of Xing Danwen's series of photographs entitled *dis*CONNEXION (2002–2003), initially believed that they were seeing abstract forms, but in reality these were electronic trash, such as computer wires and plastic outlets. Millions of tons of such trash are transported from America, Japan, Korea, and other developed countries to the beaches of Fujian province in China, where they are melted down and recycled. Thousands of peasant workers come to the beaches for temporary jobs in spite of the dangerous pollutants created through this process. Danwen Xing does not use overtly critical language, but rather the beautified forms, or the illusion of beauty, to delay recognition of the ugly truth. Her work *Urban Fiction* investigates the nature of urban modernity from yet another perspective. From the end of 2004 to early 2005, Xing visited numerous real estate sales agents in cities such as Beijing and Shanghai, and photographed architectural models of each housing complex, from which she made realistic urban scenes using digital computer technology. Each of these images appears to be an actual urban scene, to which she adds fragments of her

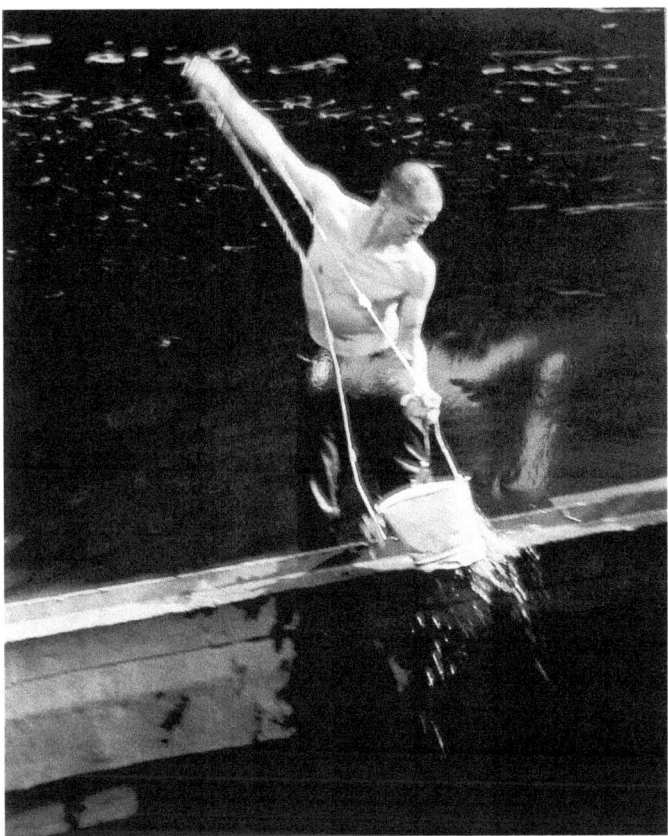

He Yunchang, *Diary on Shanghai Water,* 2003. Performance, Souzhou Creek
and Huangpu River, Shanghai. Courtesy of the artist.

real life or other's lives, such as the image of a lonely woman drinking coffee on
a balcony, or a pair of passionate lovers in a courtyard. These urban landscapes
become fictions. Virtual space becomes a site for narrative. The fragmentation
of space, and the insertion of characters into that space, brings these cold model
vistas to life. In such constructed environments, an ugly housing development
can be transformed into an apparently rosy utopia, or vice versa.

Another interesting phenomenon in Chinese contemporary art associated
with urbanization is that some artists use Modernism as a visual form to
comment on the issue of urbanization. One of the methods used for this purpose
is what I call "Maximalism." I coined this term not to characterize an art style, or
school, but to illuminate a particular artistic phenomenon, a kind of "Chinese
abstract art" that a number of artists have created since the late 1980s.[27] Since
these artists are not interested in either producing Chinese exoticism or repre-

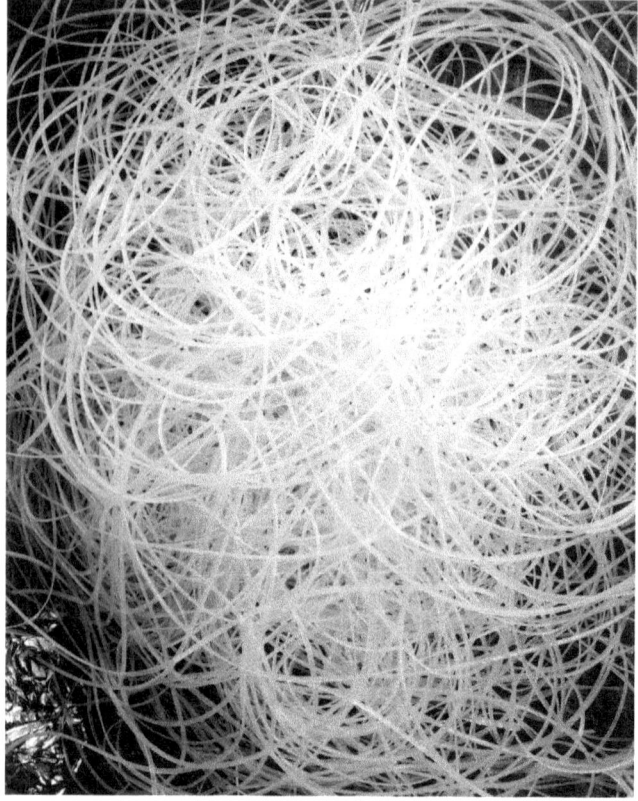

Xing Danwen, *disCONNEXION*, 2002–3. Photographic series. Courtesy of the artist.

senting the appearance of the ongoing globalization of China, their works have been underrepresented both in China and abroad. Maximalist artists use modernist modes, especially Minimalist-like forms, to address a totally different purpose from Minimalism in the West: they are antimodernist. Their practice of making artworks in a labor-intensive and time-consuming way neither shares the utopian aims of early Western Modernism nor attempts to focus on the material or process itself as in later twentieth-century Modernism.[28] What they wish to do is to unify the process of making art with daily life, in the manner of traditional Chan meditation. This is an effective response to the challenges of current Chinese modernity, rather than a purely artistic engagement in any form of modernism.

The best example is Li Huasheng's *Diary*, produced between 1999 and 2004. An ink painter well versed in traditional literati painting, in recent years Li has created many "abstract paintings" in ink and wash, in a style similar to Mini-

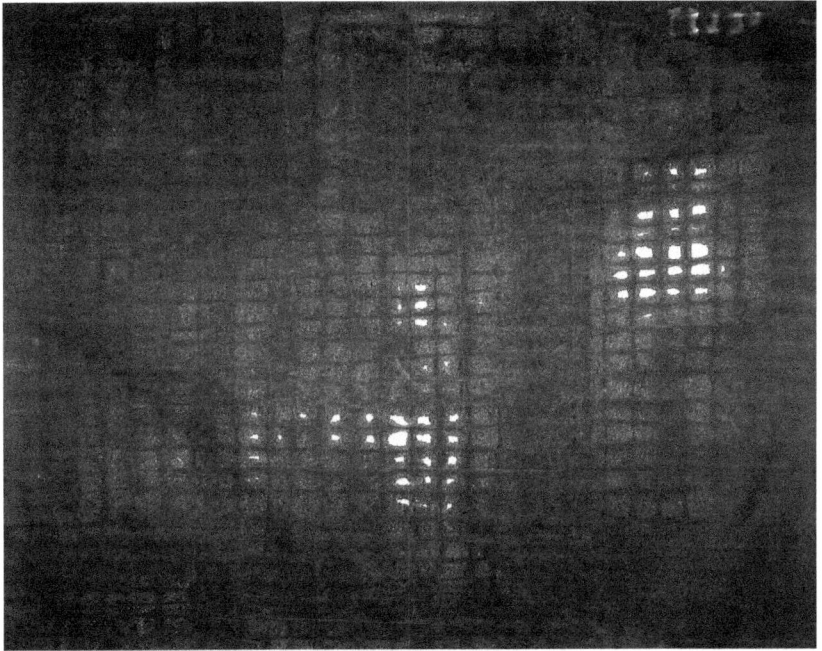

Li Huasheng, *Diary*, 1999–2004. Ink and wash series. Courtesy of the artist.

malist painting. Instead of applying light touches, or painting without any apparent control, the lines are "written" out with considerable force focused on the tip of the brush, as if he were writing Chinese calligraphy not in the form of self-expression, but rather like a monk's meditation in a meaningless process. The extremely abstract form that results has, however, nothing to do with the early European abstract art that presents a utopian world, the "material utopia."[29] Nor is it the same as the self-expression in traditional literati painting. Rather, it is a direct representation of the artist's personal surroundings. During the period of its creation Li Huasheng was fighting with the city government for the preservation of his four-hundred-year-old house located in an old district and targeted by the new city construction plan. The district finally was leveled in 2005.

The other approach within contemporary Chinese Maximalism is the deliberate use of abstract form to portray urban landscape in a style either very much like traditional ink landscape painting, or in a manner similar to Western modernist abstract painting. For example, Ding Fang uses a combination of abstract expressionism and surrealism to make his commentary on current materialism and urbanization. Wu Jian's elegant "abstract expressionist" oil painting is, in fact, a "life drawing" of a mountain of city trash. In the context of

Chinese modernization, the artist relocates artistic Modernism to undermine the meaning of modernity itself.

The methodology of dislocation is, perhaps, most fully achieved by Huang Yongping in his work *Made in China*. A huge topographical map of China, thirty-six feet by twenty-six feet and made of iron, stands on the floor. It declines from the west to the east, as does the actual topography of China. The surface of the map, however, consists not of mountain ranges, rivers, and plains, but rather of innumerable tiny iron factory models. The artist implies that we are now, and always have been, in a globalized situation: we should, perhaps, turn the phrase "Made in China" into "Made in the World."[30]

WOMAN AS CITY

I would like to discuss the important issue of Chinese women's art by examining the relation between gender space and urban space in the Chinese context of modernity. There are two tendencies in the study of Chinese women's art. Some critics attempt to employ general feminist theory to analyze contemporary Chinese women's art, treating it as a part of the international feminist community. Others see it as based on purely personal experience, their priority being to distinguish it from Chinese men's art, which is understood by this group of critics to be predominantly a public-sphere, social, and political discourse. Both of these approaches, I would argue, pay insufficiently close attention to the local context of Chinese women's art.[31] Rather than viewing Chinese women's art solely as the art of a "minority," or the product of unique individuals, or the result of feminist pursuits, we should read Chinese women's art as a particular way of responding to Chinese modernity as a whole, and therefore take it together with men's art. Chinese women's art since the 1990s does not pursue merely a gendered space, but rather one that reflects the whole city as itself feminine. Its catch-cry might be "woman is the city."

Women's art has been an indivisible part of the whole project of Chinese modernity throughout the twentieth century. In the 1920s, a great deal of literature, film, and painting emerged from the "new women's movement" in China. These works were a rebellion against traditional Confucian ethics. At that time, the term "new woman" (*xinnuxing*) was synonymous with revolution, progress, and modernity as well as women's liberty.[32] In the 1980s, a decade marked by activism and enthusiasm for the pursuit of modernity and of ideological liberation, female artists became involved in the '85 Movement. Their emergence, however, was not catalyzed by feminism. Rather, their concepts and ideals paralleled those of their male colleagues. Furthermore, their work appeared to take on what some consider stereotypically masculine qualities. A clear claim that Chinese women's art was an independent art phenomenon did not come about until the 1990s. Then, Chinese women's art grew out of the context of globalization and urbanization, and it was influenced by Western postmodern theory and artistic approaches. Nevertheless, the central issues of Chinese women's art are primarily those of housing, living quarters, marriage, children, and the harmonious cohabitation of couples—issues that arose in the face of the emergence of the urban middle class and the stresses triggered by this social transition.

When the feminist movement emerged in the West in the 1970s, many Euro-American women had already gained economic independence and access to advanced education. The movement was mostly a political advance in the evolution of women's social freedom and equality to man. Independence and individualism were the basic principles. Although the issue of gender entered into discussions of the social and public sphere in China as early as the end of the nineteenth century, it has been shaped by China's status as a third world country with profound traditions. In contemporary China, women have not gained independence, nor have Chinese men. Both face the same crisis as the Chinese people move into a process of reconfiguring social rank and class. Family, rather than the individual, is the unit that bears the main brunt of this transition. Gender unification rather than a gender split is what is most needed in this historical moment. On the other hand, the traditional philosophy of family and community has also affected Chinese women's art. While it is true that Chinese women have always formed an integral part of Chinese modernity, and that "sex" or gender is tightly linked to modernity and nationality, what social progress there has been might, at best, be labeled "womanism" rather than feminism.

"Womanism" is a term coined by the African American writer Alice Walker, with particular reference to the situation of the genders in the third world.[33] Its goal does not lie in the confrontation between male and female, but in the harmonious coexistence of humanity in general. Perhaps this is why, unlike Euro-American feminist artists, many female artists working in China today favor the use of everyday household materials including thread, yarn, cotton, cloth, quilts, clothing, and the like in their work. These domestic materials may effectively demonstrate an individual woman's particular emotions and interests. In general, however, their use shows the artists' awareness of the intimacy of family relations.

On the other hand, one cannot overemphasize the personal secret of the artworks and thus fall into the trap of positing a "female personality," one framed by male elite discourse since the beginning of modern history. Liao Wen, an active female critic of Chinese women's art, argues that the kind of women's art that heavily employed household materials indicated a unique, individual "woman's voice" that differentiated their art from that of men in the 1990s. Yet the emergence of such art by women in the early 1990s paralleled the flourishing of Apartment Art at that moment, itself an artistic movement centered on the private sphere. In Beijing, Apartment Art was created in the residences of several artist couples, including Zhu Jinshi and Qin Yufen, Wang Gongxin and Lin Tianmiao, Song Dong and Yin Xiuzhen, and Ai Weiwei and Lu Qing, among others. The women artists among them have since become some of the most significant contemporary Chinese artists. In this period, as I argued in *Chinese Maximalism*, it was not only women's art that was process-oriented, concerned with labor and an intimacy with domestic materials; so, too, was male artwork. Perhaps the only gender distinction that can be usefully made is that male and female artists generally worked with different kinds of domestic materials. Even so, their art style generally conformed to the overall movement of avant-garde art at the time. Female consciousness overlapped or shared with the contemporary consciousness of men within the same context, and vice versa.

What is the social critique in Chinese women's artwork? In other words, how can we see their works within the local context of Chinese modernity? The current boom of the "beauty industry" in Chinese urban culture is a new economy that sees women as objects for consumption. Many women artists imitate the visual strategies of this mass culture and utilize them as a new vocabulary in their own work. Chen Qiulin is an artist from Sichuan Province, who grew up in Wangzhou, a city subsequently submerged by the rising water of the Yangzi River due to the construction of the Dam of Three Gorges. Many of her works in the forms of performance, video, and photography had been done in the town before it disappeared. In one of them, Chen Qiulin is seen applying her makeup in a ruined airy factory space instead of in private living quarters, while striking a provocative and enchanting posture. In another of her performances, *I Exist, I Consume, and I Am Happy*, eight men compete to pull the shopping cart in which Chen sits, applying makeup. The winner, who received the cake placed in the distance, was allowed to pretend to be Chen's bridegroom. The performance is thus a metaphor not only for consumers of female beauty, but also for women seen as the slaves to men who represent masculinity and consumer culture. Chen positions herself, however, in a more neutral way to transcend pure gender issues and to target the current "city image project" (*chengshi xingxiang gongcheng*) in general. In order to understand

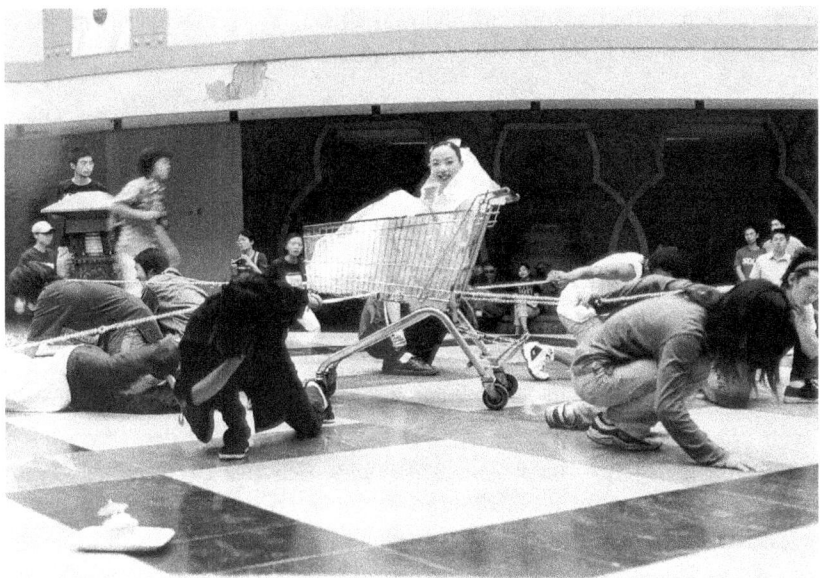

Chen Qiulin, *I Exist, I Consume, and I Am Happy,* 2003. Performance, Wangzhou. Courtesy of the artist.

Chen's neutral stance, we have to know the term *fenzi*, a term used by the people from the Southwest region, such as Sichuan province, as well as in the Northeast in Manchuria, to describe pretty women. It is a neutral or even complimentary word, accepted by both the men and the women whom it describes. At the core of what can be called fenzi culture is sexual harmony rather than gender conflict and splitting. Its foundation is the relationship between the sexes in the folk culture of these Chinese regions, rather than the feminist critique used by contemporary intellectuals. The work of Chen Qiulin, a woman artist from Sinchuan who herself is a fenzi, attempts to use the metaphor of fenzi to make her commentary on the issue of "woman as city" rather than focusing on a more confrontational feminist approach.

During the last decade, stereotypically female descriptors such as "beautiful," "lively," and "stunning" have come to be used to describe urban centers in China. In the same way that masculinity was an expression of the cultural temperament of the 1980s, femininity has now come into fashion. Both are features of the larger culture, of movements in modernity related to the resurgence of Chinese nationalism. Since the end of the 1990s, however, a petitbourgeois lifestyle has become the cultural penchant of a new generation of urban young people, and has adopted as its style a strange femininity. One of its key traits is a mixture of romanticism and degeneration that makes it a fenzi culture. In my interpretation, highlighting this change is exactly the context as well as the content of Chen's works.

OTHER MODERNITIES

Chinese modernity in art, as in other non-Western parts of the world, always remains alternative and mutable. Indeed, there may never have been a steady, shared universal modernity. We need other criteria for reading Chinese modernity and contemporary art. It may, in reality, have produced a new kind of visual space that merges aesthetic experiences, cognitive connections, and political interventions distinct from those familiar in the Euro-American world. Only by establishing these criteria can a genuinely non-Western, modern, and contemporary art come into being. Although contemporary art has rapidly changed in the last three decades, modernity in art in China throughout the twentieth century seems to remain steadily committed to the principle of transcending time and reconstructing space. It is this intrinsic, self-defined, "total modernity," following its own historical logic, that has, I believe, established the permanent condition of contemporaneity in Chinese contemporary art.

NOTES

1 Gao, "Toward a Transnational Modernity," 16.

2 Habermas has shown that the term "modern," which first emerged in fifth-century Rome and was closely associated with the origin and traditions of Christianity, again and again expresses the consciousness of an epoch that relates itself to the past of antiquity, in order to view itself as the result of a transition from the old to the new, from the past to the future. Continuing this in more secular directions, the Western modern period began in the period of the Renaissance. See Habermas, "Modernity— An Incomplete Project," 3–4.

3 An early example: Bonnie McDougall, in her influential 1971 book *The Introduction of Western Literary Theories into Modern China*, first describes the major trends of the Chinese literary world of the 1920s and 1930s, and discusses how the writing of Chinese writers such as Guo Moruo, Yu Dafu, Shen Yanbing, and others was influenced by Western avant-garde movements such as Expressionism, Futurism, and even Dadaism. She argues that the Chinese New Culture Movement of the 1920s and 1930s was essentially not an avant-garde movement, because it did not reject tradition, and because Chinese littérateurs and artists were too socialized and too politicized and did not promote the idea and practice of the autonomy of art, which was the major characteristic of the Western avant-garde in its original meaning. McDougall's argument also represents the thinking of a number of other Western scholars and critics about Chinese avant-garde art. See McDougall, *The Introduction of Western Literary Theories,* 196–213.

4 See Bürger, *Theory of the Avant-Garde;* Calinescu, *Five Faces of Modernity*; and Habermas, "Modernity—An Incomplete Project."

5 Social modernization is also called rationalization by Max Weber, who characterized cultural modernity as the separation of the substantive reason expressed in religion and metaphysics into three autonomous spheres: science, morality, and art. See Bürger, "Literary Institution and Modernization."

6 The earliest text on the topic of the postmodernist phenomenon in Chinese architecture of the 1980s is Wang, "Postmodernism in China," 455–66.

7 See Gao, "Material Utopia."

8 Cai, "Yi meishu dai zongjiao shuo."

9 Hu, "Pragmatism," 211–12.

10 See Gao, "Lun Mao Zedong de Dazhong Yishu Moshi." On the collaboration between the Russian avant-garde and Bolsheviks, and the Italian Futurists and Fascists, see Golomstock, *Totalitarian Art.*

11 See Gao, "Inside and Outside the Political Walls."

12 See Tsong-zung, *The Stars.* For the "China/Avant-Garde" exhibition, see Gao, "Post-Utopian Avant-Garde Art in China" and "Fengkuangde yijiubajiu."

13 Poggioli, *The Theory of the Avant-garde,* 25.

14 Bürger, *Theory of the Avant-Garde.*

15 Bürger, *Theory of the Avant-Garde,* lii. In the endnote of his introduction, Bürger quotes B. Lindner's comment: "In its intention to sublate art in the praxis of life, the avant-garde can thus be understood as the most radical and consistent attempt to maintain the universal claim of autonomous art vis-à-vis all other social spheres and to give it practical meaning. In that case, the attempt to liquidate art as an institution does not appear as a break with the ideology of the period of autonomy but as a reversal phenomenon on the identical ideological level" (Bürger, *Theory of the Avant-Garde,* 106).

16 Poggioli, *Theory of the Avant-Garde,* 25–26.

17 I first used the term "Apartment Art" in "From Elite to Small Man," in Gao, *Inside Out,* not knowing that the term had already been applied to aspects of sots art and other conceptualist art of the 1970s and 1980s in the Soviet Union. In China, I believe, people did not know about this Soviet avant-garde phenomenon until the late 1990s because of the lack of knowledge of the Soviet art of that period. I discuss Chinese Apartment Art extensively in Gao, *The Wall,* 63–83. See also Feng, "From 'Underground' to 'Above Ground,'" which discusses some exhibitions that occurred in alternative spaces, some of which were orchestrated by independent curators, and many publications that circulated unofficially.

18 See the chapter "Reconstructing Historical Memory: The Great Wall in Twentieth Century Chinese Art," in Gao, *The Wall.*

19 He Chengyao, "Lift the Cover from Your Head," 22.

20 Author's interview with He Chengyao, Beijing, June 30, 2001.

21 Giddens, *Modernity and Self-Identity,* 1.

22 Huntington, *The Clash of Civilizations.* Despite the author's conservative, America-centric stance, we should acknowledge his anticipation of the facts, and support his view that the best response is to learn how to coexist in a complex, multipolar, diverse world.

23 Yardley, "In a Tidal Wave, China's Masses Pour from Farm to City."

24 Song Dong, interview with the author, October 4, 2002, quoted in Gao and Wang, *Harvest*, 5–26.

25 Zhang Dali, interview with the author, Beijing, December 26, 2004.

26 He Yunchang, interview with the author, July 20, 2004.

27 Gao, *Chinese Maximalism.*

28 "My painting is based on the fact that only what can be seen there is there. It really is an object. Any painting is an object and anyone who gets involved enough in this finally has to face up to the objectness of whatever it is that he's doing. He is making a thing. . . . All I want anyone to get out of my paintings, and all I ever get out of them, is the fact that you can see the whole idea without any confusion. . . . [W]hat you see is what you see" (Frank Stella, quoted in Stella and Judd, "Questions," 158).

29 Bois, "Material Utopia."

30 Shown in the exhibition "Harvest," held in the Chinese National Agricultural Museum in Beijing in 2002. See Huang, "About *Made in China*," in Gao and Wang, *Harvest*, 36.

31 For a detailed discussion of this topic, see the chapter "The Marginalized 'Modern Man' and Chinese Women's Art," in Gao, *The Wall*, 249–63.

32 See Jia, "Chinese Women Artists of the 20th Century"; Liao, *Feminism as a Method*; Li and Tao, *The Lost History*; and Xu, *Female.*

33 Walker, *In Search of Our Mothers' Gardens.*

9

THE PERILS OF UNILATERAL POWER:

NEOMODERNIST METAPHORS AND THE

NEW GLOBAL ORDER

SYLVESTER OKWUNODU OGBECHIE

The contemporary era after postmodernism has returned to modernist commitments and strategies with a vengeance, a process hereby identified as *neomodernism.*[1] This process is evident in the reemergence of avant-garde strategies of
representation in art, in aesthetics and sociology through the search for alternative modernities, and in politics through the return of absolutist discourses of
power. It is represented in the imperial ambitions of the United States and the
reemergent division of the world into civilization and barbarism. The language
of contemporary politics is increasingly a language of religion and the rise of
fundamentalist faiths all over the world accompanies a Manichean interpretation of temporal and spiritual values that is profoundly antirational. At the start
of a new century that was long imagined as a utopia of unbridled technological
and social development, the contemporary era instead reflects more of what Carl
Sagan once bemoaned as a "demon-haunted world."[2] The return of the modernist sublime in contemporary culture is however most evident in the impact of
recurrent Western aggression on non-Western populations whose attempts to
redefine contemporary global power relations are interpreted as a direct threat
to the supremacy of the West, represented in this instance by the transatlantic
alliance of white, Western European nations. Supported by the unilateral power
of the United States, which acts as a grotesque in the contemporary era, the
transatlantic alliance signals the rebirth of occidental imperialism, which uses

the discourse of globalization to inscribe new spaces of political and cultural domination of non-Western societies, as is evident in the recent invasion of Iraq by the United States. The political justification and media coverage of the Iraq invasion in the United States echoes Joseph Conrad's narrative of primordial savagery in *Heart of Darkness*. Once again, the West invokes primitivism to justify its imperial project, under the guise of bringing "democracy" and "civilization" to the literally dark peoples and places of the earth.

Neomodernism's global formations contrast with the idea of "alternative modernities," which attends to those formations of modernity outside the normative space of white Western culture (in the case I will discuss, modern and contemporary African art). The quest for alternative interpretations of modernity evaluates how non-Western interpretations of modernity relate to canonical discourses and how these in turn inscribe new discursive formations in the contemporary era.[3] It represents an attempt to step outside the mythos of the contemporary global order and thereby validate the engagement of modern and contemporary African artists with local and international contexts of modernist practice. In the past, art history has defined all such attempts as "provincialism," addenda to the primacy of white, Western European constructions of modernity. However, it is becoming increasingly clear that the ethnic practice of white, Western European artists can no longer stand in for the experience of modernity in Africa, Asia, and other parts of the world. The assumption of universality that supports this earlier hegemonic interpretation of global culture is increasingly discredited, although its spirit persists. International resistance to its claims of preeminent authority manifests itself politically as a struggle against occidental colonial domination, but also culturally as resistance to occidental control of technologies of discourse. Although the project of an alternative modernity provides a platform for resistance to the current imperial hegemony, it however needs to confront the unilateral power of the West, represented in the contemporary era by American power, and evaluate its impact on attempts to inscribe alternative discourses of modernity (for example, in art). In what ways have previous imperial powers circumscribed similar acts of resistance? Is such an alternative even possible, given the increasingly totalitarian control of the global order by the West?

NEO/MODERNISM: SHADOWS OF THE OTHER

Neomodernism's affirmation of an essentialist Eurocentric interpretation of modernity confirms Norbert Elias's argument that Western nations tend to consider the process of civilization as completed within their own societies, from which it follows that the consciousness of their own superiority serves at least those nations that have become colonial conquerors, and therefore an upper class to large sections of the non-European world, as a justification of their rule.[4] Modernity in this sense is a chronotrope, a space-time of possibility for the location of agents, actions, and events. The quest for alternative modernities is an attempt to reconfigure this chronotrope, to locate African agents, actions, and events in modernist space-time. Modernist discourses had mostly used African culture as a backdrop for narratives about the supremacy of Western art, celebrating the genius of Western artists who adopted African conventions of representation while denigrating similar appropriations by African artists during the same period. This narrative has proven remarkably resilient and it does not entertain the possibility of an African interpretation of modernity in art. However, modern African art sustained unique forms of representation and produced unique artists in the twentieth century. We can find traces of these artists in the archival record, as in a photograph of Ben Enwonwu working on a sculpture of Queen Elizabeth II, monarch of the British Empire, as if under the gaze of David Livingstone and Franklin D. Roosevelt— one, the archetypal "discoverer/explorer" of Africa, bringing European enlightenment to those peoples who, according to Conrad, dwelled in the heart of darkness; the other, emblematic of the march of American military and political supremacy in the period after World War II, which transformed into a unilateral power after the Cold War.

Conrad's Darwinian account of the march of civilization sets up a representation of Africa as *terra nullius* in modernist discourses. Although he acknowledged that Europe was once also "one of the dark places of the earth," it was only as a way to locate contemporary Africa in Europe's past.[5] In this Conrad was more charitable but ultimately more damaging than Hegel, who considered Africa no part of history and deemed it absent at the unfolding of the world spirit. Hegel's contention can be challenged simply by pointing out that, were Africans less enterprising than he gave them credit for, there would have been no Europeans to produce such smug comments as those he validated. One could point to the now confirmed scientific fact that all humans emerged from Africa, which places African accomplishments in culture making within a hundred-thousand-year span of history upon which all later models of human culture were constructed.[6] The Western incursion into Africa in the modern era constitutes barely five hundred years of this history. But somehow this recent incursion is assumed to be more significant to Africa's political and cultural past and future than the previous millennia of cultural development that brought Africa into proven historical contact with Europe, the Islamic world, and Asia.

Also, by situating Africa (and the world outside of Western culture) as always existing in the historical and cultural past of the West, both Hegel and Conrad forestall the possibility that African cultures will ever occupy a coeval contemporaneity with Western cultures. Both individuals thus prove to be direct forebears of the Jansons and the Stokstards who relegate the history of African, Asian, and Oceanic art to a few pages stuck between Romanesque and Gothic art in teleological tomes that glorify Europe's miraculous self-invention.[7] European mythology (and its claims to sole invention and ownership of modernity in art) is full of such self-inventions: the claim of Greek uniqueness in the history of civilization; Athena springing fully formed from the forehead of Zeus; Botticelli's Venus embodying herself from the waves; and, most evidently, the Nazarene born of a virgin mother, who accomplishes transfiguration, the most poignant self-invention of all. African cultures abjured such obviously narcissistic preoccupation: Igbo peoples say, "Ife kwulu, Ife akwukwasi ya" (Things exist with their opposites); in this, they channel the wisdom of the Yoruba deity Eshu, who cautioned society about the instability of signs and signifiers, and specifically warned against any kind of belief in absolutes.[8]

And it is this belief in absolute political and discursive supremacy that constitutes the great failing of the West, although this kind of cultural arrogance is not restricted to Western culture by any means. All cultures have at one time or another entertained the illusion that they are the apexes of creation. Anthropological studies confirm that most human societies feel that they have been specially chosen to unfold the cosmological imperatives set in motion by their maker. Their narratives of history inscribed in whatever favored form (through writing, or images, or through oral traditions) subscribed to this ideal and interpreted socially constructed processes as if they reflected absolute cosmological imperatives. African societies (for example, the Igbo peoples of Nigeria) have been very wary of these kinds of narratives. Igbo peoples distinguish between the power of deities and those powers accruable to humans in their interaction with the gods. Each of these powers is sacrosanct: humans may not intrude on the domain of the gods. In turn, the gods may act in mysterious ways that defy human understanding of reality, but such actions must not be mysteriously irrational. Igbo peoples thus have a democratic relationship with their deities and have been known to literally dismiss a higher power whose utterances and actions become capricious.[9]

Western societies (those societies originating in Europe and their clones created through the vast European diaspora) buck the above trend by setting themselves above the usual norm of transcultural relationships. This attitude can be traced to Western interpretation of the biblical injunction about human dominance over all nature as a mandate for totalitarian control of the world. It has yielded a history deeply invested in "the fabrication and maintenance of a modernity that linked Europe to an ethically superior aesthetics [and politics, morality, and religion] grounded in erotic relations, thereby allaying the anxieties of cultural relativism, such that Europe (and Christendom), in their expanding encounter with alien cultures, might be saved from reduction to but one reality among many."[10] This tendency is clearest in art history and the narratives of European cultural autonomy that posit an internal European development for modernity in general. Western narratives of modernity strictly excludes the Other, except for the customary reference to the role African and other non-Western art played as sources for new ideas about the image and new conventions of representation (and even this is lacking in many narratives). Similarly, Western appropriation of these other art traditions was accompanied by a meticulous attempt to separate African art from the body of Western artists, and use this division of bodies from artistic models to cleanse African art of its danger and thus allow it into what Rasheed Araeen called "the citadel of modernism."[11] This quasi-religious construction of the modernist project as a fortified enclosure precisely defines the intention of the discourse: it narrates the enclosure of modernity as something to be guarded against the inclusion of non-Western artists as subjects, who are in turn represented as hordes of invading barbarians. It also hints at the role of raw power in maintaining the ensuing historical and discursive order.

The ideology of Modernism depended on this strict distinction between the European self that dominates and appropriates non-Western culture while dismissing the reality of non-Western interpretations of cultural practice. Its narratives thus "[impose] conceptual limitations on our aesthetics [and political] thinking and our tastes and judgment, and in its own way projects an utterly distorted model of history."[12] In the sphere of art, it has been accompanied (as Simon Gikandi puts it) by a "need to minimize the role of the Other (African art) in the emergence of Modernism as a style and, in particular, the significance of Africa as an artistic model, even when acknowledging their overall effect."[13] The citadel of art history's selective narrative about modernity provides only false security since it already includes the Other within its walls, especially in its inability to elide African contributions from its narratives of Modern art. What it fails to acknowledge is that the Modernism of European avant-garde artists in the twentieth century was a specific response to the challenge of modernity. Its appropriation of African aesthetics was an appeal to the ultimate fetish, the idea of Africa as a primitive and exotic culture whose primal energies could be metaphorically consumed to empower European modernity.

However, "modernity is always and everywhere a global phenomenon." The European encounter with African art was coeval with an African Modernism that used Western conventions of representation (among other influences) to construct identity for indigenous African populations faced with the explicit violence of European colonization. In this respect, as Carol Appadurai Brecken-ridge notes, "what is distinctive about any society is not the fact or extent of its modernity, but rather its distinctive debates about modernity, the historical and cultural trajectories that shape its appropriation of the means of modernity, and the cultural sociology . . . that determines who gets to play with modernity and what defines the rules of the game."[14]

At the beginning of the twenty-first century, this struggle for inclusion into the discourses of modernity and contemporaneity provides the clearest evidence for the return of modernist strategies in art and contemporary politics. It is a continuation of the modernist attempt to exclude the Other (black and brown peoples of the earth) from its narrative of history. We should note that the counternarrative of these "Others" always engages the conjunction of Modernism and violence, because for each society, the coming of the West (with its ideas about civilization, modernity, and social change) was coeval with explicit violence. The history of modernity in each of these locales is literally written in the blood of "the natives." For this reason, I propose that we should reinterpret the term "alternative modernities" as a historical narrative of *alter/natives* that describes the violent process of altering the worldview of native societies to conform to Western prescriptions about social and cultural organization. The West has been guided by a sole imperative in this quest: its search for additional resources of all kinds to feed a voracious and ever increasing appetite, backed by a refusal to acknowledge the rights of black and brown peoples of the world to their own bodies or resources. Neomodernism defines the resurgence of this ideal in the contemporary era, after a period of global illusion in which the existence of a rival superpower forced the West to pay lip service to the idea of international equality, even as it subscribed to the Orwellian dictum that all animals are equal, but some animals are more equal than others. Like Modernism, its discourses are supported on a framework of violence. The main difference is that the destructive abilities of Western power today dwarf those available at the turn of the twentieth century. However, there has barely been any change in the reasons given for its use and the propensity of the West to unleash this power against non-Western populations.

THE PERILS OF UNILATERAL POWER

Modernity is a shifting signifier that is probably incapable of being defined and, in this sense, it is sublime. John D. Kelly writes that "against a sublime, something so big, significant, and awesome that it cannot be defined or described, but only evoked, the Bakhtinian antidote is a grotesque, an inextricably embodied, living reality, undisguisably ugly and undeniably fertile." In the contemporary era, the grotesque is represented by American power, which, as Kelly suggests, means that "contemporary cultural initiatives, local and global, [are] situated in their relations with and against a grotesque actuality, the American plan for the postwar world, not with, against, post, or alternative to 'modernity.' "[15]

American power is the grotesque of the contemporary age. It confronts the modernist sublime with its antidote, rejecting Modernism's attempt at abstract contemplation with a gritty focus on the lived consequences of brutal force. Against the assumed benevolence of change celebrated by theories of modernization, it reveals the corruption and destruction that accompanies such changes. Against ideals of political emancipation, it reveals naked aggression, unbridled greed, and an undisguised attempt to appropriate the natural resources of non-Western societies. Against the lofty ideals of international law, it reveals the crass manipulations of each *hegemon du jour* in their outlaw disregard for international law. This very real power shows how America uses its military might to dominate the world through a vast network of military bases on all continents. These bases constitute America's version of the former imperial colonies and testify to its own growing imperial ambitions, which it successfully masks under the rhetoric of spreading "freedom" and lately, fighting a "war against terror." George Orwell famously warned against the rise of totalitarian government and the emergence of a political culture in which language serves only to communicate propaganda, in which paradoxical statements distort reality. He called this kind of language "Newspeak," whose principal utterances ("War is Peace," "Freedom is Slavery," and "Ignorance is Strength") combine with totalitarian control of all spheres of life ("Big Brother is Watching You") to produce the ultimate Fordist society, an endless replication of sameness masquerading as difference. American military power reflects the perfection of coercive totalitarian governance through its ability to deploy overwhelming force and also control what discourses are permitted. In the period after the Cold War, this force has been indiscriminately deployed against non-Western peoples in an attempt to assert America's role as the sole remaining superpower.

Nothing more graphically illustrates the nature of American power than its thirteen naval task forces, built around aircraft carriers each with enough destructive power to wipe out the major urban centers of most countries. Named after major American presidents and military figures, these aircraft carriers each carry average troop deployments of five thousand soldiers, and some carry as many as fifty warplanes. America's arsenal contains enough nuclear weapons to destroy the world, and American diplomacy is built around the clear statement of this capability. Its military "footprint" around the world includes more than seven hundred military bases encircling the globe, a number that grows daily. Although it is often denied in public discussions, the fact is that these military bases map the imperial ambitions of the United States, and have actively been used as a stepping-stone for the systematic invasion and overt colonization of non-Western countries. In the contemporary era, American military might is a unilateral power, extremely self-centered, and answerable only to a minute clique within the broad oligarchy of the military-industrial complex.

The fact of America's military might is impressive, but not as impressive as the lack of awareness exhibited by an American society for whom much of their country's military engagements remain rather abstract.[16] In a country with a supposedly free press, the media often disseminates military propaganda disguised as objective news.[17] This propaganda has spawned a militaristic culture in America itself, a pure identification of the populace with the country's imperial ambitions. In the field of visual culture, it is reflected in the rise of sport utility vehicles as the dominant form of mobility, and the reconfiguration of military vehicles (such as personnel armored carriers) into civilian conveyances like the Hummer. It is accompanied by the return of grand narratives (Huntington's clash of civilizations and Fukuyama's earlier declaration about the end of history) and the revalidation of canonical Modernism in art after a couple of decades of challenge to its narrative ideal of insular Western development. The latter explains the return of blockbuster exhibitions of canonical figures of Modern art—Picasso, Monet, Matisse, and so on—all of which avoid any discussion of the role of non-Western art on their practice as artists. In film and cinema, this tendency is evident in the resurgence of epic sword-and-sandal cinema, all conveniently located in times and places that allow the movies to be cast without a single black or non-Western actor.[18] It is also reflected in the rise of superhero mythologies, whose plots feature vigilante behavior that mimics current American policy of meting out unilateral and collective punishment to countries that it finds objectionable.[19] The irony of the present moment is that in each instance, the hegemon violates reams of international law in the name of upholding international law. Christoph Cox identifies one other consequence of this culture: "it is reflected in the revival of modernist strategies of abstraction, reduction, self-referentiality, and attention to the perceptual act itself."[20] Many contemporary artists achieve this last aspect through the inter-rogation of the works of an earlier generation of modernist painters.

American military power was meant to provide Western control of global affairs after the Cold War. However, the expected apotheosis of the West in the post–Cold War era was rudely halted by the rise of militant ethnicity and the proliferation of fundamentalist ideologies all over the world. The marked in-crease in ethnic and ideological conflicts in this new world order is a form of resistance to the hegemonic aspirations of occidental military and corporate imperialism, and the desire of the West that the other simply surrender to the temptations of Western consumer culture. Societies at the forefront of this struggle confront issues of life and death in which millions indeed lose their lives, either as victims of the occidental military order or as "collateral damage" crushed by the *hegemon de jour* in its campaign for world domination. This collateral damage takes the form of periodic slaughter of non-Western popula-tions by ever more sophisticated weapons of mass destruction, principally de-ployed through air power. As a mark of disdain for these unfortunate dead, the American military almost never produces a formal calculation of the damage inflicted on subject populations, even though it keeps meticulous account of any and all American life (both military and civilian) lost in such conflicts. This refusal of accountability masks the horrendous bloodletting that is needed to sustain imperial power in all times and manifestations. It is a favored mode of engagement used by colonial powers to subjugate local resistance.[21]

The neomodernist moment was instigated by the unilateral power of the West, and both were in turn confronted with another grotesque—the assault on New York's World Trade Center towers, the Pentagon, and elsewhere on the morning of September 11, 2001, which radically changed the structural land-scape of the politics of violence. The struggle for the history of September 11, 2001, already unfolds as a form of mythopoesis, an active process of mythmak-ing through visual and verbal narratives. Documentary analysis of the event has been superseded by the official report of the congressional committee charged with explaining the events to the American people.[22] The report holds the government blameless for the events and celebrated American heroism in the face of adversity. The political nature of this instant-history project and the tight control over how the events were narrated affirms the Manichean orienta-tion of government utterances after the event, when the United States de-manded that the world choose sides in an apocalyptic battle of civilization against barbarity. One does not wish to minimize the suffering of all the Ameri-cans who died in the attack on the Twin Towers, but it is pertinent to ask how many people in other parts of the world have died, been imprisoned without trial, had their homes destroyed or their countries invaded, and generally been reduced to nonhumans in the current American crusade against terrorism. The mastermind of this attack on America, Sheik Usama bin Muhhammad bin Awad bin Ladin (or Osama bin Laden, as he is more widely known), has been reconstituted as a demonic figure in the American media, which refuses to acknowledge that the terrorist attack, though dastardly, nevertheless fits well into the wanton disregard for human life that accompanied the advent of Western modernity and its neomodernist incarnation. In the weeks after the towers fell, American public sentiment echoed a plaintive cry too often heard around the world at sites of organized brutality directed against native populations by the West: "Why did *they* do this to us?" Here in the West, however, this cry was often accompanied by outrage: "Who *dared* do this to us? We are after all exceptional."

The peril of unilateral power is thus that narratives of Western culture that support a notion of Western exceptionalism (especially for the United States, in its current position as the preeminent military power on the planet) tend to define the imperial powers as if they were exempt from the rules of the community of nations, in the same way that it narrates human beings as being exempt from the laws of nature. The constant struggle to maintain this assertion of superiority is sustained by violent erasure of the Other, by acts of violence to the historical record, and is reflected in a discursive violence enabled by active control of technologies of discourse. The paradox of this occidental control is its insistence on universalized humanism, which prompted Fanon's criticism of "this Europe where they are never done talking of Man, yet murder men everywhere they find them, at the corner of every one of their own streets, in all the corners of the globe."[23] It is not surprising that imperial powers resort to disproportionate violence in their dealing with perceived enemies. Violence resolves the contrary presence of the Other by physically effacing its material existence or recontextualizing it to accord with hegemonic narratives about the contemporary world.

IMPERIAL HEGEMONY: THE PAST IS PRESENT

The invasion of Iraq in 2002, the second U.S. invasion of that country in a decade, provides the clearest evidence of the march of American hegemony, as well as a model of imperial behavior comparable to similar acts from previous centuries. The struggle that now unfolds in Iraq against the American occupation is an example of resistance to the march of occidental imperialism. It is obvious to the Iraqi insurgents and everyone else that the United States cannot be defeated in open battle. However, the logic of guerilla warfare is not to defeat the stronger opponent, but to bog it down in a low-intensity conflict that saps resources and fuels anger against the occupation. Sooner or later, the occupiers leave, even though they may destroy the entire country beforehand. We will return to the Iraq invasion soon enough. For now, it seems more profitable to revisit the site of an earlier struggle against another grotesque, the power of the European colonial empires, under whose global reach the discourse of modernity played out in the early twentieth century.

The example of British imperial ambitions in West Africa can be used to illustrate the resilience of colonial tropes, what Annie Coombes described as "the endless currency of certain received notions about racial difference."[24] In February 1897, an elite British force of about twelve hundred men (supported by several hundred African auxiliary troops and thousands of African porters) besieged Benin City, capital of the Edo Kingdom of Benin, whose ruler, Oba Ovonramwen, sat on a throne that was a thousand years old. The British Punitive Expedition used Maxim machine guns to mow down most of the oba's 130,000 soldiers and secure control of the capital city. They set fire to the city and looted the palace of five hundred years' worth of bronze objects that constituted the royal archive of Benin's history, an irreplaceable national treasure. The king and his principal chiefs fled into the countryside, pursued by British forces who lay waste to the countryside as a strategy to force the people of Benin to give up their fugitive king. According to Richard Gott:

> For a further six months, a small British force harried the countryside in search of the Oba and his chiefs who had fled. Cattle were seized and villages destroyed. Not until August was the Oba cornered and brought back to his ruined city. An immense throng was assembled to witness the ritual humiliation that the British imposed on their subject peoples. The Oba was required to kneel down in front of the British military "resident" of the town and to literally bite the dust. Supported by two chiefs, the king made obeisance three times, rubbing his forehead on the ground three times. He was told that he had been deposed.[25]

Oba Ovonramwen finally surrendered to stem the slaughter of his people. Many of his soldiers considered his surrender an unbearable catastrophe and committed suicide, rather than see the king humiliated. A significant number, led by some chiefs, maintained guerilla warfare against the British for almost two years, until their leaders were captured and executed. The remaining members of the resistance thereafter gave up their arms and merged back into the general population.

The invasion of Benin in 1897 came on the heels of the Berlin conference that partitioned Africa among a handful of European colonial powers (and this followed three hundred years of social damage done to Africa by the European slave trade).[26] The invasion of Iraq in 1991 marked the emergence of the doctrine of a new world order that legitimized America's self-assumed duty to serve as the sole arbiter of international law, while being exempt from it. However, the invasion of Iraq in 2002 (after ten years of crippling sanctions that left hundreds of thousands of Iraqis dead) marks the resurgence of full-fledged colonialism, which uses the logic and tactics of modernist colonialism as the central operating strategy of an American "new world order." The reasons given by Britain for its invasion of Benin and those provided by the United States for its invasion of Iraq bear comparison. The similarities are sobering, as are the aftereffects of both invasions, principally in the destruction of the social structure of each society, the humiliation of its leaders, and finally, the looting of each society's cultural treasures that now find their way to Western museums and markets.[27] These reasons included accusations of savagery from Benin and Iraq (with British and American power justifying the invasion as an act to protect human rights): the Benin king was accused of engaging in human sacrifice, and the Iraqi leader of sanctioning the deaths and torture of the Kurds. There was an obvious but unspoken need to appropriate the resources of both countries, masked by the idea that toppling each one would advance the cause of civilization: the forests of Benin were appropriated for rubber plantations after the war, while the Americans have been unable to extricate themselves from the accusation that they invaded Iraq simply to seize control of its oil. Treaties signed by each leader (the Edo-British protectorate treaty and the Iraq–United Nations disarmament treaty) were used as an excuse for invading each country. Both the British and American invaders assumed that they would be greeted as liberators and that loot from each country would help defray the costs of the invasion. Both invasions involved massive destruction of the invaded country (the British burnt the capital of Benin, while the Americans are, even as we speak, trying to "bomb Iraq back to the stone age"). The leaders of both countries were captured and publicly humiliated. The art treasures of each country were looted and Western companies granted exclusive license to exploit local resources. The above motivations were summed up in the words of the British acting consul general, James Phillips, entreating Whitehall to sanction an invasion of Benin in 1897:

> The whole of the English merchants represented on the river have petitioned the government for aid to enable them to keep their factories (trading posts)

open, and last but not least, the revenues of this Protectorate are suffering. . . . I am certain that there is only one remedy. That is to depose the King of Benin. . . . I am convinced that pacific measures are now quite useless, and that the time has now come to remove the obstruction. . . . I do not anticipate any serious resistance from the people of the country—there is every reason to believe that they would be glad to get rid of their King—but in order to obviate any danger, I wish to take up sufficient armed force. . . . I would add that I have reason to hope that sufficient ivory may be found in the King's house to pay the expenses incurred.[28]

The invasion was sanctioned, and as punishment for the death of nine British soldiers and about eighty of their African porters, the British killed more than seventy thousand Benin people, burnt the capital of a thousand-year-old kingdom, and looted its art. The archival record has not been able to show that Iraq ever inflicted any injury to the United States, except perhaps for its leader's defiance of American power. Despite this fact, it has been used essentially as a theater for testing new weapons, and new ideas about how to remake the world in an image acceptable to America's imperial ambitions. For about fifteen hundred or so American/coalition deaths recorded (at the time of writing) in its two invasions of Iraq (all of which were engendered by warfare resulting from the invasion in the first place), perhaps two hundred thousand Iraqis have lost their lives, either from direct combat or as collateral damage from the relentless aerial bombardment of the country.[29] To this we can add at least another half million or so infant and young-child fatalities resulting from the American-led sanctions against the Iraqi regime.[30]

The most problematic aspects of both invasions are that imperial violence was repackaged as a media spectacle for the home audience of the invading countries. In the British case, as Annie Coombes reports, the *Illustrated London News* "ran a series of stories on Benin which built up an ever-increasing store of depravities," ultimately leading to a designation of the Edo capital as a "City of Blood."[31] In the Iraqi case, the American media has simply repackaged warfare coverage as a kind of pornography, in which the death and destruction of Iraqi lives is used to titillate an audience ravenous for ever more explicit representations of violence in popular culture. The complete capitulation of the American media to American military propaganda, and its raucous projection of war as entertainment will go down in history as one of the great tragedies of the new century. Given its long history of recasting violence as spectacle, there is no sign that this kind of imperial bloodletting will abate in the future.

The arrival of the Benin bronzes in London and their subsequent dissemina-

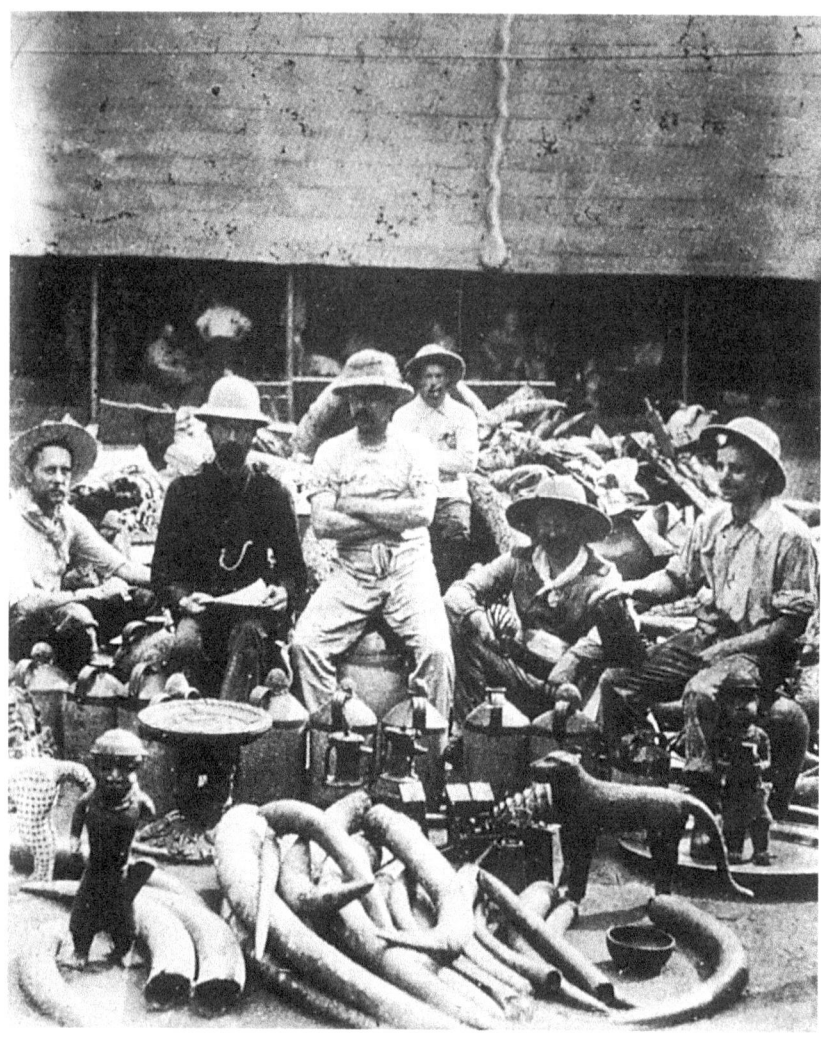

Members of the 1897 British Punitive Expedition posing with artworks and other loot removed from the palace of the king of Benin. The items constituted a national treasury of the Benin Kingdom encompassing more than five hundred years of national history. Photograph. Courtesy of the author and Collection of British Museum, London.

tion to major European museums shattered Western assumptions about African art and culture. The exquisite sculptures confounded Western audiences precisely because they exhibited the kind of internal aesthetic, historical, and stylistic development that were taken for granted in the history of Western art but assumed to be absent from the art of "primitive" peoples. By September 1897, the looted artworks were already on display at the British museum and being used to bolster the emergent fields of anthropology, aided by representations of Africans at the ubiquitous world fairs of that era. European artists subsequently appropriated the formal logic of African art as a challenge to formal and pictorial norms in Western art. Above all, the representation of the Benin kingdom as a bloodthirsty, savage environment, and its spectacular destruction by British forces, largely influenced Conrad's narrative of African primordiality and savagery in *Heart of Darkness*. The colonial project in Africa in turn acted out the prescription of Conrad's antihero, Kurtz, who asserted the imperial power's need to "exterminate all the brutes."[32] In this single sentence, the fictional Kurtz captured the European impulse toward genocide in its interaction with African and other non-Western peoples since the start of the European ascendancy in 1492, when the African Moors lost Granada, their last stronghold in Spain.[33]

ALTER/NATIVES: THE MIRROR OF MODERNISM

The centrality of violence to the project of modernity (and its reemergence in the contemporary era) is often occluded in Western histories of Modern art and culture. It is almost completely absent in art history's inscription of modernity in art and visual culture, which makes only cursory references to the impact of non-Western art (in this case, African art) on the development of European Modernism at the turn of the twentieth century. Art history, as Coombes observes, narrates "the European avant-garde's appropriation of African and Oceanic culture as a more or less opportunistic adventure in self-renewal (which none the less always puts the European in the privileged position of seer and visionary)."[34] African cultures and art were considered the outcome of savage sensibilities, thus deflecting the violence of the colonial encounter onto the populations most impacted by imperial brutality. However, in Gikandi's words, "savagery and artistic sensibility would intimately be connected in the aesthetics of modernism," although the reaction of European modernists to their dependence on artistic models from the "savage sensibility" engendered equal measures of adoration and repugnance.[35] Thus although it is acknowledged that artists like Picasso used the forms and structural logic of African art to reconfigure Western conventions of representation, Gikandi adds, "in order for modernism to claim its monumentality, that is, its enshrinement in the very institutions of Western culture that it had set out to defy and deconstruct, it had to shed the contaminants of the Other."[36]

The voice and aspirations of this "savage" Other have also been carefully edited out of art history's inscription of modernity, since the Other was imagined to exist in relation to Europe's past, and thus could not be allowed to occupy a coeval contemporaneity with European culture. Thus while the Benin bronzes contributed to a reappraisal of Western ideas about African creativity, they were reinterpreted as an anomaly in African art, which continued to be seen as the product of a degenerate sensibility.[37] African artworks were also imagined as the products of a dead culture, the invasion of Benin usually taken to mark the end of "precolonial" African art, a phase in which Africans supposedly lived in complete isolation from one another and from European influences. Neither this narrative of African primitivism nor the use of the supposed primitive art of Africa as a basis for European Modernism allows for the presence of modern African art. Thus, even though the archival record clearly shows major reconfiguration of African conventions of representation coeval with similar experiments in Western art, the resultant modernist practices were assumed to be mere imitations of Western Modernism. Modern African artists were deemed irrelevant to the discourse of Modern art in general.

When Ben Enwonwu was photographed in 1956 working on a sculpture of Queen Elizabeth II, under the stern gaze of David Livingstone and Franklin D. Roosevelt, he had spent a decade of international practice affirming the modernist nature of his paintings and sculptures against what was already a visible effort to efface him from the history of Modern art.[38] The jarring juxtaposition of historical figures and cultures in the photograph encapsulates the historical context in which Enwonwu and other modern African artists confronted the discourse of modernity in art history. It captures the violence of their negation in that discourse. It is also a document of imperial succession representing the changing of the guard, the demise of European colonial power and rise of American power after World War II. John D. Kelly suggests U.S. foreign policy in the post–World War II era was largely responsible for constructing the modern nation-state as a political ideal within which modernist transformations were possible.[39] Before that, European imperial power made possible colonial environments that trafficked in "the endless currency of certain received notions about racial difference," ideas on which European Modernism constructed its fortress of exclusions. Neomodernism casts back to a period when the identity and power of Western culture was more certain and secure.

Today, American power is global, but the terrorist attacks of September 11, 2001, and the quagmire in Iraq shows that it is far from certain or inevitable.

Enwonwu was the first African to achieve international acclaim as a contemporary artist. His artworks defined an emergent African modernist sensibility in art, with its unique vision of significant form achieved by amalgamating African and European conventions of representation. His art, like that of other African modernists, is often dismissed for the very reason for which European modernists are celebrated—the appropriation and domestication of a foreign visual language.[40] Art history's narrative of Picasso's appropriation of African sculpture (specifically masks from the Fang and Grebo peoples, among others) does not provide a space for Fang discourses about art. It assumes that the Fang and Grebo producers of the masks that inspired Picasso do not have anything useful to say about their own aesthetic processes. In fact, it doubts the existence of any indigenous interpretation of these masks.[41] The reverse of this process is that African artists who adapt aspects of their indigenous art for contemporary practice are often seen as parochial and unoriginal.

Enwonwu confronted such criticism over his famous sculpture *Anyanwu* (bronze, 1955), whose head was entirely derived from a sixteenth-century Benin bronze sculpture of the head of a queen mother. Enwonwu's exploration of Benin art and culture (he served a one-year apprenticeship with the Benin royal guild of sculptors in 1943) provided a foundation for his subsequent amalgamation of African and European conventions of representation. *Anyanwu* is the best example of such amalgamation in Enwonwu's art: it melded naturalistic and abstract forms into a numinous image. When Enwonwu first presented *Anyanwu* in a public exhibition, European critics made no attempt to understand the structure and meaning of this artwork. Instead, they compared it unfavorably to Alberto Giacometti's attenuated sculptures and accused Enwonwu of imitating the style of this artist. Enwonwu rejected the comparison and noted that his work used different structures of representation and symbolism derived from his Igbo and Edo heritage. He also asserted that Giacometti and other European modern artists appropriated the form of African sculpture without knowledge or understanding of its conceptual meanings. His own use of indigenous African aesthetics could not be defined as imitating Giacometti, Enwonwu insisted, since it was European modernists who were obviously copying forms from African art.[42] In her review of this debate, Nkiru Nzegwu noted that Enwonwu knew Giacometti personally, and she points out that these critics never even once considered that Giacometti might have been influenced by Enwonwu's sculptures in the first place. This question does not arise because the African experience of Modernism is not acknowledged in art history.

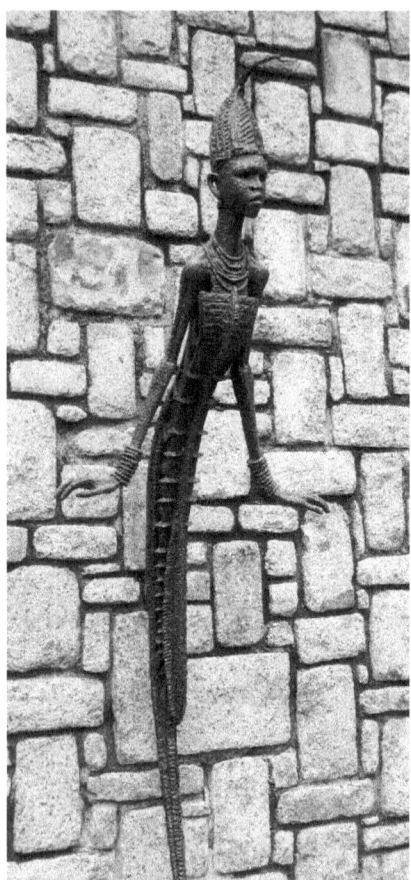

Ben Enwonwu, *Anyanwu,* bronze, 1955. Collection of the Nigerian National Commission for Museums and Monuments. Photograph courtesy of the author, 2005.

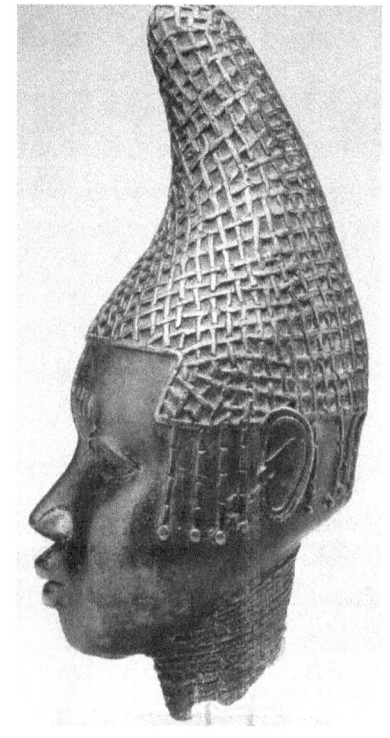

Edo Kingdom of Benin, *Head of a Queen Mother,* brass, c. 1500–50. Collection of the British Museum, London. Photograph courtesy of the author.

CONCLUSION: EVERYTHING OLD IS NEW AGAIN

The critic Arthur Danto has referred to the end of art history as a time when art does not end, but continues in a new realm that is characterized by non-patriarchal, non-Eurocentric ideals.[43]

The quest for alternative modernities in African art maps the attempt to locate African agents, actions, and events in modernist space-time and thereby achieve a coeval contemporaneity, which discredits the Hegelian assumption that Africa exists outside of history. Its call to revisit art history's narrative of modernity does not merely aim to insert African artists into the historical space of European modernist practices. Rather, it challenges the racial underpinnings of art history's interpretation of modernity, thus destabilizing the basis upon which occidental culture sustains itself as the prime engine of historical change. Modern African artists and the archival record of their practice ultimately confront art history with questions about the parameters of modernity, of "what is entailed by the process of being modern."[44] African artists accomplished significant interpretations of modernity in painting, sculpture, printmaking, and other arts. They invented new formal languages and produced highly experimental artworks that interrogated the role of art and visual culture in their emergent modernity. However, the paradigm of European primacy that structures this narrative makes it impossible for these artists to emerge as active subjects of modernity in art history. Since they (as Africans) are assumed to exist in the past of Europe, their practice is always deemed superfluous and their very existence belated. The discursive violence of this assumption is supported by the actual subordination of African and other non-Western subjects in the contemporary global order, as a reflection of imperial violence that continues unabated.

The above issues highlight the difficulty of inscribing an alternative narrative of modernity in which African and other non-Western artists achieve a coeval contemporaneity with white, Western artists. However, my analysis shows that we cannot make modern African artists emerge as art historical subjects simply by inserting them into existing narratives of Modern art in art history. The epistemological structure of art history excludes the possibility of their practice and within its historicist models, locates Modern African art in a position inferior to similar European practices. Ikem Okoye suggests that in order to unfold an African art history that does not simply replicate a projection of European intellectual desire for the art of Africa, such a history must suggest (if not execute) the possibility of an art history that is constituted by a radically different alignment.[45] A crucial first step in this realignment is to use the archival record to interrogate the practice of modern African artists and their pursuit of a modernist idiom as a response to global formations of modernity. This process restores modern African artists to the site of their creative endeavors by situating them within the historical time and contexts of their engagements with Modern art.

Ultimately, the search for alternative modernities confronts the unilateral power of the United States, whose control of technologies of discourse undermines the claims of autonomous agency on which such theories depend. The reality of imperial power (of the United States, in this instance) to shape contemporary global discourses hobbles recent attempts (by postcolonial theory, for example) to decenter the West and reshape its narratives of political and cultural supremacy. The questions it raises about non-Western modernity and contemporaneity have less to do with the cultural and aesthetic capabilities of the Other than with how it discursively positions the Other in a global interpretation of Western power.

NOTES

In this chapter I have chosen to retain the wording and interpretation of events based on the best knowledge available in 2004 at the time of the "Modernity ≠ Contemporaneity: Antinomies of Art and Culture after the Twentieth Century" conference, rather than update it to reflect contemporary realities. By 2006, however, it was clear that the Iraq war had produced the disastrous results predicted and had pushed the country toward civil war. Osama bin Laden was still at large, and the financial impact of the Iraq campaign ($290 billion and counting) was beginning to generate dissent in the American media.

1 The term "neomodernism" is generally described as a return to the certainties of formalist Modernism in art and design. An early use of the word appears in Grauer, "Modernism/Postmodernism/Neomodernism." My use of "neomodernism" focuses on the political implications of the modernist sublime in relation to African discourses of modernity in art. For a manifesto detailing its principal objectives, see Armando Bayraktari and André Durand, "Neomodernism: The Manifesto" (London, 2001), available online at http://www.armando.co.uk/manifesto.htm.

2 Sagan, *The Demon-Haunted World.*

3 For a close examination of the literature on this subject, see Knauft, *Critically Modern.*

4 See, for example, Elias, *The Civilizing Process.*

5 Many African intellectuals accuse Conrad of racism because of his enthusiastic support of the colonization project (despite his narrator's—Marlowe's—revulsion for its cruel violence) and his amoral sense of its inevitability. For example, see Achebe, "An Image of Africa."

6 See Wells, *The Journey of Man,* which proves the above contention through examination of human genetics. The search for the origins of modern humans not only locates

the emergence of man in Africa, it clearly demonstrates that there is no scientific basis for the idea of "race."

7 Janson (with A. Janson), *History of Art;* Stokstad et al., *Art History.* These and other canonical art history surveys either omit mention of African art altogether or reduce its history to a few pages of text.

8 Eshu, a trickster figure, is the Yoruba deity in charge of divination. For analysis of Ifa divination, see Bascom, *Ifa Divination;* and Witte, *Ifa and Esu.* For analysis of Eshu as an alternative interpretative model for African American literary practice, see Gates, *The Signifying Monkey.*

9 For analysis of Igbo cultural and religious practices, see Cole and Aniakor, *Igbo Arts.*

10 Preziosi, *Brain of the Earth's Body,* 41.

11 Araeen, *The Other Story,* 16–50.

12 Jameson, "Beyond the Cave," 117.

13 Gikandi, "Picasso, Africa, and the Schemata of Difference," quotation from 468.

14 Breckenridge, *Consuming Modernity,* 16.

15 Kelly, "Alternative Modernities or an Alternative to 'Modernity,' " 265.

16 For analysis of the actual history of U.S. military engagements (since the inception of the republic) and lack of public awareness of this history, see Dowd, *The Broken Promises of America.*

17 For analysis of the ethics and techniques of war coverage by the Western media and the adroit manipulation of the American media by the U.S. military during its second invasion of Iraq in 2003, see Hoskins, *Televising War.*

18 The classic example of this tendency is the *Lord of the Rings* trilogy. This story of global conflict written by a South African–born author, whose descriptions of supernatural domains drew extensively from actual South African landscapes, was filmed in New Zealand but centered exclusively on Hitlerian models of Aryan perfection. The film effects a literal reinscription of landscape by interpreting New Zealand as "Middle Earth," and the tourist industry generated by the New Zealand locales of these movies further dispossesses the Maoris (whose lands have already been seized by European colonization) of their memory of place.

19 See Reynolds, *Superheroes.*

20 Cox, "Return to Form," 67.

21 The use of torture by American soldiers and the government's attempt to dismiss this horrendous development echoes similar practices by the French in Algeria, the Belgians in the Congo, the British in Africa, and the Americans in Vietnam.

22 See National Commission on Terrorist Attacks, *The 9/11 Commission Report.*

23 Fanon, *Wretched of the Earth* (1963), 311–13.

24 Coombes, *Reinventing Africa.*

25 Richard Gott, "The Looting of Benin," *The Independent,* February 22, 1997, available online at the ARM (Africa Reparations Movement) Web site, http://www.arm.arc.co .uk/lootingBenin.html.

26 The invasion of Benin in 1897 was the latest in a string of invasions of other West African countries by the British, which had already destroyed the Ashanti empire and sent its leader into exile in 1895. From 1897 to 1914, the British Empire invaded several West African states and subsequently organized the conquered territories into colonial possessions by amalgamating then into news states with arbitrary borders.

27 This process highlights a long-standing criticism of Western museums (and museums in general) as repositories of imperial plunder that deculturize looted objects to render them amenable to reinvention within Western discourses. See Fisher, *Making and Effacing Art.*

28 Quoted in ARM, "The British and the Benin Bronzes," available online at http://www.arm.arc.co.uk/britishBenin.html. See also Coombes, *Reinventing Africa.*

29 See statistics Bovard, "Iraqi Sanctions and American Intentions: Blameless carnage? Part 1." See also Bovard, *Terrorism and Tyranny.*

30 International organizations estimate much higher figures, as much as 210,000 Iraqis dead in the 1991 U.S. invasion, and more than 800,000 dead from the sanctions, mostly children. Human rights organizations eventually complained to the United Nations that the Iraq sanctions constituted a weapon of mass destruction (see United Nations Commission on Human Rights, 52d session, agenda item 20, "Children and war Catastrophe in Iraq," available at http://www.webcom.com/hrin/parker/c96–20.html).

31 See Coombes, *Reinventing Africa,* 11. *Benin the City of Blood* was the title of a book by the intelligence officer to the British Punitive Expedition, Commander R. H. Bacon.

32 For an account of European acts of genocide in Africa, see Lindqvist, *Exterminate All the Brutes.* For analysis of Belgian acts of genocide in the Congo (Conrad's site of primordial savagery) see Hochschild, *King Leopold's Ghost.*

33 Ferdinand V and Isabella I, rulers of Spain after the Moorish defeat of 1492, that same year bankrolled the voyages of Christopher Columbus to the Americas, which resulted in the conquest of the Americas with its horrifying legacy of genocide against native peoples.

34 Coombes, *Reinventing Africa,* 5.

35 Gikandi, "Picasso, Africa, and the Schemata of Difference," 458.

36 Gikandi, "Picasso, Africa, and the Schemata of Difference," 458.

37 On this subject, see Coombes, *Reinventing Africa,* 43–64.

38 For other representations in the Western media of Enwonwu as a modern artist, see *Ebony* (Chicago), "Africa's Greatest Artist"; *Daily Herald* (London), "Africa's Ben Challenges Epstein"; *Time,* "Out of Africa"; and *Times* (London), "Nigerian Statue of the Queen."

39 Kelly, "Alternative Modernities or an Alternative to 'Modernity,'" 258–86.

40 See Bhabha, "Of Mimicry and Man."

41 On this subject, Robert Farris Thompson berated the arrogance of Western art historians who failed to consider that African peoples might have something of intellectual substance to contribute to this question of European appropriation. Thompson, "Fang Mask," 190.

42 See Nzegwu, *Contemporary Textures,* 175–76.

43 Suzi Gablik, "Towards an Ecological Self," 26.

44 Knauft, *Critically Modern,* 1.

45 See Okoye, "Book Review," 390–98. Under review were Suzanne Preston Blier, *African Vodun: Art, Psychology and Power* (Chicago: University of Chicago Press, 1995); Sarah C. Brett-Smith, *The Making of Bamana Sculpture: Creativity and Gender* (Cambridge: Cambridge University Press, 1994); and Coombes, *Reinventing Africa.*

10

ZOE LEONARD, *ANALOGUE*, 1998–2007

INTRODUCED BY HELEN MOLESWORTH

Zoe Leonard was an artist-in-residence at the Wexner Center for the Arts, Columbus, Ohio, during 2003. The *Analogue* Project was already well under way by the time of this residency and scheduled for exhibition at the Wexner Center in the summer of 2007. The residency was comprised of two significant parts: a paid trip for Leonard and her assistant to Uganda, so that Leonard could take pictures there, and a summer-long stay in Columbus, where the Wexner Center was able to provide studio space large enough to encompass the spatial demands of *Analogue*. These notes were written while the work was still very much in progress, and as such should be taken less as a definitive account of the work's ultimate appearance and structure, and more as an assessment of its fundamental concerns and problematics as they were understood by the author while *Analogue* was in the process of being made.

Zoe Leonard's *Analogue* is composed of roughly four hundred color and black-and-white photographs taken from approximately 1998 to 2004. Since then, these images have been presented in grids of varying size, forming installations in exhibitions around the world. The work is both vast and intimate, as individual images take hold of the viewer's attention with such alacrity that the encompassing nature of the whole is at first difficult to comprehend. The work begins with images taken as Leonard walked the streets of her native New York City. Closed storefronts, shutters drawn down tight, the city is asleep, empty, but also, we realize, slowly fading. In this opening chapter we see the city in a state of transition, as the small shops of traditionally working-class and immigrant neighborhoods—the Lower East Side prime among them—were slowly forced out of business in the 1990s due to the increasing gentrification of Manhattan. With this initial gesture we begin to glean that the leitmotif of this magnum opus will be the disappearing face and texture of twentieth-century urban life.

Yet things never disappear all at once: cities retain, against all odds and the urban planners, an organic dimension. So the second chapter of *Analogue* begins with images of open storefronts, many of them serving dwindling immigrant communities, onto which signs for food stamps and lotto adhere, like barnacles. There are stores with hodgepodge displays in windows, handwritten signs grace the doors, and the arrangements of goods speak of the individual hands that did the work of their placement. *Analogue* is brimming with images of shop windows and their commodity objects. Yet far from the glistening allure of the commodity in the artificial light of shopping malls or the digitally manipulated photography of mail-order catalogues, these objects are slightly frayed around the edges, holding on doggedly to their disappearing place. Their perseverance is displayed in part by the way these commodities often migrate onto the street, acting like so many ready-made sculptures, claiming for themselves a kind of extra value as ad hoc art. The tension between disappearance and tenacity is at the heart of the pathos of Leonard's project; the images in *Analogue* are a testament to what history is currently in the process of leaving behind. As the artist has said, "New technology is usually pitched to us as an improvement. . . . But progress is always an exchange. We gain something, we give something else up. I'm interested in looking at some of what we are losing."

The dynamic and churning forces of globalism have brought many of us closer together. A globalized art world and intellectual circuit has rendered a select group of us more consistently available to one another. A far less glamorous version of "globalism" is the homogenization of difference through the emergence of hegemonic brand-name chain establishments that have collapsed time and distance. This has occurred to such an extent that one can find a Starbucks at the Brandenburg Gate (on what was formerly the East German side, no less). The regional differences that once defined American life are now largely lacking, as we increasingly eat and shop at the same restaurants and stores. While this homogeneity has its creature comforts, something else is being lost. Again, I quote Leonard: "It was only as these old shops began disappearing that I realized how much I counted on them—that this layered, frayed, and quirky beauty underlined my own life."

In this sense, *Analogue* is a walking tour of the end of the twentieth century, a poignant testament to a fading way of doing business, a document of a slowly evaporating way of life, evidence of the shift in our daily rituals of exchange.

Indeed, it is possible that one hundred years from now *Analogue* will be used much the way Eugene Atget's or August Sander's or Robert Frank's work is used—as a record, an encompassing document, a witness to the end of "New York, Capital of the Twentieth Century." It is, in a sense, an early, comprehensive, and self-conscious document of the twentieth century as a historical period.

If *Analogue* is elegiac about the ramifications of the transformation of urban life by multinational corporations, it is also a requiem for traditional photography in the face of the advancements in digital technology. In this regard, Leonard's *Analogue* is an attempt to preserve the photographic realm of the analogic —the photograph's distinctive ability to record physical data in a corresponding image—in the face of digital technology, which transforms physical data into a binary system. *Analogue* is a dual testament to the increasing obsolescence of both locally owned shops and straight photography. As each image is meticulously composed, and richly printed, the individual works evoke such renowned photographers as Walker Evans and William Eggleston. The squared-off format of the Rolleiflex is ever apparent, mirroring, extracting, and exponentially focusing our attention on the machined, tooled, and gridded nature of the built human environment. Far from a snapshot aesthetic, the viewfinder of the Rolleiflex is one in which the photographer looks down at the camera as opposed to directly at the subject. Furthermore, the photographer views the potential image through a graphic matrix of a grid superimposed on the viewfinder itself. Here it would seem that Modernism is indeed an incomplete project, as Leonard quite consciously deploys a modernist idiom in her framing and composition, allowing the work to resonate with previous modernist images.

Analogue offers much more than a weak form of reference to the recognizable style of Modernism's famous authors, because it also mobilizes the modernist strategy of a self-reflexive "formalism" in which the process of making and the final product speak of the same structuring devices. *Analogue* gestures toward the typologies of Bernd and Hilla Becher, the failure of the photographic regime found in Martha Rosler's *The Bowery in Two Inadequate Descriptive Systems*, and the image saturation of Gerhard Richter's *Atlas*. While *Analogue* is rhythmically organized in chapters (the prototypical nineteenth-century art form?), its use of the grid to organize suites of photographs with like subject matter disallows a purely modernist play with photography. The importance of seriality and difference, and the staging of the problem of representation as such (for instance, it is quite rare to find a person in any of these images) point to what might be called postmodernist concerns. To some extent, the relatively equal measure of call and response to both modernist and postmodernist artists and methodologies suggests that, even as *Analogue* acts as an active agent of recording the present for posterity, it also treats the historical as a kind of fossil. In *Analogue,* history is embedded in things and images, and it is this very embeddedness that allows it to act upon the present.

The third chapter in this gently unfolding progression comprises photographs of large, colorful bundles of cloth, bound with rope in ways that squeeze their excessive forms like so many whalebones in a corset. Oblique and odd, they are nonetheless quite beautiful, and Leonard photographs them in a somewhat anthropomorphic fashion, as if they were individuals posing for a portrait. This is partly due to their labored quality, as each bundle has clearly been gathered and composed by human hands. But I also think this intimate address, directed toward these particularly inanimate objects, comes from the specificity of the Rolleiflex camera. With the camera held against, and at the height of, the artist's torso, the ensuing photographs of the bundles enact or instantiate the high degree of subjectivity found in these pictures. So, although the photographs are acting as document, as witness, to some kind of inalienable truth, they are also enormously subjective, as they are taken from a very precise point of view, which is a representational plane that emanates from the scale of the artist's body. Upon careful looking, Leonard can be seen, reflected again and again in windows, a silent partner, an interested party, the curious agent of the work. The scope of the work is historic, the scale of the piece is global, but the gesture is continually one of intimacy, proximity, a kind of tender apprehension of the world from the position of a person, a subject, an artist both implicated in and distanced from the socioeconomic and aesthetic conditions within which she finds herself.

Westerners are all too familiar with the process of donating their unwanted clothes to charity. Yet we remain largely unaware that the vast majority of those clothes are not subsequently donated to people in need; rather, they are sold for profit to American middlemen, who subsequently sell them to other middlemen in South American and African countries. This twenty-first-century rag trade has had many effects; two of which are the decimation of indigenous textile production in the countries it impacts and the institution of new forms of identity and commerce in relation to Western clothing. Leonard photographed the bundles in her Brooklyn neighborhood for approximately two years, assuming they were destined for thrift shops, before she learned of the foreign trade in used clothing. The penultimate chapter of *Analogue* follows the bundles of used clothing from their clearing house in Brooklyn to the used clothing markets of Kampala, as well as to smaller rural towns in Uganda.

It bears stating, given the history of photography's objectification of "others," that Leonard explicitly follows a group of commodities through their dispersal through time and space, so the uncannily depopulated streets of New York are echoed in similarly sparsely populated images from Uganda. Rather, the clothing in *Analogue* is shown to have what Arjun Appadurai has called a "social life."[1] The portrait–like quality of the bundles transform, like so many chrysali, into the multitudinous forms of so many jackets, T-shirts, and pants, now found—like hung with like—in emergent rather than disappearing markets. It is, perhaps, ironic that by tracing the life of one set of commodities, rather than concentrating on individual lives, Leonard is able to show the ways in which we are linked globally, allowing us to understand, perhaps, the enormity of our urban and economic systems. In this regard, *Analogue* is not only a document of a passing moment—the end of an era or century—but it is also a window onto the ways the forces of globalization have begun to shape the present, both far away and close to home.

The Uganda photographs shift the emotional tenor of *Analogue*. The novelistic aspect of the work, in which things take on the attributes of characters (the major players are New York, gentrification, the bundles, Africa, and photography), means that a kind of historistic sentimentalizing (or worse, moralizing) about the good old days is disallowed. We realize the story is not only about a massive socioeconomic transition (and it is the emphasis on transition that counteracts the undertow of nostalgia), rather, it is an attempt to register, to understand, to track the ways in which a life in Brooklyn is connected to a life in Kampala, to see how exchange at the very fringes of the United States economy dictates major avenues of production and consumption in numerous African countries.

One way to talk about what is happening in *Analogue* is to say that the bundles started out as a kind of anthropomorphic formal enterprise, one that through curiosity is transformed into a full fledged "biography" of a commodity. Rather than objectifying persons, Leonard dignifies the commodity with its own story. This is a story in which the great migration of globalism is told through the changing regimes of value placed on things—as the clothes go from being discards to coveted, from a putatively philanthropic gesture to a mode of petty profit for countless middlemen. That most of the clothes were undoubtedly made in subaltern countries, to ensure their cheap and disposable status in the States, only to be converted into a commodity good after they have been "used up" is a brutal irony to say the least. As Leonard searches out this, now nearly excruciating, point of contact between Brooklyn and Kampala, another one appears. Everywhere one can find used Western clothes, and everywhere one can find Coca Cola. That in the United States these economies appear to be antithetical to one another and that in Kampala they are part of the

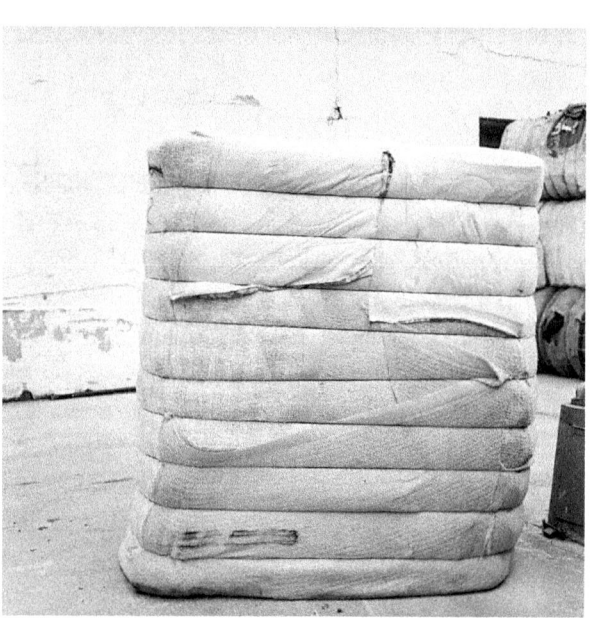

All illustrations in this chapter: Zoe Leonard, images from the series *Analogue,* 1997–2004. C-print, dimensions variable. Courtesy of the artist.

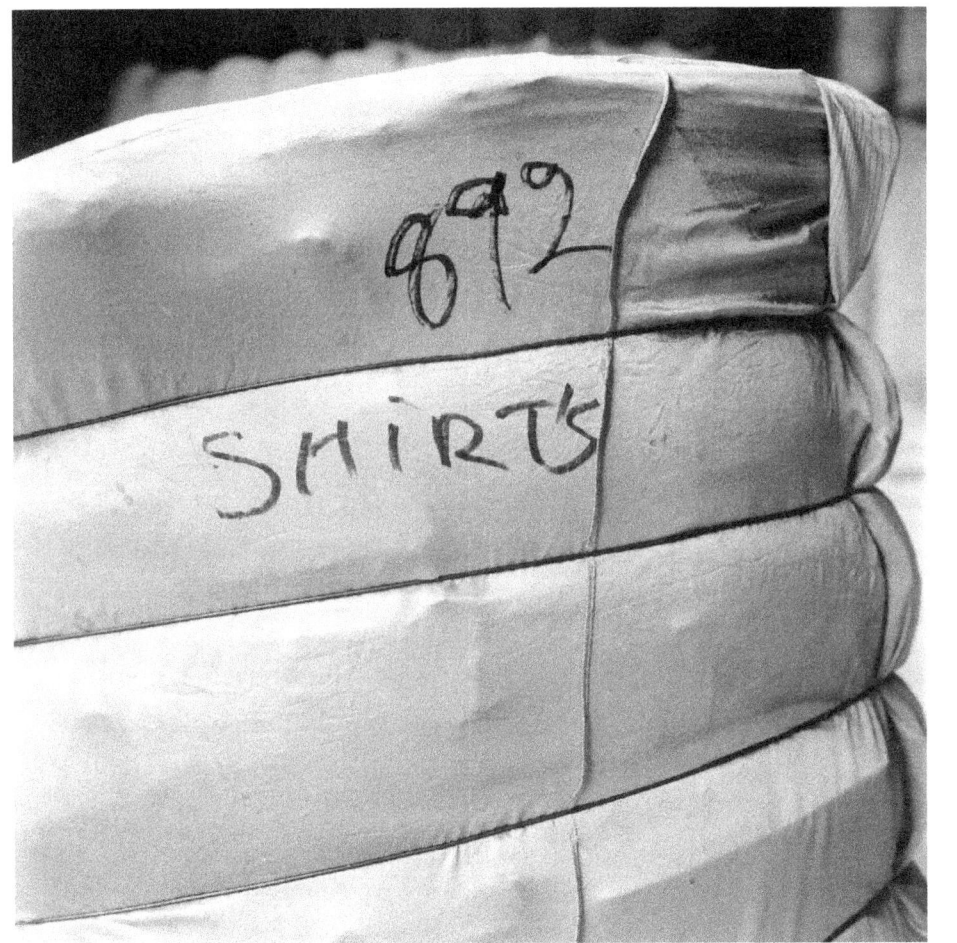

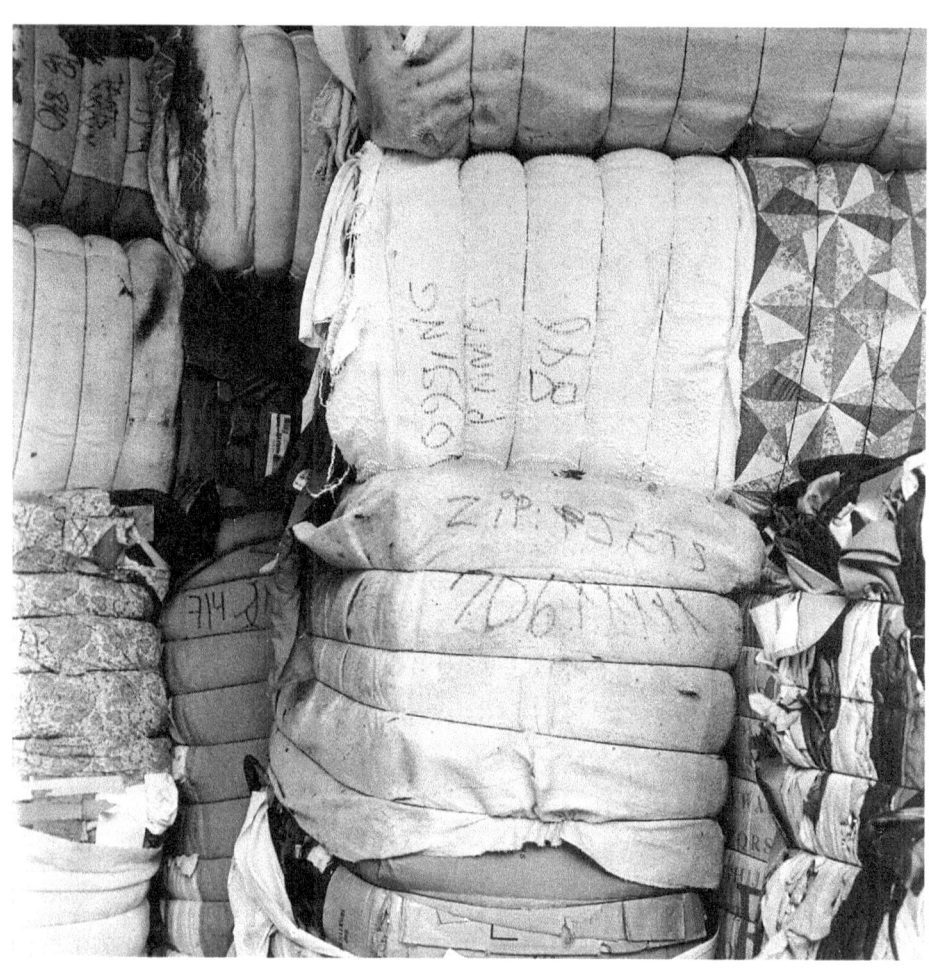

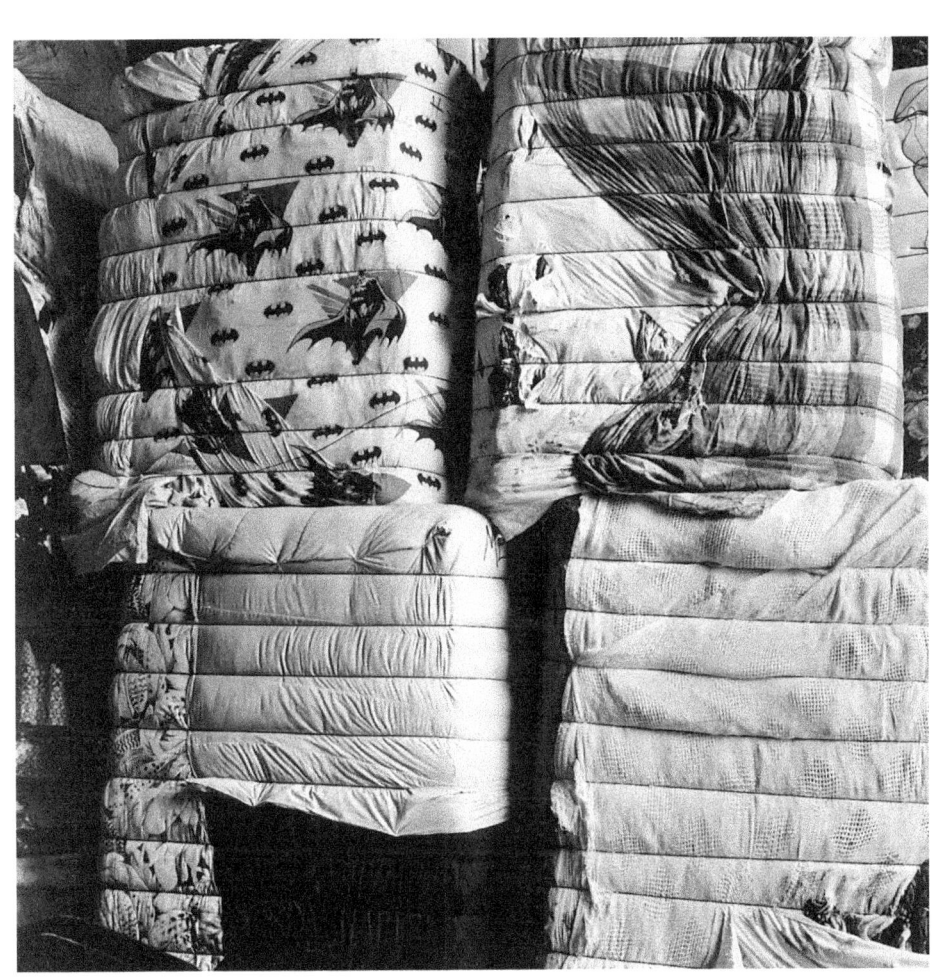

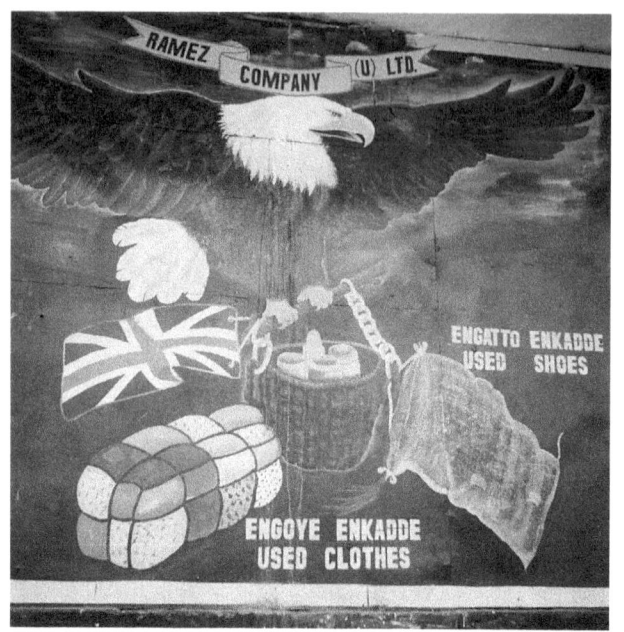

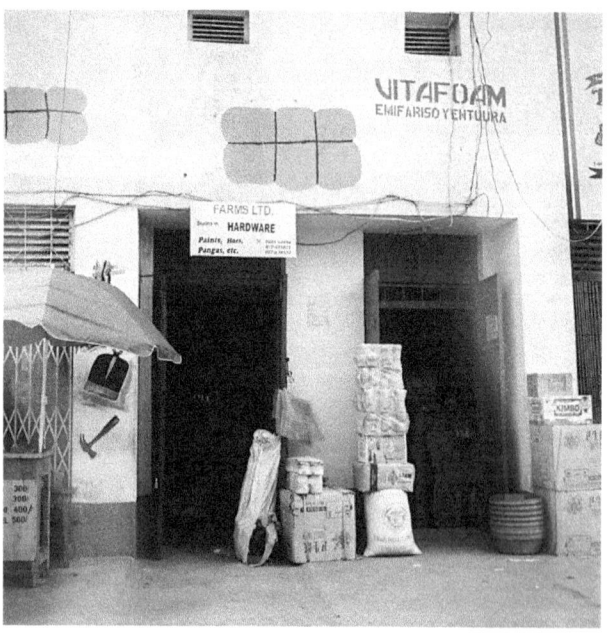

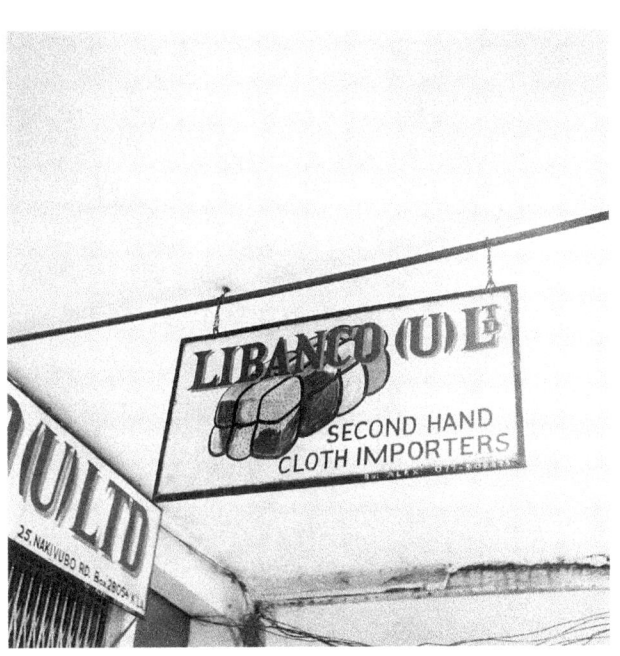

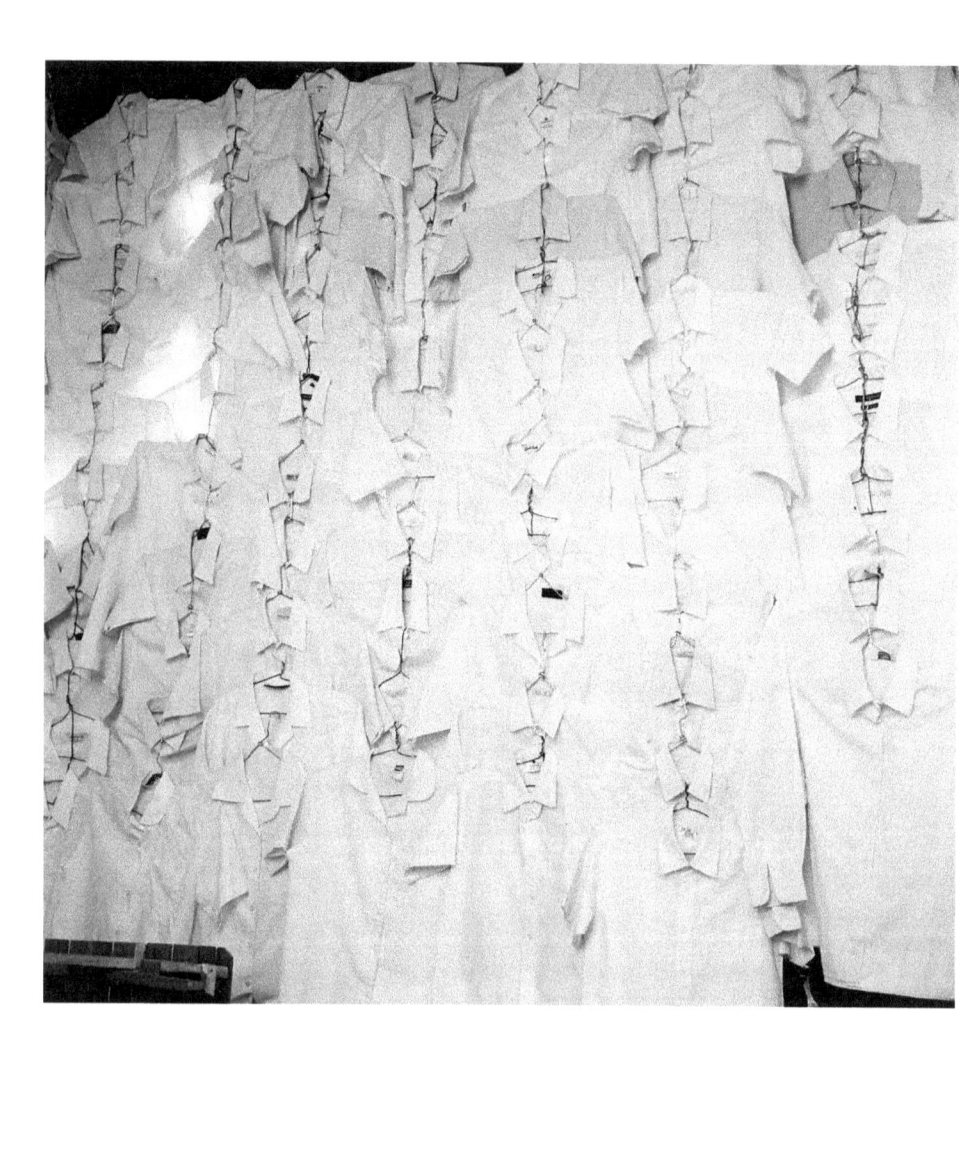

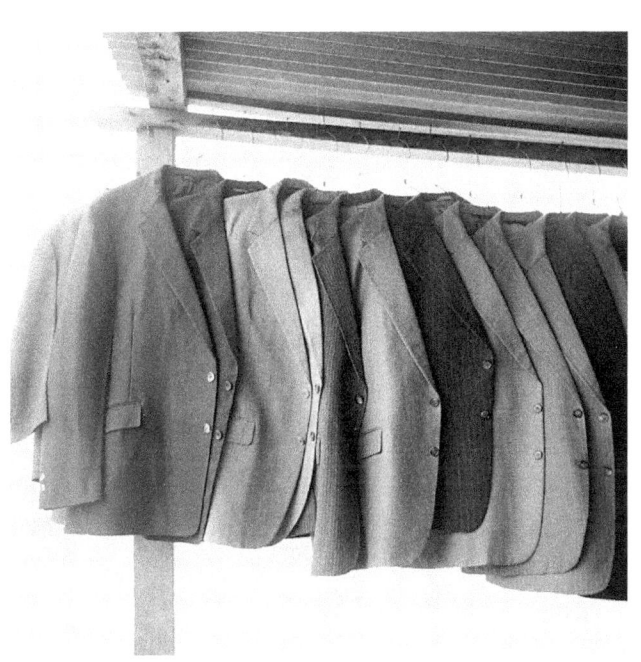

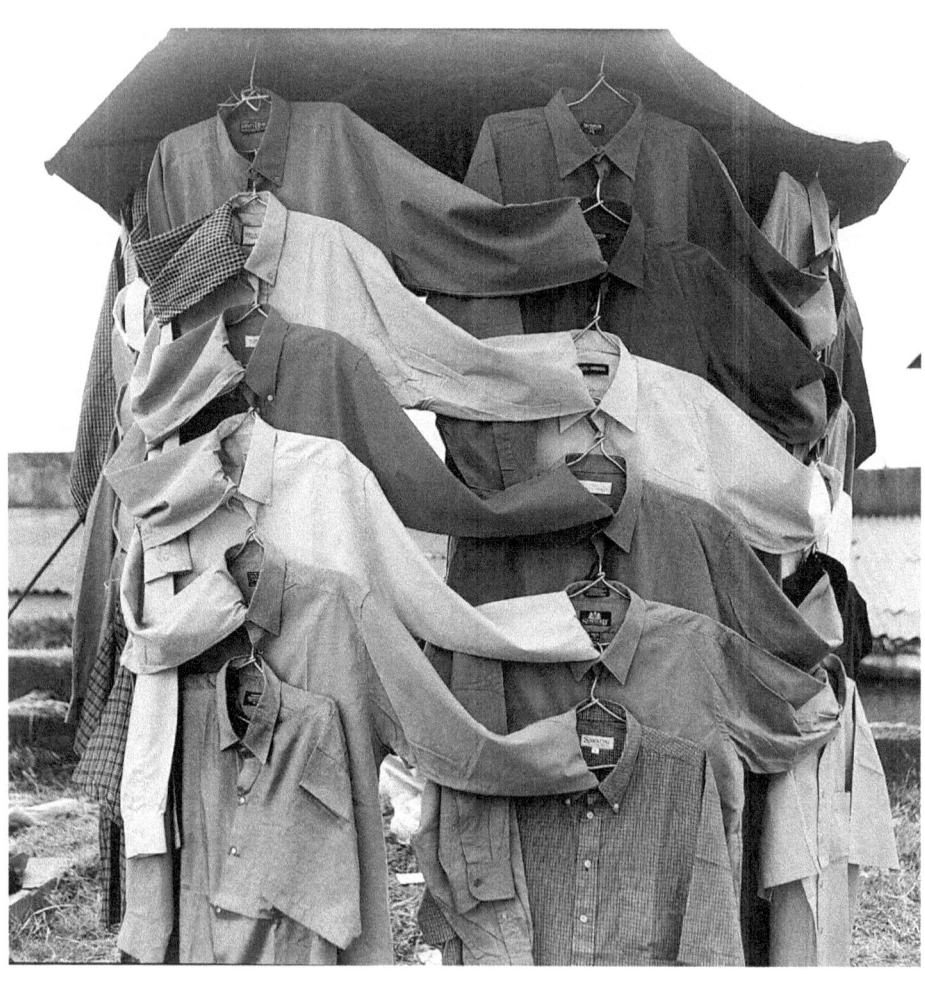

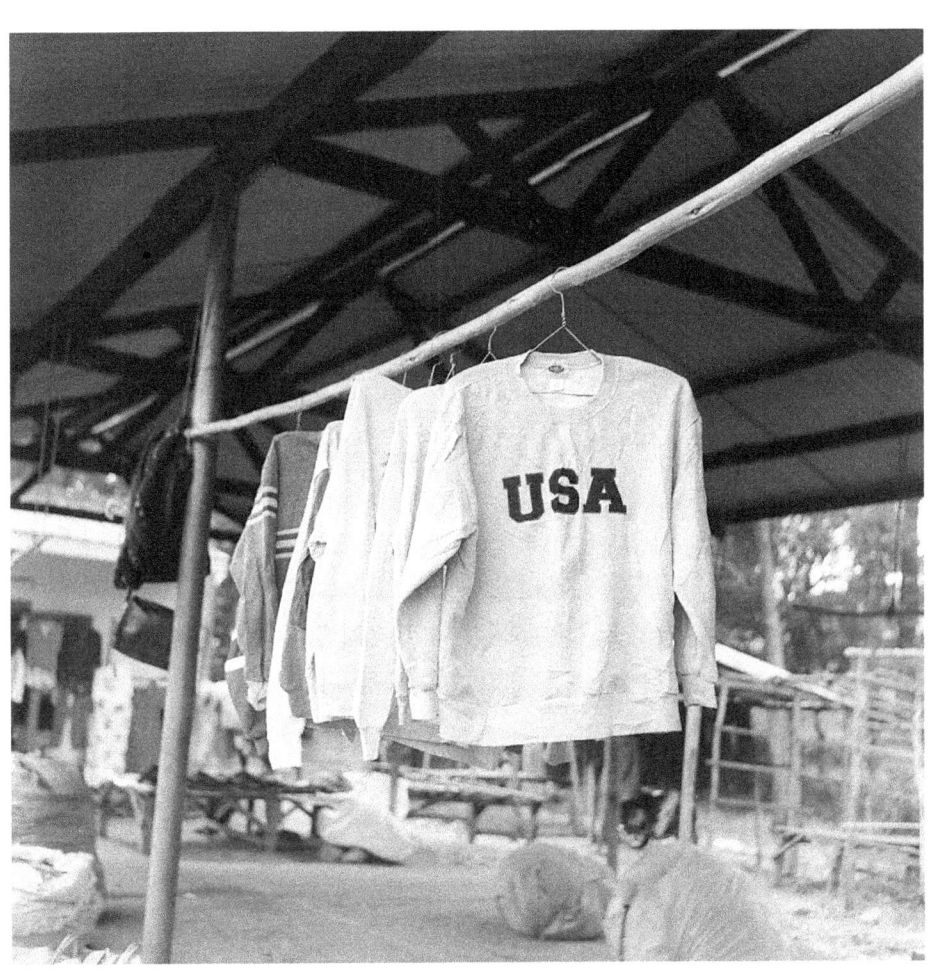

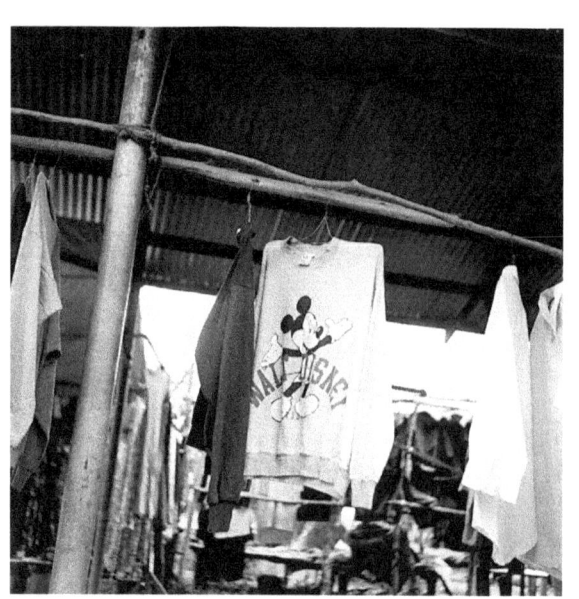

same postcolonialist regime of economic oppression is one of *Analogue*'s lessons, a lesson both learned and taught.

There remains, however, an instructive difference between the ways the signs for these global corporate behemoths are imaged in *Analogue*. In Uganda the squared-off format of the Rolleiflex is in place. Rooted firmly to the ground, the photographer shows us the uniformity of Coke's trademark, assembled in a collage-like style, one that is in keeping, despite the bright white teeth of its model, with the bricoleur tendencies exhibited in the presentation of the clothes and the hand-painted signs directing one toward the trade in bundles and used clothes. In the States, however, these logos are seen from the window of a moving car. Tilting vertiginously in an expanse of blue sky, they appear to slide out of the frame, unable to hold center court. Leonard refers to these images as "drive-bys," which is an innocent enough description of the process through which they were made, although it is hard not to be struck by the double entendre of the phrase, redolent as it is with the violence of American urban crime. In these images the camera is no longer located near the sternum of the artist's body, as if the alienation of this kind of corporate production and consumption can only be imaged in a mimetic state of disembodiment.

These skyscapes, with their fleeting avatars of enormous global power masquerading as so many aleatory stops on the way, punctuate *Analogue,* acting as dingbats in a story ostensibly about something else.

Analogue ends with a coda of sorts. One last grid of closed shops returns us to New York, returns us to the inevitably cyclical nature of exchange, returns us to a city littered with the relics of the past and shot through with the complications of the present, returns us to a geographical place, a nation state, a global economy, within which it is increasingly difficult to live one's daily life according to one's own internal moral or ethical code. Indeed, *Analogue* in many ways is an attempt to articulate the space in between the forces of extraordinary loss and plentitude where so many find themselves at the beginning of the twenty-first century.

NOTE

1 Appadurai, *The Social Life of Things,* 3.

PART 3: AFTERWORLDS

THE POSTCOLONIAL CONSTELLATION:

CONTEMPORARY ART IN A STATE OF

PERMANENT TRANSITION

OKWUI ENWEZOR

The proper task of a history of thought is: to define the conditions in which human beings
"problematize" what they are, what they do, and the world in which they live.
—Michel Foucault, *The History of Sexuality*

This flood of convergences, publishing itself in the guise of the commonplace. No longer
is the latter an accepted generality, suitable and dull—no longer is it deceptively obvious, exploiting common sense—it is, rather, all that is relentlessly and endlessly reiterated by
these encounters.
—Édouard Glissant, *Poetics of Relation*

I.

It is a commonplace of current historical thinking about globalization to say
there are no vantage points from which to observe any particular culture because the very processes of globalization have effectively abolished the temporal
and spatial distances that previously separated cultures.[1] Similarly, globalization is viewed as the most developed mode, the ultimate structure of the singularization, standardization, and homogenization of culture in the service of
instruments of advanced capitalism and neoliberalism. In the face of such
totalization, what remains of the critical forces of production which, through-

out the modern era, placed strong checks on the submergence of all subjective protocols to the orders of a singular organizing ideology, be it the state or the market? If globalization has established, categorically, the proximity of cultures, can the same be said about globalization and art? When we ask such questions, we must remember that the critical division between culture and art has, for centuries, been marked by art's waging of a fierce battle for independence from all cultural, social, economic, and political influences.

At the same time, the modern Western imagination has used the apotropaic devices of containment and desublimation to perceive other cultures, in order to feed off their strange aura and hence displace their power. Today, the nearness of those cultures calls for new critical appraisals of our contemporary present and its relationship to artistic production.

I start with these observations in order to place in proper context the current conditions of production, dissemination, and reception of contemporary art. Contemporary art today is refracted, not just from the specific site of culture and history but also—and in a more critical sense—from the standpoint of a complex geopolitical configuration that defines all systems of production and relations of exchange as a consequence of globalization after imperialism. It is this geopolitical configuration, its postimperial transformations, that situates what I call here "the postcolonial constellation." Changes wrought by transitions to new forms of governmentality and institutionality, new domains of living and belonging as people and citizens, cultures and communities—these define the postcolonial matrix that shapes the ethics of subjectivity and creativity today. Whereas classical European thought formulated the realm of subjectivity and creativity as two domains of activity, each informed by its own internal cohesion—without an outside, as it were—such thought today is consistently questioned by the constant tessellation of the outside and inside, each folding into the other, each opening out to complex communicative tremors and upheavals. Perhaps, then, to bring contemporary art into the context of the geopolitical framework that defines global relations—between the so-called local and the global, center and margin, nation-state and the individual, transnational and diasporic communities, audiences and institutions—would offer a perspicacious view of the postcolonial constellation. The constellation is not, however, made up solely of the dichotomies named above. Overall, it is a set of arrangements of deeply entangled relations and forces that are founded by discourses of power. These are geopolitical in nature and, by extension, can be civilizational in their reliance on binary oppositions between cultures. In this sense, they are inimical to any transcultural understanding of the present context of cultural production. Geopolitical power arrangements appear in the artistic context along much the same Maginot line. The terrible tear at the core of these arrangements lends contact between different artistic cultures an air of civilizational distinctions predicated on tensions between the developed and the underdeveloped, the reactionary and the progressive, the regressive and the advanced, shading into the avant-garde and the outmoded. This type of discourse is a heritage of classical modernity, which, through these distinctions, furnishes the dialectical and ideological agenda for competition and hegemony often found in the spaces of art and culture.

The current artistic context is constellated around the norms of the postcolonial, those based on discontinuous, aleatory forms, on creolization, hybridization, and so forth, all of these tendencies operating with a specific cosmopolitan accent. These norms are not relativistic, despite their best efforts to displace certain stubborn values that have structured the discourse of Western Modernism and determined its power over Modernisms elsewhere in the world. Édouard Glissant, whose classic work *Caribbean Discourse* made us aware of the tremor at the roots of the postcolonial order, interprets the current understanding of global modernity as essentially a phenomenon of the creolization of cultures. He shows us that in global processes of movement, resettlement, recalibration, certain changes and shifts in modalities of cultural transformations occur, changes that by necessity are neither wholly universal nor essentially particular. Contemporary culture, for Glissant, is cross-cultural, reconstituting itself as a "flood of convergences publishing itself in the guise of the commonplace."[2] In the modern world, he intimates, all subjectivities emerge directly from the convergences and proximities wrought by imperialism. Today, they direct us to the postcolonial. The current history of Modern art, therefore, sits at the intersection between imperial and postcolonial discourses. Any critical interest in the exhibition systems of Modern or contemporary art requires us to refer to the foundational base of modern art history: its roots in imperial discourse, on the one hand, and, on the other, the pressures that postcolonial discourse exerts on its narratives today.

From its inception, the history of Modern art has been inextricably bound to the history of its exhibitions, both in its commodity function through collectors in the economic sphere and in its iconoclasm evidenced by the assaults on formalism by the historical avant-garde. It could, in fact, be said that no significant change in the direction of Modern art occurred outside the framework of the public controversies generated by its exhibitions.[3] Fundamental to the historical understanding of Modern art is the important role played through the forum and medium of exhibitions in explicating the trajectory taken by artists, their supporters, critics, and the public in identifying the great shifts that have marked all encounters with Modern art and advanced its claim for enlightened singularity amongst other cultural avatars. For contemporary art, this history is no less true, and the recent phenomenon of the curator in shaping this history has been remarkable. Nevertheless, a number of remarkable mutations in the growing discourse of exhibitions have occurred. At the same time, art has been persistently presented as something wholly autonomous and separate from the sphere of other cultural activities. Exhibitions have evolved from being primarily the presentation of singular perspectives on certain types of artistic development to become the frightening *Gesammtkunstwerk* evident in the global megaexhibitions that seem to have overtaken the entire field of contemporary artistic production. If we are to judge correctly the proper role of the curator in this state of affairs, the exhibition as form, genre, or medium, as a communicative, dialogical forum of conversation between heterogeneous actors, publics, objects, and so on, needs careful examination.

2.

Today, most exhibitions and curatorial projects of contemporary art are falling under increasing scrutiny and attack. More specifically, they have been called into question by two types of commentary. The first is generalist and speculative in nature. Fascinated by contemporary art as novelty, consumed by affects of reification as a pure image and object of exhibitionism, with spectacle culture, such commentary is itself sensationalist, and lacks critical purpose. It tends to equate the task of an exhibition with entertainment, fashion, and the new thrills and discoveries that seasonally top up the depleted inventory of the "new." It haunts the response to so-called megaexhibitions such as documenta, biennales, triennales, and festivals, as well as commercial gallery exhibitions of the omnibus type. It easily grows bored with any exhibition that lacks the usual dosage of concocted outrage and scandal. Impatient with historical exegesis, it contents itself with the phantasmagoric transition between moments of staged disenchantment and the incessant populist renewal of art.

The second type of commentary is largely institutional, divided between academic and museological production. It is one part nostalgic and one part critical. Adopting the tone of a buttoned-up, mock severity, it is actually based on a pseudocritical disaffection with what it sees as the consummation achieved between art and spectacle, between the auguries of pop-cultural banality and an atomized avant-garde legacy. For this kind of commentary, art has meaning and cultural value only when it is seen wholly as art, as autonomous. On this view, every encounter with art must be a scientific, not a cultural, one, the priority being to understand the objective conditions of the work in question. In modernity, the inner logic of the work of art is marked by art's removal from the realm of the social-life world that positions it as an object of high culture. Yet there is a price to be paid when it wins its autonomy from any accreted social or ideological baggage. For critics with this viewpoint, the task of the curator is to pay the greatest possible fidelity to a restrained formal diligence in artworks, one derived from values inculcated and transmitted by tradition, a flow that can only be interrupted through a necessary disjuncture, one marked by innovation. The paradox of a disjunctive innovation that simultaneously announces its allegiance and affinity to the very tradition it seeks to displace is a commonplace in the entire history of Modernism, especially in the discourse of the avant-garde.

For curators and art historians the central problematic between art and the avant-garde occurs when there is a breach in the supposed eternality of values that flow from antiquity to the present, when the autonomy of art suddenly has to contend with the reality of the secular, democratic public sphere—itself the result of a concatenation of many traditions.[4] Even more problematic are breaches in the very conditions of artistic production. One example is what has been called elsewhere the "Duchamp effect"; another is highlighted in Walter Benjamin's much-referenced essay "The Work of Art in the Age of Mechanical Reproduction," which famously traced the changes in the dissemination of art that transform and question traditional notions of originality and aura.[5] Yet another is the encounter between modern European artists and the African and Oceanic sculptures at the turn of the twentieth century, one that resulted in the birth of cubism and much else.

Of these, the Duchamp effect was the most traditional view, because what it purports to do is delineate the supremacy of the artist: the artist as not only a form giver but also a name giver. It is the artist who decides what an object of art is or what it can be, rather than the decision being a result of progressive, formal transformation of the medium of art. For Duchamp, it is not tradition, but the artist who not only decides what the work of art is but also controls its narrative of interpretation. This idea found its final culmination in the tautological exercises of conceptual art, whereby the physical fabrication of art could, ostensibly, be replaced with linguistic description. From this perspective, artistic genius emerges from a subjective critique of tradition by the artist, against all other available data, not from an objective analysis of the fallacy of tradition.

The confrontation with African and Oceanic sculptures by European artists was a striking example from the "contact zone" of cultures.[6] This encounter transformed the pictorial and plastic language of modern European painting and sculpture, hence deeply affecting its tradition. What is astonishing is the degree to which the artistic challenges posed by so-called primitive art to twentieth-century European Modernism have subsequently been assimilated and subordinated to modernist totalization. Therein lies the fault line between imperial and postcolonial discourse, for to admit to the paradigmatic breach produced by the encounter between African sculptures and European artists would also be to question the narrative of modern art history. Nor should we forget that the non-Western objects in question were required to shed their utilitarian function and undergo a conversion from ritual objects of magic into reified objects of art. The remarkable import of this conversion is that the historical repercussion of the encounter has remained mostly confined to formal effects and thus formalist aesthetic analysis.

I cite these examples because they are material to our reading and judgment of contemporary art. The entrance into art of historically determined questions of form, content, strategy, cultural difference, and so on establishes a ground from which to view art and the artists' relationship to the institutions of art today. This breach is now visible, because it no longer refers to the eternal past of pure objects, nor to the aloofness from society necessary for autonomy to have any meaning. In his *Theory of the Avant-Garde* Peter Bürger makes this point clear: "If the autonomy of art is defined as art's independence from society, there are several ways of understanding that definition. Conceiving of art's apartness from society as its 'nature' means involuntarily adopting the *l'art pour l'art* concept of art and simultaneously making it impossible to explain this apartness as the product of a historical and social development."[7]

The concept of *l'art pour l'art* as part of the avant-garde formulation of artistic autonomy was described by Benjamin as a *theology of art,* which "gave rise to what might be called a negative theology in the form of the idea of 'pure' art, which . . . denied any social function of art."[8] Based on this denial, Bürger's analysis advances a claim for a socially determined theory that stands at the root of two opposing traditions of art historical thought found amongst certain key practitioners today. Not surprisingly, the two opposing traditions match the rivalry discernible in the second type of commentary on curatorial procedures mentioned earlier. This is the domain most struggled over by conservative (traditionalist) and liberal (progressive) groups, both of whom have increasingly come to abjure any social function of art, except when it fits certain theories.

Two recent examples will demonstrate my point here. A roundtable discussion on the state of art criticism in 2000, published in the one-hundredth issue of the influential art journal *October,* was typically reductive.[9] Although the panelists' attack against certain populist types of criticism was indeed cogent and necessary, one could not help but detect a tone of condescension in their irritation. The composition of the speakers of the roundtable was illustrative of the way in which the modes of elision and discrimination that are recurrent in most mainstream institutions and conservative academies pervade even this self-styled progressive intellectual organ. It is, of course, universally known, that this journal, despite its revolutionary claims, remains staunchly and ideologically committed to a defense of Modernism as it has been historically elaborated within the European context and updated in postwar American art. There is nothing inherently wrong with such commitment, were it not elevated to the height of being the universal paradigm for the in fact uneven, diachronic experience of modernity. There is very little acknowledgment of the radical political strategies and social and cultural transformations developed since the decolonization projects of the postwar period outside the West. These have shaped the reception of Modernism in the work of artists outside of Europe and North America, as well as that of many within these spheres. To ignore or downplay this, after one hundred issues of continuous publication, is a grave error.

The second example highlights the conservatism of traditional museums of Modern art in their treatment of Modernism. For its opening in 2000, the Tate Modern museum presented an overarching curatorial viewpoint, one that straddles a large expanse of historical developments in Modern art. The relationships between Modern art and the European artistic tradition, and between contemporary art and its modernist heritage, were central. To demonstrate these relationships and at the same time transform the methodology for rendering them in a public display, the museum moved actively between a synchronic and diachronic ordering of its message. The press was filled with speculation about the effectiveness of the museum's "radical" attempt to break with the outmoded chronological emphasis of modernist art history, its effort to inaugurate a far more dialectical exchange and adopt a discursive approach, above all in the display of the permanent collection, which was arranged according to genre, subject matter, and formal affinities. The goal was to present the history of Modern art and the transformations within it in a way that would be readily read by the general public, especially if, for example, a Monet landscape were demonstrated to be an immediate ancestor to the stone circle sculptures and mud wall paintings of Richard Long. What are we to make of this juxtaposition? It shows us, certainly, that both Monet and Long are deeply interested in nature as a source for their art. It could also evoke for the viewer aspects of spirituality and the metaphysical often connected to nature, as well as the conception of landscape as a genre of art from which artists have often drawn. Despite being a curatorial gimmick, these are interesting enough propositions for the average, unschooled museum visitor.

The rooms housing the permanent collection were divided into four themes: Still Life/Object/Real Life, Nude/Action/Body, History/Memory/Society, Landscape/Matter/Environment. The decisive idea was to break with a conception of modernist historiography entrenched at the Museum of Modern Art in New York since its founding more than seventy years before. Never mind that many professional visitors, namely curators and historians, whispered that this apparent boldness owed more to the lack of depth in its collection of Modern art than any radical attempt to redefine how the history of Modern art was to be adjudicated and read publicly. The rooms were divided, like stage sets, into the four themes, such that they read much like chapters in a textbook. The resultant sense of Modern art's undisturbed progression—absent the contradictions, frictions, resistance, and changes that confound and challenge conventional ideas of Modernism—is in itself a historical conceit. Anything that might challenge this most undialectical of approaches was sublated and absorbed into the yawning maws of the Tate Modern's self-authorizing account.

One example, and by far the most troubling, of the curatorial reasoning behind this account will suffice. The Nude/Action/Body theme suggests a series of transformations in the manner in which the body has been used in Modern and contemporary art. The series of passages from *nude* to *action* to *body* suggest an image of contingency, internal shifts in the development and understanding of the human form and subjectivity as it moves from Modern to contemporary art. The image that presides over this shift is corporeal and mechanical, symbolic and functional, artistic and political, from the *nude* as an ideal to the *body* as a desiring machine.

The first gallery opens out to an eclectic selection of paintings by Stanley Spencer, John Currin, Picasso, and others. This is not an auspicious introduction. The selection and arrangement of the works in the gallery is striking, but more for its formal sensibility than in authoritatively setting out any radical thesis of the nude and the body. In the second gallery two large-scale, genuinely imposing, black-and-white photographic works, one by Craigie Horsfield and the other by John Coplans, face each other. Horsfield's picture *E. Horsfield (1987)* (1995) is in the tradition of classical modernist reclining nudes reminiscent of Cézanne's bathers and Matisse's odalisques. It is an outstanding, ponderous picture, heavy like fruit, with the graded tones of gray lending the mass of flesh a stately presence. Coplans's *Self-Portrait (Frieze No. 2, Four Panels)* (1995) is typical of his performative and fragmentary, multipaneled, serial self-portraiture, often representing his flabby, aging body. The seriality of the depicted parts reveals a body seemingly laying claim to its own sentient properties. Formal echoes of the nude from its early modernist treatments of the nude are to be found in contemporary photography, but the difference between the two lies in the idealization of the former and the self-conscious subjectivity of the latter. Modernist photography of the nude focused on forces of nature trapped in classical culture, whereas the contemporary nude is closer in spirit to Deleuze and Guattari's notion of the desiring machine consumed in the process of expressing itself.[10]

When we enter the next gallery, we find a small ethnographic vitrine embedded into one of the walls of the room. To the left is a discreetly placed LCD monitor playing extracts from two films; one by Michel Allégret and André Gide, *Voyage to the Congo,* 1928, the other an anonymous archival film, *Manners and Customs of Senegal,* 1910. The two extracts evince a theme common to travel documentary. Although temporally and spatially separated, we can place these two films within a well-known genre, in the system of knowledge that belongs to the discourse of colonial, ethnographic film studies of "primitive" peoples. (We already know much about the Western modernist fascination with "primitive" peoples' bodies, along with their Orientalist correlatives. We know that the concept of alterity was not only important for Western Modernism; it was also a focus of allegorical differentiation.) Allégret and Gide's film, and the more structurally open archival footage, provide us with much to think about in regard to Modernism, spectacle, otherness, and degeneracy. In each of the two films, we see the setting of the African village and its social life: villagers self-consciously working on their everyday chores such as grinding grain, tending fires, minding children, or participating in a village festival of dance and song. Most striking about Allégret and Gide's film, however, is that it highlights nakedness; the nakedness of black African bodies under imperial observation. Here, nakedness as opposed to nudity yields a structure of critical differentiation between the primitive and the Modern, between the savage and the civilized, between ideas of nature and culture.

The method of the camera work in both films appears to be objective, aiming to show "primitive peoples" as they are, in their natural space. Nevertheless, one can detect that part of its conscious structure was to show the degree to which primitive man is not to be confused with the modern man. This differentiation lends what we are viewing a quality not of empathy exactly, but, as James Clifford puts it, "a more disquieting quality of Modernism: its taste for appropriating or redeeming otherness, for constituting non-Western arts in its own image, for discovering universal, ahistorical 'human' capacities."[11] This observation, taken *in toto* with Modernism's relationship to other-

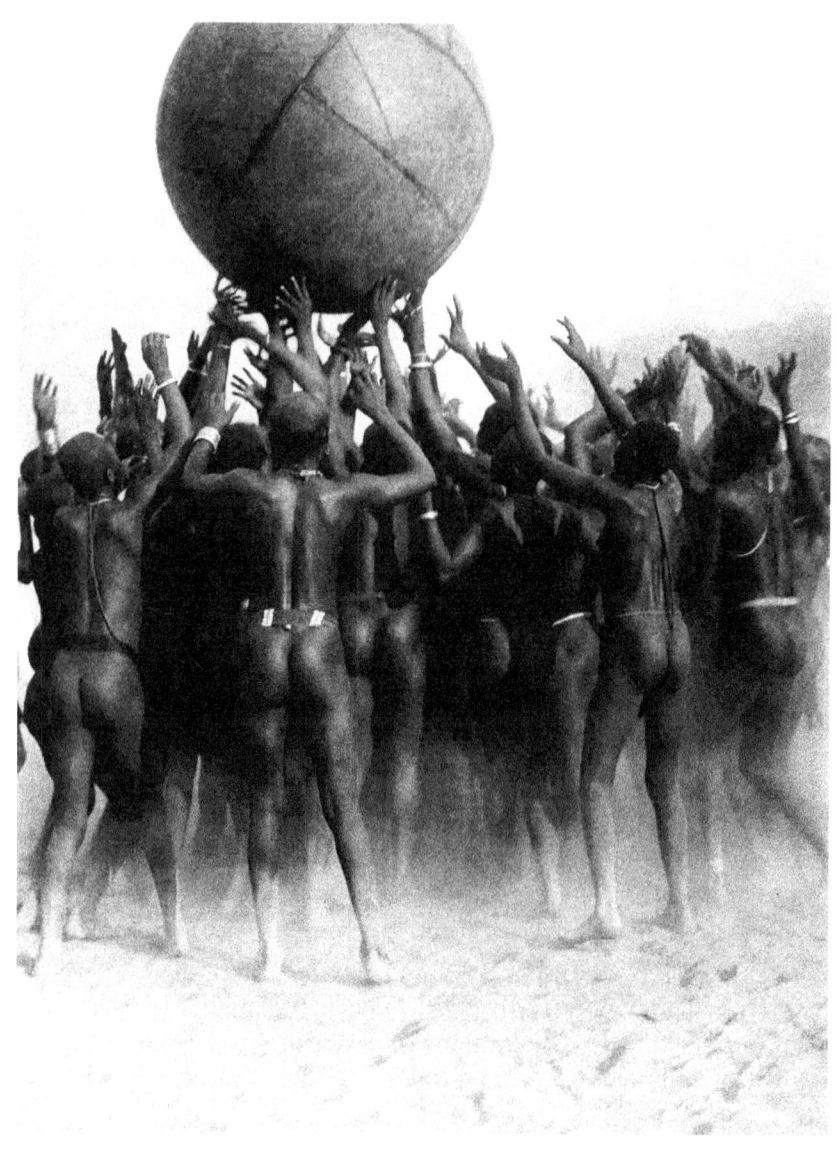

Michel Allégret and André Gide, *Voyage to the Congo,* 1928. Film still. Public domain.

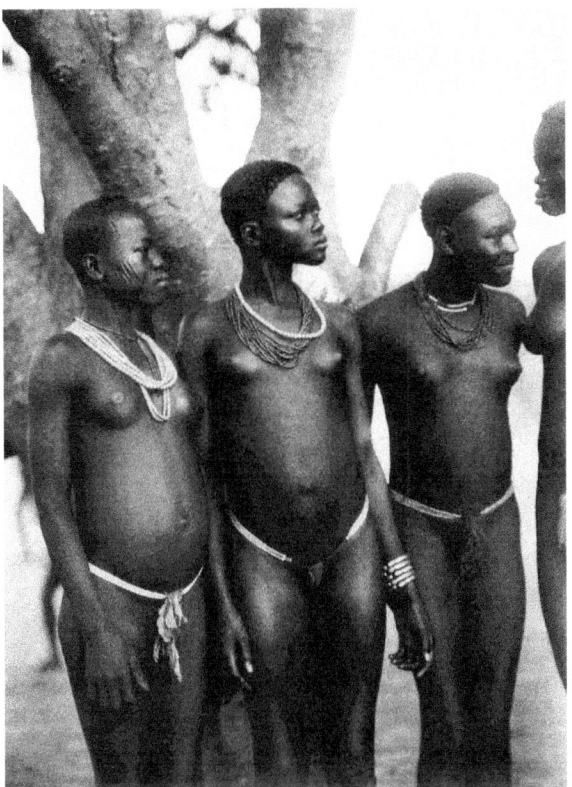

Michel Allégret and André Gide, *Voyage to the Congo,* 1928. Film still.
Public domain.

ness, the primitive and the savage, bears on the distinction between the nude's
formal, aesthetic status within Western modernist art and the picturing of
simple nakedness with no redeeming aesthetic value commonly found in ethnographic discourse.

If the Tate Modern were an institution working beyond the smug reflex of
Western museological authority it would have found right in its own context
artists such as Rotimi Fani-Kayode, the Nigerian-British photographer whose
work—formally and conceptually—involves a long, rigorous excursus into the
distinction between the nude and nakedness as it concerns the African body.
The analytic content, not to say the formal and aesthetic contradictions that
Fani-Kayode's photographic work introduces us to about the black body in
contrast to the modernist nude is quite telling. More substantial is its awareness
of the conflicted relationship the black body has to Western representation and
its museum discourse.[12] This makes the absence of works like his in the Nude/

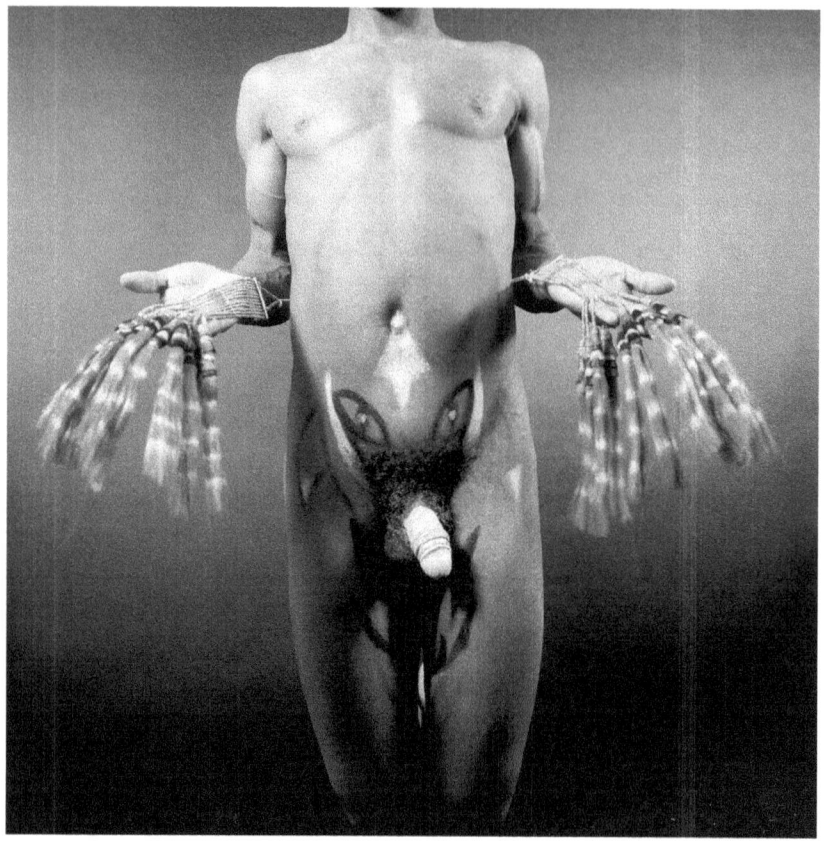

Rotimi Fani-Kayode, *Untitled,* 1987–88. Photograph. Courtesy of the artist.

Action/Body section of the Tate Modern the more glaring. Many other practitioners deal with these issues, but Fani-Kayode is important for my analysis for the more specific reason of his Africanness, his conceptual usage of that Africanness in his imagery, and his subversion of the fraught distinction between nakedness and the nude in his photographic representation. Fani-Kayode's pictures also conceive of the black body (in his case the black male body with its homoerotic inferences) as a vessel for idealization, as a desiring and desirable subject, and as self-conscious in the face of the reduction of the black body as pure object of ethnographic spectacle. All these critical turns in his work make the Tate Modern's inattention to strong, critical work on the nude and the body by artists such as he all the more troubling, because it is precisely works like his that have brought to crisis those naturalized conventions of otherness that throughout the history of modern art have been the stock-in-trade of Modernism.

Whatever its excuses for excluding some of these artists from its presenta-

tion, there are none for Tate Modern's monologue on the matter of the ethnographic films. Alongside the screen, the wall label expounds on the matter of
the films' presence in the gallery, uttering its explanation in a characteristic
double-speak: "European audiences in the early 20th century gained experience
of Africa through documentary films. Generally these conformed to stereo-
typed notions about African cultures. An ethnographic film of 1910, for instance, concentrates on the skills and customs of the Senegalese, while *Voyage to
the Congo,* by filmmaker Marc Allégret and writer André Gide perpetuates
preconceptions about life in the 'bush.' However, the self-awareness displayed
by those under scrutiny, glimpsed observing the filmmakers subverts the supposed objectivity of the film."

These words impute both the manufacture and consumption of the stereotype to some previous era of European documentary films and audiences,
which is to imply that the business of such stereotypes lies in the past, even if it
has now been exhumed before a contemporary European audience for the
purposes of explaining Modernism's penchant for deracinating the African
subject. But if the discourse of the stereotype is now behind us, is its resuscitation an act of mimicry, or is it, as Homi Bhabha has written elsewhere, an act of
anxious repetition of the stereotype that folds back into the logic for excluding
African artists in the gallery arrangement as a whole?[13] Does the repetition of
the stereotype—caught, if you will, in a discursive double-maneuver—posit an
awareness of the problem of the stereotype for contemporary transnational
audiences? Or does the museum's label present us with a more profound question in which the wall text causally explains and masks what is absent in the
historical reorganization of the museum's memory cum history? One conclusion can be drawn from this unconvincing explanatory maneuver: more than
anything it entrenches European modernist appropriation and instrumentalization of Africa into the primitivist discourse of which the Tate Modern in the
twenty-first century is a logical heir.

As we go deeper into the matter, our investigation has much to yield as we
look further into the ethnographic desublimation (an uneasy conjunction, no
doubt, between colonialism and Modernism) taking place in the museum.
Beside the film screen, inside the vitrines, we find, casually scattered, postcards
with the general title "Postcards from West Africa," and a small, dark, figurative
sculpture, untitled, undated, identified simply as *Standing Figure.* The label tells
us of the sculpture's provenance: it is from the collection of Jacob Epstein, thus
conveying to us the sculpture's aesthetic aura through the synecdoche of ownership. The implication is obvious: the ownership of such a sculpture by one of
Britain's important modernist artists means that he must have appreciated the

sculpture first and foremost as a work of art, for the important aesthetic qualities that recommend it to the modern European sculptor. But if this is so, why then is the sculpture not more properly displayed along with other sculptures installed in the gallery? Or does its namelessness and authorlessness disable it from entering into the domain of aesthetic judgment necessary for its inclusion as an authoritative work of art?

It is no use speaking about the lyrical beauty and artistic integrity of this powerful sculpture, now so pointlessly compromised by the rest of the detritus of colonial knowledge system crammed in the vitrine. The sculpture's presence is not only remote from us, it seems to connote, not art, above all not autonomous art, but merely the idea of artifact or, worse still, evidence. Nearly a hundred years after the initial venture by Western modernists (and I do not care which artist "discovered" what qualities in African or Oceanic art first), it should have been clear enough to the curators at Tate Modern that in terms of sheer variety of styles, forms, genres, plastic distinctiveness, stylistic inventiveness, and complexity of sculptural language, no region in the world approaches the depth and breadth of African sculptural traditions. In the Congo, from where Gide and Allégret gave us deleterious impressions of their *voyage,* we find distinct traditions of sculpture such as Yombe, Luba, Mangbetu, Kuba, Teke, Lega, Songye, and Dengese. These traditions of sculpture—like many others— are as distinctly unique as they are historically different in their morphological conception of sculpture. The expressive and conceptual possibilities in the language of artists working within each group have produced sculptural forms of extraordinary anthropomorphic variety and complexity. Whether of the mask or figure, the statue or relief, a simple comparative study between them yields the active field of artistic experimentation and invention that many a modernist recognized, understood, and appreciated. But this is not communicated at all in the lugubrious gathering at the museum. What this installation communicates is neither a history nor even a proper anthropology of Modernism. Rather, the task of this "historical" instruction is more the repetition of what has become a convention in a variety of museums of Modern art. This type of instruction more obfuscates than enlightens. In fact, along with museum collections, most Western modernist museology is predicated on the repetition and circulation of disparate apocrypha and objects connected to this obfuscation.[14]

The very idea that there might be an African conception of modernity does not even come up. Nor does the possibility that between Western modernist artists in correspondence with their African contemporaries there existed and now exists an affiliative spirit of mutual influence and recognition. Instead, the vitrines as a whole posit a mode of instruction as to what is modern and what is not. On display are Carl Einstein's well-known book *NegerPlastik* and Marcel Griaulle's accounts of the Dakar-Djibouti expedition published in the journal *Minotaure*, contemporary to Michel Lieris's famous book *L'Afrique Fantome*. This is a pantomime of "the Modern" opposed to "the primitive," which the Tate Modern has now upgraded to the most astonishing form of ethnographic ventriloquism. Having emptied and hollowed out the space of African aesthetic traditions, the rest of the gallery was filled in—with customary care and reverence—with carefully installed, "autonomous" sculptures by Brancusi and Giacometti, and paintings by the German expressionists Karl Rotluff and Ludwig Ernst Kirschner. A Kirschner painting of a cluster of nude figures with pale elongated limbs and quasi-cubist, conical, distended midsections is noteworthy and striking in its anthropomorphic resemblance and formal correspondence to both the sculpture in the vitrine and what we had been looking at in the film of the naked Congolese women and children in Gide and Allégret's film.

Given the large literature on the subject, one should take Tate Modern to task by asking whether it could not have found African artists from whatever period to fit into their dialectical scheme? The evidence emphatically suggests a larger number of candidates. The reality is that they did not do so. Not because they could not, but most likely because they felt no obligation to stray from the modern museum's traditional curatorial exclusions. So much for the claim to be mounting a dialectical display, as indicated by the titles of the rooms. In fact, what was concretely conveyed was an untroubled attitude, a singular point of view, a sense of sovereign judgment.

We should, nonetheless, concede the fact that Tate Modern was merely operating on well-trodden ground. When, for example, Werner Spies reinstalled the galleries of the Centre Pompidou, Paris, in 1999, he applied a curatorial flourish to the museum's cache of modernist paintings and sculptures, mixing them with postwar and contemporary art while assigning classical African sculpture and masks to a garishly lit vitrine wedged into a hallway-like room. A more serious example of this sort was the curatorially important, widely influential, and superbly scholarly exhibition "Primitivism and Modern Art: Affinities of the Tribal and the Modern" of 1984–1985 at the Museum of Modern Art, New York, which treated the African and Oceanic works as it did the most highly refined modernist objects. But even this valuing of them as autonomous sculptures was achieved through a sense of reification that all but destroyed the important symbolic power of the objects and the role they played in their social contexts.

In 1989, Jean-Hubert Martin curated "Magiciens de la Terre" at the Centre

Pompidou, an exhibition that remains controversial. It set a different course in its response to the question that has vexed the modernist museum from its earliest inception, namely the status and place of non-Western art within the history of Modern and contemporary art. To evade this conundrum Martin elected to eliminate the word "artist" from his exhibition—mindful of the fact that such a designation may be unduly burdened by a Western bias—choosing instead the term *magicien* as the proper name for the object and image makers invited to present their art. If the MOMA and Centre Pompidou exhibitions—in New York and Paris respectively, two bastions of the history of Modern art in the world—responded critically to the controversial and unresolved aesthetic and historical debates within modernist accounts concerning art and artists from other cultures, Tate Modern, in its own attempt to further the rewriting of the modernist reception of the Other and of non-Western art, proved both unevolved and unreflexive. The entire installation was ahistorical, with no semblance of the critical content of what Habermas calls the "the philosophical discourse of modernity."[15] In fact, it was marked by a subjugation of historical memory, a savage act of epistemological and hermeneutic violence.

3.

If I have dwelt on elucidating this particular view it is only to frame what is at stake for artists and curators who step into the historical breach that has opened up today within the context of contemporary art. As regards modernist historiography, that is another matter. But we do know that Modernism has many streams that do not all empty into the same basin. Equally evident is the fact that the rising tide of institutional interest in other accounts of artistic production will never lift all the boats into the dialectical position of tradition and continuity so beloved by museums such as the Tate Modern. This is the nub of the current skepticism toward a globalized reception of contemporary artistic practices from far-flung places with little historical proximity to the ideas transmitted from within the legacy of the Western historical avant-garde. In today's complex conditions, the legacy of the Western historical avant-garde seems inadequate to the job of producing a unified theory of contemporary art. Because of its restless, unfixed boundaries, its multiplicities, and the state of "permanent transition" within which it is practiced and communicated, contemporary art tends to be much more resistant to global totalization. Yet the last two decades have witnessed an exponential rise in the fortunes of curators, who, with their portmanteau of theories neatly arranged—befitting of their status as the enlightened bureaucrats of modernist totalization—travel the world scouring it for new signs of art to fill the historical breach.

Deftly packaged multicultural exhibitions seem, today, to be mere responses of convenience and strategy aimed at keeping at bay certain social forces that demand greater inclusion of art that reflects the complexity of societies in which museums exist. To be sure, the responses by museums and academies to the troubling questions of inclusion/exclusion have a historical basis, most obviously imperialism and colonialism. The rupture in continuity to which imperialism and colonialism subjected many cultures continues to have contemporary repercussions on matters such as taste and judgment. It provides many artists with an important point of disputation, and hones their capacities for figuring new values of truth within the field of contemporary art. Modern and contemporary art has demonstrated the utter impossibility of the one true judgment of art, however authoritative such judgment may seem to be.

It has long been recognized that postcolonial processes have increasingly highlighted the problematics of Western judgment over vast cultural fields in the non-Western world. Many curatorial practices today are direct responses to postcolonial critiques of Western authority. The conditions of production and reception of contemporary art evince a dramatic multiplication of its systems of articulation. This has occurred to such a degree that no singular judgment could contain all its peculiarities.

The curatorial responses to the contestations initiated both by postcolonialism and expanded definitions of art seem directed at assimilating certain historical effects that became clear only in the last three decades, especially in the 1980s and 1990s, and have accelerated since the late 1990s. I will delineate the five effects that, to me, are the most salient. They are outcomes not so much of the value system of the old world of Modernism but the postcolonial conditions of the contemporary world as such. Because modernist formalism has tended to respond to contemporary culture with hostility, the effects I am speaking of are marked, therefore, not so much by the speed of their transposition into networks and teleologies of organized totality (that is, they do not share the theology of universal history common to all modernist effects), rather, they are founded on the impermanent and aleatory. Impermanence here does not mean endless drift, or the evacuation of specificity. Rather, the structure of contemporary art's relationship to history is more transversal, asynchronous, and asystematic in nature, thereby revealing a multiplicity of cultural procedures. Contemporary art today cannot be defined by simple, singular models.

The first effect of contemporary complexity is the proliferation of exhibition forms—such as blockbusters, large-scale group or thematic exhibitions, cultural festivals, biennales, and so on—and their constant mutation. All of these have significantly enlarged the knowledge base of contemporary thinking about art and its commonplaces in museums and culture at large. This enlargement is crucial, because it has created new networks between hitherto separated spheres of contemporary artistic production, in both the everyday engagement with the world and its images, texts, and narratives, and in what I have called Modernism's dead certainties. Even though this phase is still in a developmental stage, it has already oriented the transmission of contemporary art discourses toward a deeper confrontation with what Carlos Basualdo has called the "new geographies of culture."[16] Curatorial and exhibition systems are confronted with the fact that all discourses are located, that is, they are formed and begin somewhere, they have a temporal and spatial basis, and they operate synchronically and diachronically. The located nature of cultural discourses, along with their history of discontinuities and transitions, confronts curatorial practices with the fragility of universalized conceptions of history, culture, and artistic procedures.

The second effect initially appeared as an allegory of transformation and transfiguration, then subsequently as a mode of resistance and repetition. It is easy to underestimate today the force of the dissolution of colonialism on art and culture until we realize that, not so long ago—barely half a century—the majority of the globe (covering almost two-thirds of the earth's surface and numbering more than a billion people) were places and peoples without proper political rights. Now, with the decay of colonial state structures, it is again easy enough to mock the utopian aspirations of self-determination, liberation from colonialism, and political independence that began to see off the imperial discourse that had characterized global modernity in its early phase. Indeed, global modernity powerfully sustained the plethora of fictions on which the idea of a national tradition in art and culture was founded. In the guise of the modern nation-state, it furnished the political identity of the modern artist, and continues, by and large, to do so. Decolonization and national identity, therefore, represent the bookends of two concomitant projects of late global modernity. On the one hand, decolonization portends to restore sundered traditions to their "proper" pasts, whilst national identity through the state works assiduously to reinvent and maintain them in the present and for the future. This is what has been called the roadmap to nation building and modernization. Decolonization, qua the postcolonial, transforms the subject of cultural discourse, while the nation-state reinvents the identity of the artist and transfigures the order of tradition for posterity. If the mode of the postcolonial is resistance and insubordination through transformation, that of the nation is consolidation and repetition through transfiguration. Out of each, the figure of the new becomes the emulsifier for either tradition and restoration, or tradition and continuity. The antinomies of the Modern and contemporary can be plainly seen. Contemporary curatorial practice is keenly aware of the uses, abuses, and usefulness inherent in this situation.

Nowhere is this discourse more palpable than in the fiery debates concerning cultural identity. Representation becomes not merely the name for a manner of practice, but, quite literally, the name for a political awareness of identity within the field of representation. In the context of decolonized representation, innovation is as much about the coming to being of new relations to cultures and histories, to rationalization and transformation, to transculturation and assimilation, and new practices and processes, new kinds of exchange and moments of multiple dwelling as it is about the ways artists are seen to be bound to their national and cultural traditions. Here, political community and cultural community become essentially coterminous. As well, beyond nationalism and national cultures, decolonization is more than just the forlorn daydream of the postcolonial artist or intellectual, for it has, attached to it, something recognizable in the ideals of modernity: the notion of progress. In the postcolonial constellation, therefore, the new in art has different kinds of self-affirmative content.

How does this square with the postmodern critique of what is derogatively referred to as "identity-based" or "multicultural" art? Notice the conflation of the terms: identity and multiculturalism. The weakness of all identity-based discourse, we were told, lay in its self-contradiction, in its attempt to conflate the universal and the particular, self and other, into the social site of artistic production. Another critique saw identity-based practices as presuming cultural and political grounds that were too reductive and simplistic, specific and limited; and, because of their incapacity to deal with abstraction, incapable of transcending that specificity and aspiring to universal culture. Commenting on the fragmentation of modernist totalization introduced by Postmodernism, art historian Hal Foster posed the following questions: "Is this fragmentation an illusion, an ideology of its own (of political 'crisis,' say, versus historical 'contradiction')? Is it a symptom of a cultural 'schizophrenia' to be deplored? Or is it, finally, the sign of a society in which difference and discontinuity rightly challenge ideas of totality and continuity?"[17]

Putting aside for the moment the fact that identity-based discourses have been eviscerated, are we to take it that identity discourse—understood in all of its oppositionality, contingency, and discontinuity—is the specter that haunts Modernism? Further, was there a false consciousness in the belief that identity-based discourses, along with their multicultural correlatives, working in alliance with postmodernism's critique of grand narratives and universal history (including those elaborations on paradigms of asymmetrical power relations unleashed by postcolonial studies), could bring about the possibility of a decentered global cultural order? Certainly, global culture is thoroughly decentered, but its power can hardly be said to be contained. Through an unsentimental reading of Marxism and cultural ideology, Foster offers a view that permits us to pursue this question. He writes of how:

> new social forces—women, blacks, other "minorities," gay movements, eco-logical groups, students—have made clear the unique importance of gender and sexual difference, race and the third world, the "revolt of nature" and the relation of power and knowledge, in such a way that the concept of class, if it is to be retained as such, must be articulated in relation to these terms. In response, theoretical focus has shifted from class as a subject of history to the cultural constitution of subjectivity, from economic identity to social differ-ence. In short, political struggle is now seen largely as a process of "differen-tial articulation."[18]

No museum or exhibition project, even if it might wish to avoid addressing the consequences of this "differential articulation," can remain critically blind to the importance of multicultural and identity-based practices, however wrong-headed and regressive they may appear. One guiding reason for this vigilance amongst cultural institutions has to do with both the politics of enlightened self-interest and the changing of the cultural and social demo-graphics of many contemporary societies due to large-scale immigrations of the twentieth century. In the case of the United States and Europe, the civil rights movement, antiracist movements, and the struggle for the protection of minor-ity rights have increased the level of this vigilance. There is also the recognition of the role of the market in the institutionalization of national identity in recent curatorial projects, especially in exhibitions designed to position certain na-tional or geographic contexts of artistic production. What is often elided in the excitation of these new national or geopolitical spaces, however, is the politics of national representation that recommends them through various national fund-ing and promotional boards, cultural foundations, and institutions.[19] Increas-ingly, curators have become highly dependent on the patronage of such institu-tions. The neoexpressionist market juggernaut of the late 1970s and 1980s led Benjamin Buchloh to identify a similar curatorial symptom, one that trades on the morbid cliché of national identity: "When art emphasizing national identity attempts to enter the international distribution system, the most worn-out historical and geopolitical clichés have to be employed. And thus we now see the resurrection of such notions as the Nordic versus the Mediterranean, the Teutonic versus the Latin."[20]

The third effect is the explosion of and the heterogeneous nature of artistic procedures immediately at variance with the historically conditioned, thereby conventional understanding of art within the logic of the museum. Such procedures have been theorized, quite correctly, as neoavant-garde, rather than as true ruptures from their academic obverse. However, it can be said that institutional canniness has often found inventive ways to absorb the energies of even the most insurrectional positions in art. The emergence of new critical forces has all too often become cashiered as another instance in the positivist ideology of advanced art's claim of *engagement* set forth by the institution.

The fourth effect results from the mediatization of culture, especially in the transformation of the museum form into the realm of the culture industry of mass entertainment, theatricality, and tourism. The most exact expression of the passage of museums into the concept of mass culture has been achieved through the fusion of architectural design and the museum's collection whereby the collection and architecture become one fully realized *Gesammtkunstwerk* and understood as such.[21] The fusion of the art collection with the architecture of the museum is as much a value-supplying feature as any other purpose. Out of town visitors can visit the Frank Lloyd Wright–designed Guggenheim Museum in New York or Frank Gehry's Guggenheim Bilbao, treating each as a unique work of art in its own right, or they may travel to see the buildings and visit the collections at the same time. Despite their universalist aspirations, most contemporary museums exist with the dark clouds of nationalism or ideologies of civic virtue hovering over them. Even if the aspiration of the museum is not specifically nationalist, in order to attract funding and state support, its discourse in today's competition between global cities must be decidedly nationalist in spirit.

The fifth effect, which I believe ultimately subtends the previous four, is the globalization of economic production and culture, and the technological and digital revolution that has fused them. Two factors about globalization make it fascinating in relation to this discussion: its limit and reach. While the compression of time and space is understood as one of the definitive aspects of the globalization of art and culture, the access of artists to its benefits is massively uneven. Having abandoned the values of "internationalism," there is now the idea in art discourse that the globalization of art opens the doors to greater understanding of the motivations that shape contemporary art across Europe, North America, Asia, Africa, South America, across the world at large. Paradoxically, it is globalization that has exposed the idea of a consolidated art world as a myth. Rather than a centered structure, what is much in evidence today are networks and cross-hatched systems of production, distribution, transmission, reception, and institutionalization. The development of new multilateral networks of knowledge production—activities that place themselves strategically at the intersection of disciplines and transnational audiences—has obviated the traditional circuits of institutionalized production and reception. These emergent networks are what I believe Basualdo means by "new geographies of culture." By emphasizing emergence, I wish, especially, to foreground not so much the newness of these territories (many of which, in fact, have extraterritorial characteristics) but their systematic integration into mobile sites of discourse, which only became more visible because of the advances in information technology as a means of distributing, transmitting, circulating, receiving, and telegraphing ideas and images.

4.

How does the curator of contemporary art express her intellectual agency within the state of "permanent transition" in which contemporary art exists today? How does the curator work both within canonical thinking and against the grain of that thinking in order to take cognizance of artistic thought that slowly makes itself felt, first in the field of culture, before it appears to be sanctioned by critics and institutions? I do not have specific answers to these questions. But I do have a notion or two about how we may approach them.

From the moment exhibitions of art assumed a critical place in the public domain of social and cultural discourse amongst the political classes—within the bourgeois public sphere that first emerged actively in Europe in the aftermath of the French Revolution—exhibitions have been constituted within the history of thought.[22] This field, as Foucault showed, is shaped above all by institutionalized power and systems of legitimation. Despite the evident fact that the institutions of art moved, inexorably, from the private, courtly domain of the feudal state to the increasingly public salons of the democratic secular state, fundamental instruments of power were still disproportionately held through patronage by the bourgeois elite in alliance with the aristocracy. Today, this process of social differentiation has entered another sphere, one dominated by capital, and contested by the forces of the so-called avant-garde. As Pierre Bourdieu puts it, "The literary or artistic field is at all times the site of a struggle between the two principles of hierarchization: the heteronymous principle, favorable to those who dominated the field economically and politically (e.g. 'bourgeois art') and the autonomous principle (e.g. 'art for art's sake'), which those of its advocates who are least endowed with specific capital tend to identify with a degree of independence from the economy, seeing temporal failure as a sign of election and success as a sign of compromise."[23]

This kind of struggle between the strategic utility of failure or success also confronts curators, and influences their judgment. For contemporary artists, the role of curators in the adjudication of success or failure—the principle between academicism and avant-gardism, between tradition and innovation—remains a key factor in public and institutional legitimation. Yet the emergence of exhibitions as a cultural activity of public institutions has been informed and governed by aesthetic criteria, disciplinary and artistic norms that designate the historical relationship of the public to all of art. While these standards are said to derive from nothing less than the ontological facture of art as an autonomous drive of artistic creativity—hence the apparently universal dimension of our grasp of art's meaning, and, as a supplement, its history—we know, as a fact of experience, that the constitutive field of art history is a synthetically elaborated one, that it is a history made by humans. Thus transcendental categories of art, including those works that seek to highlight this synthetic elaboration and as such obviate its foundational principle, still come under the putative influence and exertion of the epistemes of historical thought. Even the most radical exhibitions are constituted in this general field of knowledge and define themselves within or against its critical exertion, which is both historical and institutional. As we see in many contemporary exhibitions, the dispersed, fragmentary, and asymmetrical state of economic capitalization now endemic in all global systems has foreshortened the horizon of art. In this situation, the radical will of the curator is no less compromised. Therefore, all exhibition procedures today call for a new kind of assessment, grounded in the historical reality of the current episteme, especially if we view the task of an exhibition and the work of the curator as fundamentally contiguous. What exactly do exhibitions propose and curators organize, if not the alliance of historically and institutionally ordered experience governing the reception and relations of art and its objects, concepts, forms, and ideas by a heterogeneous and culturally diverse public? The avidity with which critics seek to confine the task of the curator and the curator's relationship to the one true history of art makes this reach for openness a pressing imperative.

5.

All curatorial procedures that are grounded in the discursive mechanisms of "the history of art" have an optics, that is to say a lens, a way of looking, seeing, and judging art and its objects, images, texts, events, activities, histories, and the intermedia strategies that define the artwork's public existence through institutions, museums, galleries, exhibitions, criticism, and so on. Yet the power, if not necessarily the import, of curatorial judgments are limited by the almost Orwellian dispensation on the part of certain art academics toward constructing a viewpoint that is overarching in terms of its conclusions about certain artistic skills and competencies, concepts, and meanings. As a specific discipline of the Western academy, the "history of art," having taken as its charter the oversight of all artistic matters, tends to surreptitiously adopt and incorporate into its discursive field a bird's-eye, panoptic view of artistic practice. This, in turn, appropriates and subverts subjective judgment into a sovereign assessment of all artistic production within a general framework. The curator, therefore, is not quite the sovereign we earlier made her out to be. Nonetheless, she operates (with the unambiguous sanction of historical and imperial precedent) like a viceroy, with the role of bringing the nonbelievers under the sovereign regard of the great Western tradition. It is the sovereign judgment of art history, with its unremitting dimension of universality and totality, that leads us to question whether it is possible to maintain a singular conception of artistic modernity. It also raises the question of whether it is permissible to still retain the idea that the unique, wise, and discriminating exercise of curatorial taste—or what some would call, ambiguously, "criticality"—ought to remain the reality of how we evaluate contemporary art today. Foucault's call for the problematization of the concept of thought in relation to critical praxis remains pertinent. The fields of practice in which relations of production, acculturation, assimilation, translation, and interpretation take place confront us immediately with the contingency of the contemporary norm of curatorial procedures that spring from the sovereign world of established categories of art inherited from "the history of art."

The museum of Modern art as an object of historical thought has a social life, as well as a political dimension, and its function cannot be dissociated from the complex arena of society and culture within which its discourse is imbricated. To that end, then, it is of significant interest to see in the curator a figure who has assumed a position as a producer of certain kinds of thought about art, artists, exhibitions, and ideas and their place amongst a field of other possible forms of thought that govern the transmission and reception of artistic production—someone, that is, who thinks reflexively about museums. Interestingly, in recent decades, it is artists more than curators who have interrogated the institution of the museum with considerable rigor. Even if "institutional critique," which inaugurated this critical intervention into the discursive spaces of the museum, has made itself redundant in light of the parasitic relationship it developed within the institution, it nonetheless opened up a space of critical address that few curators rarely attempt.

The challenge here is for the curator to grasp her work as a mode of practice that leads to particular ways of aligning thought and vision through the separation and juxtaposition of a number of models within the domains of artistic production and public reception. This method shows how the curator reflexively produces an exhibition, while allowing the viewer to think, see, appreciate, understand, transform, and translate the visual order of contemporary art into the broader order of knowledge about the history of art.

6.

If we were to attempt a definition of the status of the artwork in the current climate of restlessness and epistemological challenges, it would not be a restrictive one, but an understanding of the artwork as being produced and mobilized in a field of relations.[24] A field of relations places contemporary art and its problematics within the context of historical discourses on modernity, and elucidates the challenges to, and potentialities of, curatorial work today. The incandescence of Foucault's splendid definition of the idea of "work" provides a true insight into the problem. This is how he defines work: "that which is susceptible of introducing a meaningful difference in the field of knowledge, albeit with a certain demand placed on the author and the reader, but with the eventual recompense of a certain pleasure, that is to say, of an access to another figure of truth."[25]

Situated, as curators and art academics are, on the other side of the line from which the public faces institutions of legitimation, how might we achieve this other figure of truth, especially in an exhibition context? With what aesthetic and artistic language does one utter such truth? In what kind of environment? For which public? How does one define the public of art, particularly given the proliferation of audiences? Finally, in the circumstances of the contemporary upheaval of thought, ideas, identities, politics, cultures, histories, what truth are we talking about? The upheaval that today defines contemporary events is a historical one, shaped by disaffection with two paradigms of totalization: capitalism and imperialism, and socialism and totalitarianism. If the disaffection with these paradigms did not shift significantly the axis and forces of totalization, it did shape the emergence of new subjectivities and identities. But the dominant description of this emergence has crystallized into a figure of thought that is radically enacted in oppositional distinctions made on civilizational and moralistic terms, such as "the clash of civilizations," "the axis of evil," and the "evil empire."[26] During the late 1980s and early 1990s the culture wars in the United States were waged on similarly reductive terms, which in time cooled the ardor of those institutions tempted to step beyond their scope.[27]

My conception of the postcolonial constellation is an outcome of the upheaval that has resulted from deep political and cultural restructuring since World War II, manifest in the liberation, civil rights, feminist, gay/lesbian, and antiracist movements.[28] The postcolonial constellation is the site for the expansion of the definition of what constitutes contemporary culture and its affiliations in other domains of practice; it is the intersection of historical forces aligned against the hegemonic imperatives of imperial discourse. In conclusion, I would like to reaffirm the importance of postcolonial history and theory for accurate understanding of the social and cultural temporality of late modernity. If I recommend the postcolonial paradigm for illuminating our reading of the fraught historical context from which the discourses of Modernism and contemporary art emerged, it is only to aim toward a maturity of the understanding of what art history and its supplementary practices can contribute today toward our knowledge of art. The postcolonial constellation seeks to interpret a particular historical order, to show the relationships between political, social, and cultural realities, artistic spaces and epistemological histories, highlighting not only their contestation but also their continuous redefinition.

NOTES

An earlier version of this essay appeared in *Research in African Literature* 34, no. 4 (2003), 57–82.

1 See Fernand Braudel's discussion of the structural transformation of the flow of capital and culture by distinct temporal manifestations, the paradigmatic and diagnostic attribute of historical events in relation to their duration, in his *Civilization and Capitalism,* esp. 3:17–18 and 3: chap. 1.

2 Much like Gilles Deleuze and Felix Guattari, in their use of the idea of the rhizome, Glissant employs the metaphor of the prodigious spread of the mangrove forest to describe the processes of multiplications and mutations that for him describe the tremor of creolization as a force of historical changes and ruptures brought about by changes in the imperial order.

3 Admittedly, the advent of mass culture has muted the ability of exhibitions to be truly seminal in the wider cultural sense manifest in the controversies around the French salons of the nineteenth century, or the Armory Show of 1917 in New York. Dada was defined as a new artistic movement primarily through its many exhibitions and

happenings. Recent art world miniscandals—such as the lawsuit brought against the Contemporary Art Center of Cincinnati upon its exhibition of Robert Mapplethorpe's homoerotic photographs in 1990, or the controversy surrounding Chris Ofili's painting of a Madonna, which used elephant dung for one of her breasts, in the Brooklyn Museum's exhibition "Sensation" in 1999—indicate the degree to which exhibitions of art remain culturally significant.

4   The Nobel economist Amartya Sen has recently given many examples of the cross-pollination of ideas between cultures—particularly in language, mathematics, and the sciences—which has continued unabated for two millennia. See his "Civilizational Imprisonments."

5   See Buskirk and Nixon, *The Duchamp Effect;* and Benjamin "The Work of Art in the Age of Mechanical Reproduction."

6   See Pratt, "Arts of the Contact Zone."

7   Bürger, *Theory of the Avant-Garde,* 35.

8   Benjamin, "The Work of Art in the Age of Mechanical Reproduction," 224.

9   See *October,* "A Special Issue on Obsolescence," particularly the roundtable on art criticism, 200–28.

10 See Deleuze and Guattari, *Anti-Oedipus.*

11 Clifford, *The Predicament of Culture,* 193.

12 For a thorough account and brilliant analysis of this issue, see Thelma Golden's groundbreaking exhibition catalogue *Black Male.*

13 Bhabha, "The Other Question."

14 The same holds true for most museums of contemporary art in Europe and the United States. I have often found it curious how contemporary collections seem exactly identical, irrespective of the city in which the museum is located. The unconscious repetition of the same artists, objects, and chronology in both museums and private collections should make curators less sanguine about the independence of their judgment in connection with art and artists who may not fit easily into the logocentric logic of seriality.

15 See Habermas, *The Philosophical Discourse of Modernity,* for an extensive treatment of the discourse of modernity and modernization, and of Modernism as their artistic and aesthetic corollary. In the chapter "Modernity's Consciousness of Time and Its Need for Self-Reassurance" he draws attention to Max Weber's contention that the concept of modernity arose out of a peculiarly "Occidental rationalism."

16 Carlos Basualdo, "New Geographies of Culture," statement on a flyer accompanying a series of public seminars organized by Basualdo at the Jorges Luis Borges National Library, Buenos Aires, Argentina, 2002.

17 Foster, *Recodings,* 139.

18 Foster, *Recodings,* 139.

19 Some of the most active institutions are foreign policy instruments of the given countries. These include the British Council (United Kingdom), Association Française d'Action Artistique (France), Danish Contemporary Art (Denmark), Institut für Auslandsbeziehungen (Germany), Mondriaan Foundation (The Netherlands), and the Japan Foundation. They employ the export of artists and exhibitions as an active tool of cultural diplomacy, often organize curatorial tours in their respective

countries, fund artists for overseas projects, support exhibitions in highly visible international cities, and tour exhibitions of art from their national collections to other parts of the world.

20 Buchloh, "Figures of Authority, Ciphers of Regression," 123.

21 The Centre Pompidou, Paris, designed by Richard Rogers and Renzo Piano; the Guggenheim Museum, Bilbao, designed by Frank Gehry; and the Milwaukee Art Museum by Santiago Calatrava are examples of this conjunction. Yet no other museum achieves this fusion most thoroughly and with such audacious rhetorical panache as Daniel Libeskind's Jewish Museum in Berlin. Libeskind's architectural narrative is so forceful and complete that any visit through the museum is nothing less than an architectural guided tour, one in which the experience of the displays is always mediated by the stronger narrative of the building.

22 See Habermas, *The Structural Transformation of the Public Sphere.*

23 Bourdieu, *The Field of Cultural Production,* 40.

24 My idea of field of relations recapitulates Bourdieu's own assessment (in *The Field of Cultural Production*) of the artistic sphere as one enmeshed in a field of activities in which various agents and position takers collaborate in an ever expansive set of relations that define, conceive, conceptualize, and reformulate norms and methods within the field of cultural production.

25 Foucault, "Des Travaux," in *Dits et écrits* (Paris: Editions Gallimard, 1994), 4:367, quoted by Paul Rabinow in "Introduction: The History of Systems of Thought," in Michel Foucault, *Essential Works of Foucault,* 1:xxi.

26 Respectively, Huntington, *The Clash of Civilization and the Remaking of World Order;* George W. Bush, State of the Union Address, January 29, 2002, in which he outlined a stark distinction between states that belong to the moral universe of the civilized [*sic*] world, and those others, especially Iran, Iraq, and North Korea, who, he stated, exist in the pool of darkness and are motivated by evil intentions against the peaceful, civilized world; and then U.S. president Ronald Reagan characterizing the Soviet Union in a speech to the British House of Commons, June 8, 1982.

27 Conservative critics such as Hilton Kramer, Allan Bloom, and others made fodder of any cultural form or concept seen to want to relativize the obvious categorical and empirical truth of the great Western tradition with a cultural insight that deviates from the superiority of the Western canon. Postmodernism, and latterly postcolonial theory, became the easy route to show that the emperor of multiculturalism has no clothes and must be exposed as such with the most strident ideological attacks. Political subjectivity or social awareness of the dimension of multiplicity in any creative work was not only seen as fraudulent but also anti-Western. The culture wars destroyed any vestige of dissent within the intellectual field and exposed the weaknesses of the liberal academy. Part of the terrible legacy of this civilizational discourse is a return to consensual opposition between the Left and the Right, each pitched in its own historical bivouac. Today, to speak a measure of truth about art that contradicts the retreat back into rampant academicism is indeed a dangerous, yet occupational hazard.

28 Elaborated in Enwezor, "The Black Box."

12

FROM EMIGRATION TO E-MIGRATION:

CONTEMPORANEITY AND THE FORMER

SECOND WORLD

NANCY CONDEE

Nothing unusual today. I watched a rerun of *The Rich Also Cry.*
—Evgeniia E., Brighton Beach. Email correspondence, July 1, 2005

THE PAST

Efforts to capture the various divergences from first world models of modernity
have resulted in a broad range of contending adjectives to signal those differences, among them "alternative," "parallel," "multiple," or (following the trope
of the language tree) "vernacular" modernities.[1] Largely missing from these
terminological debates has been the Soviet example, both in itself and as an
agent present in the third world.[2] The socialist bloc as a set of economic and
cultural practices was a system whose foreign aid and exchanges left a massive
social imprint beyond its borders, yet Western assessment of it remains to this
day subject to much scholarly amnesia and silence. As Hardt and Negri quaintly
put it, "we continually find the First World in the Third, the Third in the First,
and the Second nowhere at all."[3]

Unlike the first world modernity, modernity in the second world was less a
vernacular or patois than a distinct, if ultimately truncated limb of modernity's
tree. Among the questions teasing out its singularity is this: what did it mean to
operate in a developed modernity that sustained no functioning identification

with the sovereign nation-state, liberal democracy, or capitalism among its operating assumptions? The question bears thought not least because it was posed by the largest country in the world, one-sixth of the world's land, one of two global superpowers, a country armed with nuclear warheads and maintaining an extensive external empire that bordered on Western Europe. Instead of those features of first world modernity, *this* modernity bore other features—democratic centralism, the one-party monopoly, the vanguard class, the five-year plan, Marxism-Leninism, state ownership of land and the means of production, the party-state apparatus, participatory politics without democracy (as the West would understand it), an emphasis on collective rather than individual subjectivity, and so forth—unrecognizable and alien to Western modernity.

Is Hardt and Negri's blind eye ("nowhere at all") mere provocation? Perhaps, though this ocular condition is certainly symptomatic of left academia's more general blindness to the messy issues of the second world. With few exceptions, such as Fredric Jameson in his writings on Tarkovskii and Sokurov, as well as in his comments on Soviet science fiction, few major cultural theorists outside the disciplinary limits of Slavic have attempted any integration of the cultural symptoms of Soviet socialism into larger accounts of globalization, the postcolonial constellation, and so forth.[4] This stubborn incuriosity about Soviet socialism is intriguing principally because for many years it had coexisted with—indeed, was surely conditioned in part by—intense anticommunist preoccupations from the early 1950s onward, for which the USSR's Sputnik launch on October 4, 1957, was confirmation that a fear of communism was justified. The intellectual Left's silence about the second world and the Right's anticommunist preoccupations were interrelated processes, mutually enforcing constraints. More relevant here, they operated silently through much otherwise thoughtful writing in the tradition of the Centre for Contemporary Cultural Studies, Birmingham, UK, and continue in the writings of today.

The reasons for the academic Left's resistance to a postcolonial theory that might more adequately account for the existence of the second world are, of course, complex, but underlying them surely were two unresolved questions: first, was the second world experiment a modernity at all; second, if it were granted the status of a modernity, what relation did it bear to that of the first world? Implicit in the necessary paralysis of thought during the Cold War era, too, was the nagging anticipation of the second world's own emancipation—reflexively, "from itself," as it were, rather than as a third world emancipation from the first—a question inescapably sovietological and therefore (with few exceptions) conservative in intent. Cold War debates concerning the second world tended instead, therefore, to revolve around different issues (such as the coherence and ideological investments of the totalitarian model) and engaged a different kind of interdisciplinarity, a stable one more suited to area studies than to cultural studies.[5]

Still, to return to these two questions—was the Soviet experiment a modernity? If so, what was its relation to the modernity of the first world?—any serious answer would require at some stage a comparative ordering of features, not only in the schoolroom sense of similarities and differences, but also as an account of which features were in fact epiphenomenal but emergent from radically different social formations—on the one hand (let us say, for simplicity's sake), a market-driven instrument and, on the other, a state-driven one, constitutive not just of socialism but also of *dynastic* Russia's history and heritage.

It is perhaps for this reason, in the aftermath of the Sputnik launch, that the U.S.-Soviet space race had such evocative international appeal. As an arena within which the second world was often foregrounded in the media, the space race provided a spectacle of two contesting modernities, otherwise so different in appearance, competing as visual twins, symptomatic in its English-language rhyme ("space race"), in the controlled laboratory of space. Abandoning to planet Earth the messier contrasts of real-existing socialism and capitalism, these sleek, metal rockets pushed the edge of their respective empires outward into unclaimed space, as empires are meant to do. In this act, a kind of interplanetary NASCAR, similar and comparable elements of two otherwise contrasting modernities—technology, science, education, militarization—could be isolated and tracked in a project of spectacular, high-concept minimalism, a streamlined posing of the question: what kind of modernity is this?[6]

Not surprisingly, the Soviet path to modernity and its economic and ideological systems were one: Bukharin's *Path to Socialism* [*Put' k sotsializmu*] was perhaps the earliest articulation that the politically specific was at the same time the (true) path to modernity.[7] This Soviet argument held fast through the tremendous cultural differences of the 1920s and 1930s to the 1970s and 1980s, containing within itself a number of glaring contradictions. First among these contradictions was the anti-imperialist empire: this pureblood legatee of tsarist imperialism fought imperialism abroad while retaining core features of its forebear: composite, yet hierarchical, highly centralized, yet uneven and expansive at its borders.[8] At the railway stations and airports of its outermost periphery from Kamchatka to Kaliningrad, the state clocks told Moscow time; railway and air tickets listed Moscow time for departures and arrivals. Throughout the empire, on Sunday mornings at 9:00 AM Moscow time and 10:00 AM Moscow time, the radio program *Good Morning* [*S dobrym utrom*] and the television program *Morning Post* [*Utrenniaia pochta*] were unfailingly introduced with reference to the capital, the same metropolitan center where, even today, 80 to 90 percent of financial resources are concentrated.[9]

To identify this chronological measure as imperial time is not therefore to imply—first and foremost—that it was imperious time; at issue here is structure, not affect. Given the immense hypertrophy of the USSR, the practice was first and foremost the utilitarian, convenient, and even necessary administration of space and time. Utilitarianism, convenience, and necessity are not counterevidence of empire; they *are* empire, scripted across the contiguous expanse in the only "sensible" way possible: Moscow time.

And within this chronotype, from at least the 1930s onward, the "equality of Man to Man" saw no contradiction in positioning the Russian at the center, with the others—the "nationalities," as we have misleadingly been determined to call them, rather than ethnicities—encircling the Russian, as the geography itself confirmed. Hence, whether we are speaking of the dynastic empire, of the Soviet empire of fifteen republics (with or without the informal empire beyond its borders), or of the shrunken polity of today's Russia, this polity's relationship to the trope of the nation-state has largely remained one of distance and relative antagonism.[10]

THE PRESENT

From this set of fundamental differences in the structures of two modernities one can perhaps understand that any talk of "a crisis of modernity" has a very different resonance in the East. The socialist crisis of modernity might reasonably be dated from 1953 or 1956, and any number of cogent accounts are now in circulation that address the rich terrain of late socialist postmodernism, which in its lengthiest span might be said to have stretched over nearly forty years (1953–1991).[11] Let us move ahead, however, to a later and—for our purposes here—a more relevant domain, the period 1989–1991, when the Soviet empire's collapse left behind a rich site—in places, a demolition site; elsewhere, a site where whole palace complexes and their holdings remained intact—for an imaginative sorting-out of what this Eastern modernity and its period of final volatility had meant.

In most such deliberations, it is customary to assert that one superpower fell and the world became unipolar. While the first assertion holds true across many social fields, the second is a military judgment with lesser explanatory power beyond that realm. In her Brighton Beach apartment, Evgeniia E.—an ex-Soviet

citizen and Jewish émigré from what used to be Leningrad—watches her favorite TV rerun, *The Rich Also Cry,* a Mexican soap opera broadcast by satellite
from Moscow with Russian voice-over. How do we make sense of her? What
"locality" does she inhabit? Does the category of unipolarity adequately capture
the complexity of this banal, quotidian event? An adequate corrective would
not substitute a different locale or seek a reconfigured regionalism and nomenclature (as does area studies today), but look instead to more fluid models of
migration and electronic flows to understand how the contemporary of space
and time is figured in this profoundly ordinary and familiar moment.[12]

For populations who had inhabited the site we now call Eurasia, emigration
and exile—the two major twentieth-century tropes of displacement—have
themselves been displaced. Within a culture long accustomed to internal as well
as external passports, to mandatory city residence permits, to hotel access only
in cities where one was not officially registered to live, migration was a deeply
alien concept, except as state-mandated work assignment, resettlement, colonization, Russification, or sedentarization of nomadic peoples.[13] Emigration,
now no longer absolute, terminal, and politically marked, takes on a truncated
form, simultaneously primordialist and futuristic: migration with the ever
present contingency of renegotiation as resources allow.

Compounding the magnitude of this shift, the 1990s witnessed a second,
fantastic kind of migration. On the Soviet periphery, extending from Lithuania
to Kazakhstan, twenty-five million "Russians"—that is to say, ex-Soviet citizens
of Russian ethnicity—had their territory pulled back from under them as the
empire receded. They had not migrated; their country had. Without having
moved, they experienced deterritorialization: if, for example, the sovereign
border of the United States were to retract, leaving residents of California,
Maine, Minnesota, and Florida no longer U.S. citizens—and therefore arguably
no longer "Americans"—this would perhaps approximate the scope, if not the
precise content, of the event.

After 1991, a return to the USSR was (again) not an option, but for a set of
reasons different from those in the period of Soviet emigration and exile: the
homeland to which the émigré and exile might have returned no longer existed,
and migration to the (new) Russian Federation was a journey to a familiar, but,
in many respects, foreign country.[14] The always unstable meaning of "Russian"
took on a newly destabilized quality: Was it a citizenship? An ethnicity? A native
language? A set of canonical texts, underpinned by (former Soviet) state education? Whatever it was, it was not a nation, in the sense of a homogeneous
community, a "deep, horizontal comradeship," an imagined community, lim-

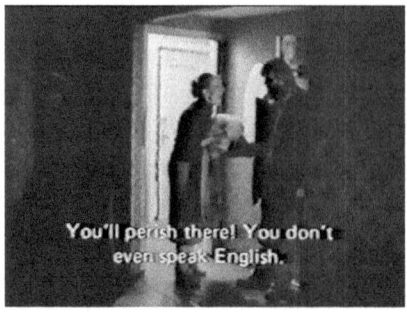

You'll perish there! You don't even speak English.

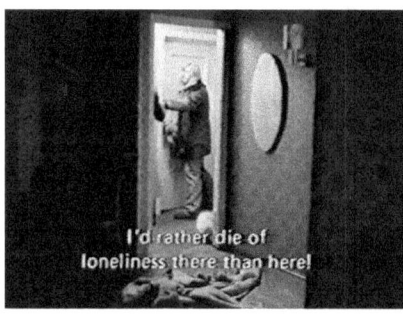

I'd rather die of loneliness there than here!

Gleb Panfilov, *Tema/Theme*, 1979. Film still. Courtesy of the artist.

Gleb Panfilov, *Tema/Theme*, 1979. Film still. Courtesy of the artist.

ited and sovereign.[15] This mutual deterritorialization—now simultaneously of émigrés from land, and of land from would-be citizens—marked the 1990s as a decisive break in the familiar coordinates of space and time.

Could we find evidence of these shifts in some sense embodied in the visual texts of this era? I choose here three brief examples over a quarter century. First, at a purely figurative level—perhaps the least interesting, but the most readily accessible—the image of the refusenik (or would-be émigré) is the trace of that past era, discernable in Soviet culture almost exclusively by the impossibility of representation: for official Soviet cultural politics, in an administrative *and therefore* artistic sense, the émigré and refusenik could not exist.[16] Gleb Panfilov's *Theme* [*Tema*, Mosfil'm, 1979; released 1986] was a rare exception that resulted in the film's shelving for seven years. Its refusenik, an intellectual and erstwhile gravedigger named Borodatyi ("the Bearded One"), was a figure in limbo, caught between Soviet life and death—such, after all, was non-Soviet life—this latter implying alternatively Israel and the United States. Awaiting his exit visa to the other world, beyond the graves he himself had dug, the Bearded One was by no means the central protagonist of the film, yet the very inclusion of the refusenik ensured that the film met the same fate as this character: having been refused release for seven years, the film appeared in 1986 only because of the early liberalizations of the perestroika era.[17]

A second example: by 1995, in Dmitrii Astrakhan's *Everything Will Be All Right* [*Vse budet khorosho*, Lenfil′m, 1995], the émigré, having enriched himself, now returns from the other world (now, explicitly the United States) to build a local Russian Disneyland in the small town where he grew up. No longer a figure associated with death and oblivion, he is associated with mere contamination and opportunism, a disruptive force in the small-town microcosm for the late Soviet Union.

Third, in 2005, a decade later, Pavel Lungin—himself a part-time Muscovite, part-time Parisian—released the Russian-French coproduction, *Roots* [*Bednye rodstvenniki*, Onix, 2005; literal translation, "Poor Relations"]. In Lungin's film, the Soviet émigrés, arriving back to the former Soviet region from the United States, Canada, Switzerland, and Israel, are now figured as unsuspecting victims of a local scammer. This charming grifter finds for the naive émigrés their "long-lost relatives," who are in fact paid accomplices trafficking in expatriate loneliness and nostalgia. And yet this shady business (the film's redemptive closure suggests) draws a global humanity together through commerce.

As objects of cinema production, these three films over a quarter century (1979–2005) oddly recapitulate the fates of their pivotal figures, the bearded gravedigger, the Disney-style opportunist, and the nostalgic transnational émigré. That is to say, respectively, Panfilov's 1979 "refusenik film" was released only in 1986; Astrakhan's film was the opportunistic blockbuster of 1995; and Lungin's 2005 film was commercially heralded as a model for Franco-Russian coproduction.

In his chapter "On Soviet Magical Realism" in *The Geopolitical Aesthetic: Cinema and Space in the World System*, written before the fall of the Soviet Union, Fredric Jameson offers an unusual reading of Aleksandr Sokurov's science fiction film, *Days of the Eclipse* [*Dni zatmeniia*, Lenfil′m, 1988]. The film, loosely based on the Strugatsky brothers' 1976 science fiction novel, *A Billion Years to the End of the World*, is imbued with an unexplained alien force that thwarts all scientific, philanthropic, or cultural efforts by the inhabitants of this god-forsaken Soviet periphery, to which the characters had been sent for reasons that are never clear. Indeed, one of the constant indeterminacies is whether the film's educated Russian visitors are *themselves* the aliens, or whether some larger, colonizing outside force ("the SF enemy," in Jameson's words) is the alien. In a sense, both interpretations are correct. Toward the end of his analysis Jameson suggests: "For in a period in which the Soviet Union, while hoping for promotion from Second to First World status, is more likely to find itself degraded to the condition of a Third World country, the SF enemy turns around, and what blocks socialism is no longer 'socialism' itself, or Stalinism, or communism or

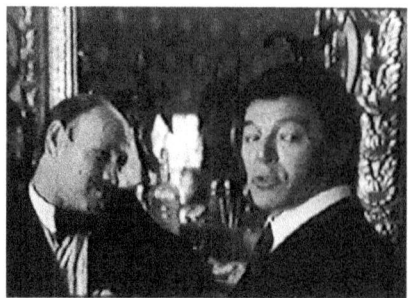

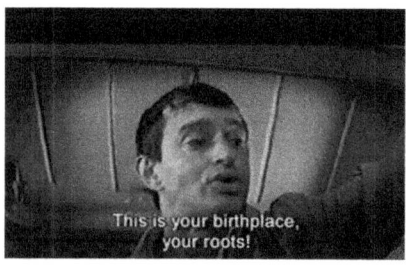

Dmitrii Astrakhan, *Vse budet khorosho / Everything Will Be All Right*, 1995. Film still. Courtesy of Lenfil'm Studios, Leningrad.

Pavel Lungin, *Bednye rodstvenniki / Roots*, 2005. Film still. Courtesy of the artist.

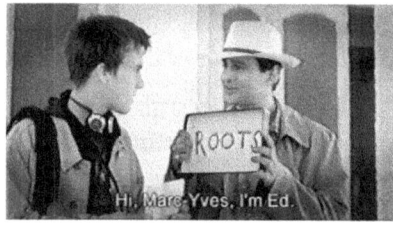

Pavel Lungin, *Bednye rodstvenniki / Roots*, 2005. Film still. Courtesy of the artist.

the Communist Party—it is the capitalist world system into which the Soviet Union has decided to integrate itself."[18]

In the midst of this argument, Jameson throws up a series of equivocations ("But of course one cannot propose so vulgar or unmediated an allegoresis without specifying the more indirect mediations," and so forth).[19] These hesitations, intended perhaps to gesture at mediations that Jameson is quite reasonably not prepared to give in a work of this scope, do not efface the fact that he is on to something important, and that his reading of Sokurov is extraordinarily prescient both of the filmmaker's work and of the cataclysmic events (then still) to come.

The Soviet empire, historically lacking a developed nationhood, provides at first glance only the most awkward fit with Jameson's paradigm of the national allegory, national subalternity, and so forth. Let us, all the same, read his remarks as an attempt to get at the following idea: the "mysterious alien power" that haunts the colonial space is indeed, as Jameson suggests, the emergence of a new global system, but one that threatens to displace *not* the "paradigm of national allegory within which [national artists] used to work," but rather the paradigm of the Soviet *imperial* allegory that functions as a tenuous and inconsistent homology to the global imperial order that hovers over this colonial outpost. If my impetuous recasting of Jameson is correct, let us return to his analysis, marking for the time being that moment when his language does not identify this metaimperial relation. Jameson writes, "In particular [intellectuals] find themselves keenly aware of the external damage to that paradigm of national [*sic*] allegory [in which it is] reduced and forcibly devalued into the regional and the nativist. . . . Power . . . becomes the mysterious, unknowable outside power (from some higher plane of civilization and technology) that incomprehensibly sets limits to the praxis of those neo-colonial subjects the Soviets are in danger of becoming."[20]

Jameson is, on the one hand, exactly right; on the other hand, the "external damage" he identifies above is damage by an emergent empire on an older, smaller one, forcibly devalued into the regional and nativist. Indeed, Sokurov's enduring preoccupation with Empire as a model of overweening hubris, both political and—ultimately, in his value system—spiritual, is increasingly evident in his later cinema, including the first three films of his (still unfinished) tetralogy, on Hitler, Lenin, and Hirohito, respectively: *Moloch* [*Molokh,* Lenfil'm, 1999], *Taurus* [*Telets,* Lenfil'm, 2001], and *Sun* [*Solntse,* Lenfil'm, 2005]. Their three structures—the Third Reich, Russia's collapsed empire and its Soviet reconfiguration, and the Japanese imperial court, three empires ruled by three fragile psyches—provide Sokurov with a political set within which to comment visually on the ambitions of human secular power, its arrogant disregard of moral boundaries, and the magnificent, flawed complicity of elite culture in shoring up a reprehensible polity. Moving outward from Lenin—initially, the first of the tetralogy—to Hitler, to Hirohito, and then to (the as yet incomplete) Mephistopheles, Sokurov points toward a structural abstraction of domination, a way of being in the world, that moves beyond the historically specific empire of the past, with its unstable boundaries of an outmoded sovereignty. As a resident in transit between Germany and Russia, Sokurov might well understand how the global system "into which the Soviet Union has decided to integrate itself" was *itself* profoundly changed as a result of that massive integration from the East.[21] The rupture in the second world had consequences for both the first and third worlds with which we have yet to come to terms. And precisely here might be initiated an argument concerning a different register in the organization of time and space.

THE CONTEMPORARY?

These variously configured deterritorializations imply a very different experience of globalization from that figured, for example, in Habermas's provocative "Postnational Constellation."[22] In the years after 1989–1991, the nation-state—as that arena had been conceived in the West where globality and modernity encounter and interdetermine one another—was massively affected by this newly migratory flow of citizens, to whom the nation-state was an unfamiliar and peripheral model of statehood. From across the anti-imperialist empire, a hermetic modernity was destabilized by its sudden access, both "live" and electronic, to a vast diversity of possible life styles, identities, and imaginative practices. In a socialist culture with a highly educated, metropolitan intelligentsia for whom the rare and antiquated photocopy machine had always been kept under lock and key, where photocopies had been individually recorded, where much letterhead stationery had been numbered and logged, where in some metropolitan enterprises the office typewriters were routinely locked away during long holidays and new typewriters were supposed to be registered with the police, the Internet and the digital universe more broadly provided the conditions for a profoundly different global consciousness.

Given these conditions, who would anticipate that, even as socialism collapsed, Russia would lead the world in electronic piracy? How did a country so utterly unprepared to manage its technological affairs manage to circumvent digital media restrictions in cinema, music, computer programs, and virtually all other forms of electronic encryption? The most public hue and cry arose from the Motion Picture Association, rightly fearful for the integrity of its international copyright interests. These responses from the MPA, the Motion Pictures Association of America, and other U.S. cultural trade organizations were swift, but not swift enough: by the time the MPA announced its boycott of the 1991 Seventeenth Moscow International Film Festival, as well as a halt on the sale to Soviet distributors of U.S. films produced by the seven major studios, video piracy was already well established as the dominant delivery system for spectatorship in the USSR.[23]

Few scholars today would still equate globalization *tout court* with the twin nightmares of Americanization and homogenization. Nowhere are the internal contradictions of these terms more evident, more subject to internal differentiation, than in the realm of cinema. I would cite two examples of this internally contradictory dynamic. First, in the Russian cinema industry today, U.S. films command 88 percent of screen time, with only 7 percent available to domestic cinema.[24] At the same time, the critical feature of resuscitation for a cinema that had ceased functioning—that is to say, that had had to contend with a video market and cable network that was 98 percent criminal activity,[25] and that had sunk from a steady Soviet output of 120 to 150 films a year in the 1960–1980s to 34 films in the mid-1990s—was, paradoxically, the influx of U.S. cinema, which required of Russia's theaters massive infrastructural and technological upgrading.[26] Even Hollywood's fiercest Russian critics and competitors acknowledge that "Hollywood . . . has created our spectator," fortuitously opening up a space for a redefined local constituency with a more internally diverse profile, including the niche for auteur cinema in precisely the conditions where the dollar called the tune.[27] These countercurrents of the industry cannot be satisfactorily contained within earlier models of globalization. Neither "homogenization" nor "Americanization" does justice to these contradictory, interdependent functions in the volatility of the global.

Second, at a time when the U.S. film industry itself is increasingly oriented toward the domestic marketing and sales of DVDs through retail outlets such as Wal-Mart;[28] at a time when the boundaries dividing cinema, television, and the computer are increasingly blurred; and when "film" is an anachronistic term for what has increasingly become a handheld object, watched in intervals on a small screen in private, domestic space, U.S. entrepreneurs and their Russian partners in the former second world have begun—oddly and counterintuitively, it would seem—to build extensive theater exhibition space, rising from thirty new venues in 2000 to seven hundred new venues in 2005.[29] Gone are the vast cinema halls, seating as many as eight hundred spectators for a single Soviet film that ran for weeks; instead, multiplex theaters and small clubs provide an initially unfamiliar diversity of choice, including outlets for digital auteurs working in video. What accounts for this local shift to exhibition space construction in a global age of Wal-Mart-style sales of DVDs?

In a region where piracy still precludes any meaningful profit from DVD and video sales, theatrical exhibition remains a formal placeholder until such time as the U.S. technology deadlock over the next medium—be it Sony's Blu-ray discs or Toshiba's HD-DVD—provides sufficient encryption to counteract the entrenched piracy.[30] Beneath the pull and tug of individual choice—an evening at the cinema? a DVD purchase?—lies a catacomb of corporate strategies that must increasingly reckon with the stochastic movement of an electronic globalism in no sense oriented toward a single territorial pole. While the process of Hollywood script selection may still often proceed from a primary U.S. audience (with global export as a secondary project), increasingly—since the unanticipated global success of *Titanic* (1997), according to the industry analyst Lynn Hirschberg—an alternate model assesses as its primary market the global draw for films that are, for economic reasons, increasingly shot abroad and scripted to draw upon new configurations of loyalty in a postnational context.[31]

All claims of rupture are a matter of argument, at least as much as a matter of verifiability. If, indeed, one can now speak of the onset of a new temporal register, one that in this volume is conditionally referred to as contemporaneity, it would engage many of the shifts that have been described here with respect to the former second world: the disjuncture and copresence of incompatible legacies of modernity; multiple and unfamiliar forms of deterritorializations, both of people from their homeland and of the homelands themselves; a sense of planetary time that evades synchronicity; and a stream of electronic media representations that facilitate a wildly more divergent set of identity projects than had been possible before the watershed of 1989–1991.

Some of this is already known. A decade ago Arjun Appadurai, with particular attention to South Asia, wrote about the impact of electronic media and mass migration as the two major, interconnected diacritics that had shaped the cultural dimensions of globalization.[32] Since that time, the concept of navigation has gained currency as a way of understanding the coextensivity and simultaneity of travel through physical and virtual orders, two ecosystems that may be coinhabited through a range of electronic media—the video game, the cell phone, the computer. This coextensivity of the virtual and the physical already implies that our physical world might merely be the "white noise" or background interference to virtual reality as the "new spatial order."[33] While no transnational state yet exists to mediate these flows of people, places, and times, nonetheless a rich and turbulent transnational culture, sustained by a broad array of global nongovernment organizations, navigates improvisational pathways through a planetary network as a working "state of contingency," providing unreliable and scarce entitlements in the space where a formal polity may or may not ever emerge. How these changes in movement and media access will affect what has until recently been conceived of as local loyalties is impossible to anticipate, in no small measure because the very category of loyalty—disembodied from older notions of time and place—may be undergoing such shifts as to render it unrecognizable to the loyalists themselves.

NOTES

Support for this research was generously provided by the University of Pittsburgh Russian and East European Studies Center and the organizers of "Kinotavr" (the Sochi International Film Festival). I wish to thank Ilya Goldin, Jonathan Harris, Ruth Levine, and Vladimir Padunov for comments on earlier drafts of this essay.

1 See, for example, Canclini, *Hybrid Cultures,* and Eisenstadt, *Patterns of Modernity,* as well as the special issue of *Daedalus* on multiple modernities, vol. 129, no. 1 (Winter 2000).

2 The term "third world," the origins of which are much debated, is most often ascribed to French demographer Alfred Sauvy (*L' Observateur,* no. 118, August 14, 1952, 14), who compared third world countries to the Third Estate: "ce Tiers Monde ignoré, exploité, méprisé comme le Tiers État" ("this ignored Third World, exploited, scorned like the Third Estate"). The most common competing attribution of the term is to Charles de Gaulle. The term "second world" is an extrapolation that refers to the (former) socialist states of the Soviet bloc, but also (often) including China, Albania, Cuba, North Korea, Mongolia, and North Vietnam. I use the term "third world" with some caution, in partial agreement with Aijaz Ahmad and others ("So does India belong in the first world or the third? Brazil, Argentina, Mexico, South Africa?"). At the same time, I disagree with Ahmad's notion that "second world" is adequately captured as "simply [*sic*] the name of a [socialist] resistance that saturates the globe today," the date of Ahmad's "today" being 1987. As Gulag returnees and former Soviet border guards, among others, might elaborate better than I, the second world of 1987 was both more material and more local than this model of global resistance suggests. See Ahmad, "Jameson's Rhetoric of Otherness and 'National Allegory,' " quotations from 7 and 9.

3 Hardt and Negri, *Empire,* xiii.

4 Jameson, *The Geopolitical Aesthetic,* and "SF Novel/SF Film."

5 The most cogent analysis of totalitarianism as a Western scholarly project (as distinct from its empirical practices in the second world) is Gleason, *Totalitarianism.* As for the differences between the interdisciplinarity of area studies and the interdisciplinarity of cultural studies, principal among these are the various *internal* disciplinary destabilizations that cultural studies would claim as conditional to its core project. By contrast, area studies would claim no investment in this issue one way or the other, though in fact it has traditionally been grounded in a fairly stable notion of discipline, which comes to the table to encounter other stable disciplines.

6 One might argue that earlier versions of this same impulse could be seen in a number of other arenas, including record-breaking polar flights and air ballooning, as well as the Soviet automobile rallies of the 1920s and 1930s. See, for example, Osinskii's article "American Automobile or Russian Cart?" For an excellent analysis of this early competition for modernity, see Siegelbaum, "Soviet Car Rallies and the Road to Socialism." One of the more interesting of recent publications on this score is Hoffmann and Kotsonis, *Russian Modernity.*

7 Bukharin, *Put' k sotsializmu.* On the ideological trope of the "path to socialism," see Siegelbaum, "Soviet Car Rallies," as well as Lih, "The Soviet Union and the Road to Communism," 706–31.

8 I take as the basis of this discussion some of the foundational texts on empire, including Doyle, *Empires,* and Pagden, *Lords of All the World,* as well as those more relevant to this region, principally Suny and Martin, *A State of Nations,* and Tolz, "Conflicting 'Homeland Myths' and Nation-State Building in Postcommunist Russia."

9 *Moscow Times,* June 15, 2005, 11.

10 The continued imperial orientation of Russia is a longer argument that will not be taken up in full here, other than to cite several brief examples from Russian Federation president Vladimir Putin's April 25, 2005, annual Address to the Federal Assembly [Poslanie Federal'nomu Sobraniiu], Russia's State of the Union speech, in which he describes the collapse of the Soviet Union as "a major geopolitical disaster of the [twentieth] century," in itself a remark redolent of a certain imperial nostalgia. Further, in the speech's foreign-policy section, Putin assures his listeners "that Russia should continue its *civilizing mission* on the Eurasian continent. This mission . . . enriches and strengthens *our historic community*" (my emphasis). Consistent with this notion of a historically conditioned *mission civilisatrice* is his astonishing characterization of El'tsin's August 31, 1996, ceasefire agreement with Chechen nationalists at Khasaviurt (Dagestan)—bringing a (temporary) peace to the first (1994–1996) Chechen war—as "the Khasaviurt *capitulation*" (my emphasis). See http://kremlin.ru.

11 Among them is the work of Groys, *The Total Art of Stalinism,* who has contributed to this volume. See also Brown, *Russian Postmodernism*; Chuprinin, "Drugaia proza"; Condee and Padunov, "Pair-a-Dice Lost"; Epstein, "After the Future" and *Re-Entering the Sign*; Erjavec, *Postmodernism and the Postsocialist Condition*; Eshelman, *Early Russian Postmodernism*; Lipovetsky, *Russian Postmodernist Fiction*, in particular chap. 10; Kruzhkov, *Fire and Ice*; Malukhin, "Post bez moderna"; Man'kovskaia, *Estetika postmodernizma*; McCann et al., "Symposium on Russian Postmodernism"; Murav, "The Post-Modern and the Post-Utopian"; Skoropanova, *Russkaia postmodernistskaia literatura*; and Sussman, "The Third Zone."

12 I refer here to the renaming efforts of the Russian and East European Studies Centers (REES), part of the U.S. National Resource Centers and funded by the provisions of the Title VI Higher Education Act. From the mid-1990s on, the REES Centers sought to reconfigure their research goals and nomenclature in response to three shifts: first, some of Eastern Europe "graduated" to Europe *tout court;* second, "Eastern Europe" became perceived as a dated and offensive term; third, Russian and East European Studies Centers gained increased funding opportunities in Central Asia, especially after September 11, 2001.

13 Among the most valuable recent analyses of colonization and empire is Sunderland, *Taming the Wild Field.*

14 Responses to 1992 and 1993 opinion polls, for example, conducted among ethnic Russian minorities abroad (Kyrgyzstan, Lithuania, Moldova) by the Center for the Study of Inter-Ethnic Relations (Institute of Ethnology and Anthropology, Russian Academy of Sciences), as well as in June 1995 in Ukraine by the Institute of Sociology and the Democratic Initiative (both located in Kiev) and elsewhere, consistently confirmed a homeland identification with the Soviet Union; a much smaller percentage considered the Russian Federation to be their homeland (Tolz, "Conflicting 'Homeland Myths,'" 292–93).

15 The reference as usual is to Anderson, *Imagined Communities.*

16 Note the paradox, however, that it was always a "he" who did not exist.

17 See Condee and Padunov, "Reforming Soviet Culture," for a discussion of this film in the context of the cultural politics of this era.

18 Jameson, *Geopolitical Aesthetic,* 109.

19 Jameson, *Geopolitical Aesthetic,* 110.

20 Jameson, *Geopolitical Aesthetic,* 110–11.

21 Jameson, *Geopolitical Aesthetic,* 109.

22 Habermas, *The Postnational Constellation,* 58–112.

23 Motion Picture Association of America, representing the interests of the seven ma-
    jor U.S. studios—Disney, MCA/Universal, MGM/UA, Paramount, Sony, Twentieth-
    Century Fox, and Warner Brothers—is responsible for issuing film ratings, lobbying
    the federal government, and protecting the copyright interests of its member studios.
    The Motion Picture Association (changed in 1994 from its original 1945 name, the
    Motion Picture Export Association of America) is the international arm, handling
    issues of foreign exhibition of U.S. films, as well as protectionism and piracy issues.

24 Roundtable discussion with Nikita Mikhalkov (president, Twenty-fourth Moscow
    International Film Festival), producers Aleksandr Atanesian, Leonid Vereshchagin,
    Sergei Sel'ianov, Sergei Sendyk, Sergei Chliiants, critics Lev Karakhan and Daniil
    Dondurei, and others on the economics of the Russian film industry. Published as
    Mikhalkov et al., "Rossiiskoe kino: kak vernut' den'gi?" Quotation from 6.

25 Dondurei, "Kinodelo na puti k rynku," 133.

26 Russia is not a unique case in this regard; a similar tendency can be observed in China,
    which vies with Russia for leadership in global piracy. There, too, Western investors
    such as Time-Warner look to exhibition rather than DVD sales for revenue growth:
    anticipating the rise of Chinese domestic box-office revenues from $500 million in
    2004 to an expected $1.2 billion in 2007, Time-Warner and other corporations are
    actively speeding up joint-venture construction of exhibition space throughout the
    country; see Barboza, "Hollywood Movie Studios See the Chinese Film Market as
    Their Next Rising Star." See also http://ercboxoffice.com/, the Web site of the enter-
    tainment research and data firm Exhibitor Relations.

27 Producer Sergei Sel'ianov in the roundtable with Mikhalkov et al., "Rossiiskoe kino," 16.

28 U.S. DVD sales, which accounted for 28.7 percent of studio revenue for feature films in
    1996, rose to 47.9 percent in 2004, according to Adams Media Research. See Belson,
    "DVD Fight Intensifies: Microsoft and Intel to Back Toshiba Format," and "A DVD
    Standoff in Hollywood." See also http://www.adamsmediaresearch.com/.

29 Mikhalkov et al., "Rossiiskoe kino," 10.

30 Blu-ray discs, developed by Sony and Panasonic, are supported by Hewlett-Packard,
    Dell, Matsushita Electric, Samsung, and Philips; HD-DVD, developed by Toshiba, is
    supported by Warner, Universal, and Paramount, as well as Microsoft and Intel.
    Belson, "A DVD Standoff"; Hirschberg, "What Is an American Movie Now?"

31 Hirschberg, "What Is an American Movie Now?" cites Nina Jacobson, president of the
    Buena Vista Motion Picture Group at Disney, who compares *Titanic*'s meager U.S.
    box-office draw of $28 million to its record international rental profits of $900 million
    (19), a key moment in a critical shift to the global market as a point of departure for
    selected films.

32 Appadurai, *Modernity at Large,* 3, 19.

33 Joselit, "Navigating the New Territory." Quotation from page 276.

13

AFTERMATH: VALUE AND VIOLENCE IN

CONTEMPORARY SOUTH AFRICAN ART

COLIN RICHARDS

Being inextricably tied to human proximity, morality seems to conform to the law of optical perspective. It looms large and thick close to the eye. With the growth of distance, responsibility for the other shrivels, moral dimensions to the object blur, till both reach a vanishing point and disappear.

—Zygmunt Bauman, *Modernity and the Holocaust*

The cover of Frantz Fanon's incendiary book *The Wretched of the Earth*, arguably the greatest masterpiece of the anticolonial struggle, shows a photograph by Paul Strand. Titled *Sleeping Man, Makola Market, Accra, Ghana* (1963), it pictures a white-clad, barefooted man resting on a concrete ledge.[1] But the title deceives. The man's eyes are not closed. He seems less asleep than turned away from the camera. Perhaps he turns away from the intrusive gaze of the cameraman?[2] If this sleeping man is metonymic for Africa, it is Africa misunderstood. Or mistranslated, if we follow Homi Bhabha's characterization of Postmodern art as a site for translation rather than transcendence.[3]

How do we translate this vast conundrum of a continent? Achille Mbembe and Sarah Nuttall provide some direction in arguing that the sign "Africa" "so often ends up epitomizing the intractable, the mute, the abject, or the otherworldly. So over-determined is the nature of this sign that it sometimes seems almost impossible to crack, to throw it open to the full spectrum of meanings and implications that other places and other human experiences enjoy, provoke and inhabit."[4]

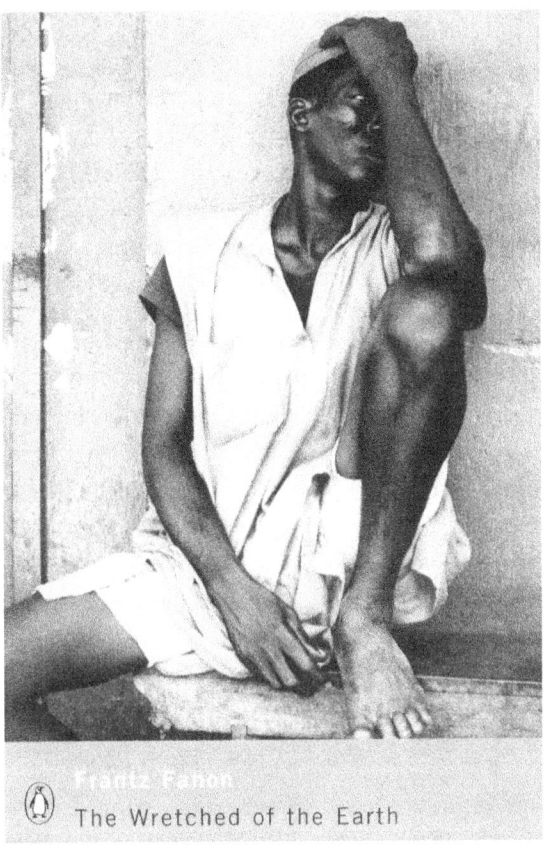

The Wretched of the Earth

Frantz Fanon

Paul Strand, *Sleeping Man, Makola Market, Accra, Ghana,* 1963.
Photograph. Courtesy of Penguin Classics, London.

Opening Africa "to the full spectrum of meanings and implications" of human joy and provocation—surely this is, in part, what art does—has always already been upon us. Such an opening process is at the heart of constituting a revitalized, even new African imaginary.[5] It may be that we in Africa seem always to be struggling in the half-life of some aftermath that cannot move beyond the catastrophes that occasioned it. But perhaps it is here that a distinctive value lies. Africa—a semiotic complex if ever there was one—seems to occupy a fertile, violent, human space untidily bound by two ancient oppositions: one expressed by Ecclesiastes, "and there is no new thing under the sun," and the other by Pliny, "ex Africa semper aliquid novi" (always from Africa comes something new).[6]

SPECTERS OF EXORBITANCE

In refashionings of Africa, rhetorical and otherwise, it is important to query the spectacularity often associated with this continent. South Africa provides one form of this spectacularity and its supercession in the current moment.[7] Locally, "spectacle" references what Njabulo Ndebele calls the "obscene social exhibitionism" of apartheid:

> Everything in South Africa has been mind-bogglingly spectacular: the monstrous war machine developed over the years; the random massive pass raids; mass shootings and killings; mass economic exploitation the ultimate symbol of which was the mining industry; the mass removals of people; the spate of draconian laws passed with the spectacle of parliamentary promulgations; the luxurious life-style of whites; servants, all-encompassing privilege; swimming pools, and high commodity consumption; the sprawling monotony of architecture in African locations, which are the very picture of poverty and oppression. The symbols are all over: the quintessence of obscene social exhibitionism.[8]

South African art under apartheid was shot through with this phenomenon. We can trace its passage through any number of artworks: in the saturated bloodiness of Alfred Thoba's *Riots* (1977), in the late Billy Mandindi's chilling *Necklace of Death* (1986), and in the congested, distressed spaces of Makgabo (Helen) Sebidi's *Mother Africa* (1988). Spectacle also reaches a kind of ironical apotheosis in a cluster of key works from the mid-eighties, including Jane Alexander's *The Butcher Boys* (1985–1986), Penny Siopis's *Melancholia* (1986), and William Kentridge's *The Boating Party* (1985).[9] In each of these extraordinary works we find that "the thick lines of spectacle were drawn with obvious relish," to borrow Njabulo Ndebele's evocative phrasing.[10]

Perhaps the most significant icon of the harrowing decade of the 1980s was the burning tire. Winnie Mandela uttered her incendiary words then, words that echoed around the world: "We have no guns—we have only stones, boxes of matches, petrol. Together, hand in hand, with our boxes of matches and our necklaces we will liberate this country."[11] The burning tire associated with necklacing branded South Africa's liberation struggle in its final decade and is seared into the consciousness of millions.[12] The tire has become part of our traumatic imaginary. Tracing this spectacular icon of violence is not difficult. Any list would include Kentridge's *The Boating Party*, mentioned above; the painted clay figure made by a nine-year-old of "something seen recently," documented in Sue Williamson's *Resistance Art in South Africa*; Billy Mandindi's

Necklace of Death (1986); and Kendell Geers's *Eeny Meeni Miny Mo* (1988). This icon survived deep into the last decade of the twentieth century, as evidenced in, for example, Minette Vári's pristine, ex-sanguinated *Firestone* (1995) and Geers's inflammatory *The Terrorist's Apprentice: Bastard* (2002).[13]

In one now notorious account heard at the Truth and Reconciliation Commission, a mother beside herself in anguish cries "They braaied [barbecued] my son while they drank and laughed."[14] Jacques Pauw recounts this scene: "In a dry ditch on the slightly elevated river bank, a shallow grave was dug with bushveld wood and tires. The two corpses were lifted onto the pyre and as the sun set over the Eastern Transvaal bushveld, two fires were lit, one to burn the bodies to ashes, the other for the security policemen to sit around, drinking and grilling meat. . . . It was just another job to be done. In the beginning it smells like a meat braai, in the end like the burning of bones. It takes about seven to nine hours to burn the bodies to ashes. We would have our own little braai and just keep on drinking."[15]

Artist Johannes Segogela produced a small carved and constructed tableau titled *The Devil's Party* (1991), which presents a religious and secular horror of hell, all the more harsh because the piece seems most like a quaint three-dimensional cartoon.[16] A figure is tied to a spit being turned by two other-worldly night figures, the fire burning below. The subtext is most likely a version of Christian eschatology in infernal intersection with history in the form of Vlakplaas, the notorious farm near Pretoria used as a base and "rest and recreation" killing ground for police hit squads.

For Ndebele the "hegemony of spectacle" had "run its course" in the 1980s, not least because it did not permit "itself the growth of complexity. . . . The entire ethos permits neither inner dialogue with the self, nor a social public dialogue. It breeds insensitivity, insincerity and delusion."[17] Approaching the phenomenon from a different and wider continental perspective, Mbembe writes of the postcolony as having a "specific system of signs, a particular way of fabricating simulacra or re-forming stereotypes. . . . The postcolony is characterised by a distinctive style of political improvisation, by a tendency to excess and lack of proportion."[18] Peter Wollen speaks of how an excess of display (spectacle) has "the effect of concealing the truth of the society that produces it, providing the viewer with an unending stream of images that might best be understood, not simply detached from a real world of things, as Debord implied, but as effacing any trace of the symbolic, condemning the viewer to a world in which we can see everything but understand nothing—allowing us viewer-victims, in Debord's phrase, only 'a random choice of ephemera.' "[19]

In an important sense, terms such as "specularity" and "spectacle" suggest a certain spatialization of time and an understanding of temporality as eternally present duration. Seeing the phenomenon this way entails that we recognize a risk: that of reducing culture to a present in which history is compromised or erased. I would argue that this has a particular meaning for South African art, especially in its crucial and surely desirable entanglements with global art discourses. The South African (perhaps even African) presence in the Fiftieth Venice Biennale of 2003 exemplifies this risk.

Francesco Bonami, director of this biennial, framed his project under the heading "Dreams and Conflicts: The Dictatorship of the Viewer," stating "I feel very strongly about advocating creative irrelevance to attack the absurdity of war, violence and discrimination. I am for producing dreams to contain the madness of conflicts."[20] Picking up a particular spectatorial orientation, Bonami also suggested that "the realm of art has become a huge panorama." Accordingly, he identified a shift in the role of the curator: he or she had become "a kind of visual anthropologist—no longer just a taste-maker, but a cultural analyst."[21]

This is a large ambition for curators. How was it met by "Fault Lines: Contemporary African Art and Shifting Landscapes," curated by Gilane Tawadros, one of the eleven sections of the overall biennial? How did Bonami's highly charged rhetoric find expression at the level of practice? But, perhaps more important, what happened to history in what Bonami characterizes as an "anthropological gaze"? The curators were apparently given complete autonomy to produce their part of what was to be, in Bonami's words, "a grand show." One of the artists included in "Fault Lines" was Moshekwa Langa, who had also made an installation work for an important South African exhibition entitled "Fault Lines: Inquiries around Truth and Reconciliation" and presented in the Cape Town Castle in mid-1996. This earlier show was a rare, focused cultural response to the Truth and Reconciliation Commission (TRC).[22] Established in 1995, the TRC was initially expected to complete its work by June 1997. The deadline was extended to October 1998, with the exception of the Amnesty Committee, which was given an indefinite period to complete its work. This committee published its report in 2003.[23]

By almost all accounts, the far from uncontroversial TRC, preoccupied as it was with restorative rather than retributive justice, was a historical event of great moment in the wider world.[24] Yet there is no mention made of the earlier "Fault Lines" exhibition in the text edited by Tawadros and Sarah Campbell for the Venice Biennale.[25] This amounts to a critically serious form of erasure, a form of violence. It is almost as if we must see the "anthropological gaze" as a kind of terrorism—a much abused word, certainly, and such abuse is not less-ened by my use of it here.

Part of the problem here is artistic agency, intellectual continuity, and crit-icality in history, and in the development of a postapartheid archive of art.[26] For inasmuch as curators are public intellectuals rather than merely cultural bro-kers, establishing accurate histories and recognizing key creative and intellec-tual continuities are surely important principles to follow. Erasing history, whether through omission or commission—both of which, ironically, are fa-miliar to us through our experiences of different forms of colonialism—is an act of violence. Yet, while we might be critical of this violence and should challenge it, there is another dimension of violence that bears further reflection and critical meditation.

VIOLENCE AND ITS VICISSITUDES

In the "Historical Context" section of the TRC report (the first volume) we find the following paragraph: "Violence has been the single most determining factor in South African political history. The reference, however, is not simply to physical or overt violence—the violence of the gun—but also to the violence of the law or what is often referred to as institutional or structural violence."[27]

In an exchange that appeared in 2004 in a major publication on contemporary South African art, the idea was mooted that the South African art world needed some sort of TRC process. Thembinkosi Goniwe supported David Koloane's prop-osition that we conduct a Truth and Reconciliation Commission of the visual arts. Amongst other things, Goniwe suggested that such a process "could help us evaluate in context how those who control and are controlled by the institu-tion/infrastructure which determines visual art productions, exhibitions, market-ing, dissemination, curating, writing, teaching continue to do so. Evaluation not for the sake of evaluating, ridiculing institutions and individuals, but to under-stand problems that inform our continuing struggle to transform art institutions. In that exercise . . . we would be able to make sense of all the continuing tension and conflict between black and white, Europe and South Africa."[28]

The fact that this call was taken seriously enough to print suggests that violence—expressed in the terms "control," "determination," and "struggle," along with reference to the institutional art world—remains a key dimension of our creative and intellectual lives.

Violence is a complex, protean notion.[29] In their introduction to a collection they edited, Nancy Scheper-Hughes and Philippe Bourgeois write:

Violence is a slippery concept—non-linear, productive, destructive, *and* re-productive. It is mimetic, like imitative magic or homeopathy. "Like produces Like," that much we know. Violence gives birth to itself. So we can rightly speak of chains, spirals, and mirrors of violence—or, as we prefer—a continuum of violence. Violence can never be understood solely in terms of its physicality—force, assault, or the infliction of pain—alone. Violence also includes assaults on the personhood, dignity, sense of worth or value of the victim. The social and cultural dimensions of violence are what give violence its power and meaning. Focussing exclusively on the physical aspects of torture/terror/violence misses the point and turns the project into a clinical, literary or artistic exercise, which runs the risk of degenerating into a theatre or pornography of violence in which the voyeuristic impulse subverts the larger project of witnessing, critiquing, and writing against violence, injustice, and suffering.[30]

Included in our understandings of violence would be what the late Pierre Bourdieu described as "symbolic violence." This is a key idea in Bourdieu's analytical architecture and one he sought to protect from critical misunderstanding. For Bourdieu and Loïc Wacquant, "Symbolic violence, to put it as tersely and simply as possible, is the violence which is exercised on a social agent with his or her complicity. . . . *Misrecognition* [is] the fact of recognizing a violence which is wielded precisely inasmuch as one does not perceive it as such."[31] This, in turn, returns us to the complex question of complicity in maintaining repressive structures. Mark Sanders, on the subject of intellectuals and apartheid, after discussing Gramsci and Sartre, argues that "just as critical independence can only be a regulative ideal because of the implications of the mental worker in institutions and policies, any theory that privileges oppositionality or resistance is an incomplete account of complicity. To have any meaning, responsibility requires a motivated acknowledgement of one's complicity in injustice."[32] In another discussion of gender and symbolic violence, Bourdieu is anxious to avoid certain assumptions that bedevil the use of these two terms, warning that "people sometimes assume that to emphasize symbolic violence is to minimise the role of physical violence. . . . Understanding 'symbolic' as the opposite of 'real, actual,' people suppose that symbolic violence is a purely 'spiritual' violence which ultimately has no real effects."[33]

Noting the definitional difficulties of the concept of violence and also noting its deep ambiguity, John Keane argues that as long as it continues to be used, it will "remain controversial, especially under democratic conditions," principally because of its ethically problematic selectivity in relation to reality.[34] The reference to democracy here is telling. Writing of "explanations that trace violence to the openness and pluralism characteristic of civil societies," Keane notes: "Modern civil societies have . . . provided handsome opportunities for certain power groups tempted by dreams of expansionism. This has ensured in turn that the whole of modern history of colonisation and bullying of the 'uncivilised' has been riddled with violence, to the point where it may be said, with bitter irony, that the current world-wide appeal of civil society is the bastard child of metropolitan civility."[35]

In a more general way, violence and democracy might be linked to the idea of trauma. In a discussion of extreme body art, Martin Jay makes the following observation: "If . . . trauma involves a kind of 'unclaimed experience' in which the wound doesn't heal, but remains still festering beneath the scar, then the deeply troubled art we have been discussing expresses the belatedness of a traumatic event or events that have not yet been assimilated or reconciled. As such, it brings to the surface those moments of founding violence that even the most democratic polity has difficulty in fully acknowledging."[36]

We do have difficulty in acknowledging this phenomenon, and our confidence in locating the difference between an image and what that image is about, in locating the violence in representation, is severely compromised.

The question of violence is implicated in a crisis in the stability of the relation between a sign and what it signifies. Jean Baudrillard provides one instance of this crisis: "our society" (presumably Euro-American culture), he says, "has expelled violence (at the same time as it has expelled evil, illness, negativity and death—I don't mean it has eliminated them, but it has expelled them from its system of values). All forms of wildcat, spontaneous violence, historical and political, has been stifled or neutralised. . . . The system has the monopoly of violence: a monopoly of the extermination of any singularity, any negativity, of death itself, and of the real violence in the virtual violence of generalized pacification, fundamentalist [intégriste] violence (the only violence, that of system, not that of terrorists, which remains small-scale and blind)."[37]

Another perspective on contemporary violence and art is offered by Paul Virilio: "Avant-garde artists, like many political agitators, propagandists and demagogues, have long understood what TERRORISM would soon popularize: if you want a place in 'revolutionary history' there is nothing easier than provoking a riot, an assault on propriety, in the guise of art. Short of committing a real crime by killing innocent passers-by with a bomb, the pitiless contemporary author of the twentieth century attacks symbols, the very meaning of a 'pitiful' art he assimilates to 'academicism.' "[38]

Virilio seems to yearn for a stable, durable, almost ahistorical distinction between symbolic violence and actual violence. Certain European intellectuals, it appears, cannot come to terms with a reality familiar to most of the postcolonial world. They fail to grasp the omnipresence and intricately discursive dance of physical violence. They also seem to avoid full recognition of the relation between violence and the origins and perpetuation of democracy.

In contrast, throughout his book *On the Postcolony* Achille Mbembe refers to its distinct regime of violence, and emphasizes the determining power of violence in the postcolonial world. Further, Mahmood Mamdani begins his work *Good Muslim Bad Muslim* on this note: "We have just ended a century of violence, one possibly more violent than any other in recorded history," and goes on to observe that while "the magnitude of this violence is staggering, it does not astound us. The modern political sensibility sees most political violence as necessary to historical progress."[39]

South African violence and art often converge in moments framed by arguments about freedom of expression and proscriptions against hate speech.[40] There is foundational violence in both. The key element missing from defenses of free expression is recognition of the problem of violence: the violence of representation and then the violent consequences of disseminating these representations in the public sphere. The last line in a postscript of a recent publication entitled *Free Expression Is No Offence* reads: "Free speech is one of the core values in a democracy and it should be championed with a vengeance."[41] The use of the word "vengeance" suggests, perhaps, a kind of violence not intended by the author of the postscript.

By way of specifics we might recall here the first "protodemocratic" South African instance of this kind of violence: the removal of some offending photographs by Steve Hilton-Barber.[42] On a larger scale, there is the controversy that exploded in 2006 around cartoons of the prophet Muhammad published in a right-wing journal in Denmark.[43] In an amusing and ironical cartoon (*Mail and Guardian*, February 10–16, 2006) the South African cartoonist Zapiro linked the power of artistic expression (broadly understood) with weapons of mass destruction: a forlorn and bemused cartoonist is seen clutching papers in one hand and brushes in the other. The words "Weapon of Mass Destruction" float in the white space above his head.[44] A point worth noting here is the quite distinctive relation between cartooning, politics, and democracy in Africa.[45] Achille Mbembe refers to cartooning in the context of the postcolony, and, more specifically, the violence of fantasy in the imaging of a figure of "the autocrat": "The universe of crude, laughable, and capricious things is also the universe most suited to the out-and-out deployment of that very specific faculty that is the faculty of imagining. The problem that these figurative expressions seek to resolve is how to write and give image to the arbitrariness that has all the hallmarks of magic, that lends itself to experimentation as caprice, and that has violent effects provoking suffering and laughter at the same time."[46]

The violence of simultaneous suffering and laughter provokes profound questions. In such cases, as in many of the other examples I have touched on, we always risk a collateral confusion of the precarious, shifting boundary between actual and symbolic violence. But what is clear is that violence is omnipresent in many parts of our cultural life, however complex and mediated that violence might be.

A wider perspective supports this point. Violence and art have a long, entwined history. This is clear, for example, in Valentine Groebner's study of violence and defacement in the visual culture of violence in the late Middle Ages. Groebner importantly includes the spectating body in defacement, asking what happens when you "cannot look away" from "the violence of the picture" staring back.[47] Defacement in contemporary cultures is taken up by Michael Taussig, who addresses public secrecy and our capacity for "knowing not to know," which is for him a singularly potent form of social knowledge.[48] Cultures have been iconophobic and iconophilic, and rarely indifferent to the diabolic terror and possibility of transcendence that material images seem to hold.[49] The fact that bouts of iconoclasm are still common enough within both secular and religious communities points to the continuing vitality of such questions. The imagery surveyed in the spectacular 2002 exhibition "Iconoclash" makes this plain.[50] This exhibition reminded us of the peculiar and complex agency of pictures in both secular and religious worlds. It is a contemporary commonplace to identify violent internal passions and affect with art, an identification against which neither reason nor irony inoculates us.[51] In this space, the "magic," the terror, the trauma, and the violence of the visual lies.

ONLY HUMAN

A fuller recognition of violence, of the trauma it occasions in our artmaking, is part of what it means to be human. This recognition presents both obstacle and opportunity. Obstacle in the sense of being tied to, fixated on, enslaved by a particular historical trauma, unable to move beyond it, as we must. Opportunity in that consciousness of this obstacle opens a space for movement.[52]

Being human in South Africa is commonly expressed by the indigenous term *ubuntu*.[53] Artist and writer David Nthubu Koloane offers a definition that would be widely accepted: "Ubuntu, simply put, is an age-old African term for humanness, incorporating the values of caring, sharing and being in harmony with all creation. As an ideal, Ubuntu espouses selflessness and fairness to all. Broadly, it promotes cooperation between individuals, families, communities, culture and nations. Ubuntu empowers all to be valued for them to reach their full potential in accord with all that is around them. It is within every human being."[54]

"Ubuntu" describes the humanism underpinning the TRC, and, in fact, our new constitution. As the TRC report states, "*Ubuntu,* generally translated as 'humanness,' expresses itself metaphorically in *umuntu ngumuntu ngabantu*— people are people through other people."[55] The link between the TRC and humanism can be demonstrated in different ways, one being Susan Stewart's suggestion that the TRC and similar tribunals for crimes against humanity reflect "an acknowledgement of the *specificity of mankind* and possibility of *universal consensual judgements* oriented toward the future" (my emphasis).[56] The capacity to recognize "the specificity of mankind" and engage the possibilities of "consensual judgements," even if conditioned by agonistic confrontation, is pivotal to the prospects for humanism.[57]

Scholar Mark Sanders, like many others, refers to the loss of ubuntu during apartheid, the loss of truth, and the presence of evil. He understands ubuntu as "an ethics of human reciprocity," where "the relation to the other is prior to the selfhood of the self," and that "relation is a condition of possibility for the selfhood of the self." Ubuntu is thus not fixed but mutable, "a commutarian alternative to human rights," which would mitigate against charges of fundamentalist identity politics, be they religious or secular. Ubuntu takes place between members of a community, but also, critically, between strangers. Because of its "ability to alter itself" the notion allows for a powerful, if always provisional, stability.[58]

We need to be critical and cautious in our appreciation of this term; it can and has been manipulated to service just about any purpose: ahistorical, "precolonial" nostalgias, suspect solidarity politics, currents of cultural correctness, and overheated fantasies about free markets. The term is a magnet to the triumphalist hubris we often find in ideas of an African Renaissance, of "Rainbowism," and, indeed, democracy.[59]

Richard A. Wilson, noting that "ubuntu" represents "an expression of community" and "a romanticised vision of 'the rural African community' based upon reciprocity, respect for human dignity, community cohesion and solidarity," cites Alfred Cockrell's argument that ubuntu "is indicative of 'the saccharine assertions of rainbow jurisprudence' in the new South Africa, which state blandly that *all* competing values can, mysteriously, be accommodated within the embrace of a warm fuzzy consensus."[60] For Cockrell, "human rights and constitutionalism require hard choices by citizens who will inevitably disagree about the common good." For Wilson, ubuntu is really "an ideological concept that conjoins human rights, restorative justice, reconciliation and nation-building within the populist language of pan-Africanism."[61] There is no protection against the less persuasive and more conformist aspects of this idea, but it should not be abandoned simply because of the risk of ready trivialization.[62]

Most adult South Africans can trace formative parts of their lived experience to the apartheid epoch. Apartheid was, after all, a crime against *humanity*, an institutionalized violence that places the human at the center of our recent history and living memory.[63] Indigenous forms of humanism can be found in the writings of the late Steve Biko and Es'kia Mphaphele, among others, and these forms are continuous with notions in circulation elsewhere in Africa as well as those surviving from earlier moments in its decolonization.[64] The thought of Julius Nyerere comes to mind here, and of course Frantz Fanon's coruscating attack on European humanism.[65] For Fanon, Enlightenment humanism went hand in hand with rapacious European imperialism, signaling enslavement and death for millions: "an avalanche of murders."[66] African humanism seeks something different, shaped as it is by the peoples of the continent's own complex background of internal violence and social strife.[67] Edward Said observes that Fanon's attack on European humanism "was to include the edifice of European humanism itself, which proved incapable of going beyond its own invidious limitations of vision. As Immanuel Wallerstein described so well, subsequent critics of Eurocentricism in the last four decades of the twentieth century furthered the attack by taking on Europe's historiography, the claims of universalism, its definition of civilization, its Orientalism, and its uncritical acceptance of the paradigm of progress that placed 'the West' at the centre of an encroaching mass of lesser civilizations trying to challenge the West's supremacy."[68]

However we might understand it, a humanist project in Africa would be a contingent, historically specific, lived, and critically inflected discourse of human being and relatedness. It would be neither essentialist nor universalist in its ambitions.

I have already pointed to the decisive role that the TRC—in its broad sense and with specific reference to violence—has had in the development of contemporary South African art of the last decade. More broadly, there are a number of indigenous terms that offer resources for our understanding of humanism. I have already mentioned "ubuntu" frequently invoked in South Africa. Elsewhere in Africa we find the KiSwahili precept "Mtu ni Watu" (a person is people).[69]

In a different context Julia Kristeva presents some thoughts on humanity and care that resonate here:

In our modern world, we do not really have a positive definition of what characterizes humanity. . . . We are even led to ask what humanity is, if only when we are confronted with crimes against it. My personal experience leads me to think that the minimum definition of humanity—the "degree zero," as Barthes would say, of humanity—is precisely the capacity for hospitality. The Greeks were not mistaken when they chose the word "ethos" to refer to the most radically human aptitude, now called ethics, which involves making a choice between good and evil but also all other choices. The word "*ethos*" . . . means "the dwelling-place or resting-place of animals."[70]

This squares rather precisely with Clifton Crais's point that the negative energy and destruction—indeed, the evil—associated with (in the case he discusses) witchcraft is "the very opposite of *ubuntu*, of *hospitality and sharing* and of those virtues that make one human and good and life worth living" (my emphasis).[71] The idea of ubuntu retains a certain currency, especially if we keep in mind the violence that structures, and has structured, our social relations, our senses of community, our history. This consciousness of violence—which the TRC both reenacted and commented on—includes both idealizations and criticisms of the idea. It is a consciousness that supports ideas of humanism as provisional, contingent, and culturally specific.

There are signs in the past decade of various developments in our consciousness of the human. Okwui Enwezor, director of the Second Johannesburg Biennial in 1997, touched on the project of humanism in his framing essay for that event: "When we examine South Africa's history, we find, like in many other places of trauma, that through the critical practice of culture history is not only brought alive and given urgency, but is, most importantly, a vital way these societies *humanise* and define their common interests, even if those interests rest on the daily reality of unbridgeable differences" (my emphasis).[72]

Enwezor's reference to trauma suggests a common experience with people from other parts of the globe and runs counter to the parochial notion of "exceptionalism" that South Africans are so vulnerable to evoking in regard to themselves.[73] Trauma is clearly a contemporary reality and almost the master trope of our time.[74]

Meditating on 9/11 (which has become *the* sign of trauma in much of the West) and its aftermath, Judith Butler traces relations between violence, vulnerability, and humanness. Her project has other objectives, but her perspective on humanism and its relation to violence seem especially relevant here. One of her most salient observations is that *corporeal vulnerability* is, in fact, "one precondition for humanization."[75] Corporeal vulnerability links to trauma, which, as I note above, may well be, today, the most common experience across the globe. There is a strong solidarity here between Butler's and Kristeva's comments about hospitality, corporeal vulnerability, and the desire to reach experiences that go beyond other forms of identification.

In a similar vein to Enwezor, Themba Sono argues that "for African intellectuals to be truly intellectual they will need to accept that *human experience* transcends the parochialism of collective existence or the eccentricity of individual preoccupation" (my emphasis).[76] For Sono, critical reflexivity, robust subject-object openness on a wide, "non-exclusive" cultural front is a key to our view of "the human." Ideas of human identity that are radically relational and resolutely dialectical bear on the actual artistic challenges facing us. The TRC and the African humanism that guided it created conditions for facing these dilemmas and resituating our critical and cultural horizons.[77] To reject these recent efforts to rearticulate "the human" is critically and culturally myopic.[78] Ideas of human identity-in-relation that are radically relational and resolutely dialectical bear on the actual artistic challenges facing us.

How does the question of proximity bear on the idea of ubuntu? Ann Bernstein criticizes the conception of ubuntu promoted by Makgoro and others as not being adequately qualified by a point John Mbiti emphasizes. For Mbiti, ubuntu is "a powerful spirit of mutual support and accountability but *one that applies within face-to-face traditional communities.*"[79] This criticism suggests a rather static and unduly literalist notion of what "face-to-face" means in a rather fixed economy of proximity and temporality. Here, "face-to-face" functions like a form of eye-witnessing requiring overtly direct access to others, events, and objects. But directness is a complex construction, and cosmopolitan space is, in fact, more intricate than is allowed by this approach, especially in the vast and speedy communication circuits in what we sometimes call "the global village." The subjectivities and identifications that operate in contact, communication, and exchange in post-1994 South Africa are entirely more pliable. Proximity is an elastic relation, and variably mediated. It is possible, therefore, to speak coherently of an instrumentally and mechanically mediated intimacy, one that enables a critically responsive, reflexive human agency, and that operates both up close and at varying kinds of distance.

BEING HUMAN (AGAIN)

In his book *Humanism and Democratic Criticism,* published in 2003, Edward Said makes a powerful case for a new humanism, a project he relates to democracy. In spite of the often justifiably bad press humanism has attracted, it is, for

Said "to some extent, a resistance to *idées reçues,* and . . . offers opposition to every kind of cliché and unthinking language."[80] This remarkable intellectual's view of humanism is thus intensely oppositional and critical, being "more attuned than any before it to the non-European, genderized, decolonized, and decentred energies and currents of our time." A new generation of humanist scholars, argues Said, situates *"critique* at the very heart of humanism, *critique as a form of democratic freedom* and as a continuous practice of questioning and of accumulating knowledge that is open to, rather than in denial of, the constituent historical realities of the post–Cold War world, its early colonial formation, and the frighteningly global reach of the last remaining superpower of today" (my emphasis).[81]

Humanism, in this view, has profound possibilities for understanding the critical force of creativity and the work of the imagination in developing a democratic civil society.[82] Said emphatically understands humanism in a critical way, and more pointedly, as a process of self-understanding: "it is possible to be critical of humanism in the name of humanism, and . . . , schooled in its abuses by the experience of Eurocentrism and empire, one could fashion a different kind of humanism that was cosmopolitan and text-and-language bound in ways that absorbed the great lessons of the past."[83]

In a discussion of Said's central thoughts about humanism, Saree Makdisi selects some qualities that are at the core of Said's critical project. Makdisi cites Said's insistence on using one's mind "historically and rationally for the purposes of reflective understanding." In addition, humanism gains strength through a sense of community with other interpreters, societies, and temporalities, there being no (strictly speaking) "isolated humanism." Makdisi reiterates Said's provocative comment that humanism is "the only and [he] would go so far as saying the final resistance we have against the inhuman practices and injustices that have disfigured human history."[84] Resistance, communality, and commitment to communication all characterize Said's humanism.

Distinctive and provocative in Said's position regarding the art world is his insistence on the integrity of the aesthetic.[85] It is difficult to overstate this aspect of his humanist thinking. Concurring with T. W. Adorno, Said writes that "there is a fundamental irreconcilability between the aesthetic and non-aesthetic that we must sustain as a necessary condition of our work as humanists. Art is not simply there: it exists intensely in a state of unreconciled opposition to the depredations of daily life, the uncontrollable mystery on the bestial floor."[86]

Said's "uncontrollable mystery on the bestial floor" (a kind of radical alterity) speaks to the risky interaction between humanism, art, and violence that, I suggest, is distinctive in contemporary South African art.[87] Part of this risk rises from associating violence with this part of the world, an association haunted by the ancient specter of primitivism and stereotypical views of Africa.[88] But we need to break the continuity with prior forms of the primitivist stereotyping that seems to be the curse of this continent. This risk is itself part of the phenomenon I am trying to grasp here. Not to engage it, to ignore the violence this discourse embodies, would be a failure of critical nerve in postapartheid South Africa. Seen this way, the pursuit (even if impossible to achieve) of humanism both strengthens and sets limits—partly by being historicized—on any purportedly universalizing ambitions that might attend arguments for "new," contemporary humanisms.

A dynamic, unstable, contingent form of humanism, one that faces violence in an aesthetic of an insistent materiality, has become an increasingly visible thread in South African contemporary art. Many works stage "humanness" in a way that does not deny the violence that conditions such works, their production and reception, their modes of representation, and, importantly, the violence out of which such powerful desires for the humane are born.

Interest in human-beingness has, of course, been a constant of human thought.[89] Kwame Appiah, for example, has argued for an agonistic humanism within the postmodern moment: "What I am calling humanism can be provisional, historically contingent, anti-essentialist (in other words postmodern) and still be demanding. We can surely maintain a powerful engagement with the concern to avoid cruelty and pain while nevertheless recognising the contingency of that concern. Maybe, then, we can recover within postmodernism the postcolonial writers' humanism—their concern for human suffering, for the victims of the postcolonial state . . . while still rejecting the master narratives of modernism."[90]

THE ART OF BEING HUMAN

Created at the intersection of art, violence, and being human, a number of recent and contemporary works offer us insights into the uneven, sometimes hesitant but always urgent unfolding of a postapartheid imaginary. There are a number of ways we might articulate this intersection. Most familiar is the picturing or performance of violent threat, risk, or action. One could speak here of the iconographies of violence, of pain, of wounding and death. There is now a well-established literature on the place of pain in creativity.[91] The artworks mentioned earlier that deal with the theme of necklacing are part of a persistently spectacular archive of this iconography.

We are alerted to a second current in art's articulation of violence and human being by Mbembe's argument that there is a level of discourse on Africa that is "almost always deployed in the framework (or in the fringes) of a meta-text about the *animal* . . . about the *beast.*"[92] When we combine this with Edward Said's reference to the link between aesthetics and the "uncontrollable mystery on the bestial floor," another condition of being human becomes clear: our relation to animality.[93] This could be put in different terms, for example, the more familiar relation between what we call culture and what we call nature. Sexualities and the body become the focus. There is a distinct, developing interest in animality—referenced in iconography and in choice of medium—at work in contemporary practices in South Africa, where a violent discursivity attends questions of "perverse" sexualities and provocative (ab)uses of the body.

Linked to this violent discursivity is the recent development of ritualized performativity focused on the body in art. There are a number of examples where not only this subject but also its reception has evoked forms of violence. These include the forcible removal of Steve Hilton-Barber's work from a Johannesburg gallery, mentioned above, and the controversy over photographs displayed at the "Sex and Secrecy" conference held at Wits University in Johannesburg in 2004.[94] These events bracketed other critical moments in our discourse on representational violence.[95]

Amongst the most notable of these events was the so-called black vagina controversy of 1996 that went all the way to parliament. The controversy was sparked by an unobtrusive three-dimensional work titled *Useful Objects* by student Kaolin Thomson and exhibited in the annual Martienssen exhibition at the Gertrude Posel Gallery, University of Witwatersrand. What ignited the debate was actually the critical framing of the work by *Mail and Guardian* critic Hazel Friedman.[96] Her implication that this work showed a black vagina provoked a stinging response from Baleka Kgositsile, then deputy speaker of the National Assembly. After noting her objections in a mass circulation newspaper, Kgositsile pointed to the specific dynamics of South African culture:

> These debates take place at a particular time in this country which has a specific history. . . . Historically black women have been the most oppressed and exploited, always having been regarded as "useful objects," which people could abuse and dispense with as they pleased. As a country we are still faced with the challenge of nation-building. In the process a number of factors have to be accommodated. Our values, sensitivities and those traditions that enable us to move towards a prosperous future need to be taken cognisance of. . . . People's pride and dignity cannot be trampled on in the name of freedom of expression. If need be, legislation must protect our people from

degradation that is likely to continue in the name of trying to keep up with some arbitrary artistic ideals not set by the majority of those affected by these academic debates.[97]

A third shaping of the intersection between art, violence, and humanism relates to technology, to machines and an interest in mechanical animality. Our response to these animate and inanimate "objects" and their worldly habitats bears directly on how we understand and engage our humanness. The spaces and the stuff of the human and animal body, along with animality and technology more generally, crucially shape human *being,* and are deeply enmeshed in much current South African photographic practice.

A fourth configuration of violence and being human occurs in and around language. I have mentioned Bhabha's claim that there was, in the postmodern moment, a shift from transcendence to translation. Translation can be considered a form of violence that occurs as we try to coordinate and correlate one language to another in a volatile public sphere. Much is lost as well as gained in the transfers we call translation. The politics of language ignited one of the turning points in the struggle for liberation, namely the Soweto Uprising of 1976.[98] Profound questions of epistemology and power underpin conflicts about language. Often these conflicts are expressed in terms of lococentric forms of knowing and experience: for example, in the battles over Afrocentricism, Eurocentricism, what is indigenous, what alien.[99]

Discursively driven artwork reiterates the violence of a certain kind of generic, abstract, linguistic interpretation. The ruling illusion here is that of radical translatability, of the transparency of the visual, especially as it travels global art circuits. Another illusion is a conceptualism in which idea dominates materiality.[100] Linguistic imperialism takes on an extra edge in polylingual South Africa. The scriptovisual violence of irony, parody, mimicry, and the counter-nostalgias for lost causes, roots, and futures are all relevant. The works of artist Moshekwa Langa, and in some measure Willem Boshoff, are exemplary instances.

But language also relates to different modes of sensory perception. The title of Sandile Zulu's artwork *Sahara Sands: (Main Theme from Kinda Music)* (1995) evokes its musical inspiration. The five panels of the piece function as five visual beats, while the markings structure spontaneities and improvisations. The optical and auditory are not mutually exclusive. I will discuss further meanings in this work below. Its references to music continue a long tradition in South African art. Music is an important subject in some early paintings by Gerard Sekoto, for example *Song of the Pick* (n.d.); the assemblages of David Koloane,

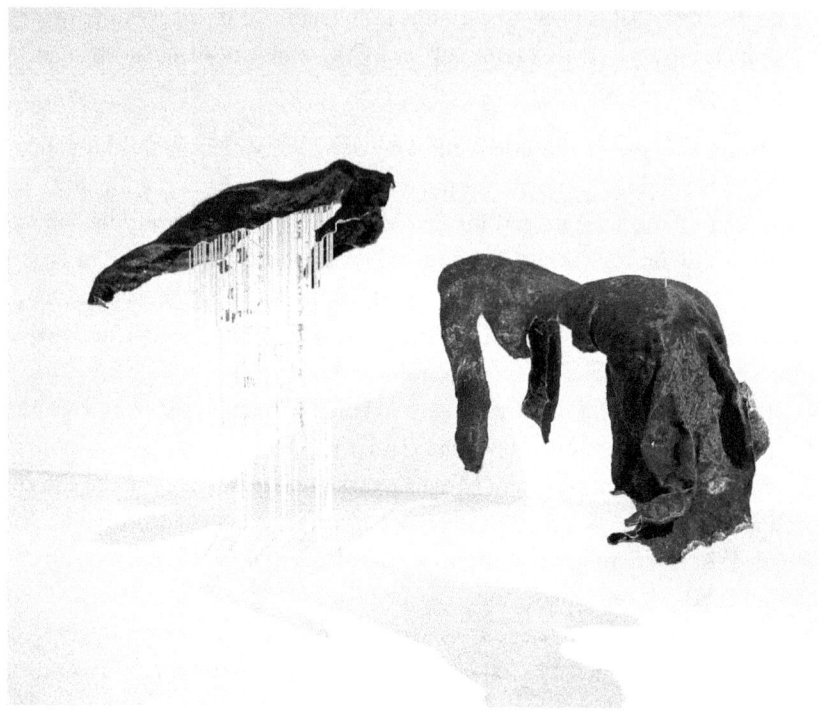

Nandipha Mntambo, *Stepping into Self* and *Purge,* both 2005. Collection of Iziko: South African National Gallery. Photograph by Kathy Comfort-Skead. Courtesy of Michael Stevenson, Cape Town.

such as *Saxophone on Wheel* (2001); and a number of Sam Nghlengethwa's collages.[101]

An interest in incarnated animality seems to inform some of the work of Nandipha Mntambo, whose key concern is with the contemporary female body, especially in its stereotyping. Her primary medium is cowhide, and she tends not to obscure or sanitize the carnality of this skin: its smell, its fattiness, its hairiness. The connotations of cowhide are diverse, but are, perhaps, most powerfully associated with power, wealth, and sexual exchange. Some of Mntambo's work is also emphatically processual, a quality captured by her titles, such as *Purge* (2005) and *Stepping into Self* (2005).[102] According to Gabi Ngcobo these works "question oppressive notions of femininity," while others "evoke a sense of beauty and release from physical restrictions." For Mntambo, race "informs appearance, language and geographical locality, which impact on access to educational resources, which in turn influences individual experiences of the South African milieu."[103]

An important trend in contemporary South African art involves specifically

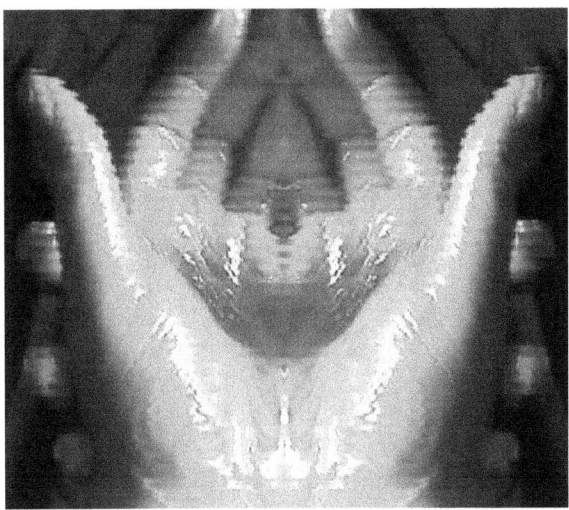

Churchill Madikida, *Blood on My Hands,* 2004. Courtesy of Michael Stevenson, Cape Town.

ritualized violence to the body. This has been the focus of a number of works on male initiation by Churchill Madikida.[104] Madikida reflects on what male circumcision practices might mean for our emerging present, and explicitly positions himself and his art making within the heavily traded terrain of self and identity. His art, he says, is "autobiographical" and engages his "Xhosa heritage as a form of positive identity and self-imagery."[105] It is "through making images" that he feels he can "connect the past to the present." These imaginative enactments are "my way of knowing what I know, a way to uncover how, where, and why I learned it, and a way to unlearn."[106] Rituals of this sort are at once forms of social cement and social control, of communal and individual self-assertion and self-limitation. Madikida is sensitive to the complexity and potency of such rituals in the modern moment. The absence of such practices is for him "unthinkable," yet they are also risky; "every year a vast number of initiates . . . go under the spear," some die, some are "maimed for life." The memorial dimension of Madikida's project moves to the fore here, and he dedicated his body of work on circumcision "to all those initiates that lose their lives and their manhood undergoing this ritual." Nevertheless, the artist is at pains to insist that his "works are not only about the horrors of circumcision . . . but . . . also interrogate issues around representation/presentation of 'private' or 'sacred' rituals." He seeks to educate "the general public" about these practices, and so contribute to the building of a civil society that acknowledges the cultural integrity of the performance of heritage in a properly critical way. Seen

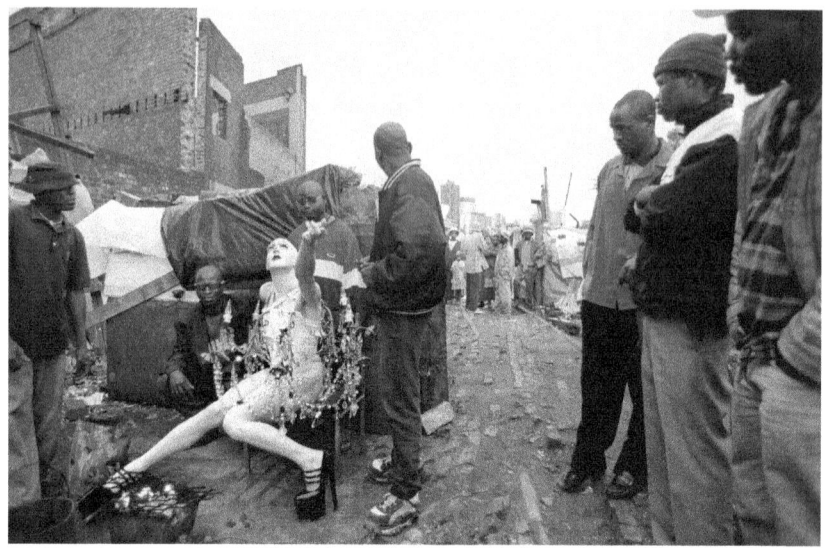

Steven Cohen, *Chandelier,* 2001–2. Performance, Newtown, Johannesburg. Photograph by John Hogg. Courtesy of David Krut Publishing.

from another perspective, Madikida's work is part of more general reworking of masculinity in our first decade of democracy.[107]

A number of male artists are involved in this reworking. Steve Hilton-Barber has been mentioned. Others include Kay Hassan in his *Ritual Crossings* (2004), an ongoing, photo-based articulation of social rituals, and Zwelethu Mthethwa, in his somewhat earlier *Black Men and Masculinity* (1999).[108] Violent trauma— socially sanctioned or otherwise—is not simply located in the personal and collective experience of circumcision, but also in the disfiguring violence of representation, a question that animates our human present.[109] Steven Cohen's metro-melancholic photo documents *Limping into the African Renaissance* (2001–2002) and *Chandelier* (2001–2002) both elaborate the performance of vagrant masculinity and take it to the edge.[110]

Sexuality, maleness, femaleness, and sexual orientation and violence against women (and children) are subjects central to the work of Nicholas Hlobo and Zanele Muholi. Muholi is a self-identified black lesbian and activist. Her often frank and disquieting photographs are included in a major recent publication that documents same-sexuality in eastern and southern Africa.[111] They also illustrate material published by the Forum for the Empowerment of Women (FEW). In her work *Virgins,* according to Gabi Ngcobo, Muholi has tackled another taboo subject, namely "the controversial 'revival' of the practice of virginity testing, presently occurring in certain areas of Kwa-Zulu Natal and Gauteng."[112]

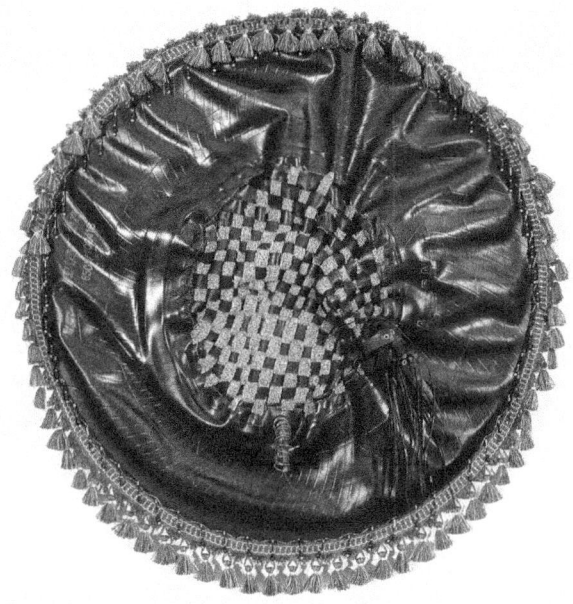

Nicholas Hlobo, *Hermaphrodite*, 2002. Photograph by Kathy Comfort-Skead. Courtesy of Michael Stevenson, Cape Town.

There is a disturbing and unforgiving intimacy in many of her works, one that compels reflection on how the difficult processes of love and objectification are being enacted. In an article by Sean O'Toole, Muholi speaks of the "violence against women who practice same sex relationships" as a major challenge.[113]

For his part, Nicholas Hlobo focuses on sexual desire and sexual destiny in a calm, sometimes campish, often amused aesthetic.[114] Of *Umtya Nethunga* (2005), he writes: "rubber . . . relates to the masculine status symbol because it comes from cars; it also relates to industrialisation which is largely male dominated. The rubber has sexual connotations as well." Rubber made an appearance in his earlier *Hemaphrodite* (2002) and is becoming something of a signature. While there is wit at work in this piece, for Hlobo the "thought of creating these works . . . made me feel like my head was going to explode." A work titled *Vanity* (2005) comprises various materials, including rubber inner tube strips, eyelets, red ribbon, and green Sunlight soap. The soap is of some moment: "This kind of soap is commonly used in South African households for washing dishes, clothes and bodies. It is the same soap most Xhosa initiates use to wash on the morning of their graduation ceremony. Like rubber, it has a strong link to industrialisation. In relation to colonisation . . . it is one of those early products that were brought to Africa by Europeans. . . . The soap has a smell that is distinctly Sunlight, cheap and very close to Africa. It is there to suggest the idea of cleansing."[115]

Sunlight soap is, as Hlobo intimates, an olfactory icon for many South Africans. It possesses something of the somatic and cultural pungency of Jeyes Fluid, which Moshekwa Langa used to such good effect in a process work for the exhibition "Fault Lines: Inquiries around Truth and Reconciliation," which I mentioned earlier.

A kind of devil-may-care, autographic (freehand), reprographic (technological), mix-and-match campishness is central to a number of Moshekwa Langa's works. In *Archive* (2002) and *I Love My Pashmina* (2002) Langa's militantly magpie approach results in collages of photographic fragments, often of faces and bodies, embedded in autographic texts and drawings. Langa also documents his body in his *Far Away from Any Scenery He Knew or Understood* (1998), a work that speaks in an affecting if obscure rhetoric of urban nomadism.[116] The hard edge of urban drift, mobility, and migration develops when movement is forced. This is the condition of unwanted exile, estrangement, and alienation. Langa's performances or stagings (mostly what we see is the residue of an actual living-time performance) are cryptic and diaristic, his aesthetic one of wit and whimsy, a sharp feel for the game and a devotion to keeping on the move. Shannon Fitzgerald remarks on conflicting senses of seriousness and playfulness in Langa's work, linking this to diasporic experience. She comments further that "Langa's epic landscapes are, on the one hand, unconventional release, and on the other, a prosaic but probing look at authorship, ownership, and cultural hegemony as these concepts figure in world literature and mythology. With an uncanny sense of levity, Langa's explosive animations of what can only be described as Darwinism gone awry, relive the empirical weight of history and science, and replace them with absurd fictions that ironically, seem much more reasonable."[117]

Young artist Thando Mama's works *Back to Me* (2002) and *Mind-Space* (2004) address African identity embedded in and interfered with by technology, while at the same time exploring the limitations of an identity that is more prescribed and fixed than self-articulated and fluid.[118] An intense, mesmeric singularity characterizes his video installation *(u)hea(r)d* (2002).[119] In this work, the space is completely evacuated save for the body of the viewer and a TV monitor on the floor. Sound lends a simultaneously sentimental and sinister tone to the whispering face on the screen, a screen that is the only source of light. Graininess, flared halos of light around forms—all contingencies of the medium and process—produce an eerie banality.[120]

Perhaps the most sustained elaboration of the relation of human body and techno-machine is to be found in the works of Nathaniel Stern and Marcus Neustetter. Stern's *Compressionism* is a digital performance that invokes a "complex conversation between artist, performance, mediation tool, art object(s) and viewer," while Neustetter, Stern's sometime partner in art, has produced "digital frottage" in which he scanned, photocopied, and photographed the screen of his laptop.[121] A more recent work is site-specific, where he used photo-sensitive paper to record the fall of light and the shape of space in the Franchise Gallery in Johannesburg. This is sly work, and both artists seem to shove a digit in the air at the cybermyths of boundless, dematerialized, "democratic" connection and communication, without rejecting the myth of a borderless global community and the boundless processes or radical interconnectivity.[122] Theirs is not the techno-utopia or dystopia promised and warned against by apologists for globalization and its opponents; one senses instead a slightly perverse smile that knows it is in the thrall of some kind of retro-materialist libido on a humane and doggedly human scale.[123]

The increasing technologization and administration of social life has led to newer if sometimes ambiguous forms of human *being* where the machine is not always antagonistic to *humanness* but rather extends its reach. This is often expressed in certain photographic practices in contemporary South African art. The distance between the body before and behind an increasingly incarnated camera is now being calibrated differently. And insofar as new technologies have an intelligent life of their own, they create risks and possibilities for human being in a posthuman age.[124]

The relation between mechanism and magic, between the automatic indexicality of the photograph and its magical mimetic function, is part of our broader understanding of the relations between bodies and technologies. The photographic image is a magical illusion, an enchanted visuality. Marina Warner, for example, argues that "running through the history of magic and its attendant anxieties runs a parallel history of optics."[125] Following the elastic logic of what "face-to-face" might mean and recognizing the magical energies bound up in photographic processes and objects, we can begin to understand the photograph as an expansion of human being and self-in-relation.

During 2003 Senzeni Marasela produced a set of photographs of her mother in which her mother is only present as a shadow. The shape of this shadow shows her carrying a baby on her back, while she leans on a grass broom. Marasela explains that her mother was reluctant to be photographed because her shadow was captured. Shadows are "windows to the soul" and once someone possesses your shadow, her mother believed, "s/he can cast evil spells on you." Photography is here a traumatic trap.[126] Evil is the absence of ubuntu.

Susan Sontag commented long ago on the enchanting, contaminating, and ruthless intimacy of photographs: "Few Americans share the primitive dread of cameras that comes from thinking of the photograph as a material part of themselves. But some trace of the magic remains: for example, in our reluctance to tear up or throw away the photograph of a loved one, especially of someone dead or far away."[127]

The presence of the magical in everyday life is not a uniquely African phenomenon, but a human one.[128]

Sandile Zulu's five-panel work *Sahara Sands: (Main Theme from Kinda Music)* (1995) addresses this complex of ideas.[129] The visual field is reminiscent of an aerial view of recently bombed desert, or some unending alien landscape. The paper surface of the work is scorched and scored by controlled fire. The surface is most suggestive of parchment, of skin, giving a powerful sense of embodiment to that surface. The surface is also slightly curved. A leather strip separates each panel and each is varnished with a light-reflecting gloss that destabilizes the surface. Zulu's use of fire points to the intense materiality of his creative response. Using fire, he reenacts the primordial capture and domestication of this powerful natural phenomenon. Fire is both destructive and creative, and is a signal aspect of the shifting boundary between nature and culture. It is not an "autonomous substance," but a "phenomenon that derives from its circumstance."[130] It also has special resonance for Africa and our part of the world: "Fire runs like a metaphor through Southern Africa's centuries. It illuminates events and casts shadows we recognise only too well."[131] For Stephen Pyne, "captured fire . . . resembles a caught animal. . . . Its 'wild' properties are what make it valuable. . . . People let it loose, like a cheetah trained to the hunt, and allow it to roam. Its success depends on timing . . . and setting."[132] Animals, wildness, habitats, wilderness also draw our attention to the shifting borderland between human and animal. This zone of difference, this interplay of the animal and the human, has been enormously productive in contemporary South African art.

There is a direct echo of this interplay in the patterning that Zulu achieves through fire, and the equation of surface as skin. Skin features prominently in his *Indluyengwe* (1998) and *Indluyengwe Yokuqala (Leopards Den 1)* (2000), in which Zulu references the leopard directly. With its ability to camouflage itself, as well as in its speed and guile, the leopard is a symbolically saturated creature in South Africa. In this iconography a kind of panhuman animism seems at work.[133] Fire and predatory cunning suggest to us the sense of violence that underpins our relations: between the animate and inanimate, between the human and the nonhuman, between culture and nature. Using fire, Zulu explores a shifting line, or edge, or, a frontline—to use Zulu's own combative language—

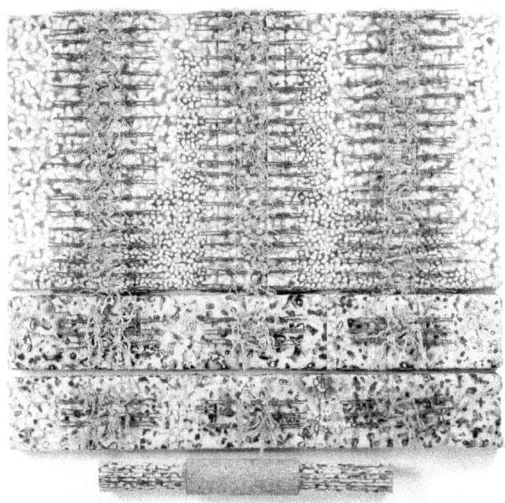

Sandile Zulu, *Indluyengwe (Leopard's Lair)*, 2000. Fire, water, air, barbed wire, canvas, and string. Photograph by Wayne Ossthuizen. Courtesy of David Krut Publishing.

between animal and human realms. Animality can be construed as a condition of being human, and vice versa. Zulu's recycling of natural and manufactured materials, industrial castoffs and grass, for example, in an aesthetic process of cutting, layering, and burning, assimilates the cultural to the natural and the natural to the cultural. This is, perhaps, the conservationists' strategy of wasting nothing, and resisting obsolescence in both our social and natural worlds.

In an important way, Noria Mabasa's *Deluge* (1994) also engages with the entanglements of the animal and human as electronically mediated forces of nature. Her imagery is drawn as much from television as it is from other sources at her disposal. But, again, here the point is the entanglement and codependency of the animal and the human realm, suspending any idea of a stable separation between the two. It also aims to underscore the volatility and violence of the forces that impact on this relation, rendering all equal under the iron law of nature. The wood used for such work is often chosen for symbolic or spiritual reasons. Carving, cutting, and shaping occurs in sympathy with the form of the material, and its own symbolic logic.[134]

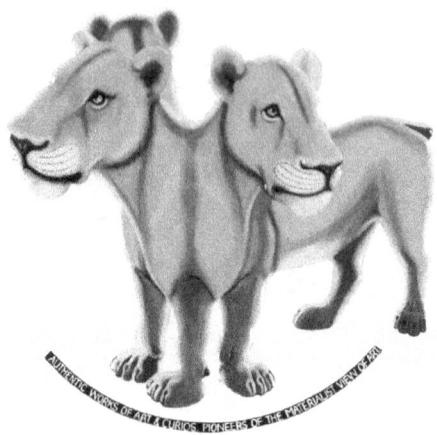

Joachim Schönfeldt, *Pioneers of the Materialist View of Art*, 1998. Painted embossments on paper. Courtesy of the MTN Collection.

Joachim Schönfeldt's mock-pedantic, lightly ironical *Pioneers of the Materialist View of Art* (1998) is a complex, multipart work that deals with different economies of the creativity and representations of the animal, or the wild. In this work five stacks of thick, round, gray disks, each disk smaller than the one immediately below, float above groups of three-headed cows, lionesses, and peahens. These solid, dull disks picture social data, reducing life to datum and cipher, and compounding complexity into gray slabs of information: optical phenomena that hover like haloes over the animals below.

These are more artifacts than actual animals. There is something curious here, indeed, a "curio aesthetic" that suggests sentiment and aesthetic simplification. A high-gloss surface of enamel paint supports the evident artifice of each image. The animals are all embossed, and hence more assertively material than might otherwise have been the case. Here, nature becomes culture, animal becomes curio, and the artist's creativity economically ambiguous. The artist looks rather laconically at the incompatibilities of different economic fields and the artificial division of particular forms of creative labor.

Jeremy Wafer's *Red Disc* (1994) is part of a series in which the human figures in diverse ways. The disk is human in scale, recalling the circle in Leonardo's so-called Vitruvian Man (1485–1490), but of course the disk is a primary form.[135] The disk of our sun rises and sets, our moon waxes and wanes. Each calibrates time. The form of the circle is unhierarchical, apart from its center and circumference, which bring into play the ranked spatialities of middle and margin. The colors Wafer uses are those of the earth, reminiscent of the actual earth colors raw or burnt umber or sienna. Here the red earth pigment (*ubomvu*) is from the local sources, and considered by Zulu-speaking South Africans as "transformational."[136] The surface of the work is studded and patterned with small orbs—one of the stronger references here is to the patterning on functional objects and treatments of the body in many indigenous cultures in Africa. As in Zulu's work, there is an equation between surface and skin, the most visible and the largest organ of the human body.[137] The overall aesthetic ecology Wafer produces suggests that the separation been the animal and the human, the earth and its inhabitants is complex, dynamic, and mobile.

Another kind of relation between "culture" and "nature" can articulate a further dimension of what makes us "human." What I have in mind here is the current interest in prosthetics, cyborgs, and other manufactured or heavily technologized dimensions of being human.[138] In *Alien* (1998), Minette Vàri morphs the animal and human within urban settings and habitats of mechanical life. Vàri's medium is digital video, and her language that of pixilated simulation, bringing her closer to the realm of the cyborg and Donna Haraway's characterization of the human and the inhuman. Haraway is fascinated with the "inhuman," the cyborgiastic hybrid of machine and organism, with the radical expressive possibilities of new, technologically enabled channels of communication, imaging, and body modification that seems to be the material of Vàri's hall of mirrors. The "self" in this work becomes polymorphous, perverse, and prosthetic. The image we see is intensely "self"-directed, almost narcissistic in its self-fashioning, the virtual version—seamless and immaterial save for the physical screen and its surrounds—of the entirely more material "machines" or pictorial automata of, for example, Willie Bester. This is an odd connection, to say the least. Vàri appears to entertain the notion that animals and aliens are not so different, and that we are all morphologically part of the same genus. Or, perhaps, she evokes the urban, middle-class fantasy that we can be anything we want to be.

Penny Siopis has recently produced two distinct streams of work.[139] The first, which she calls "the shame series," usually comprises intense, warm, small paintings that together make a field. Siopis seems to be working on the very edge of making matter form. Pools of semi-translucent pigment, swathes and drips of a very fluid medium, are organized into scenes that are, often, primal. Repeated words—catchphrases and clichés—produce visual structure in a relentless restlessness. Intense red, white, and off-black darkness is handled with looseness and freedom, a sense of the power of the contingent that is belied by the lacerating subject being painted. Shadows loom, the large tower over the small, while innocence drowns in burgeoning bad faith. Each work is an ode to violence, domestic entrapment, and bodies that leak and spill.

Siopis's second interest is in a quasi-mystical character called Pinky Pinky, a subject at the center of a number of her works. Violence, here, lies within monstrosity and a nightmarish alienation. *Who Is Pinky Pinky?* (2002) shows a strangely sexed body that lies somewhere between a mass grave and a diabolical hatchery. Perhaps grave and the incubator are not so far apart, and perhaps we are indeed born astride a grave (as Samuel Beckett would have it). The figure's body is barely formed, brutish and naive in the way a young child might be. But the face implies a sinister sexuality. A detached hand rests near to where the heart should be. Below this amputated hand, the belly is pregnant with an infestation of small, tiny plastic babies. Like a rash. The pink skin does not cover this spawn, this swarm of human life in its almost exquisite monotony. All the plastic pink babies are mass-produced and struck from the same mould. They are commodities, and commodities infiltrate almost every corner and every moment of much of our lives. Commodities are foundational to that secular religion we call, in capitalism, the "open economy." *Pinky Pinky* plays fast and loose with fundamental boundaries between the sacred and profane, nature and perversion, normality and aberration. The smeared, variegated pinkness of the figure is profoundly alien, profoundly strange in its sly sexuality. Progeny, babies, seem mere by-products of some dubious technical processes. We are reminded that we play at being God with our genetic engineering and biological tampering. The order of nature and of the divine appear mocked by what Roger Shattuck would call the "human itch to overreach."[140]

Pinky Pinky is a fright. The pink infestation suffered by the underformed figure could be anything. What threatens in the belly of *Pinky Pinky* is a humanoid cancer dividing and multiplying incessantly, colonizing and consuming everything. The creature's incontinent fertility suggests the metastasis of devilish growth. The figure is flanked on each side by a simplified, bare face. One has static, bloody tears in its blind pearlescent eyes. The eyes are sunk into scar tissue. The other face is dominated by resigned eyes that peer pensively into the space we occupy.[141]

BECOMING HUMAN

Achille Mbembe tackles the "problem of Africa" from this angle within the present:

African human experience constantly appears in the discourse of our times as an experience that can only be understood through a *negative interpreta-*

tion. Africa is never seen as possessing things and attributes properly part of "human nature." . . . It is this elementariness and primitiveness that makes Africa the world par excellence of all that is incomplete, mutilated, unfinished, its history reduced to a series of setbacks of nature in its quest for humankind. At another level, discourse on Africa is almost always deployed in the framework (or in the fringes) of a meta-text about the *animal*—to be exact, about the *beast:* its experience, its world, and its spectacle. In this meta-text, the life of Africans unfolds under two signs (emphases in the original).[142]

Mbembe is describing the familiar and persistent condition of being "African" from the perspective of what he calls the "discourse of our time." We can readily see a conjunction here between animality and brutishness, a conjunction that invokes, as it has for others, the question of violence, but with a twist. For Nancy Scheper-Hughes and Philippe Bourgeois, for example, violence as "brute force is a misnomer." In their project, "the very *human* face of violence" is a key preoccupation.[143]

The condition of being African and being human that these artists and authors present is not a terminus, a symbolic obstacle against which we are condemned struggle in perpetuity. It could just as well be—and perhaps should be—the occasion of originary moments, and the imagining of other futures in the contemporary moment. This is especially urgent on a continent that has had more than its fair share of false starts. Beginnings are important. They partake of what Michael Taussig refers to as "the magic of origins" within modernity.[144] In this sense, "magic" constitutes an unruly momentum and range *within* modernity, which may offer us a way of thinking through Mbembe's otherwise pessimistic account of Africa's condition of "negative interpretation." It may also enable us to think through complex relations between violence, modernity, and contemporaneity within a complex intersection of the "human," the "animal," technology, and violence in the work of contemporary South African artists.[145] Far from being frigid and fixed, the condition described by Mbembe is a living possibility in our present state of contemporaneity. The spatial aspect of the agitated temporality embedded in the contemporary lies in part in the movement of doubling, the "two signs" identified by Mbembe.

Doubleness means the many, the multiple, the heterogeneously different, and nonsingular alterity. Doubleness is fundamental to allegorical structures of reading, which Fredric Jameson, among others, has considered very relevant to postcolonial worlds. We might also discern it at work in Paul Gilroy's seminal and nuanced articulation of double consciousness and modernity in "the Black

Atlantic."[146] But doubleness is structurally ambiguous, symmetrical and serial, at least in potential. It may turn either way: return to indivisible singularity or explode into asynchronous, polymorphic simultaneity. From the perspective of South Africa, the temporal repetition and spatial multiplicity underpinning Mbembe's words are as much part of a unique historical transition as it is a second take, a repetition. Orientating our experiences entails responsibility as to how we address the present in time, our place in space, and the relevance and currency of our artistic responses to our ever collapsing/expanding times and locations. There is something important, if fugitive, going on here, something threaded through with the terror and excitement of risk, an animated beginning yet again in a context of increasing openness.

Africa is not sleeping. It is not simply the site of savage, surplus suffering. Nor is Africa the enduring sign of spectacularly self-inflicted woundings, famine, poverty, plagues. . . . It certainly is not the origin or destination of soft-focus, primitivist romances about being "naturally" human. The luxury of slumbering in the comforting bleakness of Afropessimism or global cynicism is not ours.[147] Hence the currency of Strand's *Sleeping Man* on the cover of Fanon's *Wretched of the Earth*. Contemporary artistic practices in South Africa face the challenge of both demystifying the condition of which Strand's title is a symptom, and imagine new possibilities for human being, agency, and relatedness in art. This can only really be built if we do not deny the violences within which we live.

The imaginative perspectives opened on our art cultures by thinking through violence and the possibilities and disappointments of being human promise a great deal. This perspective will never say all that needs to be said about any artistic work or event, but right now it says much. To adopt a critical aesthetic attitude seems to me to be essentially a form of intense noticing, mobilizing, and sharpening different forms of attention. If this attitude is historically robust but engaged and open—as it should be—the tendencies toward assimilating and homogenizing difference in art, toward capitulating tamely to national or global artcultural agendas and dynamics, are resisted. But more: the value and possibility of emancipating various forms of commonality within and across our differences cannot be overstated.

NOTES

1 This photograph appears on the cover of the 1990 Penguin edition. It was in Accra that Kwame Nkrumah's All Africa's Peoples Conference was held in 1958, at the beginning of "the golden age of high pan-African ambitions and towering intellectual aspirations in Africa." See Ali Mazrui, "Pan Africanism and the Intellectuals," 58.

2 Strand practiced a kind of "collateral photography" early in his career, using a trick camera that persuaded subjects that he was shooting in another direction. Strand wrote that he "did 'the Blind Woman' [*Woman with Sign that reads "Blind,"* published in *Camera Work,* June 1917] and all those things with the idea of photographing people without them being aware they were being photographed." Quoted in Hill and Cooper, *Dialogue with Photography,* 4. In a way he did not mean and with an irony he did not intend, Alfred Steiglitz allegorized colonialism when he described Strand's early work as "brutally direct" and "devoid of trickery." Quoted in Marien, *Photography: A Cultural History,* 202.

3 See Bhabha "Postmodernism/Postcolonialism." In these contexts, translation is perhaps a more serviceable idea than, say, interpretation, as it entails a consciousness of loss, gain, and untranslatability: see Maharaj, "Perfidious Fidelity"; Steyn, *Act 2: Beautiful Translations;* Coombes, "The Object of Translation"; Ndebele, "Multi-Lingual Fictions"; and Sommer, *Bilingual Aesthetics.* South Africa is a polylingual country with eleven official languages, a fact that bears on our aesthetic practices.

4 Mbembe and Nuttall, "Writing the World from an African Metropolis," 348. In a remarkable attempt to connect critical intellectual work and everyday life, Ari Sitas observes that as "Africa has been constructed through racialised categories, through slavery and violence, and through geographic randomness, any category in use is marked by history and oppression" (Sitas, *Voices That Reason,* 21).

5 Taylor, *Modern Social Imaginaries.* The concept is used in de Kock, Bethlehem, and Laden, *South Africa in the Global Imaginary.*

6 Ecclesiastes 1:9; Pliny quoted in Schipper, *Imagining Insiders,* 2.

7 See Richards, "New Humanisms in Contemporary South African Art."

8 Ndebele, "The Rediscovery of the Ordinary," 37.

9 For Thoba, Sebidi, Alexander, and Kentridge, see Williamson, *Resistance Art in South Africa,* 106, 38, 43, 31 respectively. For Mandindi, see Younge, *Art of the South African Townships,* 17. On Siopis, see Smith, *Penny Siopis,* 13.

10 Ndebele, "The Rediscovery of the Ordinary," 40.

11 Ndebele, *The Cry of Winnie Mandela,* 74.

12 Necklace: A petrol-filled car tire used to burn political opponents, especially collaborators and informers. The tire was usually forced over the head and shoulders of victims, immobilizing them, and then doused with petrol or paraffin. The tire was then lit. This method was widely used by both pro- and antigovernment groups from the 1980s. See Krog, *Country of My Skull,* 284; South Africa Truth and Reconciliation Commission, *Report,* 3:108–12; Wilfried Schärf and Baba Ngcokoto, "Images of Punishment in the People's Courts of Cape Town, 1985–7," 360ff. and n. 43. Gill Straker et al. link the necklacing of *impimpi* (collaborators) in urban areas to practices involving accusations of witchcraft in rural areas. What was common to all these events were situations of profound social upheaval and violent disruption of communities; see Gill Straker, et al., *Faces in the Revolution,* 114. The link is also made in a liberation song of the 1980s transcribed by Krog: "Informers, we will kill you. Hayi! Hayi! / Witches, we will burn you. Hayi! Hayi!" Quoted in Krog, *Country of My Skull,* 188.

13 See Williamson, *Resistance Art in South Africa,* 123. Mandla Sibanda's *Life in Flames* (1986) is discussed in Williamson, *Resistance Art in South Africa,* 31, 69, 109, 120, 123.

Mandindi made two other images relevant here, namely *Homage to Township Art* (1989) and *Lifebuoy* (1995), reproduced in Younge, *Art of the South African Townships*, 17. See also Elliot, *Art from South Africa*, 62. On Vári, see Hug and Vogel, *Colours*, 116, 142. For Geers, see Richards, "Kendell Geers," 122. See also *Art South Africa* 1, no. 3 (Spring 2002).

14 Pauw, *Into the Heart of Darkness*, 153.

15 The reference is to Vuyani Mavuso and Nkosinathi Dlamini, both earmarked to "disappear." Each was poisoned and then shot in the head; "one of the policemen stepped forward, placed his foot against the neck of one of the captives, pressed the barrel of the Makarov against his head and pulled the trigger. . . . Seconds later, the other man was executed in the same manner" (Pauw, *Into the Heart of Darkness*, 154). Notorious death squad operatives including Dirk Coetzee, Almond Nofomela, and Joe Mamasela participated in the activities of Vlakplaas, a farm near Pretoria used as a base for hit squad activities (Pauw, *Into the Heart of Darkness*, 151).

16 Ndebele, *Johannes Mashego Segogela*, fig. 2.

17 Ndebele, "The Rediscovery of the Ordinary," 47.

18 Mbembe, *On the Postcolony*, 102.

19 Wollen, "Introduction," 9. Annie Coombes cites John Atkinson Hobson's concept of "spectatorial lust," so deeply entwined in imperialism, and argues that it survives in contemporary "blockbuster" art exhibitions such as "Africa: Art of a Continent" held at the Royal Academy of Arts, London, October 4, 1995–January 21, 1996; see Coombes, *Reinventing Africa*, 63.

20 Bonami, *Dreams and Conflicts*.

21 Kuoni, *Words of Wisdom*, 32.

22 See Law, "Performing on a Fault-Line"; and Hill, "Iconic Autopsy."

23 Jeffrey, *The Truth about the Truth Commission*, 7. The final report of the Amnesty Commission was published as vol. 6 of the *Truth and Reconciliation Commission Report* in 2003. For a chronology of the sessions of the TRC, see Meiring, *Chronicle of the Truth Commission*, 380–84.

24 See Soyinka, "Reparations, Truth, and Reconciliation"; and Rose, "Apathy and Accountability." On different forms of justice, see Wilson, *The Politics of Truth and Reconciliation in South Africa;* and Murphy, *Getting Even.*

25 Tawadros and Campbell, *Fault Lines.*

26 For critical reflections on the archive in South Africa, see Carolyn Hamilton et al., *Refiguring the Archive.*

27 South Africa Truth and Reconciliation Commission, *Report*, 1:40.

28 Perryer, *10 Years 100 Artists*, 9.

29 See Vries and Weber, *Violence, Identity, and Self-Determination;* Schröder and Schmidt, introduction to *Anthropology of Violence and Conflict;* and Foster et al., *The Theatre of Violence.*

30 Scheper-Hughes and Bourgeois, "Introduction," 1.

31 Bourdieu and Wacquant, "Symbolic Violence," 272.

32 Sanders, *Complicities*, 8.

33 For Bourdieu, this distinction is "characteristic of a crude materialism, that the materialist theory of the economy of symbolic goods, which [he has] been trying to

build up over many years, seeks to destroy, by giving its proper place in theory to the objectivity of the subjective experience of relations of domination" (Pierre Bourdieu, "Gender and Symbolic Violence," 339).

34 Keane, *Violence and Democracy,* 39.

35 Keane also questions "boredom theories of violence" that, in considering violence symptomatically "ignore the dynamics of both psyches and social institutions" (Keane, *Violence and Democracy,* 98–99).

36 Jay, *Refractions of Violence,* 175.

37 Baudrillard, *Paroxysm,* 65.

38 Virilio, *Art and Fear,* 31.

39 Mamdani, *Good Muslim, Bad Muslim,* 3.

40 See Ndung'u, *The Right to Dissent.* For a history of apartheid censorship, see Merrett, *A Culture of Censorship.*

41 Appignanesi, *Freedom of Expression Is No Offence,* 246.

42 See Richardson, "Whose Subject?" and "Our Giftedness." See also the statement by Steve Hilton-Barber at http://www.axisgallery.com/exhibitions/circumcision/barber.html.

43 See *Mail and Guardian* 22, no. 6 (February 10–16, 2006), devoted to "The Great Cartoon Debate." See also Henkel, "The Journalists of *Jyllands-Posten* Are a Bunch of Reactionary Provocateurs."

44 *Mail and Guardian* 22, no. 6 (February 10–16, 2006), 23. See also Zapiro, "A Decade of Cartoons," 260–67.

45 See Nyamnjoh, *Africa's Medi,* 219–30.

46 Mbembe, *On the Postcolony,* 164.

47 Groebner, *Defaced,* 125.

48 Taussig, *Defacemen,* 6.

49 For contemporary "iconoclasm," see Walker, *Art and Outrage;* and Julius, *Idolizing Pictures* and *Transgressions.* For more historical approaches, see Freedberg, *The Power of Images;* Gamboni, *The Destruction of Art;* and Goody, *Representations and Contradictions.*

50 Latour and Weibel, *Iconoclash.*

51 See Meyer, *Representing the Passions.*

52 Despite its insistence on "non-position," the strongest statement I have yet encountered of what going "beyond" might mean in this context is Ashraf Jamal's extraordinarily ambitious *Predicaments of Culture in South Africa.*

53 "Ubuntu" is used by the Nguni peoples of southern and eastern Africa to express the mutuality of human existence. The same concept is named "botho" in Sotho, a Bantu language used in the same region. Moekestsi Letseka argues that the indigenous humanism of Africa finds expression in Nguini phrases such as *umuntu ngumuntu ngabantu* and in such Sotho phrases as *motho ke motho ka batho.* See Letseka, "African Philosophy and Educational Discourse," 182. See also Es'kia Mphahlele, "I Am Because We Are: Baccalaureate Address University of Pennsylvania—May 16, 1982" and *Education, African Humanism and Culture, Social Consciousness, Literary Appreciation.* This is explored in the exhibition "Motho ke motho ka batho (a person is a person because of other people): Art and Craft Heritage from the Limpopo Province,"

curated by Anitra Nettleton, Rayda Becker, Johnny van Schalkwyk, and Sam Moifat-
swane, assisted by Simon Raletjena, and held at the National Cultural History Museum, Pretoria, July 27, 2002–November 30, 2003.

54 David Koloane, exhibition invitation, *Ubuntu* (Kuala Lumpur: National Art Gallery,
2002); see also his catalogue essay for that exhibition, "The Spirit of Ubuntu as a
Creative Dynamic." See also *Ubuntu: Arts et Cultures d'Afrique du Sud* (Paris: Musée
National des Arts d'Afrique et d'Océanie, 2002). For Sue Williamson and Ashraf
Jamal, "It was the spirit of *ubuntu* that pulled South Africa from the brink, and it is
the spirit of *ubuntu* which has led many artists into projects aimed at empowering an
ever-widening circle of people through creative action"; see Williamson and Jamal,
Art in South Africa, 7. We might also understand ubuntu as part of a continuing
project of the humanization of rights: see Holkeboer, "Out of the Crooked Timber of
Humanity." Also relevant are Kaphagawani, "Some African Conceptions of Person";
and Ramose, "The Philosophy of *Ubuntu* and *Ubuntu* as Philosophy" and "Globalization and *Ubuntu*." For an account of Archbishop Desmond Tutu's essentially Christian ubuntu, see Battle, *Reconciliation;* and Tutu, *No Future without Forgiveness.*

55 South Africa Truth and Reconciliation Commission, *Report*, 1:126. The postscript to
South Africa's new constitution contains this reference; see Simpson, " 'Tell No Lies,
Claim No Easy Victories,' " 222. For Justice Yvonne Makgoro of the Constitutional
Court, the spirit of ubuntu "emphasises respect for human dignity, making a shift
from confrontation to conciliation," while Justice Pius Langa speaks of its absence as
part of a crisis in civil society: "During violent conflict and times when violent crime
is rife, distraught members of society decry the loss of ubuntu. Thus, heinous crimes
are the antithesis of ubuntu. Treatment that is cruel, inhuman or degrading is bereft
of ubuntu. . . . We have all been affected, in some way or other, by the 'strife, conflicts,
untold suffering and injustice' of the recent past. . . . But all this was violence on
human beings by human beings. Life became cheap, almost worthless" (South Africa
Truth and Reconciliation Commission, *Report*, 1:127). For a critical account of ubuntu
and the TRC, see Wilson, *The Politics of Truth and Reconciliation in South Africa*, 9–13.

56 Stewart, "Thoughts on the Role of the Humanities," 99. Stewart goes on to observe,
"When the Truth and Reconciliation Commission was established, its stance against
revenge was, I believe, as world-shaking as the previous transformation of the Furies
into the Eumenides that is recorded in the *Oresteia*." Revenge in the context of the
TRC is considered by Murphy, *Getting Even*, 15–16.

57 The phrase "agonistic confrontation" is Chantal Mouffe's; see her *On the Political*
(London: Routledge, 2005), 29–34.

58 Sanders, *Complicities*, 126. He goes on to note that, with "*umuntu ngumuntu ngabantu*
or as *umuntu ngumuntu ngumunte ngabanye* . . . one must, in effect, speak of the
attainment of human-being through an other and not one's own" (126–27).

59 For Pitika Ntuli, the "spirit of *ubuntu* and its practice have disappeared. . . . That is
why Africa must have a renaissance" (Ntuli, "The Missing Link between Culture and
Education," 184). For background to the "African Renaissance," see Makgoba, *African
Renaissance;* and Mbeki, *Africa*, 31–32. See also "Interviews: African Renaissance," in
Nuttall and Michael, eds., *Senses of Culture;* and Ramose, "African Renaissance." The
"Rainbow nation" was a much-touted national emblem in the 1990s. Nelson Mandela,

in his inauguration speech, spoke of a "rainbow nation at peace with itself and the world." Quoted in J. Cameron-Dow, *South Africa, 1990–1994,* 165. For a brief discussion of this idea in art at the time, see my "Tropics of Ice." A number of artists have engaged the idea critically, mostly as a form of counterfeit feeling and surface seduction. Obviously the idea of ubuntu, no less than "rainbowism" or the idea of an "African renaissance," is vulnerable to sentimental appropriation. But it is also easy to be cynical about such an idea. The TRC asserted that it is *against* the background of the loss of ubuntu, illustrated by the TRC process, that a spontaneous call arose amongst the people for a return to ubuntu. For an understanding of ubuntu as it informed the TRC, see Nabudere, "Ubuntu"; and Bhengu, *Ubuntu.*

60 Wilson, *The Politics of Truth and Reconciliation,* 12. See also Bernstein, "Globalisation, Culture and Development," 206–8.

61 Wilson, *The Politics of Truth and Reconciliation,* 13.

62 The trivialization of the concept of ubuntu is exemplified by the number of commercial companies using the word. In the current Johannesburg phone directory we find it naming an investment company, a security company, a financial services company, a company producing uniforms, and another producing paper. There is even an Ubuntu School of Philosophy in Tshwane (Pretoria), directed by Johann Broodryk, author of *Ubuntu: Life Lessons From Africa* (Tshwane: Ubuntu School of Philosophy, 2002).

63 See Coleman, *A Crime against Humanity.*

64 See also Biko, *I Write What I Like,* 103–4; Halisi, "Biko and Black Consciousness Philosophy"; Koloane, "Moments in Art"; and Oliphant, "A Human Face."

65 To Anthony Bogues, Nyerere's "elaborated political theory today stands as the result of a heretic [*sic*] practice that attempted to overthrow the Western framework about the natural nature of the human, one in which individual material wants trump the social. In the end his heresy made him a consistent theorist of the Swahili precept that a human being is a human being because of other human beings" (Bogues, *Black Heretics, Black Prophets,* 123).

66 Fanon, *The Wretched of the Earth* (2005), 236. See also "Section IV: Fanon's Quest for a New Humanism," in Gibson, *Rethinking Fanon,* 369–446. On humanism and (postmodern) antihumanism, see Malik, "The Mirror of Race."

67 See Mbembe, *On the Postcolony.* See also Manganyi et al., *Political Violence and the Struggle in South Africa;* and Gutteridge and Spence, *Violence in Southern Africa.* For a discussion of violence and South African literature, see Jolly, *Colonization, Violence, and Narration in White South African Writings.*

68 Edward Said, *Freud and the Non-European,* 22 and 17ff.

69 "Mtu ni watu" means "A human being is a human because of other human beings," according to Bogues, *Black Heretics, Black Prophets,* 95, 118–20.

70 Kristeva, *Intimate Revolt,* 257.

71 Crais, *The Politics of Evil,* 4.

72 Enwezor, "Introduction—Travel Notes," 8.

73 See Mamdani, *Citizen and Subject.*

74 There is a large recent literature on trauma and modern culture. See, for example, Farrell, *Post-Traumatic Culture;* and Miller and Tougaw, *Extremities.* A barbed consciousness of

this "community" is embodied in photographer Santy Mofokeng's documentation of Holocaust sites in Europe, for example, his *Birkenau—KZ2* (1997–1998).

75 Butler, *Precarious Life,* 42–43. Butler writes: "Perhaps there is some other way to live such that one becomes neither affectively dead nor mimetically violent, a way out of the circle of violence altogether. This possibility has to do with demanding a world in which *bodily* vulnerability is protected without therefore being eradicated and with insisting on the line that must be walked between the two. *By insisting on a 'common' corporeal vulnerability, I seem to be positing a new basis for humanism.* That might be true, but I am prone to consider this differently" (my emphasis).

76 Quoted in Noyes, "The Place of the Human," 57.

77 The literature on the impact of the TRC is vast; among more recent publications, see Boraine, *A Country Unmasked;* James and van de Vijver, *After the* TRC; Wilson, *The Politics of Truth and Reconciliation in South Africa;* Bell, *Unfinished Business;* Villa-Vincencio and Doxstader, *The Provocations of Amnesty;* and Sarkin, *Carrots and Sticks.*

78 See Hassan, "The Modernist Experience in African Art," 50.

79 Bernstein, "Globalisation, Culture and Development," 207. See also Mbiti, *African Religions and Philosophy.*

80 Said, *Humanism and Democratic Criticism,* 43.

81 Said, *Humanism and Democratic Criticism,* 47.

82 The production of human communities independent of the nation-state is becoming increasingly important. "At its best, civil society is the story of ordinary people living extraordinary lives through their relationships with each other, driven forward by a vision of the world that is ruled by love and compassion, non-violence and solidarity. At its worst, it is little more than a slogan" (Edwards, *Civil Society,* 112). See also Chabal and Daloz, *Africa Works.*

83 Said, *Humanism and Democratic Criticism,* 11–12. See Amin, *Eurocentrism;* and Buruma and Margalit, *Occidentalism.*

84 Makdisi, "Said, Palestine, and the Humanism of Liberation," 451–52.

85 Mitchell, "Secular Divination," 467.

86 Said, *Humanism and Democratic Criticism,* 63.

87 The source of the phrase "uncontrollable mystery on the bestial floor" is not acknowledged in Said's book, but many will recognize it as from the poem "The Magi" by W. B. Yeats. Said acknowledges the source in his early essay "Yeats and Decolonisation," 20–21.

88 For important discussion of the long and tortured phenomenon of "primitivism," see Hiller, *The Myth of Primitivism;* Torgovnick, *Primitive Passions;* Campbell, *Western Primitivism;* Ellingson, *The Myth of the Noble Savage;* and Flam and Deutch, *Primitivism and Twentieth-Century Art.*

89 K. Gyekye, for example, argues that if we "were to look for a pervasive and fundamental concept in African socioethical thought generally—a concept that animates other intellectual activities and forms of behaviour, including religious behaviour, and provides continuity, resilience, nourishment, and meaning of life—that concept would most probably be humanism" (Gyekye, *Tradition and Modernity,* 158). Humanism suffered a largely poor press prior to the publication of Said's *Humanism and Democratic Criticism,* driving some to the notion of "posthumanism"; see, inter alia,

Badmington, *Posthumanism;* and Pepperell, *The Posthuman Condition.* For useful overviews of humanism, see Davies, *Humanism;* and Norman, *On Humanism.*

90 Appiah, "The Postcolonial and the Postmodern," 155.

91 The literature on pain and death, culture and creativity is extensive. See, for example, Scarry, *The Body in Pain;* Morris, *The Culture of Pain;* O'Dell, *Contract with Skin;* Spivey, *Enduring Creation;* Burns, Busby, and Sawchuk, *When Pain Strikes;* and Elkins, *Pictures of the Body.*

92 Mbembe, *On the Postcolony,* 1.

93 The literature on "the animal" is growing apace; see Coetzee, *The Lives of Animals;* and Pickover, *Animal Rights in South Africa.* For a broader treatment, see Baker, *The Postmodern Animal;* Fudge, *Animal;* Atterton and Calarco, *Animal Philosophy;* Agamben, *The Open;* and Pollock and Rainwater, *Figuring Animals.*

94 On the "Sex and Secrecy" debate, see Mametse, "Pictures Arouse Stiff Opposition"; and Mothibi, "Racism Charges Erupt at Sexuality Conference." See also Mbembe, "Sex after Liberation"; Reid and Walker, "Coming out of the Closet: Sex and Secrecy in Africa"; and http://wiserweb.wits.ac.za/conf2003/social.htm. As discussed in the Mametse article, Nokuthula Skhosana, a South African delegate to the conference, denounced the photographs (available online at http://www.gmax.co.za).

95 Photography is itself deeply implicated in representational violence. See, for example, Landau, "Empires of the Visual," 147; Ryan, *Picturing Empire;* and Sontag, *Regarding the Pain of Others.*

96 Hazel Friedman, "On the Verge of Optimism," 29.

97 Kgositsile, "Poor Taste Must Not Pose as Art." The debate about representational violence had a reprise in the following year at a conference associated with the Second Johannesburg Biennial. See Atkinson and Breitz, *Grey Area;* and Enwezor, "Reframing the Black Subject." See also Oguibe, "Beyond Visual Pleasures."

98 See Hlongwane, Ndlovu, and Mutloatse, *Soweto '76.*

99 See Higgs et al., *African Voices in Education;* and Seepe, *Towards an African Identity in Higher Education.*

100 Richards, "The Thought Is the Thing."

101 Koloane, *Sam Nhlengethwa.*

102 Sophie Perryer, "Nandipha Mntambo," in *In the Making: Materials and Process.*

103 Gabi Ngcobo, "What Do We See When We Look at Us?"

104 See Smith, "Churchill Madikida"; Richards, "Walking Wounded"; and Greslé, "Ndyindoda!"

105 Madikida, "Statement," 48.

106 Madikida, "Statement," 49. On masculinity and fatherhood, see Richter and Morrell, *Baba.*

107 On circumcision and masculinity, see Morrell, *Changing Men in Southern Africa.*

108 Goniwe, "Kay Hassan's *Shebeen* and *Ritual Crossing,*" 172. See also Mosaka, "Kay Hassan," 141. On Zwelethu Mthethwa, see Murinik, *Intersection.*

109 See Mosaka, "Circumcised/Circumscribed." One of the earliest works to deal directly with circumcision is Lucas Seage's *African Circumcision* (n.d.), reprinted in de Jager, *Images of Man,* 189. For more recent images, see Siphiwe Sibeko's photographs of Xhosa initiates from Cofimvaba in Waller, *A Bigger Picture,* 192–200.

110 See also van der Watt, "Imagining Alternative White Masculinities"; and de Waal and Sassen, *Stephen Cohen.*

111 Morgan and Wieringa, *Tommy Boys, Lesbian Men and Ancestral Wives*; and Muholi, *Only Half the Picture.*

112 Ngcobo, "What Do We See When We Look at Us?" 49. See also Lewis, "Against the Grain: Black Women and Sexuality," 11–25; and Friedman, "Visual Odes to Intimacy," 2.

113 Sean O'Toole, "Zanele Muholi," 12.

114 For an account of gay and lesbian history in South Africa, see Hoad, Martin, and Reid, *Sex and Politics in South Africa;* van Zyl and Steyn, *Performing Queer;* and Gevisser and Cameron, *Defiant Desire.*

115 Hlobo, quoted in Sophie Perryer, "Nicholas Hlobo," in *In the Making,* unpaginated.

116 Law, "Performing on a Fault-Line."

117 Bedford, *Moshekwa Langa,* 7, 12, 13.

118 Fitzgerald and Mosaka, *The Fiction of Authenticity,* 27.

119 See "Thando Mama," in Smith, *Knap! KKNK Visuele Kunst,* 38.

120 See Sudheim, "Thando Mama," 71.

121 See Khwezi Gule, "Thando Mama," in Perryer, *10 Years 100 Artists,* 225–29.

122 See Sassen, "Nathaniel Stern," 77. See also http://nathanielstern.com. Stern makes "paintings" by acting on a field with a digital device functioning as a "brush."

123 See Marcus Neustetter, "Switch On/Off," 5. See also http://onair.co.za/mn. Neustetter was also a contributor to a "node" in a network connecting artists in Lubjlana, Lima, Berlin, Johannesburg, Vienna, and Donostia-Gasteiz to produce an ongoing collective work called *Tester: Nodes at Work;* see http://www.e-testernet and *Tester,* edited by Fundación Rodríguez (Arteleku).

124 See Donna Haraway, "Ecce Homo, Ain't (Ar'n't) I a Woman, and Inappropriate/d Others: The Human in a Posthuman Landscape," in *The Haraway Reader.* On relations between technology and the human, see Mackenzie, *Transductions;* and Simon, *Dark Light.*

125 Warner, "Camera Ludica," 13–14.

126 Richards, "Senzeni Marasela," 230.

127 Sontag, "On Photography," 354.

128 See Hankins and Silverman, *Instruments and the Imagination;* and Davis, *TechGnosis,* 206–10.

129 See Richards, *Sandile Zulu.*

130 Pyne, "Fire," 108.

131 Morris, *Every Step of the Way,* 3.

132 Pyne, "Fire," 108.

133 There is also a link with fire here; a myth from Sierra Leone, for example, links the spots of the leopard with fire. "Since then the Leopard . . . have been marked all over their bodies with black spots where the fingers of Fire touched them" (Parrinder, *African Mythology,* 126); see also Tembo, *Legends of Africa,* 29. For Sandile Zulu, the leopard connotes royalty, and he references a nineteenth-century imperial Zulu regiment named after the leopard. For a brief account of the significance of the leopard and leopard skin pattern in various forms, see Klopper, "Mobilisation of Cultural

Symbols in 20th century Zululand," 20–22. Artist Dan Rakgoathe speaks of the leopard in a work about initiation: "The leopard has significance. Maybe it is regarded as a symbol of grace. If you look at Zulu traditional dress, you will never miss a leopard skin." Quoted in Langhan, *The Unfolding Man*, 10.

134 See Struaghan and Becker, *Noria Mabasa.*

135 Popham, *The Drawings of Leonardo da Vinci*, 215.

136 Frost, *Jeremy Wafer*, 33–34.

137 As Michael Sims points out, thinking about skin returns us back to the many narratives of Marsyas and the loss of his skin, which demonstrate "how [skin] wraps us and contains us" (Sims, *Adam's Navel*, 9).

138 Perhaps the most significant writing here remains that of Donna Haraway, for example, "Cyborgs to Companion Species: Reconfiguring Kinship in Technoscience," and "Cyborgs, Coyotes, and Dogs: A Kinship of Feminist Figurations," in *The Haraway Reader.*

139 For images and information, see Smith, *Penny Siopis.*

140 Shattuck, *Forbidden Knowledge.*

141 See Nuttall, "The Shock of Beauty."

142 Mbembe, *On the Postcolony*, 1.

143 Scheper-Hughes and Bourgeois, "Introduction," 3.

144 Taussig, *The Nervous System*, 161–62.

145 See Heywood, "Modernism and Violence," 58.

146 Gilroy, *The Black Atlantic.*

147 See Sitas, "Beyond Afropessimism," 15–24.

14

A CASE OF BEING "CONTEMPORARY":

CONDITIONS, SPHERES, AND NARRATIVES OF

CONTEMPORARY CHINESE ART

WU HUNG

Several years ago, after I gave a talk on contemporary Chinese art, I was asked how "Chinese art" could also be "contemporary." The person who asked the question obviously found these two concepts incompatible. To him, China or Chinese art was intuitively—and necessarily—situated in a time/place outside the realm of the contemporary. I pointed out the falsehood of this presumption, but also confessed that a systematic explanation was yet to be worked out to account for the creation and operation of a "local" or "national" contemporary art in today's world—not only contemporary Chinese art but also contemporary Iranian art, contemporary Indian art, contemporary Mexican art, and contemporary Algerian art—to name just a few.

To develop this explanation is the purpose of my essay. It is a case study meant to shed light on a larger issue. The direct subject of my discussion is a kind of Chinese art that self-consciously defines itself as "contemporary" (*dangdai yishu* in Chinese) and that is also accepted as such by curators and art critics worldwide, judging from their inclusion of this art in the many exhibitions they have organized to showcase recent developments in visual art. To be sure, many brands of "Chinese art" are produced today, but those in traditional mediums and styles (whether literati ink landscape or realist oil portraiture) are not conceived—nor do their creators label them—as *dangdai yishu*. "Contemporary art" in Chinese thus does not pertain to what is here and now, but refers to an intentional artistic/theoretical construct that asserts a particular temporality and spatiality for itself. The first step of my study is therefore to map such temporality and spatiality in terms of art medium, subject matter, exhibition, and circulation, and to trace the people and institutions involved in its creation and promotion. This initial investigation leads me to define certain general spheres for the production, exhibition, and collection of contemporary Chinese art, and to propose a model for interpreting this art in its various contemporary contexts.

The need for a new interpretation of contemporary Chinese art naturally arises from dissatisfaction with earlier interpretations, which have often approached this art (and, in a broader sense, any contemporary art from the so-called second and third worlds) either exclusively in its domestic context or as a straightforward manifestation of globalization. The first approach follows a traditional art historical narrative defined by nations. The second privileges a totalizing, global perspective that stymies local angles of observation.[1] To this end, even the notion of a "local" contemporary art already implies this dilemma and demands reconsideration. Deconstructing the global/local dichotomy is a vital component of the new understanding of contemporary Chinese art I am pursuing.[2] In this essay, I argue that contemporary Chinese art is simultaneously constructed in different yet interrelated spaces, and that it subtly changes its meaning when artists and curators (or their works) traverse and interact with these spaces. Tracing such permutation enables us to develop a spatial model for contemporary Chinese art. This model further helps us interpret a burgeoning "international contemporary art" in today's world, which encompasses various "local" or "national" brands of contemporary art, as a unified field of presentation and representation. Generally speaking, instead of assuming that this type of contemporary art is linked with Modern (and Postmodern) art in a linear, temporal fashion and within a self-sustaining cultural system, this interpretative model emphasizes heterogeneity and multiplicity in art production, as well as the creativity of a new kind of artist, who creates contemporary art through simultaneously constructing his or her local identity *and* serving a global audience.

A "CONTEMPORARY" TURN IN CHINESE ART

The Chinese art critic Lü Peng is the main author of two comprehensive introductions to new Chinese art (also known as avant-garde or experimental art), which emerged after the Cultural Revolution (1966–1976).[3] The first book, which he coauthored with Yi Dan and published in 1992, is *A History of Modern*

Chinese Art: 1979–1989 (*Zhongguo xiandai yishu shi, 1979–1989*). The second book, which he authored alone, came out in 2000 under the title *A History of Contemporary Chinese Art: 1990–1999* (*Zhongguo dangdai yishu shi, 1990–1999*). The change in the titles from "modern" (*xiandai*) to "contemporary" (*dangdai*) was no accident. It is symptomatic of a general (but so far unnoticed) shift in the Chinese art world from the 1980s to the 1990s, which I call a "contemporary turn." Simply put, throughout the 1980s, Chinese avant-garde artists and art critics envisioned themselves as participants in a delayed modernization movement, which aimed to reintroduce humanism and the idea of social progress into the nation's political consciousness.[4] From the 1990s onward, however, many of them abandoned, or at least distanced themselves, from this collective undertaking. Looking back at Chinese avant-garde art of the 1980s, some of its original advocates contrasted that exhilarating but chaotic era with the much more practical and diffuse period following it.[5] According to Li Xianting, a major voice of new Chinese art in both the 1980s and 1990s, artists of the 1980s "believed in the possibility of applying modern Western aesthetics and philosophy as a means of revitalizing Chinese culture." Starting from the early 1990s, however, many of them turned "against heroism, idealism, and the yearning for metaphysical transcendence that characterized the '85 New Wave movement."[6] Other critics and curators share this view and have used "Modern" and "contemporary" to encapsulate the many differences between these two periods. For instance, they wrote books and articles in the 1980s to promote "Modern art," and titled the enormous exhibition that concluded the '85 New Wave: "A Grand Exhibition of Modern Art" ("Xiandai meishu dazhan").[7] In contrast, many books, art journals, and exhibitions since the early 1990s have used "contemporary art" in their titles.[8]

Underlying this change was a major shift in conceptualizing new Chinese art over the past twenty-five years. Most important, the two terms indicate two different ways to contextualize this art, one temporal and diachronic, the other spatial and synchronic. When avant-garde Chinese artists and critics called themselves "modern" in the 1980s, they identified themselves, first of all, as participants in a historical movement that had been interrupted in China by communist rule. Lü Peng and Yi Dan thus opened *A History of Modern Chinese Art: 1979–1989* with a passionate introduction, linking new Chinese art to the May Fourth movement that started in 1919. In their view, although this early twentieth-century "cultural revolution" had the correct goal of bringing China into a modern era of democracy and science, its heavy emphasis on the social function of art and literature finally led to an extreme pragmatism, as realism willingly turned itself into political symbolism in the 1960s and 1970s to assist a "proletarian dictatorship." To regain the spirit of a genuine cultural revolution, therefore, their introduction exhorted "modern artists" of the 1980s to not only uphold humanism as their fundamental ideology, but to also take upon themselves the role of cultural critic, "reexamining the relationship between art and society, religion, and philosophy in all possible ways."[9] Similar claims characterize many other writings from that period.[10]

In contrast to such spirited discussion of "modern art" in the 1980s, no particular discourse has qualified 1990s art as "contemporary," even though the term has gained wide currency among Chinese artists and critics. What the term indicated in the early 1990s was, above all, a sense of rupture and demarcation—the end of an era as well as the kind of historical thinking associated with it. This meaning is made clear in Li Xianting's writing cited above. But as veterans of the 1980s art movement, Li and his colleagues perceived the art of the new era pessimistically as visual forms without genuine historical, political, and social engagement. Other writers explained the artists' break with history and ideology in terms of China's changing political situation. For example, Chang Tsong-zung, who sponsored and coorganized the first major international exhibition of contemporary Chinese art in 1993, attributed this change to the ill-fated June Fourth movement (the prodemocratic demonstrations in Tiananmen Square in 1989).[11] He observes: "In shock, artists came to a sudden realization of their impotence in the face of real politics. The idealism and utopian enthusiasm so typical of new art in the 1980s met its nemesis in the gun barrels in Tian'anmen."[12] Applying this understanding to visual analysis, he pointed out that two major styles in post-1989 Chinese art—Cynical Realism and Political Pop—both translated idealism into sarcasm.

Chang's observation has a broader significance in alluding to a general pattern that distinguishes the development of postwar Chinese art from that of the West. It is a "pattern of rupture" caused by violent intrusions of sociopolitical events such as the Cultural Revolution and the Tiananmen incident. The result has been a series of deep ruptures as a general historical/psychological condition for artistic and intellectual creativity. Each rupture has forced artists and intellectuals to reevaluate and reorient themselves. Instead of returning to a prior time/space, the projects they have developed after each rupture often testify to a different set of parameters and are governed by different temporality and spatiality.

This pattern of response explains the sudden change in artists' attitudes after 1989, and also enables us to see 1980s "modern art" and 1990s "contemporary art" not as two consecutive trends, but as disconnected endeavors conceived in separate temporal/spatial schemes. Earlier I mentioned that avant-garde artists and critics of the 1980s linked themselves with the May Fourth movement, a cultural movement that aimed to transform China based on a Western, Enlightenment model. It is therefore not surprising that these artists and critics also developed a strong desire for cosmopolitanism and eagerly sought inspirations in Western Modern art, art theory, and philosophy. This desire became both the cause and the result of an "information explosion" in the 1980s. From the start of the decade, all sorts of "decadent" Western art forbidden during the Cultural Revolution was introduced to China through reproductions and exhibitions; hundreds of theoretical works, from authors such as Heinrich Wölfflin to Ernst Gombrich, were translated and published in a short period. These images and texts aroused enormous interest among younger artists and greatly inspired their work. It was as if a century-long development of Modern art was simultaneously restaged in China. The chronology and internal logic of this Western tradition became less important; what counted most was its diverse content as visual and intellectual stimuli for a hungry audience. Thus, styles and theories that had long become past history in the West (such as surrealism or Wölfflin's categorization of artistic styles) were used by Chinese artists as their direct models. The meaning of their works as "Modern art" was located, therefore, not in the original historical significance of the styles and ideas, but in the transference of these styles and ideas to a different time/place.

Like any transference, this dislocation of Modern art was based on the idea of precedents. Although separated by time and historical experience, Chinese artists of the 1980s saw themselves as direct followers of great modern philosophers and artists in the West. A historian of Western contemporary art may be shocked to find that in Lü Peng and Yi Dan's *A History of Modern Chinese Art: 1979–1989*, the most influential figures on Chinese artists in the 1980s were, in fact, "Arthur Schopenhauer, Friedrich Nietzsche, Jean-Paul Sartre, Sigmund Freud, Carl Jung, Albert Camus, and T. S. Eliot."[13] But it makes perfect sense if we understand these artists' longing to rediscover their modernist roots. This situation changed completely after 1989. These grand names suddenly became infinitely remote, and few Chinese artists, if any, continued to seek guidance from them. Rather, the sharp historical gap created by the Tiananmen incident distanced them from the previous era, enabling them to develop a radically different relationship with history and with the surrounding world. In this process, they also disengaged themselves from *yundong*, the Chinese term for large-scale political, ideological, or artistic "campaigns" or "movements."

Although seldom analyzed by historians and sociologists, yundong had been one of the most fundamental concepts and technologies in modern Chinese political culture until the 1990s. This was especially true for the period from the

1950s to the 1970s. Upon ascension to power, the Chinese Communist Party mobilized various yundong to realize both short and long-term projects, and to unify the "revolutionary masses" against internal and external enemies. Three major characteristics of a yundong include a definite and often concrete political agenda, a propaganda machine that helps define and spread this agenda, and an organization that helps forge a cohesive "front" among participants. Yundong became the norm. It is therefore not surprising that a yundong mindset continued to control artists' ways of thinking even after the Cultural Revolution had ended. The persistence of a yundong mentality is clearly seen in 1980s avant-garde art: while attacking official ideology and art policies, the advocates of this art tried hard to galvanize experimental artists into a unified front and to develop this art into an organized "movement." (In fact, they called their collective activities a yundong.)

It took a hit as hard as the Tiananmen tragedy to disengage Chinese artists from this yundong mentality. Almost overnight, they were transformed from soldiers in a heroic struggle into lone individuals facing an alien world. The unfamiliarity of the world in the early 1990s, however, had less to do with the Tiananmen incident as with two simultaneous, contemporary happenings. First, China had now entered a new stage in a profound socioeconomic transformation. Beginning in the late 1970s, a new generation of Chinese leaders led by Deng Xiaoping had initiated a series of socioeconomic reforms, but the consequences of these reforms were fully felt only in the 1990s. Major cities such as Beijing and Shanghai were completely reshaped. Numerous private and joint-ventured, including private-owned, commercial art galleries had appeared. Educated young men and women moved from job to job in pursuing personal well-being, and a large "floating population" entered metropolitan centers from the countryside to look for work and better living conditions. As I will discuss below, many changes in 1990s art were related to this larger picture.

Second, China also entered a new stage of globalization. If 1980s "modern art" was predominately a domestic movement closely linked with the country's internal political situation at the time, "contemporary art" since the 1990s has unfolded across multiple geographical, political, and cultural spheres. Consequently, my discussion will now turn to the three most important spheres of this art, which overlap but do not constitute a coherent framework for a continuous narrative. These are: (1) China's domestic art spaces, (2) the global network of a multinational contemporary art, and (3) individualized linkages between these two spheres created by independent artists and curators.

THE CONTEMPORANEITY OF CONTEMPORARY CHINESE ART

Contemporary Art as a Domestic Avant-Garde

In the domestic sphere, the term "contemporary art" conveys a strong sense of avant-gardism and signifies a range of experiments that aspire to challenge established art institutions, systems, and forms. Over the past ten to fifteen years, most such experimentation has been conducted in three areas: art medium, subject, and exhibition.[14]

A simple but powerful strategy employed by many avant-garde Chinese artists to make their works explicitly "contemporary" is to subvert traditional art mediums. The trend of subverting painting emerged in the 1980s. (Before this, independent artists, even the most radical ones, still worked in the domains of painting and sculpture). But it was only from the mid-1990s onward that new art forms, such as installation, performance, site-specific art, and multimedia art, prevailed. An increasing number of younger artists abandoned their former training in traditional or Western painting, or only made paintings privately to finance their more adventurous but less marketable art experiments. One can draw interesting parallels between them and an earlier generation of Westernized Chinese artists, who abandoned the traditional Chinese brush for the "Modern" medium of oil painting. But if those artists in the early twentieth century chose between different types of painting, their successors in the present choose whether to abandon painting altogether.

As I will discuss in the following section, new, experimental art forms provide contemporary Chinese artists with an "international language." Inside China, however, these forms have served to forge an independent field of art production, exhibition, and criticism outside official and academic art. In denouncing painting, artists can effectively establish an "outside" position for themselves, because what they reject is not just a particular art form or medium, but an entire art system, including education, exhibition, publication, and employment. Such a break is sometimes related to an artist's political identity. But it can also be a relatively independent artistic decision, as these artists find the new art forms both liberating and challenging. On this level of individual experimentation these artists negotiate with painting in different ways: some of them squarely reject painting; others subvert painting and calligraphy from within; still others reframe painting as components of installation or performance.

Also in the domestic sphere, contemporary Chinese artists have distinguished themselves through developing site-specific projects and "experimental exhibitions." One type of site-specific project can be called a countermonument

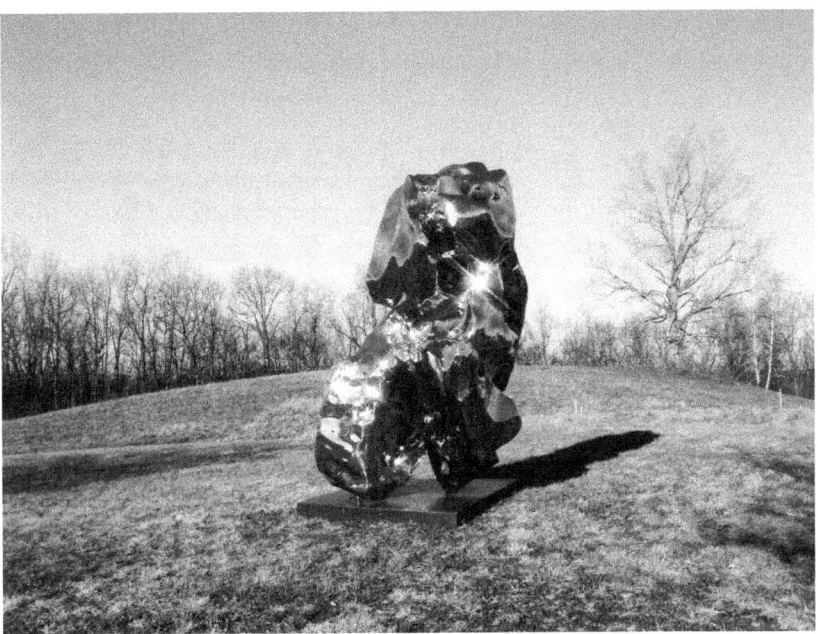

Zhan Wang, *Artificial Rock*, 2004. Site-specific installation. Private collection. Courtesy of Chambers Fine Art, New York.

or antimonument. Set in important political spaces such as the Great Wall or Tiananmen Square, a countermonument or antimonument transforms such space into a stage for individual expression. Pursuit of contemporaneity has also given rise to many "ruin images," which comment on or interact with the drastic transformation of the Chinese city. A striking aspect of a major Chinese metropolis like Beijing or Shanghai over the past ten to fifteen years has been the never ending destruction and construction that goes on there. This situation furnishes both the context and the content of a large group of works that represent "demolition sites" or take place in such locations. I have discussed elsewhere some chief characteristics of these images and site-specific projects, especially the skewed temporality and spatiality contained in them.[15] A demolition site in real life is a place that belongs to everyone and to no one. It belongs to no one because the breakdown it effects between private and public space does not generate a new space. Captured by contemporary artists, a demolition site signifies a kind of "nonspace" outside normal life. Its suspended spatiality is further linked to its suspended temporality. The contemporaneity of these ruin-related projects should be distinguished from the concept of the present, conceived as an intermediary, transitional stage between past and future. As the

subject of contemporary art, demolition sites break the logic of historical continuity, as "time" simply vanishes in these "black holes." The past of these places
has been destroyed and few people know their future. Unlike war ruins, however, demolition sites inspire not only anxiety but also hope.

Some artists and curators have staged exhibitions at demolition sites. In so
doing they have identified their projects as "experimental exhibitions," which
shift the focus of experimentation from the content of an exhibition to the
exhibition itself: its site, form, and social function.[16] These issues loom large in
present-day China because of an intensified conflict between a rapidly developing, aggressively active contemporary art and a backward official system of
exhibition. Since the late 1990s, independent curators and artists have tried to
discover new exhibition spaces and to transform old exhibition spaces into
venues for contemporary art. Most significantly, they have organized a considerable number of contemporary art exhibitions that have taken place in ver-
satile, nonexhibition spaces, bringing works of contemporary art to the public
in a dynamic, guerilla fashion. That many such site-specific exhibitions have
used commercial spaces reflects the curators' interest in mass commercial culture, which in their view has become a major force in contemporary Chinese
society. While affiliating contemporary art with this culture, their exhibitions
have also provided channels for artists to comment on it.

Decontextualization as Contemporaneity
The close relationship between the development of contemporary Chinese art
and China's sweeping transformation has encouraged the compilation of a kind
of macro history, which interprets this art in light of domestic social and
political movements. This history, however, fails to document or explain the
global presence of contemporary Chinese art and its growing contribution to a
burgeoning international contemporary art. We cannot simply expand the
domestic context of contemporary Chinese art into a global one, because different forces and present different problems govern these two spheres. Neither
can we study contemporary Chinese art in either sphere in complete isolation.
Our task, I propose, is to observe and analyze how this art negotiates with these
two spheres and how it changes its roles and aims in responding to different
spaces and audiences.

Most important, as part of an international contemporary art, the relationship between contemporary Chinese art and contemporary China becomes
submerged. Such decontextualization is coupled with a recontextualization of
this art in a different socioeconomic network. The beginning of this twofold
process of decontextualization and recontextualization can be dated precisely to

the early 1990s, when contemporary Chinese artists first appeared in the Forty-fifth Venice Biennale and were featured in mainstream Western art magazines.[17] Around the same time, contemporary Chinese art became a global commodity, promoted by transnational commercial galleries and collected by foreign collectors and museums. Direct ties between Chinese artists and Western art institutions were then forged both inside and outside China, as international curators flocked to the country to search for new talent, and as Chinese artists increasingly participated in international exhibitions and workshops; some of them emigrated abroad for good.

These facts are well known and need little elaboration, but their impact on the meaning of contemporary Chinese art remains a question. In other words, the recontextualization of this art should be thought of as a reconstruction of its definition and identity. While the term "contemporary Chinese art" remains the same, its purposes and strategies have undergone crucial changes. On the most basic level, displacement and translation already alter a work's significance. For example, I discussed earlier how in China, new art forms such as installation, performance, and site-specific art convey a strong social message to subvert established norms. This significance largely disappears when these works are displayed in international exhibitions (such as the many biennials and triennials staged extravagantly around the world) that feature endless installations and multimedia works. Contemporary artists from China contribute to these events, first of all, through immersing themselves in the kind of "international contemporary art" that these transnational exhibitions promote. Unlike oil and ink paintings, installation, performance, and multimedia art defy a rigid cultural identity. What they provide to Chinese artists on these occasions is an "international language," which not only confirms their own contemporaneity but also allows them to incorporate indigenous art forms, materials, and expression into contemporary art. In so doing, they can maintain their identity as Chinese artists within international contemporary art.

Such immersion inspires creativity as well as simplification and misinterpretation. On the one hand, some of the most compelling works of contemporary Chinese art have been created in the global sphere, where they reflect on current international and intercultural issues through genuine artistic innovation.[18] On the other hand, international art exhibitions encourage the tendency to reduce a local tradition into ready-made symbols and citations. The wide circulation of contemporary Chinese art brings contemporary Chinese art to a global audience, but such circulation also removes this art from its roots and erases its original, historical significance. On the one hand, the new context challenges Chinese artists to contend with comparisons to the best contemporary artists around the world. On the other hand, they can seldom avoid the audience's expectation to find Chineseness in exotic, self-orientalizing forms.

The advantage and disadvantage of such decontextualization and recontextualization is best demonstrated by the changing meaning of Cynical Realism and Political Pop, two contemporary Chinese art styles that are best known in the West. As discussed earlier, both styles were invented in the aftermath of the Tiananmen incident to express, among other things, artists' disillusionment with their own political engagement. But when paintings in these two styles appeared in a series of international exhibitions in the early 1990s (including the Forty-fifth Venice Biennale, the "China Avant-Garde" exhibition in Berlin's Haus der Kulturen der Welt, and "China's New Art, Post-1989" in Hong Kong, all organized in 1993), they were immediately taken as representatives of an "underground" or "dissident" art under a communist regime. Ironically, such interpretation based on a Cold War logic led to the artists' commercial success and changed their status in their home country. Soon thereafter, some of these artists built large villas outside the Chinese capital to live an affluent lifestyle in a tightly guarded environment, painting largely for an unfamiliar, overseas audience.

On a methodological level, the decontextualization and recontextualization of contemporary Chinese art implies a shift in interpretation from historical context to broad theoretical implication that can be applied to works created anywhere. The numerous self-portraits by contemporary Chinese artists lend themselves to both types of interpretation. Historically, these images signify a desire to reconstruct the self through visual representation. This desire comes from an absence: self-portraiture disappeared entirely in China during the Cultural Revolution. In a period when every action and thought had to be directed by a collective ideology, self-portraiture was naturally identified with bourgeois self-indulgence and was therefore counterrevolutionary. On the other hand, the art of portraiture was given an exaggerated importance by reducing it to the mass production of the image of one man.

The desire to represent the self resurfaced after the Cultural Revolution was over. But the form and logic of these representations have been conditioned by both the country's recent past and present. Instead of representing one's personal appearance and emotional state, a more common tendency among contemporary Chinese artists has been a conscious denial of explicit self-display. Numerous "self-portraits" by these artists demonstrate a voluntary ambiguity in their self-images, as if they felt that the best way to realize their individuality was to make themselves simultaneously visible and invisible. These ambiguous, fragmentary images express their anxiety, frustration, and dilemmas in a rapidly changing society, and are therefore still about the authenticity of the self. Displayed in an international exhibition, however, these images are given a broad rhetorical significance related to a general redefinition of the self in the contemporary world, and are used to exemplify how in our time the traditional view of a fully integrated, unique, and distinctive individuality has been increasingly compromised, causing the fragmentation of the self and decline in the belief that the individual is a legitimate social reality.[19]

Artists as Mediators of Contemporaneity

This section focuses on the third sphere of contemporary Chinese art, comprising individualized spaces and channels generated by artists and curators through their independent projects and physical movement. Although the domestic and global spheres of contemporary Chinese art are connected on the institutional level, either through a transnational commercial network or through government-sponsored art exhibitions, the main linkage between the two spaces, I would suggest, is provided by contemporary Chinese artists themselves. They thus function not only as creators of contemporary Chinese art but also as mediators between the multiple identities of this art. Many of these artists have become world travelers in the past decade. Some of them have returned to China after spending several years abroad. Others maintain a residence in New York or Paris but have become increasingly involved in domestic exhibitions. The majority of artists never officially emigrate, but it is not unusual for them to spend several months a year outside China, traveling from one exhibition to another. Some thoughtful artists have created site-specific works for locations outside China, or have expressed their experience as global travelers in their works.[20]

Because of the unsystematic nature of such movement and activity, it is difficult to generalize about them. The channels opened up by these activities remain highly fluid and flexible. The "sphere" that they constitute vaguely encompasses the domestic and international spaces of contemporary Chinese art, but again in an unsystematic and undefined way. Despite its elusiveness, however, this sphere is most intimately connected with individual artistic innovation, the result of his or her internalization of broad social and cultural issues. This recognition demands close analyses of individual artists and their works. Unlike traditional "biographical" studies in art history, however, such analyses must show how contemporaneity is constructed through an artist's personal engagement with the domestic and global spheres.

Many Chinese artists can and should be discussed this way. My example here is Zhang Dali, the only graffiti artist in Beijing and certainly the most famous graffiti artist there in the 1990s.[21] Like many other contemporary Chinese artists, his life is filled with unexpected turns. To make a long story short, he grew up in northeast China and studied traditional painting at a top art school in Beijing. He graduated in 1987 and then emigrated to Italy in 1989, after the prodemocratic student movement in Tiananmen Square ended in bloodshed that year. In Italy he first made Oriental-style commercial paintings for a living, but later became a spray-can graffiti artist and forged the image of a bald head as his trademark. He continued to paint the same head after moving back to China in 1995, and by 1998 he had sprayed more than two thousand such images all over Beijing. These images, which he created secretly at night, eventually became the focus of a public controversy and were widely discussed in Beijing's newspapers and magazines. It was only then that Zhang Dali revealed his identity as the creator of these images. In one interview he explained his art: "This head is a condensation of my own likeness as an individual. It represents me to communicate with this city. I want to know everything about this city—its state of being, its transformation, its structure. I call this project *Dialogue*."[22]

Zhang Dali's basic technique to develop such "dialogue" was to fill a half-demolished, empty house with his own image(s). He was therefore able to "reclaim" an abandoned site, however temporarily. The locations he selected for such a performance/photograph project always highlighted certain contrasts between different political identities and social spaces. Sometimes he juxtaposed the graffiti head with an official monument; other times he juxtaposed a preserved traditional building (a palace) with a half-demolished one (an ordinary residence). But most of the time he contrasted urban destruction and construction. This mode is forcefully demonstrated in this 1998 performance/photograph. In the foreground of the picture, standing amid scattered garbage, are some broken walls as the remnants of a demolished traditional house, on which Zhang Dali has sprayed a row of his famous heads. Two huge modern buildings rise behind this wasteland. Still surrounded by scaffolding, one of them already advertises itself as the future "Prime Tower" and offers the telephone number of its sales department.

Many aspects of Zhang Dali's artistic experiments in the 1990s are related to the notion of contemporaneity. These aspects include art medium and form (he abandoned painting in favor of performance, site-specific installation, and photography); social function and audience (his graffiti images became part of Beijing's public space, encountered by Beijing residents everyday); and identity. Regarding this last aspect, by inscribing his own image on old Beijing houses, Zhang Dali defined a specific space around which he could construct his identity as a "local artist" opposed to globalization and commercialization. But this identity contradicted his other identity as an "international artist" working for

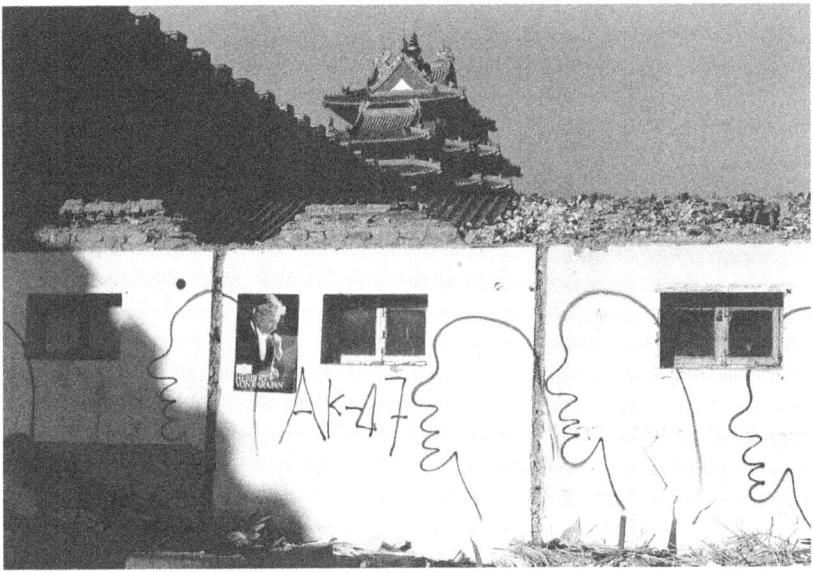

Zhang Dali, *Self-Portrait, Jinmao Tower, Shanghai,* from the series *Dialog with Demolition,* 1995–2003. Graffiti, photograph. Courtesy of the artist.

a global audience. (Since 1999, his photos have been shown in many art exhibitions outside China and collected by foreign collectors and institutions.) We should not simply consider such contradiction negatively. As I have suggested, the tensions between various spheres of contemporary Chinese art problematize straightforward answers to complex problems. Partly responding to the commercialization of his "graffiti" images, Zhang Dali has developed a new project in recent years, making sculptures directly from the bodies and faces of migrant workers from the countryside—people who are rebuilding Beijing but who remain anonymous, deprived laborers in the Chinese capital.

Zhang Dali's example supports one of my methodological proposals, that a general sociological contextualization does not automatically reveal the *contemporaneity* of contemporary Chinese art. If such contemporaneity has anything to do with China's social transformation and globalization, these external factors must be *internalized* as intrinsic features, qualities, intentions, and visual effects of specific art projects. This interpretative strategy discourages the broad reduction of contemporary Chinese art to either its domestic or global contexts, but encourages us to forge micronarratives that emphasize artists' individual responses to common social problems.

CODA: CONTEMPORANEITY AS INTENSIFICATION

In a seminar held in Beijing in 1999, a well-known European curator confessed that he actually knew little about the history of contemporary Chinese art; but he nevertheless decided to include some twenty young Chinese artists in his forthcoming exhibition because he found "the intensity of creative energy in their works irresistible." I told him that although I did know something about the cultural background and sociopolitical circumstances of this art, I was attracted to contemporary Chinese art for exactly the same reason. I then wondered what this "intensity of creative energy" actually meant—a feeling shared by two observers with very different backgrounds and experiences that seemed to capture the essence of new Chinese art at that moment.

If intensity results from intensification, then contemporary Chinese art is a consequence of a double intensification. In other words, this art not only responds to China's startling transformation over the past ten to fifteen years, but further enhances the feeling of speed, anxiety, and theatricality inherent in this external transformation through artistic representation. The strength of this art certainly does not depend upon the solitary perfection of individual masters over a prolonged time span. What makes it "irresistible" is the speed and depth of the artists' *internalization* of the sweeping changes around them— changes that in a short period have altered Chinese cities and the country's economic structure, transformed people's lifestyles and self-identities, and made China a major economic power in the world. Similar transformations took place years ago in other parts of the world; China's ambition is to accomplish a century of development in the West in one or two decades. The same desire and urgency, often combined with self-doubt and uncertainty, is found in many works created by contemporary Chinese artists. As a result, many of these works strike viewers as containing something "real" and raw: ambition, rage, struggle, yearning, hope. The rapidly changing art medium, style, and subject further generate a sense of constant happening. All these characteristics contribute to a particular kind of contemporaneity in art, which is often lacking in works produced in peaceful, "normal," and more individualized societies.

His observation, however, also implies a predicament: as China's explosive development eventually slows down and as contemporary Chinese art is eventually "normalized" to become a routine aspect of social life, the "intensity of creative energy" in this art will diminish. From such a historical perspective, therefore, the kind of contemporaneity described in this essay can only be a momentary quality of contemporary Chinese art. But this only proves that instantaneity and simultaneity are inseparable from the conception of contemporaneity, which inevitably involves the condensation of time.

NOTES

1   The need to develop a "polycentric perspective to describe a polycentric situation" in studying industrial relationships is addressed in Kristensen and Zeitlin, *Local Players in Global Games,* 1–23.

2   I pursue this understanding not only through research and writing but also through actual intervention, mainly organizing exhibitions and discussions in multiple geographical and cultural spheres. For example, I have organized several exhibitions of contemporary Chinese art outside China. Some of these exhibitions introduced this art to a global audience (e.g., "Transience: Experimental Chinese Art at the End of the Twentieth Century" and "Between Past and Future: New Photography and Video from China"). Others focused on particular issues such as the meaning of art media, cross-cultural communication, contemporary aesthetics, or censorship (for example, "Canceled: Exhibiting Experimental Art in China," "Visual Performance: Five New-media Artists from Asia," "Intersection: Contemporary Photography and Oil Painting from China," and "About Beauty"). My three major exhibitions in China have taken place in different spaces, including a large public museum (the First Guangzhou Triennial), a nonexhibition space ("Tui-Transfiguration"), and a commercial gallery ("Tobacco Project: Shanghai").

3   For a brief discussion of the applications of these two terms to contemporary Chinese art, see Wu, "Introduction," 11–12. Here I use them interchangeably in referring to the kind of new Chinese art discussed in this essay.

4   For example, Gao Minglu, a key organizer of the avant-garde movement in the 1980s, describes this movement in humanist terms. See his *Zhongguo dangdai meishu shi.*

5   See, for example, Gao, "From Elite to Small Man: The Many Faces of a Transitional Avant-Garde in Mainland China," in Gao, *Inside Out,* 149–66; especially 154–56.

6   Li, "Major Trends in the Development of Contemporary Chinese Art." For a short introduction to the '85 New Wave movement (85 Yishu xinchao) and its political context, see Wu, *Transience,* 17–22. For a detailed documentation and analysis of this movement, see Gao, *Zhongguo dangdai meishu shi.*

7   This exhibition is known in English as "China/Avant Garde," a name fabricated later for the convenience of a foreign readership. For an introduction to the exhibition, see Lü and Yi, *Zhongguo xiandai yishu shi,* 325–53.

8   As in the West, these two terms are often used interchangeably by Chinese artists and critics. But in China, such mixed uses became especially frequent from the late 1980s to the early 1990s. Toward the mid- and late 1990s, however, "contemporary art" clearly became *the* term for new Chinese art.

9   Lü and Yi, *Zhongguo xiandai yishu shi,* 2–4; quotation from 4.

10 A representative book is Lang Shaojun's *A Discussion of Chinese Modern Art,* which starts from the introduction of Western art to China and ends with the '85 Art New Wave.

11 Entitled "China's New Art, Post-1989," this show opened in January 1993 in Hong Kong and subsequently traveled throughout the world for several years.

12 Chang Tsong-zung, "Into the Nineties," in Chang, *China's New Art, Post-1989,* i–vii; quotation from i.

13 Lü and Yi, *Zhongguo xiandai yishu shi,* 4.

14 I discuss such domestic experimentations in greater detail in "Contemporaneity in Contemporary Chinese Art," forthcoming.

15 See Wu, *Transience,* 79–126.

16 I have discussed "experimental exhibitions" in a number of places, including *Exhibiting Experimental Art in China;* " 'Experimental Exhibitions' of the 1990s"; and "Tui-Transfiguration."

17 Fourteen Chinese artists participated in this Venice Biennale, including Wang Guangyi, Zhang Peili, Geng Jianyi, Xu Bing, Liu Wei, Yu Hong, Feng Mengbo, Yu Youhan, Li Shan, Wang Ziwei, Ding Yi, Sun Lang, and Song Haidong. For introductions to contemporary Chinese art in mainstream art journals in the West, see Chan, "Ten Years of the Chinese Avant-Garde"; and Solomon, "Their Irony, Humor (and Art) Can Save China."

18 Some of these works are created by, among others, Xu Bing, Cai Guoqiang, Huang Yongbing, Chen Zhen and Wenda Gu.

19 One such exhibition was "Between Past and Future: New Photography and Video from China," which I cocurated in New York (International Center for Photography) and Chicago (Smart Museum of Art, University of Chicago). It included a section entitled "Reimagining the Self."

20 One example is the Beijing artist Yin Xiuzhen, who has created a series of "suitcases" with fabric, representing a dozen or so cities around the world where she has shown her work. Ironically, all these miniature cities look alike. Instead of representing reality, here Yin expresses her experience as a global traveler.

21 For Zhang's works, see Borysevicz, *Zhang Dali.* For a discussion of his site-specific project called *Dialogue,* see Wu, "Zhang Dali's *Dialogue.*"

22 Leng Ling, *Shi wo* [It's me], 168.

PART 4: COTEMPORALITIES

15

EMANCIPATION OR ATTACHMENTS?

THE DIFFERENT FUTURES OF POLITICS

BRUNO LATOUR

Some conjunctions of the stars are so ominous, astrologers used to say, that it would be safer to stay at home in bed and wait for a better message from Heaven. It is probably the same with political conjunctions. They are presently so hopeless that the prudent advice would be to remain as far away as possible from anything political and to wait for the passing of all the present leaders, terrorists, commentators, and buffoons who strut upon the public stage. As-trology, however, is as precarious an art as political science and behind the nefarious conjunctions of hapless stars other, much dimmer alignments might be worth pondering. It is, perhaps, just when the political period triggers such desperation that the time is right for shifting our attention to other ways of considering public matters. And "matters" are precisely what might be put center stage. Yes, public *matters,* but how?

While successive German Reichs have given us two world wars, the German language has offered the word *Realpolitik* to describe a positive, materialist, no-nonsense, interest-only, matter-of-factual way of navigating through power relations. Although this "reality," at the time of Bismarck, might have been more efficient than the cruel idealisms of romanticism it aimed to replace, it strikes us now as deeply *unrealistic.* To invoke "realism" when talking politically is something that one should not do without trembling and shaking. The beautiful word "reality" has been damned by the so many crimes committed in its name. In contrast, by the German neologism *Dingpolitik,* we wish to designate a risky and tentative set of experiments that probe just what it could mean for political thought to turn around "things" and to become slightly more *realistic* than what has been attempted so far. A few years ago, computer scientists invented the marvelous expression "object-oriented software" to describe a new way to write programs. Instead of writing every time all the variables corresponding to the functions they wanted to activate, they could define objects at the beginning and, later in the program, they would simply designate those objects and all the functions and variables would be calculated anew, without writing any new line of code. We wish to use this metaphor to ask the question: "What would an object-oriented democracy look like?"

The general hypothesis is so simple that it might sound trivial—but being trivial might be part of what it is to become "realist." It is this: we might all be much more connected by our object of worries, our matters of concern, the issues we care for, than by any other set of values, opinions, attitudes, or principles. The experiment is certainly easy to make: think of any set of contemporary issues—the entry of Turkey into Europe, the Islamic veil in France, the spread of genetically modified organisms in Brazil, the pollution of the river near your home, the breaking down of Greenland glaciers, the diminishing return of your pension funds, the closing of your daughter's factory, the repairs to be made in your apartment, the rise and fall of stock options, the latest beheading by fanatics in Falluja—and for every one of those objects you will feel, spewing out of them, a different set of passions, indignations, opinions, as well as a different set of interested parties and different ways of pursuing their partial resolution.

Each object, each issue, generates a different pattern of emotions and disruptions, of disagreements and agreements. Each object gathers around itself a different assembly of relevant parties. Each object triggers new occasions to passionately differ and contest. Each object may also offer new ways of coming to a closure without having to agree on much else. In other words, objects taken as issues bind all of us in ways that trace a public space deeply different from what is usually recognized under the label of "the political." It is this space, this hidden geography, which we wish to explore.

It is not unfair to say that political philosophy is marked by a strong object-avoidance tendency. From Hobbes to Rawls many procedures have been devised to assemble the relevant parties, to authorize them to contract, to check their degree of representativity, to find the ideal speech conditions, to detect the legitimate closure, to write the good constitution, but about *what* is at issue, *which* is the object of concern that brings them together, not a word is uttered. In a strange way, political science is mute just at the moment when the objects of concern should be brought in. Procedures to authorize and legitimize are important, to be sure, but it is only half of what it is to assemble: the other half lies in the issues themselves, in the matters that matter. And they too need to be represented, authorized, legitimated, brought to bear inside the relevant assembly.

What we call an "object-oriented democracy" tries to redress this bias in much political philosophy, that is, to bring together two entirely unrelated meanings of the word "representation." The first, so well known in schools of law and political science, designates the ways to gather the relevant people around some issue. The second, well known in science, technology, and the arts, presents or *represents* what is the object of concern to the eyes and ears of those who have been assembled around it. Realism certainly implies that the same degree of attention be brought to bear on the two aspects of what it is to represent an issue. The first question draws a sort of place, sometimes a circle, that might be called an assembly, a gathering, a meeting, a council; the second question brings *into* this newly created locus, a topic, a concern, an issue, a topos. *Who* is to be concerned, *what* is being considered?

When Thomas Hobbes instructed his engraver how to sketch the famous frontispiece for his *Leviathan* he had his mind full of optical metaphors and illusion machines.[1] A third meaning of this ambiguous and ubiquitous word "representation" had to be called for to solve, this time visually, the problem of the composition of the "Body Politik."[2] To this day, it remains a puzzle: how to represent and through which medium, the sites where people meet their matters of concern? It is precisely what we are tackling here. But Shapin and Schaffer summarized the problem even better than Hobbes when they redrew his monster for *their* frontispiece and equipped his left arm not with a bishop's cross but with Boyle's air-pump.[3] From that point on, the powers of science were as important to consider: how do they assemble, and around which matters of concern? The Body Politik is not made of people alone—look at the engraving: clothes, a huge sword, immense castles, large cultivated fields, crowns, ships, cities, and an immensely complex technology of gathering, meeting, cohabitating, enlarging, reducing, focusing. Objects, objects everywhere, in addition to naked, powerless people. Where has political science turned its distracted look while so many objects were drawn under its very nose?

Two vignettes will help us focus on those sites. The first one is a fable proposed by Peter Sloterdijk.[4] He imagined that the U.S. Air Force should have added to its military paraphernalia an "Inflatable Parliament," which could be parachuted at the rear of the front, just after the liberating forces of the Good had defeated the forces of Evil. On hitting the ground, this parliament would unfold and be inflated just like your rescue boat is supposed to do when you fall

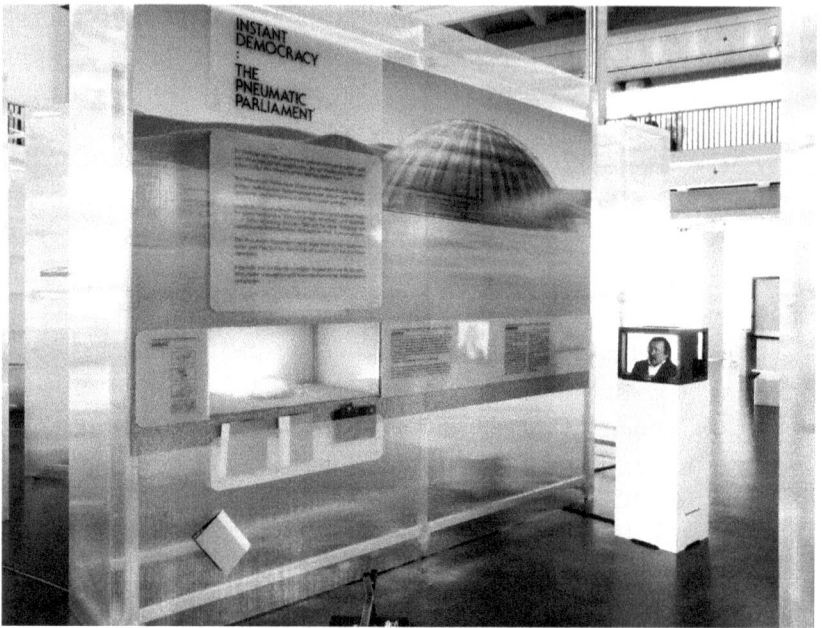

Peter Sloterdijk, *The Pneumatic Parliament,* 2004. Installation view. Photograph by Franz Wamhof. Courtesy of the artist and the Center for Art and Media (ZKM), Karlsruhe.

in the water . . . and here you are, ready to enter and to take your seat, your finger still red with the indelible ink that proves you have exerted your voting duty: Instant Democracy would be thus delivered! The lesson of this simile is easy to grasp. To imagine democracy without its material set of complex instruments, "air-conditioning," local ecological requirements, material infrastructure, long held habits, is as ludicrous as trying to parachute such an inflatable parliament in the middle of Iraq. By contrast—to pursue Sloterdijk's inquiry into spheres and globes—probing an object-oriented democracy is to research what the material conditions are that make the air breathable again.

The second vignette is the terrifying one offered by the now infamous talk U.S. secretary of state Colin Powell delivered to the United Nations on February 5, 2003, about the unambiguous and indisputable fact of the presence of weapons of mass destructions in Iraq.[5] No doubt, the first half of the representation —namely the assembly of legitimate speakers and listeners—was well taken care of: all of those around the U.N. Security Council had a right to be there. But the same cannot be said of the second half: namely, the representation of the facts of the matter presented by the secretary of state. Every one of the slides was a

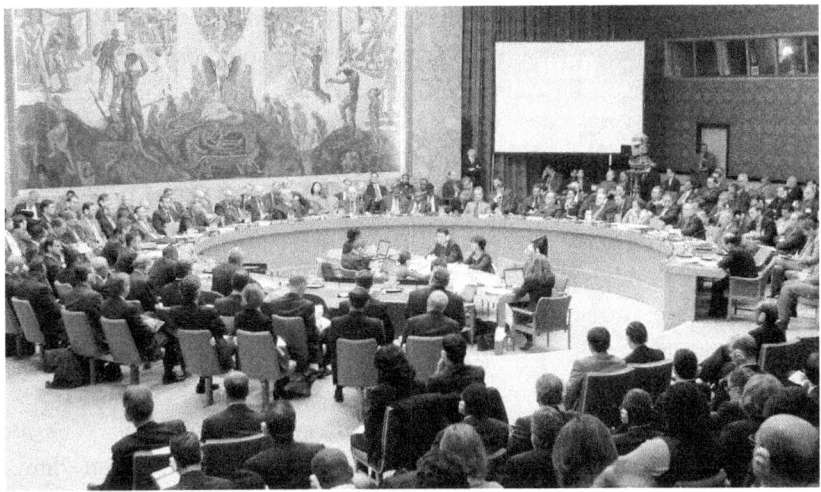

The United Nations Security Council meets at the U.N. headquarters to hear evidence of Iraq's weapons program presented by U.S. secretary of state Colin Powell Wednesday, February 5, 2003. © AP Images / Richard Drew.

blatant lie—and the more the time passes the more blatant they become. And yet their showing was prefaced by these words: "My colleagues, every statement I make today is backed up by sources, solid sources. *These are not assertions. What we are giving you are* facts *and conclusions based on solid intelligence*" (my emphasis). Never has the difference between facts and assertions been more abused than on this day.

To assemble is one thing; to represent to the eyes and ears of those assembled what is at stake is another. An object-oriented democracy should be concerned as much with the procedure to detect the relevant parties as with the methods to bring into the center of the debate the proof of what is to be debated. This second set of procedures to bring in the object of worry has several old names: *eloquence,* or more derogatory, *rhetoric,* or even more pejorative, *sophistic.* And yet these are just those poor, despised labels that we might need to rescue from the dustbin of history.[6] Mr. Powell tried to distinguish the rhetoric of assertions from the undisputable power of facts. He failed miserably. Having no truth, he had no eloquence either. Can we do better? Can we trace again the frail conduits through which truths and proofs are allowed to enter the sphere of politics?

Unwittingly, the secretary of state put us on a possible track: the abyss between assertions and facts might be a nice rhetorical ploy, but it has lost its relevance. It implies that there would be, on the one side, matters of fact, to which some enlightened people would have an unmediated access, and, on the other, disputable assertions that would be good for nothing except to feed the subjective passions of interested crowds. On the one side, truth and no mediation; on the other side, opinions and too many obscure intermediaries. With this classical argument, the Inflatable Parliament is now equipped with a huge screen on which thoroughly transparent facts are displayed . . . and those who remain unconvinced prove by this resistance how irrational they are. They have fallen prey to subjective passions.

The problem is that such transparent, unmediated, and undisputable facts have recently become increasingly rare. To provide a proof has become a rather messy, pesky, risky business. And to offer a *public* proof, big enough and certain enough to convince the whole world of the presence of a phenomenon or of a looming danger, seems now almost beyond reach.[7] The same American administration that was content with a few blurry slides "proving" the presence of nonexistent weapons in Iraq, is happy to put many brackets around the proof of the much vaster, much better validated, most imminent threat of global climate change, diminishing oil reserves, increasing poverty. Is it not time to say: "Mr. Powell, given what you have done with facts, we would much prefer you to leave them aside and let us instead compare mere *assertions* with one another. Don't worry, even with such an inferior type of proof we will come to a conclusion nonetheless."[8] Either we should despair of politics and abandon the hope of providing public proofs altogether, or we should abandon the all-too-worn-out cliché of incontrovertible matters of fact.

Good! This is just what we wish to attempt: where matters of fact have failed, let us try matters of concern. What we are trying here to register is the huge sea change in our conceptions of science, our grasps of facts, our understanding of objectivity. Objects have been wrongly portrayed as matters of fact. This is unfair to them, unfair to science, unfair to objectivity, unfair to experience. They are much more interesting, variegated, uncertain, complicated, far-reaching, heterogeneous, risky, historical, local, material, and "networky" than the pathetic version offered for too long by philosophers. Rocks are not simply there to be kicked at, desks to be thumped at. "Facts are facts are facts"? Yes, but they are also a lot of other things *in addition*. For those who, like Mr. Powell, have been long used to banishing all opposition by claiming the superior power of facts, such a sea change might be welcomed with cries of derision: "relativism," "subjectivism," "irrationalism," "mere rhetoric," "sophistry." They might see the new life of facts as so much subtraction. For sure! It subtracts a lot of their power and may render their life more difficult. Think of that: they might have to enter into the new arenas for good! They might actually have to publicly prove their assertions *against other assertions,* and come to a closure without thumping and kicking. . . . We want to explore realist gestures other than thumping and kicking. Is that asking too much?

Our notions of politics have been corrupted for too long by an absurdly unrealistic epistemology. Accurate facts are hard to come by and the harder they are, the more they entail complex equipment, a longer set of mediations, more delicate proofs. Transparency and immediacy are bad for science as well as for politics and would make both suffocate. What we need is to be able to bring inside the assemblies issues with their retinue of complicated proof-giving equipment. No unmediated access to agreement; no unmediated access to the facts of the matter. After all, we are used to rather arcane procedures for voting and electing; why would we suddenly imagine an eloquence so devoid of means, tools, tropes, tricks, and knacks that it would bring the facts in some uniquely transparent idiom? If politics is earthly, so is science.

It is exactly to underline this shift from a cheapened notion of objectivity to costly proofs that we want to resurrect the word "Ding" and use the neologism "Dingpolitik" as a substitute for "Realpolitik." The latter lacks realism when it talks about forces as well as when it talks about facts.

As every reader of Heidegger knows, or as every look in the English dictionary under the heading "thing" will certify, the old word "thing" or "Ding" originally designated a certain type of archaic assembly.[9] Many parliaments in Nordic, Icelandic, and Saxon nations still activate the old root of this etymology: Norwegian congressmen assemble in the *Storting*; Icelandic deputies called "thingmen" gather in the *Althing*; Isle of Man seniors used to gather around the Ting; the German landscape is dotted with *Thingstatten,* and you can see in many places the circles of stones where the Thing used to stand.[10] Thus, long before it was used to designate an object thrown out of the political sphere, standing there objectively and independently, the Ding or Thing referred to the issue that brings people together *because* it divides them. The same etymology lies dormant in the Latin *res*, the Greek *aitia*, and the French or Italian *cause*. Even the Russian *soviet* still dreams of bridges and churches.[11] Of all the eroded meanings left by the slow crawling of political geology, none is stranger to consider than the Icelandic Althing, since the ancient "thingmen" had the amazing idea of meeting in a desolate and sublime place that happens to sit smack in the middle of the fault line that separates the Atlantic from the European tectonic plates. Not only do they manage to remind us of the old sense of "Ding," but they also dramatize to the maximum how much political questions have also

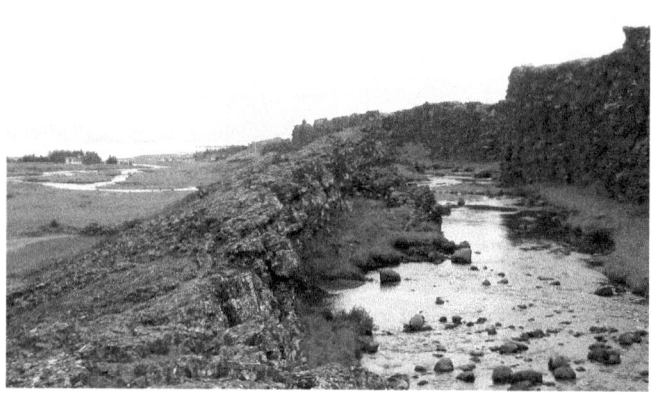

Sabine Himmelsbach, *Althing in Thingvellir (fiingvellir), Iceland* [930–1799], c. 2004. Photograph. Courtesy of the Center for Art and Media (ZKM), Karlsruhe.

become questions of nature. On how many fault lines of how many different sorts of tectonic plates do we reside today? Are not all parliaments now divided by the natures of things as well as the din of the crowded Thing?

We do not assemble because we agree, look alike, feel good, are socially compatible, wish to fuse together, but because we are brought by *divisive* matters of concern into some neutral, isolated place to come to some sort of provisional makeshift (dis)agreement. If the Ding designates both those who assemble because they are concerned as much as what causes their concerns and divisions, it should become the center of our attention: *Back to Things!* This could be our political slogan.

Through some amazing quirk of etymology, it just happens that the same root has given birth to those twin brothers: the *Demon* and the *Demos*—and those two are more at war with one another than Eteocles and Polyneices have ever been.[12] Yes, the word "demos" that makes up half of the much vaunted word "democracy" is haunted by the demon, yes, the devil, because they share the same root *da*—to divide.[13] If the demon is such a terrible threat, it is because it divides in two.

We might be familiar with Jesus' admonition: "Every kingdom divided against itself is laid waste, and no city or house divided against itself will stand; and if Satan casts out Satan, he is divided against himself; how then will his kingdom stand?"[14] But the same power of division is also what provides the division, namely, the *sharing* of the same territory, hence the *people*, the demos made simultaneously of those who share the same space and are divided by the same worries. How could an object-oriented democracy ignore such a vertiginous uncertainty? When the knife hovers around the cake to be divided in shares, it may divide and let the demon of civil strife loose or it may cut equal shares and leave the demos happily apportioned. Strangely enough, we are divided and yet might have to divide, that is to share, even more. Yes, the demos is haunted by the demon of division.

But it is also haunted—this is what is so devilish—by the demon of unity, transparency, and immediacy. "Down with intermediaries! Enough spin! We are lied to! We have been betrayed!" Everywhere resonates those cries and everyone seems to sigh: "Why are we being so badly represented?" One answer is certainly that we are badly represented because we are asking from representation something it cannot possibly give, namely, representation *without* any *re*presentation . . . without any provisional assertions, without any imperfect proof, without any opaque layers of translations, transmissions, betrayals, without any complicated machinery of assembly, delegation, argumentation, negotiation, and conclusion. There might exist, as columnists, educators, militants never tire of complaining, a "crisis of representation." The people no longer feel at ease, they rightly say, with what its elites are telling them. An abysmal gap has opened between the "political sphere" and the "reality that people have to put up with." Surely, no Dingpolitik can ignore a situation where politics has become unreal, surrealistic, virtual, alien.

But it might also be the case that half of such a crisis is due to what has been sold to the people under the name of a faithful, transparent, and accurate representation. In an exhibition called "Iconoclash," we tried to explore the roots of a specific form of Western fanaticism: if only there was no image—that is, no mediation—the better would be our grasp of Beauty, Truth, and Piety. We visited the famous iconoclastic periods from the Byzantine to the Reformation, from Mao's Red Square to Malevich's Black Square, but we also added the less well-known struggle among iconoclasts and iconodules in mathematics, physics, and the other sciences.[15] All are striking forms of iconoclasm since at the same time, scientists, artists, clerks were multiplying imageries, intermediaries, mediations, representations that they never tired of tearing down and resurrecting with even more forceful, beautiful, inspired, objective forms. Hence the neologism "Icono*clash*" to point at this double bind, this other demonic division: "Alas, we cannot do anything without the image"; "Fortunately, we cannot do anything without the image."

This was not an iconoclastic show, but a show *about* iconoclasm, not a critical show, but a show *about* critique. The urge to debunk was no longer a resource to feed from but a topic to be carefully examined. We tried to force an angel to come down and stop in mid-air the arm that held the hammer and that could mutter in our ear: "Beware, what are you striking at with so much glee? Look first at what you might destroy!" Saint George, we thought, looked more interesting without his spear.[16] Our aim was to move the collective attention, as the subtitle indicates, "*beyond* the image wars in science, religion and art." This "beyond" was drawn, very simply, by taking into consideration the other half of what they were all doing: those we were following were never simply tearing down idols, burning fetishes, debunking ideologies, exposing scandals, breaking down old forms, but *also* putting ideas onto pedestals, invoking deities, proving facts, establishing theories, building institutions, creating new forms. Hence, a new respect for mediators. Obviously, there is something in the way flows of images build the access to Beauty, Truth, and Piety that has been missed by the idol breakers of all ages. To summarize in one vignette, I proposed to say that Moses might have been hard of hearing and that is why he had confused the commandment "Thou shall not make graven images" with "Thou shall not freeze frame. . . ."

"Iconoclash," however, carefully excluded politics. This was on purpose. There is no representation where it is more difficult to pay due respect to mediators, no activity more despised than that of politicians, no sphere more inviting to irony, satire, debunking, derision than the political sphere, no idols more inviting for destruction than the Idols of the Forum; no discourse is easier to deconstruct. On political rhetoric, critique has a field day. Even toddlers are already cynical on all political matters. In a show that was *about* critique, adding politics would have skewed the whole project and visitors would have left even more iconoclastic than they had entered . . .

Is it possible, now, to tackle the question of political representation with care and respect? Once we are *beyond* the image wars could we extend the same attention to mediators of the most despised activity? This is the new question we wish to deal with.

What is the social theory that can help do this best? A good political epistemology is one that keeps open the recalcitrance—that is to say, the objections and objectivity of all its participants. I have always been puzzled by the critiques made by people who claimed to be "progressive." It seems to me, on the contrary, that they have tied themselves to the social theory least able to accommodate their various programs. If there is no way to inspect and decompose the content of social forces, if they remain unexplained, overpowering, then there is not much to be done. To insist on the presence behind all objects of the same

System, the same Empire, the same Totality that claims to explain all their movements, has always struck me as an extreme case of sadomasochism, a perverted way to look for a sure defeat while enjoying the bittersweet feeling of superior political correctness. Nietzsche traced the immortal portrait of the "man of resentment"—by which he meant a Christian, but a critical sociologist would do just as well.

Is it not obvious, on the contrary, that only a skein of weak ties, of constructed, artificial, assignable, accountable, surprising connections is the only way to begin contemplating any kind of fight? Of the Total there is nothing to say. All one can do is genuflect toward it. Or, worse, dream of occupying the place of total Power—but this, too, has been tried in the recent past and the results, to put it mildly, have not been terribly encouraging. . . . I think it would be much safer to claim that action is possible only in a territory that has been opened up, flattened down, cut to size, in which formats, structures, globalizations, totalities, circulate inside tiny conduits and where for each of their applications they need to resort to masses of hidden potentialities. If there is no possibility, then there is no politics either. No battle has even been won without resorting to new combinations and surprising events. *One's own action "makes a difference" only in a world made of differences.* But is this not the topography of the social that emerges once we take seriously the Ding? When pointing out things, do we not discover a reserve army whose size is astronomically bigger than what it has to fight? At least the chances of winning are much better—the occasions to nurture sadomasochism much more rare.

So in the end, what is Dingpolitik's political project? It is nothing more, I claim, than a complicated way to go back to the primitive surprise at seeing the social unravel—an experience that has been somewhat dulled by recent history of the social sciences—the only way to register again what we mean by politics is to get even closer to the original experience. I propose to say that when we encounter the social, it is always through a feeling of crisis in what it is to belong.

During the nineteenth century this feeling was constantly refreshed by the surprising emergence of masses, crowds, industries, cities, empires, microbes, media, inventions of all sorts. Strangely enough, this insight should have been even stronger in the next century of catastrophes and innovations, of increasing numbers of threatened humans and ecological crises. That this was not the case was due to the very definitions of Society and of social ties that tried to mop up a few elements, while excluding vast numbers of candidates. Where naturalism reigned, it was very difficult to scrutinize the composition of the social with any seriousness. What we try to do, instead, is to render ourselves sensitive again to the oddity of assembling collectives made of so many new members *once Nature and Society have been simultaneously put aside.*

How could we believe that we still have to absorb the same type of actors, the same numbers of entities, the same profiles of beings, the same modes of existence, in the same types of collectives as Comte, Durkheim, Weber, or Parson? Especially after science and technology have so massively multiplied the participants to be cooked in this melting pot. Yes, sociology is the science of immigrant masses, but what do you do when you have to deal with electrons and electors, GMOs and NGOs all at once? For the new wine of new associations, any dusty older flask will not do. This is just the reason why I have defined elsewhere the collective as an expansion of society and the sociology of associations as the resumption of the sociology of the social. This is what I take to be the "nonmodern" political project. This is what I mean by a search for political relevance. Once the tasks of gathering the collective are completed, another question can be raised: what are the *assemblies* of those *assemblages?*

We should be careful here not to confuse this formulation with another one that has a strong resemblance to it, but which would lead us back to an entirely different project. To raise a political question most often means to reveal behind a given state of affairs the presence of forces hitherto hidden. But then you risk falling into the same trap of providing social explanations and do exactly the opposite of what I mean by politics. You use the same old repertoire of already gathered social ties to "explain" the new associations. Although you seem to speak *about* politics you do not speak *politically.* What you are doing is simply the extension, one step further, of the same small repertoire of already standardized forces. You might feel the pleasure of providing a "powerful explanation," but that is just the problem: you yourself partake in the *expansion* of power, not in the recomposition of its content. Even though it resembles political talk, it has not even begun to address the political endeavor, since it has not tried to assemble the possible candidates into a new assembly adjusted to their specific requirements. "Drunk with power" is not an expression fit only for generals, presidents, CEOs, mad scientists, and bosses—it can also be used for those commentators who are confusing the expansion of powerful explanations with the composition of the collective. This is why another slogan might be "Be sober with power," that is, abstain as much as possible from using the notion of power in case it backfires and hits your explanations instead of the target you are aiming to destroy. No powerful explanation without checks and balances.

So, in the end, there is a conflict (no need to hide it) between doing critical sociology and being politically relevant, between Society and the Body Politik. One retraces the repetitive iron ties of necessity; the other explores new paths for the possible. To be politically motivated, now, begins to take on a different and more specific meaning: look for ways to register new associations and explore the manners of assembling them in a satisfactory form. The problem is that there is no longer one way to assemble the collective but as many as the circulating entities we have begun to detect. A social made of humans only is one specific way to draw together the whole, but science, religion, law, economics, art, organizations, and so on are also able to gather the associations and to make them proliferate in another specific ways. "Social" is no longer the name of what assembles all of them, but only one possible way to describe associations. To look for political relevance may thus take on several different meanings: either it designates the expansion of the calibrated social as far as possible—as is often done by critical sociology—or we mean by this term the general question of assembling the collective made of different types of ties; or, in still another sense, it means the highly specific way in which the Body Politik is being drawn.

As John Dewey had shown in his own definition of the public, the two key elements have been, first, its capacity to refresh itself—a quality impossible if a society is supposed to be "behind" or "after" political action—and, second, if it is able to loop back from the few to the many and from the many to the few, a process often simplified under the terms of representation.[17] So the test for political relevance is now fairly easy to draw: do sociology in such a way that the ingredients making up the collective are regularly refreshed; free the path for the composition so that it can go through the complete loop and take it up again; make sure that the number, modes of existence, and recalcitrance of those that are thus assembled are not thwarted too early. Everyone may now judge for him- or herself what sort of social theory is best able to fulfill those goals. The practical effect of studying the social is to be able to pursue the *event* of the assemblages in a document—whatever its form. Our distinctive touch is simply to highlight the stabilizing mechanisms so that the premature transformation of matters of concern into matters of fact is counteracted.

Positivism—in its natural or in its social form, in its "reactionary" or in its "progressive" form—is not wrong because it forgets "human consciousness" and decides to stick to "cold data" instead; it is wrong politically. It has reduced matters of concern into matters of fact *too fast, without due process*. It has confused the two tasks of realism: multiplicity and unification. It has blurred the distinction between deploying the associations, and collecting them into one *collective*. This is what the advocates of a hermeneutic sociology have rightly felt, but without knowing how to get out of the trap, so bizarre were their ideas about natural sciences and the material world. They have misunderstood what it means for a science—social or natural—to have a political project; hence the false alternative between being, on the one hand, a "disinterested" scientist, and, on the other, "socially relevant." It is, on the contrary, the sociology of the social, which has alternated feverishly between a disinterested science it could never deliver, and a political relevance it could never reach.

Instead, two other sets of procedures should be brought into the foreground: (1) a first set that makes the deployment of actors visible; (2) a second set of procedures that make the unification of the collective into a common world acceptable explicitly by those who are thus unified. It is because of the first set that this attention to Things looks more like a disinterested science and combats the urge of critique for legislating in the actors' stead. It is because of the second set that it most resembles political engagement while criticizing the production of a science of Society that is supposed to be invisible to the eyes of the "informants," as well as the claim of some avant-gardists to know better. We wish to be more disinterested than was possible with the sociurgic, or society-building, project of traditional critique since we pursue controversies much further, but we also wish to be much more engaged than what was possible with the scientistic dream of a disinterested gaze. And yet, something like disinterestedness is offered to help assembling in part the collective, that is to give it an arena, a forum, a space, a representation through the very modest medium of some risky account, most of the time a fragile documentation, sometimes only a text.

What we bet on is that it should be possible to clarify this confusion, to redistinguish the two tasks of deployment and unification, to spell out the procedures for due process, and thus to modify what it means for a critique to be more politically relevant *and* more scientific. This is almost the same balance as the one offered by the tradition, although it diverges from it because of the way the deployment is accepted and the way the collection is achieved. So far, the critical mind has not been especially interested in proposing explicit procedures *to distinguish the two tasks of deployment and collection.* We simply claim to be a tiny bit better at those two opposed and complementary moves precisely because the conception of what science and society are has been modified in step.

If we were still modern we could of course ignore all this head scratching and hair splitting, we could simply continue the earlier tasks of modernization and strive for a disinterested science and/or a scientifically based politics. There is a strong link, in my view at least, between the diagnostic of modernization and the definition I gave of Dingpolitik. If you really think that the future common world can be better composed by using Nature and Society as the ultimate metalanguage, it is of course useless. It becomes interesting only if what was called in the recent past "the West," realizing its sudden weakness, decides to rethink what it is, how it should present itself to the rest of the now more powerful world, and has thus to explore again ways to establish connections with the others that cannot possibly be held in the Nature/Society collectors. The critical mind has always been very strongly linked to the superiority of the West—including of course its own shame at being so overpowering and so hegemonic. For me, Dingpolitik is just the opposite; feeling the weakness of the former Occident, and trying to imagine how it could survive a bit longer in the future to maintain a small place in the sun, it has to redefine what is holding it together. This is the reason why it cannot be content with its earlier definitions of natural and social ties. To survive longer in the next phase of world history, it has to restudy itself and to reopen what it means by association and social ties. It has to finally do, in other words, its own anthropology. Or, to use another ambiguous term, it has to engage at last in cosmopolitics.[18]

NOTES

Elements of this text are further developed in the author's "From Realpolitik to Dingpolitik, or How to Make Things Public," in Latour and Weibel, *Making Things Public,* 4–31.

1   Nicéron, *La perspective curieuse à Paris.*
2   Bredekamp, *Thomas Hobbes Visuelle Strategien;* Schaffer, "Seeing Double."
3   Shapin and Schaffer, *Leviathan and the Air Pump.*
4   Sloterdijk, *Sphären III* and "Atmospheric Politics."
5   See http://www.whitehouse.gov/news/releases/2003/02/20030205–1.html.
6   Cassin, *L'effet sophistique* and "Managing Evidence."
7   Schaffer, "Seeing Double."
8   See the complex set of assertions offered by Blix, *Disarming Iraq.*
9   The *Oxford English Dictionary:* "ORIGIN: Old English, of Germanic origin: related to German *Ding.* Early senses included "meeting" and "matter, concern" as well as "inanimate objects." See also Heidegger, *What Is a thing?;* and Harman, "Heidegger on Objects and Things."
10 Respectively, Palson, "Of Althings!"; Edwards and James, "Our Government as Nation"; and Doelemeyer, "Thing Site, Tie, Ting Place."
11 Kharkodin, "Things as *Res Publicae.*"
12 Détienne, *Qui veut prendre la parole?*
13 Lévéque, "Repartition et démocratie."
14 Matthew 12:26–27.
15 Latour and Weibel, *Iconoclash.*
16 Brotton, "Saints Alive," 155.
17 Dewey, *The Public and Its Problems.*
18 Stengers, "The Cosmopolitical Proposal."

THE RETURN OF THE SIXTIES IN CONTEMPORARY

ART AND CRITICISM

JAMES MEYER

Just as Proust begins the story of his life with an awakening, so must every presentation of history begin with an awakening; in fact, it should treat of nothing else.
—Walter Benjamin, *The Arcades Project*, 1927–1940

Felix Gmelin's *Color Test: The Red Flag II* is an installation of side-by-side projections of identical size. The film on the left was shot in Berlin in 1968; the right projection is a reenactment staged by Gmelin in Stockholm in 2002. At first glance, the films appear to be the same. A young person runs down an urban street, disporting a large red flag. After a few minutes, he relinquishes his charge to another runner, and then another. And yet the more closely we compare the films we discern they are not equivalent. Is it the runners' haircuts and clothes, or the automobiles they pass, which date the first film to the sixties? Their boundless enthusiasm? (The runners in the second film appear listless.) The work's conclusion confirms these suspicions. In the earlier film, the final runner storms the Berlin city hall, emerging on the building's balcony: he waves the red flag triumphantly. The later run ends at the Stockholm City Hall steps: the dramatic ending of the original *Color Test* is foreclosed.

Renée Green's *Partially Buried* (1996) is yet another reflection on the counterculture. Whereas Gmelin has managed to retrieve an archival film, Green searches for an earthwork that no longer exists. Robert Smithson completed his *Partially Buried Woodshed* at Kent State University in Ohio shortly before the

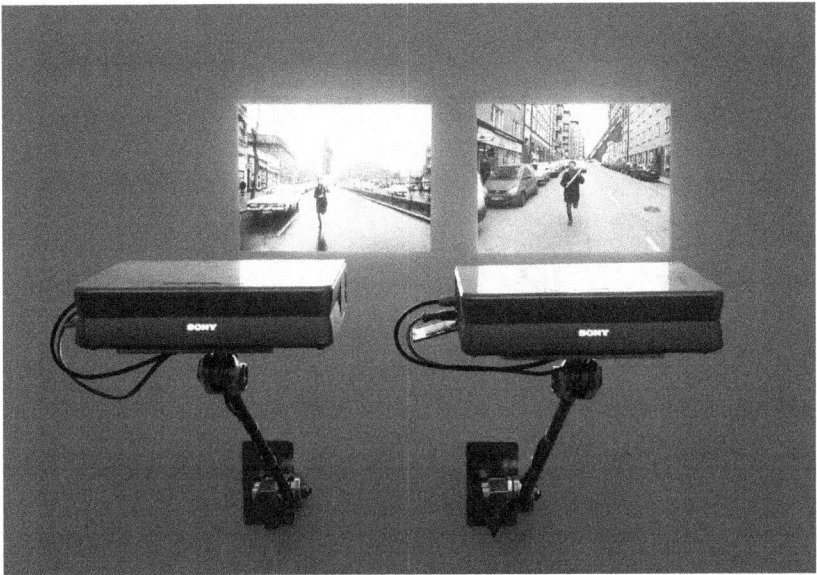

Felix Gmelin, *Farbtest: Die Rote Fahne II*, 2002. DVD video in two projections. Installation view, Portikus Gallery, Frankfurt am Main. Courtesy of Milliken Gallery, Stockholm.

riots that left four students dead in the spring of 1970. Green's unearthing of Smithson's project took multiple forms.[1] Her installation *Partially Buried*, at Pat Hearn Gallery in New York, consisted of a vintage table with paperbacks by James Michener, author of a 1971 book on the riot; shards of concrete—among the few physical remnants of Smithson's work—displayed under glass; and framed photographs documenting a recent visit by the artist to Kent State. The gallery beyond, painted an early seventies acid orange, was filled with period furniture and LPS. Video monitors presented an interview with Brinsley Terrill, the art professor who hosted Smithson at Kent State, in which Terrill describes the *Woodshed*'s history and eventual destruction; clips of interviews with the Weathermen from the 1975 film *Underground;* a Super 8 "home movie" of Cleveland, Ohio, where Green grew up; and a video of the artist's search for the woodshed's foundation. Probably the most dramatic detail of the installation was a recreation of the set of *Underground,* which included a banner bearing the text "The future will be what we the people struggle to make it." A mere twenty-five years old, the Weatherman's revolutionary slogan could not have seemed more unfamiliar, more distant.

Both *Color Test: The Red Flag II*, and *Partially Buried* exemplify the "return" of the sixties in contemporary art and criticism (not to mention curatorial practice). This tendency is indubitably, excessively pervasive. Artists revisit the forms

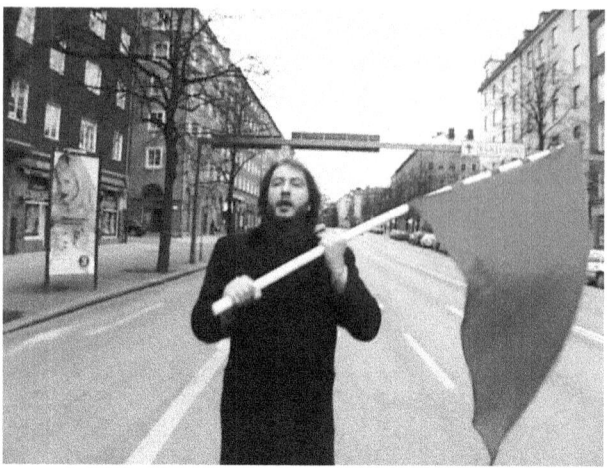

Felix Gmelin, still from *Farbtest: Die Rote Fahne II*, 2002. DVD video in two projections. Courtesy of Milliken Gallery, Stockholm.

associated with that era, and make the history of the sixties, and of sixties art, their subject. (Christopher Williams's *Homage to Bas Van Ader and Christopher D'Arcangelo,* Kerry James Marshall's homages to the civil rights movement, Tacita Dean's recent film *Mario Merz,* Andrea Fraser and Helmut Draxler's *Services,* Christian Philipp Müller's documenta 10 "homage" to Joseph Beuys and Walter de Maria, the paintings of Matthew Antezzo, and the work of Sam Durant could be discussed in these terms.)[2] Retrospectives of sixties movements and canonical sixties artists have become ubiquitous: 2003–2004 brought us Ann Goldstein's survey "A Minimal Future?" at the Los Angeles Museum of Contemporary Art, and major retrospectives of such figures as Donald Judd, Robert Smithson, Dan Flavin, Lee Bontecou, and Ed Ruscha. The Whitechapel Gallery, under Iwona Blazwick's direction, recently organized a series of significant performances from the period.[3] Major survey exhibitions, such as Catherine David's documenta 10, Okwui Enwezor's "The Short Century," and the 2004 Whitney Biennial each traced a different narrative of the contemporary to the sixties.[4] Younger art historians have taken it upon themselves to write the history of the period's artistic practices internationally, although it should be observed that the preponderance of these studies deal with the art of the West—a myopia that efforts like "The Short Century" have done much to redress. This impulse to historicize sixties practice entails a revival of such traditional art historical formats as chronological narrative and the monograph, the gathering of testimonial (interviews with artists, dealers, and critics), and intensive archival research. The rapidly rising market values of sixties practice, and the spec-

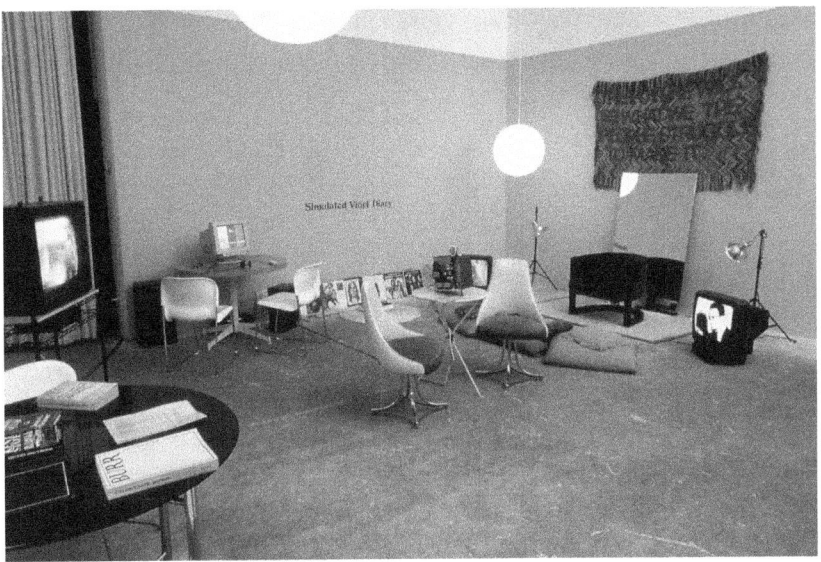

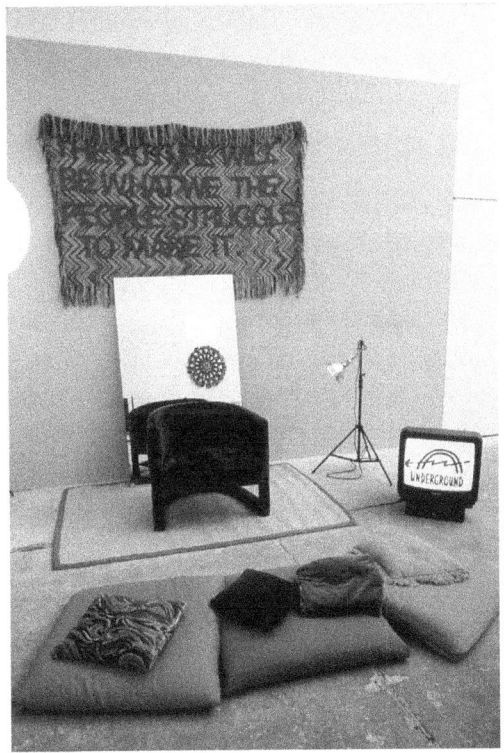

Renée Green, *Partially Buried*,
1996. Video, mixed media.
Installation views, Pat Hearn
Gallery, New York. Courtesy of
the artist.

tacularization of the minimal and postminimal installation at Dia: Beacon, the largest contemporary art museum in the world, suggest a further integration of these once radical tendencies.

This phenomenon gives us pause: what is the significance of this embrace of "the sixties" across these various sites of art world practice (art making, curation, art history, the market)? The meaning of this tendency—how "the sixties" signifies within contemporary art and criticism—is insufficiently understood. Could it be that "the sixties," in becoming history, returns to us as a trope of contemporaneity—as an object for present-day use? How does the current sixties return relate back to previous such returns, such as the postmodernist construction of a sixties "without apology," theorized by the editors of *Social Text* two decades ago?[5] What are the current forms of artistic engagement with sixties practice? A fundamental reference for progressive cultural politics, does the sixties risk becoming an object of nostalgic longing, indeed affirmation?

It is, I think, important to establish a distinction between the sixties as a period, a set of historical conditions such as Fredric Jameson has mapped in his essay "Periodizing the Sixties," versus the sixties as figure, as *effect;* our concern is the latter.[6] The second point is that the present sixties return reflects a broader historicist tendency constitutive of modernity itself, such as Jameson, Hayden White, and many others have described.[7] The condition of being modern, Matthew Arnold observes in "The Modern Element of Literature" (1910), is one that compels us to compare the present to the past, and ourselves to our predecessors. "No single event, no single literature, is adequately comprehended except in relation to other events, other literatures," Arnold writes.[8] Historical awareness, for Arnold, is a form of "deliverance" (the word is his).[9] Recalling the Latin root de-*liberare,* to free, Arnold conceives of historical consciousness as a kind of liberation. We are "delivered" by our understanding of the past. For Arnold's contemporary Friedrich Nietzsche, in *The Use and Abuse of History* (1873), in contrast, the past is hardly a deliverance, but a burden. Human beings "cannot learn to forget, but hang onto the past." The past is a "chain" that "runs" with us.[10] Nietzsche does not deprecate history per se. History is a shackle, but it is something we need.[11] The pertinent question of this text is how history is used. Nietzsche objects not to history, but to historicism—to history as a burden, to use Hayden White's term. History should inspire life; a fixation on the past leads to inaction, to nostalgia, which are against "life" in the philosopher's sense. He distinguishes three historical models. Monumental history, a "preoccupation with the rare and classic," can leave us feeling that major achievement is possible, but also perhaps impossible for us.[12] Antiquarian history is embodied by the "mad collector" of artifacts, who breathes a "moldy air"; the antiquarian knows how to "preserve" life, but not how to create it.[13] Critical history, the philosopher's third model, suggests neither the monumentalist's celebration of the past, nor the antiquarian's archival obsession. It interrogates, indeed judges the past; it uses history for the present; it is, Nietzsche observes, "in the service of life."[14]

Nietzsche's model is far more inflected than this extremely schematic account suggests. The philosopher's concepts of history are relative; each has its benefits and its costs.[15] Suffice it to say that Nietzsche's schema, generated at a previous moment of historicist intensity, the fin de siècle, is extremely suggestive.[16] As the projects by Gmelin and Green, with which I began, imply, the sixties has come to signify as monumental history in turn-of-the-century culture. If for the postmodernist artist Modernism occupied this monumental status (the early work of Sherrie Levine comes to mind) now it is the sixties that represents the possibility—and, following Nietzsche, the impossibility—of artistic and social transformation. *Color Test: The Red Flag II* captures the heady ebullience of 1968, yet suggests that this feeling of freedom is irretrievably a thing of the past (recall the slightly bored affect of the runners in the second film). *Partially Buried* suggests that Smithson's woodshed has itself become an art historical monument, a particularly ironic outcome when we recall Smithson's brilliant equation of monumentality and entropy: setting out to make a work that would destroy itself, Smithson ended up making a monument, one we now dutifully recall through the mediation of photographs and the recollections of those who witnessed its making. At the same time, Green's project suggests the antiquarian nature of this retrieval. For what is *Partially Buried* but an archive of the year 1970? Much like the philosopher's mad collector, Green is not a maker of the new so much as a scavenger of the old, a gatherer of artifacts, and in this resembles the legions of "younger" art historians who compulsively ransack the archives of sixties practitioners and critics for fresh materials and insights. Gmelin also performs an "antiquarian" role. The idea for *Color Test: The Red Flag II* came about when the artist inherited the archive of his father, a former art professor who organized the first flag run and who, in fact, appears in the original film with his students. The film Gmelin did not make would have consisted of shots of an inherited archive of sculpture.[17] Instead, Gmelin appropriated his father's film and then remade it, engaging his own students to reenact the piece.

But it is perhaps the idea of critical history that these projects most evoke; it is from this position that Gmelin and Green interrogate the other models. Both works point to the longing that attends present-day monumentalist and antiquarian constructions of the sixties. The monumental historian pines for a glorious past he himself did not experience; the antiquarian salvages and organizes its remnants. Much of the art writing on the period, my own included, bespeaks the melancholy of having not been present at the happenings and the exhibitions and the demonstrations we so assiduously describe; we can only imagine these events. Green interrogates this longing for a past that is not one's own. "Did people have more fun then?" she writes. "Burying buildings with dirt, pouring glue down hills, making islands out of broken glass? Allan Kaprow gave students dollar bills to pin on trees at Kent State then."[18] Green's search for the woodshed allegorizes this longing, this feeling of having not been there, of "living on within the force field of a past not yet over and done with" (Jameson).[19] At one point in his *The Arcades Project,* Walter Benjamin observes that "in order for a part of the past to be touched by the present instant, there must be no continuity between them."[20] The Paris of the arcades becomes knowable only as that Paris which has become historical, when it can only be accessed through archival means. Certainly, the works of Gmelin and Green construct the sixties *as* irretrievably past: the old furniture, the worn LPs, the black-and-white film footage of *Underground* look hopelessly dated; *Color Test: The Red Flag II* underscores the temporal gap between its two parts. And yet these projects speak of a particular kind of past, a past that is *recent,* that is not entirely past. Conceiving of the sixties effect in this way—as a force field or delayed reaction—makes sense when we recall that both artists were born during this period; their memories of their childhoods are memories of the sixties. The histories they recall are in this regard their own. The narrator of *Partially Buried* recalls her mother's attendance at a music class at Kent State during the months of Smithson's visit. She remembers waiting for her mother to return home the evening of the riots.[21] Gmelin recalls having "only a vague idea" of his father's activities during the sixties.[22] Recall Nietzsche's insistence that critical history "interrogates" the past; it uses *and* abuses history. And what is *Color Test: The Red Flag II* but a judgment of *Color Test: The Red Flag I?* Gmelin's remaking of his father's film exposes the inadequacy of its revolutionary narrative. "I think my father was pretty naive in his dream about ruling the world. . . . [He] was convinced that revolution would be the method by which the world would change."[23] But the revolution did not come; the world did not change in the way Gmelin senior imagined. The countercultural signifiers of *Color Test I* were appropriated for a different use. Revolution, Gmelin asserts, has become a kind of fashion. "You can see revolution on almost every poster, selling Nike shoes,"[24] (Indeed, the Yippie Jerry Rubin's exhortation "Do It!" now adorns the Nike "swoosh.") Similarly, Green observes in *Partially Buried:* "Everywhere she goes she encounters echoes" of the early seventies. "The seventies are in vogue now."[25] For Gmelin and Green, present evocations of the sixties and early seventies are deeply ambivalent; as the prior moment recedes into the past, it returns as commodity. The aftermath of the sixties, the sixties effect, thus stands as a conclusion to the periodized sixties mapped out by Jameson, conceived as the historical point of transition into advanced capitalism. Let us recall the concluding remarks in "Periodizing the Sixties": "The simplest yet most universal formulation remains the widely shared feeling that in the sixties, for a time, everything was possible: that this period . . . was a moment of universal liberation, a global unbinding of energies. . . . Yet this sense of freedom and possibility —which is for the sixties a momentary objective reality, as well as (from the hindsight of the eighties) a historical illusion—may perhaps best be explained in terms of the superstructural movement and play enabled by the transition from one infrastructural and systemic stage of capitalism to another."[26]

The cultural logic of the sixties is here conceived as a dialectical process of " 'liberation' and domination"; new forms of freedom—the end of colonialism, the emergence of black, women's, third world, gay and lesbian rights—are themselves the manifestation of capitalist expansion on a global scale. Sixties returns suggest an extension of this contradictory logic of the historical sixties into subsequent periods. One could venture that the sixties returns most forcibly as a signifier of freedom, becomes most meaningful, when the freedoms it unleashed are put at risk. Bearing this in mind, we could imagine various periodizations of different sixties returns. We could point to the sixties return of the Reagan-Thatcher eighties, manifest in neoconservative trashings of that era and, conversely, in the recovery of the sixties in such progressive ventures as *The Sixties without Apology;* or the commoditized sixties return of our globalist moment, that has developed alongside the antiglobalization movement. If *Color Test: The Red Flag II* and *Partially Buried* register the present integration of the sixties, these projects also posit a sixties that holds within itself the idea of future transformations: we are induced to imagine less romanticized forms of opposition. Dismantling the sixties effect, these practices instead construct a periodized sixties, a sixties without illusion, a sixties we can use.

NOTES

1 For another discussion of *Partially Buried,* see Wallis, "Excavating the Seventies."

2 On Williams, see Crow, "Unwritten Histories of Conceptual Art"; on Müller, see Baker and Müller, "A Balancing Act"; on Marshall, *Kerry James Marshall;* on Durant, Meyer, "Impure Thoughts."

3 "A Minimal Future?" Los Angeles Museum of Contemporary Art, March 14–August

2, 2004; "Donald Judd," Tate Modern, February 5–April 25, 2004; "Robert Smithson," Los Angeles Museum of Contemporary Art, September 12–December 13, 2004; "Dan Flavin: A Retrospective," October 17–January 2, 2005; "Lee Bontecou: A Retrospective," UCLA Hammer Museum, October 5, 2003–January 11, 2004; "Cotton Puffs, Q-tips, Smoke and Mirrors: The Drawings of Ed Ruscha," Whitney Museum of American Art, June 24–September 26, 2004; "A Short History of Performance, Parts I and II," Whitechapel Gallery, April 15–21, 2002, and November 18–23, 2003.

4 documenta 10, June 21–September 28, 1997; "The Short Century: Independence and Liberation Movements in Africa, 1945–1994"; 2004 Whitney Biennial Exhibition, March 11–June 13, 2004.

5 Sayres et al., *The Sixties without Apology.*

6 Jameson, "Periodizing the Sixties," in Sayres et al., *The Sixties without Apology.*

7 Jameson, *A Singular Modernity;* and White, "The Burden of History."

8 Arnold, *Essays in Criticism,* 40.

9 Arnold, *Essays in Criticism,* 37.

10 Nietzsche, *The Use and Abuse of History,* 5.

11 "Every man . . . needs a certain knowledge of the past" (Nietzsche, *The Use and Abuse of History,* 22).

12 Nietzsche, *The Use and Abuse of History,* 14.

13 Nietzsche, *The Use and Abuse of History,* 20.

14 Nietzsche, *The Use and Abuse of History,* 20.

15 For example, Nietzsche obviously favors critical history over the other models, yet not entirely: those who condemn the faults of their forebears cannot themselves "shake off" history's chain. Monumental history may dwell too much in the past, yet its celebration of the past allows us to imagine that we can achieve monumentality.

16 My invocation of Nietzsche's historical model is indebted to the work of Yve-Alain Bois. See Bois, *Susan Smith's Archaeology.*

17 See the Gmelin's remarks in "Rene—NE-E—Felix Gmelin + Ronald Jones."

18 Green, "Partially Buried," 43.

19 Jameson, *A Singular Modernity,* 25.

20 Benjamin, *The Arcades Project,* 470.

21 "The girl watched the news and waited anxiously, often. That's part of what she recollects of childhood. Waiting. Seeing the running text of news reporting students shot at Kent State moving across the bottom of the TV screen. Waiting. TV programs were interrupted, and her mother was late returning home from there. . . . Finally her mother did arrive, but she can't now remember what either said. It was May 4, 1970." Green, "Partially Buried," 43.

22 Gmelin, "Rene—NE-E—Felix Gmelin + Ronald Jones."

23 Gmelin, "Rene—NE-E—Felix Gmelin + Ronald Jones."

24 Gmelin, "Rene—NE-E—Felix Gmelin + Ronald Jones."

25 Green, "Partially Buried," 40.

26 Jameson, "Periodizing the Sixties," 207–8.

17

INTRODUCTION TO INFO-AESTHETICS

LEV MANOVICH

THE PROBLEM

I would like to introduce a new paradigm for understanding contemporary culture: *info-aesthetics*. Unlike concepts such as modernism or postmodernism, this paradigm does not aim to be all-inclusive. In other words, I do not have the ambition to understand all new features of contemporary culture as manifestations of a single logic, or a small set of principles. Nevertheless, as I will try to show in my forthcoming book *Info-aesthetics: Information and Form,* if we adopt an info-aesthetics filter, this will allow us to relate together a wide range of cultural phenomena, including some of the most interesting and important projects in a variety of areas of contemporary culture: cinema, architecture, product design, fashion, Web design, interface design, visual art, information architecture, and, of course, new media art. So while info-aesthetics should not be the only tool you would want in your conceptual toolbox, it comes in very handy. This essay, then, may be read as an introduction to the future book and, at the same time, a summary of some of the key ideas of the info-aesthetics project that has preoccupied me since 2000.

To explain what I mean by info-aesthetics, let me start by noting something simple but nevertheless quite significant: the word "information" contains within it the word "form." For some time now social theorists, economists, and politicians have been telling us that we are living in a new "information society." The term was first used in the 1960s, even before the computer revolution got under way. I will discuss below certain theories of information society, as well as related concepts of postindustrial society, knowledge society, and network society. Since this project is about the culture of information society, the arguments of economists and sociologists are no more important than the changes in people's everyday lives. What we do, what objects we use, how we communicate and interact with others and the kind of spaces we dwell in or pass through—all this is bound to change existing cultural patterns and aesthetic preferences as well as create new ones. The fact that we can observe significant changes in all these dimensions of everyday human experience, and that they are converging around "information," requires us to explore corresponding cultural responses.

When the term "information society" was first introduced in the 1960s, few people, even in the United States, had ever seen a computer. (In my own case, having grown up in Moscow in the 1970s, I came face to face with a working computer only after I came to New York in 1981.) Of course, a few perceptive artists such as Jean-Luc Godard in his brilliant *Alphaville* had already understood that the computer was becoming a new god of our times, but they were exceptions. Even such a visionary as Marshall McLuhan—who seemed to predict with precision most features of contemporary cyberculture about three decades before they came into existence—ignored computers. In *Understanding Media* (1964), which presents a systematic analysis of all key historical and modern media technologies, McLuhan does devote the very last section to data processing, but in general computation plays no role in his theories. This is so, probably, because McLuhan was thinking of media as above all a means of communication and/or representation. In the 1960s computers were not yet involved in any of these functions in a way that would be visible to the public.

If in that decade only a very small number of computer scientists—Ted Nelson, Alan Kay, and a few others—understood that the computer was bound to become an *engine of culture* rather than remain merely a data-processing machine, similarly, only a few social scientists were able to perceive that dealing with information was replacing industrial manufacturing in importance. Today, however, what was once an academic hypothesis has became an everyday reality that can be easily observed by the majority of citizens living in the developed and the developing countries. All kinds of work are reduced to manipulating data on one's computer screen, that is, to the processing of information. As you walk or drive past office buildings in any city, all offices, regardless of what a company does, look the same: they are filled with rows of computer screens and keyboards. Regardless of their actual profession, financial analysts, city officials, secretaries, architects, accountants, and pretty much everybody else engaged in white-collar work are doing the same thing: processing information.

When we leave work, we do not leave information society. In our everyday life, we use search engines, we retrieve data from databases, and we rely on "personal information appliances and personal information managers." We complain that there is too much information to keep track of, to make sense of; meanwhile, libraries and museums around the world constantly add to the global information pile by systematically digitizing everything they have. We turn our own lives into an information archive by storing our emails, chats, smss (short message services), digital photos, gps data, favorite music tracks, favorite television shows, and other "digital traces" of our existence. One day, we get tired of all this so we start planning to take "email free" holidays. But even this requires information work: for example, searching for the best deals on the Internet, comparing fares, inputting credit card information into a reservation Web site, and so forth. Even on a largely activity-free vacation, the moment we open a cell phone to make a call or check messages, we enter the world of information. In short, the "information society" is where most citizens of the developed and developing world live today, experiencing it in their everyday practice. While those living outside this world themselves are not using computers on a daily basis, the companies, ngos, and governments of the developed countries, which play the decisive role in deciding what happens in fourth world countries, are all of course computerized. Information processing shapes the lives and fates of citizens of these countries even though themselves may not experience it directly.

Information processing has, in these and other ways, become the key dimension of our daily lives. Yet, since we are physical beings, we have always required and continue to require various physical forms in order to house and transport our bodies, our information-processing machine, and information itself. These forms range from those that are very large (buildings, bridges, airplanes) to those that are very small (iPods, mobile phones), from the rarely changing (architecture) to the periodically updatable (clothes). Just as a person needs clothing, a computer needs a case to protect its insides and to allow us to enter and manipulate information in a convenient way (that is, a human-computer interface, typically a keyboard and a screen). Text needs to be displayed in ways suitable for us to be able to read it, be it on a screen, paper, or e-paper. Therefore, although the word "information" contains the world "form" inside it, in reality it is the other way around: in order to be useful to us, information always has to be wrapped up in some external form.

We need to design forms for ourselves, and also for information that we create, record, and manipulate. We may have become an information-processing species, but we also remain a form-creating species as well. If, for Marx, humans separated themselves from other species when they first designed tools for work, we can add that humans became humans by becoming *designers,* that is to say, the inventors and makers of forms.

INFORMATION AND FORM

If information processing is the new defining characteristic of our world, what is the effect of this situation on the forms we design today? This is the question in which I have been most interested after finishing my book *The Language of New Media* in 1999. It is important to differentiate between two lines of influence in the ways information shapes the forms we design. On the one hand, we may think about how the centrality of dealing with information in our daily lives may affect our aesthetic preferences as manifested in trends in architecture, industrial design, graphic design, media design, cinema, music, fashion, theater, dance, exhibition design, and other cultural fields. On the other hand, we also need to remember that most forms we encounter today are designed on computers. This, of course, is likely to have at least as much of an effect on what forms the designers are going to come up with. In sum, information processing acts both as a force outside a form, so to speak (that is, the new habits of perception, behavior, work, and play), as well as being the very method through which the forms are designed.

There is another fundamental effect that is worth articulating immediately. In the information society the design of forms becomes intricately linked with the concept of interface. As I mentioned above, we need to give some visual form to what will appear on the screens of computers, mobile phones, PDAs (personal digital assistants), car navigation systems, and other devices—as well as to buttons, trackballs, microphones, and various other input tools. Human-computer interfaces that involve a set of visual conventions—such as folders, icons, and menus (the graphical user interface), audio conventions (as in voice recognition interface), and particular material articulations (such as the shape, color, material, and texture of a mobile phone)—represent a whole new category of forms that need to be designed today. Even more important, as computation becomes incorporated into our lived environment (a trend described by such terms as "ubiquitous computing," "pervasive computing," "ambient intelligence," "context-aware environments," "smart objects"), the interfaces slowly leave the realm where they have lived safely for a few decades (think of stand-alone computers and electronics devices) and start appearing in all kinds of objects and on all kinds of surfaces, for example, interior walls, furniture, benches, bags, clothing, and posters.[1] Consequently, the forms of all these objects that previously lived "outside of information" have now to address the likely presence of interfaces somewhere on them.

This does not mean that from now on "form follows interface." Rather, that the two have to accommodate each other. Beyond the traditional requirements that the material forms had to satisfy—a chair has to be comfortable for sitting, for example—their design is now also shaped by new requirements. For instance, we have been accustomed to interacting with text that is presented on flat and rectangular surfaces, so if a screen is to be incorporated somewhere, a part of the object needs to be reasonably flat. Which is easy to do if an object is a table but not as easy if it is a piece of clothing or a section of Frank Gehry's Disney Hall in Los Angeles, a building that was specifically designed not to have a single flat area. Of course, given that new technologies such as rapid manufacturing may soon enable easy printing of an electronic display on any surface of any object while it is being produced, it's possible that we will be able to quickly adjust our perceptual habits, to the point that moving and shape-changing display surfaces will be accepted much more readily than I can imagine. In fact, computer-controlled graphic projections onto the bodies of dancers, as in *Apparition* by Klaus Obermair or in the *Interactive Opera Stage* system by Art+Com, already show the aesthetic potential of displaying information over a changing, nonflat, nonrectangular form.[2]

October 18, 5:04 p.m.–5:33 p.m.
I am looking at the show of student projects from the Department of Industrial Design at Eindhoven Technical University in Netherlands. The department is only three years old, so instead of designing traditional objects, students are working on "smart objects." Every project in the show starts with an everyday familiar object and adds some "magical" functions to it via electronics and computers—more examples of solid objects and media/interface surfaces coming together. In one project, a canopy placed diagonally over a child's hospital bed becomes an electronic canvas. By tracking the position of a special pen that does not need to touch the drawing surface, the canvas allows the child to draw on it without having to move from the bed. In another project, a special mirror allows one person to leave a message for somebody else—for instance, a different member of a household. A rectangular block containing a camera is built into a mirror frame. You take the block out, record a video message, and place the block back into the frame. After the video is automatically "loaded" into the magical mirror, a small picture appears somewhere on the mirror surface: when you click on the picture it plays the message. Yet another project adds magical interactivity to a vertical plastic column. The lights inside the column turn it into an ambient

light source. The column is covered with a special interface: a net. Depending on how you touch the net, the position, quality, and tint of the light changes. How exactly the light will change is not directly predictable, and this is what makes interaction with the light column fun.

Together, these three projects show us different ways in which an object, an interface, and a display can be put together. The first two projects rely on already familiar behaviors—drawing with a pen or making a recording with a video camera. The last one calls for the user to develop a new vocabulary of movements and gestures to which the light will respond. And the ways in which each of these "smart objects" talks back to us are also different: a canvas canopy shows a drawing, a mirror plays video, and a light glows in different ways. In short, the surface of an object can become at once an output and input medium, bringing the physical and the screen-like—that is to say, form and information—together in surprising ways. There is, indeed, magic in these "smart objects": we see familiar, usually passive objects literally coming to life and responding to our interactions with them.

Screen Forms
The forms used in design and architecture are not only material in character, but they are also ways to structure data in order to make it meaningful and useful for human users by presenting it on some kind of display. A cinematic narrative, an interactive information visualization, a Web search engine, the user interface of Nokia phones, or Spotlight (a new search/file management tool in Apple os x) are also forms, which organize data, whether audiovisual recordings in the case of a film, or documents on a hard drive in the case of Spotlight. To distinguish these kinds of forms from the material ones, I will refer to them as "screen forms"—keeping in mind that the actual displays can also include paper (as in illustrations and graphs that appear in journals), as well as augmented reality displays where information is seen superimposed against the real world.

Since the info-aesthetics project is about form and information, I am focusing on the new screen forms that either offer us fundamentally new ways to manage information or respond to the dramatic increase in its quantity. This last fact may appear trivial: we all know that every day fifteen thousand new blogs are created.[3] And that is not all (insert your own favorite statistic that is likely not to get completely obsolete soon). All this is familiar and therefore not very interesting; and yet our daily habits of work and entertainment, the ways in which we understand ourselves, others, and the world around us are being deeply reshaped through this purely quantitative growth of information being produced, exchanged, stored, and made available.

This is another reason why I chose the term "information society" over any other as indicating most acutely the context for this inquiry. I believe that the exponential growth of information available to us is one of the main pressure points on contemporary culture and that this pressure will only continue to increase. The cultural effects of this information glut are diverse. By situating my investigation within the context of the "information society" I want to highlight a new cultural dimension that so far has not been part of our critical vocabulary: scale. In other words, while normally we think of culture using qualitatively different categories such as authorship, collaboration, reception, media type, ideology, and so on, we also now need to start considering something purely *quantitative:* the dramatic increase in the amount of media available. We no longer deal with "old media" or "new media." We now have to think through what it means to be living with "more media."

Some effects of this quantitative change are already visible. Our new standard interface to culture is a search engine. Although by now we have become completely used to this, imagine your reaction in the early 1990s if somebody had told you that soon, if you wished to access information, you would first search through millions of documents, and only then begin listening, watching, or reading. A related development is the shift from a single media object—usually one that physically existed as an entity and was appreciated in isolation—to a sequence or a database of digital media. For instance, rather than fetishizing a particular physical music record or a particular photographic print, we now deal with music playlists or catalogues of digital photographs.

But what do these effects mean? Will the increase in the amount of available mediums, and the advent of new tools and conventions used to access them, lead to a new aesthetics in artworks themselves and to new patterns in their reception? These kinds of question are much harder to answer. There are some new cultural practices, even new fields, that address the exponential growth in the quantity of information in creative ways. I see this growth of information not as a cultural threat but as an opportunity. New cultural strategies are often invented as a response to a real social crisis or simply a perceived change in social order. Industrialization during the nineteenth century provoked a number of creative responses such Art Nouveau and the Arts and Crafts movement. World War I and revolutionary fever in Europe led to Constructivism, the development of the Russian montage school in cinema and photomontage, Surrealism, and so on. Today, "informationalization" puts pressure on society to invent new ways to interact with information, new ways to make sense of it, and new ways to represent it. Social software such as Wikipedia, work in information visualization and information design such as the projects by Benjamin Fry, exceptional database narratives such as *Bleeding Through: Layers of Los Angeles* by Norman Klein, Rosemary Camella, and Andreas Kratky, and cultural analysis such as *Rhythm Science* by DJ Spooky are all examples of approaching the new information environment creatively. Instead of trying to defend ourselves against an information glut, we need to approach this situation as an opportunity to invent new forms appropriate for our world. In short, we need to invent info-aesthetics.

METHOD

I began by observing that the word "information," which defines our era, contains within it the word "form." What are these forms? Or, to put this differently: what is "the shape of information"?

This formulation may sound cute but not in itself informative. Let me, therefore, unfold it into a set of more specific questions. Has the arrival of information society been accompanied by a new vocabulary of forms, new design aesthetics, new iconologies? Can there be forms specific to information society, given that software and computer networks redefine the very concept of form? After all, instead of being solid, stable, finite, discrete, and limited in space and time, the new forms are often variable, emergent, distributed, and not directly observable. Can information society be represented iconically, if the activities that define it—information processing, interaction between a human and a computer, telecommunication, networking—are all dynamic processes? How can the superhuman scale of our information structures—from sixteen million lines of computer code making Windows os, to the forty years it would take one viewer to watch all the video interviews stored on the digital servers of the Shoah Foundation, to the Web itself, which cannot even be mapped as a whole—be translated to the scale of human perception and cognition? In short, if the shift from industrial to information society has been accompanied by a shift from form to information flows, can we still map these information flows into forms meaningful to a human?

When I started looking at contemporary culture from the perspective of these questions, I decided that I needed a term to label my future findings. I adopted "info-aesthetics" as this term. The info-aesthetics project scans contemporary culture to detect emerging aesthetics and cultural forms specific to a global information society. I do not want to suggest that there is some single "info-aesthetics style" that already exists today or may emerge in the future. Rather, "info-aesthetics" refers to *those contemporary cultural practices that can be best understood as responses to the new priorities of information society: making sense of information, working with information, producing knowledge from information.* While I think that these practices already occupy a prominent place, and that it is one that will steadily grow, I should make it clear that the whole ecosystem of diverse styles and forms in contemporary aesthetics should not be simply correlated to the shift to information society and the key role played by information management in the social, economic, and political life of contemporary societies. Various other factors are all equally important: these include economic globalization, global aging, the ideas of complexity, emergence, and evolution, the ecological thinking manifested in such paradigms as "cradle-to-cradle" manufacturing, recyclable and sustainable design, new materials and manufacturing processes, new distributed production networks and logistics of their coordination, and even the changing political and social climate of different decades (the post–Cold War euphoria of the 1990s versus the obsession with security after 9/11).

The method that I decided to use in my research is comparative. I look at the culture of information society by comparing it with the culture of industrial society. The period that is particularly relevant here is the beginning of the twentieth century, when modernist artists formulated new aesthetics, new forms, new representational techniques, and new symbols of industrial society. I believe that by systematically asking what can be their equivalents in information society, we can begin to see more clearly the specificity of our own period.

This method is different from the one used in my book *The Language of New Media.* There my question was "What is new about computational media?" I analyzed new media primarily in relation to post-Renaissance visual culture including Modern art, and so-called old media, that is, the dominant media technologies of nineteenth and twentieth centuries (photography, cinema, video.) My use of history in that book was pragmatic and deliberately varied: since each chapter focused on a particular technique or convention of new media, I constructed the particular historical trajectory that I felt was best to illuminate this technique. In this way, every chapter traced a different path through the modern history of visual culture and media.

In the info-aesthetics projects both my subject matter and my use of history are different. Rather than approaching the question of computational media specificity in relation to the histories of various media, I am looking at the key differences between the cultural logic of our computer-based culture and that of the earlier cultural period: Modernism. I hope that such an approach will help to bring the emerging discipline of media studies closer to other fields in the humanities: art history and criticism, literary studies, cinema studies, as well as architecture and design history. All these fields rely on a concept of Modernism that is by now very familiar and well understood, but they have only begun to seriously deal with contemporary computer-based culture. I hope that by showing how the problems that animated the work of modernist artists can also be seen at work in contemporary information culture a bridge will be built between the people focused on these seemingly unrelated domains of study.

Another standard concept widely used in recent humanities and cultural criticism—the idea of postmodernism—also appears in info-aesthetics, although in ways that may displease many of its users. I suggest that some of the new aesthetics of the 1970s and 1980s, which were at the time described as "postmodern," were in fact only *an intermediary stage between the Modern and the informational.* In other words, in the cultural sphere, postmodernism represented only the very beginning of the computer and information revolution. It did not constitute a fundamental paradigm as important as that of Modernism.

Info-aesthetics does not require us to use the term "new media." Why is this so? In the *Language of New Media* I was interested in the emerging languages of "new media," which I defined as the cultural forms that required a digital computer both for their production and consumption: computer games, Web sites, CD-ROMs, virtual environments, interactive installations, and so on. In other words, if you want to know if something is "new media" or not, simply ask if you require a computer to experience it. If the answer is yes, you are dealing with "new media." Regardless of your particular experience, what you are really doing is interacting with a software program that is currently running. If the user is navigating an interactive multimedia presentation in a museum, browsing the Web, or playing a computer game, some program or programs make it all possible: a director program generating multimedia screens, a Web browser interacting with the server to pull the data and put it on the screen, a code controlling NPCs (nonplayer characters) or calculating the physics necessary to represent a realistic collision between two cars in a computer game, and so on.

Since finishing my analysis of software-based media forms I have started to expand my investigation "horizontally" to include as many other areas of culture as I am able. It was clear that the adoption of digital networked computers in almost all cultural areas was to continue, and therefore in a few years the distinction I was still able to maintain in *The Language of New Media* between "new media" and other cultural practices would become less and less useful. At the same time, as both computer-based design and production techniques were becoming more standard in the fields responsible for our material culture—industrial design, architecture, fashion, experience design, brandscaping—these fields started to attract me more and more. If the "new media" of the 1990s, as all the examples in the preceding paragraph illustrate, was primarily "screen media," from now on computers were likely to have equally significant effects on the aesthetics of our material environment. Add to this the slow but steady rise in importance of the new computing paradigms of ubiquitous computing/ambient intelligence/smart objects, and it was becoming clear to me that if we are to follow the effects of computers on culture, we need to seriously start looking outside the screen. In the years that followed, I spent endless hours in airports, visited many cities on four continents, attended numerous media festivals, architecture reviews, design exhibitions, and industry events, met so many people that my brain now often refuses to release even the names of my friends, and spent more time on orbitz.com and hotel.com than on any other Web sites. I do not think I could have done my research in any other way, and certainly not by Web surfing alone.

Info-aesthetics, therefore, does not examine "new media" specifically. Rather, it examines the various cultural fields (as many as I can keep track of) where the use of computers for design and production gives rise to new forms. Some of these forms are "screen-based"—for instance, information visualization—but many others are material. In the end, I feel that my own shift of interests parallels the shift to where what was once called "new media" really happens today. Ten years ago, an interaction designer would produce something that played on a computer screen alone. Today the common understanding of this profession is very different: according to Wikipedia, interaction design "examines the role of embedded behaviors and intelligence in physical and virtual spaces as well as the convergence of physical and digital products."[4] The cultural sites where the digital and the physical meet is also the key subject of info-aesthetics. But rather than think only in terms of convergence, as a cultural historian of the present I am also thinking about other relationships: those of conflict, contradiction, borrowing, hybridization, remix.

NOTES

The author has been developing these thoughts since 2000 on INFO-AESTHETICS, a "semi-open source book/Web site in progress," at http://www.manovich.net/IA/.

1 Takashi Hoshimo reports: "Posters in Japan are being embedded with tag readers that receive signals from the user's 'IC' tag and send relevant information and free products

back" (Hoshimo, "Bloom Time Out East," http://www.mobile.ent.biz, accessed November 20, 2005).

2 *Apparition,* choreographer Klaus Obermair, production Ars Electronica Future Lab, presented at Ars Electronica festival, 2004. Art+Com assisted in staging Andre Werner's production of Marlowe's *The Jew of Malta* at the Muffathalle, Munich, May 2002. For other interactive environments and similar projects see http://www.artcom.de.

3 Statistics from "How Much Information" report; http://www.sims.berkeley.edu/research/projects/how-much-info-2003/. Data current at time of publication (October 2005).

4 Wikipedia (English), "Interaction Design," available online at http://en.wikipedia.org/wiki/Interaction—design (accessed October 16, 2005).

18

THE GIFT SHOP AT THE END OF HISTORY

MCKENZIE WARK

The sorcerer's apprentices, the members of the revolutionary proletariat, are bound to wrest control of modern productive forces from the Faustian-Frankensteinian bourgeoisie. When this is done, they will transform these volatile, explosive social forces into sources of beauty and joy for all, and bring the tragic history of modernity to a happy end. Whether or not this ending should ever come to pass, the *Communist Manifesto* is remarkable for its imaginative power, its expression and grasp of the luminous and dreadful possibilities that pervade modern life. Along with everything else that it is, it is the first great modernist work of art.
—Marshall Berman, *All That Is Solid Melts into Air: The Experience of Modernity*

Well I'm just a modern guy. Of course I've had it in the ear before . . .
—Iggy Pop, "Lust for Life"

01. The linguistic turn, the reign of the signifier, the art of simulation, the semiotics of everyday life, the society of the spectacle: the postmodern seems to come down to a wild proliferation of signs. Perhaps this is just a misdiagnosis. Perhaps it is just a matter of taking one's in-tray to be representative of the zeitgeist. Eagleton argues: "cultural theory's inflation of the role of language [is] an error native to intellectuals, as melancholia is endemic among clowns."[1]

02. The postmodern proliferation of the sign is not so much a symptom as a syndrome. It is itself a cluster of heterogeneous signs, which all have what Wittgenstein would call a "family resemblance" to one another, yet which cannot be reduced to a unity or dismissed as a random collection of differences.[2] Some, but not all, may have a common organic cause, but this common cause

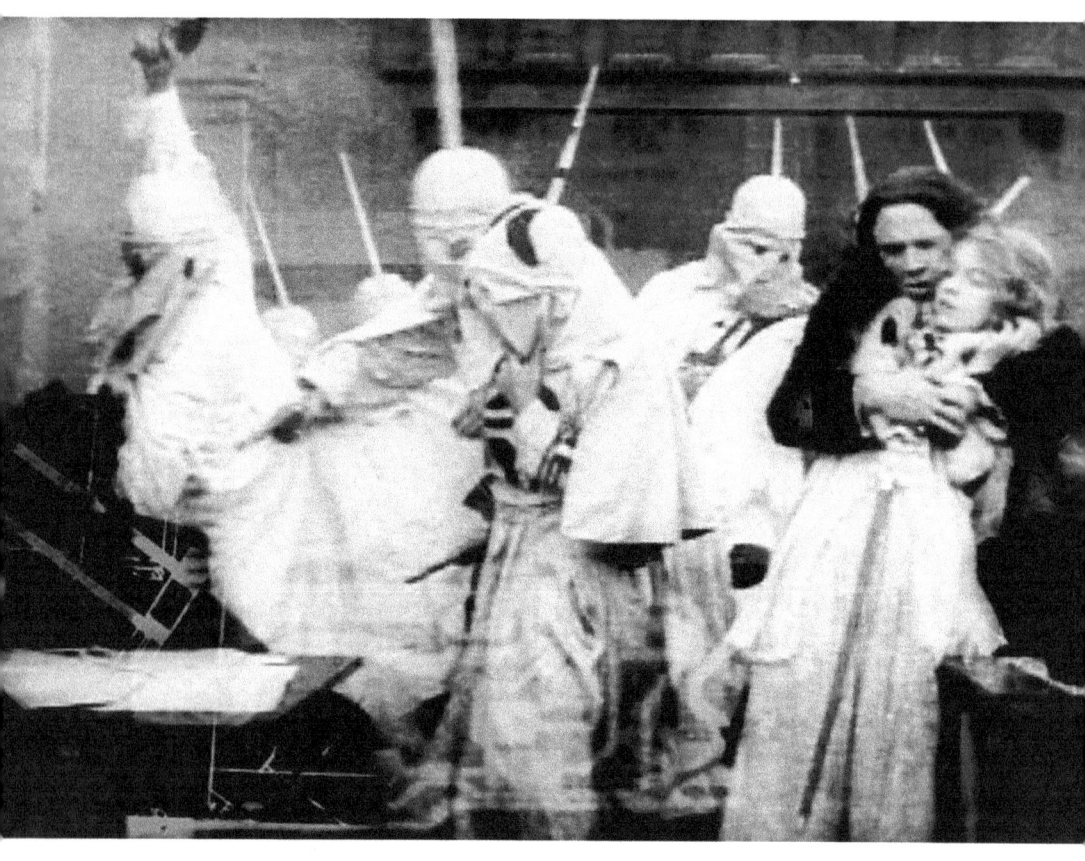

Paul D. Miller, aka DJ Spooky, that subliminal kid, *Rebirth of a Nation* ("Klan Attack"), 2005. Performance still. Courtesy of the artist.

has yet to receive a correct diagnosis. It has something to do with a mutation in the commodity form. The intellectual's obsession with the significance of signification might point to a mutation of the commodity from thing to image. But is this just a further extension of capital, its subsumption of the social, its colonization of nature and the unconscious? Or is it rather a mutation in the commodity form itself? Maybe the times are not late capitalism but early something else.

03. There is no shortage of Postmodern takes on the modern, which proceed by reducing it to an array of surfaces, which are then treated as having formal equality, thus dethroning the formerly central or canonic figures. All well and good, except that this Postmodern style tends to linger all too lovingly over its new heap of broken images, and rarely even attempts to produce the concept that might account for this production of surfaces, including the mere surface that criticism itself has become.

04. What the times call for might not be a Postmodern take on the Modern but a Modern take on the Postmodern, which restores to it some consistency as the figure for a global and historical moment of transformation. In this other reading the old powers are not simply dispersed to make way for a new dispensation. The new cultural order is in turn subjected to a critical scrutiny. Perhaps it is time again for the destructive spirit to gaily sweep away the received ideas of the times.

05. The Modern is only a figure, a rather peculiar type of sign, as Jameson says, "a way of possessing the future more immediately within the present itself."[3] Any return to it can only be tactical, a way of displacing the fragmentation of temporality urged by that other figure, the Postmodern. The tactical return of the Modern might have one and only one task to perform, which is to overcome both itself and its epigones. The great virtue of the Modern is that it decays and disappears through mere temporal succession. Debord: "But theories are made only to die in the war of time."[4]

06. The sine qua non of a sophisticated, postmodern theory is to have nothing to do with any vulgar talk of base and superstructure. Which would seem to be enough reason on its own to insist on a return to this allegedly most retrograde figure—in this case a spatial rather than a temporal one. It is not hard to fathom the displeasure intellectuals and artists must have felt for a figure that renders their own significance marginal, floating in the superstructures, waiting for history. Theologians did not want to believe that everything revolves around the sun and not the earth. Likewise intellectuals do not like being told that history is driven not by them but by the transformation of the relations of production, driven in turn by the development of the means of

production. If an essential belief for any intellectual is that the sun shines out of one's own ass, one can imagine the heresy of a heliocentric view of the universe.

07. It is by letting go of the centrality of one's own narrative and studying the transformation of the economic relations of modern society that one finds, paradoxically enough, a renewed centrality of the intellectual vocation, or something like it. Perhaps it is not late capitalism that ails us, but a whole new stage, emerging out of the contradictions of the last. Perhaps our diagnosis can move on from "post" this and "late" that to "early" something else. Perhaps we were merely waiting for a new subject of history to emerge and find its voice. And perhaps that subject is not unrelated to ourselves.

08. Flynt argues: "To defend modern art is precisely what a hopeless mediocrity would consider courageous."[5] The modern, as a unitary conception of history, has been subjected more to a process of destruction than of deconstruction. The various flavors of thought and art that replace it settle on far more modest ambitions, as if it were enough to supplement the ruins of the Modern with nothing more than a gift shop. And yet, almost in spite of itself, contemporary thinking about culture in historical time returns again and again to the big picture, but without the intellectual tools for saying much about it critically. The postmodern may have pulled the categories of history and totality apart, but what has filled the void is merely a lingering resentment of globalization.

09. Thought and art find themselves occupying niches in the university and the museum without adequate ways of creating curious distances from the relentless pressures of the institutional imperative. What were once critical or at least alternative currents find themselves recruited as mere updates on the modern form of bourgeois culture. While the avant-gardes of the Modern era may in the end have been little more than a loyal opposition within bourgeois culture, at least they were an opposition, and at least they drove it forward to new and more adequate forms, concordant with their historical moment. This necessary tension may no longer exist. What was once critical theory becomes hypocritical theory.

10. It seems timely to inquire how the current situation came to pass. Out of the remains of Modern narratives of history and totality perhaps one can at least cobble together something more ambitious than a gift shop in the ruins. This would reverse the usual method. Rather than pull apart the Modern from the vantage point of a sense of the contemporary that remains unthought, one could think the contemporary with the toolbox of theoretical and rhetorical styles the Modern bequeaths to us.

11. Another reversal may also be of service, one that is spatial rather than temporal, and that uses—or misuses—the resources of the postcolonial rather

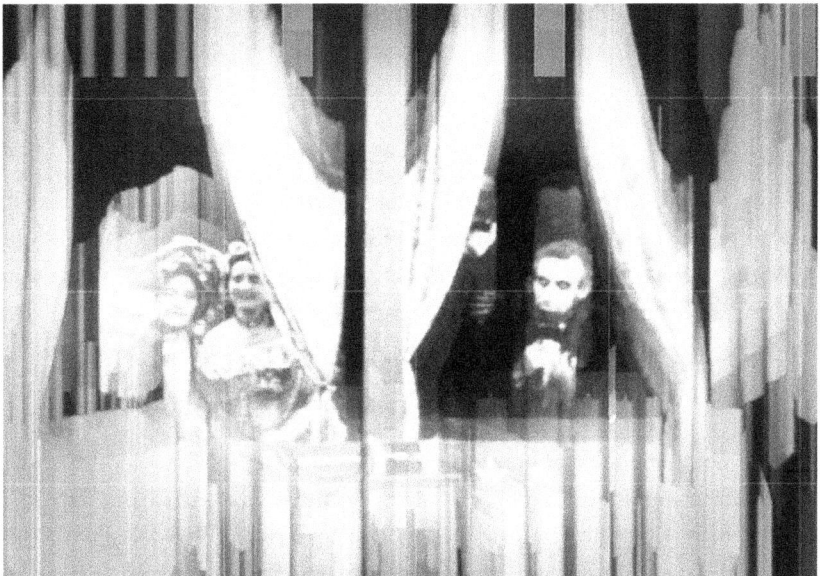

Paul D. Miller, aka DJ Spooky, that subliminal kid, *Rebirth of a Nation* ("Lincoln Blur"), 2005. Performance still. Courtesy of the artist.

than the postmodern. The postmodern moment in the overdeveloped world presents itself as one of exhaustion. The grand narratives—code word for Marxism—are over. History is no longer a unitary movement centered on the over-developed world; therefore there is no unitary history. To each its own history. Let a thousand fragments bloom. But there is a certain hubris still lurking in this formulation. If history no longer centers on the overdeveloped world, then history is simply assumed no longer to exist. The task is now to relieve ourselves of the burden of thinking critically by accepting the formal equality of the doings and sayings emanating from any place at this time. The contemporary is then a purely formal concept. It appears as a liberal gesture, making the periphery the equal of the old centers, when in actuality it masks the insignificance of the old centers. Among the old peripheries arise new centers, coordinates through which world history now passes.

12. What if history still existed, but was elsewhere? What if the overdeveloped states were merely a historical cul-de-sac, and what really mattered was driven by the decisions of the 80-odd million industrial workers of China, busily building the world? Or what if history had a whole new kind of spatiality? One that, more than ever, constructed circuits that cut across a divided world, without, for all that, uniting it or rendering all things equal? These questions

call for a return of critical thought about the transformations of space and time that is quite contrary to the institutional instincts of the academy and the art world.

13. Within art and academic institutions the pressure is always to segment the world into chunks that can be managed as if they were the property of this or that specialist. The overturning of the modern grand narratives (Marxism again) made the institutional world safe again for business as usual, for the specialists. The struggle over inclusion in this traditional field-coverage model is a real one and not to be slighted. It matters whether the arts of Asia, Africa, or the other Americas are included as fragments of a world picture within the technology of the institution. But that this is a critical project any more is clearly in doubt. Perhaps it provides the resources for a return to historical thinking, but it is not in itself that alternative. Hence the lingering prefixes—postmodern, postcolonial—and the hesitation to name the emerging world (dis)order.

14. The institutional world of the arts and humanities offers few alternatives to the rhetoric of the end of history. The triumph of the liberal capitalist model and the universal bourgeois culture that attends it is not exactly embraced in this world, but is hardly refuted. The implicit policy has become "if you can't beat 'em, join 'em." By pressing universal bourgeois culture to live up to its global pretensions, difference claims its crumbs from the table and offers itself up in trinkets of legitimation.

15. There is at least one major alternative synthetic view of this timid new world, which sees it as a grand struggle that pits empire against the multitude. Hardt and Negri correctly identify the postmodern as a syndrome, and quickly move on to a diagnosis of the new historical formation.[6] But they do so at rather a high price. Neither the materiality of the new modes of communication that make this new historical formation possible, nor the new class formations that arise out of it and drive it toward new points of conflict appear clearly in this renewed narrative of history.

16. Negri suggests: "The revolution is running extremely, extraordinarily late."[7] In many ways this seems to be the same revolution Negri and his comrades were waiting for in Italy in the 1970s, only transposed onto a global terrain. Where the nonarrival of the revolution was met by Lyotard with disillusion, and was dismissed as a fantasm by the relentless inward turn of critical thought by Baudrillard, Negri opts instead to raise the stakes and bet again. The optimism of this gesture is preferable to the shrug of indifference of Lyotard or Baudrillard and sometimes even of Deleuze. But then in the Deleuze and Guattari of *Anti-Oedipus* one finds something miraculous. Another historical narrative awaits, one that carries the struggle on, into another time, into other spaces.

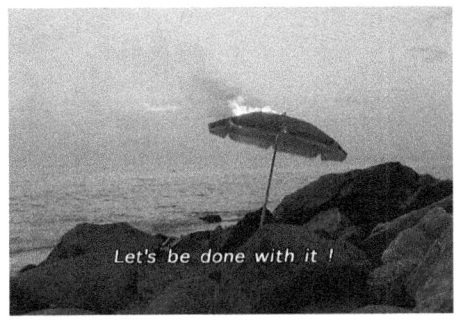

Let's be done with it !

Bernadette Corporation, still from *Get Rid of Yourself,* 2003. Video still. Courtesy of the artists.

Deleuze and Guattari insist: "One can never go far enough in the direction of deterritorialization: you haven't seen anything yet—an irreversible process . . . we cry out, 'More perversion! More artifice!'—to the point where the earth becomes so artificial that the movement of deterritorialization creates of necessity and by itself a new earth."[8]

17. It is tempting in such circumstances to abandon the historical materialist framework altogether and try to think the historical moment in other terms, but the difficulty lies in the inevitable collapse into the fragmented thinking of disciplinary specialty. Critical theory is itself in decline. The promotion of revolutionary agitation may have become revolutionary agitation for promotion. But it retains the charm of at least notional adherence to a world historical project.

18. Perhaps one could go shopping for other brand names, other styles. Latour offers a striking example of how to think outside historical materialist categories while retaining a commitment to a larger project, in this case one that is ecological.[9] The Modern, in his reading, is a dual constitution, of subjects ruled by political discourse, and of objects ruled by a scientific discourse. These two constitutions are at once formally separate and surreptitiously intertwined in strange hybrids and chimeras. The prohibition on human embryonic stem cell research enacted by President George W. Bush might then stand as an example of the contradictions and tensions between these two constitutions. This striking and timely line of thought extracts itself from the follies of European radicalism to think soberly about big-picture problems. The irony is that it could be used to enrich rather than overturn a historical materialist account of the world. One's Marxological instincts might be peaked particularly by this word "constitution," and one might want to sniff out in Latour's intellectual history of the dual constitution exactly what social forces might give rise to it.

19. The separation Latour finds between the political and the technical constitution might be a special case of the separation Guy Debord finds as the

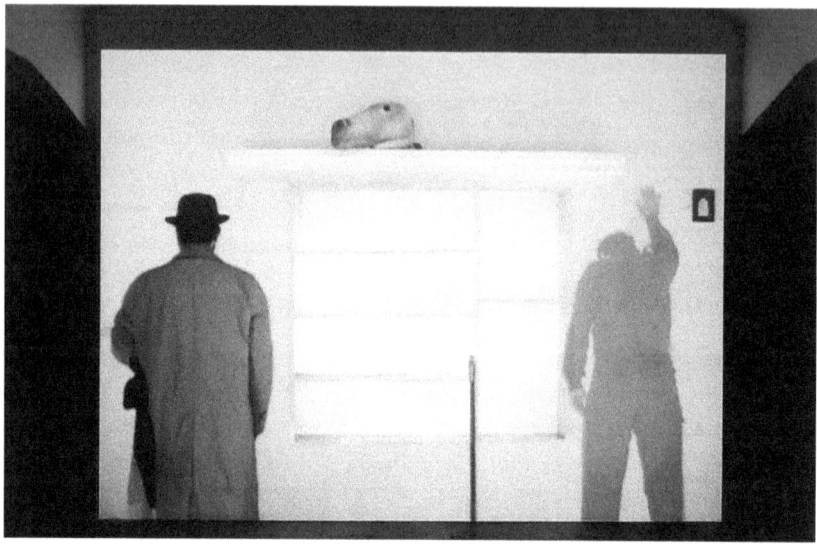

Raqs Media Collective, *They Called It the XXth Century,* from *The Impostor in the Waiting Room,* 2004. Installation view at Künstlerhaus, Stuttgart. Photograph by Marijan Murat. Courtesy of Marijan Murat and Raqs Media Collective, Delhi.

constitutive principle of what he named the society of the spectacle.[10] Whatever the flaws and follies of Debord's thought, he at least had the impertinence to propose a historical mode of thinking that embraced, negated, and overcame the prevailing currents of his time. One could do worse than take up the conflict where he left off and ask how one might in turn embrace, negate, and overcome his own now ruined edifice.

20. The movement required at the moment may be to take two steps back to take three steps forward. The step back is from Negri to Debord; the step forward might involve taking the category of spectacle seriously, and asking how it poses a transformative question to historical materialist thought, of a kind that Negri and Hardt miss. The transformative power of communication (of which art is merely a special case) is posed in Debord's theory and his practice, even if the question of how it transforms class power and the productive process is inadequately answered.

21. One of the famous Situationist slogans is "Leaving the 20th century." At the moment it might suffice to leave the 1960s. The return to Debord might be a way of extracting hypocritical theory from the 1960s, or rather from a certain concept of the 1960s. Let us not forget that the 1960s were also the time of the Cultural Revolution in China and the massacre of the Indonesian Communist Party and the rise of Suharto. Neither of these are versions of the 1960s about

which one could now feel any romanticism. Not the least of the charms of Debord is his rejection of the spectacle on both the East and West sides of the iron curtain, and his strong distrust of postcolonial strongmen.

22. The costumes and language of revolt, as Marx says, occur first as tragedy, then return as farce.[11] But if one wants to make a connection between the revolts in the overdeveloped world of the 1960s and the series of events that cluster around the year 1989, perhaps it is the other way around: first as farce, then as tragedy. The year 1989 might mark not only the popular transformation of the front-line states of the Soviet empire, particularly Poland, Hungary, Czechoslovakia, and East Germany. It might also mark a parallel transformation of the front-line states of the American empire: Taiwan, South Korea, the Philippines, and Indonesia. To this one could add the failed popular uprising in Beijing, the end of apartheid in South Africa, and the "transition to democracy" in some key parts of the Americas.

23. That would be the good news. The two halves of the spectacle are torn apart at the edges, leading to the integrated spectacle. Debord: "Yet the highest ambition of the integrated spectacle is to turn secret agents into revolutionaries and revolutionaries into secret agents."[12] The tragedy might be that the ending of the state of cold war emergency cracks open a space for a whole new kind of spatiality. The breaching of authoritarian state envelopes opens them up to the vectoral flow of information that paves the way for a whole new stage of the commodity economy. These popular democratic revolutions threw out all of the existing political economic models, including capitalism. Odd as it may seem, capitalism succeeds at the end of the Cold War by superseding itself. But then there has already been a transition within the commodity economy from one phase, the agricultural, to another, manufacturing and capital proper. So why not another? Perhaps it is time to step back and imagine again a narrative for modern times that might pass through these unanticipated coordinates. Here goes . . .

24. A class arises—the working class—able to question the necessity of private property. A party arises, within the workers' movement, claiming to answer to working-class desires: the communists. As Marx writes, "in all these movements they bring to the front, as the leading question in each, the property question, no matter what its degree of development at the time." This was the answer communists proposed to the property question: "centralize all instruments of production in the hands of the state."[13] Making property a state monopoly only produced a new ruling class, and a new and more brutal class struggle. But is that our final answer? Perhaps the course of the class struggle is not yet over. Perhaps there is another class that can open the property question

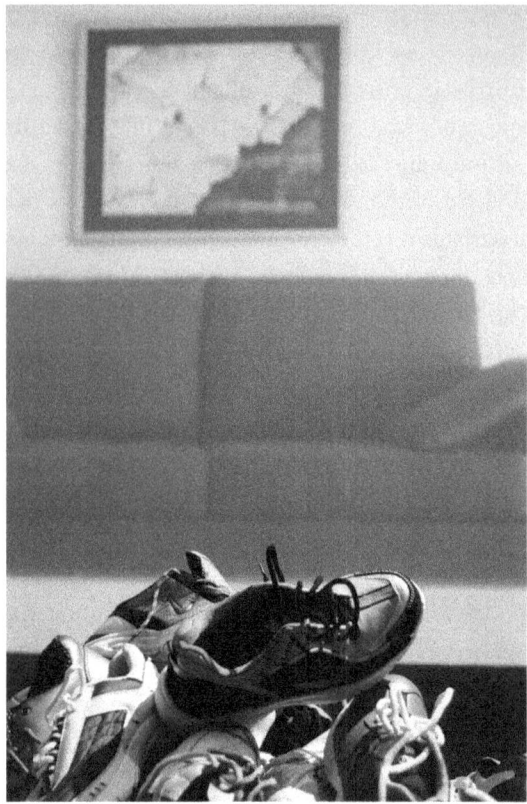

Raqs Media Collective, *Lost New Shoes,* 2005. Installation view
at PM Gallery and House, London. Photo by Monica Narula.
Courtesy of Monica Narula and Raqs Media Collective, Delhi.

in a new way—and in keeping the question open end once and for all the
monopoly of the ruling classes on the ends of history.

25. There is a class dynamic driving each stage of the development of this
post-post world in which we now find ourselves. The ruling class of our time is
driving this world to the brink of disaster, but it also opens up the world to the
resources for overcoming its own destructive tendencies. In the three successive
phases of commodification, quite different ruling classes arise, usurping different forms of private property. Each ruling class in turn drives the world
toward ever more abstract ends.

26. First arises a pastoralist class. They disperse the great mass of peasants
who traditionally worked the land under the thumb of feudal lords. The pastoralists supplant the feudal lords, releasing the productivity of nature that they
claim as their private property. It is this privatization of property—a legal

hack—that creates the conditions for every other hack by which the land is made to yield a surplus. A vectoral world rises on the shoulders of the agricultural hack.

27. As new forms of abstraction make it possible to produce a surplus from the land with fewer and fewer farmers, pastoralists turn them off their land, depriving them of their living. Dispossessed farmers seek work and a new home in cities. Here capital puts them to work in its factories. Farmers become workers. Capital as property gives rise to a class of capitalists who own the means of production, and a class of workers, dispossessed of it—and by it. Whether as workers or farmers, the direct producers find themselves dispossessed not only of their land, but of the greater part of the surplus they produce, which accumulates to the pastoralists in the form of rent as the return on land, and to capitalists in the form of profit as the return on capital.

28. Dispossessed farmers become workers, only to be dispossessed again. Having lost their agriculture, they lose in turn their culture. Capital produces in its factories not just the necessities of existence, but a way of life it expects its workers to consume. Commodified life dispossesses the worker of the information traditionally passed on outside the realm of private property as culture, as the gift of one generation to the next, and replaces it with information in commodified form.

29. Information, like land or capital, becomes a form of property monopolized by a class, a class of vectoralists, so named because they control the vectors along which information is abstracted, just as capitalists control the material means with which goods are produced, and pastoralists the land with which food is produced. This information, once the collective property of the productive classes—the working and farming classes considered together—becomes the property of yet another appropriating class.

30. As peasants become farmers through the appropriation of their land, they still retain some autonomy over the disposition of their working time. Workers, even though they do not own capital, and must work according to its clock and its merciless time, could at least struggle to reduce the working day and release free time from labor. Information circulated within working-class culture as a public property belonging to all. But when information in turn becomes a form of private property, workers are dispossessed of it, and must buy their own culture back from its owners, the vectoralist class. The farmer becomes a worker, and the worker, a slave. The whole world becomes subject to the extraction of a surplus from the producing classes that is controlled by the ruling classes, who use it merely to reproduce and expand this spiral of exploitation. Time itself becomes a commodified experience.

31. The producing classes—farmers, workers, hackers—struggle against the expropriating classes—pastoralists, capitalists, vectoralists—but these successive ruling classes struggle also amongst themselves. Capitalists try to break the pastoral monopoly on land and subordinate the produce of the land to industrial production. Vectoralists try to break capital's monopoly on the production process, and subordinate the production of goods to the circulation of information. Each successive ruling class rules in a more abstract way. The vectoral class rules through control of abstraction itself: "The privileged realm of electronic space controls the physical logistics of manufacture, since the release of raw materials and manufactured goods requires electronic consent and direction."[14]

32. That the vectoralist class has replaced capital as the dominant exploiting class can be seen in the form that the leading corporations take. These firms divest themselves of their productive capacity, as this is no longer a source of power. They rely on a competing mass of capitalist contractors for the manufacture of their products. Their power lies in monopolizing intellectual property—patents, copyrights, and trademarks—and the means of reproducing their value—the vectors of communication. The privatization of information becomes the dominant, rather than a subsidiary, aspect of commodified life. "There is a certain logic to this progression: first, a select group of manufacturers transcend their connection to earthbound products, then, with marketing elevated as the pinnacle of their business, they attempt to alter marketing's social status as a commercial interruption and replace it with seamless integration."[15] With the rise of the vectoral class, the vectoral world is complete.

33. As private property advances from land to capital to information, property itself becomes more abstract. Capital as property frees land from its spatial fixity. Information as property frees capital from its fixity in a particular object. This abstraction of property makes property itself something amenable to accelerated innovation—and conflict. Class conflict fragments, but creeps into any and every relation that becomes a relation of property. The property question, the basis of class, becomes the question asked everywhere, of everything. If class appears absent to the apologists of our time, it is not because it has become just another in a series of antagonisms and articulations, but on the contrary because it has become the structuring principle of the vectoral plane that organizes the play of identities as differences.

34. The hacker class, producer of new abstractions, becomes more important to each successive ruling class, as each depends more and more on information as a resource. Land cannot be reproduced at will. Good land lends itself to scarcity, and the abstraction of private property is almost enough on its own to protect the rents of the pastoral class. Capital's profits rest on more easily

reproducible means of production, its factories and inventories. The capitalist firm sometimes needs the hacker to refine and advance the tools and techniques of production to stay abreast of the competition. Information is the most easily reproducible object ever captured in the abstraction of property. Nothing protects the vectoralist business from its competitors other than its capacity to qualitatively transform the information it possesses and extract new value from it. The services of the hacker class become indispensable to an economy that is itself more and more dispensable—an economy of property and scarcity.

35. As the means of production become more abstract, so too does the property form. Property has to expand to contain more and more complex forms of difference, and reduce it to equivalence. To render land equivalent, it is enough to draw up its boundaries, and create a means of assigning it as an object to a subject. Complexities will arise, naturally, from this unnatural imposition on the surface of the world, although the principle is a simple abstraction. But for something to be represented as intellectual property, it is not enough for it to be in a different location. It must be qualitatively different. That difference, which makes a copyright or a patent possible, is the work of the hacker class. The hacker class makes what Bateson calls "the difference that makes the difference."[16] It is this difference that drives the abstraction of the world, but which also drives the accumulation of class power in the hands of the vectoral class.

36. The hacker class arises out of the transformation of information into property, in the form of intellectual property, including patents, trademarks, copyright, and the moral right of authors. These legal hacks make of the hack a property-producing process, and thus a class-producing process. The hack produces the class force capable of asking—and answering—the property question, the hacker class. The hacker class is the class with the capacity to create not only new kinds of object and subject in the world, not only new kinds of property form in which they may be represented, but new kinds of relation, with new properties that question the property form itself. The hacker class realizes itself as a class when it hacks the abstraction of property and overcomes the limitations of existing forms of property.

37. The hacker class may be flattered by the attention lavished upon it by capitalists compared to pastoralists, and vectoralists compared to capitalists. Hackers tend to ally at each turn with the more abstract form of property and commodity relation. But hackers soon feel the restrictive grip of each ruling class, as it secures its dominance over its predecessor and rival, and can renege on the dispensations it extended to hackers as a class. The vectoralist class, in particular, will go out of its way to court and coopt the productivity of hackers,

but only because of its attenuated dependence on new abstraction as the engine of competition among vectoral interests themselves. When the vectoralists act in concert as a class, it is to subject hacking to the prerogatives of its class power.

38. The vectoral world is dynamic, struggling to put new abstractions to work, producing new freedoms from necessity. The direction this struggle takes is not given in the course of things, but is determined by the struggle between classes. All classes enter into relations of conflict, collusion, and compromise. Their relations are not necessarily dialectical. Classes may form alliances of mutual interest against other classes, or may arrive at a historic compromise, for a time. Yet despite pauses and setbacks, the class struggle drives history into abstraction and abstraction into history.

39. Sometimes capital forms an alliance with the pastoralists, and the two classes effectively merge their interests under the leadership of the capitalist interest. Sometimes capital forms an alliance with workers against the pastoralist class, an alliance quickly broken once the dissolution of the pastoralist class is achieved. These struggles leave their traces in the historical form of the state, which maintains the domination of the ruling-class interest and at the same time adjudicates among the representatives of competing classes.

40. History is full of surprises. Sometimes, for a change, the workers form an alliance with the farmers that socialize private property and put it in the hands of the state, while liquidating the pastoralist and capitalist classes. In this case, the state then becomes a collective pastoralist and capitalist class, and wields class power over a commodity economy organized on a bureaucratic rather than competitive basis.

41. The vectoralist class emerges out of competitive, rather than bureaucratic states. Competitive conditions drive the search for productive abstraction more effectively. The development of abstract forms of intellectual property creates the relative autonomy in which the hacker class can produce abstractions, although this productivity is constrained within the commodity form.

42. One thing unites pastoralists, capitalists, and vectoralists: the sanctity of the property form on which class power depends. Each depends on forms of abstraction that they may buy and own but do not produce. Each comes to depend on the hacker class, which finds new ways of making nature productive, which discovers new patterns in the data thrown off by nature and second nature, and which produces new abstractions through which nature may be made to yield more of a second nature—perhaps even a third nature.

43. The hacker class, being numerically small and not owning the means of production, finds itself caught between a politics of the masses from below and a politics of the rulers from above. It must bargain as best it can, or do what it

does best: hack out a new politics, beyond this opposition. In the long run, the interests of the hacker class are in accord with those who would benefit most from the advance of abstraction, namely those productive classes dispossessed of the means of production: farmers and workers. In the effort to realize this possibility the hacker class hacks politics itself, creating a new polity, turning mass politics into a politics of multiplicity, in which all the productive classes can express their virtuality.

44. The hacker interest cannot easily form alliances with forms of mass politics that subordinate minority differences to unity in action. Mass politics always run the danger of suppressing the creative, abstracting force of the interaction of differences. The hacker interest is not in mass representation, but in a more abstract politics that expresses the productivity of differences. Hackers, who produce many classes of knowledge out of many classes of experience, have the potential also to produce a new knowledge of class formation and action when working together with the collective experience of all the productive classes.

45. A class is not the same as its representation. In politics one must beware of representations held out to be classes, which represent only a fraction of a class and do not express its multiple interests. Classes do not have vanguards that may speak for them. Classes express themselves equally in all of their multiple interests and actions. The hacker class is not what it is; the hacker class is what it is not, but can become.

46. Through the development of abstraction, freedom may yet be wrested from necessity. The vectoralist class, like its predecessors, seeks to shackle abstraction to the production of scarcity and margin, not abundance and liberty. The formation of the hacker class as a class comes at just this moment when freedom from necessity and from class domination appears on the horizon as a possibility. As Negri suggests: "What is this world of political, ideological and productive crisis, this world of sublimation and uncontrollable circulation? What is it, then, if not an epoch-making leap beyond everything humanity has hitherto experienced? . . . It constitutes simultaneously the ruin and the new potential of all meaning."[17] All that it takes is the hacking of the hacker class as a class, a class capable of hacking property itself, which is the fetter upon all productive means and on the productivity of meaning.

47. The struggle among classes has hitherto determined the disposition of the surplus, the regime of scarcity and the form in which production grows. But now the stakes are far higher. Survival and liberty are both on the horizon at once. The ruling classes turn not just the producing classes into an instrumental resource, but nature itself, to the point where class exploitation and the exploi-

tation of nature become the same unsustainable objectification. The potential of a class-divided world to produce its own overcoming comes not a moment too soon . . .

48. And so: the thread emerges, in the visual arts as in any other domain where hackers hack the new out of the old, the leading forces are those that ask the property question—from Dada to the Surrealists to the Situationists, to Conceptual Art to appropriation to (pick your current favorites) relational aesthetics, net.art, or tactical media.[18] Where the property question is asked—and answered—there are the forces for social change.

49. Just as clearly, the property question is the defining feature of a neo-bourgeois art, which draws on exactly the same avant-garde sequence, but strips from it its questioning of the property form in the realm of the aesthetic. Neobourgeois art legitimates the new ruling class just like the old one, by producing a realm of quasi-sacred, scarce things—even if these things are no longer art objects but art installations. The difference is that these newer things lack the objective qualities of bourgeois art, its lush surfaces, its residues of the painterly hand. Art is reduced to a taut relation between property and pure information. The question of value becomes indifferent to material support.

50. The rigorous pursuit of abstraction was indeed a revolutionary project—but one that merely aided and abetted the installation of a new ruling class. It is the proof, in the realm of aesthetics, of a system of value indifferent to any material support. What the vectoral class achieves in the realm of general econ-omy, neobourgeois art achieves in the restricted realm of aesthetic economy.

51. Jameson: "Money is the last surviving absolute."[19] Yet what gives money its historical quality is its relation to two other absolutes, one modern, one more contemporary. The other side of money under capitalism is private prop-erty. The commodity appears as the object sprung from this relation. But as the vectoralist class supersedes the capitalist class as its ruling order, it brings money and private property into a relation that produces not the object, but information. The object becomes a mere support for something intangible yet invested with value. In these times, the ideological function of art is to invest information with value as property in the absence of any material attribute.

52. If the avant-garde was the loyal opposition within bourgeois culture, upon its election into the institutional apparatus of art, it became what it beheld. But one must be wary of the ideology of the death of the avant-gardes. The project of the realization and suppression of art in the world perhaps just takes new forms, even if the official project is now the realization and suppres-sion of the world in art.

53. The ideology of the contemporary perpetuates the ideology of the Mod-

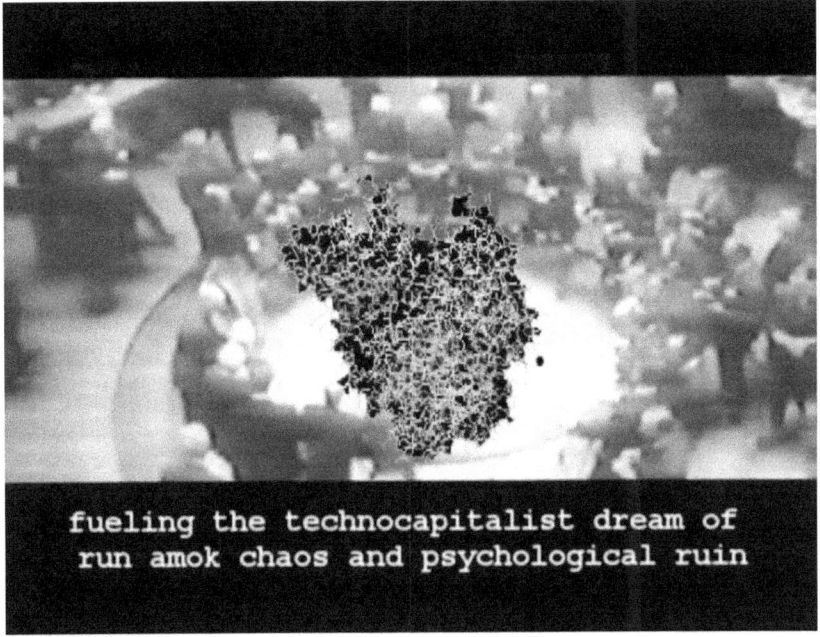

fueling the technocapitalist dream of
run amok chaos and psychological ruin

DJRABBI (Mark Amerika, Trace Reddell, and Rick Silva), *Society of the Spectacle (A Digital Remix)*, 2004. DVD still. Courtesy of the artists.

ern without the latter's claim to a historical vision of progress. Realizing that support for the concept of the Modern as progress offers bourgeois culture as a hostage to historical fortune, the art world obliges with a new idea, the contemporary, as the ever renewable mask for a new cultural constellation—the eternal bourgeois.

54. We meet the eternal bourgeois in Buñuel's films or Barthes's mythologies, but as a troubled figure, still vulnerable to attack in the name of historical obsolescence. The eternal bourgeois emerges fully only with the foreclosure of the temporal horizon. The eternal bourgeois may be legitimated by God or by Nature, in the language of theology or genetics, in a conservative or liberal guise.

55. But what is most troubling for the eternal bourgeois is the renewal of the property question, either in its traditional forms in the underdeveloped world, or in new forms in the overdeveloped world. And with this new wrinkle: that the abstraction of the property form, from land to capital to information, has indeed reached the point where a world beyond necessity emerges. The proliferation of information confounds both property and propriety. Information wants to be free, but is everywhere in chains. Progress is possible, plagiarism implies it.

NOTES

1 Eagleton, *After Theory,* 60.
2 Wittgenstein, *Philosophical Investigations,* sec. 66.
3 Jameson, *A Singular Modernity,* 35.
4 Debord, *In girum imus nocte et consumimur igni,* 24.
5 Flynt, *Blueprint for a Higher Civilization,* 185.
6 Hardt and Negri, *Empire,* 136ff.
7 From Negri's remarks at the conference "Modernity ≠ Contemporaneity"; see Negri, chap. 1 of this volume.
8 Deleuze and Guattari, *Anti-Oedipus,* 321.
9 Latour, *We Have Never Been Modern.*
10 Debord, *The Society of the Spectacle.*
11 Marx, "The Eighteenth Brumaire," 146.
12 Debord, *Comments on the Society of the Spectacle,* 11.
13 Marx and Engels, "Manifesto of the Communist Party," 98, 86.
14 Critical Art Ensemble, *The Electronic Disturbance,* 16–17. See also Critical Art Ensemble, *The Molecular Invasion.*
15 Klein, *No Logo,* 35. See also Klein, *Fences and Window.*
16 Bateson, *Steps towards an Ecology of Mind.*
17 Negri, *The Politics of Subversion,* 203.
18 Bourriaud, *Relational Aesthetic;* Stallabrass, *Internet Art;* Thompson and Sholette, *The Interventionist.*
19 From his remarks at the conference "Modernity ≠ Contemporaneity," Pittsburgh, 2004.

SPATIAL AESTHETICS: RETHINKING

THE CONTEMPORARY

NIKOS PAPASTERGIADIS

Narratives of place and displacement are now central to the definition of contemporary art. New forms of cultural practice that have transfigured the relationship between the local and the global, and mobilized the discourse of difference, are now common throughout the world. The characteristics that Lucy Lippard identified in her seminal text as a "dematerialization of art" have been extended toward a much wider spectrum.[1] The temporal dimensions, site specificity, and relational experiences in contemporary art practice present new questions for the understanding of artistic production and dissemination. If the material object of art is not only shorn of its auratic power but also displaced as the ideal destination point in the production of art, then this poses a range of questions in relation to the status of collections in the institutions of contemporary art, the role of the art historian, the function of the curator, the emergence of the "documenteur," the place of the witness, and the dynamism of social interaction. The coda for the contemporary artist is now defined by the desire to be *in* the contemporary, rather than to produce a belated or elevated response to the everyday. To be in the place of the here and now, to work with others in a simultaneous and concrete practice, to see the realization of work in the experience of connection, is to raise the value of what Scott Lash calls the "performative" aspect of practice and displace the reflexive role of cultural production.[2]

It is now plausible to defend the dual right of contemporary artists to both maintain an active presence in a local context and participate in transnational dialogues. Everyone who enters the context of contemporary art is already part of the complex process of intervention and feedback that now cuts across the world. This duality is experienced neither as an irreconcilable opposition nor as a loss of authenticity. Yet the key task is not to simply parade more signs of difference but to introduce different ways of being in the world. The Cuban curator and critic Gerardo Mosquera has stressed that expansion in the recruitment of artists from diverse countries is not the solution to the problems of exclusion and appropriation. The conundrum of choice in globalization is evident in the plethora of nonestablishment, collaborative projects and the spread of biennials to every corner of the globe. This new form of pluralism in contemporary art can be, in Mosquera's words, "a prison without walls."[3] He reminds us that the most effective labyrinth in the world is the desert. In its vast openness there is no escape. The city is also a desert.

The aim of this essay is not only to map out the interventions that artists have made in specific places, and to account for the political consequences of their gestures, but also to see how the interconnection of these actions is part of an ongoing attempt to grasp the complex forms of cultural relations that occur in everyday life. The art of placing and the place for art are always shifting. Artists stretch the boundaries of their practice by defining their context and strategies in paradoxes. Museums without walls. Cities as laboratories. Living archives. Walking narratives. These slogans are now common in the art world. They reveal a recurring desire: to stretch the parameters of art by incorporating new technologies, sites, and perspectives. As they introduce foreign tools, places, and subjects they also expand the category of the contemporary. Today, the shock of the new is not very shocking; it is just a starting point for thinking about reality. For over a century now, artists and writers have realized that art and life do not exist in separate domains. The idea that the place of art is above life is an illusion that no longer has much meaning.

SMALL GESTURES IN CONTEMPORARY CULTURAL PRACTICE

The most radical gestures in contemporary art are no longer positioned outside the dominant institutions of art or on the moral high ground from which the artist can pour scorn against the foibles of everyday life. Collaborative artists such as Lucy Orta, artist collectives such as Superflex, and curatorial projects such as "If I Ruled the World," work within the institutions of art in order to create connections with social groups and develop new political strategies of expressive resistance. Their engagement with everyday life, especially the codes and symbols of popular media culture, is not confined to invigorating the discourses of art, but is an admission that art belongs in the same time-space continuum as popular culture. Art no longer aims to be an elevated or a belated response to events already staged in the sphere of everyday life. On the contrary, there is a dual level of commitment to the aesthetic and the political. In the past decade, there has been an emergence of artistic practice that defines itself explicitly as project-based and that seeks to work across diverse community networks. These projects offer a rare insight into alternative modes of social engagement. Charles Esche goes so far as to claim that the logic of creative exchange has the potential to contest the hegemony of economic rationalism. It is this combination of pragmatic modeling and cultural experimentation that has lead Esche to argue that art is now "positioned in the territory between active political engagement and autonomous experimentation."[4]

What is the point of art if not to change our ways of seeing? I know that Ad Reinhardt warned against excessive expectations. He was right! You do have to be "out of your mind" if you think that art can serve as a weapon for foreign policy. An installation of flags by Bryndis Snaebjornsdottir and Ross Sinclair, in the exhibition "If I Ruled the World," may have political ambitions, but it is important to note that the scale of ambition is neither at the level of a resolution passed by the United Nations, nor expressed in the civic rhetoric of a local politician.[5]

The risk taken by these artistic strategies is calculated against its potential to develop new forms of collaboration. Following the example of an earlier generation such as Hélio Oiticica, Lygia Clark, Joseph Beuys, and David Medalla, these artists seek to reach new audiences, and to include their participation as part of the construction and experience of the work. The work, therefore, finds its completion in the active experience of the public. These collaborative techniques also operate on a second order. As complexity in society has led to increasing atomization, these projects have recognized the need to create new forms of exchange between intellectuals, professionals, and community groups. Lucy Orta claims that her work can only bring a certain problem to a point of clarity when there is an open debate among different people. In these collaborations the function of the museum has taken a new focus: "I don't see museums as spaces any longer, I see them as part of a larger management team which helps to co-ordinate the various collaborations of the artistic process. . . . I have found that an exhibition can form a role to both reflect upon a subject and raise concerns to another level of debate."[6]

In a project called "Fluid Architecture," Orta occupied the former Army Drill Hall at the edge of Melbourne's Central Business District.[7] The site for this project is significant. For over a decade the Australian army had chosen to

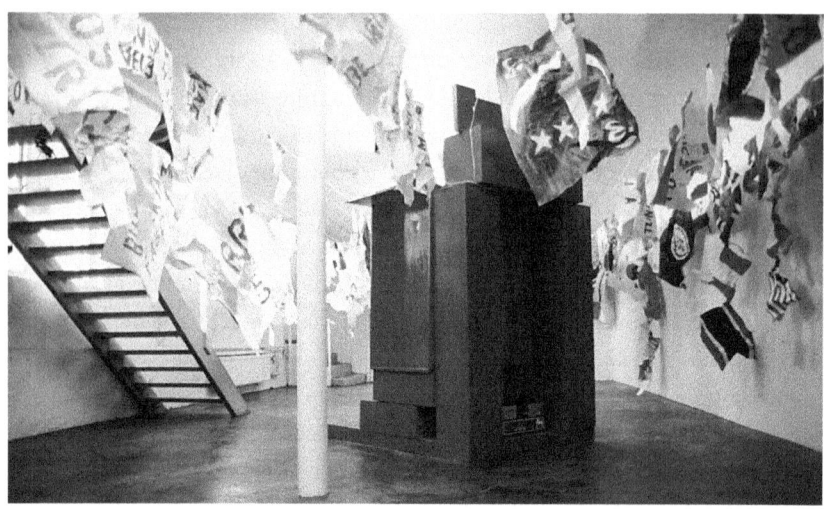

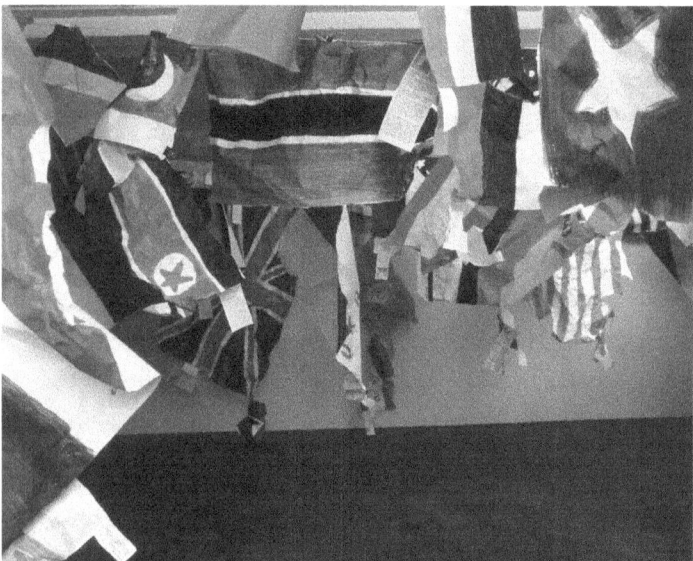

Bryndis Snaebjornsdottir and Ross Sinclair, *Flag Piece,* 1999. Mixed media. Installation view, Living Art Museum, Reykjavik, and McLellan Galleries, Glasgow. Courtesy of the artists.

Bryndis Snaebjornsdottir and Ross Sinclair, *Flag Piece,* 1999. Mixed media. Living Art Museum, Reykjavik, and McLellan Galleries, Glasgow. Courtesy of the artists.

conduct its marching and shooting exercises away from the gaze of the city. The old Art Deco building fell into disuse, its absurd decorative motifs began to crumble and peel, its decay compounded by the fading status of the neighborhood. Next to the Drill Hall stood the forlorn headquarters of a collapsed national airline, and beside it the redundant bluestone building of a brewery that has recently gone global. At a time when the world was becoming increasingly callous toward the plight of refugees, Orta proposed a project for this site with the heart as a symbol for hospitality. Her aim was not to lead a protest against the civic authorities, or present herself in a morally superior position, but rather to organize a diverse network of individuals and groups to develop its own sense of how an artistic situation could give and gain a heart from collective action.

The politics in this practice is situational. Clusters form with no specific structure. The form is found in the responsive process of working through the issues and interacting with the other participants. During the "Fluid Architecture" project the musician Tim O'Dwyer created a pulsing ambience of found sounds and improvised rhythms, while the architect James Legge worked with a design team lead by Michael Douglas and a community of activists and artists from local tower blocks and art schools. The project culminated in performances in new body suits and sculptural installations that stretched the concept of mutual support and collective movement. A comment made by Paul Virilio on Orta's practice served as the theme of this project: "One individual keeps an eye on, and protects, the other. One individual's life depends on the life of another. In Lucy's work, the warmth of one gives warmth to the other. The physical link weaves the social link."[8]

A crucial feature of this collaborative practice is the dynamic incorporation of all elements of the museum and gallery structures. This cuts against the hierarchical master role of the artist and curator, and mobilizes a horizontal integration of the so-called technical and educational support staff. Ideas are developed simultaneously in a horizontal sphere, rather than being defined from above and then executed down a vertical and sequential chain of command. The realization, fabrication, and public dissemination of the work occurs in the process of actualizing the idea, rather than being compartmentalized and distributed under the exclusive categories of creativity, production, and promotion.

The artist collective Superflex also works in the cross-disciplinary mode. Whether it is in the "Biogas" project for recycling waste in third world farming communities, or the "Superchannel" project for empowering residents in marginalized tower blocks, their goal is to create processes that do not only offer a

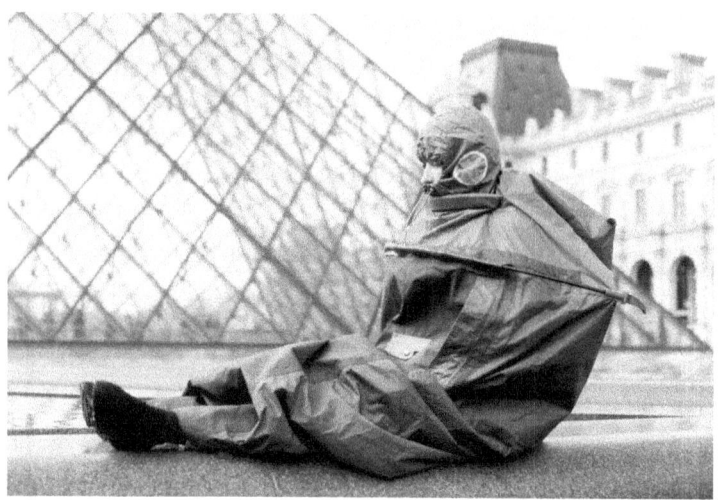

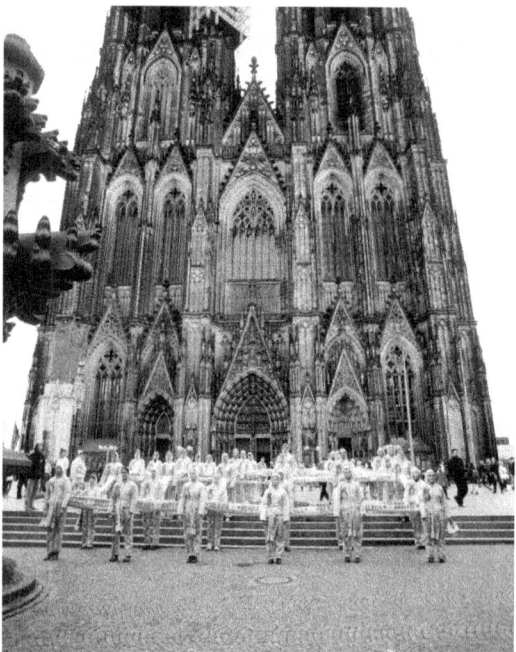

Lucy Orta, *Nexus Intervention with architecture students from the Technischen Universität Berlin,* 2001. Color photograph. Courtesy of the artist.

Lucy Orta, *Nexus Architecture x 50 Intervention Köln,* 2001. Color photograph. Courtesy of the artist.

critique of the socioeconomic conditions in the world but also generate a utility with clear aesthetic and political relevance.[9] Pierre Restany, a critic who has witnessed both the collaborative strategies of the earlier generations and Orta's most recent projects, had the perspicacity to define these multidisciplinary practices as a form of "relational aesthetics."[10]

What transpires across and within such seemingly small gestures is the larger expression of a desire for connection. They are unlikely reference points for cultural and aesthetic revolutions. If anything, they could be little reminders of things past. They are certainly not the manifestos for the future. They are far too light and slender to withstand such applied functions. What could be significant in such small gestures in specific places? At one level, alienation begins with the shutdown of communication and ends with the banalization of all exchanges. The power of the poetic gesture in art is revolutionary in that it acts as a circuit breaker in the closed system of habituated equivalence between signs. The twentieth-century discourse on art was littered with big claims about small gestures. Elaborate narratives have been articulated to expose the hidden signs, to uncover the buried processes and reveal the intended messages. At times, these stories served no other function than the hyperbolic repetition of romantic myths; in other instances, such as the recent work of T. J. Clark, there is a melancholic review of both the ruins that lurked within the grid of modernity and the ruination of the revolutionary promises of Modernism.[11]

AMONGST RUINS AND METROPOLITAN JUNCTURES

My attention to the relationship between art and place was originally provoked by the way artists located their studios in the abandoned and derelict sectors of the city. I was attracted to these places because their high levels of improvisation made them feel "homely." I was aware that this decision to dwell among the ruins of the metropolis was not always driven by economic imperatives, for even successful artists hung on to their old studios. They stayed not just for sentimental reasons, but perhaps because they found inspiration from the possibility that forgotten histories and alternative ways of being could still be found within the contradictions of these abandoned zones. There is also the possibility that these zones offered an even more general space: a location for contemplation and reflection. I imagine that these spaces prompted other unconscious connections, enabled artists to think through the unthought thoughts of our time. These were breathing spaces in which attention was allowed to wander.

At the beginning of the twentieth century, artists responded to the changes in the modern city with a mixed sense of awe and excitement. Modernity was ushered in by the power of new industrial technologies. Sweeping socioeconomic changes pushed many earlier forms of culture to the side. The damage was often justified by the promise of a higher level of liberation and emancipation. Many remained skeptical of such a blind faith in progress, but even artists who had been critical of capitalism's impact on society, still believed that the Machine Age could be harnessed to produce a new utopia. For instance, in the postwar period, Benjamin Constant constructed images, models, and maps for his imaginary city "New Babylon."[12] By the end of the twentieth century the glow of modernity was tarnished and contaminated. The promise of lifting ordinary people above the ground and onto higher levels sank into the filthy mud of accumulated waste and pollution. The radical task of the artist shifted from dreaming the new utopia to dealing with the dystopia that surrounded urban life. Artists such as Julie Bargmann and Stacy Levy began their practice in the form of a "clean-up" operation. Yona Friedman also stressed that the task of the artist shifted from invention to recycling, from expressing a new vision for the future to developing new ethical collaborations to deal with the legacies of the Machine Age.

> All living beings together produce an enormous amount of refuse. This mass is larger than the total mass of all living beings. Refuse produced by one species might be a resource for another species. Human technology starts with the conversion of things found into things useful. Architecture emerges since the original fallout of agriculture. Our present civilization produces more fallout than all previous civilizations together. Much of that fallout can be recycled. For example, by artists who turn junk into works of art. A large part of industrial fallout becomes converted by the poorest people into objects of their own use; shelter, mobiles. The huge shantytowns all around the globe are but an example of reconversion. Shanty towns are at the scale of the city, what the Merzbau was at the scale of the sculpture: both are works of art out of mainstream aesthetics.[13]

This process of reconversion also brings to the surface the complex layering of history and memories that lurk within the city. What do artists uncover when they excavate objects from the remains of the postindustrial landscape? What sorts of mental maps are made when artists wander through the streets of the city? Can artists reveal the real "face" of the city? Since the founding of Rome, the city has thrived on multiplicity.[14] The stories we find create more stories, each stratum revealing another, every journey unfolding a new route. Even ruins defy the cliché that, at last, here is a place where time and things have stood still. For ruins are like way stations, where convergence and departure operate according to a slower and rougher schedule.

To contemplate the meaning of these places is neither an opportunity for nostalgia, nor an exercise in sighing at the cruelty of fate. The visual power of ruins runs deeper in our modern unconscious. It is no coincidence that Freud used archaeological metaphors to depict the processes of the mind. The image of layers of earlier cities buried under every city was, for Freud, a powerful metaphor for describing the dynamic of change and repetition, waste and accumulation, desire and memory that also occurred in the mind. Hubert Damisch observed that Freud struggled with his own metaphor. For Freud, the traces left in cities were not just an analogy, with which the process of the mind could be compared, but also a commonplace. Knowing that Freud recognized the limits of the archaeological metaphor but refused to renounce it, Damisch speculates, "Why did he find it necessary to evoke visual images, figuration, in this connection if not because the mind itself must, at one time or another, have passed the same way, have found its place in them."[15]

From this perspective, or rather from this sense of place, we can revisit the debates on the place of art in the global city. Particularist claims that the place of art could be defined by its relationship to specific civic functions or bound to primordial forms of communal attachments have been displaced by a new discourse that stresses a new kind of universalism. I am suspicious of these broad claims and would prefer to direct my thoughts toward the way art partici-pates in the understanding of the hybrid forms of urban life. The turbulent patterns of global migration and the complex formations in new urban con-urbations have catapulted the social questions in art to new levels of urgency. The forms of exile and displacement in the contemporary city have taken harder twists and have found new jagged edges. There is a growing need to address the questions such as "How do we belong in the city?" and "What can be done in the name of art?"

If we consider the ways in which artists have not merely inhabited buildings that were abandoned by commerce and citizens, but have staged their events in these parts of the city, we can also gain a new perspective on the relationship between the available spaces in the postindustrial urban landscape and the conception, production, and display of art. Today the gallery is not just a place for the display of complete works of art, but also the mechanism for its produc-tion, and the platform for further forms of spatial engagement. The gallery needs to be involved in the unfinished processes of art. It can facilitate the realization of working processes and the conception of new engagements, rather than simply accumulate the products that have survived the tests of taste and opportunity. Artists such as Lucy Orta recognize that the institutions of contemporary art are demanding homes. However, Orta also considers that the political process of negotiation over the modes of engagement between place and perception is a central part of her artistic practice.

TOPOGRAPHICS: THE RELATION BETWEEN SPACE, WRITING, AND ART

Artists engage with everyday life, now, in a wide variety of ways. This produces new challenges for writers and curators in their work with artists. The new practices of art do not always aim to result as objects that can be collected and displayed in museums. The ultimate aim may well be the initiation of experiences that occur in everyday settings. Even these site-specific experiences, however, are not immune to the process of institutionalization. When art from the everyday returns to the museum, it is not simply a matter of balancing documentation with display. Simulacra of these events can be as moving as the proverbial dream about the most exotic bird in a cage with the door slightly ajar. You awaken from a dream but what happened? The bird has gone. Coming back to the museum must be, for the artist, like coming back to a demanding home, one that insists on new engagements between place (*topos*) and modes of perception (*tropos*). This level of engagement with everyday life, and the ambivalent relationship that it poses with the institutions of art, also presents new challenges to writers. There is a need for the writer to be there to experience the event and also be aware of the politics of institutionalization. The writer does not merely trace out the remains of the artist's dream. The written document cannot replace the feather; it must suggest another form of flight.

There is a form of writing called topography that is conventionally understood as referring to a system for mapping either a landscape or the contours and form of a place. The aim of this discipline is to provide a detailed analysis of the surface of a landscape, and to construct a story of its formation from the residual signs that are contained within its volume. It involves both observation and excavation. I refer to my writing on art as topographical because it also deals with both the imaginary and geographic role of place. I would like to extend this concept for rethinking the relationship between art and place. Art can never totally represent a specific place. Even the most comprehensive map cannot contain all the details of a territory. Art that has come from a place, and which refers to a place, must also acknowledge its own exile. It leaves, it does not remain left behind, but the success of its movement is bittersweet. The impossibility of representing a place on a map is analogous to writing about the small gestures of art. The place of art and the manner of writing have no symmetrical correspondence. There is no fixed hierarchy. No stable order. If writing just follows art, it remains a shadow. If it proceeds, it can advance like a stereotype. Only when both reach for a common space can the parallel lines of different practices find a resonance.

Topography could be a form of writing that provokes the imaginary and evokes the real sensation of art and landscape. The aim of topography is not to recount stories of previous adventures; it is more concerned with the tracks and traces that are still visible and portable. Topography is also concerned with the mapping of invented signs that have no genealogical reference but rather a phantasmagorical relationship to place. The origin of signs can be endless and melancholic. To break from this regress, topography focuses on what happens when small gestures are made in a specific place. The placement of art in the landscape and the replacing of art in the museum do not always carry the burden of a landmark statement. It is not a gesture that commands attention toward the appreciation of grand views, or simply seeks to retell the heroic stories of the past. Topography is a form of writing that could extend the artist's invitation to participate in the *en*placement of art within everyday life.

The story of contemporary art practice can no longer be told exclusively in the form of the historical survey, or as a mere cultural effect of socioeconomic changes. There are many parallel stories and competing genres that are constituted out of a shuttling between the discourse of art and the cultural politics of everyday life. To try to explain art in purely formal terms, or to assume that the highest purpose of art is to deliver a new political agenda is, as Jacques Rancière has noted, "somewhat beside the point."[16] Art cannot be explained as a social activity that fulfills the stated goals of a national agenda or an economic order. The specific place of art is now increasingly located in networks that are both above and below the reach of the nation-state. Through the process of collaborating with community networks in local places, there is the opportunity for artists to uncover countercultural pockets and forge new transnational diasporas that defy the hegemonic order of the nation-state. Rancière is correct to argue that the "life of art" is found in the shuttling between the extremes of autonomy and heteronomy. Art cannot exist in its own discursive ghetto. If it did, it would inevitably spiral down through a process of entropy. Similarly, if art is bound to serve other laws and conform to a given political order, it will also divest itself of any distinctive identity. To confine art to either extreme is a death sentence. The academic and the activist approaches to art are, in Rancière's terms, the negation of the life of art.

"Small gestures in specific places"—this could be the coda for the time when the place for art is on the move. Today the form of art bends to the circumstance, and the boundary with the everyday blurs. The placement of small gestures in specific places can at first glance be continuous with our daily stride, sight, breath, touch, and reach. And yet it might also suggest that all these actions are more complex.

In Greek, there is only a slight difference between the word for the place in which events occur (*topos*), and the manner in which they occur (*tropos*), but I would also claim that both are linked to the collaborative process of topography. To collaborate with other people, to receive them and work with them, is to be attentive to this engagement between topos and tropos. Collaboration is a way of receiving others, involving both the recognition of where they are coming from, and the projection of a new horizon line toward which the combined practice will head. I see the practice of writing on art as a form of imaginary collaboration. The practical exchange of information between the artist and the writer is not as vital as the intellectual pursuit of a common trajectory.

My writing, like all forms of art criticism, is parasitic. It occupies a separate space but also notes the trajectories in contemporary art. Artists have used specific places not as a flat stage upon which they can perform their practice but as an active site. Artists acknowledge the constitutive role that spatial forces play in our everyday experience. In this sense, place functions more like a scene. Still-life painters have always been conscious of the paradoxes of capturing the flux in time and place. The model that I am referring to goes beyond the challenge of rendering the dynamic scene in a given form, as it includes the fields of institutional distribution and social contextualization. In the past artists have concerned themselves primarily with production, while responsibility for the other domains was passed on to curators and critics. Now, however, by incorporating the responsibility of distribution and contextualization within the multispatial processes of production, the artist has effectively expanded the field of art. This enhances the artist's capacity to intervene in the institutional structures and heightens the potential for social dialogue. As art operates in an expanded field, the process of critical feedback, interruption, and transformation multiplies. The consequences of this model demand multilinear forms of engagement and an openness to unpredictable responses, for the process of dissemination and contextualization is no longer designed as an apparatus that serves and promotes the originality of the art work, but has become an active force in the construction of a field of aesthetic experiences and social meanings.

To write on the topographic relationship between art, place, and the everyday is neither a new historical approach toward particular places nor a survey of new artistic practices. This writing practice does not resemble an account of artistic representations of a specific landscape, nor does it track the artistic movements that are traversing the territories of modernity. My methodology is not based on an art historical survey of new tendencies in contemporary art, nor am I upholding a definitive sociological perspective that reveals the geopolitical characteristics of art. It requires that the writer does not simply describe and analyze the composition of the artwork. My task is not confined to authenticating artists' provenance, classifying their practice, and evaluating their achievements. It does not restrict the discussion of the context of art to a mapping of its specific geographic origins or location. My concern is not bound by the need to identify the extent of political influences or economic dependencies. It does not narrate the genesis of the work according to the fixed coordinates that are either stated in the artist's intentions or defined by prior sociological debates on the context of art. While drawing from academic disciplines that do have these aims, my goal is instead to articulate the way artistic practice is creating new levels of engagement within the available spaces of contemporary art and is expressing ideas that are part of everyday life. I am not seeking to establish a methodology that is oblivious to the discursive formation of art history or claiming a new transcendence from socioeconomic forces. Rather, I am defining an expanded field that requires a new cross-disciplinary mode of analysis.[17]

This shift in methodology is related to two parallel developments in contemporary thinking and practice. First, artists have developed strategies that are more cross-disciplinary and operate in an expanded field. They have not only destabilized the conventional boundary between art and popular culture and challenged the museum's representational frameworks, but also critiqued the institutional history of art. Second, the challenge of critical theory, feminism, and postcolonial theory has been to push writers beyond the task of recording and reflecting on the material presence of art, and into an engagement with the frameworks of perception and experience. The task of the writer is not only to reflect on art but also to see how a representation is both transformative and constitutive of subjectivity. As Rogoff rightly observes, art does not serve as either a transcendental guide or a mirror for revealing the world we are in, but offers the space of an interlocutor.[18]

PICKING UP THE PIECES OF CONTEMPORANEITY AND
THE MULTIPLE ENDINGS OF MODERNITY

If the idea of the contemporary no longer derives its saliency from spatial-temporal markers of rupture or exclusion—it is neither confined to the perimeter of the West, nor presupposes a clean break with the past—then it is probable that the conceptualization of the new and the critical is now "situated" in a more complex narrative, one that is conceived not as a linear trajectory toward a point of singular destination and based on binary distinctions but rather as entangled in multiple associations with a confounding sense of attachment that includes the double experience of displacement in the very practice of enplacement, and an awareness that tradition and innovation are not opposed but part of the cultural dynamic of renewal and continuity.

I am struck by the way commentators throughout this collection of writings have referred to the social position of the artist. There is no doubt that art is not subordinate to ideology but neither is it above society. So where is the artist? As Geeta Kapur suggests, the artist is both in the everyday spaces of society and against the normative directions of the social. The countermodern tendencies of the hacker identified by Mackenzie Wark; the dubious distinction between the artwork's original value and its practical utility that is, as Jonathon Hay observes, not only blurred by gift exchange but is also a marker of the limits of modernity; and even Sylvester Ogbechie's semijoking suggestions of global tolls that would pay tribute to our Afrocentric origins are all examples of the reactivation of traditions for short-circuiting the channels of alienation, subverting the principles of commodification, and redeeming the legacies of colonialism.

Reflecting on these discourses of hope and critique I also note disquiet over our own positioning within the national narratives and unease in the supposed fit between our internationalist aspirations and the rhetoric of globalization. Who would proudly say, "I belong here and everywhere"? It is this ambivalence over belonging and affiliation that also represents a challenge to the old avant-gardist rhetoric of detachment and provides a new starting point for radicalizing the new politics of institutionalization. Our sense of belonging may not be unequivocal, but there is still the need to be attached to something. There is no longer the self-belief that the critic or the artist can claim an outsider position. To be inside, coterminously, is not necessarily a sign of conformity and enclosure. Yet this ambivalent positioning, which is in part symptomatic of the transformed conditions for the material production of art, also requires a rethinking of the reflexive terms of agency. The idea of agency in art needs to be extended, and in particular the concept of cultural authority and responsibility needs to be distributed in all social directions. It should not privilege the ego of the artist but attend to the radial interactions that occur in all engagements with art. This implies not only a rethinking of the process by which artists communicate with the public but a critical examination of the active role—not just mediating function—of writers, curators, and technical producers. To this end, my own contribution has shifted between a reflection on the representation of contemporary practice and speculation over the critical space of theory.

Two definitions in particular have helped frame my reflections on the issues explored in this book. Peter Sloterdijk's identification of mobilization as the fundamental process of modernity contains within its own definition the propensity for the maximization of surplus in economic, cultural, and perceptual modalities.[19] To suggest that the new exceeds, extends, or transforms the old modernity does not therefore mark its ending but the beginnings of its own internal kinetics. Or, to put it in other terms, every declaration of contemporaneity introduces modernity through its own back door.

Antonio Negri's definition of contemporaneity does add a qualification to the modern idea of self-reflexivity. As he shows in this volume, the propensity of this reflexivity is not driven by neutral mobilization but by antagonism. In his conception, the multitude is not a mere accumulation of differences but a multiplicity of singularities recomposed in the immanence of antagonism. Between this conception of the extensional drive of modernity and the antagonistic composition of contemporaneity there is a strong account of the unstable grounds and uncertain trajectories of the social. There is a tempering of the spirit of revolution that also breathes faith in the signs of change and difference.

The ambition to generate a surplus movement takes many forms, and if, in its contemporary manifestation, it abuts against rival claims of plenitude and order, then we must also consider the complicities and felicities of new forms of practice that not only resist commodification but whose very existence circulates in an unending process of translation: those collaborative practices that extend the tendencies earlier identified as the "dematerialization of art," and which also resemble the characteristics in Nicolas Bourriaud's notion of "relational aesthetics."[20] In focusing more heavily on the significance of place and representation within the totality of the institutions of art, however, I am contending that the concept of place has been distorted in the mainstream discourse of art. It has been both exaggerated by nationalist accounts and entirely missed in the formalist discourses on art. A new concept of place needs to be inserted, one that addresses both the radial energies and complex junctures of the social engagement of art.

In the field of contemporary culture such forms of investigation are becoming more and more remote from the core of cultural practice. They require more dynamic exchange, intimate knowledge, and immediacy in feedback. The dynamic that mobilizes cultural practice through these expanded forms of collaboration has, I suggest, ten key characteristics.

1. Artistic practice is defined through, not in advance of, collaboration.

2. Collaboration is the socialization of artistic practice.

3. Identification of common needs is the politicization of artistic practice.

4. Critical engagement with the specificity of place involves more than using it as a stage for new ideas.

5. Mobilization of communicative networks extends and implicates both the local and transnational domains.

6. Artistic practice is inserted in the same time-space continuum as everyday life.

7. Institutions are not external objects, but resources critical for the material production of art.

8. Critique of the sovereign position of the artist in creative direction leads to a redistribution of social responsibility.

9. Horizontal models of cultural and social engagement are created.

10. Institutions shift from a singular destination to a transitional platform for dissemination.

Nicolas Bourriaud has been at the forefront of identifying these emerging formations. He has stressed the critical dynamic between everyday life, technical support, and public participation. Most recently he has suggested that in this field the artwork exists as a kind of mapping, the creation of pathways through the complex grids and labyrinths of metropolitan life.[21] The boundary between the artwork and the "rest of the world" is never secure, as Boris Groys notes in his remarks on installation in this volume. The participatory demands of the viewer also ensure that the same work never exists twice. It is literally like the river of Heraclitus, always in flow, never fixed. Every entry and even the position of each viewer can affect the view of the other. In most cases the position of another witness can not only obscure one's own view but also initiate different stimuli into the feedback system and thereby alter the narrative flow. Each person's reception creates an interference of the next. To grasp the frame of this artwork a different model of boundary and system is necessary. The work might exist in a closed space but the boundary and system operate in a relatively open-ended manner. The dynamic of interaction means that the communicative system does not proceed in a fixed trajectory but is instead enabled by its rendering of the boundary between art and life as permeable.

The perceptual and technical demands of installation art and collaborative practice have emerged at the same time as the two key unfinished tasks of modernity—negotiating cultural difference and confronting the ruins of industry—have begun to slip further away from consciousness. Amid the turbulent flows of globalization there has been growing anxiety over the status of minority communities. Not only are they seen as irritant splinters that disrupt the comfortable narrative of the nation as family, but the reconfiguration of local communities as diasporic communities—that can establish their own transnational networks—has also given succor to the paranoid delusions that global terrorism is transmitted in these information flows, and that their multiple "structures of feeling" to different places is evidence of treacherous attachments. New forms of authoritarian loyalty tests are being conjured as the academic debates on the representation of cultural identity in the form of hybridity or *creolité* are being contested. It is unclear to me whether this new political terrain will impact on the theoretical frameworks for representing difference. Even within the emergent field of critical theory, there is still division over the significance of power differentials between different constituencies, as well as a lack of consensus over the cultural consequences of displacement in relation to tradition and innovation. Throughout these pages we can read a switching between and, at times, conflation of two models of difference: difference under the sign of homogenized subsumption, where it comes under the reign of the similar; and difference as constitutive force in a heterogeneous collage, where it is unleashed in the form of the uncanny. Two questions remain unanswered: Under what conditions does difference mask the dominant structures of uniformity? How can it ever escape this oppressive logic and heighten critical awareness?

The second incomplete task is the recognition of the legacy of the ruins of the industrial age. While dominating much of the urban landscape, the abandoned spaces and ruins serve as alternative spaces for artist's studios, provide the material for art, and prompt the meditative rethinking of the significance of time and space. The material and symbolic significance of ruins has barely registered within the mainstream discourses of Modernism and contemporaneity. I have referred to these sites and their attending conceptual challenges as parafunctional.[22] Ruins not only offer the challenge as to how we can "clean up" and recycle, but also provide a spatial allegory for the function of absence. To his credit Okwui Enwezor elevated the legacies of colonialism and industrialism as the two axioms that structured the main pathways through documenta 11. Despite the fact that most critics wanted to relegate the conceptual challenge of this exhibition to what they saw as the last gasps of an exhausted link to theory, it was by no means the last word on the subject.

The challenge today is not only to recognize the difference of minority or marginal communities but also to rethink the terms of what Okwui Enwezor has called the new universalism.[23] It will involve a radical analysis of the structures that enable certain forms of agency and the opportunities for dialogue across cultural boundaries. Antonio Negri is very astute in his observations on the agency of resistance, but in response to the rise of neoauthoritarianism in the contemporary political landscape, this phenomenon is not a recurrence of an earlier form of fascism but a complex hybrid of local populism and global insecurity. To smear the opposition with epithets will only repeat the blindness of dogma that renders the Left impotent and out of touch. What is needed is honesty: to dissect one's own idealism, not with the cynical purpose of self-flagellation but in order to sharpen the lines of contemporary engagement. We can no longer avoid the more complex task of understanding the appeal of authoritarianism. The power of authoritarianism, like the power of art, is not reducible to logic: if we assume that it is defined by its intellectual value, then we miss the point. As contemporary art practice reimagines notions of place and exile, as artists trace connections that transcend the old geospatial boundaries, we not only witness new narratives of mobility and difference, but new patterns of social engagement and aesthetic production. The next challenge is to find a discourse that can articulate the complex interlocal connections that now operate in a global network.

NOTES

1 Lippard, *Six Years.*
2 Lash, *Critique of Information.*
3 Mosquera, "Alien-Own/Own-Alien," 167.
4 Esche, "Modest Proposals," n.p.
5 "If I Ruled the World," an exhibition curated by Bryndis Snaebjornsdottir and Ross Sinclair, at the Living Art Museum, Reykjavik, and McLellan Galleries, Glasgow. See Wilson, *If I Ruled the World.*
6 Lucy Orta, interview with Hou Hanru, May 1999, http://studioorta.free.fr/lucy—orta/TMP-1115468054.htm (accessed October 20, 2005).
7 Orta and Smith, *Lucy Orta.*
8 Virilio, "Urban Armor," 9.
9 Superflex, *Biogas,* Artspace, Sydney, 1998; and *Superchannel,* Liverpool Biennale, Liverpool, 1999.
10 Restany, "Social Engineering"; and Bourriaud, *Relational Aesthetics.*
11 Clark, *Farewell to an Idea.*
12 This juxtaposition between the modernist vision of utopia and the dystopic spaces of postindustrial landscapes was powerfully staged in documenta 11, Kassel, 2002, artistic director Okwui Enwezor.
13 Yona Friedman, wall panel text, documenta 11, Kassel, 2002.
14 Serres, *Rome,* 151.
15 Damisch, *Skyline,* 114.

16 Rancière, "The Aesthetic Revolution," 151.

17 See also Marsh, "The Future of Art History."

18 Rogoff, *Terra Infima*, 10.

19 Sloterdijk, "Modernity as Mobilization."

20 Lippard, *Six Years;* Bourriaud, *Relational Aesthetics.*

21 Bourriaud, *Post-Production.*

22 Papastergiadis, *Spatial Aesthetics.*

23 Enwezor, "The Black Box."

REFERENCES

Achebe, Chinua. "An Image of Africa: Racism in Conrad's *Heart of Darkness*." In Kimbrough, *Joseph Conrad*, 251–61.

Agamben, Giorgio. *The Open: Man and Animal.* Stanford: Stanford University Press, 2004.

Aijaz, Ahmad. "Jameson's Rhetoric of Otherness and 'National Allegory.'" *Social Text* 17 (1987): 3–25.

Alliez, Eric, ed. "Art contemporain: La recherche du dehors." Special issue, *Multitudes* 15 (winter 2004).

Altbach, Philip G., and Salah M. Hassan, eds. *The Muse of Modernity: Essays on Culture as Development in Africa.* Asmara: Africa World Press, 1996.

Amin, Samir. *Eurocentricism.* London: Zed, 1998.

Anderson, Benedict. *Imagined Communities: Reflections on the Origin and Spread of Nationalism.* Rev. ed. New York: Verso, 1991.

Appadurai, Arjun, ed. *Modernity at Large: Cultural Dimensions of Globalization.* Minneapolis: University of Minnesota Press, 1996.

———. *The Social Life of Things.* Cambridge: Cambridge University Press, 1986.

Appiah, Kwame Anthony. "The Postcolonial and the Postmodern." In Appiah, *In My Father's House: Africa in the Philosophy of Culture*, 137–57. Oxford: Oxford University Press, 1992.

Appignanesi, Lisa, ed. *Freedom of Expression Is No Offence.* London: Penguin, 2005.

Apter, Emily. "Comparative Exile: Competing Margins in the History of Comparative Literature." In Bernheimer, *Comparative Literature in the Age of Multiculturalism*, 86–96.

———. "Global *Translatio:* The 'Invention' of Comparative Literature, Istanbul, 1933." *Critical Inquiry* 29, no. 2 (winter 2003): 253–81.

Araeen, Rasheed. *The Other Story: Afro-Asian Artists in Post War Britain.* London: Hayward Gallery, 1989.

Arendt, Hannah. "Introduction. Walter Benjamin: 1892–1940." In Walter Benjamin, *Illuminations,* 1–58. New York: Schocken Books, 1986.

Armstrong, Carol. "This Photography Which Is Not One: In the Gray Zone with Tina Modotti." *October* 101 (summer 2002): 48–51.

Arnold, Matthew. *Essays in Criticism: Third Series.* Boston: Ball Publishing, 1910.

Atkinson, Brenda, and Candice Breitz, eds. *Grey Areas: Representation, Identity and Politics in Contemporary South African Art.* Sandton, South Africa: Chalkham Hill, 1999.

Atterton, Peter, and Matthew Calarco, eds. *Animal Philosophy: Ethics and Identity.* London: Continuum, 2004.

Augé, Marc. *The Anthropology of Contemporaneous Worlds.* Stanford, Calif.: Stanford University Press, 1999.

——. *Non-Places: Introduction to an Anthropology of Supermodernity.* London: Verso, 1995.

Augé, Marc, and Jean-Paul Colleyn. *The World of the Anthropologist.* Oxford: Berg, 2006.

Bacon, R. H. *Benin the City of Blood.* London: E. Arnold, 1897.

Badiou, Alain. "Does the Other Exist?" In Badiou, *Ethics: An Essay on the Understanding of Evil,* 18–29. Translated by Peter Hallward. London: Verso, 2002.

Badmington, Niel, ed. *Posthumanism.* London: Palgrave, 2000.

Baker, George, and Christian Philipp Müller. "A Balancing Act." *October* 82 (fall 1997): 95–118.

Baker, Steve, *The Postmodern Animal.* London: Reaktion, 2002.

Baldwin, James, Romare Bearden, Ekpo Eyo, Nancy Graves, Ivan Karp, Lela Kouakou, Iba N'Diaye, David Rockefeller, William Rubin, and Robert Farris Thompson. *Perspectives: Angles on African Art.* Edited by Michael J. Weber. New York: Center for African Art, 1987.

Barboza, David. "Hollywood Movie Studios See the Chinese Film Market as Their Next Rising Star." *New York Times,* July 4, 2005, C3.

Barthes, Roland. *Mythologies.* St. Albans, England: Paladin, 1973.

Bascom, William. *Ifa Divination: Communication between Gods and Men in West Africa.* Bloomington: Indiana University Press, 1991.

Bateson, Gregory. *Steps towards An Ecology of Mind.* New York: Ballantine Books, 1972.

Battcock, Gregory, ed. *Minimal Art: A Critical Anthology.* New York: E. P. Dutton, 1968.

Battle, Michael. *Reconciliation: The Ubuntu Theology of Desmond Tutu.* Cleveland: Pilgrim Press, 1997.

Baudelaire, Charles. "Exposition Universelle I. Critical Method: On the Modern Idea of Progress Applied to the Fine Arts, on the Shift of Vitality" (1855). In Baudelaire, *Art in Paris, 1845–1862: Salons and Other Exhibitions Reviewed by Charles Baudelaire,* 121–28. Edited by Jonathan Mayne. London: Phaidon, 1964.

——. *The Painter of Modern Life and Other Essays.* Translated by Jonathan Mayne. London: Phaidon, 1964; 2nd ed., 2001.

Baudrillard, Jean. *Paroxysm: Interviews with Philippe Petit.* London: Verso, 1998.

Bauman, Zygmunt. *Modernity and the Holocaust.* Ithaca, N.Y.: Cornell University Press, 1991.

Bazin, Andre. "An Aesthetic of Reality: Neorealism." In Bazin, *What Is Cinema?* 2:16–40. Translated by Hugh Gray. Berkeley: University of California Press, 1971.

Bedford, Emma. *Moshekwa Langa.* Cape Town: South African National Gallery, Iziko, 2003.

Bell, Terry. *Unfinished Business: South Africa Apartheid and Truth.* With Dumisa Buhle Ntsebeza. Observatory, South Africa: Redworks, 2001.

Belson, Ken. "DVD Fight Intensifies: Microsoft and Intel to Back Toshiba Format." *New York Times,* September 27, 2005, C1–2.

———. "A DVD Standoff in Hollywood." *New York Times,* July 11, 2005, C1, 6.

Benjamin, Walter. *The Arcades Project.* Translated by Howard Eiland and Kevin McLaughlin. Cambridge, Mass.: Belknap Press of Harvard University Press, 1999.

———. *Illuminations.* Edited by Hannah Arendt. Translated by Harry Zohn. New York: Harcourt, Brace and World, 1968; New York: Schocken Books, 1969.

———. "On Some Motifs in Baudelaire." 1940, in Michael W. Jennings, ed., *Walter Benjamin: Selected writings, Volume 4, 1938–1940,* 313–55. Cambridge, Mass.: Belknap Press of Harvard University Press, 2003.

———. "Rigorous Study of Art: On the First Volume of the *Kunstwissenschaftliche Forschungen*" (1933). Translated by Thomas Y. Levin. *October* 47 (winter 1988): 84–90.

———. "Surrealism: The Last Snapshot of the European Intelligensia," 1929, in Michael W. Jennings, ed., *Walter Benjamin: Selected writings, Volume 2, 1927–1943,* 207–21. Cambridge, Mass.: Belknap Press of Harvard University Press, 1999.

———. "The Work of Art in the Age of Mechanical Reproduction." In Walter Benjamin, *Illuminations* (1969), 217–52.

Berger, Peter L., and Samuel P. Huntington, eds. *Many Globalizations: Cultural Diversity in the Contemporary World.* Oxford: Oxford University Press, 2002.

Berman, Marshall. *All That Is Solid Melts into Air.* London: Verso, 1983.

Bernheimer, Charles, ed. *Comparative Literature in the Age of Multiculturalism.* Baltimore: Johns Hopkins University Press, 1995.

Bernstein, Ann. "Globalisation, Culture and Development: Can South Africa Be More Than an Offshoot of the West?" In Berger and Huntington, *Many Globalizations,* 185–249.

Bhabha, Homi K. "Of Mimicry and Man: The Ambivalence of Colonial Discourse." In Bhabha, *The Location of Culture,* 85–92. New York: Routledge, 1994.

———. "The Other Question: Stereotype, Discrimination and the Discourse of Colonialism." In Bhabha, *The Location of Culture,* 66–84.

———. "Postmodernism/Postcolonialism." In Nelson and Shiff, *Critical Terms for Art History,* 435–51.

Bhengu, Mfuniselwa. *Ubuntu: The Essence of Democracy.* Cape Town: Novalis, 1996.

Biko, Steve. *I Write What I Like.* Harmondsworth, U.K.: Penguin, 1998.

Blix, Hans. *Disarming Iraq.* New York: Pantheon Books, 2004.

Bogues, Anthony. *Black Heretics, Black Prophets.* London: Routledge, 2003.

Bois, Yve-Alain. "Material Utopia." *Art in America* (April 1988): 161–80.

———. *Susan Smith's Archaeology.* New York: Margarete Roeder Gallery, 1989.

Bonami, Francesco. *Dreams and Conflicts: The Dictatorship of the Viewer.* Venice: La Biennale di Venezia, 2003.

Boraine, Alex. *A Country Unmasked: Inside South Africa's Truth and Reconciliation Commission.* Oxford: Oxford University Press, 2000.

Borja-Villel, Manuel, ed. *Lygia Clark.* Barcelona: Fundació Antoni Tà'pies, 1997.

Borradori, Giovanna, ed. *Philosophy in a Time of Terror: Dialogues with Jürgen Habermas and Jacques Derrida.* Chicago: University of Chicago Press, 2003.

Borysevicz, Mathieu, ed. *Zhang Dali: Demolition and Dialogue.* Beijing: Courtyard Gallery, 1999.

Bos, Saskia. *Berlin Biennale 2.* Berlin: Berlin Biennale, 2001.

Bourdieu, Pierre. *The Field of Cultural Production: Essays on Art and Literature.* New York: Columbia University Press, 1993.

——. "Gender and Symbolic Violence." In Scheper-Hughes and Bourgois, *Violence in War and Peace,* 339–42.

Bourdieu, Pierre, and Loïc Wacquant. "Symbolic Violence." In Scheper-Hughes and Bourgeois, *Violence in War and Peace,* 272–74.

Bourriaud, Nicolas. *Esthétique relationnelle.* Dijon: Les Presses du Reel, 1998. English translation *Relational Aesthetics,* by Simon Pleasance and Fronza Woods (Dijon: Les Presses du Reel, 2002).

——. *Post-Production.* New York: Lucas and Sternberg, 2002.

Bovard, James. "Iraqi Sanctions and American Intentions: Blameless carnage? Part 1" (January 2004). Available online at the Future of Freedom Foundation Web site, http://www.fff.org/freedom/fd0401c.asp.

——. *Terrorism and Tyranny: Trampling Freedom, Justice and Peace to Rid the World of Evil.* London: Palgrave Macmillan, 2003.

Braudel, Fernand. *Civilization and Capitalism: The Fifteenth Century to the Eighteenth Century.* Vol. 3, *The Perspective of the World.* New York: Harper and Row, 1984.

Breckenridge, Carol Appadurai, ed. *Consuming Modernity: Public Culture in a South Asian World.* Minneapolis: University of Minnesota Press, 1995.

Bredekamp, Horst. *Thomas Hobbes visuelle Strategien: Der Leviathan; Das Urbild des modernen Staates Werkillustrationen und Portraits.* Berlin: Akademie Verlag, 1999.

Brotton, Jerry. "Saints Alive: The Iconography of St. Georges." In Latour and Weibel, *Iconoclash,* 155–57.

Brown, Deming, ed. "Russian Postmodernism." Special issue, *Russian Studies in Literature* 30, no. 1 (winter 1993–94).

Bryson, Norman. "Art in Context." In Cohen, *Studies in Historical Change,* 18–42.

Büchler, Pavel, and Nikos Papastergiadis, eds. *Random Access: On Crisis and Its Metaphors.* London: Rivers Oram Press, 1995.

Buchloh, Benjamin H. D. "Figures of Authority, Ciphers of Regression: Notes on the Return of Representation in European Painting." In Wallis, *Art after Modernism,* 107–36.

——. "Hantaï, Villeglé, and the Dialectics of Painting's Dispersal." *October* 91 (winter 2000): 25–35.

——. *Neoavantgarde and the Culture Industry: Essays on European and American Art 1945 to 1975.* Cambridge, Mass.: MIT Press, 2000.

Bukharin, Nikolai. *Put' k sotsializmu: Izbrannye proizvedeniia N. I. Bukharina.* [Path to socialism: Selected works of N. I. Bukharin]. Edited by V. P. Danilov and S. A. Krasil'nikov. Novosibirsk: Nauka (sibirskoe otdelenie), 1990.

Bürger, Peter. "Literary Institution and Modernization." In Bürger, *The Decline of Modernism*, 3–18. Translated by Nicholas Walker. University Park, Pa.: Pennsylvania State University Press, 1992.

——. *Theory of the Avant-Garde.* Translated by Michael Shaw. Minneapolis: University of Minnesota Press, 1984.

Burns, Bill, Cathy Busby, and Kim Sawchuk, eds. *Theory out of Bounds.* Vol. 14, *When Pain Strikes.* Minneapolis: University of Minnesota Press, 1999.

Buruma, Ian, and Avishai Margalit. *Occidentalism: A Short History of Anti-Westernism.* London: Atlantic Books, 2004.

Buskirk, Martha, and Mignon Nixon, eds. *The Duchamp Effect.* Cambridge, Mass.: MIT Press, 1996.

Butler, Judith. *Precarious Life: The Powers of Mourning and Violence.* London: Verso, 2004.

Cai Yuanpei. "Yi meiyu dai zongjiao shuo" [To replace religion with aesthetic education]. *Xin qingnian* [New youth] 3, no. 6 (August 1917): 11–15.

Calinescu, Matei. *Five Faces of Modernity: Modernism, Avant-garde, Decadence, Kitsch, Postmodernism.* Durham, N.C.: Duke University Press, 1987.

Cameron-Dow, J. *South Africa 1990–1994: The Miracle of a Freed Nation.* Cape Town: Don Nelson, 1994.

Campbell, Aidan. *Western Primitivism: African Ethnicity: A Study in Cultural Relations.* London: Cassell, 1997.

Canclini, Nestor Garcia. *Hybrid Cultures: Strategies for Entering and Leaving Modernity.* Translated by Christopher L. Chiappari and Silvia L. Lopez. Minneapolis: University of Minnesota, 1995.

Cassin, Barbara. *L'effet sophistique.* Paris: Gallimard, 1995.

——. "Managing Evidence." In Latour and Weibel, *Making Things Public*, 858–65.

Cavell, Stanley. *Must We Mean What We Say? A Book of Essays.* Cambridge: Cambridge University Press, 1976.

Chabal, Patrick, and Jean-Pascal Daloz, eds. *Africa Works: Disorder as Political Instrument.* Oxford: James Currey; Bloomington: Indiana University Press, 1999.

Chakrabarty, Dipesh. *Provincializing Europe: Postcolonial Thought and Historical Difference.* Princeton, N.J.: Princeton University Press, 2000.

Chan, Lauk'ung. "Ten Years of the Chinese Avant-Garde, Waiting for the Curtain to Fall." *Flash Art* 25, no. 162 (January/February 1992): 110–14.

Chandrasekhar, Indira, and Peter C. Seel, eds. *Body.City: Siting Contemporary Culture in India.* Delhi: Tulika Books; Berlin: House of World Cultures, 2003.

Chang, Tsong-zung, ed. *China's New Art, Post-1989.* Hong Kong: Hanart T Z Gallery, 1993.

——. "Into the Nineties." In Chang, *China's New Art*.

——, ed. *The Stars: 10 Years.* Hong Kong: Hanart, 1989.

Chatterjee, Partha. *Nationalist Thought and the Colonial World: A Derivative Discourse?* Delhi: Oxford University Press, 1988.

Chatterjee, Partha, and Gyanendra Pandey, eds. *Subaltern Studies*. Vol. 7, *Writings on South Asian History and Society*. Delhi: Oxford University Press, 1992.

Chengyao, He. "Lift the Cover from Your Head." *Yishu* 2, no. 3 (fall 2003): 20–24.

Chow, Rey. "Leading Questions." In Chuh and Shimikawa, *Orientations*, 189–212.

Christian, David. *Maps of Time: An Introduction to Big History*. Berkeley: University of California Press, 2004.

Christove-Bakargiev, Carolyn. *William Kentridge*. Turin: Castello di Rivoli Museo d'Arte Contemporanea, 2004.

Chuh, Kandice, and Karen Shimikawa, eds. *Orientations: Mapping Studies in the Asian Diaspora*. Durham, N.C.: Duke University Press, 2001.

Chuprinin, Sergei. "Drugaia proza" [Other prose]. *Literaturnaia gazeta* [Literary gazette], February 8, 1989, 4.

Clark, Lygia. "Objeto Relacional." In collaboration with Suely Rolnik. In Gullar, *Lygia Clark/textos de Ferreira Gullar, Mário Pedrosa, Lygia Clark*. Reprinted in Borja-Villel, *Lygia Clark: Fundació Antoni Ta'pies, Barcelona*, 48–55.

Clark, T. J., *Farewell to an Idea*. New Haven, Conn.: Yale University Press, 1999.

———. *The Painting of Modern Life*. London: Thames and Hudson, 1999.

Clifford, James. *The Predicament of Culture: Twentieth-Century Ethnography, Literature, and Art*. Cambridge, Mass.: Harvard University Press, 1988.

Clunas, Craig. *Pictures and Visuality in Early Modern China*. Princeton, N.J.: Princeton University Press, 1997.

———. *Superfluous Things: Material Culture and Social Status in Early Modern China*. Cambridge: Polity Press, 1991.

Coetzee, J. M. *The Lives of Animals*. Princeton: Princeton University Press, 1999.

Coetzee, P. H., and A. J. P. Roux, eds. *Philosophy from Africa: A Text with Readings*. Cape Town: Oxford University Press, 2002.

Cohen, Ralph, ed. *Studies in Historical Change*. Charlottesville: University Press of Virginia, 1992.

Cole, Herbert M., and Chike Aniakor. *Igbo Arts: Community and Cosmos*. Los Angeles: UCLA Museum of Natural History, 1984.

Coleman, James. *Projected Images, 1972–1994*. New York: Dia Art Foundation, 1995.

Coleman, Max, ed. *A Crime against Humanity: Analysing the Repression of the Apartheid State*. Johannesburg: Human Rights Committee; Belleville: Mayibuye Books; Cape Town: David Philip, 1998.

Colman, Julia. *Zhang Dali: Headlines*. London: Chinese Contemporary Gallery, 2004.

Condee, Nancy, and Vladimir Padunov. "Pair-a-Dice Lost: The Socialist Gamble, Market Determinism, and Compulsory Postmodernism." In Slobin, "Postcommunism," 72–94.

———. "Reforming Soviet Culture: Retrieving Soviet History." *Nation*, June 13, 1987, 815–20.

Cooke, Lynne, and Peter Wollen, eds. *Visual Display: Culture beyond Appearances*. Seattle, Wash.: Bay Press, 1995.

Coombes, Annie. "The Object of Translation: Notes on 'Art' and Autonomy in a Postcolonial Context." In Fred R. Myers, ed., *The Empire of Things: Regimes of Value and*

Material Culture, 233–56. Santa Fe: School of American Research Press; Oxford: James Curry, 2001.

——. *Reinventing Africa: Museums, Material Culture and Popular Imagination in Late Victorian and Edwardian England.* New Haven, Conn.: Yale University Press, 1994.

Cooppan, Vilashini. "World Literature and Global Theory: Comparative Literature for the New Millennium." *Symplokç* (2001): 15–43.

Cox, Christoph. "Return to Form: Christoph Cox on Neomodernist Sound Art." *Artforum* 42, no. 3 (November 2003): 67–71.

Crais, Clifton. *The Politics of Evil: Magic, State Power, and the Political Imagination in South Africa.* Cambridge: Cambridge University Press, 2002.

Christove-Bakargiev, Carolyn. *William Kentridge.* Turin: Castello di Rivoli Museo d'Arte Contemporanea, 2004.

Critical Art Ensemble. *The Electronic Disturbance.* New York: Autonomedia, 1994.

——. *The Molecular Invasion.* New York: Autonomedia, 2002.

Crow, Thomas. "Unwritten Histories of Conceptual Art: Against Visual Culture." In Crow, *Modern Art in the Common Culture,* 212–42. New Haven, Conn.: Yale University Press, 1996.

Crusz, Robert, and Priyath Liyanage. "Interview with Anand Patwardhan." *Framework* 38/39 (1992): 118–32.

Cubitt, Sean. "Bombay, Our City: Interview with Anand Patwardhan." *Framework* 30/31 (1986): 60–67.

Daily Herald (London). "Africa's Ben Challenges Epstein." August 1, 1950.

Damisch, Hubert. *Skyline: The Narcissistic City.* Stanford, Calif.: Stanford University Press, 2001.

Davies, Tony. *Humanism.* London: Routledge, 1997.

Davis, Erik. *TechGnosis: Myth, Magic and Mysticism in the Age of Information.* London: Serpents Tail, 2004.

Debord, Guy. *Comments on the Society of the Spectacle.* London: Verso, 1988.

——. *In girum imus nocte et consumimur igni.* Paris: Gallimard, 1999.

——. *The Society of the Spectacle.* New York: Zone Books, 1994.

De Jager, E. J. *Images of Man: Contemporary South African Black Art and Artists. A Pictorial and Historical Guide to the Collection of the University of Fort Hare Housed in the De Beers Centenary Art Gallery.* Alice, South Africa: University of Fort Hare, 1992.

De Kock, Leon, Louise Bethlehem, and Sonja Laden, eds. *South Africa in the Global Imaginary.* Pretoria: University of South Africa Press, 2004.

DeLanda, Manuel. *A New Philosophy of Society.* London: Continuum, 2006.

——. *A Thousand Years of Nonlinear History.* New York: Swerve, 2000.

Deleuze, Gilles, and Felix Guattari. *Anti-Oedipus: Capitalism and Schizophrenia.* Translated by Robert Hurley, Mark Seem, and Helen R. Lane. Minneapolis: University of Minnesota Press, 1983; London: Athlone Press, 1984.

Deliss, Clémentine, ed. *Seven Stories: About Modern Art in Africa.* London: Whitechapel, 1996.

Derrida, Jacques. "The Double Session." In Derrida, *Dissemination,* 173–286. Translated by Barbara Johnson. Chicago: University of Chicago Press, 1981.

——. *Specters of Marx: The State of the Debt, the Work of Mourning and the New International.* Chicago: University of Chicago Press, 1994.

Détienne, Marcel, ed. *Qui veut prendre la parole?* Paris: Le Seuil, 2003.

De Waal, Shaun, and Robyn Sassen. *Stephen Cohen.* Houghton, South Africa: David Krut Publishing, 2003.

Dewey, John. *The Public and Its Problems.* Athens: Ohio University Press, Swallow Press, 1927.

Diamond, Jared. *Collapse: How Societies Choose to Fail or Succeed.* New York: Viking, 2005.

——. *Guns, Germs, and Steel: The Fates of Human Societies.* New York: Norton, 2003.

Doelemeyer, Barbara. "Thing Site, Tie, Ting Place: Venues for the Administration of Law." In Latour and Weibel, *Making Things Public,* 260–67.

Dondurei, Daniil. "Kinodelo na puti k rynku" [Cinema business on the path to the marketplace]. In Dubrovin and Zak, *Rossiiskoe kino,* 126–40.

Dowd, Douglas F. *The Broken Promises of America at Home and Abroad, Past and Present.* Monroe, Me.: Common Courage Press, 2005.

Doyle, Michael. *Empires.* Ithaca, N.Y.: Cornell University Press, 1986.

Dubrovin, A. G., and M. E. Zak, eds. *Rossiiskoe kino: Paradoksy obnovleniia* [Russian cinema: Paradoxes of renewal]. Moscow: Materik, 1995.

Eagleton, Terry. *After Theory.* New York: Basic Books, 2003.

Ebony (Chicago). "Africa's Greatest Artist." No. 4 (March 1949): 12, 27–29.

Edwards, Michael. *Civil Society.* Oxford: Blackwell, 2004.

Edwards, Elizabeth, and Peter James. " 'Our Government as Nation': Sir Benjamin Stone's Parliamentary Pictures." In Latour and Weibel, *Making Things Public,* 142–55.

Eisenstadt, S. N., ed. "Multiple Modernities." Special issue, *Daedalus* 129, no. 1 (winter 2000).

——. *Patterns of Modernity: Beyond the West.* New York: New York University Press, 1987.

Elias, Norbert. *The Civilizing Process.* Oxford: Blackwell, 2000.

Elkins, James. *Pictures of the Body: Pain and Metamorphosis.* Stanford: Stanford University Press, 1999.

Ellingson, Ter. *The Myth of the Noble Savage.* Berkeley: University of California Press, 2001.

Elliott, David, ed. *Art from South Africa.* Oxford: Museum of Modern Art, 1999.

Enwezor, Okwui. "The Black Box." In Enwezor, ed., *Documenta 11—Platform 5: Exhibition Catalogue,* 42–55. Ostfildern-Ruit: Hatje Cantz Publishers, 2002.

——. "Documentary/Verité: The Figure of Truth in Contemporary Art." In Nash, *Experiments with Truth,* 97–104.

——. "Introduction—Travel Notes: Living, Working, and Travelling in a Restless World." In Enwezor, *Trade Routes: History and Geography,* 7–12. The Hague: Prince Claus Funds; Johannesburg: Greater Johannesburg Metropolitan Council, 1997.

——. "Reframing the Black Subject: Ideology and Fantasy in Contemporary South African Art." In Hope, *Contemporary Art from South Africa,* 20–36.

——. "Reframing the Black Subject: Ideology and Fantasy in Contemporary South African Art." Rev. ed. In Oguibe and Enwezor, *Reading the Contemporary,* 377–99.

——, ed. *The Unhomely: Phantom Scenes in Global Society.* Seville: Bienal Internacional de Arte Contemporáneo de Sevilla, 2006.

Epstein, Mikhail. "After the Future: On New Consciousness in Literature." *South Atlantic Quarterly* 90, no. 2 (1991): 409–44.

——. *Re-entering the Sign: Articulating New Russian Culture.* Edited by Ellen E. Berry and Anesa Miller-Pogacar. Ann Arbor: University of Michigan Press, 1994.

Erjavec, Aleš, ed. *Postmodernism and the Postsocialist Condition: Politicized Art under Late Socialism.* Berkeley: University of California Press, 2003.

Esche, Charles. "Modest Proposals." In Bos, *Berlin Biennale 2,* 22–26.

Eshelman, Raoul. *Slavische Literaturen.* Vol. 12, *Early Russian Postmodernism.* New York: Peter Lang, 1997.

Fabian, Johannes. "Culture, Time, and the Object of Anthropology." In Fabian, *Time and the Work of Anthropology: Critical Essays, 1971–1991.* Chur, Switzerland: Harwood Academic Publishers, 1991.

Failing, Patricia. "Ed Ruscha, Young Artist: Dead Serious about Being Nonsensical." *ARTnews* 81, no. 4 (April 1982): 74–81. Reprinted in Ruscha, *Leave Any Information at the Signal,* 225–37.

Fanon, Frantz. *Wretched of the Earth.* Translated by Constance Farrington. New York: Grove Press, 1963.

——. *Wretched of the Earth.* Translated by Richard Philcox. New York: Grove Press, 2005.

Farrell, Kirby. *Post-Traumatic Culture: Injury and Interpretation in the Nineties.* Baltimore: Johns Hopkins Press, 1998.

Feng Boyi. "From 'Underground' to 'Above Ground': On Chinese Avant-Garde Art Since the 1990s." *Yishu Pinglun* [Art criticism], no. 7 (2004): 43–47.

Fisher, Philip. *Making and Effacing Art: Modern American Art in a Culture of Museums.* New York: Oxford University Press, 1991.

Fitzgerald, Shannon, and Tumelo Mosaka. *The Fiction of Authenticity: Contemporary Africa Abroad.* St. Louis, Mo.: Contemporary Art Museum, 2003.

Flam, Jack, and Miriam Deutch, eds. *Primitivism and Twentieth-Century Art: A Documentary History.* Berkeley: University of California Press, 2003.

Flynt, Henry. *Blueprint for a Higher Civilization.* Milan: Multiphla Edizioni, 1975.

Foster, Don, Paul Haupt, and Marésa de Beer, eds. *The Theatre of Violence: Narratives of Protagonists in the South African Conflict.* Cape Town: Institute of Justice and Reconciliation, 2005.

Foster, Hal, ed. *The Anti-Aesthetic.* Seattle, Wash.: Bay Press, 1983.

——. *Recodings: Art, Spectacle, Cultural Politics.* Seattle, Wash.: Bay Press, 1985.

Foucault, Michel. *Essential Works of Foucault, 1954–1984.* Vol. 1, *Ethics, Subjectivity and Truth.* Edited by Paul Rabinow. New York: New Press, 1997.

——. *The History of Sexuality.* Vol. 2, *The Uses of Pleasure.* New York: Pantheon, 1985.

Freedberg, David. *The Power of Images: Studies in the History and Theory of Response.* Chicago: University of Chicago Press, 1989.

Friedman, Hazel. "On the Verge of Optimism." *Mail and Guardian,* August 2–9, 1996, 29.

——. "Visual Odes to Intimacy." *Mail and Guardian,* March 31–April 6, 2006, 2–3.

Frost, Lola. *Jeremy Wafer.* Houghton, South Africa: David Krut Publishing, 2001.

Frow, John. *Time and Commodity Culture: Essays in Cultural Theory and Postmodernism.* Oxford: Clarendon Press, 1997.

——. *What Was Postmodernism?* Occasional Paper 11. Sydney, Australia: Local Consumption, 1991.

Fudge, Erica. *Animal.* London: Reaktion, 2002.

Gablik, Suzi. "Towards an Ecological Self." *New Art Examiner* (January 1991): 26–30.

Gamboni, Dario. *The Destruction of Art: Iconoclasm and Vandalism since the French Revolution.* London: Reaktion, 1997.

Gao Minglu. *Chinese Maximalism.* Chongqing: Chongqing People's Press, 2003.

——. "Fengkuangde yijiubajiu: Zhongguo xiandai yishuzhan shimo" [Great social happening: China/avant-garde exhibition]. *Qingxiang* [Tendency quarterly], no. 12 (1999): 43–76.

——, ed. *Inside Out: New Chinese Art.* San Francisco: San Francisco Museum of Modern Art; New York: Asia Society Galleries; Berkeley: University of California Press, 1998.

——. "Lun Mao Zedong de dazhong yishu moshi" [The principle of Mao Zedong's mass art]. *21st Century* (Chinese University, Hong Kong), no. 4 (1993): 61–73.

——. "Material Utopia in Contemporary Chinese Architecture and Urban Design." *Time + Architecture* (Shanghai), (January 2005): 5–10.

——. "Post-Utopian Avant-Garde Art in China." In Erjavec, *Postmodernism and the Postsocialist Condition.*

——. *The Wall: Reshaping Chinese Contemporary Art.* Beijing: China Millennium Museum of Art; New York: Albright Knox Gallery of Art, 2005.

——. *Zhongguo dangdai meishu shi, 1985–1986* [The history of contemporary Chinese art, 1985–1986]. Shanghai: Shanghai renmin chubanshe, 1991.

Gao Minglu and Wang Mingxian. *Harvest: Contemporary Art Exhibition.* Hong Kong: Architecture Post Publishing House, 2002.

Gates, Henry Louis, Jr. *The Signifying Monkey: A Theory of African American Literary Criticism.* New York: Oxford University Press, 1988.

Geers, Kendell. "Sand in the Vaseline." Interview by Jerome Sans. *Art South Africa* 1, no. 3 (spring 2002): 28–34.

Gevisser, Mark, and Edwin Cameron, eds. *Defiant Desire: Gay and Lesbian Lives in South Africa.* Johannesburg: Ravan, 1994.

Gibson, Nigel C., ed. *Rethinking Fanon: The Continuing Dialogue.* New York: Humanity Books, 1999.

Giddens, Anthony. *Modernity and Self-Identity: Self and Society in the Late Modern Age.* Stanford, Calif.: Stanford University Press, 1991.

Gikandi, Simon. "Picasso, Africa, and the Schemata of Difference." *Modernism/Modernity* 10, no. 3 (2003): 455–80.

Gilroy, Paul. *The Black Atlantic: Modernity and Double Consciousness.* London: Verso, 1993.

Gladwell, Malcolm. *Blink: The Power of Thinking without Thinking.* New York: Little, Brown, 2005.

Gleason, Abbott. *Totalitarianism: The Inner History of the Cold War.* New York: Oxford University Press, 1995.

Glissant, Édouard. *Caribbean Discourse: Selected Essays.* Edited by A. James Arnold, translated by Michael Dash. Charlottesville: University of Virginia Press, CARAF Books, 1992.

——. *Poetics of Relation.* Ann Arbor: University of Michigan Press, 1996.

Gmelin, Felix. "Rene—NU-E—Felix Gmelin + Ronald Jones—04.15.04." Interview by Ronald Jones and Robert Stasinski. *16 Beaver* (April 15, 2004). Available online at http://www.16beavergroup.org.

Goedhuis, Michael. *China without Borders: An Exhibition of Chinese Contemporary Art.* London: Field Print and Graphics, 2001.

Golden, Thelma. *Black Male: Representations of Masculinity in Contemporary American Art.* New York: Whitney Museum/Abrams, 1994.

Golinski, Hans Günther, Sepp Hiekisch-Picard, and Museum Bochum, eds. *New Identities: Zeitgenössische Kunst aus Südafrika* [New identities: Contemporary art from South Africa]. Ostfildern, Germany: Hatje Cantz Verlag, 2004.

Golomstock, Igor. *Totalitarian Art in the Soviet Union, the Third Reich, Fascist Italy and the People's Republic of China.* London: Collion Harvills, 1990.

Goniwe, Thembinkosi. "Kay Hassan's Shebeen and Ritual Crossing." In Golinski et al., *New Identities,* 172–74.

Goody, Jack. *Representations and Contradictions: Ambivalence towards Images, Theatre, Fiction, Relics and Sexuality.* Oxford: Blackwell, 1997.

Grauer, Victor A. "Modernism/Postmodernism/Neomodernism." *Downtown Review* 3, nos. 1–2 (fall/winter/spring, 1981–82): 3–7.

Green, Renée. "Partially Buried." *October* 80 (spring 1997): 39–56.

Greslé, Yvette. "Ndyindoda! Initiation as a Right of Passage." *Art South Africa* 3, no. 1 (spring 2004): 62–63.

Groebner, Valentin. *Defaced: The Visual Culture of Violence in the Late Middle Ages.* New York: Zone Books, 2004.

Groys, Boris. *The Total Art of Stalinism: Avant-Garde, Aesthetic Dictatorship, and Beyond.* Translated by Charles Rougle. Princeton, N.J.: Princeton University Press, 1992.

Guattari, Félix, and Suely Rolnik. *Micropolítica: Cartografias do desejo.* Petrópolis: Vozes, 1986. Forthcoming in English as *Molecular Revolution in Brazil.* Translated by Brian Holmes. New York: Semiotext(e), MIT Press, 2008.

Gullar, Ferreira. *Lygia Clark: Textos de Ferreira Gullar, Mário Pedrosa, Lygia Clark.* Rio de Janeiro: Funarte, 1980.

Gule, Khwezi. "Thando Mama." In Perryer, *10 Years 100 Artists,* 226–29.

Gutteridge, William, and J. E. Spence, eds. *Violence in Southern Africa.* London: Frank Cass, 1997.

Gyekye, K. *Tradition and Modernity: Philosophical Reflections on the Africa Experience.* Oxford: Oxford University Press, 1997.

Habermas, Jürgen. *Die nachholende Revolution.* Frankfurt am Main: Suhrkamp, 1990.

——. "Modernity—An Incomplete Project." In Foster, *The Anti-Aesthetic,* 3–15.

——. "Modernity's Consciousness of Time and Its Need for Self-Reassurance." In *The Philosophical Discourse of Modernity*, 1–22. Cambridge: Polity Press, 1987; Cambridge, Mass.: MIT Press, 1990.

——. *The Postnational Constellation: Political Essays*. Translated by Max Pensky. Cambridge, Mass.: MIT Press, 2001.

——. *The Structural Transformation of the Public Sphere: An Inquiry into a Category of Bourgeois Society*. London: Polity Press, 1992.

Halisi, C. R. D. "Biko and Black Consciousness Philosophy: An Interpretation." In N. Barney Pityana, Mamphela Ramphele, Malusi Mpumlwana, and Lindy Wilson, eds., *Bounds of Possibility: The Legacy of Steve Biko and Black Consciousness*. Claremont, South Africa: David Philip, 1991.

Hall, Stuart, and Bram Gieben, eds. *Formations of Modernity*. Cambridge: Polity Press, 1992.

Hamilton, Carolyn, Verne Harris, Michèle Pickover, Graeme Reid, Razia Saleh, and Jane Taylor, eds. *Refiguring the Archive*. Dordrecht: Kluwer Academic Publishers, 2002.

Hankins, Thomas L., and Robert J. Silverman. *Instruments and the Imagination*. Princeton: Princeton University Press, 1995.

Haraway, Donna. *The Haraway Reader*. New York: Routledge, 2004.

Hardt, Michael, and Antonio Negri. *Empire*. Cambridge, Mass.: Harvard University Press, 2000.

Harman, Graham. "Heidegger on Objects and Things." In Latour and Weibel, *Making Things Public*, 268–71.

Harrison, Stephen, Steve Pile, and Nigel Thrift, eds. *Patterned Ground: Entanglements of Nature and Culture*. London: Reaktion, 2004.

Harvey, David. *The Condition of Postmodernity: An Enquiry into the Origins of Cultural Change*. Oxford: Blackwell, 1989.

Hassan, Ihab. *The Postmodern Turn: Essays in Postmodern Theory and Culture*. Columbus: Ohio State University Press, 1987.

Hassan, Salah. "The Modernist Experience in African Art: Towards a Critical Understanding." In Altbach and Hassan, *The Muse of Modernity*, 37–61.

Hay, Jonathan. "Adventures in Chinaspace and Transnationalism." In Goedhuis, *China without Borders*, 20–33.

——. "The Conspicuous Consumption of Time." In Hay, *Shitao*, 26–56.

——. "Culture, Ethnicity and Empire in the Work of Two Eighteenth-Century 'Eccentric Artists.'" *Res: Anthropology and Aesthetics* 35 (spring 1999): 201–23.

——. "The Diachronics of Early Qing Visual and Material Culture." In Struve, *The Qing Formation*, 303–34.

——. "The Kangxi Emperor's Brush Traces: Calligraphy, Writing, and the Art of Imperial Authority." In Tsiang and Wu, *Body and Face in Chinese Visual Culture*, 311–34.

——. "Painting and the Built Environment in Late Nineteenth-century Shanghai." In Hearn and Smith, *Chinese Arts*, 61–101.

——. *Shitao: Painting and Modernity in Early Qing China*. New York: Cambridge University Press, 2001.

——. "Toward a Disjunctive Diachronics of Chinese Art History." *Res: Anthropology and Aesthetics* 40 (autumn 2001): 101–11.

Hearn, Maxwell, and Judith Smith, eds. *Chinese Art: Modern Expressions.* New York: Metropolitan Museum of Art, 2001.

He Chengyao. "Lift the Cover from Your Head." *Yishu* 2. no. 3 (fall 2003): 22.

Heidegger, Martin. *What Is a Thing?* Translated by W. B. Barton Jr. and Vera Deutsch. Chicago: Chicago University Press, 1968.

Heiss, Alanna, Fan Di' An, Wu Jiang, and Li Xv. *2002 in Shanghai, in Yangjiang: Some Event Occurring.* Shanghai: Shanghai Shuhua Press, 2002.

Henkel, Heiko. " 'The Journalists of *Jyllands-Posten* Are a Bunch of Reactionary Provocateurs': The Danish Cartoon Controversy and the Self-Image of Europe." *Radical Philosophy,* no. 137 (May–June 2006): 2–7.

Heywood, Ian. "Modernism and Violence." In Heywood, *Social Theories of Art: A Critique.* New York: New York University Press, 1997.

Higgs, P., N. C. G. Vakalisa, T. V. Mda, and N. T. Assie-Lumumba, eds. *African Voices in Education.* Landsdowne, South Africa: Juta, 2000.

Hill, Paul, and Thomas Cooper, *Dialogue with Photography.* New York: Farrar, Straus and Giroux, 1979.

Hill, Shannen. "Iconic Autopsy: Postmortem Portraits of Bantu Stephen Biko." *African Arts* 38, no. 3 (autumn 2005): 14–25, 92–93.

Hiller, Susan, ed. *The Myth of Primitivism: Perspectives on Art.* London: Routledge, 1991.

Hirschberg, Lynn. "What Is an American Movie Now?" *New York Times Magazine,* November 14, 2004, 88–94.

Hlongwane, Khangela Ali, Sifiso Ndlovu, and Mothobi Mutloatse, eds. *Soweto '76: Reflections on the Liberation Struggles.* Houghton: Mutloatse Arts Heritage Trust, 2006.

Hoad, Neville, Karen Martin, and Graham Reid, eds. *Sex and Politics in South Africa.* Cape Town: Double Storey, 2005.

Hobbs, Philippa, ed. *Messages and Meaning: The MTN (Mobile Telephone Network) Art Collection.* Johannesburg: MTN, 2006.

Hochschild, Adam. *King Leopold's Ghost: A Story of Greed, Terror, and Heroism in Colonial Africa.* Boston: Houghton Mifflin, 1998.

Hoffmann, David L., and Yanni Kotsonis, eds. *Russian Modernity: Politics, Knowledge, Practices.* New York: St. Martin's, 2000.

Holkeboer, Mieke. "Out of the Crooked Timber of Humanity: Humanising Rights in South Africa." In Erik Doztader and Charles Villa-Vincenzio, eds., *To Repair the Irreparable: Reparation and Reconstruction in South Africa,* 149–65. Claremont, South Africa: David Philip, 2004.

Holmes, Brian. "The Flexible Personality." In Holmes, *Hieroglyphs of the Future,* 106–37. Zagreb: WHW/Arkzin, 2003.

——. "Warhol in the Rising Sun: Art, Subcultures and Semiotic Production." *Université Tangente,* August 8, 2004. Accessed online at http://www.beavergroup.org.

Hope, Marith, ed. *Contemporary Art from South Africa.* Oslo: Riksutstillinger, 1997.

Hopkins, David. *After Modern Art, 1945–2000.* Oxford: Oxford University Press, 2000.

Hoptman, Laura. "The Essential Thirty-Eight." In Hoptman, *54th Carnegie International*, 17–35. Pittsburgh, Pa.: Carnegie Museum of Art, 2004.

Hoshimo, Takashi. "Bloom Time Out East." *ME: Mobile Entertainment* 9 (November 2005). Accessed online at http://www.mobile-ent.biz/ (accessed November 30, 2005).

Hoskins, Andrew. *Televising War: From Vietnam to Iraq.* London: Continuum International Publishing Group, 2004.

Hu Shi. "Pragmatism." *Xinqingnian* [New youth] 6, no. 4 (1919). Reprinted in Hu, *Ouyangzhesheng*, 342–58.

——. *Ouyangzhesheng* [Essays by Hu Shi]. Edited by Hushi Wenji. Beijing: Peking University Press, 1988.

Huang Yongping. "About Made in China." In Gao and Wang, *Harvest*, 36.

Hug, Alfons, and Sabine Vogel, eds. *Colours: Kunst aus Südafrika.* Berlin: Herausgeber Verlag, 1996.

Huntington, Samuel P. *The Clash of Civilizations and the Remaking of World Order.* New York: Simon and Schuster, 1996.

Huyssen, Andreas. "After the Wall: The Failure of German Intellectuals." In Huyssen, *Twilight Memories*, 37–66. New York: Routledge, 1995.

Jakobson, Roman, and Morris Halle. *Fundamentals of Language.* The Hague: Mounton, 1971.

Jamal, Ashraf. *Predicaments of Culture in South Africa.* Pretoria: University of South Africa Press; Leiden: Koninklijke Brill NV, 2005.

James, Wilmot, and Linda van de Vijver, eds. *After the TRC: Reflections on Truth and Reconciliation in South Africa.* Cape Town: David Philip, 2000.

Jameson, Fredric. "Beyond the Cave: Demystifying the Ideology of Modernism." In Jameson, *Ideologies of Theory: Essays 1971–1986*, 115–32. Minneapolis: University of Minnesota Press, 1998.

——. *The Geopolitical Aesthetic: Cinema and Space in the World System.* Bloomington: Indiana University Press; London: BFI, 1992.

——. "Periodizing the Sixties." In Sayres et al., *The Sixties without Apology*, 178–209.

——. "Postmodernism, or The Cultural Logic of Late Capitalism." *New Left Review* 146 (July–August 1984): 53–92.

——. *Postmodernism, or The Cultural Logic of Late Capitalism.* Durham, N.C.: Duke University Press, 1991.

——. *The Seeds of Time.* New York: Columbia University Press, 1994.

——. "SF Novel/SF Film." *Science Fiction Studies* 22, no. 7, part 3 (November 1980). Available online at http://www.depauw.edu/sfs.

——. "Shifting Contexts of Science Fiction Theory." *Science Fiction Studies* 42, no. 14, part 2 (July 1987). Available online at http://www.depauw.edu/sfs.

——. *A Singular Modernity: Essay on the Ontology of the Present.* London: Verso, 2002.

Janson, H. W. *History of Art.* With Anthony Janson. New York: Abrams, 2001.

Jauss, Hans Robert. *Literaturgeschichte als Provokation.* Frankfurt am Main: Suhrkamp, 1970.

——. "Modernity and Literary Tradition." Translated by Christian Thorne. *Critical Inquiry* 31, no. 2 (winter 2005): 329–64.

Jay, Martin. *Refractions of Violence.* New York: Routledge, 2003.

Jeffrey, Anthea. *The Truth about the Truth Commission.* Johannesburg: Institute of Race Relations, 1990.

Jia Fangzhou. "Chinese Women Artists of the 20th Century." In Werner et al., *Die Hälfte des Himmels.*

Jolly, Rosemary Jane. *Colonization, Violence, and Narration in White South African Writings.* Johannesburg: Wits University Press, 1996.

Joselit, David. "Navigating the New Territory: Art, Avatars, and the Contemporary Mediascape." *Artforum* 43, no. 10 (summer 2005): 276–79.

Julius, Anthony. *Idolizing Pictures: Idolatory, Iconoclasm and Jewish Art.* London: Thames and Hudson, 2000.

———. *Transgressions: The Offences of Art.* Chicago: University of Chicago Press, 2000.

Kane, Cheikh Hamidou. *Ambiguous Adventure.* Portsmouth, N.H.: Heinemann, 1972.

Kanwar, Amar. " 'Not Firing Arrows': Multiplicity, Heterogeneity and the Future of Documentary." Interview by Anne Rutherford. *Asian Cinema* 16, no. 1 (spring 2005): 117–24.

———. *Notes for a Night of Prophecy.* Chicago: Renaissance Society, University of Chicago, 2003.

Kaphagawani, Didier. "Some African Conceptions of Person: A Critique." In Ivan Karp and D. A. Masolo, eds., *African Philosophy as Cultural Inquiry,* 66–79. Bloomington: Indiana University Press, 2000.

Kaprow, Allan. *Assemblage, Environments and Happenings.* New York: Abrams, 1965.

———. "The Legacy of Jackson Pollock." *ARTnews* 57, no. 6 (October 1958): 24–26, 55–57.

Kasfir, Sidney. "African Art and Authenticity: A Text with a Shadow." *African Arts* 25, no. 2 (April 1992): 41–53, 96–97.

Kaufmann, Thomas Dacosta. *Towards a Geography of Art.* Chicago: University of Chicago Press, 2004.

Kaufmann, Thomas Dacosta, and Elizabeth Pilliod, eds. *Time and Place: The Geohistory of Art.* Burlington, Vt.: Ashgate, 2005.

Kaviraj, Sudipta. "The Imaginary Institution of India." In Chatterjee and Pandey, *Subaltern Studies,* 7:1–39.

Keane, John. *Violence and Democracy.* Cambridge: Cambridge University Press, 2004.

Kelly, John D. "Alternative Modernities or an Alternative to 'Modernity': Getting Out of the Modernist Sublime." In Knauft, *Critically Modern,* 258–86.

Kerouac, Jack. *On the Road.* London: André Deutsch, 1958.

Kgositsile, Baleka. "Poor Taste Must Not Pose as Art." *The Star,* August 13, 1996, 10.

Kharkodin, Oleg. "Things as Res Publicae." In Latour and Weibel, *Making Things Public,* 280–89.

Kierulf, Ida. *Amar Kanwar—Portraits.* Oslo: Fotogalleriet, 2005.

Kimbrough, Robert, ed. *Joseph Conrad: Heart of Darkness.* New York: W. W. Norton, 1988.

Klein, Naomi. *Fences and Windows.* New York: Picador, 2002.

———. *No Logo.* London: Harper Collins, 2000.

Klopper, Sandra. "Mobilisation of Cultural Symbols in 20th century Zululand." *African Studies Forum,* no. 8 (September 1988): 20–22.

Knauft, Bruce, ed. *Critically Modern: Alternatives, Alterities, Anthropologies*. Bloomington: Indiana University Press, 2002.

Kögler, Hans Herbert. "Review of *Social Systems* by Niklas Luhmann." *American Journal of Sociology* 103, no. 1 (July 1997): 271–73.

Koloane, David. "Moments in Art." In Deliss, *Seven Stories*, 143–57.

——. *Sam Nhlengethwa*. Johannesburg: Standard Bank Foundation, 1994.

——. "The Spirit of Ubuntu as a Creative Dynamic." In *Ubuntu*, 22–33. Kuala Lumpur, Malaysia: National Art Gallery, 2002.

Krauss, Rosalind. "The Cultural Logic of the Late Capitalist Museum." *October* 54 (fall 1990): 3–17.

Krauss, Rosalind, Annette Michelson, George Baker, Yve-Alain Bois, Benjamin H. D. Buchloh, Leah Dickerman, Hal Foster, Denis Hollier, Mignon Nixon, and Malcolm Turvey, eds. "Roundtable: The Present Conditions of Art Criticism." *October* 100, no. 1 (spring 2002): 200–229.

Kristensen, Peer H., and Jonathan Zeitlin. *Local Players in Global Games: The Strategic Constitution of a Multinational Corporation*. Oxford: Oxford University Press, 2004.

Kristeva, Julia. *Intimate Revolt: The Powers and Limits of Psychoanalysis*. New York: Columbia University Press, 2002.

Krog, Antjie. *Country of My Skull*. London: Jonathan Cape, 1998.

Kruger, Barbara and Phil Mariani, eds., *Remaking History*. Seattle: Bay Press, 1998.

Kruzhkov, Grigorii, ed. "Fire and Ice: Romanticism and Postmodernism in Contemporary Russian Poetry." Special issue, *Russian Literature in Translation* 29, no. 4 (fall 1993).

Kuoni, Carin. *Words of Wisdom: A Curator's Vade Mecum on Contemporary Art*. New York: Independent Curators International, 2001.

Lal, Vinay. "Travails of a Nation: Some Notes on Indian Documentary." *Third Text*, no. 73 (March 2005): 177–87.

Landau, Paul S. "Empires of the Visual: Photography and Colonial Administration in Africa." In Landau and Deborah D. Kaspin, eds., *Images and Empires: Visuality in Colonial and Postcolonial Africa*, 141–71. Berkeley: University of California Press, 2002.

Lang Shaojun. *Lun Zhongguo xiandai meishu* [A discussion of Chinese modern art]. Nanjing: Jiangsu meishu chubanshe, 1988.

Langhan, Donvé. *The Unfolding Man: The Art and Life of Dan Rakgoathe*. Cape Town: David Philip, 2000.

Lash, Scott. *Critique of Information*. London: Sage, 2002.

Latour, Bruno. *Pandora's Hope: Essays on the Reality of Science Studies*. Cambridge, Mass.: Harvard University Press, 1999.

——. *We Have Never Been Modern*. Translated by Catherine Porter. Cambridge, Mass.: Harvard University Press, 1993.

Latour, Bruno, and Peter Weibel, eds. *Iconoclash: Beyond the Image Wars in Science, Religion and Art*. Cambridge, Mass.: MIT Press, 2002.

——, eds. *Making Things Public: Atmospheres of Democracy*. Cambridge, Mass.: MIT Press, 2005.

Law, Jennifer A. "Performing on a Fault-Line: The Making(s) of a South African Spy Novel and Other Stories." In Marcus, *Para-Sites,* 151–94.

Lazzarato, Maurizio. "Créer des mondes: Capitalisme contemporain et guerres 'esthétiques.'" In Alliez, "Art contemporain: La recherche du dehors," 229–37. Revised as "Entreprise et néomonadologie," in Maurizio Lazzarato, *Les révolutions du capitalisme,* 93–149 (Paris: Les Empêcheurs de penser en rond, Le Seuil, 2004).

Leng, Ling. *Shi wo* [It's me]. Beijing: Zhongguo wenlian chubanshe, 2000.

Letseka, Moeketsi. "African Philosophy and Educational Discourse." In P. Higgs et al., *African Voices in Education,* 179–93.

Lévéque, Pierre. "Repartition et démocratie à propos de la racine da-." *Esprit,* no. 12 (1993): 34–39.

Lewis, Desirée. "Against the Grain: Black Women and Sexuality," *Agenda,* no. 63 (2005): 11–25.

Li Shi and Tao Yongbai. *The Lost History: The History of Chinese Female Painting.* Changsha: Hunan Fine Arts Publishing House, 2000.

Li Xianting. "Major Trends in the Development of Contemporary Chinese Art." In Chang, *China's New Art, Post-1989,* x–xxii.

Liao Wen. *Feminism as a Method—Feminist Art.* Jilin City, China: Jilin Fine Arts Publishing House, 1999.

Lih, Lars. "The Soviet Union and the Road to Communism." In Suny, *The Cambridge History of Russia,* vol. 3, 706–31.

Lindqvist, Sven. *Exterminate All the Brutes.* Translated by Joan Tate. New York: New Press, 1996.

Lippard, Lucy. *Eva Hesse.* New York: New York University Press, 1976.

——. *Six Years: The Dematerialization of the Art Object, 1966–1972.* London: Studio Vista, 1973.

Lipovetsky, Mark. *Russian Postmodernist Fiction: Dialogue with Chaos.* Edited by Eliot Borenstein. Armonk, N.Y.: M. E. Sharpe, 1999.

Lü Peng. *Zhongguo dangdai yishu shi, 1990–1999* [A history of modern Chinese art: 1990–1999]. Changsha: Hunan meishu chubanshe, 2000.

Lü Peng, and Yi Dan. *Zhongguo xiandai yishu shi, 1979–1989* [A history of contemporary Chinese art: 1979–1989]. Changsha: Hunan meishu chubanshe, 1992.

Luhmann, Niklas. *Art as a Social System.* Translated by Eva M. Knodt. Stanford, Calif.: Stanford University Press, 2000.

——. "Deconstruction as Second-Order Observing." *New Literary History* 24, no. 4 (autumn 1993): 763–83.

——. "European Rationality." In Robinson and Rundell, *Rethinking Imagination,* 65–86.

Lyth, Peter, and Helmut Trischler, eds. *Wiring Prometheus: Globalization, History and Technology.* Aarhus, Denmark: Aarhus University Press, 2004.

Lyotard, Jean François. *The Postmodern Condition: A Report on Knowledge.* Minneapolis:University of Minnesota Press,1984.

——. *The Postmodern Explained: Correspondence, 1982–1985.* Minneapolis: University of Minnesota Press, 1993.

Mackenzie, Adrian. *Transductions: Bodies and Machines at Speed.* London: Continuum, 2002.

Madikida, Churchill. "Statement." In Smith, *Knap! KKNK Visuele Kunste 2004,* 49.

Maharaj, Sarat. " 'Perfidious Fidelity': The Untranslatability of the Other." In Jean Fisher, ed., *Global Visions: Towards a New Internationalism in the Visual Arts,* 38–35. London: Kala Press in association with the Institute of International Visual Arts, 1994.

Makdisi, Saree. "Said, Palestine, and the Humanism of Liberation." *Critical Inquiry* 31, no. 2 (winter 2005): 443–61.

Makgoba, Malegapuru William, ed. *African Renaissance: The New Struggle.* Sandton: Mafube; Cape Town: Tafelberg, 1999.

Malik, Kenan. "The Mirror of Race: Postmodernism and the Celebration of Difference." In Ellen Meiksins Wood and John Bellamy Foster, eds., *In Defense of History: Marxism and the Postmodern Agenda,* 113–34. New York: Monthly Review Press, 1998.

Malukhin, Vitalii. "Post bez moderna" [Post without modern]. *Izvestiia,* May 8, 1991, 4.

Mamdani, Mahmood. *Citizen and Subject: Contemporary Africa and the Legacy of Late Colonialism.* Kampala: Fountain Publishers; Cape Town: David Philip; London: James Currey, 1996.

——. *Good Muslim, Bad Muslim: America, the Cold War, and the Roots of Terror.* Johannesburg: Jacana Media, 2005.

Mametse, Dikatso. "Pictures Arouse Stiff Opposition." *Mail and Guardian,* June 27–July 3, 2003, 5.

Manganyi, N. Chabani, and André du Toit, eds. *Political Violence and the Struggle in South Africa.* London: Macmillan, 1990.

Man'kovskaia, Nadezhda. *Estetika postmodernizma* [Aesthetics of postmodernism]. St. Petersburg: Aleteiia, 2000.

Mannoni, Laurent, Werner Nekes, and Marina Warner. *Eyes, Lies and Illusions.* London: Hayward Galleries; Aldershot, England: Lund Humphries, 2004.

Manovich, Lev. *The Language of New Media.* Cambridge, Mass.: MIT Press, 2001.

Marcus, George E., ed. *Para-Sites: A Casebook against Cynical Reason.* Chicago: University of Chicago Press, 2000.

Marien, Mary Warner. *Photography: A Cultural History.* London: Lawrence King, 2002.

Marsh, Anne. "The Future of Art History: The Discipline in an Expanded Field." *Art Monthly Australia,* no. 33 (August 2001): 8–10.

Marshall, Kerry James. *Kerry James Marshall.* New York: Abrams, 2000.

Marx, Karl. "The Eighteenth Brumaire of Louis Bonaparte." In Marx, *Political Writings,* 2:143–249.

——. *Political Writings.* Vol. 1, *The Revolutions of 1848.* Edited by David Fernbach. Harmondsworth, England: Penguin, 1973.

——. *Political Writings.* Vol. 2, *Surveys from Exile.* Edited by David Fernbach. Harmondsworth, England: Pelican, 1973.

Marx, Karl, and Friedrich Engels. "Manifesto of the Communist Party." In Marx, *Political Writings,* 1:67–98.

Mazrui, Ali. "Pan Africanism and the Intellectuals: Rise, Decline and Revival." In Thandika Mkandawire, ed., *African Intellectuals: Rethinking Politics, Language, Gender and Development*, 56–77. Dakar and London: CODESRIA and Zed Books, 2005.

Mbeki, Thabo. *Africa: The Time Has Come*. Cape Town: Tafelberg; Johannesburg: Mafube, 1998.

Mbembe, Achille. *On the Postcolony*. Chicago: University of Chicago Press, 2001.

——. "Sex after Liberation." *Mail and Guardian*, July 12–July 17, 2003, 23.

Mbembe, Achille, and Sarah Nuttall. "Writing the World from an African Metropolis." *Public Culture* 16, no. 3 (fall 2004): 347–72.

Mbiti, John S. *African Religions and Philosophy*. Oxford: Heinemann, 1989.

McCann, Jerome, Vitaly Chernetsky, Arkadii Dragomoshchenko, Mikhail Epstein, Lyn Hejinian, Bob Perelman, and Marjorie Perloff. "Symposium on Russian Postmodernism." *Postmodern Culture* 3, no. 2 (January 1993). Available online at http://muse.jhu.edu/journals/postmodern—culture/toc/pmc3.2.html.

McDougall, Bonnie S. *The Introduction of Western Literary Theories into Modern China*. Tokyo: Centre for East Asian Cultural Studies, 1971.

McLuhan, Marshall. *Understanding Media: The Extensions of Man*. New York: McGraw-Hill, 1964. Reprint, Cambridge, Mass.: MIT Press, 1994.

McNeill, J. R., and William H. McNeill. *The Human Web*. New York: W. W. Norton, 2003.

Meiring, Piet. *Chronicle of the Truth Commission*. Vanderbijlpark, South Africa: Carpe Diem Books, 1999.

Merewether, Charles. "The Spectre of Being Human." *Yishu* (June 2003): 58–81. Reprinted in Turner, *Art and Social Change*, 101–43.

——. *2006 Sydney Biennale: Zones of Contact*. Sydney: Biennale of Sydney, 2006.

Merrett, Christopher. *A Culture of Censorship: Secrecy and Intellectual Repression in South Africa*. Cape Town: David Philip; Pietermaritzburg: University of Natal Press; Macon, Ga.: Mercer University Press, 1994.

Meyer, James. "Impure Thoughts: The Art of Sam Durant." *Artforum* 38, no. 8 (April 2000): 112–17.

Meyer, Richard, ed. *Representing the Passions: Histories, Bodies, Visions*. Los Angeles: Getty Institute, 2003.

Meyers, Steven Lee. "Putin Says Russia Faces Full 'War' to Divide Nation." *New York Times*, September 5, 2004, A1.

Mikhalkov, Nikita, Aleksandr Atanesian, Leonid Vereshchagin, Sergei Sel'ianov, Sergei Sendyk, Sergei Chliiants, Lev Karakhan, Daniil Dondurei, et al. "Rossiiskoe kino: kak vernut' den'gi?" [Russian cinema: How can money be returned?]. *Iskusstvo kino* [Cinema Art] 4 (2005): 4–20.

Millar, Jeremy, and Michael Schwarz, eds. *Speed: Visions of an Accelerated Age*. London: Photographer's Gallery, 1998.

Miller, Nancy K., and Jason Tougaw, eds. *Extremities: Trauma, Testimony and Community*. Urbana: University of Illinois Press, 2002.

Mitchell, W. J. T. "Secular Divination: Edward Said's Humanism." *Critical Inquiry* 31, no. 2 (winter 2005): 462–71.

Morgan, Ruth, and Saskia Wieringa. *Tommy Boys, Lesbian Men and Ancestral Wives: Female Same-Sex Practices in Africa.* Johannesburg: Jacana, 2005.

Morrell, Robert, ed. *Changing Men in Southern Africa.* Pietermaritzburg: University of Natal Press; London: Zed, 2001.

Morris, David B. *The Culture of Pain.* Berkeley: University of California Press, 1991.

Morris, Michael. *Every Step of the Way: The Journey to Freedom in South Africa.* Cape Town: HSRC Press, 2004.

Mosaka, Tumelo. "Circumcised/Circumscribed." *Art South Africa* 1, no. 3 (autumn 2003): 62–63.

——. "Kay Hassan." In Perryer, *10 Years 100 Artists,* 138–41.

Mosquera, Gerardo. "Alien-Own/Own-Alien: Globalization and Cultural Difference." *boundary 2* 29, no. 3 (2002): 163–73.

Mothibi, Nano, "Racism Charges Erupt at Sexuality Conference." *The Star,* June 26, 2003, 1.

Mouffe, Chantal. *On the Political.* London: Routledge, 2005.

Moxey, Keith. "Motivating History." *Art Bulletin* 77, no. 3 (September 1995): 392–401.

Mphahlele, Es'kia. *Education, African Humanism and Culture, Social Consciousness, Literary Appreciation.* Cape Town: Kwela, 2002.

——. "I Am Because We Are: Baccalaureate Address University of Pennsylvania—May 16, 1982." In *Es'kia Continued: Literary Appreciation, Education, African Humanism and Culture, Social Consciousness,* 286–90. Johannesburg: Stainbank and Associates, 2004.

Muholi, Zanele. *Only Half the Picture.* Cape Town: Michael Stevenson, 2006.

Murav, Harriet. "The Post-Modern and the Post-Utopian: Some Problems in Contemporary Soviet Criticism." *Contention* 2 (winter 1991–92): 47–63.

Murinik, Tracy, ed. *Intersections: South African Art from the BHP Billiton Collection.* Marshalltown, South Africa: BHP Billiton, 2002.

Murphy, Jeffrie G. *Getting Even: Forgiveness and Its Limits.* Oxford: Oxford University Press, 2003.

Nabudere, Dani W. "Ubuntu." In Villa-Vincencio and Doxtader, *Pieces of the Puzzle,* 10–16.

Nash, Mark. "Art and Cinema: Some Critical Reflections." In Enwezor, *Documenta 11—Platform 5,* 129–36.

——. "Experiments with Truth: The Documentary Turn." In Nash, *Experiments with Truth,* 15–21. Philadelphia: Fabric Workshop and Museum, 2005.

National Commission on Terrorist Attacks upon the United States. *The 9/11 Commission Report: Final Report of the National Commission on Terrorist Attacks upon the United States.* Washington, D.C.: National Commission on Terrorist Attacks upon the United States, 2003.

Ndebele, Njabulo. *The Cry of Winnie Mandela: A Novel.* Cape Town: David Philip, 2003.

——. *Johannes Mashego Segogela: "Devils, Angels and Other Things."* Johannesburg: Goodman Gallery, 1995.

——. "Multi-Lingual Fictions: Writing, Language, and Identity." In Rosalind C. Morris and Radhika Subramaniam, eds. Special issue on translation. *Connect* (fall 2000): 191–98.

——. "The Rediscovery of the Ordinary: Some New Writings in South Africa." In Ndebele, *Rediscovery of the Ordinary: Essays on South African Literature and Culture*, 37–57. Johannesburg: Congress of South African Writers, 1991.

Ndung'u, Simon Kimani, ed., *The Right to Dissent: Freedom of Expression, Assembly and Demonstration in South Africa*. Braamfontein: Freedom of Expression Institute, 2003.

Negri, Antonio. *The Politics of Subversion: A Manifesto for the Twenty-First Century*. Cambridge: Polity Press, 1989.

Nelson, Robert S., and Richard Shiff, eds. *Critical Terms for Art History*. Chicago: University of Chicago Press, 1996.

Nemser, Cindy. "An Interview with Eva Hesse." *Artforum* (May 1970): 59–63.

Neustetter, Marcus. "Switch On/Off." In *KKNK 2001*, 6. Johannesburg: Suid Afrikaanse Steenkool en Olie (SASOL), 2001.

Ngcobo, Gabi. "What Do We See When We Look at Us?" *Art South Africa* 4, no. 3 (autumn 2006): 48–51.

Nicéron, Jean-François. *La perspective curieuse à Paris chez Pierre Billaine Chez Jean Du Puis rue Saint Jacques à la Couronne d'Or avec l'Optique et la Catoptrique du RP Mersenne du mesme ordre Oeuvre très utile aux Peintres, Architectes, Sculpteurs, Graveurs et à tous autres qui se meslent du Dessein*. 1663.

Nietzsche, Friedrich. *The Use and Abuse of History*. Translated by Adrian Collins. Indianapolis, Ind.: Liberal Arts Press, 1949.

Nochlin, Linda. *Realism*. Harmondsworth, England: Penguin, 1971.

Norman, Richard. *On Humanism*. London: Routledge, 2004.

Noyes, John. "The Place of the Human." In Nuttall and Michael, *Senses of Culture*, 49–60.

Ntuli, Pitika. "The Missing Link between Culture and Education: Are We Still Chasing Gods That Are Not Our Own?" In Makgoba, *African Renaissance*.

Nuttall, Sarah. "The Shock of Beauty: Penny Siopis' Pinky Pinky and Shame Series." In Smith, *Penny Siopis*, 59–72.

Nuttall, Sarah, and Cheryl-Ann Michael, eds. *Senses of Culture: South African Culture Studies*. Cape Town: Oxford University Press, 2000.

Nyamnjoh, Francis. *Africa's Media: Democracy and the Politics of Belonging*. London: Zed Books; Pretoria: University of South Africa, 2005.

Nzegwu, Nkiru. *Contemporary Textures: Multidimensionality in Nigerian Art*. Binghamton, N.Y.: International Society for the Study of Africa, 1999.

October. "A Special Issue on Obsolescence." Vol. 1, no. 1, spring 2002.

O'Dell, Kathy. *Contract with Skin: Masochisms and Performance Art in the 1970s*. Minneapolis: University of Minnesota Press, 1998.

Oguibe, Olu. "Beyond Visual Pleasures: A Brief Reflection on the Work of Contemporary African Woman Artists." In Salah M. Hassan, ed., *Gendered Visions: The Art of Contemporary Africana Women Artists*. Trenton: Africa World Press, 1997.

Oguibe, Olu, and Okwui Enwezor, eds. *Reading the Contemporary: African Art from Theory to the Marketplace*. London: inIVA, 1999.

Okoye, Ikem Stanley. "Book Review." *Art Bulletin*, 80, no. 2 (June 1998): 390–98.

Oliphant, Andries Walter. "A Human Face: The Death of Steve Biko and South African Art." In Deliss, *Seven Stories*, 257–60.

Orta, Lucy. *Process of Transformation*. Paris: Jean Michel Place, 1999.

Osinskii, Nikolai. "Amerikanskii avtomobil′ ili rossiiskaia telega?" [American automobile or Russian cart?]. *Pravda*, July 21, 1927, 3.

O'Toole, Sean. "Zanele Muholi: Are You Feeling a Little Uncomfortable?" *Business Day Art*, March 2006, 12.

Paasche, Marit. "Sterke politiske filmportretter" [Strong political filmportraits]. *Aftenposten* (October 2005). Available online at http://oslopuls.no/kunst/article1131121.ece.

Pagden, Anthony. *Lords of All the World: Ideologies of Empire in Spain, Britain, and France, c. 1500–c. 1800*. New Haven, Conn.: Yale University Press, 1995.

Palson, Gisli. "Of Althings!" In Latour and Weibel, *Making Things Public*, 250–59.

Panofsky, Erwin. "Reflections on Historical Time" [1927]. Translated by Johanna Bauman. *Critical Inquiry* 30, no. 4 (summer 2004): 691–701.

Papastergiadis, Nikos. *Spatial Aesthetics: Art, Place and the Everyday*. London: Rivers Oram Press, 2006.

Parrinder, Geoffrey. *African Mythology*. London: Paul Hamlyn, 1967.

Patnaik, Prabhat. *The Retreat to Unfreedom: Essays on the Emerging World Order*. Delhi: Tulika Books, 2003.

Patnaik, Utsa. *Republic of Hunger*. New Delhi: Safdar Hashmi Memorial Trust, 2004.

Patwardhan, Anand. "Waves of Revolution and Prisoners of Conscience: The Guerilla Film, Underground and in Exile." MA thesis, McGill University, 1981.

Pauw, Jacques. *Into the Heart of Darkness: Confessions of Apartheid's Assassins*. Johannesburg: Jonathan Ball, 1997.

Pepperell, Robert. *The Posthuman Condition*. Bristol: Intellect, 2003.

Perryer, Sophie. *In the Making: Materials and Process*. Cape Town: Michael Stevenson, 2005.

——. *10 Years 100 Artists: Art in a Democratic South Africa*. Cape Town: Bell-Roberts and Struik, 2004.

Pickover, Michelè. *Animal Rights in South Africa*. Cape Town: Double Storey, 2005.

Pines, Jim, and Paul Willeman, eds. *Questions of Third Cinema*. London: BFI Publishing, 1989.

Poggioli, Renato. *The Theory of the Avant-Garde*. Cambridge, Mass.: Harvard University Press, 1968.

Pollock, Mary Sanders, and Catherine Rainwater, eds. *Figuring Animals: Essays on Animal Images in Art, Literature, Philosophy, and Popular Culture*. New York: Palgrave, 2005.

Popham, A. E., ed. *The Drawings of Leonardo da Vinci*. London: Reprint Society, 1953.

Posel, Deborah, and Graeme Simpson, eds. *Commissioning the Past: Understanding South Africa's Truth and Reconciliation Commission*. Johannesburg: Wits Press, 2002.

Prasad, M. Madhava. *Ideology of the Hindi Film: A Historical Construction*. Delhi: Oxford University Press, 1998.

Pratt, Mary Louise. "Arts of the Contact Zone." *Profession* 91 (1991): 33–40.

Preziosi, Donald. *Brain of the Earth's Body: Art, Museums, and the Phantasms of Modernity*. Minneapolis: University of Minnesota Press, 2003.

Pyne, Stephen J. "Fire." In Harrison et al., *Patterned Ground*, 107–9.

Rabinow, Paul. "Introduction: The History of Systems of Thought." In Foucault, *Essential Works of Foucault, 1954–1984*, 1:xi–xlii.

Rajadhyaksha, Ashish. "The Bollywoodization of the Indian Cinema: Cultural Nationalism in a Global Arena." *Inter-Asia Cultural Studies* 4, no. 1 (April 2003): 25–39.

——. *Cinema in the Time of Celluloid: Indian Evidence, 2005–1925*. Delhi: Tulika Books, 2007.

——. "Visuality and Visual Art: Speculating on a Link." In Sambrani, *Edge of Desire*, 156–69.

Ramírez, Mari Carmen, and Héctor Olea, eds. *Inverted Utopias: Avant-Garde Art in Latin America*. New Haven: Yale University Press, for the Museum of Fine Arts, Houston, 2004.

Ramose, Mogobe E. " 'African Renaissance': A Northbound Gaze." In Coetzee and Roux, *Philosophy from Africa*, 600–610.

——. "Globalization and *Ubuntu*." In Coetzee and Roux, *Philosophy from Africa*, 626–50.

——. "The Philosophy of *Ubuntu* and *Ubuntu* as Philosophy." In Coetzee and Roux, *Philosophy from Africa*, 230–38.

Rancière, Jacques. "The Aesthetic Revolution." *New Left Review*, no. 14 (March/April 2002): 133–51.

Rawski, Evelyn. "The Qing Formation and the Early-Modern Period." In Struve, *The Qing Formation*, 207–41.

Reid, Graham, and Liz Walker. "Coming out of the Closet: Sex and Secrecy in Africa." *Mail and Guardian*, December 19–31, 2003, 38–39.

Renov, Michael. *The Subject of Documentary*. Minneapolis: University of Minnesota Press, 2004.

Restany, Pierre. "Social Engineering." In Orta, *Process of Transformation*, 4–7.

Reynolds, Richard. *Superheroes: A Modern Mythology*. Jackson: University Press of Mississippi, 1994.

Richards, Colin. "Kendell Geers." In Perryer, *10 Years 100 Artists*, 122–25.

——. "New Humanisms in Contemporary South African Art." In Hobbs, *Messages and Meaning*, 88–109.

——. "Our Giftedness." In Van Wyk, *A Decade of Democracy*, 17–21.

——. *Sandile Zulu*. Houghton, South Africa: David Krut Publishing, 2005.

——. "Senzeni Marasela." In Perryer, *10 Years 100 Artists*, 230–33.

——. "The Thought Is the Thing." *Art South Africa* 1, no. 2 (summer 2002): 34–43.

——. "Tropics of Ice." In Hope, *Contemporary Art from South Africa*, 37–59.

——. "Walking Wounded." *Art South Africa* 2, no. 4 (winter 2004): 52–57.

——. "Whose Subject? Identities in Conflict in South African Visual Culture." In Büchler and Papastergiadis, *Random Accesss*, 151–74.

Richter, Linda, and Robert Morrell, eds. *Baba: Men and Fatherhood in South Africa*. Cape Town: HSRC Press, 2006.

Roberts, David. "Sublime Theories: Reason and Imagination in Modernity." In Robinson and Rundell, *Rethinking Imagination*, 171–84.

Robinson, Gillian, and John Rundell, eds. *Rethinking Imagination: Culture and Creativity.* London: Routledge, 1994.

Rogoff, Irit. *Terra Infirma: Geography's Visual Culture.* London: Routledge, 2000.

Rolnik, Suely, and Corinne Diserens. *Lygia Clark: de l'oeuvre à l'évévement.* Dijon: Les presses du réel, for the Musée des Beaux-Arts de Nantes, 2005.

Rose, Jacqueline. "Apathy and Accountability: The Challenge of South Africa's Truth and Reconciliation Commission to the Intellectual of the Modern World." In Rose, *On Not Being Able to Sleep: Psychoanalysis and the Modern World,* 216–37. London: Chatto and Windus, 2003.

Ross, David R., ed. *Between Spring and Summer: Soviet Conceptual Art in the Era of Late Communism.* Tacoma, Wash.: MIT Press, 1990.

Rowe, William T. *Hankow: Conflict and Community in a Chinese City, 1796–1895.* Stanford, Calif.: Stanford University Press, 1989.

Ruscha, Ed. "Conversation between Walter Hopps and Ed Ruscha." By Walter Hopps. In Ruscha and Bois, *Edward Ruscha: Romance with Liquids; Paintings 1966–1969.* As cited in Ruscha, *Leave Any Information at the Signal.*

——. "Ed Ruscha Discusses His Latest Work with Christopher Fox." By Christopher Fox. *Studio International,* no. 179 (June 1970): 281, 287. Reprinted in Ruscha, *Leave Any Information at the Signal,* 30–33.

——. "Interview with Ed Ruscha in His Western Avenue, Hollywood Studio." By Paul Karlstrom. California Oral History Project, 1980–81. Reprinted in Ruscha, *Leave Any Information at the Signal,* 92–209.

——. *Leave Any Information at the Signal: Writings, Interviews, Bits, Pieces.* Edited by Alexandra Schwartz. Cambridge, Mass.: MIT Press, 2004.

——. "Ed Ruscha: An Interview." By Henri Man Barendse. *Afterimage* 8, no. 7 (February 1981): 8–10. Reprinted in Ruscha, *Leave Any Information at the Signal,* 210–19.

Ruscha, Edward, and Yve-Alain Bois. *Edward Ruscha: Romance with Liquids; Paintings 1966–1969.* New York: Gagosian Gallery, Rizzoli, 1993.

Ryan, James R. *Picturing Empire: Photography and the Visualisation of the British Empire.* London: Reaktion, 1997.

Sagan, Carl. *The Demon-Haunted World: Science as a Candle in the Dark.* New York: Random House, 1996.

Said, Edward. *Freud and the Non-European.* London: Verso, 2003.

——. *Humanism and Democratic Criticism.* Basingstoke, England: Palgrave, 2004.

——. "Yeats and Decolonisation." In Barbara Kruger and Phil Mariani, eds., *Remaking History.* Seattle: Bay Press.

Saltz, Jerry. "Worlds Apart—A Meditation on Separation: Amar Kanwar Walks the Border between India and Pakistan." *Village Voice,* February 27, 2004. Available online at http://www.villagevoice.com/.

Sambrani, Chaitanya, ed. *Edge of Desire: Recent Art in India.* New York: Asia Society Museum, Queens Museum of Art, 2005.

Sanders, Mark. *Complicities: The Intellectual and Apartheid.* Pietermaritzburg: University of Natal Press, 2002.

Sarai Editorial Collective. *Sarai Reader 03: Shaping Technologies.* Delhi: Sarai/Centre for the Study of Developing Societies; Amsterdam: Society for Old and New Media, 2003.

———. *Sarai Reader 04: Crisis/Media.* Delhi: Sarai/CSDS; Amsterdam: Society for Old and New Media, 2004.

Sarkin, Jeremy. *Carrots and Sticks: The TRC and the South African Amnesty Process.* Antwerp: Intersentia, 2004.

Sassen, Robyn. "Nathaniel Stern." *Art South Africa* 3, no. 3 (autumn 2005): 77.

Sayres, Sohnya, Anders Stephenson, Stanley Aronowitz, and Fredric Jameson, eds. *The Sixties without Apology.* Minneapolis: University of Minnesota Press, 1984.

Scarry, Elaine. *The Body in Pain: The Making and Unmaking of the World.* Oxford: Oxford University Press, 1985.

Schachter, Judith, and Stephen Brockmann, eds. *(Im)permanence: Cultures in/out of Time.* University Park: Pennsylvania State University Press, 2008.

Schäfer, Wolf. "Global History and the Present Time." In Lyth and Trischler, *Wiring Prometheus,* 103–25.

Schaffer, Simon. "Seeing Double: How to Make Up a Phantom Body Politic." In Latour and Weibel, *Making Things Public,* 196–202.

Schärf, Wilfried, and Baba Ngcokoto. "Images of Punishment in the People's Courts of Cape Town, 1985–7." In Manganyi and du Toit, *Political Violence and the Struggle in South Africa,* 341–71.

Scheper-Hughes, Nancy, and Philippe Bourgeois. "Introduction: Making Sense of Violence." In Scheper-Hughes and Bourgeois, eds., *Violence in War and Peace: An Anthology,* 1–32. Oxford: Blackwell, 2004.

Schildkrout, Enid, and Curtis A. Keim. *African Reflections: Art from Northeastern Zaire.* Seattle: University of Washington Press; New York: American Museum of Natural History, 1990.

Schipper, Mineke. *Imagining Insiders: Africa and the Question of Belonging.* London: Cassell, 1999.

Schröder, Ingo W., and Bettina E. Schmidt. Introduction to Schröder and Schmidt, eds., *Anthropology of Violence and Conflict.* London: Routledge, 2001.

Seepe, Sipho, ed. *Towards an African Identity in Higher Education.* Pretoria: Vista University, Skotaville Media, 2004.

Sen, Amartya. "Civilizational Imprisonments." *New Republic* (June 10, 2002): 28–33.

Sengupta, Shuddhabrata, and Geert Lovink, eds. *Sarai Reader 01: The Public Domain.* Delhi: Sarai/CSDS; Amsterdam: Society for Old and New Media, 2001.

Serres, Michel. *Rome: The Book of Foundations.* Stanford, Calif.: Stanford University Press, 1991.

Shapin, Steven, and Simon Schaffer. *Leviathan and the Air Pump: Hobbes, Boyle and the Experimental Life.* Princeton, N.J.: Princeton University Press, 1985.

———. *Modern Art, Nineteenth and Twentieth Centuries.* New York: Braziller, 1979.

Sharma, Miriam. "Anand Patwardhan: Social Activist and Dedicated Filmmaker." *Critical Asian Studies* 34, no. 2 (June 2002): 279–94.

Shattuck, Roger. *Forbidden Knowledge: A Landmark Exploration of the Dark Side of Human Ingenuity and Imagination.* Orlando: Harcourt Brace, 1996.

Siegelbaum, Lewis H. "Soviet Car Rallies and the Road to Socialism." *Slavic Review* 64, no. 2 (summer 2005): 247–73.

Simon, Linda. *Dark Light: Electricity and Anxiety from the Telegraph to the X-Ray.* London: Harcourt, 2004.

Simpson, Graeme. " 'Tell No Lies, Claim No Easy Victories': A Brief Evaluation of South Africa's Truth and Reconciliation Commission." In Posel and Simpson, *Commissioning the Past,* 220–51.

Sims, Michael. *Adam's Navel: A Natural and Cultural History of the Human Form.* New York: Viking, 2003.

Sitas, Ari. "Beyond Afropessimism." In Sitas, *Voices That Reason,* 15–24.

——. *Voices That Reason: Theoretical Parables.* Pretoria: University of Pretoria; Leiden: Koninklijke Brill NV, 2004.

Skoropanova, Irina. *Russkaia postmodernistskaia literatura* [Russian postmodernist literature]. Moscow: Nauka, 2001.

Slobin, Greta, ed. "Postcommunism: Rethinking the Second World." Special issue, *New Formations* 22 (spring 1994).

Sloterdijk, Peter. "Atmospheric Politics." In Latour and Weibel, *Making Things Public,* 944–51.

——. "Modernity as Mobilization." In Millar and Schwarz, *Speed,* 43–52.

——. *Sphären III—Schäume.* Frankfurt am Main: Suhrkamp, 2004.

Smith, Barbara Herrnstein. "Contingencies of Value." In Von Hallberg, *Canons,* 5–40.

Smith, Kathryn. "Churchill Madikida." *Art South Africa* 1, no. 4 (winter 2003): 69.

——, ed. *Knap! KKNK Visuele Kunste 2004.* Johannesburg: Suid Afrikaanse Steenkool en Olie, 2004.

——, ed. *Penny Siopis.* Johannesburg: Goodman Gallery, 2005.

Smith, Terry. *The Architecture of Aftermath.* Chicago: University of Chicago Press, 2006.

——. "Contemporary Art and Contemporaneity." *Critical Inquiry* 32, no. 4 (summer 2006): 681–707.

——. "Creating Dangerously: Then and Now." In Enwezor, *The Unhomely,* 114–29.

——. "Time Taken, Given by Contemporary Art." In Schachter and Brockmann, *(Im)permanence,* 263–75.

——. "World Picturing in Contemporary Art; Iconogeographic Turning." *Australian and New Zealand Journal of Art* 7, no. 1 (2006): 24–46.

Snaebjornsdottir, Bryndis, and Ross Sinclair. *If I Ruled the World.* Edited by Mark Wilson. Glasgow: Centre for Contemporary Art, 2000.

Solomon, Andrew. "Their Irony, Humor (and Art) Can Save China." *New York Times Magazine,* December 19, 1993, 42–72.

Sommer, Doris. *Bilingual Aesthetics: A New Sentimental Education.* Durham, N.C.: Duke University Press, 2004.

Song, Dong. Interview by Gao Minglu, October 4, 2002. In Gao and Wang, *Harvest: Contemporary Art Exhibition,* 25–27.

Sontag, Susan. *Against Interpretation.* New York: Dell, 1969.

——. "On Photography." In Sontag, *A Susan Sontag Reader,* 349–67. New York: Farrar, Straus and Giroux, 1982.

——. *Regarding the Pain of Others.* New York: Farrar, Straus and Giroux, 2003; New York: Picador, 2004.

South Africa Truth and Reconciliation Commission (TRC). *Truth and Reconciliation Commission of South Africa Report.* 5 vols. Cape Town: TRC and Department of Justice, 1998.

Soyinka, Wole. "Reparations, Truth, and Reconciliation." In *The Burden of Memory, The Muse of Forgiveness,* 23–92. Oxford: Oxford University Press, 1999.

Spivey, Nigel. *Enduring Creation: Art, Pain and Fortitude.* London: Thames and Hudson, 2001.

Stallabrass, Julian. *Internet Art.* London: Tate Publishing, 2003.

Stella, Frank, and Donald Judd. "Questions to Stella and Judd." Interview by Bruce Glaser. In Battcock, *Minimal Art,* 148–64.

Stengers, Isabelle. "The Cosmopolitical Proposal." In Latour and Weibel, *Making Things Public,* 994–1003.

Stewart, Susan. "Thoughts on the Role of the Humanities in Contemporary Life." *New Literary History* 36, no. 1 (winter 2005): 97–103.

Steyn, Juliet, ed. *Act 2: Beautiful Translations.* London: Pluto, 1996.

Stokstad, Marilyn. *Art History.* In collaboration with David Cateforis. With chapters by Stephen Addiss et al. New York: Prentice-Hall, Abrams, 2002.

Straker, Gill, Fatima Moosa, Risé Becker, and Madiyoyo Nkwale, eds. *Faces in the Revolution: The Psychological Effects of Violence on Township Youth in South Africa.* Claremont: David Philip; Athens: Ohio University Press, 1992.

Struaghan, Kathryn, and Rayda Becker. *Noria Mabasa.* Houghton, South Africa: David Krut Publishing, 2003.

Struther, Zoe. "Gambama a Gingungu and the Secret History of Twentieth-Century Art." *African Arts* 32, no. 1 (spring 1999): 19–31, 92–93.

Struve, Lynn A., ed. *The Qing Formation in World-Historical Time.* Cambridge, Mass.: Harvard University Press, 2004.

Sudheim, Alex. "Thando Mama." *Art South Africa* 3, no. 4 (winter 2005): 71.

Sunderland, Willard. *Taming the Wild Field: Colonization and Empire on the Russian Steppe.* Ithaca, N.Y.: Cornell University Press, 2004.

Suny, Ronald Grigor, ed. *The Cambridge History of Russia.* Vol. 3, *The Twentieth Century.* Cambridge: Cambridge University Press, 2006.

Suny, Ronald Grigor, and Terry Martin, eds. *A State of Nations: Empire and Nation-Making in the Age of Lenin and Stalin.* New York: Oxford University Press, 2001.

Sussman, Elizabeth. "The Third Zone: Soviet Postmodern." In Ross, *Between Spring and Summer,* 61–73.

Taussig, Michael. *Defacement: Public Secrecy and Labor of the Negative.* Stanford, Calif.: Stanford University Press, 1999.

——. *The Nervous System.* London: Routledge, 1992.

Tawadros, Gilane, and Sarah Campbell, eds. *Fault Lines: Contemporary African Art and Shifting Landscapes.* London: inIVA, 2003.

Taylor, Charles. *Modern Social Imaginaries.* Durham, N.C.: Duke University Press, 2004.

Tembo, Mwizenge. *Legends of Africa.* New York: Friedman Fairfax, 1999.

Thompson, Nato, and Gregory Sholette, eds. *The Interventionists: Users' Manual for the Creative Disruption of Everyday Life.* Cambridge, Mass.: MIT Press, 2003.

Thompson, Robert Farris. "Fang Mask." In Baldwin et al., *Perspectives,* 190.

Time. "Out of Africa." September 4, 1950, 49–50.

Times (London). "Nigerian Statue of the Queen." November 16, 1957, 10.

Tolz, Vera. "Conflicting 'Homeland Myths' and Nation-State Building in Postcommunist Russia." *Slavic Review* 57, no. 2 (summer 1998): 267–94.

Torgovnick, Marianna. *Primitive Passions: Men, Women, and the Quest for Ecstasy.* Chicago: University of Chicago Press, 1996.

Tsiang, Katherine, and Wu Hung, eds. *Body and Face in Chinese Visual Culture.* Cambridge, Mass.: Harvard University Press, 2005.

Tsing, Anna Lowenstein. *Friction: Ethnography of Global Connection.* Princeton, N.J.: Princeton University Press, 2005.

Turner, Caroline, ed. *Art and Social Change: Contemporary Art in Asia and the Pacific.* Canberra: Australian National University, Pandanus Books, 2005.

Tutu, Desmond. *No Future without Forgiveness.* London: Random House, 1999.

Van der Watt, Liese. "Imagining Alternative White Masculinities." In Natasha Distiller and Melissa Steyn, eds., *Under Construction: "Race" and Identity in South Africa Today,* 120–33. Sandton, South Africa: Heinemann, 2004.

Van Wyk, Gary, ed. *A Decade of Democracy: Witnessing South Africa.* Boston: Sondela, 2004.

Van Zyl, Mikki, and Melissa Steyn, eds. *Performing Queer: Shaping Sexualities, 1994–2004.* Vol. 1. Roggebaai, South Africa: Kwela, 2005.

Vasudevan, Ravi S., ed. "An Imperfect Public: Cinema and Citizenship in the 'Third World.'" In Sengupta and Lovink, *Sarai Reader 01,* 57–68.

——. *Making Meaning in Indian Cinema.* Delhi: Oxford University Press, 2000.

——. "Selves Made Strange: Violent and Performative Bodies in the Cities of Indian Cinema 1974–2003." In Chandrasekhar and Seel, *Body.City,* 84–117.

Villa-Vincencio, Charles, and Erik Doxtader, eds. *Pieces of the Puzzle: Keywords on Reconciliation and Transitional Justice.* Cape Town: Institute for Justice and Reconciliation, 2004.

——. *The Provocations of Amnesty: Memory, Justice and Impunity.* Cape Town: David Philip, 2003.

Virilio, Paul. *Art and Fear.* London: Continuum, 2003.

——. "Urban Armor: Observations of the Work of Lucy Orta." In Orta, *Process of Transformation,* 45–47.

Von Hallberg, Robert, ed. *Canons.* Chicago: University of Chicago Press, 1984.

Vries, Hent de, and Samuel Weber, eds. *Violence, Identity, and Self-Determination.* Stanford: Stanford University Press, 1997.

Walker, Alice. *In Search of Our Mothers' Gardens: Womanist Prose.* San Diego: Harcourt Brace Jovanovich, 1983.

Walker, John A. *Art and Outrage: Provocation, Controversy and the Visual Arts.* London: Pluto, 1999.

Waller, Margaret. *A Bigger Picture: A Manual of Photojournalism in Southern Africa.* Cape Town: Juta, 2000.

Wallis, Brian, ed. *Art after Modernism: Rethinking Representation.* New York: New Museum of Contemporary Art in association with David R. Godine, Publisher, Boston, 1984.

———. "Excavating the Seventies." *Art in America* 85 (September 1997): 96–99.

Wang Mingxian. "Postmodernism in China." In Gao, *The History of Contemporary Art, 1985–1986,* 455–66.

Warner, Marina. "Camera Ludica." In Mannoni et al., *Eyes, Lies and Illusions,* 13–23.

Weber, Samuel. *Mass Mediauras: Form, Technics, Media.* Sydney: Power Publications; Stanford, Calif.: Stanford University Press, 1996.

Wells, Spencer. *The Journey of Man.* Princeton, N.J.: Princeton University Press, 2002.

Werner, Chris, Qiu Ping, and Marianne Pitzen, eds. *Die Hälfte des Himmels: Chinesische Künstlerinnen der Gegenwart.* Bonn: Publishing House Frauen Museum, 1998.

White, Hayden. "The Burden of History." In Hayden White, *Tropics of Discourse: Essays in Cultural Criticism,* 27–50. Baltimore, Md.: Johns Hopkins University Press, 1978.

Williamson, Sue. *Resistance Art in South Africa.* Cape Town: David Philip; London: Catholic Institute of International Relations, 1989.

Williamson, Sue, and Ashraf Jamal. *Art in South Africa: The Future Present.* Claremont, South Africa: David Philip, 1996.

Wilson, Mark, ed. *If I Ruled the World.* Glasgow: Centre for Contemporary Art, 2000.

Wilson, Richard A. *The Politics of Truth and Reconciliation in South Africa: Legitimizing the Post-Apartheid State.* Cambridge: Cambridge University Press, 2001.

Winnicott, D. W. *Playing and Reality.* London: Tavistock Publications, 1971.

Witte, Hans. *Ifa and Esu: Iconography of Order and Disorder.* Soest, Holland: Kunsthandel Luttik, 1984.

Wittgenstein, Ludwig. *Philosophical Investigations.* 1953. Oxford: Blackwell, 2004.

Wollen, Peter. Introduction to Cooke and Wollen, *Visual Display,* 8–13.

Wolmarans, Riaan, ed. "The Great Cartoon Debate." Special issue, *Mail and Guardian,* February 10–16, 2006, 22–25.

Wu Hung. "Between Past and Future: A Brief History of Contemporary Chinese Photography." In Wu and Phillips, *Between Past and Future,* 119–60.

———. *Exhibiting Experimental Art in China.* Chicago: Smart Museum of Art, University of Chicago, 2000.

———. " 'Experimental Exhibitions' of the 1990s." In Wu, *The First Guangzhou Triennial,* 83–97.

———, ed., *The First Guangzhou Triennial: Reinterpretation: A Decade of Experimental Chinese Art, 1990–2000.* Guangzhou: Guangdong Museum of Art, 2002.

———. "Introduction: A Decade of Chinese Experimental Art (1990–2000)." In Wu, *The First Guangzhou Triennial,* 10–19.

———. *Transience: Chinese Experimental Art at the End of the Twentieth Century.* Chicago: Smart Museum of Art, 1999.

———. "Tui-Transfiguration: A Site-Specific Exhibition at Factory 798." In Wu Hung, *Rong Rong and Inri: Tui-Transfiguration,* 8–43. Beijing: Timezone 8, 2004.

——. "Zhang Dali's Dialogue: Conversation with a City." *Public Culture* 12, no. 3 (2000): 749–68.

Wu Hung and Christopher Phillips. *Between Past and Future: New Photography and Video from China.* New York: International Center for Photography, 2004.

Xu Hong. *Female: Thoughts on Fine Arts.* Nanjing: Jiangsu People's Publishing House, 2003.

Yardley, Jim. "In a Tidal Wave, China's Masses Pour from Farm to City." *New York Times,* September 12, 2004, B6.

Younge, Gavin. *Art of the South African Townships.* London: Thames and Hudson, 1988.

Zapiro [Jonathan Shapiro]. "A Decade of Cartoons." In Andries Oliphant, Peter Delius, and Lalou Meltzer, eds., *Democracy X: Marking the Present / Re-presenting the Past,* 260–67. Pretoria: University of South Africa Press, 2004.

Zhang Dali. *Zhang Dali: Demolition and Dialogue.* Edited by Mathieu Borysevicz. Beijing: Courtyard Gallery, 1999.

CONTRIBUTORS

MONICA AMOR is a professor of contemporary art at the Maryland Institute College of Art. Recent publications include "Another Geometry, Gego's Reticulárea 1969–1982," *October* 113 (Summer 2005). She served as curator of the 2006 exhibition "Gego: Defying Structures" (Serralves Museum, Porto, Portugal).

NANCY CONDEE is an associate professor of Slavic studies at the University of Pittsburgh. Her publications include *Soviet Hieroglyphics: Visual Culture in Late 20c. Russia* (British Film Institute, 1995), *Endquote: Sots-Art Literature and Soviet Grand Style,* with Marina Balina and Evgeny Dobrenko (Northwestern University Press, 2000), and *The Imperial Trace: Recent Russian Cinema* (Oxford, forthcoming). Her work, with Vladimir Padunov and separately, has appeared in *The Nation,* the *Washington Post, October, New Left Review,* and *Sight and Sound,* as well as the major Russian cultural journals.

OKWUI ENWEZOR is the dean of academic affairs and a senior vice president at the San Francisco Art Institute. He was visiting professor in the Department of the History of Art and Architecture at the University of Pittsburgh 2003–2006. Artistic director of the Second Seville Biennial of Contemporary Art (2006) and of documenta 11 (Kassel, 1998–2002), he also curated "The Short Century: Independence and Liberation Movements in Africa, 1945–1994" (Museum Villa Stuck, Munich, 2001) and "Snap Judgments: New Positions in Contemporary African Photography" (International Center of Photography, New York, 2006), where he serves as adjunct curator. Among his books are *Reading the Contemporary: African Art, from Theory to the Marketplace* (MIT Press, 2000) and *Mega Exhibitions: Antinomies of a Transnational Global Form* (Wilhelm Fink Verlag, 2002). He was editor of the four-volume publication of Documenta 11 Platforms: *Democracy Unrealized, Experiments with Truth: Transitional Justice and the Processes of Truth and Reconciliation, Creolité and Creolization,* and *Under Siege: Four African Cities, Freetown, Johannesburg, Kinshasa, Lagos* (Hatje Cantz Verlag, 2002–3).

GAO MINGLU is an associate professor in the Department of the History of Art and Architecture at University of Pittsburgh. A specialist in modern and contemporary Chinese art, he has edited *Inside Out: New Chinese Art* (University of California Press, 1998) and published *History of Contemporary Chinese Art, 1985–1986* (Shanghai Peoples Press, 1990), *A Century's Utopia: Chinese Avant-Garde Art* (Artists Publishing House, 2000), *Chinese Maximalism* (Chongqing People's Press, 2003), and *The Wall: Reshaping Contemporary Chinese Art* (The Albright Knox Art Gallery and China Millennium Museum, 2005).

BORIS GROYS is a professor of philosophy and art history at the College of Design at the Center for Arts and Media (Karlsruhe), and Global Distinguished Professor at the Department of Russian and Slavic Studies, New York University. His publications include *The Total Art of Stalinism: Russian Avant-Garde, Aesthetic Dictatorship, and Beyond* (Princeton University Press, 1992) and *Ilya Kabakov: The Man Who Flew into the Cosmic Space* (Afterall/MIT Press, 2006).

JONATHAN HAY is Ailsa Mellon Bruce Professor of Fine Arts at the Institute of Fine Arts, New York University. He has written on many aspects of the art and material culture of dynastic China, principally of the period from the sixteenth to the nineteenth century. He also publishes from time to time on modern and contemporary Chinese art, and on theoretical and methodological issues in art history.

GEETA KAPUR is an independent critic and curator living in Delhi. Writings on art, film, and cultural theory in her book *When Was Modernism: Essays on Contemporary Cultural Practice in India* (Tulika Books, 2000) are further developed in *Iconographies for the Present* (Tulika Books, 2007). Her curatorial work includes "Bombay/Mumbai 1992–2001," cocurated within the multipart exhibition "Century City: Art and Culture in the Modern Metropolis" at the Tate Modern, London (2001).

ROSALIND KRAUSS is a university professor and professor of art history at Columbia University, New York, and a founding editor of *October*. Her books include *The Optical Unconscious* (MIT Press, 1993), *Formless: A User's Guide* (Zone, 1997), *The Picasso Papers* (Farrar, Straus, 1998), *Bachelors* (MIT Press, 1999), and *"A Voyage on the North Sea": Art in the Age of the Post-Medium Condition* (Thames and Hudson, 1999). Curated exhibitions include *Robert Morris: The Mind/Body Problem* (Guggenheim Museum, New York, 1994). With Yve-Alain Bois she organized "L'Informe: Mode d'emploi" for the Centre Georges Pompidou, Paris (1996), and with Benjamin Buchloh, Hal Foster, and Yve-Alain Bois she coauthored the textbook *Art since 1900* (Thames and Hudson, 2004).

BRUNO LATOUR is a professor at the Ecole des Mines in Paris and vice president for research at Sciences Po in Paris. His books include *The Pasteurization of France* (Harvard University Press, 1988) and *We Have Never Been Modern* (Harvard University Press, 1993). He has curated two major international exhibitions, "Iconoclash: Beyond the Image Wars in Science, Religion and Art" (Center for Art and Media, Karlsruhe, 2002) and "Making Things Public: Atmospheres of Democracy" (Center for Art and Media, Karlsruhe, 2005), catalogues for both of which were published by MIT Press (2002 and 2005).

ZOE LEONARD is a New York–based artist who exhibits with the Paula Cooper Gallery. She works primarily in black-and-white photography but has also engaged in sculpture, installation, and film. Her work was included in documenta 9 (1992) and documenta 12 (2007) in Kassel, Germany, and has been shown twice (1993, 1997) in the Whitney Biennial, Whitney Museum of American Art, New York. She has since presented her work at the Vienna Secession, the Kunsthalle Basel, the Centre National de la Photographie, Paris, and the Tate Modern, London.

LEV MANOVICH is a professor of visual arts, University of California, San Diego, and a director of The Lab for Cultural Analysis at California Institute for Telecommunications and Information Technology. He is the author of *Soft Cinema: Navigating the Database* (MIT Press, 2005), and *The Language of New Media* (MIT Press, 2001).

JAMES MEYER is an associate professor of art history at Emory University. He is the author of *Minimalism: Art and Polemics in the Sixties* (Yale University Press, 2001) and the editor of *Minimalism* (Phaidon, 2000); *Cuts: Texts, 1959–2004* by Carl Andre (MIT Press, 2005), and *The AIDS Crisis Is Ridiculous and Other Writings, 1986–2004* by Gregg Bordowitz (MIT Press, 2003). His study of Howard Hodgkin appears in *Howard Hodgkin*, ed. Nicholas Serota (Tate Publications, 2006).

HELEN MOLESWORTH is the curator of contemporary art at the Harvard University Art Museums, Cambridge, Massachusetts. She was chief curator of exhibitions at the Wexner Center for the Arts, Ohio State University, Columbus, Ohio, where she curated "Part Object Part Sculpture" (2005–6). From 2000 to 2003 she was curator of contemporary art at the Baltimore Museum of Art, where she organized "Work Ethic" (2003–4) and "Body Space" (2003). Her writing has appeared in *Art Journal, Documents, October,* and elsewhere.

ANTONIO NEGRI is currently a university professor at the College International de Philosophie, Paris. Among his publications are (with Michael Hardt) *Empire* (Harvard University Press, 2001) and *Multitude* (Penguin, 2004). Forthcoming publications include *Workshops of Subjectivity* (Stock, 2006), *Goodbye Mister Socialism* (Feltrinelli, 2006), and *Descartes* (Towards, 2006).

SYLVESTER OKWUNODU OGBECHIE teaches the history of arts and architecture at the University of California, Santa Barbara. He is founder and editorial director of *Critical Interventions: Journal of African Art History and Visual Culture.* His book *Ben Enwonwu: Making of An African Modernist* is forthcoming from the University of Rochester Press.

NIKOS PAPASTERGIADIS is an associate professor and reader at the University of Melbourne. His publications include *Modernity as Exile* (Manchester University Press, 1993), *Dialogues in the Diaspora* (Rivers Oram Press, 1998), *The Turbulence of Migration* (Polity Press, 2000), *Metaphor and Tension* (Artspace, 2004), and *Spatial Aesthetics* (Rivers Oram Press, 2006). He coedited with Scott McGuire *Empires, Ruins and Networks* (Melbourne University Press, 2005) and has been special guest editor of *Arena, Chronico, Third Text, Art and Design, Annotations,* and *Photofile.*

COLIN RICHARDS is an artist, curator, and personal professor in the Division of Visual Arts, Wits School of Art, at University of the Witwatersrand, Johannesburg, South Africa. His publications include *Sandile Zulu* (David Krut, 2005); "Lost in the Supermarket," *Art South Africa* 4, no. 3 (Autumn 2006); and "The Double Agent: Humanism, History and Allegory in the Art of Durant Sihlali (1939–2004)," *African Arts* (2006).

SUELY ROLNIK is a full professor at the Universidade Católica de São Paulo. She has translated Gilles Deleuze and Félix Guattari into Portuguese and, with Guattari, wrote *Micropolítica: Cartografias do desejo* (Vozes, 1986). She was the curator with C. Diserens of the related exhibition and catalogue: *Nous sommes le moule: A vous de donner le souffle. Lygia Clark, de l'œuvre à l'événement* (Musée de Beaux-arts de Nantes, 2005) and the Pinacoteca do Estado de São Paulo (São Paulo, 2006).

TERRY SMITH, FAHA, CIHA, is Andrew W. Mellon Professor of Contemporary Art History and Theory in the Department of the History of Art and Architecture at the University of Pittsburgh, and a visiting professor in the Faculty of Architecture, University of Sydney. From 1994 to 2001 he was Power Professor of Contemporary Art and director of the Power Institute, Foundation for Art and Visual Culture, University of Sydney. He is the author of *Making the Modern: Industry, Art and Design in America* (University of Chicago Press, 1993); *Transformations in Australian Art*, vol. 1, *The Nineteenth Century: Landscape, Colony and Nation*, and vol. 2, *The Twentieth Century: Modernism and Aboriginality* (Craftsman House, Sydney, 2002); and *The Architecture of Aftermath* (University of Chicago Press, 2006).

MCKENZIE WARK is an associate professor of media and cultural studies at Eugene Lang College, the New School for Social Research, in New York City. He is the author of *Virtual Geography* (Indiana University Press, 1994), *Virtual Republic* (Allen and Unwin, 1997), *Celebrities, Culture and Cyberspace* (Pluto Press, 1999), *Dispositions* (Salt, 2002), and *A Hacker Manifesto* (Harvard, 2004). He is the author of the networked book GAM3R 7HEORY, see www.futureofthebook.org/gamertheory.

WU HUNG is Harrie A. Vanderstappen Distinguished Service Professor in Chinese art history, and director of the Center for the Art of East Asia at the University of Chicago. His major books and edited volumes on contemporary art include *Transience: Chinese Experimental Art at the End of the Twentieth Century* (University of Chicago Press, 1999), *Exhibiting Experimental Art in China* (University of Chicago Press, 2000), *Chinese Art at the Crossroads: Between Past and Future, between East and West* (Hong Kong, 2001), *Reinterpretation: A Decade of Experimental Art in China (1990–2000)* (Guangzhou, 2002), and *Remaking Beijing: Tiananmen Square and the Creation of a Political Space* (University of Chicago Press, 2005). He was artistic director of the First Guangzhou Triennial (2002), a curator of the Sixth Gwangju Biennale (2006), and cocurator of *Between Past and Future: New Photography and Video from China* (International Center of Photography and Asia Center, New York; Smart Museum of Art and Museum of Contemporary Art, Chicago, 2004).

INDEX

Page numbers in italics refer to
illustrations

TERRY SMITH is Andrew W. Mellon Professor of
Contemporary Art History and Theory in the Department
of the History of Art and Architecture at the University of
Pittsburgh, and a visiting professor in the Faculty of
Architecture at the University of Sydney.

OKWUI ENWEZOR is the dean of academic affairs and a
senior vice president at the San Francisco Art Institute.

NANCY CONDEE is an associate professor of Slavic
studies at the University of Pittsburgh.

Library of Congress Cataloging-in-Publication Data
Antinomies of art and culture : modernity,
postmodernity, contemporaneity / Terry Smith, Okwui
Enwezor, and Nancy Condee, eds.
p. cm.
Includes bibliographical references and index.
ISBN 978-0-8223-4186-4 (cloth : alk. paper)
ISBN 978-0-8223-4203-8 (pbk. : alk. paper)
1. Art, Modern—21st century. 2. Modernism (Art)—
History—21st century. 3. Art and society—History—21st
century. 4. Art and globalization—History—21st century.
I. Smith, Terry (Terry E.) II. Enwezor, Okwui. III.
Condee, Nancy.
N6497.A58 2008
709.05—dc22   2008028478

www.ingramcontent.com/pod-product-compliance
Lightning Source LLC
Chambersburg PA
CBHW0721129170526
45158CB00004BA/1298